D0984592

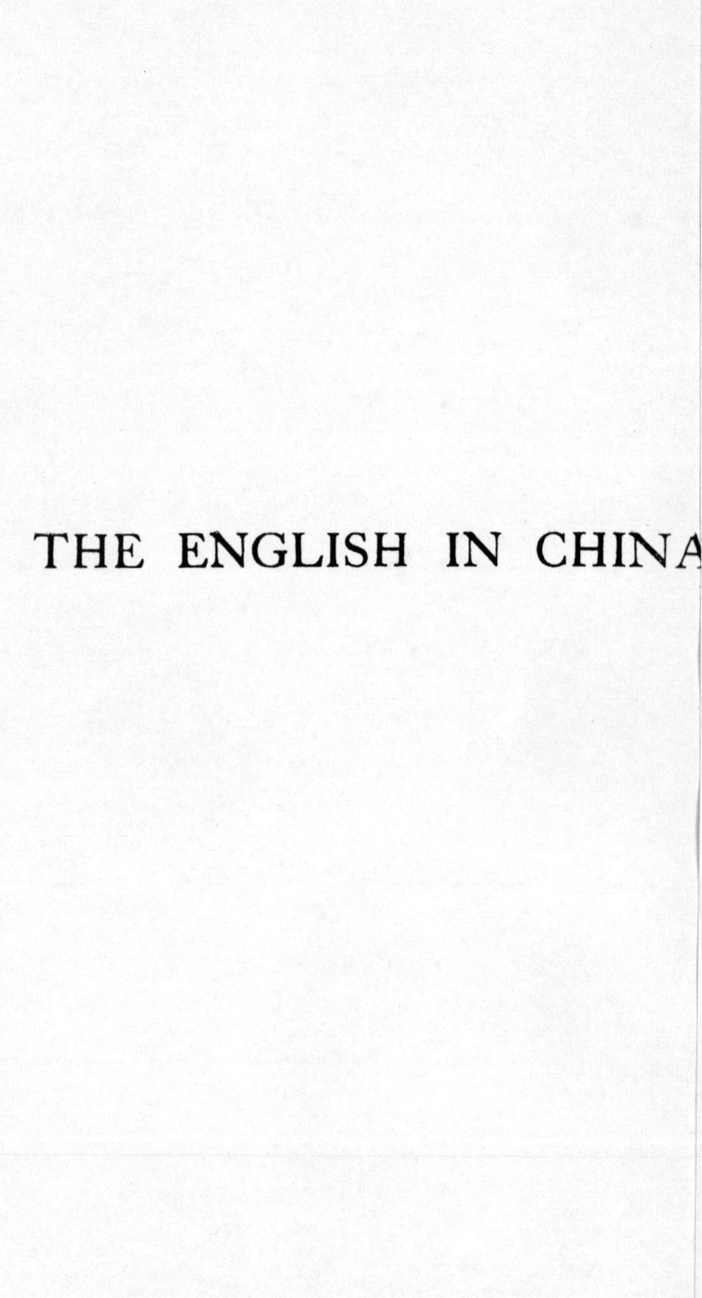

THE ENGLISH IN CHINA

MACAO IN 1637

(From an old print in Peter Mundy's Diary)

THE ENGLISH IN CHINA

BEING AN ACCOUNT
OF THE INTERCOURSE AND RELATIONS
BETWEEN ENGLAND AND CHINA FROM
THE YEAR 1600 TO THE YEAR 1843
AND A SUMMARY OF LATER
DEVELOPMENTS

BY

JAMES BROMLEY EAMES, M.A., B.C.L.

OF WORCESTER COLLEGE, OXFORD,
AND OF THE MIDDLE TEMPLE, BARRISTER-AT-LAW,
PROFESSOR OF LAW IN THE IMPERIAL TIENTSIN UNIVERSITY 1898 TO 1900,
LEGAL ADVISER TO THE TIENTSIN PROVISIONAL GOVERNMENT 1901

LONDON : CURZON PRESS
NEW YORK : BARNES & NOBLE BOOKS

First published 1909
New impression 1974

Published by
Curzon Press Ltd · London and Dublin
and
Harper & Row Publishers Inc · New York
Barnes & Noble Import Division

UK 7007 0043 9
US 06 491870 X

Printed in Great Britain
by Kingprint Ltd · Richmond · Surrey

TO

ADMIRAL SIR EDWARD HOBART SEYMOUR,

G.C.B., G.C.V.O., O.M., LL.D.,

TO WHOSE FORESIGHT AND COURAGE,

IN THE YEAR 1900,

THE PRESERVATION OF

BRITISH INTERESTS IN NORTH CHINA

IS LARGELY DUE,

I Dedicate

THIS BOOK

PREFACE

It was my original intention, in writing this work, to present to the reader a description and an analysis of our interests in China, as they exist at the present day. It soon became evident that it is impossible fully to comprehend the present position without a knowledge of the past. My original plan was therefore abandoned, and in its place has been substituted this attempt to explain the origin, growth and development of those interests. The main object has been to present facts, relying on the best authorities. The chief sources of information have been four. The records of the E. I. Company have supplied much material for the period ending 1834. The *Chinese Repository*, a periodical published at Canton from the year 1832 to 1852, is a mine of information of all sorts, furnished by the best authorities of that period, but thrown together without any special design, of which the sorting and proper arrangement have involved much labour. The chronological narrative of Auber, a former secretary of the E. I. Company, has provided some additional information in respect of the period covered by the records at the India Office. The Blue Book of 1840 has been freely utilised in discussing the events leading up to the Opium War.

Authorities have been cited in some detail, so that the reader who wishes to inquire further may know from what sources he can obtain information. Chinese edicts and other documents have been quoted in many cases *verbatim*, in order that the light thrown by them on the questions under discussion may not suffer the refraction that usually results from paraphrase.

The spelling of Chinese words has presented a difficulty. I have taken in each case that which appeared most usual, without attempting to follow any particular system.

When speaking of the rest of mankind, as distinguished from the Chinese, I have used the words "Foreigner" and

"Foreign," spelt with a capital letter on the analogy of words of nationality. When used in their strict sense, that is in relation to persons not of British nationality, these words have been written in the ordinary way.

I have to express my indebtedness to the many friends who, at various times, have indicated sources of information. In this respect my thanks are especially due to the sub-librarian at the India Office, Mr. William Foster, who first called my attention to such unpublished material as the *Factory Records of the East India Company*, the *Journal of Captain Weddell's Voyage*, and *Peter Mundy's Diary*.

J. BROMLEY EAMES.

10 King's Bench Walk,
Temple, E.C.

8 March, 1909.

CONTENTS

ILLUSTRATIONS

MAPS

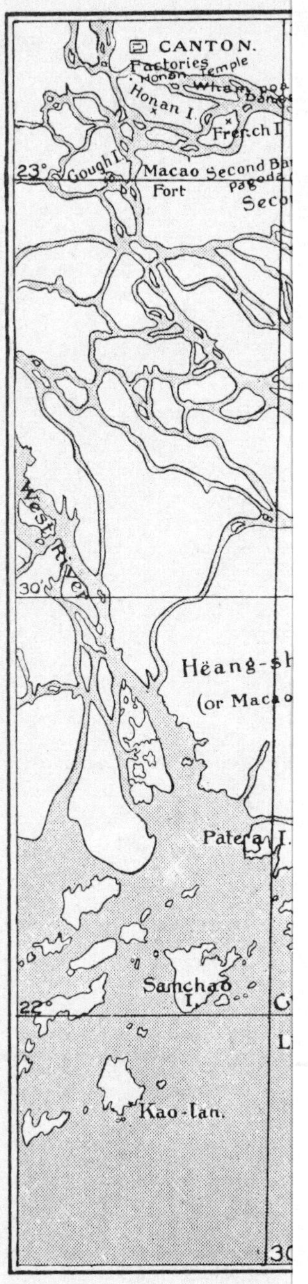

Map of the mouth of the
Kowloon Extension. The
by the dotted line and th

… Canton River, showing Macao and the … limits of British jurisdiction are the portions … the portions of coast line …

THE ENGLISH IN CHINA

CHAPTER I

THE BEGINNINGS OF OUR TRADE WITH THE FAR EAST

To the thirst for knowledge which arose on the Revival of Learning, and to the desire of the nations of Europe to find an outlet for their growing energies in fresh fields of commercial enterprise, must be attributed those voyages of discovery that led to the foundation of our trade in the Far East. When European voyagers towards the close of the fifteenth century set out to explore the unknown parts of the globe, the object of their quest was a region vaguely designated "The Indies." Of this region the islands first visited by Columbus were assumed to be part, and though the great group to which they belong continued to be called the "West Indies," it was soon discovered that the huge continent which lay beyond them formed no part of that India with which from very ancient times Europe had carried on a commercial intercourse through the little known countries of Western and Central Asia. When, however, in 1498, Vasco da Gama rounded the Cape of Good Hope and sailed to the port of Calicut, it was recognized that he had reached the goal for which all had been striving. From that time the terms "India" and "The Indies" had a significance far more precise than that in which they had before been used, a significance which became rooted and fixed, and has continued to the present day.

It was an extension of the travels of the men who opened up India that brought about direct commercial intercourse between Europe and the Far East. The founding of the trade between Europe and the countries East of the Straits of Malacca is due to the Portuguese. As early as 1493 Spain and Portugal were at variance as to their respective rights over newly discovered territories, and the controversy between them was only prevented from becoming acute by the publication in that year of the famous bull of Pope Alexander VI., which granted to the united crowns of Castile and Arragon all lands discovered and to be discovered beyond a line to be drawn from the North to the South Pole 100 leagues west of the Azores, with a reservation of all lands which had been before that date occupied by any other Christian nation. It is mainly owing to this pronouncement that from that time the operations of the Portuguese were confined to what we call the Eastern Hemisphere. Debarred from exploring the continent of America, they pushed ahead in India and in the East generally, and commenced to trade with countries of which, until then, Europeans had little or no knowledge; and thus it came about that the Portuguese were the first European nation to gain a footing in China. There is another reason, a geographical one, to which this result is in some measure due. The configuration of the land in the Western Hemisphere was soon found to be such as to make the voyage in that direction far more difficult than by the route round the Cape of Good Hope. The Spaniards, to whom this field of discovery had been assigned by the decision of Pope Alexander, instead of trying to reach India by crossing the Pacific, contented themselves with the easier task of subjugating the natives of America and appropriating their wealth, a task which well-nigh absorbed their energies for a considerable period.

As further explorations were made in the East, the names "China" and "Cathay" became identified with territories more definitely ascertained than had ever been the "Dominions of the Great Khan" of mediæval times. From the date of Vasco da Gama's famous voyage to the appearance of the Portuguese at Canton is but a short period. In 1511 d'Albuquerque, who had already gained a footing for the Portuguese in India, assaulted and took Malacca. Four years later he despatched thence a single vessel, under the command of Raphael Perestrello, to investigate the opportunities of trade with China, and this vessel succeeded in making a profitable voyage to the islands at the mouth of the Canton river.[1] This was the first voyage ever made by Europeans to the coast of China. It was followed in 1517 by a second Portuguese expedition, consisting of four ships and four Malay vessels under the command of Fernando Perez de Andrade. The gentleness of the commander and the liberal presents made by him to the imperial officials, created such a favourable impression, that the local authorities at Canton, without obtaining the sanction of the Emperor, allowed two of his ships to proceed up the river with permission to trade. Of this privilege little use could be made, for, receiving word that some of the vessels left behind had been attacked by pirates at San-shan, Andrade was obliged to leave Canton prematurely to hasten to their assistance.

When he had succoured the threatened portion of his squadron, Andrade proceeded with some of his ships to Ningpo, in the province of Fu-kien, and founded there some sort of Portuguese colony. This was the first settlement of Europeans in China. Before leaving Canton he had announced that he wished to make reparation to any who might have been wronged by his followers. Thus he gained the good opinion of the Chinese, who began to think that the reports they had heard of Portuguese violence at Goa must be without foundation. They were soon, however, undeceived, for in 1518 Simon de Andrade, brother of Fernando, arrived with one Portuguese ship and three junks. His chief aim was to establish his own authority, and he brought with him a medley of persons of doubtful character to assist in terrorizing the Chinese. Without obtaining any kind of permission, he built a fort at San-shan, and arrogated to himself the title of "Sovereign." The Chinese, incensed at so high-handed a proceeding, assembled a naval squadron and besieged the fort, which was on the verge of being reduced by starvation when a violent storm arose, which enabled Andrade to escape with three of his vessels. In 1522, Martin Alfonso de Mello Continho arrived with a commission from King Emanuel of Portugal to propose friendship with the Emperor of China.

[1] Davis: *China and the Chinese*, vol. i, p. 13.

With this expedition the Chinese managed to get up a quarrel in which nearly all the Portuguese were killed, the survivors fleeing to Lampaco, a place about twenty miles north of San-shan. In 1545 another party of Portuguese, commanded by Ferdinand Mendez Pinto, and consisting of a number of desperadoes, arrived at Ningpo.[1]

So long as the countries discovered by European explorers were those peopled by savages, no difficulty had been experienced in enforcing the principle, asserted by all the nations of Christendom and recognized in the bull of Pope Alexander, that newly discovered lands inhabited by pagans should form part of the dominions of the European sovereign whose representative first landed on their shores. But in dealing with more highly developed communities, such as China and Japan, it was soon perceived that a doctrine so illogical and so utterly wanting in any ethical foundation was altogether unworkable, and must be abandoned. Deprived of this ground for claiming an exclusive right to trade with the Chinese, the Portuguese had recourse to the plan of applying to the sovereign power for a special grant of commercial privileges. This they obtained, though not without some difficulty. The Chinese, disgusted with the excesses of the earlier expeditions, were careful to confine within very narrow limits the rights thus conferred. Later, when other European nations came seeking the liberty of trade in China, the Portuguese contended that the grants already made to them were such as debarred their rivals from obtaining any similar privilege. Neither the Chinese nor the European nations concerned took this view of the matter, and in course of time the Spaniards, Dutch, English, and others, received formal permission to engage in commerce; but in every case the

[1] There has been much dispute as to whether Pinto's narrative is correct. His story is, that after being most hospitably received by their fellow-countrymen at Liampo, a suburb of Ningpo, they set out to find an island where they were told by a Chinese pirate a great quantity of treasure lay buried. They were wrecked on the voyage, and all but fourteen of them were drowned. Wandering about they arrived at Nanking, whence they were sent to Peking as captives. Ultimately they returned to the coast and made their way to Japan. See Voyages of *Fernando Mendez Pinto* (Gent's translation, ch. xxii-xliv).

precedent was followed of limiting that permission within very narrow bounds. In this way it came about that the beginnings of commercial intercourse between European nations and China took the form of grants allowing the liberty of trade only at a few and carefully defined places.

From an early date the centre of Portuguese influence in China was at Macao, which was not far from that San-shan (corrupted into St. John's), of which mention has been made above. In 1535 permission was given by the local Chinese officials to a party of Portuguese to erect temporary sheds for drying some goods, which the latter alleged had been brought as tribute but had been damaged in a storm. Acting on this permission, the new arrivals landed and put up dwellings, in which they stored their merchandise. By a skilful use of presents these first settlers succeeded in establishing a form of government to administer the territory occupied, which consisted of a small peninsula connected with the mainland, or more correctly speaking, with the island of Hëang-shan, by a very narrow neck of land. For twenty or thirty years little attention was paid to this colony. Across the isthmus the Chinese, in 1573, built a barrier, pierced with a single archway, through which alone access from the land side could be obtained to the Portuguese settlement. In this archway was set a gate, and on the Chinese side of the gate guards were stationed perpetually, to prevent the Portuguese from passing the limits within which they were thus confined.

In 1582 the Viceroy of Canton summoned before himself the Governor, Captain, and Judge of Macao, these being the Portuguese officials who exercised authority in the colony, and having upbraided them for forming a settlement without permission, announced that they were to be expelled for ever. This was probably done merely from the usual Chinese motive, a desire to extort money ; at any rate, by a judicious use of their resources, the Portuguese obtained an informal permission to reside at Macao, subject to the laws of China. No deed of grant was ever executed, and the tenure on which the Portuguese were allowed to remain was at best a tenancy at the will of the local Chinese officials. A ground rent was paid for the use of the land on which the settlement stood, varying in amount from 500 to 600 taels per annum.[1] At an early date a Chinese official, called the *tsotang*, was appointed to reside in the settlement and to keep watch on behalf of the Emperor over the Portuguese inhabitants, who in other respects were allowed to govern themselves. The Chinese population continued to be under the jurisdiction of the Chinese district in which Macao was situated, as though they had been living in a Chinese town.[2]

Throughout the sixteenth century the influence of the

[1] From 1649 to 1740 it was 600 taels ; in 1835 it was 500 taels. In 1848 the Governor, Ferreira do Amaral, refused to pay the ground rent, and forcibly expelled from Macao the Chinese officials who had up till then exercised authority there. For this he was waylaid and barbarously murdered near the Barrier by Chinese assassins, and his head was taken to Canton. No rent was paid after 1849, but the rights of the Portuguese on this point remained undefined until 1887.

[2] In 1732 the Viceroy of Canton commanded the Portuguese authorities at Macao to report to a civil mandarin the arrival of every foreign ship, giving particulars as to her force, nationality, and business. This troublesome duty was not willingly performed, so the Chinese authorities stationed on the Praya Grande a subordinate Hoppo (see *post*, p. 48 chap. iii), called the *Keun-min-foo*, whose function it was to lay an arbitrary tax on all persons and goods leaving or entering a ship. In all cases of importance, however, the Portuguese Governor made his own report to the Chinese officials at Canton.

In 1862 a treaty was negotiated, by which the supremacy of the Chinese within the Barrier was implied rather than declared, and it was mutually agreed that consular officers should be appointed ; but the Chinese, finding that this stipulation might be taken to be an acknowledgment of the independence of Macao, refused to ratify the treaty. In 1887 a new treaty was signed, in which China confirmed to Portugal the " perpetual occupation and government of Macao and its Dependencies by Portugal as any other Portuguese possession," the Portuguese undertaking never to alienate it without the consent of the Chinese Government. From this it will be seen that Macao is now Portuguese territory, having a status altogether different from that of a Concession or Settlement at one of the Treaty Ports. (See *post*, p. 544, chap. xxiv). From the terms of the lease under which Great Britain holds Wei-hai-wei, it would appear as if the Chinese had had in their minds the precedent of the Portuguese occupation of Macao when that lease was drawn up. See *Correspondence respecting the Affairs of China* (Blue Book, No. 1, 1899), p. 199.

For further information as to the early history of Macao, see Ljungstedt, *Historical Sketch of the Portuguese Settlements in China* ; and Davis, *China and the Chinese*, chap. i.

Portuguese in the Far East was practically supreme. Except that Magellan [1] landed in the Philippine Islands in 1521, of which Spain took *de facto* possession in 1565, no other European nation but the Portuguese could claim before 1600 to have obtained a footing in that part of the world. But political changes in Europe were destined to have a far-reaching effect in the East. In 1581 the Duke of Alva, who had harried the Netherlands, invaded Portugal and reduced it on behalf of his master, Philip of Spain. [2] The promise given by Philip, that he would administer Portugal and her dependencies quite separately from Spain and her possessions, resulted in the interests of the two countries in the Far East being kept quite distinct. This, however, did not prevent the Dutch from attacking the Portuguese colonies, now ruled by Holland's hated foe, with as much ardour as if they had been completely Spanish. To this development in Europe is mainly attributable the fact that at the close of the sixteenth century the Dutch appeared in the East to challenge the Portuguese monopoly. Before long they were followed by the English, who adopted a not less hostile attitude. It was soon apparent that before the vigour and enterprise of these newcomers Portuguese supremacy could not long endure.

In 1595 Dutch merchants despatched from Holland a great expedition to Java by way of the Cape of Good Hope. As Queen Elizabeth was anxious to extend English trade in that direction, it is not surprising to find that English merchants organized the first English expedition to China in the following year. This consisted of three vessels, the *Bear*, the *Bear's Whelp*, and the *Benjamin*, fitted out at the expense of Sir Robert Dudley. In the company were two merchants of the City of London, by whom Queen Elizabeth sent to the Emperor of China a letter of introduction, written in Latin, asking that "when they shall come for traffique's sake unto

[1] Magellan, although in the service of Philip of Spain, was a Portuguese. For an account of Spanish operations in the Philippines see *Chinese Repository*, vol. vi, p. 171 ; vol. vii, pp. 290, 462, 525 ; vol. viii, pp. 101, 169, 246.

[2] Portugal remained under the Spanish dominion till the rebellion of John of Braganza in 1640.

any the stations, ports, towns, or cities of your Empire, they shall have full and free libertie of egresse and regresse and of dealing in trade of marchandize with your subjects, may by your Highnesse clemency most firmly enjoy all such freedomes, immunities and privileges as are usually granted to the subjects of other Princes which exercise traffic in your dominions: and we on the other side will not only perform all the offices of a well-willing prince unto your Highnesse, but also for the greater increase of mutuall love and commerce between us and our subjects, by these present letters of ours doe most willingly grant unto all and every your subjects (if it shall seem good unto your Highnesse) full and entire libertie unto any of the parts of our dominions to resort there to abide and traffique, and thence to returne."[1] Of this unfortunate expedition no one ever returned to give an account. Whether it reached China is not known, but it is practically certain that it never got so far.

In 1598 the Dutch fitted out a second expedition to Java,[2] whereupon the merchants of the City of London held a meeting at Skinners' Hall to consider the situation. At this meeting a resolution was passed that a petition be presented to the Crown, asking for a grant of exclusive trading privileges with India and the East. It was in response to the petition presented in accordance with this resolution that in December, 1600, the charter was granted which incorporated the East India Company.[3] By this charter the Company obtained a monopoly for fifteen years of the trade between England

[1] This translation is given with the original Latin version in Hakluyt's *Voyages, Travels, and Discoveries of the English Nation*, vol. iv, p. 372 (1810 edition).

[2] As a result of these voyages the Dutch East India Company was incorporated in 1602 for the purpose of conducting the trade between Holland and the East. This Company held sway over the Dutch East Indies for nearly two centuries.

[3] A copy of the charter will be found in Ilbert's *Government of India*, p. 464. The real name of the Elizabethan Company was "The Governor and Company of Merchants of London trading into the East Indies." Throughout this work it is called the East India Company in accordance with a common usage, for reasons of convenience. See *post*, chap. ix, p. 172.

and all countries lying East of the Cape of Good Hope as far as the Straits of Magellan. In 1609 James I granted a perpetual monopoly by a fresh charter. For this reason it happened that in England, as in Holland and Portugal, the same men who opened up commerce with India also founded the commercial intercourse with China and Japan. The connection between our establishments in India and those in China remained unbroken until the Act of 1833[1] abolished the Company's monopoly at Canton; even at the present day some traces of it still remain.

It would be impossible to discuss here the vicissitudes of the East India Company.[2] Suffice it to say that the Company soon found that in practice the monopoly conferred by its charter could not always be enforced. Indeed, on more than one occasion rival associations were able seriously to threaten its predominance. From the date of its incorporation to 1612, the Company's operations consisted of twelve separate voyages, of which the expense was borne and the profit shared by individual subscribers. Determined opposition was offered by the Portuguese, but in 1602 Sir James Lancaster, who was knighted for his services in this connection, succeeded in establishing commercial relations with the King of Achin,[3] with the Moluccas, and with Bantam.[4] This was the first of the twelve voyages; it lasted from February, 1601, to September, 1603. In 1604 the second voyage was undertaken. So great was the success of the initial venture that in 1604 Sir Edward Michelborne and others applied to James I for a licence to trade to "Cathay, China, Japan, Corea, and Cambaya," which they obtained notwithstanding the Company's monopoly. Michelborne, however, so far from using his privileges for the advancement of the renown of England, imitated the malpractices of the Portuguese, and contented himself with plundering the native traders among

[1] See *post*, chap. ix, p. 176.

[2] For a history of the development of the East India Company, see Ilbert, *Government of India*, chap. i.

[3] In Sumatra.

[4] In Java. See *Voyages of Sir James Lancaster to the East Indies*, p. 56. (Hakluyt Society's edition, 1877.)

the islands of the Archipelago. The result was that the English name was brought into disrepute, and the business of the Company seriously impeded.

From the first the East India Company found the Portuguese its declared enemies. It was in the attempt to found factories in India that the Company experienced this enmity in its greatest bitterness. Much desperate fighting took place before that attempt met with success; but in 1612, after the overwhelming defeat of the Portuguese in four successive naval engagements, the first English factory in India was established at Surat. This reverse marks the commencement of the decline of Portuguese influence in Asia, as well as the beginning of that rivalry between the English and Dutch which later developed into active hostility. A little before the successful attempt to gain a footing in India, the Company succeeded in obtaining permission to trade in Japan. In 1613 John Saris, the first Englishman to trade in that country, arrived at Firando, a small island north of Nagasaki, with a letter from James I to the retired shogun Iyeyasu.[1] Here again the English met with the opposition of the Portuguese, who had first visited Firando as early as 1545, and had shortly afterwards received permission to trade.[2] The Englishman, Will Adams, through whose good offices the Dutch had two years previously obtained permission to engage in commerce in Japan, rendered to Saris all the assistance in his power. After visiting Yeddo, Saris obtained a grant of substantial privileges from the shogun, who sent a written reply to the letter of King James.[3] This was the commencement of intercourse between England and Japan.

Though the East India Company's earlier efforts in the Far

[1] For further particulars of this expedition, see *Voyage of Captain John Saris to Japan* (Hakluyt Society, 1900).

[2] On the introduction of Christianity into Japan by Francis Xavier the Portuguese looked round for fresh centres of trade, and in 1573, or thereabouts, obtained leave to trade at Nagasaki, which from that date to their final expulsion was the chief seat of their operations in Japan.

[3] A translation of the grant is given by Hildreth, *Japan as it Was and Is*, p. 169. The shogun's letter is given in Appendix I of the same work.

East were directed to establishing a trade with Japan, the desirability of opening up communication with China was kept in mind. A letter dated 1612 from James I to the Emperor of China has recently been discovered,[1] which in all probability was sent out with John Saris to be forwarded to China at a suitable opportunity. That the Company's factors in the East were not unmindful of the advantage of establishing a trade with China is evident from the frequent allusions to this topic in their letters.[2] The following extract is taken from a letter sent by George Bell, Thomas Spurway and John Byndon from Bantam to the Directors of the East India Company in London, dated 19th January, 1617 [3] :—

"Touching his Majesty's (of England) letters to the Emperor of China here we can get none to translate them much less to convey them, and have therefore sent them to Mr. Cocks in Firando if haply he through his friend Captain Dettis can get them done and sent. This Dettis is a Chinaman and the only he upon whose promise Mr. Cocks depends, and as it were makes himself sure of trade in China he having (as he saith) travailed any time these three years in the business at his own cost and charges in the end like to prove nothing but the plot of a nimble brain to serve his own turn, while Mr. Cocks having his imagination levelled beyond the moon, hath the eyes of his understanding so blinded with the expectation of incredible wonders that it is to be feared that he will feel the loss before he will be made to see his error. No Chinese dare translate and send those letters, it being death by the laws of their country, or give passage to any Christian that shall carry them, neither is there any security to send otherwise thither. It was revealed by oracle unto the Emperor that his country should be subdued by a gray-eyed people, and so therefore forbid all Christians his country. If letters be so

[1] The original was discovered by the Historical Manuscripts Commission.

[2] See particularly the *Diary of Richard Cocks*, vol. ii, p. 298 (Hakluyt Society, 1882-3), where it is stated that Cocks received two letters sent by James I to the Emperor of China.

[3] The original of this is in the records of the East India Company preserved in the library of the India Office.

hard to be delivered trade will be more harder to be procured, and consequently not to be expected by any fair course, and the sooner you begin with them in the way of force (I mean taking) the better, and the most reasonable course of dealing with them, and the best way to enable us to keep markets with the Flemings."

As the English trade in the East Indies and Japan became more firmly established, the hostility of the Dutch grew more intense, until it culminated in the massacre of Amboyna.[1] For this barbarity the feeble English Government of those days was unable to obtain reparation. The East India Company, finding its commercial operations unsupported by a sufficiently strong foreign policy, abandoned its more distant factories, and withdrew from Japan. Deprived in this way of a most valuable market, it became still more desirous of entering into commercial relations with China. For some time, however, the whole of the Company's energies were engaged in warding off the attacks of the Portuguese and Dutch; but in 1634 a "truce and free trade to China" was entered into between the Company and the Portuguese viceroy at Goa, and this opportunity was used by merchants in England to examine the possibilities of trade at Canton. In that year Sir William Courteenes obtained the royal licence

[1] Amboyna was a port in the Moluccas (or Spice Islands), where the East India Company had a large factory. In 1623 ten or twelve English factors and traders were massacred by the Dutch, on the charge of having conspired with some thirty Japanese residents to seize the Dutch fortress. At that time there was peace between England and Holland, so that the massacre was absolutely indefensible. Cromwell in 1654 extracted £80,000 from the Dutch Government as compensation for this outrage.

The Dutch East India Company, who were the authors of the massacre, had by this time grown into a powerful body, having a monopoly of the trade between Holland and the East, and the right to exercise sovereign powers in the country where it formed settlements. Its affairs were administered by the Governor-General in Council at Batavia, subject to a Council of XVII in Holland. The ordinances issued from Batavia form the foundation of the Roman-Dutch Law which still obtains in Cape Colony and Ceylon, both of which were originally settled by the Dutch East India Company. (See *Law Quarterly Review*, vol. xxiv, No. 94, p. 164.)

to fit out a commercial expedition to China, and to him is due the credit of initiating our intercourse with that country.

This expedition, commanded by Captain John Weddell,[1] consisted of four ships, the *Dragon*, *Sun*, *Catherine*, and *Planter*, and two pinnaces, the *Anne* and the *Discovery*. It appears to have been organized not by the East India Company, but by one of the rival associations which existed at that time. It was not merely an expedition fitted out to make geographical discoveries, but was particularly constituted with the object of ascertaining what were the possibilities of establishing a trade with China. For this reason Captain Weddell was accompanied in his flag-ship, the *Dragon*, by Nathaniel Mounteney, a "Cape merchant,"[2] and by his brother, John Mounteney, "an accomptant," while on the *Planter* were Peter Mundy and John Fortescue, two merchants specially entrusted with the duty of making commercial investigations at Canton. Peter Mundy entered the chief events in a diary, illustrated by himself as he went along, to which and to a Journal in the nature of a log we turn for particulars of the voyage.[3] That the expedition enjoyed the especial favour of King Charles is shown by a passage in Peter Mundy's diary, where it is recorded that "His Majesty of Great Britain, taking into consideration that this action tended to the future good of the Commonwealth, hath out of his princely favour been pleased to countenance further and protect the same against all opposers who were not a few (and those not of the meanest), giving thereto most large commissions licence to wear the Union Flag: proponly to the Navy Royal; appointing also a rich seal of arms for the employment, viz., a lion passant gardens between three imperial crowns as by the figure thereof

[1] John Weddell had commanded the English fleet that defeated the Portuguese off Surat in 1625. (See Clowes, *History of the Royal Navy*, ii, 41–4; and the life of John Weddell in the *Dictionary of National Biography*.)

[2] i.e., a head merchant, or supercargo. The word appears to have been used in both senses. (See Murray's *Dictionary of the English Language*.)

[3] The first part of the Journal is in the Record Office. The latter part is at the India Office, where there is also a transcript of Peter Mundy's Diary; the original of Peter Mundy's Diary is in the Bodleian Library at Oxford. (Rawlinson MS., A. 315.)

hereto annexed." This expedition set sail from the Downs on the 14th April, 1636. It arrived at Goa on the 8th October of that year, where it was favourably received by the Portuguese viceroy. Leaving Goa on the 17th January, 1637, it proceeded to Malacca, where Peter Mundy came across an Englishwoman, who appears to have been the first subject of the King of England to visit China. Of her he says :—

"Here is also an Englishwoman married to a Portugal Mestizo : of some quality : are well to live and have between them one pretty boy. She came from England some eighteen or nineteen years since ; when Captain Carter (now Commander of the *Catherine*) was master of the *Unicorn* bound for Japan : then she was maid-servant to one Furbisher a carpenter : who with his family was passing thither to remain in the country as chief carpenter. . . . The said ship *Unicorn* in her voyage thither was cast away on the coast of China : and with what they saved from her they bought China vessels : and proceeding on their voyage : were taken by the Portugalls near unto Macao : we then being at difference with them in these parts : her master was afterwards slain."

On the 25th June, 1637, Captain Weddell with his expedition arrived at the mouth of the Canton river, and anchored about three leagues from Macao. Having saluted the place with ordnance, he was shortly afterwards informed that he must proceed no further until he received permission from the "General of the City." John Mounteney, Thomas Robinson and Peter Mundy thereupon took the King's letter to the Captain-General of Macao, and were received with much respect. They were entertained at a feast at the Jesuits' College, where they tasted for the first time the fruit called "Leichea," of which Mundy says, "to speak my mind it is the prettiest and pleasantest fruit that ever I saw or tasted." From all this it seemed as though the Portuguese were disposed in the most friendly way towards the English expedition, but it very soon became manifest that they intended to do their utmost to prevent the new arrivals getting any sort of footing in China.

At this time the Portuguese fleet of six vessels, which traded from Macao to Japan once in every year, was waiting for the arrival of the "caphila," that is, a flotilla of lighters, which brought from Canton the goods that were to form the cargoes of the six vessels. The "caphila" had been detained by the Chinese on the pretext that the Portuguese had built a bigger vessel than was allowed by their licence to trade. Even at this early date the Chinese showed those tendencies to impose on commerce oppressive burdens, such as hampered our own trade in later years. On the 12th of July the "caphila" arrived. It consisted of five long lighter-like vessels which had to be unloaded immediately. The English at once perceived that they could not hope to trade until the Portuguese fleet had sailed for Japan. On the 27th July the General of Macao sent word that "the Chinois would not permit any other nation to traffic with them. No, not even the Spaniards themselves, although the same King's subjects."[1] Peter Mundy very shrewdly suspected that the opposition was due not so much to the Chinese as to the Portuguese, of whom he writes that "our coming would quickly eat them out of all trade."

At the beginning of August it was noticed by the English that the number of Chinese war junks was being gradually increased. On the 6th of that month a Chinese official came aboard and desired them not to proceed further up the river, but to turn aside into a place called Lantao, where they might get provisions; he also informed the English that he would endeavour that they should have admittance of trade, and that ships had been sunk in the river to prevent their further passage. To this the English replied that they "wished them no hurt; but desired their friendship and good will to have merchandize for their money, and then they would depart; and that they only would go a little further up towards the river mouth to secure their ships; and that there they would stay their answer." The warlike preparations continued on the part of the Chinese, till at last matters came to

[1] This was quite untrue. The Spaniards had obtained in 1598 permission to trade from Manilla to a port which they called the Pinal, twelve leagues from the city of Canton. See De Morga, *The Philippine Islands* (Hakluyt Society, 1868), p. 114.

a crisis. Peter Mundy thus states his version of what happened :—

"However it came to pass that whether through the Portugal bribery ; or whether the Chinois observing an ancient custom reported of them in not permitting strangers to traffic in their country I know not ; but they seem also very unwilling of our company : and much discontented at our coming up so near to the river's mouth at Canton. . . . The 9th we sent ashore to the fort and receiving some bad answer to our peaceable demand we fitted ourselves as well for offence as defence, displaying our bloody ensigns on our poopes : taking in the white ; putting on our wasteclothes and the King's colours in our main-top : taking down Saint George, which the Chinois perceiving sent immediately a messenger from the said fort desiring us to have patience for six days more."

In the meantime the Chinese constructed a platform on which they mounted several pieces of ordnance commanding the English ships. On the 12th August a barge, sent by Captain Weddell to take soundings, got near this platform and was fired on by the Chinese three several times. The narrative continues :—

"Then out went again our King's colours, wasteclothes and bloody ensign. And the tide of flood serving, we came up : anchored near unto it and beset it with our four ships. Then from the platform they began to discharge at us also, near a dozen shot before we answered one. By their working we perceived what good gunners they were ; and how well they were fitted : for many of their own shot dropt out of the mouth of the piece close under the wall : others were shot at random haphazard ; quite another way : giving fire to them with wet vents : even as the pieces lay on the round wall : without aiming or traversing them at all. However one shot came and cut a little of the Dragon's main halliards a little above a man's height, the Admiral then walking on the half-deck.

"At length we began to discharge our ordnance on all hands ; first the Admiral, then the rest, with sound of drums and trumpets. Some of our shot so lighted and frighted them that within half an hour there ran out at the gate near a score of them, along the strand, and so got behind a point. We conceiving there were yet some remaining within continued shooting: but hearing no more from them (for I think when they had once discharged those guns of theirs that were laden, they had no mind to charge them again), our boats well manned were sent ashore: but by the time they were gotten half away there came forth out of the fort about a dozen more: but none of any quality that we could perceive. Our people being landed and finding the gates open; entered the fort, took down the China flag: hung it over the wall and thereon advanced our King's colours."

The English captured several Chinese junks, by which they sent letters to Canton stating that their only object was to have friendship and free commerce. In August a petty mandarin arrived to know what was the request of the English, to whom the concise answer was given, "Free trade, a commodious place for our ships, and a house on shore for ourselves to inhabit in." On the 21st August a mandarin arrived bringing "a patent or firman in China writing; pasted on a great board: such as are usually carried before men of office. The effect thereof (as he himself interpreted unto us) was that in regard the Portugal had denied us trade at Macao, and that we had been forced to seek for it hither: and willing to pay the King's duties, they granted us free leave to buy and sell any commodity in their country: appointing us the choice of three several places for ships to ride in."

Another account of this affair is given in the Journal mentioned above as being in the India Office, from which account the well-known passage given below is taken. It should be remembered that the conduct of the Portuguese on this occasion was no exceptional instance of bad faith, but was in accordance with their usual practice of vilifying any nation that attempted to establish a trade at a place where they had already found a commerce. When the Spaniards, in 1598, had attempted to open negotiations with the Chinese for trade at Canton, they had experienced at the hands of the Portuguese exactly the same sort of treatment as was now meted out to the

English. It is useful to compare the account of the Spanish negotiations with that of Captain Weddell's, from which it is abundantly manifest that there was no degree of servility to which the Portuguese would not descend to obtain favour with the Chinese. Indeed, when the Spaniards' request for permission to trade was being heard by the Viceroy of Canton, the Portuguese present were subjected to corporal punishment for interrupting the proceedings.[1]

The narrative is thus continued in the pages of the Journal :—

" The procurador of Maccow soon repaired aboard the principal ship of the English, and said, that for matter of refreshing, he would provide them ; but that there was a main obstacle to their trading, which was the non-consent of the Chinesoos, who, he pretended, held his people in miserable subjection. The English determined, however, to discover the river of Canton ; and fitted out a barge and pinnace with above fifty men, which, after two days, came in sight of the mouth of the river, being a very goodly inlet, and utterly prohibited to the Portugalls by the Chinesoos, who do not willingly admit any strangers to the view of it, being the passage and secure harbour for their best jounckes, both of war and merchandize ; so that the Portugal traffic to Canton was only in small vessels, through divers narrow shoaled straits, amongst many broken islands adjoining to the main. The barge anchoring for a wind and tide to carry them in, a jouncke of those that accustom to fish was descried early in the morning, whom Thomas Robinson followed, (a tedious chase by reason of their many oars) hoping to have found some aboard that might have stood either of a pilot or interpreter ; but finding neither, having used them with all courtesy, dismissed them, contrary to their timorous expectation ; and afterwards for the same causes, and with the same success, spake with another ; but after a delay of several days a small boat made towards the pinnace ; and having sold some refreshing, signs were made to carry some of the English to Canton and bring them to the

[1] See De Morga, *The Philippine Islands* (Hakluyt Society, 1868), p. 114.

speech of the mandarines; which the boatmen accepted of: but the next day, the pinnace being under sail with a fair wind and tide, after having passed by a certain desolate castle, a fleet of about twenty sail of tall jounckes, commanded by the admiral of the sea's deputies, passing down from Canton, encountered the English; and in courteous terms desired them to anchor, which accordingly they did; and presently John Mounteney and Thomas Robinson went aboard the chief mandarine, where were certain Negroes, fugitives of the Portugalls, that interpreted.

"At first the Chinese began somewhat roughly to expostulate what moved them to come thither, and discover the prohibited goods, and concealed parts and passages of so great a prince's dominions? Also, who were their pilots? Thomas Robinson replied that they were come from Europe, to treat of such capitulation as might conduce to the good of both princes and subjects, hoping that it might be lawful for them, as well as for the inhabitants of Maccow, to exercise a free commerce, paying duties as the others; and as for pilots, they had none; but every one was able, by his art, to discover more difficult passages than they had found. The Chinese hereafter began to be more affable, and, in conclusion, appointed a small jouncke to carry up Captain Carter, John Mounteney, and Thomas Robinson, or whom else they pleased to the town, if the English would promise that the pinnace should proceed no further; for though each of these vessels was well furnished with ordnance and treble manned, yet durst they not all to oppose her in any hostile way. The same night Captain Carter, Thomas Robinson and John Mounteney left the pinnace, with order to expect their return; and, being embarked in a small jouncke of thirty tons, proceeded towards Canton, with intent to deliver a petition to the viceroy for obtaining of licence to settle a trade in those parts. The next day they arrived within five leagues of Canton, whither it seems the rumour of their coming, and fear of them, was already arrived; so that they were required in a friendly manner to proceed no further, but to repair aboard their own ships, with promise of assistance in the procuring of licence for trade, if they should seek it at Maccow by the solicitation of some they should find there; and would instantly abandon the river: the which (having satisfied themselves with this discovery, and willing to remove the anxiety which their long absence might breed in the rest of the fleet) they readily performed. In a little time the Portugalls' fleet of six small vessels set sail for Japan; upon whose departure it was expected that licence of trade would have been permitted, according as they still had borne in hand the English; but being then freed of their conceived fear lest Captain Weddell and his men should have surprised their vessels, they instantly flouted the simple credulity (the inseparable badge of folly) of the nation; and at last, having assembled a council of purpose, sent the English a flat denial."

"The same day, at a consultation called aboard the admiral to that purpose, Captain Carter, John Mounteney and Thomas Robinson delivered to the whole council, together with a draught of the river, the sum of their attempts, success and hopes; which being well pondered, it was generally consented that the whole fleet should sail for the river of Canton. They arrived in a few days before the forementioned desolate castle, and being now furnished with some slender interpreters, they soon had speech with divers mandarines in the king's jounckes, to whom the cause of their arrival was declared, viz., to entertain peace and amity with them, to traffic freely as the Portugalls did, and to be forthwith supplied for their monies with provisions for their ships; all which those mandarines promised to solicit with the prime men resident at Canton; and in the meantime desire an expectation of six days, which were granted; and the English ships rode with white ensigns on the poop; but their perfidious friends, the Portugalls, had in all that time, since the return of the pinnace, so beslandered them to the Chinese, reporting them to be rogues, thieves, beggars, and what not, that they became very jealous of the good meaning of the English; insomuch, that in the night time they put forty-six of iron cast ordnance into the fort lying close to the brink of the river; each piece being between six and seven hundred weight, and well proportioned;

and after the end of four days, having, as they thought, sufficiently fortified themselves, they discharged divers shot, though without hurt, upon one of the barges passing by them, to find out a convenient watering place. Herewith the whole fleet, being instantly incensed, did, on the sudden, display their bloody ensigns; and weighing their anchors fell up with the flood, and berthed themselves before the castle, from whence came many shot; yet not any that touched so much as hull or rope. Whereupon, not being able to endure their bravadoes any longer, each ship began to play furiously upon them with their broadsides; and after two or three hours, perceiving their cowardly fainting, the boats were landed with about one hundred men; which sight occasioned them, with great distractions, instantly to abandon the castle and fly; the boats' crews, in the meantime entering the same, and displaying his Majesty's colours of Great Britain upon the walls, having, the same night, put aboard all their ordnance, fired the council house and demolished what they could. The boats of the fleet, also, seized a jouncke laden with boards and timber, and another with salt. Another vessel of small moment was surprised, by whose boat a letter was sent to the chief mandarines at Canton, expostulating their breach of truce, excusing the assailing of the castle, and withal, in fair terms, requiring the liberty of trade. This letter, it seems, was delivered; for the next day, a mandarine of no great note, sometime a Portugal Christian, called Paulo Noretty, came towards the ships in a small boat with a white flag, to whom the English, having laid open the injuries received, and the sincerer intent they had to establish a fair trade and commerce, and were no way willing (but in their own defence) to oppose the China nation, presented certain gifts, and dismissed him to his masters, who were some of the chief mandarines, riding about a point of land not far from the ships, who being by him duly informed thereof, returned him again the same night, with a small jouncke and full authority to carry up such persons as should be appointed to Canton, there to tender a petition, and to conclude further upon the manner of their future proceedings."

The striking passage just cited from the Journal[1] is a *locus classicus* on the subject of our trade with China. The conduct of the Chinese as there described is characteristic, and the account gives as perfect an impression of the Chinese of to-day as it is meant to give of those who, nearly three hundred years ago, put off Captain Weddell with fair words and promises intended to be broken as soon as the cause of fear which inspired them had been removed. It is a curious trait of the Chinese mind, and one that appears not to have been affected by the long experience of Europeans which they have now had, that it is absolutely devoid of foresight. The Chinese have no faculty of looking ahead and counting the ultimate cost of any course of action that may present itself as expedient for the time being. As soon as they had quieted Captain Weddell, and were assured that, owing to the departure of the Portuguese fleet for Japan, there was nothing to be feared from any other quarter, the officials of those days showed as changed a demeanour as we are accustomed to experience in like circumstances from their descendants at the present day.

[1] Staunton gives it at p. 5 of the account of Macartney's Embassy as being taken from a manuscript which he does not identify. Succeeding writers have copied it, apparently without investigating its origin.

CHAPTER II

EARLY EFFORTS OF THE EAST INDIA COMPANY

FROM the time of Captain Weddell's visit to Canton the best part of a century was to elapse before the English established a regular trade at that port. The reasons for this delay are not far to seek. The East India Company were prevented by more than one potent cause from prosecuting their enterprises in fresh regions with that vigour which one would expect from the possessors of a monopoly such as theirs. To begin with, they had to face the enmity and rivalry of very powerful persons in England, who were not seldom successful in extracting from the Crown a grant purporting to give the right to make a voyage or voyages to countries over which the East India Company's monopoly in theory extended. To such a grant Courteene's Association,[1] which sent out Captain Weddell, owed its existence. Private merchants, too, did not scruple to fit out ships to trade with the East, without leave or licence of any kind. These adventitious traders, commonly referred to in the records of the Company as "interlopers," did not hesitate to make use of the opportunities thus obtained without regard to the permanent commerce that others might wish to establish. In this way it more than once happened that at some port where the Company had been steadily working with the object of obtaining a permanent trade, some interloping ship would arrive and, content to make an immediate profit on that one venture, trade on such terms as completely spoilt the market for the Company, who had been obliged to incur a large capital expenditure in obtaining permission to trade at all. Another source of difficulty was the insecurity of the tenure on which the Company held its trading privileges. Not only did experience show that their monopoly existed merely in name, but even the validity of the grant, by which that monopoly had been conferred, was

[1] Courteene's Association was amalgamated with the Company in 1649.

called in question,[1] and this happened not once nor twice. Cromwell was one of those who expressed doubts as to whether the Company had in law a monopoly, and the Company only maintained its privileges by obtaining from him a fresh grant. His financial necessities, too, were a source of weakness to the Company, and when he obtained from the Dutch £85,000 as compensation for the massacre at Amboyna, he insisted on being allowed to borrow £50,000 of that sum. At the Restoration a fresh charter was obtained from Charles II, and the Company fondly supposed its difficulties were at an end; but when the *Quo Warranto* proceedings were instituted against the Corporation of the City of London, it was perceived that no charter could be regarded as safe from the hands of the King. In 1689 a further confirmation of the Company's privileges was obtained from James II, and in 1693 yet another charter was granted by William and Mary. On this last occasion, however, the House of Commons intervened by passing a resolution declaring that the trade to the East was free. Nothing could have shown more clearly that the Company's presumed monopoly rested on a very unsubstantial foundation. To meet this fresh attack, the Company offered to lend £700,000 to the public treasury at 4 per cent. interest, if Parliament would confirm the exclusive privileges granted by the Company's charters; but they were at once outbidden by a rival company, which offered a loan of £2,000,000, at 8 per cent. interest, on the condition that a grant was made to them of the sole right to trade to India, with a proviso that they should not be obliged to trade as a joint stock concern.[2] Thus there were from this time in existence two rival Companies,[3] each doing its utmost to thwart the enterprise of the other, and it was not until 1702, when through Godolphin's exertions the two were amalgamated, that the East India Company can be said to have enjoyed a monopoly of trade to the East.

[1] See *Skinner's Case* (1666), 6 State Trials, 710; *East India Co.* v. *Sandys* (1683) 10 State Trials, 373.

[2] Introduction to the *Index of the Factory Records of the East India Company*, p. vii (India Office).

[3] The official title of this second company was "The English Company trading to the East Indies."

Another source of difficulty, which was encountered more especially in opening up a trade with China, was the hostility of the Portuguese and Dutch. The former, after they ceased to be under the dominion of the King of Spain, became less demonstrative in their opposition to English enterprise, though not less assiduous in seeking to counteract any favourable impression that English merchants might make at ports where the Portuguese were already established. Misrepresentation and calumny were the least of the weapons employed by them for this purpose. As to the Dutch, the constant wars between England and Holland frequently gave them a legitimate excuse for seeking to crush their rivals ; but over and above this we find, on examining the records of the East India Company, that acts of hostility were indulged in by the Dutch traders towards Englishmen without any regard to whether it was a state of peace or war that existed between the two countries in Europe. Indeed, as we read the accounts of our early experiences as a trading nation, we are forced to confess that it is not through the friendliness of foreign competitors that we have gained our pre-eminence in commerce. The attempts made at the present day to destroy the trade of England, strenuous though they be when judged by an economic standard, fade into comparative insignificance beside the physical efforts to the same end that were put forth in the sixteenth and seventeenth centuries.

Another influence adverse to the success of the Company was civil war. In England, the struggle between the King and the Parliament, which began some six years after Captain Weddell set out for Canton, of necessity enfeebled all commercial organizations, the lack of money alone making it impossible to launch out into new enterprises. But not only in England did civil war paralyze the Company's efforts ; in China the same scourge produced chaos throughout the whole of the Eighteen Provinces. It was a misfortune for England that, at the time when Captain Weddell arrived in China, the struggle between the Chinese and the Manchu Tartars had already begun.[1] Until that struggle should be determined, it

[1] In 1618, a Manchu chieftain, by name Tien-ming, published a

was in the nature of things improbable that such a radical change could be brought about in the policy of China as must be involved in granting the liberty of trade to Englishmen. Indirectly, as we shall see, these civil dissensions in China were the cause of the Company being able to found a trade at Taiwan and at Amoy, but this was no compensation for the failure to gain a footing at Canton. The scene of the Company's earliest efforts to conduct a trade with the Chinese was in Formosa, an island which, though lying close to the mainland of China, had never been under the dominion of

manifesto, in which he announced before Heaven seven things which, as he said, he intended to avenge against the House of Ming, which then held sway over the Chinese Empire. He assumed the title of "Emperor," and "vowed to celebrate the funeral of his father with the slaughter of 200,000 Chinese." In his endeavours to accomplish this purpose, he laid waste and ravaged the whole of north-eastern China, but died in 1627 before his object was attained. His son, by name Tien-tsung, carried on the struggle in his stead, and being assisted through the internecine strife that was waged between the many Chinese claimants to the Throne, gradually established his power in the North. Hwai-tsung, the last of the Ming Emperors, despairing of success when he heard that Peking had been captured by a rebel leader, Li Tsze-ching, stabbed his daughter and hanged himself, lest a worse fate should befal. Thus the Ming dynasty came to an end in 1643. The Chinese general, Wu San-kwei, refused to acknowledge the claim to the title of Emperor which Li Tsze-ching now put forward, and making peace with the Manchus, invited Tien-tsung to assist him in driving Li from the capital. The united Chinese and Manchu forces, being thus joined in the same enterprise, speedily recaptured Peking, which by this time had been reduced to a heap of ruins. Whilst the Chinese forces went in pursuit of Li, Tien-tsung, who had changed his name to Tsung-teh, remained at Peking, and being in possession of the capital, announced that he intended to assume the control of the Empire. At this juncture, however, he died, and his son, Shun-chi, who was then six years old, was at once proclaimed Emperor by the Manchus. Thus the Ta-tsing dynasty, which still rules China, was established at Peking. Wu San-kwei was forced to assist the invaders against his countrymen; all of whom were ordered to shave the head to the poll, and to wear the hair in a cue in token of submission to the new dynasty. In this way originated the fashion of wearing the hair as it is worn to-day in China, and it is curious to observe that what was once the badge of servitude has now become the most cherished distinction known to the Chinese. The civil war did not end with the proclamation of Shun-chi as Emperor, but for another half a century China was a prey to the most frightful carnage and rapine consequent on the attempts of the Manchus to subdue the whole country. (See further *Chinese Repository*, vol. iii, pp. 521-525.)

the Emperor. Since the year 1530 it had been ruled by a Chinese pirate, who had fled from the Emperor's wrath. From the time of his arrival many Chinese must have crossed from the mainland and settled in the island, but it continued to be an independent state.[1] In 1622 the Dutch, having failed in an attack on the Portuguese at Macao, sailed to the Panghoo Islands, at the mouth of the Formosa Channel, and captured them from the Chinese, in revenge, as they said, for the Chinese having assisted in the defence of Macao. From these islands they organized an expedition against the coast of China, which met with such success that in 1624 the Emperor, pretending to have jurisdiction over Formosa, promised them liberty of trade and permission to settle there, if they would evacuate their newly acquired possession. Accepting this promise, the Dutch crossed to Formosa, and meeting with no resistance from the natives, or from the small Japanese colony which retired before them, they took possession of a harbour on the south-western portion, called Ta-keang or Tai-wan, and there built a fort, which they named Fort Zealandia. Operating from this as a base they expelled the Spaniards from a fortified position at Kelung in 1626, and shortly afterwards made themselves masters of the whole island.

During the civil wars, consequent on the attempt of the Manchus to seize the Throne, large numbers of Chinese sought the protection of the Dutch, and as many as 25,000 Chinese families are said to have settled in Formosa alone. Among the Chinese who refused to submit to the Manchus was a half-patriotic, half-piratical, naval chief, named Ching-ching-kung, better known to Europeans by his Portuguese name of Koxinga, or Koshinga. His father, from being a petty trader at Macao, had grown, by means of the trade with Europeans at that port, to be the richest merchant in China, and with the riches thus acquired had equipped a small fleet against the Tartar invaders. This fleet he handed over to his son in order that he himself might accept an invitation from the new Emperor to visit Peking. On his arrival at the capital he was thrown

[1] *Chinese Repository*, vol. ii, pp. 403-420.

into prison, where he spent the remainder of his life. Koxinga, not more favourably disposed towards the new dynasty by this turn of events, continued the struggle against the invaders. In time he came to have under his command a fleet of 1,000 ships, with which he made many successful descents on the coast. Finding, however, that his efforts to gain a footing in the maritime provinces were unavailing, he cast his eyes towards Formosa. For the time being he took no active measures for the conquest of that island, but contented himself with carrying on a secret correspondence with the Chinese residents. The Dutch, foreseeing danger, strengthened their garrison at Fort Zealandia in anticipation of future hostilities.

Meanwhile the East India Company had not lost sight of the desirability of opening up a trade with China, and they instructed their factors at Surat to report on the chances of commerce becoming possible. The factors, in reply, thus wrote in 1648 :—

" The experiment you desire we should make with one of our small vessels for trade into China, we are certainly informed by those that know the present state and condition of that country very well, cannot be undertaken without the inevitable loss both of Ship, Men and Goods ; for as the Tartars overrun and waste all the inland country without settling any Government in the places which they overcome ; so some of their Great Men in China with a mighty fleet at sea of upwards 1,000 sail of great ships (as is confidently reported) rob and spoil all the sea coasts, and whatsoever vessels they can meet with ; and how one of our feeble vessels should be able to defend themselves against such forces is easy to suppose. As for the Portugalls in Macao, they are little better than mere rebels against their Viceroy in Goa, having lately murdered their Captain-General sent thither to them ; and at Macao itself so distracted among themselves that they are daily spilling one another's blood. But put the case, all these things were otherwise, we must needs say we are in a very poor condition to seek out new discoveries ; while you will not allow us either Factors, Shipping, or Sailors, scarce half sufficient to maintain the Trade already you have on foot ; and therefore the Dutch but laugh at us, to see us meddle with new undertakings, being hardly able to support the old."[1]

This is not the only reference in the contemporaneous records of the East India Company to the question of establishing a trade with China. Similar passages occur in several letters from the factors to the Court of Directors in London. In a letter dated in 1654, it was suggested that a factory might be established in Cambodia, as a place from which there would be small difficulty in getting a trade to China, and this suggestion was carried out.[2] In 1654 the Company's opportunities of trading at Macao, and so at Canton, were improved by the treaty negotiated between Cromwell and John IV of Portugal, which provided that the subjects of both countries should have free access to any of the ports of the East Indies, and in 1657 its general position was strengthened by Cromwell's confirmation of the charter.

The ratification of Cromwell's confirmation of the charter which took place in 1661 on the restoration of Charles II, encouraged the Company to extend the scope of its activity abroad. Just at this time Koxinga, who had suffered a severe defeat at Nanking, determined to make a descent on Formosa, and in his stronghold at Amoy he prepared a formidable expedition for this purpose. In 1661 he appeared before Fort Zealandia with 25,000 of his best troops, and the Dutch, whose garrison had been increased to 1,500, were forced to engage in hostilities. After sustaining a siege of nine months Zealandia capitulated in the face of overwhelming odds, and the Dutch retired to Java, leaving Koxinga in undisputed possession.[3]

Koxinga constituted himself king, and fixed his palace and court at Zealandia, distributing garrisons through all the western portions of the island. He introduced Chinese laws and customs, and the Chinese system of government, and generally did everything that lay in his power to establish

[1] *East India Company's Factory Records.* (MSS. in the India Office under *China Materials*, vol. i, p. 63.)

[2] *Ibid.*, pp. 63–67.

[3] *Chinese Repository*, vol. ii, p. 415.

peace and security in his newly acquired dominions. He even meditated foreign enterprises, and was actually preparing an expedition against the Spaniards at Manilla, when he died two years after his success over the Dutch. He was succeeded in the government of Formosa by his son, referred to below as King of Taiwan, the title by which he is designated in the records of the Company.

This young king, seeing the advantages to be gained from intercourse with Europeans, gave a general invitation to merchants of all nationalities to come and trade in his dominions, promising them a friendly reception. The Company's factors at Bantam, who had lately received more letters from the Court of Directors urging them to fresh efforts to open up a trade with China, seeing that little could be hoped for in that country whilst the civil wars continued, determined in 1670 to accept this invitation, and accordingly sent the *Bantam* pink and a sloop under Ellis Crisp to Taiwan, to ascertain the nature of the advantages to be obtained at that port. Crisp was careful on his arrival to inform the King of Taiwan that the English were quite a distinct nation from the Dutch. In response to his request for a residence and trading privileges a written agreement was entered into between the King and the Company, by which it was declared that the latter might sell or truck their goods with whom they pleased. The terms of this agreement, which are set out in full in the Company's records,[1] were very liberal, and included a lease to the Company of the old Dutch staat house " with a Godown which is to be built more to it." When this agreement was submitted to the Court of Directors, they disapproved certain of its provisions, by which every ship belonging to the Company, which should come to Taiwan, was bound to bring a specified quantity of arms and ammunition and some other kinds of goods, which were to be sold to the King at specified prices. In writing to the King to express their approval of the other terms of the agreement, the Court stated that the treaty the King of England had made with his allies prevented the

[1] *East India Company's Factory Records.* (MSS. at the India Office under *China Materials*, vol. i, pp. 76–82.)

Company from carrying out the stipulations as to the supply of arms. They also asked for the rescission of the degrading conditions by which the Company's ships had to yield up their guns on coming into port.

The opportunity thus offered of trading at Taiwan was eagerly welcomed by the Court of Directors, not so much on account of the advantages that might accrue from a trade with Formosa, as because they hoped to form there a base from which to carry on a trade with China, and to renew the commercial intercourse with Japan. The Directors determined to fit out a ship from London itself, and in 1673 the *Experiment* was despatched to Taiwan with instructions to proceed thence to Nagasaki and to endeavour to re-open trade at the latter port. When they reached Formosa the supercargoes of this vessel found that the privileges actually enjoyed under the King of that island were very much smaller than the terms of the grant and the letters of the Company's factors at Bantam had led the Directors to suppose. Immediately on their arrival at Taiwan difficulties arose with the King, who was jealous of any infringement of his own monopoly of the trade between Japan and Formosa. He appropriated the sugar and hides brought by the *Experiment*, which were the principal portions of the cargo intended for Nagasaki, sold them himself in Japan, and used the proceeds to discharge the arrears of pay due to his army. In this position of affairs the factors decided to ship the remainder of the *Experiment's* cargo on a smaller vessel, the *Return*, which had arrived from Bantam, and to send the *Experiment* back to London. This they accordingly did, but no sooner had the *Experiment* left Taiwan than she was captured by the Dutch. The *Return* proceeded to Nagasaki as arranged, but finding it impossible to trade there sailed for Macao. On her arrival at the latter port the Portuguese did all in their power to prevent the English getting any trade, and so churlish were they in their behaviour that they even refused permission for the English ship to take shelter under the guns of the fort, if she should be attacked by the Dutch. As a last resource the factors sailed to Lampaco, "the only free place of free trade amongst these islands," where they managed to sell some of their cargo.[1]

By this time the Manchus had subdued the whole of China. The provinces of Fukien and Kwang-tung, which had been reduced in 1650, had been allowed to preserve their old status as kingdoms. This concession had not the effect, however, of securing their allegiance to the new dynasty, and in 1674 they revolted against the Emperor Kanghi, who in 1662 had succeeded Shunchi. Thereupon the King of Taiwan made overtures to the Kings of Fukien and Kwang-tung, with the object of forming an alliance with them against the Manchu dynasty, but he was met with the response that they could not recognize in him a sovereign prince. Angered at this slight, the King of Taiwan turned his arms against the King of Fukien, who, being defeated by him in several battles, was obliged to submit again to the Emperor and to receive the tonsure.[2] The provinces of Fu-kien and Kwang-tung were at once subdued, and were placed under the jurisdiction of Viceroys appointed by the Emperor. At this juncture the King of Taiwan took possession of Amoy, and with a view to gaining adherents and strengthening himself with European aid, he issued a proclamation inviting Chinese and foreign merchants to trade thither, promising them exemption from customs and other duties for a period of three years. In this way he attracted crowds of Chinese to Amoy, from whom he was able to enlist recruits ; but no sooner had he strengthened his army in this way, than he revoked the proffered exemption and insisted on customs being paid on all goods brought by traders into the port.

Just at this time the East India Company's factors at Bantam had despatched the *Flying Eagle* to Taiwan to improve the opportunity of trade there offered. On their arrival, however, the factors found the King ready to use almost any means to supplement his own resources with those of the Company. He

[1] *East India Company's Factory Records.* (MSS. in the India Office under *China Materials*, vol. i, pp. 144–148.)

[2] *Chinese Repository*, vol. ii, p. 415.

compelled the supercargoes to supply him with a gunner for the purpose of instructing his men in the use of their big guns, and endeavoured unsuccessfully to obtain from them other kinds of assistance. Hoping to cajole them into acting as his allies, he offered them special permission to trade at Amoy; but fearing that he would seize both men and ship if they went thither, the supercargoes declined the offer. They obtained, however, two chops, or official permits, granting them liberty of trade at Amoy, which they sent on to Bantam with a message that they could get a similar chop for Hockchew (Foo-chow) where the Dutch had been trading for some considerable time. These chops were forwarded to London, and in 1676 the Directors wrote to the factors at Bantam that they should make use of this opportunity of opening a trade with the mainland. In 1677 the Directors again wrote in a similar strain, and in this letter they asked that the trade in tea should be encouraged. This letter may be regarded as making the beginning of the great trade in tea, which later became of such vast importance.

The factors had in the meantime composed their differences with the King of Taiwan, and a new agreement had been drawn up, by which they were authorized to carry on a regular trade, though not on such advantageous terms as were conferred by the first agreement, and the old Dutch staat house was granted to them as a factory. But the budding hopes of a general trade with the mainland of China, hopes which had been fostered by the many successes that the King of Taiwan had obtained over the Tartar troops on the mainland, were destined to be blighted. Early in 1677 the King met with such reverses that he was compelled to abandon all his conquests in China except the island of Amoy, a misfortune to which the factors thus adverted in a letter written in November of that year:—

"By this sudden mutation of Govt. ye hopes we had of ys. trade is much abased, & if may calculate from ys. years of experience, doe see, if affaires continue in ye posture, but little probabilitie of vending any quantitys of Merchandize proper for China, for all passages with ye islands are so narrowly watched, yt. no grosse goods can be imported or exported."[1]

From this time the conditions under which trade was in fact carried on, both at Taiwan and at Amoy, steadily grew worse. In 1679 the King granted a monopoly of the trade at the latter port to one Sinkoe, who in the King's name seized the principal part of the Company's goods. For this wrong the factors at Taiwan endeavoured to obtain redress, but in vain. Finding that their efforts to secure fair treatment were of no avail, they were forced to the conclusion that it was useless to persevere with the project of establishing a permanent trade. The Court of Directors adopted the same view, and by letter dated February, 1681, ordered the factory to be finally withdrawn from the King of Taiwan's dominions. To the King himself they sent a letter giving as their reasons for this step, that they had continued to trade for some years at a loss in the hope of making a market, but without any prospect of success having showed itself; that they could obtain no satisfaction for debts due from the King himself; and that their factory at Amoy had been betrayed by Sinkoe and plundered by the King's own soldiers.

During the years 1678 and 1679 the King of Taiwan had captured a town or two on the mainland, and so had regained some of the ground he had lost. But his success was not long lived. In 1683 he lost in two pitched battles with the Manchus and was compelled to withdraw all his forces to Formosa. The Manchus were not slow to follow him up. In June of that year a fleet of 400 Imperial junks was sighted off the island. A "stiff engagement" ensued in which the Chinese were victorious, but with the loss of 1,000 men. The Manchus retired with the loss of several junks burnt and sunk, but receiving a reinforcement of 200 sail early in July, they again attacked Taiwan. The Chinese, being "borne down by the irresistible multitude of the enemy," were obliged to beg for quarter, which was granted. The King's troops in the other parts of the island, on the receipt of the news of the

[1] *East India Company's Factory Records.* (MSS. in the India Office under *China Materials*, vol. ii, pp. 204–5.)

defeat at Taiwan, " cut ye haire a la mode the Tartar," and refused to fight for a master who could not pay them. The Tartar general, Sego, thereupon sent ambassadors to propose the surrender of the whole of Formosa, and " swore by his wooden god that if they lay down their arms he would not touch a sole of them."

The terms thus offered were accepted without the royal sanction by those of the King's ministers who were opposed to war, whereupon Sego sent word that the rebels were to " shave all the hairs off, save enough to make a monkey's tail pendent from the very noddle of their heads." The majority of the people at once complied with this order, and the King was constrained to follow suit.[1] In this way Formosa became a part of the Chinese Empire under the dominion of the Manchus, and so it remained until it was ceded to Japan in 1895.

Hoping that the conditions of trade in Formosa might be improved under the new government, the factors of the East India Company began to reconsider their resolve to withdraw from Taiwan and Amoy, and to make advances towards Sego with a view to continuing the factory. The encouragement they received from this official was of the smallest. He roundly charged them with having supplied arms and ammunition to " this nest of thieves," and generally with having aided Koxinga and his son to make war against the Emperor. He demanded from them a list of all articles then in the factory at Taiwan. and threatened the severest punishment against all the Company's servants for the offences with which they were charged. In this predicament the factors cast about for some other method of negotiating with the enraged general, and it was not long before they discovered that a Manchu official was not less amenable to bribery than a Chinese. To appease the wrath of Sego they made him a present of 3,090 taels, which they supplemented with a further present of 200 taels to his servant, the latter precaution being one that is still observed

[1] *East India Company's Factory Records.* (MSS. in the India Office under *China Materials*, vol. ii, p. 293.) For an account of Formosa at the present time, see *Proceedings of the Japan Society*, vol. vi, p. 30.

towards Sego's countrymen at the present day by all who hope to obtain any advantage with officials in China. But then, as now, the Emperor's servants proved insatiable, for as the factors wrote home to the Directors, "5 or 600 taels were in his eyes like the phil of a farthing." It soon became apparent that trade could not be carried on at a profit under such a *regime*, and the factors reluctantly withdrew from Formosa. This course was approved by the Directors, who, in 1686, wrote, "Taiwan is good for nothing now, and we will not have you settle any factor there again."[1]

During all the years that the Company had been making efforts to build up a trade in Formosa, the Court of Directors had not lost sight of the desirability of getting a footing at Canton. To understand what had been done in this direction it is necessary to go back some quarter of a century. In 1658 the *Surat* frigate was sent from Batavia to Macao, but when her supercargoes attempted to get permission to trade, difficulties arose owing to the fact that some two years before two English ships, the *King Ferdinand* and the *Richard & Martha,* which must have been sent thither by some interloper, had left the port without paying the measurement duty. This measurement duty was a charge imposed by the Imperial authorities on all ships that traded in Cantonese waters. It stood in place of the customs on goods with which we are more familiar, and so was regarded by the Chinese as of the utmost importance. Its amount was determined in accordance with the length, breadth, and depth of the ship measured, which dimensions had to be ascertained by Chinese officers before the vessel could begin to trade. This duty was destined to be an ever recurring source of trouble between the English merchants and the Chinese officials until 1843, when it was abolished by the treaty of Nanking, and a system of tonnage dues substituted in its place.[2]

The civil wars had produced commercial stagnation at Canton, as at other ports. In February, 1664, the factors

[1] *East India Company's Factory Records.* (MSS. in the India Office under *China Materials*, vol. iv., p. 457.)

[2] See *post*, p. 526.

wrote home that owing to the troubles in China, there had been no trade at Macao for two years, "also yt. ye Tartars were soe base that any ship that did come under command of the Towne forts was not permitted to go out again, but must lie rotting within; as is to be seen by sad experience, 15 of their own (Portuguese) good ships and 4 of the King of Spain lying by the walles and dare not budge forth upon great penalties." The factors went on in this letter to describe the difficulties encountered by the *Surat* in attempting to trade. First of all the Portuguese attempted to levy a duty of 6 per cent. on her whole cargo, pretending that the Tartars demanded a tax of that amount from the city on all ships that entered Macao, because of the bad conduct of the *King Ferdinand* and the *Richard & Martha*. This imposition the supercargoes refused to pay, on the ground that the last-named ships did not belong to the Company, and so their evil deeds could not legitimately be visited on the Company's ships. The Portuguese thereupon used all their influence with the Chinese to prevent the English getting a trade. The trouble about the measurement duty was renewed, and the supercargoes, who had taken a house on shore, over which the Chinese now placed a military guard, were forced to deposit with the Chinese officials 2,926½ rials of pepper and lead as security for the payment of this impost. Having thus gained permission to trade, the factors found it impossible to use the privilege, as the Portuguese refused to let the English have a house in Macao to use as a factory. The *Surat* was obliged to return to Bantam, having accomplished nothing. The factors in their letter remark: "Under ye Tartar's govte. little security of persons; any trade or dispatch there, nor is there any certainty of trade in any part of China under ye Tartar; who is an enemy to trade and hath depopulated all ye vast quantityes of islands on ye Coaste of all maritime parts of Chyna 8 Leagues from ye Sea merely not to have a trade with any."[1]

The peace patched up between the English and the Dutch

[1] *East India Company's Factory Records.* (MSS. in the India Office under *China Materials*, vol. i, p. 75.) Auber's *China*, p. 137.

in 1667, after Van Tromp's famous exploits in the Thames, did little to help the East India Company in the prosecution of its enterprises. The Portuguese, emboldened to take still stronger measures to prevent the English trading at Canton, petitioned their sovereign and also the Viceroy of Goa against giving to any strangers leave to come to Macao. Thus the English found that the only means of getting a trade at Canton was to get special permission from the King of Portugal to go to Macao. The English Government under Charles II, was so weak that no help could be hoped for from diplomacy, and when our ambassador at Lisbon had asked that our merchantmen might have good treatment, if they were forced to touch at Goa or Macao, the utmost had been accomplished of which England under the Stuarts was capable.

In this state of things the East India Company had to rest content for some years, at least as far as China was concerned, with the precarious opportunities of trade at Taiwan and Amoy already described. In other directions they managed to extend their activity, and opened up a trade with Tonquin and with Siam. Attention was still, however, given by the Directors in London to a trade with China ; in 1681 they decided to change the method of carrying on that trade, by conducting it in freighted ships, as the expense of the country trade was so great ; in the following year they transferred the superintendence of the China trade from Bantam to Surat. Twenty-one days before the letter was received, by which this change was ordered, the Dutch wantonly attacked Bantam, and having captured the town expelled the occupants of the English factory, who were obliged to retire to Batavia, and finally to Surat. As England was then at peace with Holland this catastrophe was altogether unforeseen. Shortly after this the Company sustained a further detriment by the loss of the *Johanna*, outward bound with £70,000 in bullion. These misfortunes, combined with a total failure of credit in the City of London consequent on the *Quo Warranto* proceedings against the Corporation, frustrated for the time being all attempts to found a trade at Canton. It was not until 1683 that any further efforts were made in this direction.

In that year the Court of Directors resolved to send out a ship from London, and accordingly despatched the *Carolina* to Macao. On her arrival, the Portuguese authorities proved as recalcitrant as ever, and refused to allow her to trade without an order from the Viceroy of Goa. They further claimed to have purchased from the Emperor, who now held China in entire subjugation, the sole liberty of trading at Canton. The supercargoes found the Chinese impoverished by the exactions of the Tartar officials, who had taken over the collection of all duties, to such a degree that trade had been killed. The outlook being hopeless, the *Carolina* sailed for Lantao, and thence to Lampaco, but failed to do any trade. Two months later the Directors sent out the *Delight* to Amoy, to attempt to re-open a commerce there. Her supercargoes spent large sums of money in bribes and were compelled to give up their arms and ammunition as a present, but never succeeded in doing any real trade.[1]

In 1684 the affairs of the Company in the Far East took a turn for the better. Bantam had been restored by the treaty concluded between England and Holland in 1674, and the Directors resolved to make another attempt to re-open the trade at Amoy by sending out the *China Merchant*. On her arrival at her destination, the supercargoes found that the Company's old factory had been turned into a custom-house, that the whole trade had been put under the control of a customs' official, whom they called the Hoppo, and that all ships were compelled to send their sails ashore before being allowed to trade. The *China Merchant*, while at Amoy, was joined by another of the Company's ships, the *Loyal Adventure*, which had been despatched by the factors at Madras, to which Presidency the China trade had by this time been transferred. Considerable trouble was experienced by both ships owing to the Chinese interpreters, or *linguists*, as they were wont to be called, insisting on having a share of the profits of the trade. Ultimately it was agreed that the charge for *linguists* should be one per cent. on the transactions carried through

[1] *East India Company's Factory Records.* (MSS. in the India Office under *China Materials*, vol. iii, pp. 307–336.)

for the ship on whose behalf they acted. This is the first recorded instance of the charge for *linguists*, which afterwards became a fruitful source of trouble at Canton. Trading operations were further hindered by the demands of the Hoppo, who insisted on customs being paid on all goods either carried out of or brought into port. Nevertheless, the supercargoes managed to do considerable trade, and to leave with their vessel, to use their own expression, "chock full."[1]

From this time till the year 1757, when all trade between the Chinese and Foreigners, except the Russians, was confined by Imperial decree to Canton, the Company continued to keep up a regular trade with Amoy. In 1687, three ships, the *Loyal Merchant*, the *Cæsar*, and the *Moulsford*, left the port with full cargoes. Moreover, in that year the *New London* and *Worcester* from Bombay, and the *George* and *Moulsford* from Madras, were all at Amoy together. These four vessels found the revenue regulations more strictly defined than had hitherto been the case, and that the measurement duty had been introduced at Amoy in place of the customs which had caused so much trouble to the *China Merchant* and *Loyal Adventure*. The factors, who knew of the difficulty that had been experienced at Canton with regard to measurement duty, tried to discover the rate of duty before the ships were measured, in order to ascertain the expenses that must be cleared before they could make a profit on their goods. But to their inquiries no definite answer could be obtained, the only reply being that the duty would not be greater than that paid by the Dutch at Canton and Foochow. After some days the Hoppo, who at first demanded delivery up of the guns and ammunition, but later waived the demand, announced that the measurement duty would be 1,073 taels for the *New London*, and 1,250 taels for the *Worcester*, with an additional 18 per cent. as percentage for the officers who made the measurements. These exorbitant demands the supercargoes refused to pay, with the result that after much haggling the total charges were agreed for the two vessels respectively at 1,073 taels

[1] *East India Company's Factory Records.* (MSS. in the India Office under *China Materials*, vol. iii, pp. 355–378.)

and 572 taels. When these difficulties had been surmounted, a good trade was done, there being plenty of cargo available owing to the Chinese merchants having lost their trade with Manila and Japan.[1]

In connection with the visit of these two vessels to Amoy, we have the first instance of the exercise of exterritorial jurisdiction in China.[2] One of the English sailors when drunk broke into the custom house at night, " where concerns of the Emperor lay," an offence that would have been punishable with death in a Chinese. The factors, alarmed at what might result, at once repaired to the " Cung-po," and offered to make reparation. This official " was kind and civill, & all he desired was a due punishment might be given to him [the offender] by ourselves, accordingly as [in our opinion] the crime meritted ; which was inflicted in Publick view ashoare by 100 Stripes with a catte of nine tailes and Pickle, to their satisfaction."[3] On this occasion the Chinese voluntarily waived the right to inflict punishment on an Englishman found guilty of committing a crime within their territory. As English merchants continued to visit China, the practice grew up of allowing the supercargoes of the ships to punish any of the ship's company guilty of offences against the local law. This privilege was never granted as a right, though the English traders came to regard it as such, and later the Chinese, on more than one occasion, claimed the power to punish Englishmen for offences committed on Chinese territory. This question remained unsettled on any definite basis until the Treaty of Nanking was signed in 1842. Most writers on China think that our difficulties in gaining permission to trade were due to a determination on the part of the Manchus to secure their conquest by prohibiting all intercourse between the Chinese and other nations.[4] For this opinion there

[1] *East India Company's Factory Records.* (MSS. in the India Office under *China Materials*, vol. iv, pp. 467–478.)

[2] As to exterritorial jurisdiction, see *post*, pp. 521, 559.

[3] *East India Company's Factory Records.* (MSS. in the India Office under *China Materials*, vol. iv, p. 471.)

[4] Until their conquest was consolidated the Manchus feared that Foreigners might assist the Chinese. After that period they showed no particular hostility to subjects of other nations.

appears to be no real foundation. The policy of the Manchus at this time seems to have been directed towards encouraging foreign commerce. This may be inferred both from the favourable reception accorded to the Company at Amoy, and from the fact that it was owing to an invitation from the Viceroy at Canton, that the Company were at last able to realize their dream of obtaining liberty to trade at that port. As early as 1679 the Viceroy had invited the Company to send a ship thither, but the Directors, discouraged by the unsettled state of affairs at Bantam, and apprehensive as to what might happen whilst the fighting between the Manchus and the Chinese continued, without sending a refusal abstained from accepting.[1] Some nine years later, however, the invitation was acted upon, and the *Rebecca* made a prosperous voyage to Macao from Madras, though not without experiencing the difficulties which seemed to be inevitable to Englishmen who visited that port. The next year, in 1689, the *Defence* arrived from Madras at Macao, and some days after her arrival managed to obtain leave to go right up the river. The supercargoes, on reaching Canton, were well received by the Hoppo, who requested them to bring up their vessel to the city itself. In response to this invitation they sent word to Macao for the *Defence* to enter the Bogue, but her master, Captain Heath, in disobedience to the orders of his superiors, refused to stir. There was the usual difficulty about the measurement duty, but the supercargoes, " after hot dispute and a bribe to the measurers, got the Hoppo's consent to measure her from before the mizzenmast to the after part of the foremast which otherwise would be from stem to stern, and so amount to a vast sum." At first 2,484 taels were demanded as measurement duty, but the factors threatening to depart and going on board " bagg and baggage," the amount was reduced to 1,500 taels for the Emperor and 300 taels for the Hoppo.[2] The precedent thus set up was followed by all ships that afterwards came to Canton, and it was not until 1842 that the present to the

[1] *East India Company's Factory Records.* (MSS. in the India Office under *China Materials*, vol. iii, pp. 225–230.)

[2] *Ibid.*, vol. iv, p. 41–90.

Hoppo, or "cumshaw," as it was called, was abolished as a regular charge.

Whilst the supercargoes of the *Defence* were up at Canton, the master, Captain Heath, was the cause of a serious affray at Macao. Contrary to all orders he insisted on going ashore and trading on his own account, with the result that the Chinese, according to their usual custom, insisted on detaining the mast until all such operations should have come to an end. Captain Heath, however, took twenty of his men and seized the mast by force of arms, in spite of the opposition of the Chinese. Having tied it to the longboat, he began to tow it to the ship, whereupon the Chinese threw showers of stones at the boats' crews. This so enraged the Captain that he ordered his men to open fire, the result of which was that one Chinaman was killed and another wounded. The Chinese returned the fire and wounded the pilot, and, what was worse, attacked the doctor, the third and fifth mates, and seven of the seamen who were on shore unarmed. The doctor was cut down within sight of the boats, and his companions, having been seized and bound by the Chinese, were carried off to prison and treated with the utmost barbarity. The Chinese, who had witnessed the affray, carried their dead countryman round the streets of Canton in order to incense the mob against the British, an object in which they did not fail to succeed. The supercargoes, who at the news of the trouble had hastened down from Canton, attempted to settle the difficulty by a money payment, but the officials demanding at least 5,000 taels, they departed with the *Defence* to Madras, leaving their countrymen in the hands of the Chinese. What ultimately became of these poor fellows history does not record. We only know that the trade with the British was not stopped on account of this incident, for in the following year we find that the *Loyal Merchant* visited Canton from Madras and came away with a full cargo.[1] When in later years the residents in Canton were kept under close surveillance, the Chinese gave as their reason for adopting such a mode of treatment that

[1] *East India Company's Factory Records.* (MSS. in India Office under *China Materials*, vol. v, p. 602.)

experience had shown that the Foreigners were without reason and like to brute beasts, that must be kept in subjection. The foundation for this opinion of Foreigners seems to have been laid by incidents of the kind just described, which seem, however, to have been much less common in connection with Englishmen than with other nationalities.

CHAPTER III

THE TRADE AT CANTON MADE PERMANENT

THE signing of the Peace of Ryswick in 1697 at once produced in England a revival of commercial activity. In the case of the East India Company this revival was manifested in a determination to reorganize and extend the trade with China and to obtain a permanent footing at Canton. The difficulties experienced in achieving this object were somewhat different in character from those which previously had been encountered, and bear a strong resemblance to the obstacles to successful trading which are met with in China to-day. The grant of a monopoly of the trade with Europeans at a port to a single individual or body of individuals ; a combination of Chinese merchants to keep down the prices at which imports should be bought and to raise the prices at which exports should be sold ; fraudulent practices on the part of Chinese traders, by which goods deficient in quantity or quality were delivered under their contracts ; the imposition of heavy duties and the exaction of illegal charges by the Chinese officials ; the futility of appeals to Chinese tribunals for the redress of grievances ; these were the hindrances to a successful trade that took the place of the hostility of the Dutch and Portuguese.

Apart from the troubles due to causes such as these, the operations of the East India Company were further retarded by difficulties that sprang from defects in its own internal organization. These arose mainly from the vagueness of the instructions given by the Directors to the Company's superior officers, and from the lack of powers by which the latter could compel obedience on the part of their subordinates. Indeed, at the commencement of the eighteenth century, the commissions which the Company issued, even for trading purposes, were so indefinite in their terms, that frequently it happened that the supercargoes by bidding in rivalry against one another, in the desire to do as well as possible for their respective ships, raised the prices of commodities to such a figure that they could not be bought with any profit to the Company. In course of time these defects were remedied. More precise instructions were issued by the Court of Directors; statutory powers for compelling obedience to the orders of the supercargoes were obtained from Parliament; and the right to exercise jurisdiction over the Company's servants on Chinese soil was conceded by the Chinese authorities to the supercargoes trading at Canton.

Another source of weakness to the Company was the practice of private trading indulged in by the Company's servants. The captains and supercargoes of ships frequently purchased large quantities of goods on their own account, conveyed them in the Company's vessels to England or other markets, and there sold them at such a price as to compete with the Company's goods to the disadvantage of the latter. This evil at last reached such a pitch, that some of the captains brought home on their own account as much as 20,000 pounds of tea in a single ship. To remedy this abuse of the privilege of private trading, the Court of Directors in 1714 restricted the captains to bringing an amount not greater than 3 per cent. of the gross tonnage of the vessel; and they further enacted that in any case the Company should be entitled to a charge of 15 per cent. on any tea so brought, in addition to 2 per cent. for general charges and to the duty payable to the Government. The penalty for an infringement of this regulation, as provided by statute, was confiscation of the tea and the infliction of a fine equivalent to double the value of the cargo seized. Various expedients were tried from time to time with the object of fixing the remuneration of the supercargoes in such a way that two necessary but antagonistic conditions would be satisfied, viz., that the supercargoes would receive such remuneration as would place them beyond the temptation to engage in private trading, whilst the Company would be safeguarded in case of a voyage proving unprofitable. In the year 1721 a scale of allowances was drawn up, ranging from £3,000 to £800 according to the respective ranks of the officers concerned, supercargoes "to be paid out of the return cargoes, and in the event of any one or more ships being lost, a proportionate deduction to be made." In 1725 a fresh plan was adopted; an allowance of 5 per cent. on the whole cargo of each ship was made to the officers of that ship collectively, which sum was divided among them in proportions determined by their respective rank, whilst each had liberty to ship bullion and engage in private trade to a limited and carefully specified extent.[1]

By sturdy resolution, combined with tact and diplomatic skill, the English supercargoes at Canton soon placed themselves on a more independent footing than was enjoyed by the traders of any other nation. Thus after a very short period they acquired the foremost place in the estimation of the Chinese, as well as of the other Europeans who were trading at that port. As a result, the East India Company very soon acquired a preponderant share in the trade. When, however, that stage of development had been once reached, the old methods were discarded and a less resolute policy adopted. Thenceforth the Directors were animated by the fear that any course of conduct which savoured of boldness would place in jeopardy the results achieved. It would have been better had the Directors instructed their servants in China to maintain a resolute front against official arrogance and oppression. Such a course must speedily have produced one of two consequences. Either the Chinese officials would have remitted the illegal exactions and heavy impositions under which the trade laboured from the middle of the eighteenth century to the close of the Opium War in 1842; or else matters would have come to a crisis and China have been compelled to accord to English traders a fitting reception a century or so before such treatment was in fact conceded. It is probable that the first of these consequences would have ensued. As it was, the supercargoes who had the control after the Company's position had been firmly established, observing the wishes and behests of the Court of Directors, adopted an attitude of compliance and subservience. It was directly

[1] *East India Company's Factory Records.* (MSS. in the India Office under *China Materials*, vol. viii, pp. 1302, 1397, 1465.)

owing to this mistaken policy that they were subjected to degradations at the hands of the Chinese officials at Canton, which never would have been tolerated by the men who founded the trade. In brief, the Company sought to strengthen itself against dangers from without by adapting itself to its local environment, a course which in China must result in deterioration.

The real foundation of the permanent trade at Canton dates from the voyage of the *Macclesfield*, which arrived off Macao on August 26th, 1699. The Portuguese on this occasion, in strong contrast to their previous behaviour, showed great courtesy to the English traders, and invited them to bring their ship into the harbour under shelter of the fort, a favour never before granted to any European vessel. The invitation was declined on the ground that its acceptance might be disagreeable to the Chinese authorities. The latter, however, showed themselves no less courteous than the Portuguese, and the mandarin of Casa Branca visited the supercargoes on board their ship, who "saluted him and entertained him with wine and pickles." As soon as the English arrived business questions began to be discussed, but the supercargoes refused to enter into any contracts until the question of measurement duty, which by this time was known to be a likely theme of contention, had been satisfactorily determined. The English were quick to notice that Macao itself did not offer any great commercial advantages. "This city," they wrote, "is att present miserable poor: and altho' ye Portuguese have ye name of ye government, yett ye Chinese have ye Chiefe Power, and all ye Customes of ye Port excepting some small privileges yt. ye Portuguese ships injoy."

At Canton, as at Amoy, and apparently as at all other ports where European traders were wont to come, the interests of the Emperor, with regard to the collection of measurement duty and revenue generally, had by this time been placed in the hands of a single official, who is always designated in the records as the Hoppo. There can be no doubt that this term is simply a corruption of the Chinese name Hoo-Poo, the official designation of the Board of Revenue at Peking, which is charged with the care of all fiscal matters and to which the Hoppo was responsible. At the earliest opportunity the supercargoes of the *Macclesfield* called on the Hoppo of Canton, who appears to have been in Macao at the time of their arrival. He informed them that he had given all merchants liberty to trade with them, but explained that "his commission did not extend to compell or constraine any Merchant to any Contract but what they judged for their own interest."

It was agreed by the Hoppo that the measurement duty should be determined on a measurement taken from the centre of the mizzen to the centre of the foremast, which the Chinese measures made out to be 62½ cubits of 14 inches each. As showing how like their modern descendants were the Chinese of that day, it is interesting to notice that the supercargoes record that "the true cubit is $14\frac{8}{10}$ but the true standard is never observed, either in weight or measure; and scarce any two merchants use the same, but they have all two or three weights or measures, which they use according as they meet with customers upon whom they can impose, and are not the least ashamed if discovered."[1] The measurement duty should have been assessed at 1,200 taels as on a first-rate ship, but wishing to encourage the English to found a permanent trade, the Hoppo not only promised to reduce it to 600 taels, as on a third-rate ship, but to remit a fifth of that amount, saying at the same time: "You are strangers and come from a distant country; therefore to encourage your trading hither, I do not wish to gain anything by you; my only ambition is to obtain a good name in the discharge of my duty." He further promised a chop to the effect that they should have liberty of trade, that their *linguist*, or interpreter, should not be molested, and that they themselves should be civilly treated. These privileges came to be regarded at a later date as usual, and to be claimed as a matter of right; but at this time they were known to be dependent on the favour of the Hoppo.

[1] A detailed account of the voyage of the *Macclesfield*, as described by the supercargoes, is given in the *East India Company's Factory Records*. (MSS. in the India Office under *China Materials*, vol. v, pp. 647-756.)

In the meantime the supercargoes found a Chinese Christian to act as their *linguist*, and obtained leave to go up to Canton. There they called on the French agent, M. Bonac, and met Pere Basset, the chief of the French Jesuits, who acknowledged their indebtedness to the English for having for many years given them free passage to China both in times of peace and of war, no ship of their own country having traded to those parts till the preceding year. From their statement we are able to fix the commencement of the trade of the French at Canton as being in the year 1698. The kindly sentiments of the French agent and the Jesuit fathers were very different from those manifested by the captain of a French ship which happened to be at Canton. This man, with several of his seamen, attacked some of the Company's servants, whom they outnumbered in the proportion of four to one, and beat them unmercifully. The English were forced to complain to the Hoppo, because, as they pointed out, they could not avenge themselves so long as they were within the jurisdiction of the Chinese Government. They also explained that they had come to Canton to trade and not to fight, for they "had given the French enough of that at home." M. Bonac and the Jesuits did all in their power to make amends for the ill conduct of their compatriots, and ultimately peace and harmony were restored.

Whilst they were in Canton, the supercargoes stayed in the house of a Chinese merchant who had been "King's Merchant" in the days when Canton was a kingdom. With this man they made a contract that he should buy all their goods and buy them at fixed rates, and that all goods sold by him to them should be at prices which were fixed and free of customs and duties. In this way the supercargoes were able to estimate their profit as soon as the agreement was concluded. It was drawn up in writing and provided that treble damages should be paid in case of a breach by either party. The supercargoes soon found, however, that it was impossible to get delivery of cargo which had been agreed to be sold to them, unless they were prepared to advance before delivery at least part of the price. For this reason they advanced as much as 1,442 taels before they went up to Canton at all. Thus was initiated that practice of advancing what are now called "bargain moneys," which is followed to-day by all European merchants in China who wish to do any considerable export trade. The Chinese are so poor and there is such a lack of currency for commercial purposes, that it is found in practice to be difficult to obtain export cargo unless such advances are made.[1]

When it came to paying the measurement duty, the supercargoes of the *Macclesfield* met with the same difficulties as their fellow-countrymen had experienced on previous visits. A great deal of time was spent in discussing matters of this kind. The outcome was that the measurement duty itself was fixed at 480 taels, and in addition 48 taels were paid to the measuring officers as their percentage, 7 per cent. discount was paid for sycee with which to make these payments, 24 per cent. was paid as a present to the Hoppo, 16, 17, and 18 per cent. were paid to the Hoppo's officers respectively, whilst further sums were paid as presents and port charges. From this list it will be seen that the Chinese of those days were not less ingenious than their successors of later years in devising grounds for demanding money, such grounds being very similar to those which were the subject of so much contention at the beginning of the nineteenth century. Still the supercargoes seem to have been pleased with the general result, doubtless feeling thankful to have got an opportunity of trading on any terms at Canton.

Encouraged by this success, the Court of Directors in London now resolved to establish in China a Presidency similar to the Presidencies which had been constituted in India. As the Company's first President in China, they chose Allen Catchpole,

[1] This practice of making advances on the faith of cargo, to be bought in the interior on account of the British exporter, being delivered to him at the port where he carries on business, frequently leads to trouble owing to the difficulty of deciding in whom is the ownership before delivery. In 1900 the losses suffered by British merchants, arising out of the Boxer movement, consisted to a large extent of moneys so advanced, for which no cargo was ever delivered, it having been lost or destroyed whilst in transit to the coast.

for whom they obtained from William III, who had recently ascended the English throne, a commission appointing him the King's Minister or Consul for the English nation. This is the first occasion on which England was represented in China by any kind of agent appointed by the Crown.[1] Catchpole appears never to have attempted to exercise diplomatic functions, but to have contented himself with discharging his duties to the Company as their President. In the latter capacity he was assisted by a Council of five, of whom one, Lloyd, was chosen "on account of his long residence in China and knowledge of the language." This Council was to manage all the Company's affairs in China, and was to record all its deliberations in a "Consultation Book," a copy of which was to be sent every year to London. The Company's establishment also comprised a minister, a surgeon, two factors and five writers. All were to live in the Factory and eat at the Company's table. The salaries were fixed at £60 a year for each of the mercantile members, £40 for factors, £20 for writers, £50 to the minister with an additional gratuity of £50, and £30 to the surgeon with an allowance of £10 for a servant. The merchants, factors and writers might engage in exchange business by remitting gold to England and receiving silver in return. Five years' service in any one of these capacities was to entitle the servant to promotion. To the Council was given power to dismiss any of the Company's servants for unfaithful service, or "any heinous crime such as murder, theft, blasphemy or the like," for renting farms or duties of the Emperor, whereby they might be subjected to the arbitrary power of Chinese officials, or for marrying a Mahommedan, Gentoo, or Pagan.

The limits of the Presidency were to include the whole Empire of China and the neighbouring islands, but the seat of the Presidency was left to be chosen by the Council at their discretion. They were to proceed to Liampo (Ningpo) and,

[1] It has been stated that at this time there were two King's Consuls in China, each representing a rival Company; but for this statement no authority is to be found in the records. See *Parliamentary Paper on the Affairs of the East India Company* (1830), p. 2.

if they found it possible, settle there or at some convenient port thereabout, "where you can be permitted by the Government and is most likely to introduce you directly into the Trade of the City of Nankin, or rather at Nankin itself, if it be practicable and best for the interest of our commerce." If they could not get a full cargo in those parts before the easterly monsoon set in, they were to sail to Amoy or Canton and take in a full cargo there. With these instructions, which bear date 23rd November, 1699, Catchpole sailed from London. It was thought that the more northerly the port at which the Factory was settled, the more likelihood there was of getting a trade with Japan, which was an object still cherished by the Court of Directors. Catchpole accordingly proceeded straight to Chusan. On his arrival he found the *Macclesfield* and one of the Company's ships from Bombay. Here again difficulties arose over the question of measurement duty. To his inquiries as to the prospect of establishing a permanent trade, the reply was given that to obtain such a privilege an embassy must be sent direct to the Emperor.

During the first year of his stay at Chusan, Catchpole experienced all sorts of troubles. The promises of liberty to trade made by the "Chumpein," or Viceroy, very soon turned out to be worth nothing. Large sums of money had to be advanced as bargain money on the security of cargo, which he found was not delivered after six or seven months had elapsed, though by their contracts the bargainers had agreed to deliver in a much less time. His appeals to the Chinese officials to assist him in enforcing these contracts were unavailing. The position became so desperate, that Catchpole wrote home advising the Directors that the island of Pulo Condore should be occupied in the King's name, and held as security for the debts due to the Company arising from the advances so made, which altogether amounted to as much as £60,000. He also suggested that an application should be made to the King for conditional letters of reprisal, authorizing him to seize and detain Chinese ships if necessity should arise. Having made these recommendations to the Court of Directors, he remained at Chusan trying to recover his bargain moneys, or goods to their value. He soon found, however, that his attempts to enforce the fulfilment of the contracts were arousing the resentment of the Chinese officials. Relations became so strained that in January 1702 the Governor ordered him and his Council to leave Chusan.

This untoward development, not due solely to the altercations with regard to bargain moneys, was largely the result of the intrigues of Captain Roberts and one Gough, the supercargo of the *Sarah* galley, who, having been sent to Liampo by the Directors, came on to Chusan. Out of jealousy of the President's powers, they represented to the Chinese that no other ships would come thither so long as the Council remained, as " the President was here over the English as a mandarin, and had an Awe upon all ships that should come hither." This statement stirred up the enmity of the " Mandarin of Justice," who tried to compel Catchpole to receive in satisfaction of the debts owing from the merchants, goods of a kind not contracted for, and to receive them at prices that were altogether unreasonable. During the negotiations that ensued over these proposals, the factors were kept in confinement by the Tartar General, who pleaded the Hoppo's orders in justification of this fresh outrage. Then the subordinate officials demanded that the guns, sails and rudders of the ships be sent ashore. The General could easily have put a stop to demands of this kind, but though professing to be friendly he " unworthily held his tongue till they had squeezed some small presents out of us."[1] Unable to endure the treatment that was being meted out to them, Catchpole and his Council withdrew from Chusan to Batavia, and there awaited further orders from the Directors.

On August 6th, 1702, the *Macclesfield*, *Robert & Nathaniel* and the *Union* all arrived at Batavia bound for China, and the President used the opportunity to proceed again to Chusan. He found Roberts and Gough still there, and dissensions at once arose. He also found that during his absence the Emperor's second son had sent his merchant from Peking to

[1] This is the first time that we find the English word "squeeze" used in the sense that it now has all along the China coast.

trade with the English, with orders that the officials should assist him in every possible way. This monopolist was very soon followed by the merchant of the Emperor's fourth son, and the two combined to prevent any trade being done by the English with the ordinary merchants. As neither of them had brought any stock, business soon came to a standstill. The factors complained bitterly to the Directors in England that all chance of a profitable commerce was destroyed, and explained that these Emperor's Merchants, as they styled them, " were too great for the Mandarins to dare meddle with. They will deliver no goods, but what they please ; no force can be used against them ; and for the arguments of Justice and Reason, they laugh at us." Further trouble ensued with the captains of the other English ships, which again prejudiced the President and Council, " the Chinese much doubting where the rules and powers of Government lay." A captain named Smith went so far as openly to insult the President and actually struck him in public. Catchpole promptly had Smith arrested and carried on board his ship, the *Liampo*, " which although it raised a great uproar in the Town and amused the Mandarins, yet it convinced them that the English Company's President had some power ; and they did not venture to meddle in it, although Captain Smith made some efforts towards it, promising one of our linguists a good sum of money if he would stand by him."

Early in 1703 a fresh Hoppo arrived, and it looked as though the trade might be successfully carried on, this new official making the most attractive promises. But the factors now began to experience a fresh source of trouble, though but a minor one, in which again the Chinese of those days showed how like they were to the Chinese of to-day. This was the desire to obtain curious birds and animals. The factors were so plagued for rarities of this kind, that they managed to pay the measurement duty on a whole ship with " one great Irish dog." The hope of a change for the better in the conditions of trade speedily disappeared. The difficulties with which the factors had to contend grew in number and magnitude. Ultimately in February, 1703, the President put in execution the plan he had outlined to the Directors, and sailed away to Pulo Condore. There he built a fort, which was nothing better than "an inclosure with two ranges of stakes, with hurdles fastened to them and in some places filled with sand." With the object of building a permanent fort and establishing a settlement he wrote to the Court asking that bricklayers, sawyers, and carpenters might be sent out from England. For a year or two serious efforts were put forward to make Pulo Condore[1] a trading centre, but as a firmer footing was obtained at Canton, these efforts were relaxed. In the end the Directors definitely ordered in 1703 that no more ships be sent to Chusan, because of the impositions and hardships which had been there endured.

In the meantime the Company had not neglected Canton. There, too, their servants had to face difficulties similar to those encountered by Catchpole at Chusan. In 1704 the Company's representative at Macao heard "of a new monster sprung up, called an Emperor's Merchant, who having given 42,000 taels at Court for his employment, is invested with an authority to engross the whole trade with the Europeans, and that no China merchant shall presume to interfere with him, unless for a valuable consideration he shall admit him to the partnership." This report turned out to be true, and further details were obtained and forwarded to the Court of Directors in a letter which thus described the new official :—

"He is a man who formerly sold salt at Canton, and was whip't out of the province for being caught defrauding the Emperor of his dutys on that commodity, but not being whip't out of all his money, he had found means to be introduced to the Emperor's son and successor, who for a sum of money, reported to be 42,000 taels, has given him a patent of trade with all Europeans in Canton, exclusive of all other Merchants, forbidding anyone to interfere with him, without his special licence first obtained, and that this is done without the Emperor's knowledge. The Hoppo is in course his declared enemy, because he can't drain him by unwarranted impositions

[1] Pulo Condore is an island off the coast of Cochin-China.

as he does other Merchants, for he will pay no more than the Emperor's Customs to a nicety."[1]

The care of the Company's interests at Canton was entrusted to the supercargoes of the various ships that were sent thither to trade. Thus it happened that in successive seasons the Company was represented by a different set of agents. This explains the lack of continuity in the Company's policy, and the seeming failure to learn from experience. The supercargoes who arrived in 1704 found the Chinese traders equally desirous with themselves of destroying the monopoly of the Emperor's Merchant. At first this task was attempted by means of secret trading operations. Not finding these of much help, they determined to apply to the Hoppo, who was already sufficiently hostile to the new official. The Hoppo, having heard the complaints of the merchants, to the effect that the trade was being ruined, that the Emperor's Merchant had no stock, and that if matters continued in this state the new and lucrative trade with the English would come to an end, made an order that if the Emperor's Merchant did not provide himself with a sufficient stock of goods within three days, the ordinary merchants should be allowed to do business with the English. Finding his monopoly threatened, the Emperor's Merchant complained to the Viceroy, who ordered an investigation to be made by the *kwang-chow-foo*.[2] Whilst this inquiry was proceeding, no trade could be done. Each party had recourse to the expedients usual in China. The ordinary merchants bribed the *kwang-chow-foo*, so that he reported in their favour; the Emperor's Merchant offered the Viceroy's son a half interest in his monopoly. In the end the Viceroy upheld the order of the Hoppo, but commanded those merchants who had taken business out of the hands of the Emperor's Merchant to pay him a valuable consideration. Thus the "monster in trade" was destroyed.

[1] *East India Company's Factory Records*. (MSS. in the India Office under *China Materials*, vol. vii, pp. 1025-6.)

[2] The *kwang-chow-foo* was the official responsible for the government of Canton city, corresponding somewhat to the mayor of an English town.

One reason that induced the Hoppo to make his order in favour of the ordinary merchants was, that he had already borrowed a large sum from them on the security of the 4 per cent. duty, which he was in the habit of levying on all goods imported from foreign countries. This duty was an altogether illegal exaction, and as it had in the first place to be paid by the English seller, the supercargoes felt that they had under this head alone a serious grievance. Hence we find them writing in the following terms to the Court of Directors :—

"This 4 per cent. is an imposition lately crept upon us by the submission of our predecessors the two preceding seasons. One per cent. of the four is what has usually been given by the China Merchant to the Linguist upon all contracts, and the Linguist was used to gratify the Hoppo out of this sum, for his employment. The other three were at first squeezed from the China Merchant as a gratuity for upholding some particular men in monopolizing all the business, and this used to be given in a lump, so that by undervaluing the goods, and concealing some part, they used to save half the charge, but to show how soon an ill precedent will be improved in China to our disadvantage, the succeeding Hoppos, instead of persuasive arguments such as their predecessors used, are come to demand it as an established duty. If the China Merchant scruples to pay, the English Merchant shall pay, or nobody shall dare to load upon him ; and ye poor Linguist shall part with all his one per cent., and be thankful he is not bamboo'd into the bargain."[1] One could hardly wish for a more striking proof that the Chinese of the twentieth century are very like the Chinese of the eighteenth century.

Some sort of trade was still being carried on by the Company with Amoy. There, too, the supercargoes met with the kind of difficulties that had been experienced at Chusan and Canton. An Emperor's Merchant, the nominee of the son of the Emperor, put in an appearance and exacted a percentage from the ordinary merchants, whilst the Hoppo inaugurated a new kind of monopoly by compelling the English to trade only

[1] *East India Company's Factory Records.* (MSS. in the India Office under *China Materials*, vol. vii, p. 1038.)

with eight particular merchants. The general result was that Amoy rapidly deteriorated as a trading centre. The Hoppo of Canton seems to have attempted to imitate this plan of granting a monopoly of the English trade to a few favoured Chinese merchants, but did not meet with success for some years. The impositions and exactions at both ports gradually increased in amount and variety. Matters came to a crisis at Amoy in 1714. In that year the *Ann* from Madras arrived for the purpose of trading. Bargain money was advanced in the usual way, but when the supercargoes came to demand their cargo, they experienced the greatest difficulty in enforcing their contracts. The officials sided with the defaulting merchants, and at length, whilst 8,000 taels were still owing to the Company for goods brought in the *Ann*, that vessel was expelled the harbour. Not willing to endure treatment of this kind, her captain seized a junk, which he met on coming out of the port, and this junk he announced he should hold as security for his debt. The "Tytock"[1] promised that the debt should be paid, if the junk were released, so the *Ann* came to anchor to await the fulfilment of this promise. When the captain had been lulled into a false security by these means, the Chinese, treacherous as when Captain Weddell first arrived at Canton, suddenly attacked the *Ann* with forty war junks and forty fire-ships. The English vessel with the greatest difficulty managed to get away and escaped to Madras. Later the Company made complaint of the treatment which had been meted out to the *Ann*, although she was a private trader and not a Company's ship, and news of the outrage having reached the Emperor, two of the responsible officials were dismissed from office.[2]

At Canton from the year 1704 onwards the Company's supercargoes were busy building up a permanent trade. The supercargoes of newly arrived vessels waited on the Hoppo and demanded "the usual privileges," and as these were

[1] That is, the *tituh*, a Chinese official whose title is euphemistically rendered into English by the word "Admiral."

[2] *East India Company's Factory Records.* (MSS. in the India Office under *China Materials*, vol. viii, p. 1312.)

granted year after year, they came to be regarded as obtainable as of right rather than by favour. In 1716 the "usual privileges," as obtained by the supercargoes of the *Susanna*, are thus enumerated in a letter sent by them to the Court of Directors :—

"1. That we might speak with him [the Hoppo] at all times without waiting.

"2. That we have a chop[1] affixed at our gate for a free trade and to forbid insults.

"3. That we choose our linguist, compradore, and such other servants as we think proper, and discharge them at our pleasure.

"4. That the supercargoes of the *Susanna* shall not be obliged to stop in coming from or going to the ship, at any of the Hoppo's boats: and that the flag flying shall be the signal of their being in the boat.

"5. That we have liberty to provide all naval stores without duty or any imposition whatever.

"6. That we have at our request the Grand Chop for leaving the port without delay or embarrassment."

Two years later the supercargoes of the *Carnavon* obtained other privileges, in addition to those just enumerated, which as far as can be discovered, is the first occasion on which the Chinese recognized as a permanent privilege the right of the supercargoes to exercise jurisdiction over their subordinates. These additional privileges were :—

"7. If our English servants should commit any disorder or fault, deserving punishment, that the Chinese should not take upon themselves to punish, but should complain to us, and we would see them sufficiently punished according to the crime.

"8. Liberty to fit up a tent ashore, and to refit casks, sails, and rigging.

"9. That no customs should be paid on goods landed but not disposed of."

[1] A written permit. This word is derived from the Malay "chapa," a seal or stamp.

In these nine privileges we have the constitution under which the servants of the East India Company originally carried on their trade at Canton. If observed in good faith on both sides, they were such as may fairly be described as liberal. The privilege of punishing their own servants was of the greatest value to the supercargoes, who knew how severe and unjustly administered is the law of China. For many years the trade was carried on in peace and quietude under these conditions, save for an occasional disturbance of a merely temporary nature. One of the chief sources of worry to the supercargoes during this period were the troublesome inquiries made by the officials for "Nick Nacks," for which there seems to have been an insatiable demand at Peking as well as at Canton itself. The plotting to gain a monopoly of the trade with the English still went on among groups of Chinese merchants. One reason for this was that, as the trade increased, the other officials grew jealous of the Hoppo, who got most of the benefit of the increase. "As they observe the great profits arising to him from this port and from Macao, by the vast ingress of shipping, and as he is but a petty mandarin to many of them (his Commission indeed special from the Emperor), they begin to link in parties, which may prove very prejudicial to European traders." In this strain wrote the supercargoes in 1716.

How far the development of trade with foreign nations was favoured at Peking at this time is not quite certain. But it is clear that there was no settled policy, as is commonly supposed, which involved the exclusion of Foreigners from the Empire. The encouragement given to the Roman Catholic missionaries, and the extent to which their services were used by the Emperor, would go a long way to rebut any theory of that kind. The decree of Kanghi, published in 1692, permitting the exercise of the Christian religion, is indicative of a spirit of toleration towards Foreigners. Moreover the English, Portuguese, Dutch, and Spanish were all trading at ports on the southern coast of China. This was known at Peking and was not forbidden. But it seems to have caused some uneasiness, and Kanghi, seeing the possibility of future trouble between China and the nations of Europe, gave expression to his anxiety in the year 1717 when he said: "There is cause for apprehension lest, in centuries or millenniums to come, China may be endangered by collision with the various nations of the West, who come hither from beyond the seas."[1]

One curious result of the trading operations carried on by the English and Dutch in China was the establishment of the Spanish-American dollar as the currency ordinarily used in commercial dealings between the Chinese and Foreigners. The introduction of this coinage to the notice of the Chinese had taken place as early as 1571, when Legaspi, having conquered the Philippines, compelled the Mindorans to restore to some shipwrecked Chinese property plundered from them in their misfortune. When thanked by the grateful strangers, he invited them to come and trade at the *free port* of Manilla, promising them Mexican silver in exchange for the merchandise of China. Owing to this invitation a trade was opened between Manilla and Fukien, and Chinese products were shipped from the Philippines to New Spain, for which payment was made in the manner promised.[2] In course of time the merchants of Cadiz found that the commerce thus initiated injured the export of goods direct from Spain to the Spanish colonies in America. To preserve their own trade, they obtained in 1604 a royal order to the effect that the trade between the American colonies and the Philippines should be restricted to one shipment every year from Manilla to Acapulco, in which Americans were forbidden to have any interest. The value of the cargo thus sent was not to exceed $250,000, but this limitation being evaded by false valuations, the amount allowed to be carried was raised in 1702 to $300,000.[3] The return cargoes were limited to double the amount permitted to be carried from Manilla. Owing to this restriction, the people of the Philippines built huge galleons, with a view to carrying as much as possible in a single voyage, by means of which cargo of

[1] *Chinese Repository*, vol. v. p. 394.
[2] *Ibid.*, vol. vi, pp. 267–8.
[3] This was again raised in 1734 to $500,000.

twice the value allowed by law was illicitly shipped to Acapulco in each year. But even so, the check on the commerce of the Philippines was fatal to their development, not only because of the restriction imposed, but because the demand for Chinese products in New Spain was so great, that the Dutch and English were able to dispose of large amounts at a great profit, which they smuggled into the Spanish-American markets. Thus the growth of the interests of England and Holland in the Far East was directly favoured by the disabilities imposed upon the merchants of Manilla by their own country. For the cargoes thus carried by the English and Dutch to New Spain payment was to a large extent made in dollars, which were carried to China and used as a circulating medium.[1]

[1] The importation of silver into Manilla from Spanish America from 1571 to 1821 has been computed by De Comyn at $400,000,000, a large share of which, probably one-fourth, also passed to China. The importation has continued since the revolt of the Spanish colonies, and the Mexican dollar is used to this day, though not so much as formerly, as the British mint at Hong-kong and the Chinese mints in several provinces now coin dollars of their own.

CHAPTER IV

THE MONOPOLY OF THE HONG MERCHANTS

THE year 1720 was a year of changes. By this time the China Presidency, as constituted in Catchpole's commission, had either been abolished or fallen into abeyance. From 1715 to 1720, as is clear from the records, the supercargoes arriving at Canton in each year were regarded as the Council for the time being. There is no mention of Catchpole after the year 1703. The projected settlement at Pulo Condore appears to have been abandoned, for the vessels of the French Mississippi Company, which in the year 1722 were sent thither in the expectation that they would find a fortified city and a great trade, found only the foundations of a fort. By this time Canton had become the centre of the Company's operations in China, and in 1721 the supercargoes of the ships despatched to that port in that year were formally constituted a " Standing Council," to manage the Company's affairs in China, and endowed with similar powers to those enjoyed by the councils at the settlements in the East Indies.[1]

On the part of the Chinese the new development of most importance was the organization of a monopoly under official sanction, by which certain privileged persons only were to be allowed to trade with the English. We shall see that after a short time this organization was dissolved, owing to the opposition which its formation aroused. But this dissolution appears not to have extended beyond the destruction of the written instrument which established the monopoly as a legal institution, and there can be no doubt that it never really ceased to exist after it had once been called into being.[2] That instrument took the form of an agreement in writing between

[1] *East India Company's Records.* (MSS. in the India Office under *China Materials*, vol. viii, pp. 1397, 1403.)

[2] To the organization of this monopoly the supercargoes of the East India Company, themselves the representatives of a much more powerful monopoly, took the strongest exception.

the merchants of the leading "hongs,"[1] the local name by which the chief Chinese business warehouses were known, whence comes the term "Co-hong," or "Hong Merchants," by which the members of the monopoly were commonly designated. The preamble of the agreement was worded in the flowery language in which the Chinese still delight, and was translated as follows by the Company's representatives :—

"There is no doubt but the customs of this Kingdom, paid by the merchants and the people, of right belong to the Emperor, that every honest man may expect a just and moderate profit ; that it is a great part of humanity that people dwelling in the same place should have a good agreement among themselves and be assistant to one another. We are a people renowned for fidelity and justice, deriving our principles from our two great ancestors, Kwoh and Pao, and our confiding in their maxims has always rendered the trade of the Warehouses equally beneficial to private persons, as well as the public ; all merchandize having an easy vent ; 'tis our happiness to have an Emperor who hath such a regard to the good of the people, and that of strangers, as to make them equal sharers of good and bad fortune ; the Mandarins are compassionate to the Merchants, and encouraging to Strangers, treating both with the same affection.[2] China and Foreign kingdoms are accounted here to be one house, and therefore they and we ought to have the same heart ; the Foreign ships that come here are from different Nations, which is the reason that by degrees different houses are set up, and different designs are carried on. The misfortune that attends this will be, that at last some ill-designing people will overturn everything. Goods have no fixed price, being at first very dear, at last very cheap ; Strangers also do not keep their words, nor Contracts made beforehand ; refusing what they do not like, and is not according to their fancy ; and from this proceeds the loss of our whole Stock and Merchandize ; things going on after

[1] The word "hong" is now used on the China coast to signify any of the big commercial houses founded and controlled by Foreigners.

[2] For further particulars as to the Chinese impression of the outside world see *post*, chap. vi.

this rate, there is a likelihood that the rights of the Emperor, as well as the public, may suffer. It is from these reasons that we, by our general consent, make the following regulations; not being actuated by any desire of gain, but truly to put the Merchants' houses into such a disposition that they may agree; have no diversity of opinions; and love and assist one another; and if it is allowed that this be agreeable to reason, it must necessarily follow, that everybody with his heart full of justice should endeavour to bring this affair to a good conclusion; from henceforth it is necessary that the prices of Goods should be fixed, and the Merchants receive a profit, provided they are good, of a good assortment, and the Foreigners are contented with them. Wherefore we think it proper to wait upon our Mandarins, and desire their advice; and in the presence of our Idol, to make confession of our sincerity; that if any one of us should falsify this agreement, he may not be able to avoid a just punishment."

The actual provisions of the document are of too great a length to be reproduced here *verbatim*, but their effect may be briefly summarized thus :—

1. All foreign curiosities that might arrive were to be reserved for the benefit of the Emperor.
2. Conventions of the members of the association formed by the Instrument of Agreement were to be attended by all members.
3. The members were to meet together and fix the prices at which goods should be bought from or sold to Foreigners, and anyone making a private bargain with a Foreigner should be punished.
4. Members were to meet together to fix the price at which goods brought to Canton from the interior by Chinese merchants should be sold to Foreigners, and anyone selling at a price not so fixed should be punished.
5. Dealings with Foreigners were to be honestly conducted. "To cheat Foreigners is a crime our laws never pardon; if, for the future, anyone should impose false goods, he shall be liable to punishment."

6. All shipments of commodities were to be entered in a public book.

7. Manufactures such as fans, lacquered ware, embroideries, pictures, and things "which have no relation to the grand cargo," might be dealt in by the shopkeepers, who were prohibited from being concerned in any other investments, or from meddling with the commerce in general.

8. The trade in porcelain was to be left to those who understood it, but a charge of 30 per cent. was imposed in favour of members of the association.

9. Sellers of green tea were to attest the weight of the tea sold, and were not to adulterate it.

10. Chinese merchants were to pay beforehand the price of goods sold to them by Foreigners.

11. One member might buy as much as half the whole stock of any one Foreigner, but the rest was to be sold to all the members.

12. Anyone trading contrary to the provisions of this agreement was to be punished.

The thirteenth clause set out the financial reasons for constituting the monopoly in these words :—

"To set up shops and establish warehouses is a thing of no small consequence, by reason of the great expense, and those at present have every year greatly suffered. It cannot certainly be thought fair that the new Warehouses should enjoy the same profit as the old ones ; and they would think such treatment very unreasonable : for the future, therefore, those who would set up Warehouses shall be obliged to deposit a thousand Taels towards defraying the expenses of the Community ; and then they shall have the permission to be enrolled in the Third Class of Merchants. Whosoever will not submit to this Agreement shall be liable to punishment."

For a Chinese document this agreement is unusually explicit. The recital that it had been sworn to by the parties thereto, and the statement that criminal punishment was to be inflicted upon any who disobeyed its provisions, show that it was regarded as embodying a solemn undertaking. Some of its provisions are excellent in letter ; but, as so often happens in China, such provisions were probably inserted more for ornament than because they were intended to be enforced. No Chinese would seriously contend that "to cheat Foreigners is a crime our laws never pardon" ; but the sentiment sounds excellently well, and so is inserted. Still, it would appear as though the members of the association, having organized their monopoly, had some desire that a kind of protection should be extended to the Foreigner, possibly through a fear that if nothing of this kind were done, the Foreigner might cease to come and trade. One striking feature of the agreement is especially worthy of notice, namely, the division of all traders into "hong merchants," or "warehouse keepers," who were to enjoy the commerce in the "grand cargo," and "shopkeepers," who were permitted to deal only in trumpery articles. The distinction thus introduced is one that remained right down to the year 1843. The signatories to the agreement were all hong merchants, five of whom were ranked as of the first class, five as of the second class, and six as of the third class. In addition to the intrinsic evidence of the solemnity of the engagements thus entered into, the supercargoes themselves state that "this Agreement was made in the most sacred manner, by going before one of their Idols, and there swearing and sacrificing a cock, and drinking his blood."[1] It was evident to the supercargoes that, if this monopoly were allowed to stand, they would be at the mercy of the Chinese, and profitable trading would come to an end. They at once got up an agitation and laid the matter before the "Chuntuck,"[2] who summoned the Hong Merchants before him and explained the evil results that must follow if the monopoly were enforced. After lengthy deliberations the members who had subscribed to the new arrangement resolved to tear up the Instrument of Agreement, but whether this was actually done it is impossible to say. The records go to show that the

[1] *East India Company's Factory Records.* (MSS. in the India Office under *China Materials*, vol. viii, pp. 1374–1380.)

[2] This must be the *Chientuh*, or Commissioner of Customs, who is more commonly referred to as the Hoppo.

system of confining the trade with the English to a select body of Chinese merchants took its rise from this date.[1] It did not disappear for more than a century.

Although, as we have seen, the "usual privileges," granted by the Chinese authorities to the supercargoes, included the right to exercise jurisdiction over and punish the Company's servants and seamen in respect of offences committed on Chinese territory, still this right was not enforced without difficulty in extreme cases. In 1721 a servant of the Hoppo was accidentally shot by one of the crew of the *Bonitta*, an English ship. Thereupon the Chinese seized the second officer and four of the crew of another English ship, the *Cadogan*, who happened to be on shore, and beat them after stripping them of all their clothes and belongings. The supercargoes protested against this violent proceeding, and threatened to withdraw their trade from Canton if reparation were not made. The Hoppo at once degraded the mandarin responsible for this violence, and the matter there terminated. This resolute attitude of the supercargoes was due partly to reasons of policy, as is evident from the following passage in one of their letters: "We thought it absolutely necessary to carry this point, for as they encroach upon us every year, and render the trade of the place more difficult, we took this occasion in some measure to put a stop to the growing insults, which might otherwise have come to extremities." In the following year the gunner's mate of the *King George*, firing at a bird in a paddy field, accidentally killed a boy. No violent measures were taken by the Chinese, but redress was demanded, ostensibly on behalf of the parents of the boy. Eventually the supercargoes had to pay 2,000 taels in settlement of all claims in respect of this matter. Of this sum the parents received 350 taels.

About this time the privileges enjoyed by the Company's supercargoes and servants at Canton would seem to have reached high-water mark. The "usual privileges," as granted in 1723, again provided in terms that English servants or

[1] *East India Company's Factory Records.* (MSS. in the India Office No. 11, under *Memoir: Intercourse with China*, Part I, p. 96.)

sailors committing disorders should not be punished by the Chinese, but complaint should be made to the supercargoes, and they should do justice. Further, it was conceded that provisions and stores for the ships and Factory might be freely bought, and that the supercargoes might engage what *linguists* and servants they pleased, and turn them away at their pleasure. But in the year 1723 a change was apparent in the demeanour of the Chinese officials. The Tituck[1] notified the supercargoes that he intended to send his lieutenants aboard their ships, to see what guns and ammunition they might have on board. This was an indignity to which the English had never been subjected at Canton. The supercargoes replied to the Tituck that they would not suffer such an inspection to be made. A serious controversy arose, and the Tituck insisted that, having said so much about the matter, he must carry it through, and represented to the supercargoes that, as his inspection would be merely formal, it was unreasonable in them to persist in their refusal. Thus persuaded the supercargoes reluctantly gave way, and having caused a few small arms to be disposed on the quarter-deck, allowed these to be inspected. This concession led to the imposition of further degradations, which now began to be put upon the supercargoes and their servants. The officials at the Bocca Tigris claimed the right to search for arms, and went so far as to seize and carry off the British[2] flag from a boat.

So great did the oppression of the Chinese officials become, that the supercargoes considered a plan for transferring their trade to Amoy, whither no English ship had been sent for some years. After many complaints from the English, however, the officials adopted a more reasonable attitude. Having gained sundry concessions as a result of their complaints, the Company continued to trade at Canton. In 1707 they obtained the privilege of having stores and food brought into the Factory free of customs. The next year one of the

[1] Chinese admiral.

[2] This adjective now begins to appear in the records, where previously the word English would have been exclusively used. Scotland had passed the Act of Union with England in 1707.

Company's ships put into Amoy, and was greatly welcomed by the officials at that port. The Tituck offered to reduce the port charges to one-half, and to grant " any liberty he could desire " to any English captain who would trade thither, but apparently the prospect was not sufficiently attractive to induce the Company to act on these promises. It should be noticed, in passing, that at this time the East India Company suffered severely from the competition of the Ostend Company, which was now trading to the Far East. The Court of Directors instructed the supercargoes to attempt to get the " Ostenders " excluded from Canton, but on the attempt being made, the Chinese stated in the clearest way that the privileges of the port were granted to Europeans in general, and that any design against the Ostenders would react against the English Company. In England, however, the assistance of Parliament was invoked, and statutory powers were obtained by the Company which enabled them to deal more effectually with " interlopers " generally, and to penalize any attempt to support the Ostend Company.[1]

The Chinese now resorted in a still stronger degree to a form of oppression of which the Company had already experience. This was the imposition of heavy and illegal duties on the trade at Canton. In 1727 an apparent termination of disputes on matters of this kind had been reached, by the Hoppo agreeing that no greater sum should be paid as measurage, or as duties on goods, than was set down in the " Emperor's Book." But in 1728 an additional charge of 10 per cent. was imposed on all goods sold by the Chinese merchants to ships from Europe. The reason for this, as given in the records, was that the country ships, that is to say, the ships trading from the other presidencies in the East Indies, brought raw produce on which a heavy duty was paid to the Emperor; but as the ships from Europe brought no such produce, this additional tax was imposed on them to make things even.

[1] The charter of the Ostend Company was granted by the Emperor Charles VI in 1722, but withdrawn in 1725. The statutes referred to are 5 Geo. I, c. 21; 7 Geo. I, stat. 1, c. 21; 9 Geo. I, c. 26; 5 Geo. II, c. 29.

A further sum of 1,950 taels for each ship was demanded as a present for the Hoppo. By way of protesting against this breach of faith, the Company's supercargoes, accompanied by the "Madras, Bombay, and French gentlemen," making eleven in all, proceeded in chairs to the yamên and insisted on having a personal interview with the Viceroy, claiming that they had the right to address him whenever they suffered under grievances. On this occasion they were admitted to the Viceroy's presence; but when some months later they attempted to gain a second interview, they were unsuccessful. On the latter occasion they were received by the "Chungya," who "gave them but rough treatment," and described their application for redress as "a trifling affair." This official told them that when they had anything to bring before him "they must apply to the Merchants to get them a hearing." He refused to give them a "chop" allowing freedom of entry into the city, saying that the Emperor had ordered that no stranger should have that liberty. This is the first indication we have of the practice that afterwards arose, of addressing the officials by means of a petition presented through the Hong Merchants, which became the recognized means of communication between the supercargoes and the Viceroy and other officials. It was the refusal of Lord Napier in 1824 to follow this practice that started the controversy which led to the first war between Great Britain and China.

The supercargoes did not quietly submit to the payment of these exactions. In 1730 they made representations to Peking on the subject, which, though not immediately successful, possibly had some effect in producing the edict of 1736, by which the illegal charges were abolished. This is the first instance of the Company's agents having recourse to Peking. No particulars are given in the records as to what exactly was done in order to get the grievances laid before the Throne. For a few years afterwards things remained in a state of quiescence, but in 1734 the impositions were so heavy at Canton, that only one ship, the *Harrison*, was sent thither. Under these circumstances the Company again sought to establish a trade at other Chinese ports. An attempt was made to renew the trade with Amoy, and the *Grafton* was despatched for that purpose ; but after months had been wasted in negotiations of the most futile kind, the Hoppo demanding 20 per cent. for himself alone, in addition to the ordinary duties, the *Grafton* left for Canton, having been unable to get permission to trade with any except those merchants who were in league with the officials. In 1736 the *Normanton* made an effort to open up a trade at Ningpo, but after wasting two months in attempting to obtain fair conditions, she sailed for Canton.

Just about that time the Emperor Kien-lung ascended the throne, and signalized the commencement of his long reign by remitting both the 10 per cent. duty and the present, or *cumshaw*, of 1,950 taels.[1] Notwithstanding this edict of Kien-lung, these illegal charges continued to be exacted until the whole system was abolished by the Treaty of Nanking in 1843. The other provisions of the edict, which ordered that when Foreign ships came to Whampoa all their cannon, arms, and ammunition should be delivered up to the Chinese officials, were similarly disregarded, the officials finding it more profitable to accept the bribes offered to them not to execute the law, than to put the imperial commands into force. The publication of this edict was made the occasion of an unpleasing innovation in the relations between the Chinese officials and the English merchants. The supercargoes were summoned to the Imperial Hall of Audience at Canton, to hear the Emperor's commands publicly read. On attending, in response to this summons, they found the Chinese merchants also present. When the edict was about to be read, the order was given that all present should *kotow* to the Emperor's name.[2] This the English resolutely refused to do, with the result that a lengthy dispute arose, which ended, however, in compliance on their part being waived.

The history of the trade at Canton for the next hundred

[1] The word *cumshaw*, which is the pidgin English for a *gift* or *present*, is probably derived from *kum-sëah*, the Fukien word for *I thank you*, or from the Cantonese *kumsha*, meaning *a sand of gold*. (J. R. Morrison, *Commercial Guide*.)

[2] As to the *kotow*, see chap. vi, *post*, p. 106.

years from this time is not agreeable to the patriotic Englishman. It is mainly a record of acquiescence in humiliations of every kind, put, it is true, upon all Foreigners alike, but not the less such as must have lowered the dignity of the British nation in the eyes of the Chinese. This attitude of subservience is not to be attributed to the absence of courage or resolution in the Company's representatives, but rather to the desire of the Directors in London to preserve the trade at all costs. This is plain on a perusal of the contemporaneous records. If the supercargoes at Canton showed any behaviour that the Court of Directors considered likely to imperil the continuity of the trade, they were reprimanded by despatches that indicate in the plainest manner the disapproval of the Directors. At times, however, in spite of the assiduity of the Directors in commanding a policy of acquiescence, the supercargoes revolted against some fresh indignity proposed to be inflicted on them, or some fresh exaction proposed to be levied. These assertions of right took place more particularly on those rare occasions when the arrival of some ship of the Royal Navy disturbed the atmosphere of passive obedience that was wont to prevail at Canton. The most noteworthy instance of this kind was the arrival of *H.M.S. Centurion*, under Commodore Anson, which anchored off Macao, in 1741.

This is an important epoch in the history of the English in China. The Commodore, at that time engaged in making his famous voyage round the world, put into the Canton River for the purpose of obtaining supplies. The Chinese protested against a man-of-war entering the river at all, whereupon he determined to proceed in a small boat right up to Canton itself. The Hoppo's officers, however, refused to issue a permit, and threatened the watermen with dire punishment if they should venture to proceed. Incensed at this treatment, Commodore Anson announced, that if he did not receive a permit within twenty-four hours, he would arm the *Centurion's* boats and go up to Canton in them. This threat had the desired effect, and the journey was made under permit. On arriving the Commodore announced to the supercargoes his intention of calling on the Viceroy in person. They, fearing that so unusual a proceeding would imperil the trade, begged him not to carry this intention into effect, and prevailed upon him to abandon his design, with the result that they were able to obtain, through the Hong Merchants, permission for him to purchase provisions. It was then discovered that the *Centurion* had sprung a leak, and must be laid down for repairs ; but the necessary permission was only obtained from the Chinese authorities after protracted negotiations. The *Centurion*, having been repaired, put to sea. In a very short time Commodore Anson returned to the river with a valuable prize in the shape of a Spanish ship that he had captured on her way from Acapulco and Manilla to Lisbon.

Immediately Anson re-entered the river, the Chinese officials required him to pay both on the *Centurion* and on her prize such duties as were usually levied on merchant vessels. With this demand he refused to comply. He demanded an interview with the Viceroy, and on his demand being refused, determined to go up to Canton and obtain an interview, by force if necessary. Having arrayed his boat's crew in their dress jackets, he proceeded again to Canton, and was only dissuaded from compelling the Viceroy to grant him an interview by the supercargoes, who obtained from the Chinese merchants a promise that the Chinese would see his bread baked, his meat salted, and his stores prepared with the utmost despatch, and that they would obtain permission for the same to be shipped when ready. As was only to be expected, there was a good deal of delay in the fulfilment of these promises. Growing impatient, the Commodore sent a letter by one of his officers to the Viceroy, demanding an interview. Before an answer had been received to this communication, it happened that a fire broke out in Canton city, by which a hundred shops and eleven streets of warehouses were destroyed. The fire was only checked by the exertions of Anson and his seamen, a service which so pleased the Viceroy that he appointed a day for the desired interview. At the meeting thus arranged the Commodore complained of the delays to which he had been subjected, and further asked that the grievances under which the British merchants laboured might be redressed. No promise was made, and the interview closed by the Viceroy wishing the Commodore a prosperous voyage, heartily glad, there can be no doubt, to see the last of such a pertinacious guest.

It was supposed at the time that the visit of Commodore Anson, and his vigorous measures to secure proper recognition of his dignity as a naval officer, would result beneficially in a change of attitude on the part of the Chinese towards the English residents. This hope was destined to prove absolutely unfounded. After the visit the Chinese adopted as their habitual demeanour that attitude of insolent arrogance which was continued until the close of the First War with England. Immediately Commodore Anson had taken his departure, the illegal exactions were increased, and the supercargoes found themselves involved in the old disputes. They did not tamely submit to every imposition of the Chinese authorities, and matters rapidly came to a state of tension. The temper of the two parties is well illustrated by an incident that occurred in 1747. One of the Company's officers, when embarking from the Factory, objected to having his escritoire examined, and refused to allow the Hoppo's servants to make such an examination. The Chinese authorities at once had the ship's *linguist* arrested and put in chains, demanded the surrender of the officer, and stopped the trade. The supercargoes stood firm, and refused to comply with the demand. Moreover, they informed the Viceroy that if the trade were not put on a better footing, they would have to leave the port. There is nothing to show that the supercargoes ever receded from this attitude, but the trade was at length renewed, from which it is to be inferred that they secured some modification of the Chinese contentions. That they still contemplated having to make a determined stand for fair treatment, is evident from the fact that in the following year the Court of Directors, apparently fearing a heavy loss, if they should find it necessary suddenly to withdraw their representatives from Canton, prohibited the supercargoes for the future from advancing bargain money, or paying for goods before delivery.[1]

[1] *East India Company's Factory Records.* (MSS. in the India Office under *China Materials*, vol. ix, p. 87.) Auber's *China*, p. 166.

Another incident that took place about this time shows that the Chinese populace were not more respectful than the Chinese officials, though more easily dealt with when guilty of misbehaviour. Captain Congreve, of the English ship *Onslow*, was taking a walk on French Island, one of the islands near the anchorage of the European ships, when he was attacked by Chinese, who stole all his money, his buckles, and the buttons off his coat, and would have cut off his finger to get his ring had he not pulled that valuable off and handed it over to them. Stripped of all he had, he was allowed to return to his ship. The next day, being Sunday, he armed sixty of his crew, and taking with him four cannon, attacked the town of Whampoa, near which the robbery had taken place. These summary measures soon brought the town officials to him asking for mercy. When he had explained to them his reasons for making the attack, a search was made in the town for the robbers, and four persons apprehended. These were bound before his eyes, their hands and feet being tied together, and sent to Canton for further punishment.[1]

What would clearly seem to have been an opportunity of putting the trade on a better footing than that to which it had now sunk, presented itself in 1751, when the Chief of the Factory was a supercargo named Misenor. The Hong Merchants suggested that, as the Emperor would be at Nanking that year to celebrate the "great birth-day" of his mother, the supercargoes should send thither a deputation with presents, and should petition the Emperor for the abolition of the *cumshaw* and some of the burdensome impositions under which the trade laboured. So confident were the Chinese of the success of such a mission, that they offered to pay the expense of the journey and of the presents. The opportunity was neglected by Misenor, who declined the proposal on the ground that other nations besides Great Britain might benefit if the mission were successful.[2] A more sorry reason it is impossible to imagine. This is the only occasion during the

[1] Osbeck, *A Voyage to China* (Forster's translation), vol. i, p. 322; *Chinese Repository*, vol. i, p. 215.

[2] *Chinese Repository*, vol. v, p. 127.

whole of our intercourse with China when our policy has been actuated by any fear that others besides ourselves might reap the benefit of our actions.

By this time the English had already obtained a predominant share in the trade at Canton, and held the first place among the nations trading at that port. In the year 1750, out of eighteen vessels that arrived at Whampoa, no less than one-half were British ships, eight being from Europe, and one a country ship.[1] Of the rest two were Swedish, two were French, four Dutch, and one Spanish. The Factories consisted at this time of Chinese houses, two stories high, built on the bank of the river, or on piles overhanging the water, which were let by their Chinese owners to the supercargoes of the European ships. As a rule, each ship hired a separate Factory. The ships were supposed to stay for only five months in the year, but some managed to remain a complete twelvemonth. Contemporary writers, speaking of the behaviour of the native population at Canton in those days, describe it in terms which show that it was not very different from that sometimes exhibited at the present day, in these words :—

"It is dangerous for a single person to venture too far, because he is in danger of being stripped to the very shirt. Though the curiosity of the Europeans may not be perhaps void of blame, yet the natives look as though they were glad to find a pretence to use violence against a stranger, especially when they are sure of overpowering him. . . . If you go further up into the town, they call you names, and pelt you with stones, which fly about your ears as thick as hail. If you intend to go out of town, you must have company, walk fast, and carry a good stick."[2]

"I had a mind to see the situation of the environs of the suburbs in that part where I had not yet been, and was forced to go by myself for want of company. As soon as I had passed the usual trading streets, the boys gathered about me in thousands, throwing sand, stones, and dirt at me ; and shouted

[1] A country ship is a ship, privately owned, trading from one of the Company's presidencies under licence from the Company.

[2] Toreen : *Voyage to Suratte* (Forster's translation).

altogether, *Akia, aque ya, quailo*; and with this music they followed me through the whole town. . . . As I stopped here, and only gathered now and then a plant, my disagreeable company stopped their noise, especially when I turned to them. Here was no road which carried directly into the country, nor did I venture any further, but returned whence I came. However, in the afternoon, I went out of town, in a palankin, by this means avoiding my disagreeable forenoon companions. Returning again, I went on foot about the wall of Canton on the side from the country.

"When we came to the first city gate, towards the side of the European burying-place, a mandarin, with a whip in his hand, joined us to accompany us about the city. Near this gate was a Chinese inn, where brandy and tea were sold. The people stood by the side of the round-house on the wall and stared at us; however, we got by without hurt, though not without fear, for we remembered that a person was some time before pelted with stones from this very place. When we approached nearer to the suburbs, we everywhere, and almost close up to the wall, found houses; they were all full of men, and especially children and youths, who sang their old song, of which they were put in mind by the grown people, if they did not begin it themselves. Yet we likewise found an old reverend man, who had more sense than the others, and made his children or grandchildren greet us civilly."[1]

Even at this early date, the Foreigners at Canton were insulted every year by the publication of lying placards, accusing them of horrible vices and crimes, issued by the officials for the purpose of vilifying them in the eyes of the populace. In protest against this and other indignities, the supercargoes, in 1754, refused to allow any more ships to come up to Whampoa until they received better treatment. Alarmed at the prospect of losing the profits that flowed from the Foreign trade, the Viceroy instructed the Hoppo to render the supercargoes any assistance in his power, and promised that he himself would hear their grievances if they should

[1] Osbeck, *A Voyage to China* (Forster's translation), vol. ii, p. 19; *Chinese Repository*, vol. i, pp. 216-220.

think it necessary to address him. The lack of unanimity among the different Europeans prevented them from gaining the advantage which this occasion offered. " Some gentlemen were of opinion that we ought to make a stand ; and as, by arguing the case, we seemed to be the farther from a determination, we parted without any resolve, except that every man would do as he liked best."[1]

Owing to the fact that England and France were at war, the English and French sailors were continually attacking one another at Whampoa. In one of these affrays a Frenchman shot an Englishman dead, under circumstances that showed deliberate murder. The correspondence that arose over this fatality was conducted on the French side by "Le Conseil de Direction de Canton, représentant la nation Française."[2] On an appeal from the English for justice, the Viceroy stopped the trade and demanded the surrender of the guilty person. After a time someone was seized, who said he was responsible, and imprisoned at Canton ; but in the following year he was liberated by the Emperor's orders, on the occasion of a general act of grace. As a means of preventing further disturbances, Danes' Island, which was the Danish burying-ground, and French Island, which was the burying-ground for the French, English, Swedes, and Dutch, were allotted to the English and French sailors respectively, as their places of recreation.[3]

The occasion of this appeal to the Viceroy was also used to lay before him the objections to a practice which had grown up, of requiring two Chinese merchants to go bail for the good conduct, in paying the duties and port charges, of every ship that came to Whampoa. It was only natural that the merchants who placed themselves under such an obligation expected some benefit from the trade done by the ships for which

[1] Davis, *China and the Chinese*, vol. i, p. 47.

[2] It is difficult to say what this body was. Possibly it was more or less self-constituted like the authority that administered the "Cité Meillotte" at Ching Wan Tao during the Boxer troubles of 1900 and afterwards.

[3] Davis, *China and the Chinese*, vol. i, p. 48 ; *Chinese Repository*, vol. i, p. 222.

they became sureties. Only the more wealthy could afford to undertake such a liability, and in this way the trade with Europeans had in fact become a monopoly in the hands of the very merchants who, in 1720, had attempted to form the Co-hong. Thus, in spite of the supposed dissolution of that body, the monopoly of the Hong Merchants had by this time assumed a very real existence. The entry in the records of the East India Company thus sums up the position :—

"A discussion took place at the same time with reference to the practice of naming Security Merchants for each ship, a practice which, it was stated, had not existed above twenty years, and to which the merchants strongly objected, as they thereby became responsible to the Government for all the duties and customs on all the goods imported in such ships, whether purchased by the security merchant himself, or any other person. In like manner he was also accountable for the duties on Export Cargoes. Moreover, he became subject to demands for curiosities brought out in the ship, and that for one-tenth of what the security paid for them. Hence he must be impoverished, or the Company charged excessive prices for the Commodities of Trade."

On July 29th, the supercargoes had an interview with the Viceroy to discuss this question, and, as if to show how little their representations were heeded, only ten days later it was announced that two security merchants must be named for each ship, and that any deficiency in the duties would be levied on the whole body of security merchants.[1] In the following year, that is to say, in 1755, the Emperor Kien-lung issued an imperial edict commanding that all dealings with Foreigners be confined to the Hong Merchants, that the latter should be jointly and severally sureties for the duties for which any of their number were security, and that trade with the shopkeepers should be only in small articles of no importance. Thus the monopoly of the Hong Merchants became officially established under the sanction of the Emperor himself.

[1] *East India Company's Factory Records.* (MSS. in the India Office No. 11, under *Memoir : Intercourse with China*, Part I, pp. 96-8.)

CHAPTER V

THE TRADE CONFINED TO CANTON

ONE of the most striking features of the commercial intercourse between the nations of Europe and the Chinese is, that for more than two centuries it was carried on without any adequate means of communication in the nature of a written or spoken language. In the earliest times the English traders had to use Portuguese in order to make themselves understood, that being the only foreign tongue with which the Chinese could claim any kind of acquaintance. Even so, it was with difficulty that they were able to communicate all the ideas which must necessarily come under discussion, when two nations, hitherto unknown to one another, first commence to engage in the operations of commerce. The Portuguese of which the Chinese had any knowledge, judging it by that spoken for commercial purposes in much later times at Macao, was of so corrupt a kind, that only the simplest notions could be conveyed to a Chinese who had to rely on this as a medium of communication with the English merchants. When the British trade outstripped that of all the other European nations trading at Canton, and assumed the place of first importance, the Chinese commenced to attempt to carry on their trading operations in English, and made such efforts as they were capable of to speak our language.

By the law of China it was forbidden that any Chinese should teach to " barbarians " the language of the Flowery Land. Thus it happened that from the earliest times the English traders were at the mercy of those Chinese who professed to have a sufficient knowledge of some Foreign language to enable them to act as interpreters. This class, known as the *linguists*, conducted all the trading negotiations between the Chinese and the Foreigners who resorted to Canton. To these *linguists* is due the introduction or evolution of the commercial jargon known as " pidgin English," which since the beginning of the eighteenth century has been the language used by British subjects engaged in commerce in China. A more wretched and inadequate medium for the expression of ideas it is almost impossible to imagine. The ordinary Cantonese are unable to pronounce the letters *b*, *v*, *d*, *r*, and *st*. For *b* they substitute *t*; for *d*, *r* and *st* they use *t*, *l*, and *sz* respectively. The *linguists* of early times, using these substitutions where applicable, and as regards other sounds indulging their fancy in any way they pleased, invented a number of words which they were pleased to call English. There is no alphabet in Chinese, and the only way of conveying in writing to a Chinese mind the pronunciation of an English word is to write down for each syllable a Chinese character which, when pronounced, resembles in sound the syllable of the English word. A Chinese, seeing these characters, gives them their proper Chinese pronunciation, and fondly imagines that he thus correctly reproduces the sound of the English word whose pronunciation the characters are intended to represent, oblivious of the fact that in each language there are some sounds which cannot be represented graphically in the other. Acting on these principles the *linguists* produced a number of words and taught them to their fellow-countrymen as English, which were in sound as unlike the real English they were intended to be as could well be imagined. These came into common use for business purposes. The English traders, finding how difficult a language Chinese was, and discovering that anyone who sought to learn it must construct his own grammar and dictionary, as no books of that kind were in existence in those days, quickly adopted the "business English" or "pidgin English" of the *linguists*, as being the only medium of communication that could be acquired without immense labour. For the ordinary purposes of commerce a very small vocabulary could be made to do duty, and so the number of words to be learnt was not very large. How different they were in sound from the English, which they were supposed to be, will be seen at once from the fact that the first twenty numerals were respectively pronounced, *wun*, *too*, *te-le*, *faw*, *fi*, *sik-she*, *sum-wun*, *oot*, *ni*, *teng*, *lum-wun*, *te-lup*, *ta-teng, faw-teng, fi-teng, sik-she-teng, sum-wun-teng, oot-teng, ni-teng, tune-te.*[1] Some of the words used by the *linguists* were of Portuguese origin, so that "pidgin" English at the best is but a hybrid dialect made up of mispronounced English and Portuguese terms. In the construction of sentences the *linguists* followed the Chinese language, which in this respect bears no resemblance to our own. In speaking "pidgin" the method was and is to construct the sentence in Chinese and then substitute for each Chinese word its equivalent in "pidgin English." It is not surprising that even at the present day, when "pidgin" has become somewhat more like real English than it originally was, the Englishman at first finds "pidgin" as difficult of comprehension as Chinese itself. It is only because of the small number of words and constructions employed therein, that he becomes able to use it with less effort than it would take him to obtain an equally serviceable knowledge of Chinese itself.[2]

Recognising that the intercourse between the English and Chinese was entirely at the mercy of the *linguists*, and knowing how useless for the expression of any but the simplest ideas was this jargon, on which the supercargoes had to rely, the East India Company resolved in 1753 to send out to Canton two young men to study the Chinese language and to be trained to act as the Company's interpreters. Until this time there had been no provision for securing that there should be anyone in the Factory competent to act as an interpreter. We have seen that one of those who went out with Catchpole to Chusan in 1699 was chosen because of his knowledge of the language, but between that time and 1747 the Company appears to have had no servant in China who knew Chinese. In the latter year Flint, of whom mention will be made again later, qualified himself to act as an interpreter, and it was doubtless due to his exertions that the Company in 1753 arrived at the decision to send out the two young men of whom mention has been made above. It is not surprising

[1] *Chinese Repository*, vol. iv, p. 432.

[2] For a further discussion of "pidgin English" see *Chinese Repository*, vol. iv, pp. 428–435; vol. vi, pp. 276–279.

that in these circumstances difficulties so frequently arose between the English and the Chinese. It says much for the supercargoes that they were able to conduct the trade with so little interruption during many years, when the only way of discussing a difficulty was by using as interpreter a corrupt *linguist*, who at the best could but imperfectly apprehend the views of his English employer, much less interpret them into Chinese.

The career of Flint is one of the most interesting episodes in the history of our intercourse with China. Unfortunately, the amount of information available in reference thereto is but small. He was undoubtedly a man of unusual energy and ability, and not lacking in enterprise or boldness. He seems to have made every possible effort to put the trade at Canton on a better footing, and generally to improve the conditions under which the English trade was carried on, but with no success. His failure shows how little could be done by a private individual to effect a reform, and how little desire the Court of Directors of the East India Company had that any change should be brought about. In 1753 the Court sent out instructions, that an attempt was to be made to open a trade at Liampo (Ningpo). Accordingly, in 1755, Flint, with one of the young men who had been sent out to study the language, proceeded to Ningpo and Chusan, and were favourably received by the officials at each of those places. The *foo-yuen* readily granted them permission to trade at both ports on the terms proposed by them, which included the payment of much lighter duties than those levied at Canton; but the Viceroy, hearing that the *Holdernesse*, the ship in which they had come, was attempting to act on the terms of this permission, ordered that her arms and ammunition should be delivered up, and that the same duties should be paid as at Canton. The *foo-yuen* thereupon memorialized the Throne on the subject, and it was agreed by all concerned that until an answer to the memorial should be received, half the guns and ammunition should be delivered up and the *Holdernesse* should be allowed to unload her cargo.

In answer to this memorial the Emperor Kien-lung issued

the edict which more than any other makes his reign famous in the history of the relations between Europe and China. Impressed with the difficulties that arose between his subjects and Europeans at any port where the latter determined to trade, and anxious to consolidate the control over Europeans which, in the opinion of the Chinese, a peaceful intercourse demanded, he determined to confine the trade between Europeans and Chinese to a single port. The port chosen for this purpose was that at which Europeans had first traded. In 1757 he published the famous edict which confined all trade with Foreigners, excepting the Russians, to Canton, and laid down detailed regulations for the control of Foreign commerce and the punishment of persons trading at other ports.[1] He particularly forbade European ships from trading at Ningpo or Chusan, and to enforce this prohibition, commanded that all Foreign ships entering either of those ports should deliver up all their arms, guns, ammunition and sails, and pay double duties. It is owing to this edict that the history of our intercourse with China from 1757 to the outbreak of hostilities in 1840 is the history of our trade at Canton. It is possible that Kien-lung, in taking this step, was influenced by the example of the Japanese, who some hundred years before had confined the trade with Foreigners to the single port of Nagasaki. The Japanese prohibition was much more strict, inasmuch as only a single nation, the Dutch, were allowed to engage in trade at that port, and they were confined to the small artificial island of Deshima. As soon as the imperial edict was received at Ningpo, the Viceroy ordered the English to leave. In vain Flint urged that the season was unfavourable. Forced to put to sea, he resolved to sail North, and present his case to the Emperor himself. Having reached the Pei-ho, he proceeded to Tientsin, being the first Englishman who ever set foot in that city, and persuaded one of the local officials to present his petition to the Throne.

[1] By an edict published in 1737 viceroys and lieutenant-governors had been ordered to treat with compassion all Foreigners driven ashore or into port by stress of weather, and this continued to be the law. J. R. Morrison, *Chinese Commercial Guide*, p. 25.

By kind permission *of Mr. John Murray*

THE EMPEROR KIEN-LUNG

The Emperor despatched a high official to Canton, to inquire into the matters set out in the petition. As a result of this inquiry the Hoppo was degraded and several impositions were abolished, but the cumshaw of 1,950 taels, and the 6 per cent. duty received the imperial sanction. It was further commanded that in future European ships should not be called "Devil's Ships," but should be styled "Western Ocean Ships."

Flint appears to have gone to Ningpo a second time, after the publication of the edict closing that port to Foreign trade. Late in 1759 he returned to Canton, and on the 6th of December was summoned by the Viceroy to appear before him. The supercargoes, fearing some treachery on the part of the Chinese, refused to allow Flint to attend this interview alone, and resolved to accompany him. When they had arrived at the Viceroy's yamên, the Hong Merchants proposed to them that they should go in one by one. This proposal was rejected, and the supercargoes and Flint went in together. When they reached the inner court, their swords were forcibly taken from them, they themselves were rushed into the presence of the Viceroy, and the Viceroy's attendants attempted to throw them down in order to make them *kotow*. The English made a determined resistance, and the Viceroy thereupon ordered his servants to desist. He then showed to Flint a document, which he said was an imperial edict, by which it was decreed that Flint should be banished to Macao for three years, and afterwards sent to England. The Viceroy stated that this sentence was imposed as a punishment for attempting to open a trade at Ningpo contrary to the orders from Peking; he further added that the man who had presented the petition at Tientsin had been beheaded. Flint was at once taken to a place of confinement three leagues from Macao, where he was imprisoned for three years without being allowed to have any communication with any of his countrymen at Canton.[1]

[1] As to Flint, see *Factory Records of the East India Company* (MSS. in the India Office No. 11, under *Memoir: Intercourse with China*, Part I., pp. 100-6); *Chinese Repository*, vol. v., p. 128; Davis, *China and the Chinese*, vol. i, pp. 46–50; Auber's *China*, pp. 167-172.

The whole of the European community at Canton was indignant at the Viceroy's behaviour. In self-defence the members of the French, Danish, Swedish and Dutch factories joined in a protest. Even at this early date the nations of Europe were learning to sink their differences when faced by a common danger in China. The supercargoes of the East India Company sent full particulars of what had taken place to the Court of Directors in London, who resolved to send out a special mission to inquire into and report on the situation. For this purpose they chose Captain Skottowe, the commander of the merchantman, *Royal George*, by whom in the year 1760 they despatched a letter to the Viceroy of Canton, expressing their disappointment at being excluded from Ningpo, and asking that the grievances under which their supercargoes and servants laboured might be remedied, and Flint set at liberty. In particular, they asked for the abolition of the cumshaw of 1,950 taels, of the 6 per cent. charged on imports and the 2 per cent. charged on all silver paid to the Hoppo: for leave to pay the duties themselves and not through the security merchants; that the Hoppo would consent to hear any complaint they might wish to prefer; and that they should have the right to appeal from the decision of the Hoppo to the Viceroy. This mission was in no sense a diplomatic mission from the sovereign of Great Britain to the Emperor of China, and so does not come within the same category as the embassies of Lord Macartney and Lord Amherst, which are discussed in the next chapter. Captain Skottowe was simply a special representative of the East India Company, sent out by them to inquire into certain matters and to make certain representations to the Viceroy. For the time being he superseded the supercargoes in the affairs to which his instructions related. The Company, whilst wishing not to excite suspicion in the minds of the Chinese by parading Captain Skottowe as a person of high rank, were not unmindful of the prestige which would attach to the mission, if in any way it could be shown to be acting under the sanction of the King of Great Britain. Orders were therefore given that Captain Skottowe should be addressed as Mr. Skottowe, but that it should be given out that he was the brother of the King's Under Secretary of State, who had the honour to write the King's letters. This statement was absolutely false; it was based on the fact that Captain Skottowe's brother happened to hold some sort of a post under the government in England. This piece of dishonesty met with the fate it deserved. The mission was a complete failure, not one of the requests preferred being conceded by the Chinese authorities.[1] Flint remained in prison under the same conditions as before until the year 1762, when he was carried by the Chinese to Whampoa, and there put on the *Horsendon* to be conveyed to England.[2]

The condition under which the trade between Chinese and Foreigners might in future be carried on were promulgated by imperial edict in 1760, the issuing of which was probably directly due to the efforts made by Captain Skottowe to mitigate the evils of the intercourse at Canton. These conditions were stated in the following terms :—

"1. Foreigners must not stay at Canton over the winter, gaining information respecting the prices of goods, and making purchases in order to obtain profit. If any of their affairs are not concluded at the end of the season, they may be allowed to stay at Macao.

"2. Natives must not borrow money from Foreigners, under penalty of remote transportation and confiscation of the money borrowed.

"3. Natives must not degrade themselves and the dignity of the Empire by serving Foreigners.

"4. Proper officers must be placed over ships to prevent illegalities.

"5. Foreigners may reside only with Hong Merchants. Natives may not build elegant houses, with the view of tempting Foreigners to pay large rents for them; nor may traitorous natives go into their Factories. Their intercourse must be only with the Hong Merchants and the Linguists."[3]

[1] *Factory Records of the East India Company* (MSS. in the India Office No. 11, under *Memoir: Intercourse with China*, Part I, pp. 110-112; Auber's *China*, pp. 173-4.

[2] Davis, *China and the Chinese*, vol. i, p. 50.

[3] J. R. Morrison, *Chinese Commercial Guide*, p. 47.

By this edict the intercourse between the English and Chinese was finally stereotyped into such a form that, as will be seen presently, only war broke its rigidity. Remonstrances and complaints, suspensions of trade, embassies and diplomacy, all failed to procure for the Foreigners trading at Canton any amelioration of the hard conditions imposed by the edicts of Kien-lung. But for the fact that in practice these conditions were not observed in all their strictness, the trade could not have continued. For instance, in disregard of the prohibition against Chinese acting as servants, gate-keepers and coolies were in practice permitted to be hired by the Foreign residents. But the provisions that trade should be carried on only with the Hong Merchants, except in such minor articles as the shopmen were allowed to deal in ; that security merchants must be found by every ship that came into port ; that residence at Canton should not extend beyond the trading season in each year ; that access to the officials could be had only through the Hong Merchants ; that all communications should take the form of a servile petition ; and that heavy impositions must be paid, and paid through the security merchants, as a condition precedent to trade of any kind ; these were enforced with regularity and strictness.

For the thirty years preceding the despatch of Lord Macartney's embassy, which took place in 1792, the history of the intercourse between the British and Chinese is for the most part an account of various incidents, that serve to illustrate or emphasize the difficulties under which the trade was conducted. The first of these which claims our attention is the arrival at Whampoa, in 1764, of H.M.S. *Argo*, which is the second occasion in the history of our relations with China in which one of the King's ships visited the Canton river. The man-of-war was convoying the schooner *Cuddalore*, on board of which were half-a-million dollars for the Company's treasury. A controversy at once arose over the measurement of the ship, Captain Affleck, who commanded her, claiming the same treatment as had been accorded to Commodore Anson. The supercargoes were, however, required by the Hoppo to compel

Captain Affleck to allow his ship to be measured, to which they replied that as he was a naval officer they had no jurisdiction over him. The Viceroy then intimated that he regarded the supercargoes as responsible for the conduct of all British subjects that came to Canton. Negotiations ensued which lasted over four months, during which the supercargoes offered to pay for the *Argo* the same duties as would be levied on the largest of the Company's ships, but the Viceroy refused to accede to any such proposal, on the ground that it was his duty to measure the ship and to charge a proper sum as measurement duty. The security merchants, who throughout had refused to become surety for the *Argo*, were now threatened by the Viceroy that, if his demands were not complied with, the supercargoes should be expelled the country, and they themselves bambooed and driven from Canton. At this juncture the supercargoes pointed out to Captain Affleck that if he persisted in the attitude he had taken up, the whole trade would be placed in jeopardy. Moved by these considerations the latter gave way and consented to the *Argo* being measured, after four months had been wasted in a vain dispute, by which the British had gained nothing and the Chinese officials had been exasperated. It is worthy of mention that in connection with this incident a rumour reached the Court of Directors that opium had been shipped on the *Argo*, and that the difficulty which had arisen was not unconnected with this fact. Even at this time the importation of opium was prohibited, the Company's ships alone being exempt from the search for the contraband drug, and it was therefore of the utmost importance that the Company's interest should not be injured by any attempt to trade in the forbidden article.[1]

From the time of the establishment of the Hong Merchants, the Court of Directors of the East India Company had not spared their efforts to get that monopoly abolished. In their letters they continually urged upon the supercargoes

[1] *Factory Records of the East India Company* (MSS. in the India Office No. 11, under *Memoir : Intercourse with China*, Part I, pp. 116–121) ; Auber's *China*, pp. 176–177.

the importance of working to this end, admonishing them at the same time to be particularly careful not to do anything that would give umbrage to the Chinese Government, and to treat the officials with all the respect due to their rank. They also enjoined upon the supercargoes the necessity of seeing that private traders, coming to Canton with the Company's licence, did not reside there continuously, lest the Company should be held responsible for the behaviour of persons over whom they had no efficient control. In 1770 a change was introduced by the Court of Directors into the manner of conducting the trade, an order being issued that the supercargoes, instead of departing every year with the ships that were under their care, which had been the practice up to this time, should reside permanently in China. Notwithstanding this change the body entrusted with the care of the Company's interests at Canton continued to be called supercargoes, or, to give them their full title, the Select Committee of the East India Company's Supercargoes, an appellation which was more commonly abbreviated to that of "Select Committee." It is possible that this change was hastened by the fact that in 1767 the French East India Company had appointed ten supercargoes to reside in Canton "none being sent out from France yearly." In 1771 the English supercargoes advised the Court of Directors that their efforts to get the Co-hong dissolved had been successful, an edict abolishing the Hong Merchants having been procured from the Viceroy by one of that body, named Puankhequa, at a cost of 100,000 taels, which sum the supercargoes had repaid to him.[1] It was soon found that very little real advantage had been gained by this expenditure of money, as might have been expected, seeing that the Co-hong had received the imperial sanction, and after six years, as will be shown presently, a proclamation was issued by the Emperor, stating that in future only Hong Merchants might engage in trade with Foreigners.

[1] *Factory Records of the East India Company* (MSS. in the India Office No. 11, under *Memoir : Intercourse with China*, Part I, p. 125 ; *Correspondence Relating to China* (China Blue Book, 1840), p. 277 ; *Chinese Repository*, vol. v, p. 130.

The East India Company were by this time beginning to experience serious trouble in connection with the private traders, who resorted to Canton under the special licences which the Company were empowered to grant. The ships used by these traders, which were known as "country" ships, were on an altogether different footing from the Company's own East Indiamen, in that they were not directly under the supervision of the Company's supercargoes. To what extent the supercargoes might compel, or attempt to compel, the private traders to obey their orders, without exposing themselves to proceedings in the English Courts of Law, was by no means clear. Their power to suppress interlopers was by this time clearly ascertained, but in regard to the extent of their jurisdiction, if any, over persons who were not servants of the Company, but were lawfully trading in the East Indies, there was a good deal of doubt. These private traders were behaving in a manner that might easily lead to difficulties with the Chinese authorities, particularly in the respect that they lent money to impecunious Chinese traders at very high rates of interest. In 1777 the Court of Directors again directed the supercargoes to enforce the order against the continuous residence of private traders at Canton. In the following year it was discovered that the amount of the debts, due from Chinese merchants to private traders alone, amounted to a total of 1,000,000 taels, in spite of the direct prohibition against debts being incurred to Foreigners promulgated by imperial edict in 1760. In 1780 the question of the status of private traders arose in an acute form in the case of an Englishman named George Smith, who, after having been expelled the port, had been with the Company's permission, allowed by the supercargoes in 1764 to return to Canton for two years, for the purpose of settling up his affairs. On the expiration of the two years he refused to take his departure. The Court of Directors took the opinion of the Attorney-General and of the Solicitor-General and their own standing counsel in England, all of whom were of the opinion that the Company had power to compel Smith to leave the port. Acting on this advice, the Court instructed the supercargoes that Smith was to be removed by force if necessary, but whether any such extreme measure became necessary does not appear.[1]

From time to time difficulties arose with the Chinese authorities, owing to some Chinese being accidentally killed by a Foreigner. In 1769 a Chinese was wounded by one of the English seamen of the *Lord Camden*, whereupon the officials refused to give the vessel a port clearance until the wounded man had sufficiently recovered to be out of danger.[2] On these occasions the English always insisted, with one exception that took place in 1784, to which reference will be made later, on their right to exemption from the jurisdiction of the Chinese courts, but unfortunately their example was not followed by the other Europeans who traded at Canton. In 1770 the Portuguese were guilty of a particularly flagrant act of acquiescence with Chinese demands in a case of this kind. A Chinese had lost his life at Macao, in consequence of which an Englishman named Francis Scott was arrested at that port and imprisoned. At the trial no sort of proof was forthcoming that Scott was in the least degree guilty of causing the death of the Chinese, but the Canton officials, in their usual manner, demanded that he should be surrendered, and threatened punishment on Macao if he were not given up. The matter was discussed at length in the Senate of Macao, and in the end a majority of members voted for the surrender of Scott, who was handed over to the Chinese and by them put to death. This atrocious behaviour on the part of the Portuguese was attempted to be justified by the Vicar-General of Macao with the following argument, which he put before the Senate: "Moralists decide that when a tyrant demands even an innocent person, with menaces of ruin to the community if refused, the whole number may call on any individual to deliver himself up for the public good, which is of more worth than the life of an individual. Should he refuse to obey, he is not innocent, he is criminal."[3] Needless

[1] *Factory Records of the East India Company* (MSS. in the India Office No. 11, under *Memoir: Intercourse with China*, Part I, pp. 126–9.)

[2] Davis, *China and the Chinese*, vol. i, p. 51; Auber's *China*, p. 178.

[3] Davis, *China and the Chinese*, vol. i, p. 52.

BRONZE MATHEMATICAL INSTRUMENTS AT THE PEKING OBSERVATORY

to say, this argument, however potent to the minds of the Portuguese, was far from convincing to the British community.

At this period the French nation showed considerable activity in China. We have seen that in 1767 the French East India Company had sent supercargoes to reside permanently in China. In 1776 the French Government itself first intervened by appointing a French consul to reside at Canton.[1] M. Vanquelin, the first person chosen for this post, arrived in the following year. He does not appear to have been officially recognized either by the imperial authorities at Peking or by the local authorities at Canton, for apparently no French consul was so recognized in China until 1829.[2] The French had, before this date, intimate relations with the Chinese through the Jesuit missionaries at Peking. The first French Jesuits to reach Peking were Le Comte and his companions, who left France in 1685 and arrived at the capital in 1688. They had come to China at the express command of the King of France, and some of the bronze mathematical instruments of the Peking Observatory[3] bear witness to the interest taken by " Le Grand Monarque " in Chinese affairs. But the relations thus commenced were in no sense political, and it was not until this appointment of a French Consul at Canton that the French Government officially concerned itself with the affairs of the Far East.[4] How little authority was possessed by this consul in those days is shown by an incident that occurred in 1780. A French sailor, who had killed a Portuguese, took refuge with the French consul to gain protection from the Chinese, who, he knew, would demand his surrender. The Chinese officials took their usual course and asked that he be given up to them. After many days of discussion, the consul complied with this demand in the feeblest possible way.

[1] Cordier, *La France en Chine au dix-huitième siècle*, p. 69.

[2] *Chinese Repository*, vol. v, p. 132.

[3] These were removed by the French troops in 1900. The French Government afterwards restored them.

[4] For further information with regard to the intercourse between France and China see Cordier, *La France en Chine au aix-huitème siècle ; Chinese Repository*, vol. i, pp. 251, 369 ; vol. ii, p. 294 ; vol. iv, p. 371 ; vol. v., pp. 132–7.

The Chinese, as might have been expected, paid no attention to European ideas in considering whether the man was guilty, and, having determined that he must die, publicly strangled him. This is the first instance of one European being put to death by the Chinese for the murder of another European.[1]

This bad precedent was, somewhat unwittingly, followed by the English supercargoes some four years later in the case of a gunner of the *Lady Hughes*, a country ship, who had accidentally killed two Chinese when firing a salute. When the request for the surrender of the gunner was first made, the supercargoes took up the position that they had no power over the crews of ships not belonging to the company, a contention which they had previously set up in the case of H.M.S. *Argo*. Captain Smith of the *Lady Hughes* consented, however, to go up to Canton and submit to an examination for form's sake, but on his arrival at the gate he was decoyed into the Chinese city and there detained, the Chinese refusing to set him free until the gunner should be surrendered. The supercargoes, fearing an attempt on their own liberty, sent to the French, Dutch, Danes and Americans,[2] and asked for assistance. The gunner, expressing his willingness to surrender himself on the understanding that he would be fairly treated, was handed over to the Chinese on their promise that he should be kept safe from harm. Captain Smith was set at liberty, and on his return to the Factory gave a good account of the treatment he had received.

The English supposed that the affair was now settled, but on the 8th of January they learnt that the gunner had been strangled by order of the Emperor. On the same date all the factors of the different nationalities were summoned to attend before the Viceroy, and were then informed that the Emperor was greatly displeased at the delay which had taken

[1] *Factory Records of the East India Company* (MSS. in India Office No. 11, under *Memoir : Intercourse with China*, Part I, pp. 128–9).

[2] These Americans must have been the captain and crew of the first American ship to make the voyage to China. This is the first time that Americans are mentioned in the Factory Records. See *Factory Records of the East India Company* (MSS. in India Office No. 11, under *Memoir : Intercourse with China*, Part I, p. 137) ; *Chinese Repository*, vol. v, pp. 218-231.

place in the surrender of the gunner, and that the Chinese officials had been extremely moderate in demanding only one European for the two Chinese who had lost their lives. The factors were further notified that the Chinese Government expected that, in the event of a similar occurrence happening again, the Europeans would pay a more ready obedience to the commands of the Chinese officials, and that they must abide the consequences of any disobedience on their part. It speaks volumes for the degeneracy of the supercargoes of that period that the Chinese officials should presume thus to lecture them, and that they should submit to treatment of that kind. There can be no doubt that in adopting this attitude they were seeking to act in harmony with the wishes of the Court of Directors. Submissive as they were, they were afterwards severely censured from London for having requisitioned the aid of armed boats, and for their conduct in the matter generally. They were instructed that in the case of a like casualty occurring again, they were to call in some Chinese merchant of ability, to make representations to the Viceroy and secure the life of the person in question, and if a murder had been perpetrated they were to surrender the offender to the Chinese authorities. Thus the Directors, simply from a desire to preserve the trade at any cost, expressed their willingness to abandon, without a struggle, a privilege that had been maintained for more than a hundred years. In this connection they stated that all doubts as to the power of the supercargoes to control the country ships and their seamen had been set at rest by a new statute. But an examination of the statute, to which their letter refers, shows that the Directors were mistaken and that the powers could be exercised only over interlopers, and not over persons who were lawfully trading at Canton.[1]

[1] This statute is cited in the *Records* as 26 Geo. III, c. 57, s. 35, and the terms of the section are given, which provide that all the powers exercised by the Company elsewhere over persons "being in the East Indies or other places in the Act contrary to law" may be exercised by the Council of Supercargoes at Canton. (MSS. in the India Office No. 11, under *Memoir : Intercourse with China*, Part I, p. 155). The words "contrary to law" effectually exclude from the operation of the Act all persons who were trading under the Company's licence.

It is not surprising that when the Company's policy was so subservient to the wishes of the Chinese as indicated above, the occasion should have been used by the local officials to impose fresh burdens on the trade at Canton. This they did by creating a new tax for the purpose of raising a fund, which became famous under the name of the Consoo Fund. The professed intention, in levying this exaction, was to provide a reserve to meet the liabilities of any Hong Merchant who might become bankrupt, a provision which, strictly speaking, would, if properly carried out, be of benefit to all the Foreign traders at Canton. The most influential Hong Merchant in 1779, when the Consoo Fund was instituted, was Puankhequa ; and as the articles in which he principally dealt were woollens, calicoes and iron, these were exempted from the new tax by his deliberate contrivance. It is a curious fact that these articles continued to be exempt until the tax was abolished in 1843. On all the other principal commodities dealt in at Canton was imposed a new tax of three per cent., which in times of emergency was raised to even six per cent., the various commodities taxed being assessed at a fixed value which was never altered.

For the most part the tax thus imposed never reached the Consoo Fund at all, but remained in the pockets of the Hong Merchants, through whom this, like every other duty, had to be paid. The result was that, although the Foreign merchant had to allow for it in full, in fixing the price of his commodities, and so felt the burden in all its severity, the advantages contemplated from its imposition were wholly lost. Had the tax been at once paid over to the Consoo Fund, the amount thus reserved would in a few years have amounted to an enormous sum, and the Foreign trader would have had the satisfaction of knowing that, if a Hong Merchant should become insolvent, his liabilities could be met from the Fund thus provided. Instead of this being the case, such moneys as the Hong Merchants actually paid into the Consoo were pounced upon by the imperial authorities for all sorts of expenses ; and for the rest, which amounted to the major part of the Fund, there were the mere credit entries in the books of the Hong Merchants. The cash represented by such entries was not kept in hand, but was used by each Hong Merchant respectively for any purpose for which he might need money. Thus the trade felt the full effect of the imposition of the Consoo tax, but received none of the intended benefit. When some fifty years later the insolvency of the Hong Merchants brought on a crisis, it was found that there was absolutely nothing of the Consoo Fund available to meet the liabilities that had been incurred. This was one of the many causes of the Opium War, and led to the insertion in the Treaty of Nanking of the article providing for the payment of the debts of the Co-hong by the Imperial Government.[1]

The immediate cause of the institution of the Consoo Fund was the fact that in 1779 it came to light that the paper indebtedness of Chinese traders to British merchants amounted to no less a sum than £1,000,000. None of this sum was owing to the East India Company, but the whole of it was due to private traders and others, who had advanced loans to Chinese at enormous rates of interest. Representations on the subject having been made to the Court of Directors, the Select Committee of supercargoes at Canton were instructed to investigate the matter. The supercargoes, having discovered, as a result of their inquiries, that only one-fourth of the amount owing had actually been received by the debtors, and that the remaining three-fourths were made up of accumulated interest, were reluctant to push matters to an extreme. Thereupon some of the principal creditors at Madras, who were the original lenders, complained to the Governor of Madras, and he, thinking that British subjects were being defrauded by the Chinese, instructed Admiral Vernon to despatch H.M.S. *Seahorse*, under Captain Panton, to render such assistance to the British community as a naval captain might give under the circumstances. Captain Panton, in spite of the remonstrances of the Select Committee, proceeded to Canton and insisted on having an interview with the Viceroy.

[1] See *post*, chap. xxiii, p. 533. As to the Consoo Fund, see J. R. Morrison, *Chinese Commercial Guide*, p. 33; *Correspondence Relating to China* (Blue Book, 1840), p. 292.

That official ultimately ordered the debts to be paid, and so far Captain Panton was successful. But immediately after the *Seahorse* had departed, an edict was issued again prohibiting debts from being incurred, and appointing twelve Hong Merchants through whom alone the Chinese might trade with Foreigners. From this time to 1843 the Hong Merchants preserved their monopoly unimpaired. Thus eventually it happened that, as a result of this intervention, the Foreign traders found the Hong monopoly more stringently enforced and the trade burdened with the Consoo tax.[1]

Immediately this episode had come to an end, the Company found itself involved in fresh difficulties through the private traders. In 1781 Captain McClary, of a country ship from Bengal, stopped a sloop, which was proceeding to Manilla, believing her to be Spanish. Although we were then at war with Spain, such an act was quite unjustifiable, if it took place in Chinese waters. Having landed at Macao, McClary explained to the Portuguese Governor that he had ordered his mate to bring the captured vessel into harbour for examination. Alarmed at what might be the consequence of such a proceeding, the Portuguese threw the captain into prison and there kept him until he gave orders for the release of his prize. Whilst the mate was on his way to carry out this order, a gale arose and the sloop was wrecked on the rocks. Captain McClary was thereupon imprisoned for a further two months. During that period the Portuguese extorted from him a sum of $70,000, on the ground that that was the value of the vessel, under threat of handing him over to the Chinese, if he did not pay that sum into their hands. Having been set at liberty, McClary shortly afterwards was at Whampoa, where he was lying alongside a Dutch ship, when news arrived that war had broken out between Great Britain and Holland. McClary at once seized the Dutch vessel as a prize of war. The Chinese now protested, and demanded that this prize should be restored to her lawful owners. McClary, failing to arrive at terms

[1] *Factory Records of the East India Company* (MSS. in India Office No. 11, under *Memoir: Intercourse with China*, Part I, pp. 134–5; *Correspondence Relating to China* (Blue Book, 1840), pp. 277–279; Auber's *China*, p. 179).

with the officials, dropped down the river with his ship, whereupon all the available Chinese troops, to the number of two hundred, were assembled to oppose his departure. At this juncture Puankhequa intervened, and made the suggestion that by way of a compromise the Chinese should be allowed to board the Dutch ship with cries of triumph, whilst McClary should retain for himself a chest full of gold and pearls, which had been shipped on the Dutch vessel by some Armenians. This suggestion commended itself both to the Chinese and McClary, and was acted upon. Thus the incident terminated. The property of the defenceless and innocent Armenians passed to a man who was no better than a pirate. The Chinese saved their face.[1]

On this occasion the Select Committee had found themselves confronted with the old difficulty, that the Chinese expected them to restrain and be responsible for the acts of any of their countrymen, who might be guilty of misconduct. Once more they appealed to the Court of Directors for further powers. "Long experience," they said, "has shown the Chinese that we must suffer almost anything to avoid an impediment to our trade, but country ships are every day committing some irregularity which sets aside their decrees and mortifies their pride; these they sometimes permit to pass by unnoticed and sometimes make it a pretence for oppressing the Hong Merchants, but when it becomes a matter of too great magnitude to be passed over, the Company are held responsible; for whether it be their policy or really incomprehensible to their strict notions of subordination, they will not allow themselves to believe that every Englishman who comes here is not under the control of the Chief, though every day's experience might have convinced them to the contrary."[2] In reply to this letter, the Directors again ordered that all private persons be sent away from Canton.

[1] *Factory Records of the East India Company* (MSS. in the India Office No. 11, under *Memoir: Intercourse with China*, Part I, pp. 130–133); Davis, *China and the Chinese*, vol. i, p. 55; Auber's *China*, pp. 181–190.

[2] *Factory Records of the East India Company* (MSS. in the India Office No. 11, under *Memoir: Intercourse with China*, Part I, p. 133.

These events led the Court of Directors in London to see that some change in the conditions under which trade and intercourse at Canton were carried on was extremely desirable. The burden of illegal exactions and impositions was too heavy to be removed by the fortuitous intervention of some naval officer, constrained to put into the Canton river for water or supplies. The difficulties with which the supercargoes had to contend had grown to such a strength, that they could not be cut away except by some strong hand operating from without. War was too drastic a remedy for the ills under which the British merchants laboured; and indeed it was felt that the very notion of making war on a power so inferior in strength to Great Britain, without a trial of more peaceful measures, could not be seriously discussed. In these circumstances the Directors began to turn their eyes towards Peking, in the hope that there might be found, in the will of the Emperor, the force that could bend the stubborn mandarins of Canton city. Little by little this idea took root until, encouraged by the thought that other powers had sent representatives to Peking to urge their claims to better treatment, the Directors resolved in favour of some sort of diplomatic mission being despatched direct to the Emperor himself.

CHAPTER VI

DIPLOMACY AND EMBASSIES

If we look into the origin of government, we find that the idea at the root of sovereignty is a religious one. In all primitive communities there is a belief that the sovereign is the depositary of Heaven's express commands, which he dispenses to his subjects at their need. It has been pointed out that this belief is especially manifest in the conception of the sovereign as the fountain of justice.[1] It made easier the assumption of pontifical functions by the Roman emperors, notwithstanding the diversity of the nations subject to their sway.[2] Common to European and Asiatic nations alike, in the early stages of their development, it may be regarded as one of the principles that in primitive times were universally accepted by mankind. It did not disappear from England until the Divine Right of James I was swept away in the Revolution of 1688. It survives as a common superstition in Russia, and traces of it are still found in imperial utterances in Germany. In China it is a living belief, an accepted principle of the constitution. That unfortunate country is the victim, among other things, of arrested development. The student of archæology finds existing in China to-day beliefs, customs, and institutions, that he imagined could be known only through the writings of learned antiquarians. For three or four thousand years the Chinese people have, in many respects, stood on the same spot and marked time, while nations that were sunk in barbarism, when the Chinese had fully developed the civilization in which they still live, have marched forward and got so far ahead, that it is almost impossible that they should ever be overtaken.

In ethics, in literature, and in politics, China advanced to a certain point with the other societies of ancient times, and then stopped, since when no further development has taken place. The national life suddenly became petrified, and has continued from the moment of petrifaction to the present time unchanged.

[1] Maine, *Ancient Law*, chap. i.

[2] See Bryce, *The Holy Roman Empire*, chap. iii.

In it are preserved, like the fossils of some bygone age, thoughts and conceptions that were long since abandoned by the nations that are now the leaders of the world in civilization. For instance, in religion the one practice that obtains universally, the one in which alone the Chinese show any real religious feeling, is the worship of ancestors. This same practice once coloured law and custom in Rome as it does the national life of China to-day. Now it is as extinct in Europe as is the belief in the philosopher's stone. This worship of ancestors is at the foundation of many of the distinctive features of the Chinese character, and explains many of the causes that have retarded its development. The whole Chinese people is wedded to the grave; their attention is absorbed in contemplating the past. They do not look ahead; their mental attitude is the attitude of the wry-neck. All their thoughts are for the dead; for the generations unborn they care nothing. It is the infection of the dead past, to which it is tied, that ails the body politic in China.

A very casual survey of the history of our doings in China will show that we have constantly been misled by the delusion that the ways of the Chinese are as our ways, and their thoughts as our thoughts. Nothing could be further from the truth. Their whole method of reasoning is different from ours. As a Chinese official once expressed it: "You Foreigners always think in straight lines, but we think in curves." If this is borne in mind, we shall not be surprised to learn that our attempts at diplomatic intercourse have not always had the effect intended. Still less will be our surprise when we have grasped the fact that the political and social organization of China is on lines very different from those familiar to us. In China the family is still the social unit; the individual counts as of no great importance, except as a member of his father's family. Contractual relations have not entirely supplanted those resulting from status. This idea of the family being the social unit has been copied in the construction of the political fabric. The nation is regarded as one great family, of which the Emperor is the head. Add to this the belief that he is specially chosen and favoured by Heaven, and you have the fundamental principles of the Chinese polity. To his subjects the Emperor is an object of absolute veneration, and by them he is respectfully addressed as "The Son of Heaven." "The Buddha of the present day" is his popular appellation, and "Lord of Ten Thousand Years" is the title given to him in adulatory addresses.[1] His power and position as the head of the nation is that of the Roman paterfamilias, rather than that of the father in our sense of the word. He has unbounded authority, and exacts the most servile homage. At the same time, he is responsible to Heaven for the proper exercise of his power, and if the nation suffers from famine or pestilence, it is his duty to pray to Heaven to take away the calamity, which is regarded as being due in some way to the Emperor's failings. In his own person he unites the three functions of Vice-gerent of Heaven, High Priest of the nation, and Sole Mediator between Heaven and the people.[2]

The conception that the Emperor is divinely appointed has affected Chinese ideas of geography. These are based on the supposition that China is situate in the middle of the earth, while all the other nations, grouped around in a respectful circle, make obeisance in a manner not unlike that in which Joseph's sheaf was worshipped by those of his brethren. The name by which the Chinese prefer to designate their country is the Middle Kingdom. Sometimes they improve upon this by adding the word "flowery." They seek to impress upon the outer barbarian the fact that their land is peculiarly favoured by Heaven in being bright and sunny, while all the rest of mankind have to dwell in the dark and desolate regions of the earth. In their opinion the sovereigns of other countries, ruling over lands that have not been wont to bask in the sunshine of Heaven's favour, are but vassals of the Son of Heaven, towards whom he exercises a benignant toleration. To this is partly due that feeling of contempt which every Chinese feels towards all Foreigners. That

[1] Mayers, *Chinese Government*, p. 1. For an account of the Chinese religious system see Giles, *Religions of Ancient China*.

[2] A valuable illustration of the way in which these functions are exercised will be found in the prayer for rain offered up by the Emperor Taou-kwang in 1832. See *Chinese Repository*, vol. i, pp. 236–8.

feeling is, to some extent, however, only a manifestation of a prejudice often found in other countries. The contempt of the Greek for the barbarian, the Roman for the *peregrinus*, the Jew for the Gentile, are but particular instances of a common principle. "Outlandish," which in modern English is a term of reproach, was not many centuries ago used in place of the word "foreign" in its modern sense. The conviction that the "Foreigner," or "outside man," is a barbarian, is now not less deeply rooted in the minds of the Chinese, than it was when the British Government decided to despatch its first ambassador to the Court of Peking.

The Chinese render to their Emperor the same obeisance as is paid to Heaven itself, and the ceremonial observed in his presence is suited to a ruler of a divine nature. The prostrations, which are the distinctive feature of this ceremonial, consists in thrice kneeling and in knocking the forehead nine times on the ground. This is the eighth and highest degree of obeisance in use in China, and is generally called by English writers the *kotow*, though by the Chinese that term is applied only to the fifth degree, which consists in kneeling once and knocking the forehead thrice on the ground.[1] The refusal to perform this ceremony has been a source of failure to more than one European envoy, and when in 1792 the King of England sent the first British embassy to Peking, a difficulty arose as to the right of the Emperor to demand such homage. It must be remembered that, previous to this time, the Chinese had been not without experience of ambassadors from Europe. The Russians had sent two envoys in 1567, who were dismissed because they brought no presents. A similar fate had befallen Evashko, who crossed the desert in 1619 to see the "Dragon's Face." The Czar Alexis sent his envoy, Baikoff, in 1653, to Peking, but he was dismissed because he refused to *kotow*. Before the arrival of these Russian embassies, the Emperor had been accustomed to receive ambassadors only from states that were admittedly tributary, or over which at least a nominal suzerainty was claimed. After the middle of the seventeenth century,

[1] See Williams, *The Middle Kingdom*, i, p. 801.

however, embassies were received from more than one European country, some notice of which may properly precede a discussion of the embassies that were sent from England.

In 1655 the Dutch East India Company despatched from Batavia a mission under Peter de Goyer and Jacob de Keyser, with the object of establishing a firm league with the Emperor Sung-ti, and obtaining a free trade throughout his dominions.[1] They were informed on their arrival at Peking that they could not be admitted to an audience with the Emperor unless they were akin to the prince that sent them. This objection was with some difficulty surmounted, and the Dutch obtained access to the Forbidden City, but only in the company of the ambassadors from the Great Mogul and from the Tartars. In attaining their object of seeing the Emperor face to face, de Goyer and de Keyser sacrificed every vestige of self-respect. They were compelled to give valuable presents, to make the customary prostrations to the Emperor, to *kotow* to the Emperor's name, to his throne, and to the letter which was sent by the Emperor to the Governor of Batavia. How little success attended their efforts is shown by the terms of this document, which ran as follows :—

" Our territories being as far asunder as the East from the West, it is with great difficulty that we can approach each other, and from the beginning to this present the Hollanders never came to visit us. But those who sent Peter de Goyer and Jacob de Keyser to me are a brave and wise people, who in your name have appeared before me, and brought me several presents. Your country is ten thousand miles distant from mine, but you show your noble mind in remembering me ; for this reason my heart doth very much incline to you, therefore I send to you presents." [Here a list of the presents was set out.] " You have asked leave to come and trade in my country by importing and exporting commodities, which will redound very much to the advantage of my subjects ; but,

[1] An account of this mission was written in Latin by Nieuhoff, who acted as steward, under the title, *Legatio Batavica ad Magnum Tartariæ Chamum Sungteium, Modernum Sinae Imperatorem.* It was published at Amsterdam in 1668.

in regard, your country is so far distant, and the winds on these coasts so boisterous as to endanger your ships, the loss of which would very much trouble me, therefore if you do think fit to send hither, I desire it may be but once every eight years, and no more than a hundred men in a company, twenty of whom may come up to the place where I keep my Court, and then you may bring your merchandize ashore into your lodge without bartering them at sea before Canton. This I have thought good to propose for your interest and safety, and I hope it will be well liked of by you; and thus much I thought fit to make known unto you." [1]

This letter does not seem to have encouraged the Dutch to persevere with their wish to trade at Peking. It does not appear ever to have been acted upon. The trade of the Hollanders continued to be carried on, as we have seen, at ports in the South, and a settlement was made in Formosa. After the loss of Taiwan, a splendid embassy, under Lord Peter van Hoorn, was sent to the Emperor Kanghi in 1668, but though received in perfect friendliness, it met with no particular success. From this time there was no Dutch embassy sent to Peking until after the return of Lord Macartney.

Whilst England was attempting to gain a footing in the South of Asia, another European power, destined to be her great rival in the field of Asiatic diplomacy, but then only just rising into prominence, was pressing down from the North. Russia, who had begun to rouse her national energies at the very time when England, under Queen Elizabeth, was taking her part in seeking opportunities of trade in the newly discovered portions of the earth, had by the time the East India Company was incorporated, penetrated the wilds of Siberia and arrived on the confines of China. Her explorers, a little later, built the fort called Albazin, known to the Chinese as Yaksa, right on the boundaries of the Chinese Empire. Parties of Russians came into collision with parties of Chinese, and there were present all the elements of conflict between the two countries. These border affrays were made the occasion of the despatch of a Russian embassy to China, plenipotentiaries

[1] Auber's *China*, pp. 89–90.

being appointed on both sides to delimit the frontier. The Chinese, fearing even at that early date that the Russian diplomacy might be superior to their own, set a precedent, which has often been followed since, and appointed a European to advise her representatives in performing their diplomatic duties. For this purpose was chosen a Jesuit, Father Gerbillon, who stood high in the esteem of the Emperor Kanghi. It is to him that we are indebted for our knowledge of what took place on this historic occasion, an occasion which is remarkable as having produced the first treaty between China and a Foreign power. It is interesting to observe that Gerbillon judged one member of the Russian mission "to be either an Englishman or a Dutchman, for he had nothing of the Russian pronunciation, and understood the European characters." The chief of the mission was Theodore Alexieviez Golowin, between whom and the Chinese plenipotentiaries the Treaty of Nerchinsk was signed in September, 1689.

By this treaty the boundaries between the two Empires were defined, and the Russians agreed to demolish the fort at Yaksa. It was further provided that if the subjects of either nation should cross into the territory of the other, whether to hunt, plunder, or to steal, they might be seized and punished by the governor into whose province they had intruded. Everything that had previously occurred was to be buried in everlasting oblivion, and perpetual peace was sworn between the two countries. Fugitives from either Empire were to be sent back to their own officials. The provision with which we are chiefly concerned was that which provided for a trade between Russia and China, which was expressed in these general terms: "All persons, of what condition soever they be, may go and come reciprocally, with full liberty, from the territories subject to either Empire into those of the other, provided they have passports by which it appears that they come with permission; and they shall be suffered to buy and sell whatever they think fit, and carry on a mutual trade." Two copies of the treaty in Latin were signed and sealed both by the Russian and Chinese plenipotentiaries; a copy in Russian was similarly executed by the Russians, and one in the Mongol language by the Chinese. It was provided by the treaty that it should be engraved in the Mongol, Chinese, Russian, and Latin languages, on stones "which shall be placed at the bounds settled between the two Empires, there to remain as a perpetual monument of the good understanding that ought to subsist between them." This stipulation was actually carried out, and the monuments of stone, on which the terms of the treaty were inscribed, may be seen at the present day.[1]

Russia, having once gained an entry into China, was careful that the advantages obtained should not be lost for lack of use. Everard Ysbrandt Ides was sent as an ambassador from the Czar in 1693, bearing the ratification of the Treaty of Nerchinsk, and on arriving at Peking was received and treated with marked distinction. Contrary to the experience of the Dutch ambassadors, he found he was not kept waiting all night till the Emperor's appearance on the throne in the morning. He thus describes the manner in which he was entertained at Court :—

"I was informed that I was invited to eat before the Emperor ; wherefore, accompanied by the mandarins thereto

[1] The Tartarian, or Mongol, text of the treaty will be found in the *Archives Diplomatiques*, vol. i (1861) p. 271, which also gives a French translation. Du Halde, in his great work (*Description de la Chine*, tom. iv. pp. 243–4) gives a French version received from Père Gerbillon. A complete English translation will be found in the *Chinese Repository*, vol. viii, pp. 422–4. Du Halde also describes the negotiations that led up to the signing of the treaty.

The object of the treaty, as set out in the preamble, is thus given by Du Halde : "Afin de réprimer l'insolence de certaines canailles, qui saisant les courses hors des limites de leurs terres pour y chasser, pillent, tuent, et excitent des troubles et des brouilleries, comme aussi pour déterminer clairement et distinctement des bornes entre les deux Empires de la Chine et de la Muscovie, et enfin pour établir une paix et une intelligence éternelle."

The same author thus translates the commercial provisions : "Ayant égard au présent traité de paix et d'union réciproque entre les deux couronnes, toutes sortes de personnes de quelque condition qu'elles puissent être, pourront aller et venir réciproquement, avec toute sorte de liberté, des terres sujettes à l'un des deux Empires dans celles de l'autre pourvû qu'ils ayent des patentes par lesquelles il conste qu'ils viennent avec permission, et il leur sera permis de vendre et d'acheter tout ce qu'ils jugeront à propos, et de faire une commerce réciproque."

appointed, and my retinue, I rode to Court. As soon as I entered, the Emperor mounted the Throne. . . . The Emperor sent the viceroy to me with the utmost respect, to ask after the health of their Czarish majesties; to which I returned the proper answer.

"The Emperor sent me from his table a roast goose, a pig, a loin of very good mutton, and soon after several dishes of fruit, and a sort of drink composed of boiled tea, fried meal, butter, which looked not unlike bean or coffee decoction; having received all which, his majesty ordered the viceroy to ask me what European languages I understood. To which I answered, I could speak the Muscovite, German, Low Dutch, and a little Italian. Upon which he immediately despatched some servants to the hinder parts of the palace, which done, there instantly appeared three Jesuits, who approached the throne. And after kneeling, and performing their reverence to the Emperor, he commanded them to rise. One of these was Father John Francis Gerbillon, a Frenchman; and the two others were Portuguese, one of them called Father Anthony Thomas. The Emperor ordered Father Gerbillon to me; who, coming towards me speaking Italian, asked me in the Emperor's name how long I had been travelling from Moscow to Peking, and which way I came, by waggon, on horseback, or by water; . . . The Emperor then ordered the viceroy to acquaint me that it was his most gracious pleasure that I should approach nearer the presence, by coming up to the throne; upon which I arising, the viceroy taking me by the hand, after having led me up six steps, set me at the table opposite to the Emperor. After I had paid my most humble respects to his majesty, he talked with Father Gerbillon, who again asked me how long I had been on the way hither, in what manner I had travelled, and in what latitude Moscow was situate, and how far distant from Poland, France, Italy, Portugal, or Holland. To all which I observed my answer proved very satisfactory. Upon which he gave the viceroy a gold cup of Tartarian liquor called *kumis*, in order to hand it to me; which with due respect I accepted, and having tasted, returned it. This *kumis*, according to the report of the attendants, is a sort of brandy distilled from mare's milk. After this the Emperor ordered my retinue to advance within three fathoms of his throne, and entertained them with the same liquor ; which being done, I paid my compliment in the European manner, and the viceroy took me by the hand, conducting me to my former place, where, after sitting for a quarter of an hour, I was desired to rise." [1]

Other Russian embassies followed that of Ides at short intervals, and to the efforts put forward at this time must be attributed the foundation of the Russian influence at Peking. In 1715, Laurence de Lange was sent by Peter the Great, and met with a reception not less favourable than that previously accorded to Ides, the Emperor declaring that he would "protect them not like strangers, but like his own children." Indeed, the Russians generally, whether from fear or generosity is not quite apparent, were treated by Kanghi with great liberality. When the Chinese merchants who traded with Russia were not able to pay their debts, they were assisted with advances from the Imperial treasury. Again, in 1717, when the depression of trade at Peking was so great that the Russians could find no sale for their goods, the Emperor remitted the duties paid by his subjects in connection with the Russian trade, thereby losing 20,000 taels of the Imperial revenue. [2] In 1719, Peter the Great sent Ismailoff, with a retinue of musicians and attendants, on an embassy to Peking, to which de Lange acted as secretary. To this mission a most flattering welcome was given, but Ismailoff was compelled to perform the ceremony of prostration, a fact which leads one to suspect that previous Russian envoys may have submitted to the same degradation. [3] On his departure he received from the Emperor a personal letter to the Czar, which he was informed he must regard "as a singular mark of favour to

[1] Ides, *Three Years' Travels from Moscow overland to China* (translated by W. Freeman, 1706). *Chinese Repository*, vol. viii, pp. 523–4 ; Brand, *Beschreibung der Chinesischen Reise vermittelst Einer Zaaris.*

[2] Auber's *China*, p. 97.

[3] As to Ismailoff's expedition, see Bell of Antermony, *Travels from St. Petersburg in Russia to divers parts of Asia ; Chinese Repository*, vol. viii, p. 527.

his master, as their emperors were not in use to write letters of compliment to any prince ; or indeed to write letters of any kind, except those which contained their orders to their subjects, and that the Emperor dispensed with so material a custom only to testify his respect for his Czarish Majesty."

The Russian Government was not slow to make use of the privileges conceded by the Treaty of Nerchinsk. Ismailoff actually left at Peking a Russian resident, who should see that Russian interests were not allowed to suffer, de Lange being chosen to fill this novel position. As soon as the embassy was well quit of the capital, de Lange found himself subjected to every sort of insult at the hands of the Chinese, and for the most part confined as a prisoner in his own house. Having endured treatment of this kind for seventeen months, he left Peking and retired into Russian territory. One cause of his departure seems to have been that the jealousy of the Chinese was excited by an attempt on the part of the Corean merchants at Peking to enter into negotiations with the Russian representative. This is the first occasion on which Corea came into relation with the diplomacy of Europe, and the Chinese at once perceived that such a relation could not enure to the advantage of China, which was at that time the acknowledged suzerain of the kingdom of Corea. The departure of de Lange was not the only untoward result of this jealousy. The Russians had been in the habit, since 1689, of sending every three years a caravan from St. Petersburg to Peking, which was met on the frontier by a company of Chinese soldiers, and escorted to the capital. There the whole caravan was shut up in a caravanserai, Chinese merchants being allowed to bring to them for sale such goods as they thought proper. When its trading operations were concluded, the caravan was released and allowed to return to Russia. On de Lange's departure an end was put to this practice. It was decreed that in future no transactions should be carried on between the two nations except upon the frontier.[1]

In 1727 the Empress Catharine I determined to put the relations between her subjects and the Chinese on an improved

[1] De Lange, *Journal*. Auber's *China*, pp. 102–8.

footing. For that purpose she despatched Count Vladislawitch as a special envoy to the Chinese Court, and to his efforts Russia is indebted for a fresh treaty, which was ratified by her successor, Peter II, in June, 1728. In this treaty it was provided that there should be a free trade between the two Empires, and that Russian merchants to the number of two hundred might proceed every three years to Peking for purposes of commerce. The trade carried on by them was to be exempt from taxation. When the Russian merchants reached the frontier, they were to give notice in writing to the Chinese authorities, who were to despatch an officer to receive and accompany them. Each company of Russians was to come in charge of a superintendent, who should have power to settle any differences that might arise among them, and be received by the Chinese in a manner becoming to his rank. Trade was to be permitted in every kind of goods, except such as were forbidden by the laws of the two Empires. It was further provided that at Kiakhta, the Selinga, and Nerchinsk trading depots should be established, which might be protected with hedges and palisades ; and except at these depots and at Peking, the Russians resorting thither were not to trade within the limits of the Chinese Empire.[1]

To the provisions of this treaty Russia owes the privilege which is still enjoyed by her alone, of maintaining at Peking itself a permanent trading establishment. The article of the treaty by which this is provided is so worded as to show that the mission, as it is commonly termed, was to be looked upon as a continuation of the residency to which de Lange had been appointed on the departure of Ismailoff. This mission was to be partly commercial, partly religious, no diplomatic standing being claimed or recognized in respect of

[1] Mayers, in his *Treaties between the Empire of China and Foreign Powers*, says that this treaty abrogated everything which had previously passed between the two Governments. An examination of the French translation, mentioned below, fails to reveal any such provision. Mayers must have misunderstood the Article which provides that everything which had previously passed was to be forgotten. That Article simply means that old dissensions are to be buried in oblivion. The treaty in effect re-affirms the treaty of Nerchinsk.

it. It is not unfair to say that the existence of this religious mission in the heart of the capital has been of the greatest use to Russia in her diplomacy, not the least advantage afforded by it being a constant supply of capable interpreters, well versed in the methods of the Chinese themselves. It was provided that all Russian merchants coming to Peking thereafter should be lodged in the mission; that a chapel should be built close at hand, where a head priest and three assistant priests should be allowed to reside; that the Russians should be permitted to exercise their own religion with all the usual ceremonies, and to say prayers; and that four young Russians, skilled in the Latin and Russian written and spoken languages, and two of more mature age, should reside at the mission for the purpose of learning the Chinese language, the expense being paid by the Chinese government. As these last completed their studies, they were to be succeeded by fresh batches of students subject to similar conditions. The treaty further provided that communications from the one nation to the other should take the form of letters under seal, and defined the mode in which diplomatic representatives might be sent from one empire to the other.[1]

The privileges thus obtained by Russia were forty years later confirmed by a supplementary treaty, signed in the year

[1] The Mongol Text, with a French translation, will be found in Klaproth's *Chrestomathie Manchoue*, pp. 222 *et seq.*; a French version will also be found in the *Archives Diplomatiques*, vol. i (1861), pp. 276–282. The provisions with which we are chiefly concerned are the following:—

"Art. 4.—Maintenant que la fixation de la frontière des deux empires est déterminée, et qu'aucun transfuge ne peut plus être admis, il est convenu avec le comte illyrien Sawa Wladislawitche, ambassadeur de l'empire des Oros, d'établir un libre commerce entre les deux États. Le nombre des négociants qui peuvent aller tous les trois and à Péking, ne doit pas dépasser deux cents, comme il a été fixé antérieurement. Quand ce ne seront que des commerçants, ils ne seront plus extretenus commes autrefois; mais on n'exigera aucun impôt ou taxe, ni du vendeur, ni de l'acheteur. Quand ces négociants arriveront à la frontière, ils devront en donner l'avis par écrit. Après la réception de cet avis, on expédiera un officier pour les recevoir et les accompagner à cause du commerce. S'ils achètent, pendant la voyage, des chameaux, des chevaux, et des vivres, ou ils louent des domestiques, ils les doivent acheter à leur dépens. Les négociants seront sous les ordres d'un

1768 by Kroptow, whom the Empress Catharine II sent on a special mission to China. Kroptow did not reach Peking, but was met at Kiakhta by Chinese envoys, who negotiated the treaty with him there. The chief subject of discussion on this occasion was the punishment of frontier stragglers

chef chargé de soigner leurs affaires: et s'il survient des différends entre eux, ce sera lui qui les réglera. Si ce chef négociant est un homme d'un haut rang, il sera reçu êt traité conformément à son rang. Tout espèce de marchandises peut être vendue, excepté celles que les lois des deux empires défendent. On ne permettra à qui que ce soit de rester sécrètement et sans la permission de son chef dans le pays étranger. Si quelqu'un meurt, tous ses biens, de quelque nature qu'ils soient, seront remis aux gens de son pays, comme il a été convenu avec l'ambassadeur des Oros, le comte illyrien Sawa Wladislawitche. Outre le commerce fait par les caravans des deux empires, on établira encore, sur les frontières réciproques, auprès de Kiaktou, du Selinga et de Nibtchoo (Nerchinsk), des maisons pour le commerce ordinaire qui, selon qu'on le jugera nécessaire, seront entourées de haies et de palisades. Ces qui se rendent à ces lieux pour laire le commerce doivent exactement suivre la route directe. Si quelqu'un d'eux s'éloigne de cette route pour faire le commerce en d'autres lieux, toutes ses marchandises seront confisquées au profit du gouvernement: on installera des deux cotés un nombre égal d'officiers, placés sous les ordres de chefs d'un rang égal, et chargés de protéger ces lieux. Les différends seront accommodés de la manière convenue avec l'ambassadeur de l'empire des Oros, le comte illyrien Sawa Wladislawitche.

"Art. 5.—L'habitation des Oros dans la capitale (Péking) servira dorénavant à loger les voyageurs Russes. Sur la demande du comte illyrien Sawa Wladislawitche, ambassadeur de l'empire des Oros, et avec l'assistance des grands de l'empire du Milieu, qui soignent les affaires des Oros, on a construit un temple auprès de cette habitation. Le prêtre (lama) qui réside dans la capitale, y logera avec trois autres prêtres pour l'assister. Lorsque ceux-ci arriveront ils seront entretenus comme leurs prédecesseurs et employés au dit temple. Il sera permis aux Oros d'exercer leur culte avec toutes les cérémonies et de reciter leurs prières. Quatre jeunes Oros, sachant la langue et l'écriture russe et latine, et deux autres plus âgés, que le comte illyrien Sawa Wladislawitche, ambassadeur de l'empire des Oros, a laissés dans la capitale pour apprendre la langue chinoise, doivent demeurer dans ce même lieu. Leur entretien sera payé par le gouvernement, et lorsqu'ils auront achevé leurs études ils pourront retourner dans leur pays.

"Art. 6.—Quant à la correspondance entre les deux empires, il est très nécessaire que les lettres soient munies d'un cachet. Le tribunal des affaires des provinces extérieures est chargé d'expédier au tribunal du sénat des Oros, après y avoir mis le sceau. Les lettres de l'empire des Oros pour l'empire du Milieu doivent etre expédiées au tribunal des provinces extérieures, et munies du sceau de l'empire des Oros ou du cachet du gouverneur de la ville de Tobolsk."

and brigands, provisions as to which were incorporated in the treaty.[1] In the meantime a Portuguese mission proceeded to Peking by way of Macao in 1754. The Portuguese envoys did not meet with any great success. Excepting that some impositions, to the amount of about three hundred pounds a year, were remitted, the Portuguese at Macao found themselves treated worse than before. A few years later the Viceroy of Canton, to complete the humiliation in which they lived, ordered a procession of Chinese idols to be made through the streets, a disgrace to which the governor and clergy had never before been called upon to submit.[2] From this date no embassy, except Kroptow's mission, was sent by a European power until the departure of Lord Macartney.

We have seen that hitherto the British Government had been content to allow the intercourse between England and China to be conducted by the East India Company in such manner as the Company thought best. The result was not altogether pleasing to a nation which had arrived at the highest degree of eminence in Europe and was conscious of the power to advance still further. There could be no doubt that the conditions under which trade was carried on at Canton, and British subjects allowed to resort to that port, were most unsatisfactory. Knowing something of the success that attended the efforts of Russian ambassadors, and advised by the East India Company that, to improve the relations between Great Britain and China, an appeal must be made at Peking, the British Government, in 1787, despatched Colonel Cathcart as a special envoy to the Chinese capital. Owing to the death of Cathcart when in the Straits of Sunda, this attempt to establish friendly relations proved abortive. Determined, however, to deal direct with the Emperor himself, the British Government made a second effort in 1792, and sent out the Earl of Macartney as a special ambassador, accompanied by a large staff of persons skilled in various kinds of knowledge that, it was hoped, would impress the

[1] A French version of this treaty will be found in the *Archives Diplomatiques*, vol. i, p. 282.

[2] Auber's *China*, p. 85.

Court at Peking, and add to the success of the mission. It is amusing, in the light of later experience, to read of the preparations that were made to bring home to the Chinese a sense of the might and dignity of Great Britain.

Sir Erasmus Gower was appointed to the command of *H.M.S. Lion*, in which the embassy was to sail to China. As might be expected, there were numerous applications to be allowed to serve under him, " and young gentlemen, of the most respectable families, glowing with the ardour and enterprise of youth, were admitted in the *Lion* considerably beyond the customary complement of midshipmen." A small bodyguard was chosen for the ambassador, consisting of " picked men from the infantry, as well as from the artillery, with light field-pieces, the rapid exercise of which, agreeably to the recent improvements, together with the various evolutions of the men, might, in these respects, convey some idea of the European art of war, and be an interesting spectacle to the Emperor of China." This guard was put under the command of Major Benson, assisted by two lieutenants, one of whom was a good draughtsman and made many sketches of striking objects that came under his notice. In addition, there was a professional painter and draughtsman, a physician and a surgeon, " Dr. Dinwiddie and Mr. Barrow,[1] both conversant in astronomy, mechanics, and every other branch dependent on mathematics," and two private secretaries, of whom one was " a young gentleman from the university." Sir George Leonard Staunton[2] was appointed secretary to the embassy

[1] Barrow's *Travels in China* is an account of the experiences of the embassy in China. It is remarkably accurate in its information and in its observations on Chinese institutions.

[2] Sir George Leonard Staunton was born in 1737, and when resident in the West Indies formed, with Lord Macartney, who in 1774 was appointed Governor of the Caribu Islands, a friendship which lasted throughout his life. When Macartney was made Governor of Madras in 1781, Staunton went with him as secretary. He returned to England in 1784, and lived in retirement till appointed to accompany Lord Macartney to China. He published a narrative of the experiences of the mission under the title, *An Account of an Embassy from the King of Great Britain to the Emperor of China*, which is still a standard work on China. The other works bearing the name of Staunton are the works of his son. He died in 1801.

and minister plenipotentiary, whilst his son, who was then eleven years old, accompanied the mission as page to the ambassador.

The greatest difficulty was to find a competent interpreter. There was no single person throughout the British dominions qualified to act in this capacity. It was felt that the native *linguist* of Canton, who in the course of trade had picked up a knowledge of "pidgin" English, would hardly suffice for the purpose. In those days the Chinese Government did not allow missionaries to leave the country, so it was of no avail to attempt to enlist the services of a returned missionary. In the end, recourse was had to a college which had been founded at Naples, "dedicated to the education of young Chinese, whom the European missionaries contrived to get away from China." Two of the students from this institution were engaged to act as interpreters to the embassy, with whom the young Staunton, before embarking and during the voyage, studied Chinese so assiduously, that on arriving at Peking he could speak their language with fluency, as well as read it to some extent. When the mission reached the Ladrone Islands, one of the two interpreters disappeared, afraid to face the consequences of having been absent from his native land for the purpose of studying in a college at Naples. The other, known as "Mr. Plum," remained with the embassy throughout.

The affairs of the East India Company at Canton had recently been put under the control of three commissioners, selected from among the Company's most trusted servants, to whom the Chairman of the Court of Directors, Sir Francis Baring, gave instructions to forward to the Viceroy of Canton a letter in which the despatch of the mission was announced. On receiving this information the Emperor, Kienlung, showed great satisfaction, and ordered that the port of Tientsin should be opened for the reception of the vessels employed upon the occasion. Nevertheless, the Court at Peking was not without suspicion as to the designs of Great Britain in sending the embassy. This feeling was partly due to suggestions contained in letters received from the officials at Canton, and from the Portuguese at Macao. A further cause was that the operations of the British in India, which had brought the Governor-General into direct relations with the Grand Lama of Thibet, were viewed with some alarm as being a menace to China. It was supposed that the British had even given active assistance against Chinese troops, and until an opportunity occurred of explaining that nothing of the kind had happened, it could hardly be expected that the embassy would be regarded as sent purely out of a desire to establish friendly relations. The circumstances under which this suspicion had arisen may here be fittingly noticed.

Thibet appears to have been finally reduced by the Chinese in the year 1720, during the reign of the Emperor Kanghi. The government was continued in the hands of native princes until the year 1750, when the royal dignity was suppressed and the administration vested in the Dalai Lama, assisted by a cabinet of officers who received their instruction from Peking. Two Chinese generals were appointed residents at Shigatse, and they, in conjunction with Dalai Lama, exercised the supreme control in all state matters. Not many years afterwards, the British arms penetrated to Thibet. The Teshoo Lama sent an ambassador to the Governor-General of India at Calcutta, and the latter in return sent an embassy to Lhassa. Shortly after this, the Emperor of China, who was a disciple of the religion of the Lama, invited the Lama to Peking, and received him there with great honour. The latter, on his arrival in the Chinese capital, sickened with small-pox and died. This untoward event aroused suspicion in the minds of the Thibetans, and Sumhur Lama, the brother of the deceased Lama, fled to the Rajah of Nepaul for protection. The latter, seeing an opportunity of plunder, sent troops into Thibet, who, after several encounters, defeated the Thibetan army assembled to resist them. A peace was concluded by which Thibet was bound to pay an annual tribute of three lacs of rupees to the Rajah. Thibet had in earlier times been tributary to Nepaul, and the effigy of the Rajah, as sovereign paramount, had been stamped on the Thibetan coins. In the treaty it was stipulated that this practice should be revived.

Notwithstanding the peace, the Rajah continued offensive

operations against various parts of Thibet, and in 1791 plundered the Lama's treasury at Shigatze. The Emperor of China, on hearing what had happened, despatched an army of 70,000 men to expel the Napaulese. The Rajah thereupon appealed to the Governor-General of India, as a friend and ally, for assistance; and to the same quarter the Chinese general turned, asking for aid in the name of his imperial master, "the flower of the imperial race, the sun of the firmament of honour, the resplendent gem in the crown and throne of the Chinese territories." At Calcutta there was no one with a sufficient knowledge of Chinese to translate this latter appeal, but its purport was made clear in a letter from the Dalai Lama which accompanied it. The Governor-General refused to help either party, giving as his reason that he wished to remain on friendly terms with both China and Nepaul. The Rajah, finding that he would not be assisted by the British, restored to Thibet the plunder he had received. A peace was concluded when Lord Macartney was on his way to Peking, and the Chinese general bestowed on the offending Rajah the pardon of his imperial master, on condition that the Rajah delivered up the bones of Sumhur Lama, and consented to pay tribute to the Emperor of China. It was stated by the Chinese that they had seen *hats* as well as turbans among the troops opposed to them, and these they supposed to belong to British soldiers, whom they imagined to be assisting the Nepaulese. It was this surmise that gave rise to the belief at Peking that the British Government had assisted in hostilities against the Chinese Empire.[1]

On the 5th of August, 1793, Lord Macartney and his mission reached Taku, where he was officially received by the Viceroy of Chih-li. The attitude adopted by the ambassador was hardly so firm and independent as could have been wished, his main desire being to please the Chinese rather than to assert his own dignity. This is probably the reason that

[1] Staunton, *Account of an Embassy*, etc., vol. i, pp. 50–64; *Chinese Repository*, vol. vi, pp. 493–4; *Papers relating to the East India Company's Affairs* (ordered to be printed by the House of Commons, 21st Jan., 1817).

the embassy, though received with every mark of friendliness and attention, produced little result of practical advantage to Great Britain. As the mission proceeded up the Pei-ho to Tientsin, it was remarked that the junks in which they were carried were decked with flags bearing the words : " Ambassador bearing tribute from the country of England." Lord Macartney, though apprised of the necessity of preserving his independence, thought best not to make any complaint or to attempt to get these flags removed, his reason being that if he made a complaint and obtained no redress, he would be forced to turn back and leave China without having accomplished the purpose for which he had been despatched thither.[1] On arriving at Peking the habitation of the Russian mission was pointed out, but the members of the embassy clearly did not understand its significance, for they describe it as " a dwelling-house of some Russians." [2] Passing through the city Lord Macartney and his suite were escorted out of the North-West gate to a villa close to the imperial palace of Yuen Ming Yuen. The hall of audience in this palace, which contained only the throne, some porcelain vases, and a musical clock, which played twelve old English tunes and bore the inscription : " George Clarke, Leaden-hall Street, London," was set apart for the presents brought from the King of England. These included mathematical and scientific instruments, specimens of British manufactures and inventions, field-guns, pottery, an album of engraved portraits of the nobility of England, a chariot, and a miscellaneous collection of articles that might delight or amuse the Emperor. It is interesting to observe that some specimens of Wedgwood were very much admired by the Chinese.

Whilst still at Yuen Ming Yuen, Lord Macartney was advised by the Chinese officials to practise the *kotow*, as it would be necessary for him to perform that ceremony when presented to the Emperor, who was away at Jehol. Though content to be dubbed a tribute-bearer, the ambassador was hardly prepared to humiliate himself to this extent. He offered,

[1] Staunton : *Account of an Embassy*, etc., vol. ii, pp. 130–1.
[2] *Ibid.*, p. 123.

however, to do so if a subject of the Emperor, of equal rank with himself, would perform the same ceremony before a portrait of George III, which he had brought with him. This proposal gave rise to considerable discussion, and Lord Macartney determined that, in order that there might be no mistake, his proposal should be forwarded to the Court in writing. It was then that the lack of trustworthy interpreters made itself felt. A Portuguese missionary had been appointed by the Emperor to attend the embassy as official interpreter, but as he knew no English his abilities were not of much avail. It was remembered that in days gone by a Chinese who had written a petition for an Englishman had been beheaded,[1] which did not make the task of procuring assistance easier. In this difficulty the younger Staunton proved of great service, and with his aid a letter in Chinese was written to the following effect :—

"His Majesty, the King of Great Britain, in sending an Embassy to his Majesty the Emperor of China, fully intended to give the strongest testimony of particular esteem and veneration for his Imperial Majesty; that the Embassador entrusted to convey such sentiments was earnestly desirous of fulfilling that object of his mission with zeal and effect; that he was ready likewise to conform to every exterior ceremony practised by his Imperial Majesty's subjects, and the tributary princes attending at his court, not only to avoid the confusion of novelty, but in order to show by his example on behalf of one of the greatest as well as most distant nations on the globe, the high and just sense universally entertained of his Imperial Majesty's dignity and transcendent virtues; that the Embassador had determined to act in that manner without hesitation or difficulty, on this condition only, of which he flattered himself his Imperial Majesty would immediately perceive the necessity; and have the goodness to accede to it, by giving such directions as should be the means of preventing the Embassador from suffering by his devotion to his Imperial Majesty in this instance; for the Embassador would certainly suffer heavily if his conduct, on this occasion,

[1] On the occasion of Flint's visit in 1759.

could be construed as in any wise unbecoming the great and exalted rank which his master, whom he represented, held among the independent sovereigns of the world: that this danger could be easily avoided, and the satisfaction be general on all sides, by his Imperial Majesty's order that one of the officers of his court, equal with the Embassador in rank, should perform before his Britannic Majesty's picture at large, in his royal robes, and then in the Embassador's possession at Peking, the same ceremonies which should be performed by the Embassador before the throne of his Imperial Majesty."

There is a tone of subordination about this document that Lord Macartney would have done well to have discarded. Nothing is to be gained by flattering the Chinese or accommodating oneself to their notions of what is a suitable demeanour to be observed by Foreigners. Lord Macartney would have done better to refuse to perform the *kotow* under any conditions. As it turned out, he was relieved from the necessity of performing it even under the conditions proposed by himself, for after his arrival at Jehol, he received word that the Emperor would be content if the same forms were observed in his presence as would be observed by the ambassador before his own sovereign. The journey to Jehol was performed in a four-horse carriage, specially brought from England, which was drawn by four Chinese ponies. The spectacle must have been an amusing one. Besides this carriage there was a splendid chariot, built as a present for the Emperor, which also had been brought from England. The latter vehicle was greatly admired by the Chinese when it was unpacked, but when it was put together, they insisted on the box being removed, as no one could be allowed to occupy a higher position than the Emperor in the Emperor's own carriage.

The state reception of the ambassador by the Emperor took place in a large tent in the grounds of the palace at Jehol. On this occasion the Chinese Court seems to have done its utmost to show honour to the visitors. No official wearing a button below the opaque red, that is, of lower rank than the second, was allowed to be present, and most of those in

THE EMPEROR KIEN-LUNG RECEIVING LORD MACARTNEY AT JEHOL

attendance wore the decoration of a peacock's feather. Several of the courtiers were partly dressed in garments of English cloth, instead of the customary silk, out of compliment to the ambassador's country and by special permission of the Emperor. Lord Macartney himself wore a richly embroidered velvet suit with the mantle and insignia of the Order of the Bath. Sir George Staunton was arrayed in the scarlet robe of a Doctor of Civil Law of Oxford University. The ambassador presented the letter from the King of England in a gold box, which he held in both hands above his head as he ascended the steps that led to the throne, and knelt before the Emperor. The King's letter was couched in the most flattering language, which could not fail to be construed as showing that the King of England acknowledged the Emperor's right to all the virtues and prerogatives usually claimed for him by his subjects.[1] After this ceremony was over, the embassy was sumptuously entertained at a banquet during which the Emperor sent them dishes from his own table. For several days they continued at Jehol, during which time they continued to be entertained in the most lavish style. No attempt appears to have been made to negotiate a treaty or to secure the better treatment of the British residents at Canton, the behaviour of the British ambassador in this respect being in striking contrast to that of the Russian envoys to whom reference has already been made. It is true that before being received by the Emperor, Lord Macartney had a lengthy interview with the Colao, or chief minister, and used the occasion to talk a good deal of politics, and to try to remove any misconception as to our policy in Thibet ; but there his diplomatic efforts seem to have come to an end.

The Emperor's birthday was celebrated on 17th September, whilst the British embassy was still at Jehol. As soon as the festivities were over the Tartar princes began to prepare to leave. On the 21st of the same month, Lord Macartney also took his leave and proceeded to Peking, where he was joined by Barrow and the others who had been left in charge of the

[1] Extracts from the letter are given by Staunton in his *Account of an Embassy*, etc., vol. i, p. 49.

presents at Yuen Ming Yuen. In a few days the return of the Emperor to his capital was announced, and shortly afterwards he arrived. In company with the ambassador he examined the presents, and was much gratified at seeing how the various contrivances were to be used. The novelty of the reception of the embassy being over, hints began to be thrown out that Lord Macartney need not prolong his stay. The English ambassador had hoped to remain until the festival of the Chinese New Year in February, but was told that the climate of Peking was so severe in winter that the Emperor feared his health would suffer if he remained. Shortly afterwards he was sent for to attend the Hall of Audience as soon as he could get ready, and notwithstanding that he was severely indisposed, he felt it best to obey the summons. The Emperor's answer to the letter of the King of England, wrapped in yellow silk, was placed in a chair hung with curtains of the same colour, and was afterwards carried up into the midst of the hall in the presence of the Colao and the ambassador. It was not delivered then, but was afterwards sent in state to the ambassador's hotel.

In his reply to the King's letter, the Emperor stated that the proposals of the ambassador, by which presumably were meant the contents of the King's letter and the tenor of the conversation that had passed between Lord Macartney and the Colao, went to change the whole system of European commerce so long established at Canton, and could not be allowed, neither could the imperial consent be given to any project for allowing the English to trade at Ningpo, Liampo, Chusan, Tientsin, or any northern port. The Emperor went on to say that he could not permit a British Resident at Peking, and that the Russians now only traded to Kiakhta,[1] they not having come for many years to Peking, nor could he give permission for Europeans to reside at any place near Canton except Macao. The letter concluded :—

"As the requests made by your ambassador militate against the laws and usages of this our Empire, and are at the same

[1] This is probably untrue. Certainly the religious part of the Russian Mission still continued.

time wholly useless to the end professed, I cannot acquiesce in them. I again admonish you, O King, to act conformably to my intentions, that we may preserve peace and amity on each side, and thereby contribute to our reciprocal happiness. After this my solemn warning, should your Majesty in pursuance of your ambassador's demands fit out ships with orders to attempt to trade either at Ningpo, Tientsin, or other places, as our laws are exceedingly severe in such cases, I shall have to be under the necessity of directing my officials to force your ships to quit those ports, and thus the increased trouble and exertions of your merchants would at once be frustrated. You will not then, however, be able to complain that I had not clearly forewarned you. Let us therefore live in peace and friendship, and do not make light of my words. For this reason I have so repeatedly and earnestly written to you upon this subject."[1]

Sir Erasmus Gower was still at Chusan with H.M.S. *Lion*, whither he had repaired in the belief that the embassy would stay in the north some considerable time. Having made up his mind to depart at once, Lord Macartney determined to proceed by the Grand Canal and to attempt to join the *Lion* at Chusan. On October 7th the embassy took leave of the Colao and proceeded to Tientsin. From thence they went by the canal route to Hang-chow, and from thence, instead of joining the *Lion*, they continued the journey to Canton by means of the system of inland navigation that supplies an easy route to the South. On the 16th of December, 1817, they arrived finally in Canton. That the embassy was treated with such unusual courtesy by the Chinese was only policy, they hoping by this means to encourage a repetition of such pleasing visitations. How little the position and influence of England were appreciated was shown by the contumely that continued to be heaped on the English and Foreigners generally at Canton. The only permanent effect left upon the Chinese was that England was promptly enrolled on the list of tribute-bearing nations.

[1] *Factory Records of the East India Company* (MSS. in the India Office No. 11, under *Memoir : Intercourse with China*, Part I, pp. 173-5).

Although Lord Macartney's mission produced no very useful result in China, it must not be imagined that in this respect we fared worse than other nations. The truth is, we had been treated much better. At that time the consular agent at Canton of the Dutch East India Company was one Van Braam, who conceived the notion that a mission of salutation and respect, to congratulate the Emperor Kien-lung on attaining the sixtieth year of his reign, would perhaps be more fruitful of success than the visit of the English ambassador, and might tend to efface any unpleasant impression left in the mind of the Emperor by Lord Macartney's failure to comply with all the requirements of the Chinese officials. He had a thought that, by showing a properly humble mind and by conforming to Chinese usages, he might succeed in doing great things for the trade of the Dutch. Van Braam was very desirous of being appointed to conduct such a mission, but the company chose Isaac Titsingh as chief, and himself as second commissioners. The mission set out in 1794. With them went a large staff of interpreters and assistants, one of whom has given us a full narrative of the experiences he underwent on this journey.[1] The Chinese officials at Canton, alarmed lest the visit of the English embassy should provoke inquiry into their own behaviour, assisted Van Braam in his enterprise on receiving assurances that it should be conducted in a manner agreeable to their ideas. It is always a mistake to cringe to the Chinese, and the Dutch soon learnt this. " They were brought to the capital like malefactors, treated when there like beggars, and then sent back to Canton like mountebanks to perform the three-times-three prostrations at all times and before everything their conductors saw fit, who on their part stood by and laughed at their embarrassment in making these evolutions in their tight clothes. They were not allowed a single opportunity to speak about business, which the Chinese never associate with an embassy, but were entertained with banquets and theatrical shows, and performed many skilful evolutions themselves upon their skates, greatly to the Emperor's gratification, and received, moreover, a present of broken

[1] De Guignes, *Voyages à Péking*, vol. i, p. 252.

victuals from him, which had not only been honoured by coming from his majesty's table, but bore marks of his teeth and his good appetite; they were upon a dirty plate, and appeared rather destined to feed a dog than form the repast of a human creature." Van Braam's account of this embassy is one of the most humiliating records of ill-requited obsequiousness which any European was ever called upon to pen.[1]

After Lord Macartney's return some attempt was made to initiate a diplomatic correspondence between England and China. In 1795 the King of England sent a letter to the Emperor through the Select Committee of supercargoes at Canton. At the same time Dundas, who was then Foreign Secretary, Lord Macartney, Sir George Staunton, and the Chairman of the Court of Directors of the East India Company, sent letters and presents to the Viceroy and Hoppo of Canton. These officials refused to receive either the letters to themselves or the presents, alleging that they were intended for their predecessors. The letter to the Emperor was duly forwarded to Peking. It may be mentioned here that in 1805 another letter was sent by the King to the Emperor, and at the same time Lord Castlereagh, who was then Prime Minister of England, sent a letter to the Colao at Peking. Translations of these were forwarded by the Select Committee through the Hong Merchants to the Viceroy. It was arranged that Sir George Staunton, who had returned from England to Canton, should personally present the King's letter to the Viceroy, who sent a handsomely ornamented chair for its conveyance to the yamen. The letter was received in state by the assembled officials, a salute of three guns being fired on its arrival. On the same occasion it was intimated by the Chinese that Lord Castlereagh's letter could not be forwarded, it being an invariable rule of the Empire that no official should receive letters or presents from an official of another country, and the Select Committee were desired to convey this intimation to the Court of Directors.[2]

[1] See Williams, *The Middle Kingdom*, vol. ii, p. 439.

[2] *East India Company's Factory Records* (MSS. in India Office No. 11, under *Memoir : Intercourse with China*, pp. 178, 208-220).

The Emperor replied to the King's letter in the following year. The imperial missive was couched in the language of a suzerain to a vassal, thus affording one more proof of the fact that Lord Macartney had made a mistake in observing the line of conduct adopted by him during his visit to Peking. The subsequent letters to the Emperor had only served to confirm the impression, produced on the occasion of Lord Macartney's visit to Peking, that the King of England was exceptionally desirous of showing zeal as a dutiful subject of the Son of Heaven. In the Emperor's reply occurs the following passage, which admirably sums up the views of the Chinese on the relations between the British and themselves :—

"Your Majesty's kingdom is at a remote distance beyond the seas, but is observant of its duties and obedient to its laws, beholding from afar the glory of our Empire and respectfully admiring the perfection of our Government. Your Majesty has despatched messengers with letters for our perusal and consideration. We find that they are dictated by appropriate sentiments of esteem and veneration, and being therefore inclined to fulfil the wishes and expectations of your Majesty, we have determined to accept of the whole of the accompanying offering.

"With regard to those of your Majesty's subjects, who for a long course of years have been in the habit of trading to our Empire, we must observe to you that our Celestial Empire Government regards all persons and nations with eyes of charity and benevolence, and always treats and considers your subjects with the utmost indulgence and affection. On their account, therefore, there can be no place or occasion for the exertions of your Majesty's Government."[1]

[1] *Factory Records of the East India Company* (MSS. in India Office No. 11, under *Memoir : Intercourse with China*, p. 230.)

CHAPTER VII

MORE DIFFICULTIES AND A SECOND EMBASSY

THAT the Embassy of Lord Macartney had but slightly impressed the Court and governing officials at Peking is apparent as soon as we consider the result of the effort that was made by the Foreigners at Canton, shortly after his departure, to obtain more favourable treatment than they had hitherto received. In 1796 a correspondence was begun between the Select Committee and the Viceroy, in the course of which the former preferred certain requests, to which the latter was invited to give definite answers. It was asked that a correct tariff of duties might be promulgated; that there be no undue interference with the passage of chop-boats[1] between Macao and Canton; that there be granted to the Foreigners a place for free exercise, for walking and for riding; that they might have permission to erect temporary hospitals for sick seamen; that they be allowed to remain at Canton after the last ships had sailed; that the monopoly of the Hong Merchants be abolished and free trade permitted with the shop-men; that the Foreigners be allowed to pay the duties direct to the revenue officials instead of through the Hong Merchants; that those of them who wished to learn Chinese be allowed to engage proper Chinese teachers; and that each ship be held responsible for offences committed on board, without the other ships being involved.

Nearly all these requests were refused, and for reasons of the most flimsy nature. The Select Committee were informed that they could not have a correct tariff of duties, as that request had been refused to "the tribute-bearer" two years before; that all in Canton were necessarily confined, and if Foreigners wanted exercise, they might go twice a month to

[1] Chop-boats were a kind of cargo-boats, sometimes fitted up for the carriage of passengers as well as of goods.—J. R. Morrison, *Chinese Commercial Guide*, p. 3.

the Honan temple; that permission to build hospitals would entail the result of Foreigners remaining at Canton throughout the year, and so could not be granted; that if they were allowed to pay duties otherwise than through the Hong Merchants, they would be exposed to extortion (a poor enough excuse in face of the many illegal exactions from which they already suffered); and that so far as learning the language was concerned, they might sufficiently do that from the *linguists* and compradores. The only concessions made were the permission to visit the Honan temple twice a month, and leave to remain in Canton for a period not exceeding twenty days after the ships had sailed, concessions which were joined with an exhortation to the Hong Merchants not to use their monopoly to oppress the Foreigners.[1]

The outcome of these efforts to bring about a reform was directly contrary to what had been expected. The British community found themselves bound by restrictions, definitely sanctioned by the Viceroy, which had previously been more or less a matter of usage only. Shut up within the narrow limits of the Factories and the three streets immediately surrounding them, not allowed to remain even in that confined area when the shipping season had come to an end, compelled to leave their wives at Macao, owing to the prohibition against any Foreign woman coming to Canton, dependent on the *linguists* as their interpreters and on the compradores as their purveyors, the Foreign community had to live under social conditions that were not less irksome than the commercial disadvantages under which they carried on their business. Finding that nothing could avail to improve their lot, the supercargoes for a time ceased to exert themselves to procure that express recognition of the privileges conceded to their

[1] A report made in 1799 by the supercargoes to the Court of Directors shows that there were other evils that injured the trade itself, which were not discussed in this correspondence, such as the Consoo tax, dishonesty in the weighing of commodities, excessive impositions on shipping, heavy charges for the trans-shipment of goods at Whampoa, and unfairness in measuring the country ships for the purposes of the measurement duty.—*Factory Records of the East India Company* (MSS. in the India Office, No. 11, under *Memoir: Intercourse with China*, p. 183).

predecessors of a century earlier, for which they had been contending. They were fain to rest content with the hope, that lapse of time would of itself bring some new opportunity of obtaining that freedom which was the object of their desires.

It is important to notice some of the changes which had been produced at Canton by the American War of Independence, and by the incessant wars that were waged in Europe during the latter part of the eighteenth, and the beginning of the nineteenth, centuries. The Swedes lost the importance which had been theirs in the days of Charles XII, and the Danes, Portuguese, and Dutch were rapidly sinking to the position which they still occupy in regard to Far Eastern affairs. On the other hand, the Americans were rising into prominence. They were rapidly establishing a thriving trade, not only in the produce of their own country, but as carriers of Chinese products to the continental nations of Europe. In 1798 the United States appointed the first American consul to China, some fourteen years after an American ship had first made the voyage to Canton.[1] In making this appointment the American Government established a precedent which was followed until recently, in that they allowed the consul to levy certain fees on the commerce transacted by his countrymen, and permitted him to engage in trade on his own account, a system in striking contrast to our own, by which every member of the consular service is paid a fixed salary and strictly forbidden to involve himself in commercial transactions. In 1802 the American flag was first hoisted at Canton,[2] and it is from then that we must date the real foundation of the American trade. Not only did the Americans show a determination to take advantage of the opportunity to strengthen their position in China, but France, too, now a republican state, appointed in 1802 a representative at Canton, choosing for that purpose M. Piron, the chief of the French Factory.[3] Russia, by this

[1] *Chinese Repository*, vol. v, p. 218.

[2] *Factory Records of the East India Company* (MSS. in the India Office No. 11, under *Memoir : Intercourse with China*, p. 206) ; Davis, *China and the Chinese*, vol. i, p. 65 ; Auber's *China*, p. 209.

[3] *Chinese Repository*, vol. v, p. 132.

time grown into a great European power, made one attempt to gain a footing at Canton, which failed of success. This was in 1806, when two Russian merchantmen arrived off Macao. An edict forbidding them to engage in commerce was forwarded from the Viceroy through the Hong Merchants to the Select Committee of the East India Company, with a direction to them to deliver it to the Russians, a proceeding which illustrates in a curious way the pre-eminence enjoyed by the British at that time in the eyes of the Chinese.[1] From this time until the year 1858 the Chinese resolutely refused to allow Russia to trade at Canton, giving as a reason the fact that she had already an overland trade through Kiakhta.

Another respect in which political events in Europe were reflected in the state of affairs at Canton, was that British ships of war came to Chinese waters more and more frequently, so that gradually they vindicated their claim to be allowed to anchor and to purchase provisions and stores from the compradores. The growth of the East India Company's trade at Canton, the success of their arms and the extension of their power in India, caused the commerce between England and the East to be the most valuable in the world.[2] The splendid merchant ships in which that commerce was carried on, familiar in stories of heroism and adventure as East Indiamen, though provided with means of defence that commanded respect, were not sufficiently armed to enable them to dispense with convoy when carrying their more valuable cargoes.[3]

[1] *Factory Records of the East India Company* (MSS. in the India Office No. 11, under *Memoir: Intercourse with China*, pp. 227-9). *Report of the Select Committee of the House of Commons on the Affairs of the East India Company* (1830), Evidence of C. Marjoribanks, p. 29.

[2] The trade with Canton was of considerable value. In 1780 the amount of tea carried from that port in British ships was 4,061,830 lbs. See Staunton, *Account of an Embassy*, etc., vol. ii, Appendix. By the season of 1789-90 it had risen to 18,230,720 lbs., of which the value was £1,194,498.

[3] On the 15th February, 1804, the China fleet of sixteen East Indiamen under Commodore Sir Nathaniel Dance beat off the French squadron under Admiral Linois in the China seas. The value of the property at stake on this occasion was estimated at over £16,000,000. In 1795 some of the Company's ships then being built were handed over to the British Government to be used in the Royal Navy. (See Auber's *China*, p. 211; Davis, *China and the Chinese*, vol. i, p. 67.)

Moreover, the cruisers of the Royal Navy extended their quest for enemy ships to the regions of the China seas, and thus a twofold cause operated to bring British men-of-war to Canton in increasing numbers. Over the crews of these vessels the Chinese authorities expected the supercargoes of the East India Company to exercise the same supervision as over the Company's servants and private traders. In China the civil arm is superior to the military, and the rules of English law, which placed the seamen of the Royal Navy outside the civil jurisdiction exercised by the Select Committee, were almost impossible of apprehension to Chinese minds. Hence had arisen the difficulties with H.M.S. *Centurion* in 1744, and H.M.S. *Argo* in 1765, and from the same source similar troubles were to arise in the future.

In the year 1800 one of these troublesome incidents arose in connection with H.M.S. *Providence*, a schooner which had come up to Whampoa from Lintin by order of Captain Dilkes, of H.M.S. *Madras*. The officer of the watch hailed a suspicious-looking boat, which had been anchored at the schooner's bows for some time, and receiving no reply ordered the sentry to fire. On the order being obeyed, one Chinese in the boat was wounded and another fell into the water. The Chinese officials demanded of the supercargoes that the person who had fired should be handed over to them. With this request Captain Dilkes resolutely refused to comply, stating at the same time that he was willing to accompany the man to Canton, to be there examined. This offer was not acceptable to the Chinese, between whom and the Select Committee lengthy negotiations ensued. Had the wounded man died, there would probably have been a serious controversy; but fortunately he recovered, and on the supercargoes proving that the man who had fallen into the water had jumped overboard, the matter was allowed to drop. The Viceroy on this occasion showed a more reasonable disposition than had been exhibited by some of his predecessors in like circumstances. It is pleasant to record that at about this time six Englishmen, who were serving on an American ship and had been badly treated by the captain, on being landed in Fu-kien were well received by the Chinese officials and assisted to reach Canton by an overland route.[1]

More trouble arose with British men-of-war in 1807. The armed schooner *Antelope*, being in need of supplies, violated all the regulations of the port of Macao by entering the harbour and attempting to ship provisions. The majority of the Senate, the governing body of Macao, refused to countenance any such proceeding, and complained of the ill-conduct of the captain in thus thrusting a new controversy upon them. The Chinese officials at Canton called upon the Portuguese to expel the *Antelope* from the harbour, and the Select Committee of the East India Company found themselves entangled in an embarrassing discussion as to the right of British men-of-war to come to Chinese territorial waters at all. In the end the protests of the Chinese were attended with success, and the vessel had to withdraw into the open waters at the mouth of the Canton river. From this time it became a regular practice for ships of war to anchor at Chuen-pi, and though this practice was never officially sanctioned, the ships that availed themselves of it were not prohibited from obtaining supplies. Thus the rule against men-of-war anchoring in Chinese waters gradually became a nullity, and naval captains considered they had a right to make use of more than one anchorage. The privileges thus obtained were not always used with that deference which should have been shown to the authority of the Chinese Government. The conduct of some of the captains who came to the China seas was extremely arbitrary, one of them, Captain Pellew, of H.M.S. *Phæton*, in 1809, going so far as to impress American seamen in Canton, and attempting to exercise the right of search over American vessels then in port.[2]

At this time Canton was one of the worst ports in the world in regard to the demoralizing effect produced on the seamen who landed there. The hot and sultry climate was extremely depressing during the months from April to October, when the

[1] Auber's *China*, pp. 204-6.

[2] *Factory Records of the East India Company* (MSS. in the India Office No. 11, under *Memoir : Intercourse with China*, p. 258).

ships used to load. The haunts of the sailors on shore were of the very worst type. At Whampoa there was merely a beggarly Chinese village ; at Canton the thoroughfare known as Hog Lane was the only resort for the common sailor. The result was that when ashore the seamen fell a prey to the most rascally Chinese, who made them drunk with *sam-shu*, and then robbed them of all their belongings. Disorders frequently arose, and it was due to this fact that, when by the Treaty of Nanking British subjects were allowed to frequent certain ports, special rules were made with regard to the landing of seamen that did not apply to ordinary civilians, a distinction which has been followed to this day. In 1807 an affair of an extremely serious character occurred between sailors of the Company's ship *Neptune* and the Chinese populace, which is noticeable as resulting in an unusual sort of tribunal being called into existence to inquire into the matter. In this affray the sailors were driven back upon the Factory, into which they retreated. There they were detained by their officers, who ordered the gates to be shut. The mob, who had surrounded the building, finding themselves baulked of their intended prey, spent the day in throwing showers of stones and smashed the windows of the Factory. Incensed at this attack, the sailors, eluding the officer in charge, made a sudden sally, and one of the Chinese was killed.

The Select Committee, who knew that the Chinese officials would make the usual demand for the surrender of the offender, at once held an inquiry, but the person responsible for the death of the Chinese could not be discovered. It was then arranged that a further inquiry should be held, which should be conducted by Chinese officials in the presence of British representatives according to the rules of Chinese procedure, except that torture should not be used. Captain Rolles, of H.M.S. *Lion*, Sir George Staunton, and the members of the Select Committee attended as the British representatives, whilst two British marines with fixed bayonets mounted guard at the door. Fifty-two British seamen were to have been examined, but on the inquiry being opened the Chinese offered no evidence. To prevent the trial being abortive, the British representatives agreed that Edward Sheen, one of eleven seamen who had admitted rioting, should be punished with such a fine and detained in custody for such time as the Emperor might determine. The British intended that Sheen should be confined on board ship, but when, on the ships leaving Canton, they attempted to take him to Macao, the Chinese demanded that he should be left behind. Captain Rolles refused to accede to any such arrangement, and announced that if Sheen were not taken to Macao by the Select Committee, he would be carried on board H.M.S. *Lion* and there confined. The wisdom of this determination is apparent when we remember the fate that had befallen the gunner of the *Lady Hughes*, in 1785. Captain Rolles carried his point, and Sheen was kept in custody by the Select Committee. He was taken to Macao, where he was imprisoned until 1808, when he was released by order of the Emperor after paying a fine of twelve taels. The Court of Directors appointed Sir George Staunton for his services on this occasion interpreter to the Factory at a salary of £500 per annum, and they were so pleased at the conduct of Captain Rolles that they voted him a present of a thousand pounds.[1]

An imperial edict was issued on this occasion prescribing the method of trial that should be followed in similar circumstances. It stated that in all cases of offences by contrivance, design, or in affrays happening between Foreigners and natives, whereby such Foreigners were liable, according to law, to suffer death by being strangled or beheaded, the matter should be investigated by the local magistrate, who should report to the Viceroy and *foo-yuen*. If the determination of the lower court were found to be just, the magistrate should receive orders to proceed, in conjunction with the chief of the nation, to take the offender to execution, according to his sentence. In all other instances of offences committed under what the laws declared to be palliating circumstances, which were therefore not capitally punishable, the offender

[1] *Factory Records of the East India Company* (MSS. in the India Office No. 11, under *Memoir : Intercourse with China*, pp. 236-249 ; Davis, *China and the Chinese*, vol. i, p. 73 ; Auber's *China*, pp. 224-9).

should be sent away to be punished by his countrymen in his own country.[1] The provisions of this edict were a serious curtailment of the "usual privileges" which had been granted to the supercargoes when the East India Company first traded at Canton. There is nothing to indicate that its terms were accepted by the Select Committee as binding. So far as can be gathered from the conduct of the successive Presidents, they continued to regard all British subjects as exempt from the jurisdiction of Chinese tribunals.

No sooner had the case of Edward Sheen been satisfactorily determined, than the merchants found their trade again interrupted through no fault of their own. The trouble on this occasion was due to the high-handed conduct of the Indian Government in seeking to garrison Macao against a possible attack by the French. Once before, when Lord Wellesley was Governor-General of India, a similar measure of precaution had been attempted but not carried through. This was in 1802, when the fear had arisen that the French might make a descent on the establishments in the East of our Portuguese allies, and by seizing Macao place our China trade in the gravest peril.[2] Now, in 1808, Great Britain and France were again at war, and the Peninsular Campaign had brought the Portuguese into active co-operation with the British forces. Lord Minto, the Governor-General of India, arranged with the Viceroy of Goa to throw a garrison into that place, and to send an expedition to protect Macao. For that purpose Admiral Drury was placed in command of a large naval force and despatched to China. The Portuguese authorities were pledged to the Chinese not to admit any foreign troops without the consent of the Chinese officials, but, playing a double game, they led the Admiral to understand that they were willing for him to assist them with

[1] Staunton, *Notices Relating to China*, p. 132.

[2] To guard against any such catastrophe, the Indian Government had despatched a force to Macao in 1802, but on its arrival the Chinese protested in the strongest manner against it being landed, and required the troops to be withdrawn. Fortunately at this juncture the brig *Telegraph* arrived with news of the Peace of Amiens, and the force was able to return to India without loss of dignity.

reinforcements, and he, learning in September that there was a French force off Java, landed troops at Macao on the 18th of the same month.

The Chinese were indignant at the mere thought that they might be incapable of defending their own territory against the French or any other invaders, and at once required the British troops to be withdrawn. "Knowing, as you ought to know, that the Portuguese inhabit a territory belonging to the Celestial Empire, how could you suppose that the French would ever venture to molest them ?" Thus ran the Chinese edict. The Viceroy reported the whole matter to the Throne, and prepared to expel the British by force. Roberts, the President of the Select Committee, was foolish enough to encourage Admiral Drury to persist in his project. In reply to the Viceroy the Emperor issued an edict suspending the trade with Foreigners until the troops should be withdrawn. Roberts, who was the prime mover in opposing the Chinese officials, refused to agree to any concession being made to their wishes, and threatened to withdraw the whole British community if the garrison were re-embarked. The Admiral then proposed by letter to the Viceroy that they should have a conference to discuss the situation ; but to this communication no answer was received. Indignant at the want of respect thus shown, Admiral Drury proceeded to Canton in person and threatened that if an audience were not granted he would make his way into the city by force. The Viceroy remained obdurate. The Admiral returned to his ship at Macao, where he assembled all the boats of the men-of-war and Indiamen, fully manned and armed, and announced his intention of forcing the passage of the river, which had been stopped by the Chinese with boats full of soldiers moored across the river's mouth. As soon as the Admiral attempted to proceed the Chinese forts opened fire, which was returned by the *Antelope*. One of his men being wounded, the Admiral gave the signal for attack. The signal, however, was not observed, and Admiral Drury, wavering in his resolution, ordered it not to be repeated. He then drew off his boats and returned to the fleet. Shortly afterwards a convention was concluded at Macao by which the troops were withdrawn, and the expedition returned to India. The net result is well expressed in the words of a member of the Select Committee: "A pagoda was built by the Chinese on this occasion, to commemorate the victory they had obtained over the English admiral; they cannot afford to lose an opportunity of this sort." [1]

The year 1808 is also noteworthy as the date of the commencement of Protestant missions among the Chinese, an event not much noticed at the time, but destined to have a most fateful influence on the relations between China and the rest of the world. It must not be supposed that this was the beginning of Christian missions in China. As early as the sixth century we find the Nestorians arriving and preaching their faith. In the thirteenth century Roman Catholic missionaries made their appearance, and in 1288, John of Montecorvino, who built the first Roman Catholic church at Peking, was sent out by Pope Nicholas IV. The story of the Roman Catholic missions in China, too long to be narrated here, is one of intense interest. There is ground for supposing that, had not the missionaries interfered in temporal affairs, Roman Catholicism would have become in China at least as powerful as Buddhism. Disputes, too, between Jesuits, Dominicans, and Franciscans contributed to bring about its fall, and in 1718 the Emperor Kanghi forbade any missionary to remain in his dominions without his permission. In 1724 the young Emperor, Yung-ching, expelled all missionaries except those required for scientific purposes at Peking, and this policy of repression was continued by Kien-lung. [2]

Until the beginning of the nineteenth century, the only

[1] Evidence of C. Marjoribanks. *Report of the Select Committee of the House of Commons on the Affairs of the East India Company* (1830), p. 29. See also *Factory Records of the East India Company* (MSS. in the India Office No. 11, under *Memoir: Intercourse with China*, pp. 260-278).

[2] For further information as to Christian missions, see Williams, *The Middle Kingdom*, vol. ii, pp. 275–371, and the authorities there cited. The *Lettres Édifiantes* give a particularly vivid account of the Roman Catholic missions at Peking. The exclusion of missionaries from China continued until 1860, when the Treaty of Tientsin came into force. See *post*, chap. xxv, p. 554.

clergy at Canton were the chaplains in the Factories. Then for the first time the Protestant Churches sent missionaries to China. In 1807 Dr. Robert Morrison left England and proceeded to China by way of New York, having been sent out by the London Missionary Society. On his arrival at Canton he lived quietly in one of the American Factories for more than a year, and when the trade was stopped in 1808, retired to Macao, taking care to live in seclusion there, lest he should excite the jealousy of the Roman Catholic fathers. Having in that year obtained the imperial sanction, he settled in Canton and commenced his labours. A man of high character and great ability, he speedily made friends with the British supercargoes, and at the instance of Sir George Staunton, was appointed translator to the East India Company, which was at that time seeking to stimulate the study of the Chinese language. In the service of the Company he did most valuable work, right up to the time of his death in 1834, in forwarding the study of Chinese by English students. One of his chief works was the production of a Chinese and English Dictionary, the first ever published, in which he was most generously assisted by the East India Company, which spent over £12,000 in this connection.[1] Of his thirty-one literary achievements perhaps the most celebrated was the translation of the Bible into Chinese, a task which had never before been attempted. A few years later, Morrison was joined by Milne, and it was not long before there was a considerable missionary establishment at Canton.

During the years from 1806 to 1809 the ships trading in the China seas were much harassed by pirates, commonly known by the Portuguese name of ladrones.[2] The many islands that stud the southern coasts, and the many inlets and bays that

[1] *Report of the Select Committee of the House of Commons on the Affairs of the East India Company* (China Trade). "I conceive a knowledge of the peculiar language of China to have been more materially promoted by Dr. Morrison than by any other individual whom I have ever known in China."—Evidence of C. Marjoribanks, p. 19. Auber's *China*, p. 252.

[2] From the time of Koxinga the seas had not been wholly free from Chinese pirates.

mark the coast line, are inhabited by Chinese who, at the best of times, make a precarious living by fishing and thieving. When these means of subsistence fail, they become pirates, and according as the vigilance of the Government waxes or wanes, grow less or more formidable. In 1806 a large body of freebooters of this kind had collected together, who were constantly adding to their fleet vessels captured both from the naval and mercantile marine of China. This growth in numbers was accompanied by an increase in audacity, and in December, 1806, they seized the cutter of the British country ship *Tay*, on board which was Turner, the chief mate. For five months he was detained among them, and during that period he was able to observe their organization and operations in every detail.

The total force of the ladrones was computed by Turner to be at that time about 25,000 men, and 500 or 600 sail, divided into five divisions, each of which was under the command of a separate chief and flew a distinctive flag. Each division was subdivided into several squadrons, each under an inferior chief who was responsible to the chief of division. Their vessels ranged in size from 15 to 200 tons, but most of them were between 70 and 150 tons. The largest of these carried twelve guns, the heaviest of which were 18 pounders. All ships frequenting the coasts of China were liable to be attacked by them, excepting those which, by paying tribute to one of the chiefs, obtained a pass. Similarly all villages near the coast were liable to be plundered, unless they purchased safety by the payment of money. Exemption thus obtained was scrupulously respected, and the chiefs punished their followers and compelled them to make reparation for any violation of the immunity that had been so purchased. Captives from merchant ships were detained for ransom or compelled to join the pirates ; but if capture had been resisted they were murdered. If they refused to obtain ransom money from their friends, or to join the piratical body, they were stripped naked and beaten with twisted rattans, until they changed their minds or succumbed to the torture. All captives from war-junks were put to death, some of them being first tortured in the most cruel manner. Turner saw one of these nailed to the deck by long nails driven through his feet, and flogged with four rattans twisted together until he vomited blood, after which he was taken ashore and cut in pieces. Another was fixed upright, his bowels cut open, and his heart taken out, which the pirates soaked in spirits and ate. Cruelty of this kind struck such terror into the seamen of the imperial navy, that they durst not make an attack. Consequently by 1809 the pirates had become so powerful that the seas in the neighbourhood of Macao were under their control.

The ladrones were at this time governed by a woman, the widow of their former chief, Chang Yih, who had been drowned in a typhoon in 1807. Under her hand the piratical community was ruled by a regular code, of which the governing principle was socialistic. All booty was registered and distributed in equal proportions among the ships, and embezzlement was punished with death. Money taken from captured vessels was handed to the chief of the division, who gave two-tenths to the captors, and paid the rest into the common fund. No pirate was allowed to go on shore without permission. All provisions, stores, and ammunition obtained from the country people were to be honestly paid for on pain of death. Of female captives the handsomest were reserved for wives and concubines, being sold to the highest bidder among the pirates; of the others some were held to ransom, and those of most homely appearance were put on shore. The purchaser of a wife was compelled to retain her. Each pirate kept his wife and family in a small berth about four feet square. Promiscuous intercourse was strictly forbidden, and any attempt at rape was punished with death. The pirates were great opium smokers and gamblers. They were very superstitious, and frequently consulted their priests as to when operations might be successfully undertaken.

The power of the pirates had now grown to such a pitch that orders were sent by the Emperor for their destruction. Time after time the Chinese fleet took the offensive against them, but never with any real success, and usually with great loss to the attacking force. A new method of operations was then devised, by which all vessels were ordered to remain in port, and the people forbidden to afford supplies, by which it was hoped that the pirates would be starved out. The latter, exasperated by this policy, indulged in the most atrocious cruelties. Driven to greater boldness, they appeared in the Macao roads and entered the Canton river itself. The Viceroy thereupon moved into the Portuguese settlement, to plan with the Procurador a scheme for the suppression of the common enemy. It was agreed between them that six ships should be equipped by the Portuguese, to combine with the Chinese in cruising for six months between Canton and Macao, and that in return the Viceroy should contribute 80,000 taels towards the expense, and, on the extermination of the free-booters, restore " the ancient privileges of Macao." Independently of this arrangement, the Select Committee of the British Factory sent to India to ask for protection from the ships of the Royal Navy, and as a result two cruisers were sent from Bombay under Captain Ross.

In September, 1809, another Englishman, named Glasspoole, an officer of one of the East India Company's ships, was captured by the pirates and detained for eleven weeks, until ransomed by his friends. He found that their numbers had now increased to 70,000 men, having 800 large and 1,000 small vessels under their control. All were by this time suffering from the shortage of food produced by the new policy, and Glasspoole himself was obliged for three weeks to live on caterpillars boiled with rice. Scenes of butchery, rapine, and pillage, in which innocent villagers were the sufferers, were witnessed day after day, and in some of these he was compelled to take part. The combined Portuguese and Chinese fleets did little to repress these depredations, though publishing reports of deeds of the greatest prowess wrought by their forces. In the end the decay of the ladrone power, which had commenced by the stoppage of supplies, was accelerated by internal dissensions among the chiefs. Seeing his opportunity, the Viceroy offered a general amnesty, which was accepted by one of the chiefs, named Kwo Potae, who became an imperial officer, and with his adherents devoted his energies to attacking his former friends. Weakened by this desertion, and harassed by the enemy who were now aware of the pirates' secret haunts, the chieftainess and her principal lieutenant, Paou, made their submission a few months later. Many of her followers enlisted in the imperial forces, and joined in the hunt against their old associates. Paou went to Peking and received an office at Court, being much esteemed by the Emperor.[1] For his exalted services in suppressing the ladrones the Viceroy received the imperial permission to wear a peacock's feather with two eyes ; for their assistance the Portuguese got nothing except the Viceroy's contribution towards the expense ; the British cruisers remained to complete the survey of the China seas which they had begun on behalf of the British Admiralty department.

For the six years from 1808 to 1814 the trade at Canton continued to be carried on without interruption, though subject to all the old restrictions and impositions. In 1814 the Court of Directors appointed a new Select Committee, with Sir George Staunton as President,[2] who very soon set to work to try to improve the conditions under which the intercourse between the Foreigners and Chinese was carried on at Canton. At the outset they were faced by an unforeseen difficulty that arose out of the war which was then being waged between England and the United States. Captain Patterson, of H.M.S. *Doris*, having captured an American prize off the Ladrones, brought her into the Canton river. The Chinese officials protested against any such use being made of their territorial waters, and required the Select Committee to send the *Doris* away. On receiving the reply that the King's ships were not under the Committee's control, the Viceroy,

[1] For further information as to the ladrones, see an article in the *Chinese Repository*, vol. iii, pp. 68-83.

[2] *Factory Records of the East India Company* (MSS. in the India Office No. 11, under *Memoir : Intercourse with China*, p. 310). This was Sir George Thomas Staunton, who had accompanied Lord Macartney's embassy to Peking as page to the ambassador, and had succeeded to the baronetcy on the death of Sir George Leonard Staunton in 1801. In 1798 he had been appointed a writer in the E.I. Company's Factory at Canton, and in 1804 was promoted to be a supercargo.

by way of bringing pressure to bear, withdrew all the Chinese servants from the Factory.[1] The Select Committee did all in their power to induce Captain Patterson to take his departure, and prohibited any of the Company's ships from entering the river so long as he remained. The discussion between the English and Chinese went on for some months, until the latter, finding their protests of no avail, ordered the Select Committee to expel the *Doris*, suspended the trade, and prohibited all intercourse between the Indiamen and men-of-war. They also took the unusual step of stopping Captain Patterson's boat when it was flying the British flag.

Sir George Staunton now attempted to settle the matter by negotiation with the Viceroy, but when hopeful that the matter would be thus smoothed over, he was surprised to find that the Viceroy refused to continue the negotiations. Resenting the contumelious fashion in which he had been treated, Staunton moved all the Company's ships to below Second Bar, and ordered all British merchants to join the shipping. This decisive action was not without its effect, and on the 19th of November the Chinese officials again met the Company's representative in conference. Staunton used this opportunity to discuss the whole question of the conditions under which Foreigners were compelled to carry on their trade, and to ask for a redress of grievances. The views of the Select Committee were formulated in a series of eight propositions, of which the purport was as follows [2] :—

1. That the Select Committee should be allowed to address Chinese officials in the Chinese language.

2. That no contemptuous or disrespectful language should be used in edicts addressed to the English, simply because they were Foreigners.

3. That the local magistrates and their attendants should not enter the Factory at their pleasure.

[1] The first intimation that the Foreign residents of Tientsin had in the year 1900 that the Concessions were likely to be attacked was that all the servants disappeared the night before the bombardment commenced, probably by order from the Chinese officials.

[2] J. R. Morrison, *Chinese Commercial Guide*, pp. 49-53.

4. That Captains in their boats flying their national flags should not be unnecessarily stopped by the Hoppo's boats.

5. That the English should be allowed to engage what Chinese servants they pleased.

6. That ships of war be allowed to anchor, as had been the practice for many years past, at Chuen-pi, Keaouke, Lintin, and Macao Roads, and to be supplied with provisions.

7. That communication by boat between ships of war and merchantmen be permitted.

8. That Chinese armed boats be not allowed to fire at the country ships.

To most of these propositions a favourable answer was received. The second was evaded, and as to the third it was agreed that such visits should not be paid without notice. With respect to the seventh, boats might receive passes at certain stations, and in reply to the eighth it was stated that the firing was only by way of notice to the Bogue Fort. Thus the Company acquired the privilege of presenting their petitions to the officials in Chinese, whilst all other persons, of whatsoever nationality, had to petition in their own language. This was a most valuable concession, as the *linguists* who acted as interpreters were so incompetent that nothing but the very simplest "pidgin English" was within their powers. Moreover they did not hesitate to put on a petition, which was not written in Chinese, such a construction, without regard to its real meaning, as might most please the official to whom the petition was addressed. From this time it was the right, and became the custom of the Company, to present all their requests in the form of petitions in Chinese, enclosed in a cover superscribed with the character *Pin*, or "Petition."

Some additional regulations were made by the Viceroy himself, which provided that any address intended to be laid before the Emperor should be written in English; that in important affairs petition should be made to the Viceroy, in commercial affairs to the Hoppo, and in local district affairs to the district officials; that further arrangements would be made with respect to boats passing the Bocca Tigris; that the opening or suspending of trade would not be enquired into; and that notice would be given when Chinese were about to be tried for offences in which Foreigners were implicated. These additional regulations, together with the answers given to the propositions submitted by Sir George Staunton, formed a rough code, which remained the basis of the rules governing the intercourse between the British and the Chinese until the East India Company were deprived of their monopoly in 1834.

Owing to the difficulties described above, the British Government came to the conclusion that it might be an advantageous measure to send a second embassy to Peking. In arriving at this decision they were also influenced by considerations which, until that time, had not been allowed to affect their policy in China, namely, the desirability of satisfying the Chinese Government that the Company's policy elsewhere was not intended to menace the security of the Chinese Empire. It was recognized that the extension of our power in India had by this time proceeded so far, that our policy with regard to the border states on the North directly affected Chinese interests. Moreover, fresh difficulties had arisen between the Indian Government and the state of Nepaul, which was regarded as in some degree tributary to China, such as would be likely to excite distrust and suspicion at Peking, if the attitude of Great Britain were not clearly and accurately explained to the Emperor. Hostilities against the Ghoorkha rajah were commenced by our troops in 1815, and the forts of Ramghur, Jhurjhuri, Taraghur, and Chumbull, captured in quick succession. Only the valour of Umr Sing, the Rajah's general, prevented the British from gaining all they wished. This officer, in 1815, advised his master to appeal to Peking, on the ground that the Emperor had been insulted by the British in daring to invade Nepaul, a part of the Celestial Empire. Hastings, who was then Governor-General, warned the Chinese ambans[1] against abetting the enemies of the British Government, a warning which was passed on by them to Peking. The Emperor, indignant at the demeanour of the British, despatched troops to the

[1] The Chinese Residents at Shigatze. As to the nature of the Chinese administration of Thibet, see *Chinese Repository*, vol. vi, p. 495.

frontier ; but eventually explanations were offered by the Indian Government which appeased the imperial wrath,[1] all intention of encroaching upon or obtaining access to Chinese territory being disclaimed.

When matters had come to this pass the second embassy, which had been placed under the direction of Lord Amherst, sailed from England in H.M.S. *Alceste*. Mr. Elphinstone, the chief of the Factory at Canton, and Sir George Thomas Staunton, who had acted as page to Lord Macartney but was now interpreter to the Factory, were appointed assistant commissioners, and Henry Ellis[2] was appointed secretary, with power to act as commissioner in the absence of either of the assistant commissioners. A large following of persons of all sorts and kinds accompanied the mission, whose presence can hardly be regarded as calculated to produce a favourable impression on the Court at Peking. To the Chinese secretaries, among whom were J. F. Davis[3] and the Rev. Robert Morrison, no exception can be taken ; of the rest none were distinguished, and many were merely ornamental. The narratives of Ellis and Davis are largely accounts of things that might much better have been done differently. The following incident shows how little attention had been paid to matters of ceremonial, by which the Chinese set such store. When the mission reached T'angku, at the mouth of the Pei-ho, it was received by the Chinese officials, who came on board for that purpose. It was then discovered that no means had been provided for serving tea, the beverage invariably used on such occasions in China. Thinking it best to supply some refreshment, the ambassador regaled his visitors with cherry brandy, a substitute which, it must be admitted, was drunk with no apparent dissatisfaction.

At the very outset the members of the mission were

[1] For further particulars see *Chinese Repository*, vol. vi, pp. 486–494. *Papers relating to East India Affairs ordered to be printed by the House of Commons*, Jan. 31st, 1817.

[2] Ellis's *Embassy to China* is the standard account of the mission.

[3] Afterwards Sir John Davis and British Minister to China. Davis's *Sketches in China* is an entertaining description of the various experiences undergone during the progress of the embassy.

questioned as to the willingness of Lord Amherst to perform the *kotow*, as to which great discussions ensued, the Chinese officials falsely asserting that Lord Macartney had complied with the usual forms observed in the Emperor's presence. Lord Amherst announced that he would not *kotow* on any conditions, but expressed his willingness to bow to the Emperor as many times as the Chinese officials prostrated themselves. The latter attempted to wrest this concession into a compliance with their demands, but the ambassador maintained his ground with great firmness. All the way from Tientsin to Peking the discussion over the *kotow* continued. On arriving at the capital the ambassador, fatigued and indisposed, was surprised to receive a summons to attend the Emperor forthwith, an intimation being added that this audience was not for purposes of business. Excuses were made on the ground that Lord Amherst was far from sufficiently well to attend at the palace at such summary notice. The next day the Emperor sent word that the embassy would not be received at all, and desired that it should take its departure forthwith, a desire that was at once gratified. The Emperor afterwards stated in edicts issued with reference to the visit of this embassy, that he had never been fully informed as to the circumstances under which Lord Amherst had declined the audience, and ordered that his ministers be punished for not having apprised him of the true facts.

Thus the second mission from Great Britain to China failed completely. Its want of success was due to no incompetence on the part of the ambassador, but mainly to the arrogance and ignorance of the Chinese. Had the old Emperor Kien-lung still been on the throne, it is possible that he would have accorded the mission such a reception as that extended by him to Lord Macartney. But from first to last no chance of success attended Lord Amherst's undertaking. The officials at Canton had been at great pains to misrepresent the nature of the embassy to their sovereign, in order to further their own intrigues, and the officials at Peking were either too stupid or too insolent to ascertain the true state of affairs. Whatever the cause, this opportunity of improving the relations between England and China by diplomacy had been thrown away. The Emperor, Kiaking, himself wrote in a letter to the Prince Regent: "Hereafter there is no occasion for you to send an ambassador so far, and be at the trouble of passing over mountains and passing seas." In one of those vermilion edicts, used in China to make announcements to which exceptional importance is attached, the imperial version of the departure of Lord Amherst was stated in the words: "I therefore sent down my pleasure to expel these ambassadors, and send them back to their own country, without punishing the high crime they had committed."[1]

[1] *Factory Records of the East India Company* (MSS. in India Office No. 11, under *Memoir: Intercourse with China*, pp. 361).

CHAPTER VIII

LAST YEARS OF THE COMPANY'S MONOPOLY

THE rejection of the embassy at Peking at once re-acted on the state of affairs at Canton, and produced a more hostile disposition in the Chinese officials. When the *General Hewitt*, the Company's ship which had accompanied to the North H.M.S. *Alceste*, in which the embassy had sailed from England, returned in September, she was ordered to remain at Lintin. The edict prohibiting her from passing the Bocca Tigris was not sent to the Select Committee, but was forwarded to the *linguist* in defiance of all precedent and contrary to the arrangement agreed upon in 1814. The supercargoes refused to receive the communication thus transmitted to them, and addressed a letter to the Hoppo reminding him of their right to communicate with him direct, and pointing out that the Emperor had given his permission to the vessel to come up to Whampoa, a permission they intended to use. On the 22nd of October the *General Hewitt*, by order of the Select Committee, was brought up the river. Thereupon the Hoppo refused to receive their letter, and the Hong Merchants refused to be the bearers of any further communication. The Committee were determined not to be put off, and instructed Captain Jameson to proceed in person to the city, to force his way through the gate to the Viceroy's yamên, and to deliver the letter in person. Captain Jameson so far succeeded as to reach the city gate and deliver the missive into the hands of "a mandarin of distinction." The Chinese officials showed their disapprobation of this boldness by seizing and beating the Company's compradore, an outrage which incited the Committee to announce that they would not receive any representative of the Chinese officials until the compradore should have been released.

Things had come to this pass when on the 3rd of November, H.M.S. *Alceste*, under the command of Captain Maxwell, arrived off Lintin. The Chinese refused for a time to allow him to enter the river, but when he remonstrated they promised that if he would wait a few days the necessary permission would be given. Having waited a day beyond the stipulated time and received no communication, Captain Maxwell took the *Alceste* up to Chuen-pi, where he found a flotilla of boats assembled, and was informed that, if he did not anchor, a gun would be fired. Scarcely had this peremptory message been delivered than several guns were fired. They appeared not to be shotted, and Captain Maxwell, thinking that possibly they were saluting, replied with blank cartridge. The Chinese thereupon opened fire with shot, a proceeding for which there could be no justification, as the *Alceste* was below the limit assigned to men-of-war. Captain Maxwell, having silenced the flotilla by firing a single shot over the boat of the commander, came to anchor. The Chinese immediately spread a report that their fire had compelled the *Alceste* to desist, whereupon Captain Maxwell determined to maintain the privilege accorded to H.M.S. *Lion* in 1793, and to proceed within the Bogue. As soon as he had weighed anchor to carry out this resolution, the Chinese opened a brisk cannonade with from 90 to 100 guns. One shot fell on board the *Alceste*, and two lodged in her bows. She replied with a broadside that silenced the forts on the starboard side, and it was not long before those to larboard ceased to attack. Eventually the *Alceste* anchored within the Second Bar without injury, having been piloted up by the second officer of the Company's ship *Surat Castle*.[1] The Chinese thought it prudent not to further molest either of the ships, and the incident terminated.

For the twelve years immediately following the return of Lord Amherst's mission, the trade was carried on in greater tranquillity than had been experienced for many years. The British Admiralty had issued instructions to their ships to abstain from all acts that would in the least trench upon the law of nations, or afford any colourable pretext for offence on the part of the Chinese Government[2]. The Congress of

[1] *Factory Records of the East India Company* (MSS. in the India Office No. 11, under *Memoir : Intercourse with China*, pp. 363-383).
[2] *Ibid.*, p. 318.

Vienna had settled the affairs of Europe for the time being, and the war between England and the United States had come to an end, so that the causes of dissension between the different nations that traded at Canton had been removed. Sir George Staunton had done good work in putting the relations between the Chinese officials and the Factory on a more friendly footing, albeit the conditions under which the trade was carried on would have been intolerable to any but servants of the Company who had grown up under the existing *régime*. During these twelve years only two incidents occurred of which it is necessary to make any particular mention. These serve to show how little power the consuls of the nations trading at Canton possessed, and how soon a mistake by the subjects of one nation would be used by the Chinese to attempt to obtain an advantage over another.

In September of 1821 an Italian, named Terranova, who was serving on an American merchantman as a sailor, accidentally caused the death of a Chinese woman, who was selling spirits from a boat moored alongside his ship, by throwing down a jar which struck her on the head. The woman fell overboard and was drowned. The Chinese officials demanded, as was their wont, that the man who had caused her death should be given up, and stopped the trade until their demand should be conceded. The American consul refused to make any such concession, but consented to a trial being held by Chinese officials on board an American vessel. Dr. Morrison's offer to interpret on this occasion was rejected, and not a single witness was called on behalf of the accused, who, being unable to speak more than a few words of English, never had the semblance of a fair trial. Terranova was found guilty and was put in irons on board his ship. This did not appease the Chinese, who continued to press for his surrender, and to refuse to allow the Americans to trade. At length the American captains, chafing at the delay imposed on their ships, took the law into their own hands and intimated to the Hong Merchants that they might take the prisoner. Terranova was thereupon taken into Canton by the Chinese, and there subjected to the farce of a second trial, at which no Americans or Europeans were allowed to be present. He was at once found guilty, and on the morning following his surrender was publicly strangled.

The iniquity of this proceeding was such as to lay open to the severest condemnation all who took any part in it. Apart from that, it could not fail to lessen the prestige of the whole Foreign community. Its effect on the Chinese was soon apparent. In December of the same year H.M.S. *Topaze* was watering at Lintin, when some of her crew who were on shore were attacked by Chinese with clubs and spears and placed in great danger. A party of marines was quickly sent to their assistance, and these with their fire covered the retreat of the seamen. Of the latter fourteen were carried on board the *Topaze* wounded, and it was afterwards ascertained that of the Chinese two had been killed and four wounded. Captain Richardson, who was in command of the frigate, wrote a letter of complaint to the Viceroy, which he caused to be handed in at the city gate by the officers of some of the Indiamen. The Viceroy refused to have any communication with the captain, and replied to the Select Committee, demanding the surrender of two Englishmen. The Committee refused to allow a reply to Captain Richardson to be sent through them, and Captain Richardson refused to accede to the Viceroy's proposal that a Chinese official be sent on board to examine the wounded seamen. The Viceroy thereupon stopped the trade and prohibited the *Topaze* from proceeding up the river. When the trade had been suspended some two weeks, the Select Committee wrote to the Viceroy remonstrating against the attitude taken up by him, and stating that they had no control over ships of war. Matters having come to a deadlock, the Committee announced their intention of leaving China with the whole British community. The Viceroy then withdrew the threat he had held out of making the supercargoes personally responsible, but continued the stoppage of trade. It was suggested to Captain Richardson by the Committee that he should intimate to them that the matter was one which he could not decide on his own responsibility, but would report to his Sovereign on his return to England, and that they should communicate with the Viceroy to this effect. This suggestion was carried out, and the Committee reported to the Viceroy accordingly. This proceeding somewhat mollified the Chinese, who sent an official to visit the *Topaze* and receive a full statement of the facts, which was given to him by the first lieutenant. A few days later, on the 8th of February, 1822, Captain Richardson, having received no communication from the Viceroy, put to sea and left the Chinese to take what course they pleased. Disconcerted at this manœuvre, the Viceroy, on receiving from the Select Committee a promise that the whole affair should be laid before the British Government, allowed the trade to be resumed. The Court of Directors subsequently laid the facts of the case before Lord Liverpool, who was then Prime Minister, and Lord Melville, the First Lord of the Admiralty, and instructions were sent out by the British Government to the naval commander-in-chief in India, that in future no ships of the Royal Navy should visit China in time of peace except at the request of the Governor-General of India or of the Select Committee at Canton. These instructions were strictly carried out, and so an end was put to incidents of the kind just described.[1]

For the seven years following the termination of the affair of the *Topaze* the trade was carried on in tranquillity and without interruption, under the conditions which long use had made to seem unalterable. In 1829, however, a fresh agitation arose with the object of procuring a change, caused by the discovery that more than one of the Hong Merchants was hopelessly insolvent. During these years of quietude the affairs of the Co-hong had been steadily drifting from bad to worse, and now matters came to a crisis owing to one of the members, Chungqua, absconding. Various remedies were proposed and discussed, the Select Committee using the occasion to ask for the abolition of some of the heavy imposts under which the trade laboured, and that men of substance

[1] *Factory Records of the East India Company* (MSS. in the India Office No. 12, under *Memoir : Intercourse with China,* Part II, p. 512.) *Chinese Repository*, vol. ii, p. 423, vol. v, p. 223. Auber's *China*, pp. 288-309.

should be induced to become Hong Merchants. As the East India Company's representatives were the only persons among the Foreign community who were able to command the services of competent interpreters, they took the leading part in bringing before the Chinese officials the views of the whole of the Foreign merchants. They were backed by all the private traders, as well as by the Spanish and Dutch consuls, but the other consuls seem to have stood aloof. Their views were embodied in a lengthy letter to the Viceroy, which graphically summarized the chief subjects of complaint in these terms :—

" Substantial and respectable men will not become mandarin merchants for two reasons. First, they are subjected to so heavy, so arbitrary, and such grievous extortions by the Hoppo's *kingshing* and the clerks and servants of the Hoppo's establishment, that human nature can bear no more. Rich men have declared that they would prefer being the vilest animal to being a Hong Merchant. Secondly, a man who once enters the Hong becomes a prisoner for life : he cannot retire when his fair exertions have increased his store, old age disabled him from active employment, or sickness rendered labour irksome. Some of the Co-hong have declared they would freely give up eight parts of their property to be allowed truly to retire and enjoy the other two parts. But when a merchant has paid largely to get away, he is liable to be hastily brought back again, even when he owes money to nobody. Thus no man can be induced to purchase with a large sum the hateful privilege of being insulted and ruined.

" This then must be changed ; or the Hongs now dropping severally and quickly to decay can never be replaced. Government must give sufficient assurance to the merchants that they may retire when they please : that they shall not be subject to the insult and extortion of the Hoppo and his officers ; and that they may become merchants authorized to trade with Foreigners, without paying any fee or fine on their appointment. Under these assurances we do not doubt that many outside shopmen and small traders, to the amount of twenty, thirty, or more,—and the more the safer and better—

may be induced to become merchants ; but they can be only truly useful in trade, acquire fair gains, and ensure regularity and security in providing the revenue, if established under the regulations we now propose for your excellency's approval. These points are essential :—

" 1. Chungqua's Hong must not be allowed to fail. Lew Shingshoo must come back and bring money. If this hong fails Foreigners will be clamorous, and demand instant payment of the whole amount ; they will not bear to be defrauded of their property and then told to wait for payment in five or six years.

" 2. The new hongs now created, if there be twenty, or if there be fifty, must not be responsible for any debts of Foreigners or Chinese on account of bankrupt merchants ; let each answer for his own, no one for his neighbour's debts. Then each will be trusted as far as he deserves, but no farther.

" 3. The old hongs must not be responsible for any debts contracted by them from the day on which public notice is given of the new system commencing. They must now pay off, or declare the amount of their present incumbrances.

" 4. The debts of former hongs now bankrupt must be paid by an assessment on the amount of the whole import and export trade of each : a small percentage on the total value of their transactions will suffice. The new hongs, as well as the old, must be assessed in proportion to their dealings, or the old cannot stand long. The Government may reasonably grant time for paying the duties now due, as the debts of Foreigners have been so often and so long postponed. In a few years the assessment will have paid off all : it must then cease. No fresh occasion, as will soon be shown, can ever recur for it.

" 5. Duties on import cargoes must be charged and levied daily, and the amount must be paid to government within five days, as now the case with export cargo. Responsibility for duties will thereby be destroyed, as there can be no arrears, and the revenue will be benefited by quicker receipts and increased security.

"6. Foreigners must be allowed to rent warehouses, and have such control over them as will afford ample security for property stored therein. This will be quite necessary when dealing with hongs of small capital, and which in case of failure are not secured. No smuggling can take place therefrom, because the moment the goods are landed, and the duties ascertained, Foreigners housing the articles will pay immediately to the proper government officers the amount in cash. There will be no occasion to wait for a distant period of sale, or to pay the money through the merchants and linguists.

"7. None of the hongs shall be required to secure foreign ships. Such security will be unnecessary as regards duties. It is only useful as a handle to the Hoppo's extortions for acts, or imputed acts, of Foreigners over which the merchants can exercise no control. It is vexatious to both parties. No ship shall be obliged to have a house or ship compradore appointed to it. Such people, to pay for their licences, are obliged to overcharge on their supplies. Let ship captains buy what they want through whom they please.

"8. The amount of port charges must be reduced. That remaining to be paid must be charged according to the size of the ship, a smaller ship paying less : it must be paid on board the ship, at the time she is measured, by the captain to the proper government officer, who shall give his receipt at once. That ships be rated in proportion to their size is necessary, because when the changes soon expected in Europe occur, many small private ships will come to China ; they cannot afford to pay large port duties : they will be forced to remain outside the river, where smuggling will be resorted to ; disturbances will arise ; and the revenue, in lieu of being very much increased, will be reduced to perhaps one half, perhaps less. Soon indeed no ships will come in, and there will be no revenue, but much confusion and disorder."[1]

To this letter the Viceroy replied, on the 12th of November, in a lengthy edict in which he sought to justify each of the above abuses on the ground of "old custom," that Chinese

[1] J. R. Morrison, *Chinese Commercial Guide*, p. 54.

shibboleth which has saved so many evils from destruction. The gist of his pronouncement was, that substantial Hong Merchants could not be allowed to retire; entire remission of fees would be granted to those who would become new Hong Merchants; Chungqua had been ordered to return; the practice of lending money to Chinese had long been forbidden; the tax out of which the Consoo Fund was maintained must be continued; duties on imports should be paid within twenty days of the goods being landed; Foreigners could not be permitted to have warehouses, as this would be impracticable as well as injurious to the Foreigner; the old system of security merchants and compradores would be continued, but a reduction would be made in the fees of the latter; "a want of discrimination" with regard to the *cumshaw* was admitted, but the *cumshaw* had existed so long it could not be abolished.

One can plainly trace throughout the edict the desire to increase the chance of being able to squeeze money from the merchants by granting small concessions, and to run no risk of diminishing the opportunity which the officials already enjoyed of making an illicit profit. To allow substantial Hong Merchants to retire would be folly from the point of view of a Viceroy or Hoppo,whose revenue was mainly derived from money extorted from Hong Merchants; the wisdom of inducing new Hong Merchants to come forward is equally apparent from the same point of view. That the promises made to enlist new recruits for the Co-hong would ever be performed no one for a moment expected; consequently it still remained almost as difficult as before to maintain the Co-hong at anything like a commercial strength sufficient to enable the trade to be carried on.

The Select Committee were so dissatisfied with the Viceroy's reply, that they came to the determination to memorialize the Emperor himself, and to withdraw all their ships and servants to Manilla, leaving a single vessel to guard the Factory, until a reply to their memorial should be received. On the 11th of January, 1830, they wrote to the Governor-General of India informing him of the unsatisfactory state of affairs, and suggesting that he should communicate with the Emperor in their behalf by means of two missions, one to be sent through Nepaul, and the other by way of the Yellow Sea; they also asked that ships of war might be sent to assist them in enforcing the stoppage of trade. They handed in at the city gates the memorial which they had had prepared for presentation to the Emperor, but within a few days the document was returned. At this stage differences arose between the members of the Committee; Mr. Plowden, the President, who was in favour of a more pacific policy, left Canton and returned to England. By the 8th of February the whole movement against the Chinese had collapsed, the trade being resumed on the receipt of an assurance from the Viceroy that one new Hong Merchant would be appointed, that debts would be paid or the parties punished, and that the question of the enter-port fee had been laid before the Emperor.

On considering the Select Committee's letter Lord William Bentinck, who was then Governor-General of India, came to the conclusion that he was not sufficiently informed as to the facts of the case to justify him in taking the unprecedented step of making an official remonstrance to the Chinese Government. He was also at a loss to understand the need for the presence of a ship of war, as asked by the Committee, which would involve a breach of that rule which had been previously so strongly commended to the Indian Government by the residents at Canton. For these reasons, and in view of the course taken by Mr. Plowden, he decided not to interfere without the special authorization of the Home Government. When the state of affairs prevailing at Canton was reported in London, the Court of Directors were so dissatisfied, that they unanimously appointed a new Select Committee, who embarked with all convenient speed and arrived in China on the 29th of November, 1830.[1] The residents were not by any means pleased that this should be the outcome of the controversy, and determined to petition the House of Commons, asking that their grievances might be remedied, and that a permanent British resident be appointed at Peking. On the 2nd of

[1] Auber's *China*, pp. 329–333.

January, 1831, they presented an address to the new Select Committee, enclosing a copy of this petition, and asking the Committee's aid in promoting its objects.[1]

As a result of the Viceroy's representations to the capital, the Emperor Taoukwang in 1831 published an edict which, so far from mitigating the conditions of which the Foreigners were complaining, imposed still greater restrictions upon their freedom. The spirit in which this edict was published is well illustrated by the title, "Regulations to guard against Foreigners," with which it was headed. It prohibited in terms Foreigners from remaining at Canton out of the trading season, ordering them to retire to Macao or to go home with their ships. The regulation of 1754 against the making of loans to Chinese was repeated. In the matter of Chinese servants some modification of the old regulations was introduced, but personal attendants continued to be forbidden. Military officers and soldiers were to be appointed to search and examine the ships when they anchored. The Hong Merchants were to exercise restraint and control over the Foreigners in the Factories, not allowing them to go out without permission, and seeing that all purchases of goods were made by them through a Hong Merchant. Foreigners were not to wander about the villages or market-places near Canton; they were not to bring their wives or any women up to the Factories; they were not to be allowed to use sedan chairs; and they were to be prevented from taking arms or ammunition to Canton. Foreigners were not to pass between Macao, Whampoa, and Canton, without a written permit,[2] and only boats carrying a ship's captain were to fly a flag. Matters which the Foreigners wished to bring before the notice of Chinese officials should be the subject of petitions, which should be presented through the Hong Merchants; if the Hong Merchants refused to present a petition, two or three Foreigners in person might present it at the city gates. Petitions relating to ordinary matters of trade were to be presented to the Hoppo, whilst those relating to other affairs

[1] Auber's *China*, p. 334.
[2] Commonly spoken of as a "red chop."

should go to the Macao *tung-chi*, the Hëang-shan *hien*, or the Macao *tsotang*, with a right of appeal in all these cases as before.[1]

This edict was not received in Canton until the 20th of May, by which time other troubles had arisen. In November, 1822, Canton had been devastated by a fire which in its terrible effects is only comparable with the Great Fire of London, and the Factories, with the exception of a few apartments, had been burnt to the ground.[2] In rebuilding the Factories the Foreigners had encroached on the river bank, by extending the place in front of them. The only part of the work remaining incomplete in 1831 was a small square in front of the English Factory, which it was intended should be planted with shrubs and laid out as a garden for exercise and recreation. For some inexplicable reason this projected improvement excited the hostility of the Chinese, and on the 12th of May the *foo-yuen*, in the absence of the Viceroy from Canton, suddenly presented himself at the Factory and demanded to know why the quay and wall had not been demolished. He sent for the Hong Merchants and the *linguist*, who pleaded that they were entirely innocent in the matter. The *linguist* was at once put in chains, and the senior Hong Merchant, Howqua, had to beg for his life on his knees. The command was given that the quay should be restored to its former condition on pain of death to the *linguist* and Howqua. The *foo-yuen* then ordered the cloth, which draped a portrait of George IV, to be torn down, and deliberately seated himself with his back to the picture.[3] The Select Committee, on receiving at Macao news of this occurrence, at once protested against such conduct to the Viceroy, and threatened that, if redress were not forthcoming, they would suspend the trade on the 1st of August. At the same time a letter was again sent to the Governor-General of India asking for his protection and assistance.

[1] J. R. Morrison, *Chinese Commercial Guide*, p. 57 Auber's *China*, pp. 344–9.

[2] Davis, *China and the Chinese*, vol. i, pp. 94–5.

[3] *Ibid.*, pp. 102–3. Auber's *China*, p. 343.

On the 9th of June an edict was received from the Viceroy, who was still absent in Hainan, sanctioning the conduct of the *foo-yuen*, and forwarding an imperial edict promulgating the new regulations. The Select Committee now saw that it was hopeless to expect that they could obtain any alteration in these without an appeal to Peking, a proceeding which would require some months for its performance. They therefore reconsidered their determination to suspend the trade, and decided to take no decisive action until they should hear further from India.[1] Their protest, however, was successful to this extent, that no attempt was ever made to enforce the new regulations, and business was carried on unmolested.[2] The private traders, who had been doing all in their power to help the Select Committee, were not satisfied with the Viceroy's attitude. They therefore determined to make an independent effort to obtain better treatment, and to address the Viceroy themselves. The instigators of this movement were two of the leading private traders, Jardine and Innes, who suggested that a petition be presented to the Hoppo. This course was adopted, but the result was far from encouraging. The Hoppo, in his reply, told the petitioners that if they did not like the conditions under which they carried on their trade, it was open to them to trade elsewhere, and suggested that the Chief of the Factory should punish them with imprisonment for having dared to address him. How little was likely to be obtained as the result of private effort is shown by the language in which the Hoppo framed his reply, which was worded as follows :—

" Lately the English private merchants, Jardine, Innes, and others, have presented a petition, stating that the whole scope of the regulations is at variance with the principles of justice ; thus whining, disputing, and contradicting, and also requesting to appeal to the Emperor not to permit their being put in practice. This is extreme insolence and opposition. Moreover, the affairs of the English Company have all hitherto

[1] Davis, *China and the Chinese*, vol. i, p. 104.
[2] *Ibid.*, p. 105.

reverted to the Chief's control. At present the said Chief, Marjoribanks, is profoundly intelligent, and acts with great propriety. The said Jardine, Innes, and others are merely private English Merchants, and are not at all comparable to the Company. If the said private merchants really regard their property, they ought indeed to trade on as usual; but if they dislike the restraint imposed by the orders of government, and consider their own private affairs to be disadvantageous, the said private merchants may entirely withdraw their trade, and not trouble themselves to come from a great distance through many countries of different languages. When it reaches the Hong Merchants, let them immediately take the contents of the reply made by me, the Hoppo, and enjoin them on the said nation's Chief, that he may know and act accordingly, and continue to keep Jardine, Innes, and the others under strict restraint, not allowing them to create disturbances and again dun with petitions."[1]

In November, 1831, H.M.S. *Challenger*, under Captain Freemantle, anchored off Lintin bearing the reply of Lord William Bentinck, who had written a personal letter to the Viceroy. In this letter he complained in the firmest language of the conduct of the *foo-yuen*, explaining that the occurrence had taken place in the absence of his excellency, to whose wisdom and justice he paid a diplomatic tribute. As the Hong Merchants were afraid to deliver such a missive, it was decided that Captain Freemantle should present it in person. This he did by presenting it at the water-gate, or imperial landing-place, in the city. A direct reply in writing was requested, but this the Viceroy refused to give. On the 7th of January an edict was issued to the Hong Merchants, in the usual way, stating that the Viceroy had received "an official document presented by Freemantle, a naval officer sent by the said nation,"[2] and that he had examined into the subject of the complaints. He pointed out that the Factories were not owned by the Foreigners who inhabited them, but were merely allowed to be rented by them from the Hong

[1] Auber's *China*, pp. 356–7.
[2] *Chinese Repository*, vol. xi, p. 4.

Merchants, and that the quay and wall had been built without the necessary leave having been obtained by petition. He stated that the action of the *foo-yuen* was in accordance with orders secretly received from the Emperor, that it was intended to be a punishment to the Hong Merchants, and was not directed against the British. As to the insult to the King's picture, the *foo-yuen* had repudiated any such conduct, " saying that he would not trample even on a child unless he had offended the laws, and how then could he lightly enter into the people's Factory and lightly insult the picture of their nation's king ! " In conclusion, the Viceroy mentioned the request that had been made for a direct reply to the Governor-General's letter, and absolutely refused to give any other reply than the publication of this edict.[1]

The closing years of the East India Company's monopoly were marked by renewed efforts to extend British commerce to other ports than Canton, prompted by the ill-treatment received from the Viceroy and Hoppo. The first of these was made in July, 1830, when Captain Parkyns, in the *Merope*, proceeded to the Eastern provinces with a cargo consisting of 450 chests of opium and other commodities. He got as far as Formosa, where he lost all his anchors in a typhoon, but found few opportunities of trade, selling only $15,000 worth of opium and a little saltpetre.[2] Early in 1832 a further attempt was made, organized by the Select Committee, who despatched the bark *Lord Amherst*, under Captain Rees, from Canton on the 27th of February, for the East coast. In this vessel sailed H. H. Lindsay and the Rev. Charles Gutzlaff,[3] the former representing the East India Company, and the latter to act as interpreter and to conduct such missionary work as he might find opportunities to do. When they reached Keatsze, they were requested to give the local Chinese officials particulars as to who they were and whither bound. Lindsay did not wish it to be known that he was connected with the East India Company, or that the vessel should be traced, and so

[1] *Chinese Repository*, vol. xi, pp. 2–7.
[2] Auber's *China*, p. 337.
[3] *Chinese Repository*, vol. xi, p. 7.

said that the ship was an English ship from Bengal, that he was the commander, and his name was Hamilton, and that she was bound for Japan. Whilst Lindsay kept up these pretences, Gutzlaff was busy distributing missionary literature and in preaching to the people, in whose language he was very well versed, and sometimes in giving them medical aid. Lindsay distributed several copies of a pamphlet, written by Marjoribanks, the Chief of the Factory at Canton, giving an account of the English people, which it was hoped would serve to disabuse the minds of the Chinese of their prejudices against Foreigners. The reception accorded to the expedition by the Chinese officials at the ports at which it touched was not the most cordial, nor did opportunities occur for any real trade, though frequent requests for opium were received. After visiting the coast of Fukien, the ports of Amoy, Foochow, Ningpo, Shanghai, and Wei-hai-wei, the Pescadores and the Chusan Islands, the coasts of Formosa, Corea, and the Loo Choo Islands, the *Lord Amherst* returned to Macao on the 5th of September, 1832.[1] Gutzlaff had previously made a voyage along the coast from Siam to Tientsin and Manchuria in a Chinese junk,[2] solely for missionary purposes, arriving back at Macao on the 13th of December, 1831, where he met Dr. Morrison, through whom he became known to the Select Committee. Two voyages of less importance were made in

[1] For an account of this voyage see Lindsay and Gutzlaff, *Report of Proceedings on a Voyage to the Northern Ports of China;* Gutzlaff, *Journal of Three Voyages along the Coast of China; Chinese Repository*, vol. ii, pp. 529–553, and vol. i, pp. 196–201.

[2] Gutzlaff was a German, born at Stettin, who in 1826 went out as a missionary to the East. From 1828 to May 1831 he lived in Siam, where he met many Chinese from the Eastern provinces of China, who came thither to trade. Working amongst them as a missionary, he conceived the desire to make a missionary journey along the coast of China, which he undertook in the summer of 1831. Long before leaving Siam he became a naturalized Chinese subject, being adopted into the family of Kwo, of the Tung-an district in Fukien. He took the Chinese name of Shih-lae. He sometimes wore the Chinese dress in Siam, and did so always during the journeys mentioned above. For information as to his life in Siam and the voyage along the coast of China, see the Journal published in the *Chinese Repository*, vol. i, pp. 16–25, 45–64, 81–99, 122–140, 180–196, and published as a separate work in London (1834).

1832, one by the *Jamerina*, under the direction of Innes, another by the *Sylph*, neither of which were able to trade with any degree of success.[1] The general effect produced on the minds of the Chinese in the eastern provinces by these three voyages seems to have been, that missionary enterprise and the sale of opium [2] were in some secret way connected together, as part of the general commercial enterprise of the British nation.

[1] Auber's *China*, pp. 359–362.

[2] For an account of the rise and progress of the opium traffic, see chap. xii, *post*, p. 227.

CHAPTER IX

THE SUPERINTENDENTS OF TRADE

WHEN Queen Elizabeth granted to the original "Governor and Company of Merchants trading unto the East Indies" a monopoly of the commerce between England and the countries lying east of the Cape of Good Hope and west of the Straits of Magellan, no one would have questioned the right of the Crown to create a corporation having this exclusive right; nor did the fact, that James I, by his charter of 1609, made that monopoly perpetual, excite at the time adverse criticism. The change, however, in methods of thought, that occurred in England during the reigns of the Stuart kings, led to such monopolies being regarded with particular dislike, not so much on economic grounds as because they were the creatures of the royal prerogative. When, owing to the Revolution of 1688, the supremacy of Parliament as the legislative authority had become firmly established, it was apparent that the Company held its privileges on a somewhat precarious tenure, notwithstanding that the courts of law had decided that the grant, under which those privileges were enjoyed, was one that could not be impeached.[1] By the time that William and Mary came to the throne, it was clear that Englishmen would not respect a monopoly, which depended for its validity solely on royal charters and was unsupported by statutory authority. It was then that the Company learnt that they must have recourse to Parliament to sanction the privileges which up to then they had enjoyed under royal favour.

The resolution of the 11th of January, 1693–4, by which the House of Commons declared "that all subjects of England have equal rights to trade to the East Indies unless prohibited by Act of Parliament," was but the outward sign of the change that had come over the mind of the English people. In the East Indies, notwithstanding this declaration of the Commons, the Company's monopoly continued to be enforced

[1] See the case of *East India Company* v. *Sandys*, 10 State Trials, p. 371.

by the Company's servants with just as much rigour as though its validity had never been called in question. In England, however, a rival body, which came to be known as the New or English Company, was speedily organized, and then arose that competition for the monopoly of the trade to the East, to which reference has already been made in an earlier chapter. In 1698 an Act of Parliament [1] was passed, which authorized the raising of a loan to the Exchequer on the security of certain taxes, and provided that the Crown should have power to incorporate the subscribers to such loan, or such of their number as might wish to trade in a joint-stock enterprise, and to give to such incorporated body a monopoly of trade to the East. On the 3rd of September in that year a charter was granted incorporating all the subscribers to the loan in a "General Society," and two days later another charter was granted incorporating those members of the general Society, who wished to trade on a joint-stock basis, under the name of "the English Company trading to the East Indies," and to this latter creation was given the monopoly of the trade to the East. The Old or London Company, however, had sufficient influence to enable it to get a private Act passed continuing it as a corporation on certain conditions.

In the struggle for existence the Old Company succeeded in gaining such a holding in the shares of the New Company as gave it the control of the latter. Very soon it was found that the two companies could not exist side by side, and on the 22nd of July, 1702, an indenture tripartite was entered into, to which the Crown and each of the Companies was a party, the object of which was to bring about an amalgamation. It was arranged that the Old Company should purchase a sufficient amount of stock in the New Company to give them a half interest, and that for seven years the trade should be carried on in such a way that the Old Company should have an equal voice with the members of the New Company in its management. It was further arranged that after seven years the Old Company should surrender its charter and the trade be entirely controlled by the New Company. Some difficulty

[1] 9 & 10 Will. III, c. 44.

was found in carrying out the terms of this arrangement, so in 1707 another statute[1] was passed, which, after reciting the circumstances under which the Indenture tripartite had been executed, provided that all differences outstanding between the two companies should be submitted to the arbitration of Lord Godolphin, and that after his award had been given and the Old Company had surrendered their charter, the trade should be carried on by the New Company under the name of "The United Company of Merchants of England trading to the East Indies." Godolphin's award was published in 1708, and the Old Company surrendered its charter in the following year, so that from the year 1709 the monopoly which had originally been granted to the London Company was enjoyed by the United Company.[2]

The monopoly of the United Company, having been created by Parliament, was not attacked in the manner in which the privileges of the Old Company had been assailed. In the preceding chapters the term "East India Company" has been used as though there was one single corporation, existing from the year 1600 to the year 1830, enjoying a monopoly of trade to the East Indies. Such a course is in accordance with a usage which, though common and convenient, is not accurate in law. The justification for this course is that, as appears from what has been said above, the trade was in fact carried on, and the monopoly enjoyed, as though the legal existence of the Old Company had never been interrupted. By the time that the New Company was strong enough to insist on its rights being respected, the Old Company had obtained a controlling interest in its shares; and when the two rival corporations were amalgamated in the United Company, the control of this corporation was in fact in the hands of those who had ruled the Old Company. Thus it happened that though in England the monopoly passed from one legal entity to another, in China the trade was to all outward appearance

[1] 6 Anne, c. 17.

[2] For further information as to the changes here mentioned, see Ilbert, *Government of India*, pp. 28–32; Macaulay, *History of England*, chap. xxiii.

carried on by the agents of one and the same Company, the only real change being in the legal name of the actual holders of the monopoly. For this reason there is no great inaccuracy in writing as though a single company had conducted the trade between England and the East from 1600 down to the beginning of the nineteenth century.[1]

When the charter of the Old Company was first granted, London was the only great commercial centre in England. Queen Elizabeth's grant, being a grant to the chief merchants of London, was in fact a grant to those who were the leading representatives of the whole commercial community in England. When the United Company was formed, Bristol had become sufficiently important to deserve a share in any trading privileges that might then be granted, and the opportunity was afforded to the merchants of Bristol of securing an interest in the United Company, an opportunity which, however, was lost through the mail conveying the letter of application arriving late in London.[2] During the eighteenth century the people of England were occupied politically in consolidating the advantages they had obtained over the Crown, and commercially in developing their resources under the constitutional freedom which they had gained during the reigns of the Stuarts. The internal conditions of the country being favourable to development, and the nation possessing sufficient energy to secure for itself external conditions that would allow its commerce to expand, the wealth of the people enormously increased.

As new commercial centres, far removed from London and Bristol, grew up in other parts of England and increased in wealth and population, they found themselves cramped and confined by conditions which had been laid down at a time when the development of such centres had not been foreseen. One such condition was the prohibition by which they were debarred from trading directly to those countries over which the monopoly of the East India Company extended. The key-note

[1] By 3 & 4 Will. IV, c. 85, s. 91, it was provided that the Company from that time should be known as the East India Company.

[2] Macaulay, *History of England*, chap. xxiii.

of the political controversies, which marked the opening of the nineteenth century, was a demand for the abolition of privileges in which the industrial towns had no part. The nation at large claimed the right for every man to enjoy the commercial advantages which had been gained or held by national effort. Monopolies were attacked as being economic evils, and freedom of competition was declared to be the economic ideal. Amid ideas of this sort the Company's monopoly of trade to the East could not long survive. The passing of the Reform Act of 1832, by which the industrial towns were for the first time adequately represented in Parliament, sounded the death knell of that monopoly. It is not surprising that within two years of the assembling of the Reform Parliament, the trade of China was thrown open to all British subjects alike.

We have seen that from the year 1698 the privileges of the Company rested on a statutory basis, the charter of that year being granted by the Crown in pursuance of statutory provisions. From time to time these privileges were renewed, confirmed, or strengthened by fresh Acts of Parliament, usually on condition of a fresh loan being made by the holders of the monopoly to the national Exchequer. By the Charter Act of 1813,[1] the Company were deprived of the sole right of trading with India, but the monopoly of the trade with China, and of the trade in tea generally, was carefully preserved,[2] whilst the Company's administrative powers and political functions were left unimpaired. This Act further provided that the Company's trading rights might be determined on three years' notice being given after the 10th of April, 1831. As the year 1831 approached, the great manufacturing towns became more and more vigorous in their demands that the monopoly of the trade in tea, and of the trade to China, should be abolished. Petitions poured in upon Parliament from all sides, and both in the House of Lords and in the House of Commons the Government were interrogated as to their intentions in this matter. It was pointed out that the subjects

[1] 53 Geo. III, c. 155.

[2] *Ibid.*, s. 2.

of every nation in the world, except Great Britain, might engage in carrying goods to and from China to countries other than the British Isles, whilst our own people were absolutely excluded from this source of profit. On a motion moved in the House of Commons in favour of the trade being thrown open, it was stated, without contradiction, that the value of the annual trade of the East India Company with China was on the decline, or at least stationary, whilst that of the United States of America was steadily increasing. In contrast with this our trade with the Straits of Malacca had risen from £1,000,000 in 1814 to £4,000,000 in 1829. At Singapore alone, where in 1819 not ten acres of the primeval forest had been cleared and the whole population consisted of 300 beggarly Malays, the exports for the year 1828 amounted to £1,488,599, and the imports to £1,387,201.[1] The exports to Canton in the same year were only £853,494. These figures were used to enforce the moral that free competition was more conducive to the export of British manufactures than a monopoly such as that enjoyed by the East India Company at Canton.

In the year 1830 both the House of Lords and the House of Commons decided to appoint committees to inquire thoroughly into the affairs of the East India Company. Each of these committees was independent of the other, worked on independent lines, and reported independently. With regard to the trade at Canton, the Committee of the Lords appear not to have particularly concerned itself, but in the Report of the Committee of the Commons, which was published in 1830, this question was dealt with in the most exhaustive manner. The evidence, which was ordered by the House to be published in full, is of the most detailed character and abounds in valuable information.[2] The witnesses called

[1] Hansard, *Parliamentary Debates*, vol. 21, 1348–1350. These figures were stated to be not the actual but the declared value. The figures presented to the House of Commons in 1829 show the value of the Company's trade from England for the season 1826–7 as being (taking presumably the value in China) £3,176,901. See *Papers relating to trade with India and China* (1829), p. 5.

[2] The full title of the report is *Report from the Select Committee of the House of Commons on the Affairs of the East India Company* (*China Trade*), 1830.

before the Committee on behalf of the Company were unanimous in condemning the proposals for throwing open the trade at Canton, some of them asserting that it was only by sending shipments of produce from China that India could discharge the obligations, under which she lay, to remit large sums to England, and that this cause would operate to prevent any large increase of English exports to China.

Some of the findings of the Committee are still of great interest. They reported that the only other European nations trading at Canton at that time were the French. Dutch, Swedes, Danes and Austrians; that the trade of all these was only trifling; that the Dutch trade, which had been monopolized formerly by the Dutch East India Company, but was carried on then by a modern organization called the Netherlands Association, was the most important. As to America, they found that formerly the Americans had carried on a large carrying trade from China to Holland and other countries, but of late years there had been a considerable falling off. Their tea trade, which had been very profitable, had declined owing to over-trading, induced by the practice in vogue in America of giving a year's credit for duties to importers of tea, and by an Act of Parliament passed in 1825,[1] which had robbed the Americans of the trade with Canada by making it lawful for the East India Company, or any person authorized by them, to export tea or any other commodity from China to any colony in America. It was stated in evidence that the number of American ships resorting to Canton had fallen from 42 in 1826 to 20 in 1828, and the value of American exports from $7,700,000 to $6,000,000. The Committee, in presenting their Report, did not make any recommendation on the question of opening the trade, but confined themselves to setting out the facts as shown by the evidence.

Two statutes, by which the Company's monopoly was abolished, and the trade at Canton thrown open to all British subjects alike, were passed by that Reform Parliament which added so many useful measures to the English statute book.

[1] 5 Geo. IV, c. 88.

The first was entitled, "An Act for the better government of His Majesty's Indian Territories,"[1] and is the statute by which the Government of India was organized on the basis on which it continued to rest till the year 1854, when the East India Company was dissolved. In this Act, which was of considerable length, there are two sections relating to China, one of which provided that from and after the 22nd day of April, 1834, the exclusive right of trading with the dominions of the Emperor of China, and of trading in tea, enjoyed by the East India Company, should cease, whilst by the other it was enacted that the Company should cease to carry on any trading operations at all, and should sell its property with all convenient speed.[2] The statutory provisions against Interlopers remained unrepealed, and another Act was necessary to enable British subjects to trade in China without being liable to punishment in the English Courts. In the same session of Parliament the second statute was passed, entitled, "An Act to regulate the Trade to India and China," and this provided that it should be lawful for any of His Majesty's subjects "to carry on trade with any countries beyond the Cape of Good Hope to the Streights of Magellan." [3]

The British Government, which now for the first time began to take any real interest in the question of our relations with China, was not so ignorant of the conditions that obtained at Canton as to be unaware that it would be necessary to make some provision for the control of British subjects resorting thither to trade. By the second of the statutes just mentioned, which is generally cited as "The China Trade Act," an attempt was made to meet this necessity by creating an official, called the Chief Superintendent of Trade, who should exercise over all British subjects in China a jurisdiction similar to that hitherto possessed by the supercargoes of the East India Company over the servants of the Company and persons trading to Canton under the Company's licence. The Act

[1] 3 & 4 Will. IV, c. 85.

[2] See ss. 3 and 4.

[3] 3 & 4 Will. IV, c. 93, s. 2. This section and the statutes against Interlopers have now been repealed, and British subjects trade to China by virtue of their common law rights.

provided that it should be lawful for the Crown, by commission or warrant under the sign manual, "to appoint not exceeding three of His Majesty's subjects to be superintendents of the trade of His Majesty's subjects to and from the said dominions, for the purpose of protecting and promoting such trade, and by any such commission or warrant as aforesaid to settle such gradation and subordination among the said superintendents (one of whom shall be styled the chief superintendent)," and to appoint such officers to assist them as might from time to time be expedient.[1] The Act further provided that the Crown by Order in Council might give to the Superintendents power and authority to control the trade and commerce of His Majesty's subjects within any part of China, make regulations for the government of such subjects, and create a court of law having criminal and admiralty jurisdiction, of which one of the Superintendents should be the judge, for the trial of offences committed by British subjects within Chinese territory.[2]

The British Government did not stop at merely creating this authority. In utter disregard of all rights of the Emperor of China, the Act further provided that it should be lawful for the Crown by Order in Council to create a system of dues, to be levied on British ships entering any port, where any of the Superintendents might be stationed, and so raise a fund out of which the salaries of the superintendents and the expense of their establishments in China might be defrayed. These dues were not to exceed more than five shillings per ton on shipping, and ten shillings per ton on goods, and were to be collected by officials appointed by Order in Council. To ensure that the Superintendents of Trade should not be affected by

[1] 3 & 4 Will. IV, c. 93, s. 5. This section is still unrepealed. The office of Chief Superintendent of Trade is now filled by the British Minister at Peking. See *post*, chap. xxiii, p. 522.

[2] *Ibid.*, s. 6. This section was repealed by the *Statute Law Revision Act*, 1874. The Supreme Court of China and Corea, which now exercises over British subjects in China the ex-territorial jurisdiction allowed under the Treaties was constituted by Order in Council in 1865, under the provisions of the *Act for the Better Government of H.M. Subjects resorting to China* (6 & 7 Vict. c. 80) and *The Foreign Jurisdiction Act*, 1843 (6 & 7 Vict. c. 94). See chap. xxiv, *post*, p. 560.

their own pecuniary interests in the exercise of the powers conferred upon them, the Act further provided that no Superintendent or commissioner appointed under the authority of the Act should accept for or in discharge of his duties any gift, donation, gratuity, or reward, other than his salary, or be engaged in any trade or traffic for his own benefit, or for the benefit of any other person. This provision has since been followed with regard to all British officials serving in China, in which respect the British consular service differs from those of most other countries, which include in some instances ordinary merchants.

So early as the year 1831 the East India Company had foreseen that in all probability its privileges would not be renewed, so that its monopoly of the trade with China would be taken away, and the supercargoes had notified the Hong Merchants to this effect. The latter had communicated the news to the Viceroy Li, who issued an edict requiring the Chief of the Factory to write home stating that, in the case of the dissolution of the Company, it would be incumbent on the British Government to appoint a "Chief" to come to Canton for the general management of commercial dealings and to prevent affairs from going to confusion.[1] The Chinese clearly foresaw that, if the privileges of the Company came to an end, some fresh provision must be made for regulating the intercourse between English and Chinese at Canton. In this respect they were more far-sighted than the King's ministers in England. It never seems to have occurred to Lord Palmerston, who was then Foreign Secretary, that any communication with the Chinese Government on the subject of the contemplated change was either necessary or expedient. Though destroying at a blow the fabric under which our trade with China had been carried on for so many years, the British Government made no attempt to ascertain or consult the wishes of the Chinese Government or officials as to what should be erected in its place. No treaty was negotiated, on which to found the office of Superintendent of Trade, nor was the consent of the Chinese Government ever sought

[1] *Chinese Repository*, vol. iii, pp. 186, 237.

to be obtained to the exercise of the authority which the China Trade Act purported to create. The Chief Superintendent was appointed to exercise judicial functions and to levy taxes—the two highest prerogatives of sovereignty—without leave being so much as asked of the Emperor within whose dominions those functions were to be exercised.

Within a few months of the passing of the China Trade Act, the British Government issued Orders in Council under that Act further defining the powers of the new Superintendents of Trade. The most important of these is that dated 9th December, 1833, in which it was recited that the Chinese officials at Canton had signified to the supercargoes of the East India Company the desire of the Chinese Government that effectual provision should be made for the good order of British subjects resorting to Canton. To connect the new order of things with the old, this Order in Council [1] expressly provided that all the powers and authority, which had been enjoyed by the supercargoes over and in respect of the trade of British subjects at Canton, should be vested in the Superintendents of Trade, and that all regulations then in force with regard to the trade should continue in force, save in so far as they were expressly abrogated. Thus it happens that to-day the British Minister at Peking, in whom the powers of the Superintendents of Trade have become vested, has all the authority of the old supercargoes of the East India Company, except in so far as those powers have been expressly modified. For this reason a study of our relations with China from the beginning of the seventeenth century helps to a fuller appreciation of the nature of the authority exercised at the present day by the British Minister and consuls over British residents in China. The consular services of other Foreign powers have been modelled on ours, so that it can truly be said that the powers of the supercargoes of the East India Company are not without some bearing on the ex-territorial rights enjoyed in China by all the Powers that possess such rights.

Thus was introduced that radical change in the relations

[1] For the exact terms of the Order in Council, see Auber's *China*, p. 409.

between England and China which is at the root of the present system of intercourse between the two countries. Roughly speaking, for two hundred years the policy of England in China had been determined by a body of private traders, whose chief aim was, as it naturally would be, first to create a trade profitable to themselves, and secondly to abstain from any conduct that would imperil that trade. Whatever may have been the merits of this method of initiating intercourse with an unknown people, when first it was introduced, no one can deny that by the 22nd of April, 1834, when it came to an end,[1] it was hopelessly out of date. Perceiving that some change was necessary, the British Government passed the statutes and issued the Orders in Council to which reference has been made above. Before taking any definite step they had been at great pains to ascertain the state of things that already existed, so far as it could be ascertained from English witnesses giving evidence before a committee sitting in London. The defect in their mode of inquiry was that no attempt was made to understand the Chinese point of view, or to secure that the changes introduced were such as would be acceptable to the Chinese authorities. It is possible, nay, even probable, that such an attempt would have elicited nothing from the Chinese except a statement that in their opinion no change was needed. But it would have been wiser at least to have made the attempt before setting up the machinery created by the China Trade Act, and had success attended the effort, we might have avoided the mistakes, the humiliations, and the disputes of the ten years that are discussed in the succeeding chapters.

[1] This date was fixed by the China Trade Act (3 & 4 Will. IV, c. 93, s. 1).

CHAPTER X

LORD NAPIER AT CANTON

It will help us to appreciate more fully the nature of the changes introduced by the statutes of 1833, if we pause to recapitulate the salient features of the conditions under which the trade at Canton was being conducted when the monopoly of the East India Company was abolished. In their reputation for honourable dealing, in the magnitude of their business operations, and in the princely style in which they maintained their factory, the Company surpassed all other traders at Canton. Their establishment was made up of twenty supercargoes and writers, an interpreter, two surgeons, and a chaplain, all of whom lived together in that one of the "Thirteen Hongs" which was known as the British Factory. The Select Committee, called by the Chinese *Kung-sze*, which consisted of the three or four chief supercargoes, conducted the whole of the Company's business, the work done by the writers being purely clerical. In addition to the Company's officials and servants, there were other British subjects trading at Canton. These were the "country traders," or "private traders," who carried on their businesses under special licence from the Company in hongs which were quite distinct from the British Factory.

The charter and statutes, which regulated the constitution of the Company, had vested in the supercargoes ample powers of control over all servants of the Company, but had left the question of the authority that might be exercised over the private traders in an extremely vague and unsatisfactory condition. In practice the private traders were brought under the control of the Select Committee by means of a condition inserted in their licences, which provided that the licence should cease and be void if the person to whom it was issued should disobey the Company's regulations or the instructions of the supercargoes. In the eyes of the Chinese the Select Committee were responsible for the acts and omissions of all

British subjects that came to Canton or any of the places thereabouts. This was a burden that the Company never accepted, and indeed openly repudiated so far as ships of war were concerned. Nevertheless, the Chinese adhered to the opinion that the President of the Select Committee, who was more commonly known as the Chief of the Factory, was a sort of headman, having rights and duties in respect of the control of the other British subjects at Canton similar to those exercised by the headman in a Chinese village community. To some extent, as has been already indicated, the Select Committee were regarded as representing the whole of the Foreign community at Canton.

All the Foreigners who traded at Canton were confined to the Thirteen Factories, or "Hongs," the total frontage of which was not more than seven or eight hundred feet. Excepting two small islands, one of which was used as a place of recreation, and the other as a cemetery, there was no part of the country round Canton that they were allowed to frequent, The Factories occupied a strip of land by the side of the river, in a miserable suburb that swarmed with filthy Chinese. No Foreigner was allowed to enter the city itself. No Foreign woman was allowed to come up the river, so those members of the Foreign community who were married were obliged to rent houses at Macao, where their wives and families might reside. Thither the husbands retired during the period of the north-east monsoon, which lasts from October to April, when no sailing ships could make their way into port, and trade came to a standstill. During that part of the year Foreigners were forbidden to remain at Canton, but some of the private traders evaded this prohibition and remained there all the year round. The Foreigners who went to Canton, went there to make money, and in accomplishing their purpose they put up with privations that only the magnitude of the possible commercial reward made tolerable.

The Chinese merchants, with whom the Foreigners were allowed to trade,were divided into two classes, Hong Merchants and shopmen. The law was that the latter might trade only in the minor articles of commerce, whilst the former had a complete monopoly of the more lucrative branches of business.[1] In practice, however, this restriction was more or less disregarded, but inasmuch as the landing and shipping of goods could only be done through a Hong Merchant, the monopolists had the trade in their control. The Hong Merchants, of whom, in 1834, there were seven, were jointly and severally liable for the whole of the debts incurred by any one of their number; but inasmuch as very few of them were men of any capital, this legal liability was of little value to the Foreign merchants who traded with them. In theory there was a fund, called the Consoo Fund, raised by means of a tax called the Consoo tax, which was held as a reserve out of which the liabilities of insolvent Hong Merchants might be paid; but the duty of deducting the tax, which lay on the Hong Merchants themselves, was not strictly performed. Such fund as was in fact raised was resorted to by the imperial officials for all sorts of payments that had no connection with the trade, and so this pretended reserve was of no value at all to the foreign merchant. The monopoly of the Hong Merchants was conducted as a sort of partnership business, in which the senior Hong Merchant held four shares, the second, third, fourth, and fifth Hong Merchants three shares each, and the sixth and seventh, commonly known as the junior Hong Merchants, two and a half shares each. Nobody could become a Hong Merchant without the licence of the Imperial Government.

Every ship coming to trade at Canton had to find a Hong Merchant, who would go security that the shipping dues, customs, and other impositions would be paid. Hence the Hong Merchants are frequently styled "security merchants." There were several other formalities that had to be observed before a vessel was allowed to discharge her cargo. First of all, as soon as she sighted the islands at the mouth of the Canton river, she had to take on board a pilot, who for a fee of $10 or $12 piloted her to Macao. There the captain had

[1] For a list of the articles in which shopmen and Hong Merchants might trade at this time, see J. R. Morrison's *Chinese Commercial Guide*, p. 59.

to make a formal application for a river pilot, licensed by the *keun-min-foo*,[1] give a description of the cargo and the number of men and guns on board, and pay a fee of one dollar for each box landed at Macao. When the total charges had been paid, which amounted to $60 or $70, a permit would be issued for the ship to proceed to the Bogue, or Bocca Tigris, the Portuguese name of the entrance to the river itself. Those passengers, who wished to make the journey to Canton as quickly as possible, proceeded from Macao by the European "passage boats" at a charge of $20 per head. On arriving at the forts at Chuenpi, which guarded the Bogue, the pilot went ashore to make his official report. If it were night the ship had to wait till daylight before proceeding. The pilot, on his return, was accompanied by two customs' officials, who fastened their boats to the ship and remained with her to prevent smuggling. A local pilot having been taken on board, the ship proceeded up the river to Second Bar, and thence to Whampoa, where the pilot's duties came to an end. If the ship wished to go up the remaining twelve miles to Canton, "dollar boats," propelled with oars, might be hired to assist her in making headway against the stream. The Hong Merchant was engaged to act as security merchant as soon as the vessel entered the river. *Linguists* were engaged to act as interpreters and as middlemen in the negotiating of contracts; compradores were hired to act as purveyors of provisions and to engage coolies.

The Hong Merchants were not merely licensed traders. They occupied an official position as the recognized intermediaries between all Foreigners and the Chinese officials. If any Foreigner wished to address a Chinese official, he had to do so by means of a petition which he handed to the Hong Merchants, whose duty it was to present it to the particular official to whom it was addressed. These petitions were in all cases couched in terms that would be employed by an inferior towards a superior. They were written in the language

[1] The *Keun-min-foo* was the Chinese official who had charge of pilots and all matters relating to the coast. His office was at Casa Branca, near Macao.

of the petitioner, excepting in the case of the East India Company, which had obtained the special privilege of using the Chinese language and of presenting their petitions under sealed cover. The Company, however, had been obliged to superscribe on these covers the Chinese character *Pin*, in token that the petition contained therein came from a suppliant. The answers to the petitions were never sent direct to the petitioners ; they were embodied in edicts, which were issued to the Hong Merchants with an injunction that they should be made known to the persons whom the petitions concerned.

For purposes of local government the fifteen of the eighteen provinces of China are divided into viceregal districts, each having its own staff of local officials.[1] The Foreigners who traded in China all resided within the jurisdiction of the Viceroy of the Liang-Kwang, who is more usually known as the Viceroy of Canton. He is spoken of by various titles, being called sometimes the Governor-General, sometimes the Isontock, and sometimes the Tsung-tuk or Chungtuk, the last title being a local form of his official designation of *Tsung-teh.* Next to him came the lieutenant-governor, known in Chinese as the *fu-tai* or *foo-yuen.* A subordinate official, known as the *kwang-chow-foo*, presided over Canton city in somewhat the same capacity as a mayor presides over an English borough. All matters of trade and commerce were under the control of the Superintendent of Customs, or Hoppo, as he was generally called by the Foreign community. The Hoppo was appointed direct from Peking, and was always a Manchu of the imperial clan. Enjoying a salary of but 2,500 taels (£800) per annum, he used his position to supplement his official income by such illegal exactions as he thought fit to impose. This is the usual

[1] Chih-li, the metropolitan province, has its own Viceroy. Kiangsu, Kiang-si and Anhui are under the Viceroy of the Liang-Kiang ; Shensi and Kansuh are under the Viceroy of Shen-Kan ; Fukien and Chêkiang under the Viceroy of Min-chêh ; Hupeh and Hunan under the Viceroy of Hukuang ; Kwangtung and Kwangsi under the Viceroy of the Liang-Kwang ; Yünnan and Kweichow under the Viceroy of Yün-kuei ; and Sze-chuan has a Viceroy of its own. See Mayers, *Chinese Government*, p. 34.

practice in China, but the Hoppo carried the practice to such lengths as were regarded with wonder even by the Chinese. His head clerk, called the Hoppo's *king-shing*, was regarded as the incarnation of corruption and extortion. The whole of his subordinates imitated the example set by their chief, and thus the Foreign trade became the prey of a horde of underlings, who "squeezed" from the Chinese merchants engaged therein such sums as they felt to be due to their official rank.[1]

One would have expected the British Government carefully to instruct its newly created representatives with regard to their behaviour under the conditions described above, and to have taken some steps to acquaint the officials at Canton, if not the Court at Peking, with the nature of the functions intended to be exercised by the Chief Superintendent of Trade. It is therefore astonishing to learn that no formal announcement of any kind was made to the Chinese authorities. Rumour was left to do the work of diplomacy, and jealousy sprang up where confidence should have been most carefully nourished. Lord Napier, who had been chosen as the Chief Superintendent, seeing that difficulties might arise on his arrival in China, requested before he left England that he might have authority to treat, in case of necessity, with the Imperial Government

[1] The Hoppo still exists at Canton, but shorn of much of his glory. By the Chinese he is styled the Hai-kuan Chien-tu, or Superintendent of Customs. At the present time he has control only of the native trade, for since the establishment of the Imperial Maritime Customs, of which Sir Robert Hart is the Inspector-General, all trade carried on in Foreign bottoms has been placed under the control of that department. The Hoppo is always a member of the Imperial Household, and has to pay heavily for the privilege of holding his office by remitting to Peking large sums of money, as well as pianos, musical-boxes, gramaphones, telescopes, and any other articles of a like nature for which the Court may exhibit a fancy. He receives his appointment direct from the Emperor, and is always allowed the privilege of wearing the yellow jacket. He usually contrives in a few years to amass a very considerable fortune.

There is a similar office at Foo-chow, which is filled by the Manchu General-in-Chief. At the custom-house of Huai-an a special appointment is likewise made. At Tientsin there has been for some years a "Customs' Taotai," whose duties are similar to those formerly exercised by the Hoppo at Canton, and to whom the Foreign consuls prefer all complaints relating to commercial matters.—See Mayers, *Chinese Government*, p. 43.

at Peking; and when this request was denied, he asked that some communication from the British Government be addressed to the Viceroy at Canton. For some inexplicable reason it was not thought expedient that any preliminary message should be sent, and Lord Napier was left to announce his own arrival. The preamble of the China Trade Act set out that one of the objects of appointing the Superintendents of Trade was to secure between England and China an amicable intercourse. If the object of the British Government had been to engender lasting jealousy and hatred, it could hardly have chosen a different line of conduct.

The Right Honourable William John Lord Napier was a descendant of that John Napier who invented the system of logarithms which bears his name, and like his ancestor was a keen student of religion and mathematics. He was a man of broad sympathies, generous views, and high courage. At the age of sixteen he had become a midshipman in the Royal Navy, and during his naval career saw some hard fighting: he was present at the battle of Trafalgar, and afterwards served under Lord Cochrane during the period of that nobleman's most brilliant achievements. In 1815 he left the Navy, and having married, settled down on the family estate in the county of Selkirk in 1816. In 1823 he rejoined the Navy and served on the South American station as captain of H.M.S. *Diamond*, but returned home in 1827. In his absence he had been chosen to sit in the House of Lords as one of the representative peers of Scotland, a position which he retained until the year 1833. Whilst in the House of Lords he voted in favour of the Reform Bill and of Catholic Emancipation. He was strongly in favour of the abolition of slavery, and proposed to the Lords that a commission should be sent to the West Indies to study the conditions under which the slaves lived, offering to act himself as one of the commissioners, if the unhealthiness of the climate should make it difficult to constitute such a body. So far as personal qualifications went, there could be no doubt that the Chief Superintendent was well chosen.[1]

[1] For a short biography of Lord Napier, see *Chinese Repository*, vol. iii, pp. 272–4, and the *Dictionary of National Biography*.

The commission appointing the first Superintendents of Trade was dated the 10th December, 1833. In it Plowden, who had been Chief of the Factory, and J. F. Davis were associated with Lord Napier as second and third superintendents respectively.[1] Lord Napier, immediately on receiving his commission, sailed for China. He arrived off Macao on the 15th of July, 1834, and at once landed with his wife and family. It was then found that Plowden had in the meantime returned to England, so Davis was promoted to be second superintendent, and Sir George Best Robinson, another old member of the Factory, was made third superintendent. J. H. Astell was appointed secretary to the commission, Dr. Morrison, Chinese interpreter and secretary, and A. R. Johnston, private secretary to the Chief Superintendent. Captain Charles Elliot, R.N., who now for the first time appeared on the scene where later he was to play so prominent a part, was appointed to the office of master-attendant.

As soon as Lord Napier had anchored off Macao, word was sent by the local Chinese naval officer to the Viceroy at Canton, "that an English war vessel, having on board a barbarian eye"[2] had arrived. By this time it had become generally known at Canton that the new official coming out from England claimed a much higher position than that formerly occupied by the supercargoes of the East India Company, and that Lord Napier was of higher rank than any British subject who had hitherto resided at Canton. The Viceroy was at a loss to know the best course to be pursued in these circumstances, as it was clear to him that, if he received a British official of a rank and position not hitherto recognized, he might bring himself into disgrace with the authorities at Peking. He therefore published an edict, stating that if the "barbarian eye" wished to come to Canton, it would be necessary to make first a report to the Throne and ascertain the Imperial will, and ordering the Hong Merchants to find out for what purpose Lord Napier had come to China. He further instructed

[1] For the commission, see *Chinese Repository*, vol. iii, p. 143.

[2] *Eye* appears to have been used to denote that Lord Napier was more than a headman (*tai-pan*), and was in the nature of an envoy.

the Hong Merchants to acquaint the "barbarian eye" with the laws of the Celestial Empire, by which, "with the exception of the tai-pans (supercargoes) and other barbarian merchants trading to Canton, none can be permitted to come to Canton without a report having been made, and the mandate received." If, said the Viceroy, Lord Napier wishes to come to Canton, he must petition me through the Hong Merchants, and I will send a memorial to the Throne; when a reply has been received, the proper orders will be issued; but until then he must not come beyond Macao.[1]

Lord Napier saw at once that it was impossible for him, as the King's representative, to conform to the Viceroy's instructions and petition through the Hong Merchants, even had his personal dignity allowed him to take such a course. Recognizing that it would be necessary to show at the outset that he did not intend to be bound by the old usages of the East India Company, he treated the Viceroy's edict as of no account, and determined to act with that freedom which his position demanded. Without waiting for a permit, or obtaining the usual "chop" from the *keun-min-foo*, he went straight up to Canton, where he arrived on the morning of the 25th of July, 1834. Having taken up his quarters in the old British Factory, he at once hoisted the Union Jack on the flag-staff in the square. The news of his arrival was conveyed to the Viceroy by the Chinese tide-waiters, who announced "the arrival of a barbarian ship's boat, bringing four English devils who went into the barbarian factories to reside,"[2] and gave it as their opinion that this was "a clandestine stealing into Canton," which could not have been brought about without the privity of the Hong Merchants and *linguists*, a suggestion for which there was no foundation whatever. The Chinese officials had no desire to see the Superintendent of Trade settled at Canton. On the contrary, they had made up their minds to harass him in every possible way, regarding him as an intruder who had no right to come within the Emperor's dominions without their express permission. Technicalities

[1] *Chinese Repository*, vol. iii, p. 187.
[2] *Ibid.*, p. 190.

which were of no real importance were now made out to be of the greatest moment. The fact that Lord Napier had not waited for an official permit was insisted on as an offence against the laws of China, though for years past such permits had been dispensed with in the case of ships coming from Europe.[1] The old procedure of the *Pin*, presented through the Hong Merchants, was declared to be the only possible means by which the Chinese officials could be approached, though on more than one occasion, as shown in the preceding chapters, viceroys of Canton had received direct from British officers letters written in the language of equality.

From the date of his arrival at Canton, Lord Napier was engaged in one long wrangle as to his right to be there at all, and as to whether he should be treated as a person of equal rank with the provincial officers. He had been instructed to do everything in his power to cultivate such relations with the Chinese as would be generally favourable to an extension of British trade, which was recognized as being the primary object of our intercourse with China. At the same time he had to take great care that he did not frustrate his object by allowing the Chinese officials to draw him into such a position, that he would be impotent to effect anything to the advantage of his countrymen. His instructions were thus set out in a letter from Lord Palmerston, which shows in the clearest possible way the intentions of the British Government in sending out the Superintendents of Trade :—

" Your lordship will announce your arrival at Canton by letter to the Viceroy. In addition to the duty of protecting and fostering the trade of His Majesty's subjects with the port of Canton, it will be one of your principal objects to ascertain whether it may not be practicable to extend that trade to other parts of the Chinese dominions. And for this end you will omit no favourable opportunity of encouraging any disposition which you may discover in the Chinese authorities to enter into commercial relations with His Majesty's Government. It is obvious, with a view to the attainment of this

[1] *Chinese Repository*, vol. iii, p. 325.

object, the establishment of direct communications with the imperial court at Peking would be desirable ; and you will accordingly direct your attention to discover the best means of preparing the way for such communications ; bearing constantly in mind, however, that peculiar caution and circumspection will be indispensable on this point, lest you should awaken the fears, or offend the prejudices, of the Chinese Government ; and thus put to hazard even the existing opportunities of intercourse, by a precipitate attempt to extend them. In conformity with this caution, you will abstain from entering into any new relations or negotiations with the Chinese, except under very urgent and unforeseen circumstances. But if any opportunity for such negotiations should appear to you to present itself, you will lose no time in reporting the circumstance to His Majesty's Government, and in asking for instructions ; but, previously to the receipt of such instruction, you will adopt no proceedings but such as may have a general tendency to convince the Chinese authorities of the sincere desire of the King to cultivate the most friendly relations with the Emperor of China, and to join with him in any measures likely to promote the happiness of their respective subjects.[1]"

Acting on these instructions, and with the best possible intentions, Lord Napier, the day after his arrival at Canton, sent the following letter to the Viceroy, which was carried to the city gates by Mr. Astell :—

" In pursuance of orders from my most gracious sovereign, William IV, King of Great Britain and Ireland, I have the honour of notifying to your excellency my arrival at the city of Canton, bearing a royal commission constituting and appointing me Chief Superintendent of British trade to the dominions of his imperial majesty the Emperor of China. By this commission are associated with me John Francis Davis, esq. ; and Sir George Best Robinson, bart., late of the honourable East India Company's factory at this place. The object of the said royal commission is to empower us,

[1] *Correspondence Relating to China* (Blue Book), 1834, p. 4.

his majesty's superintendents, to protect and promote British trade, which, from the boundless extent of his majesty's dominions, will bear the traffic of the four quarters of the world to the shores of the Emperor of China,—the exclusive privileges and trade hitherto enjoyed by the honourable East India Company of merchants having ceased and determined, by the will and power of his majesty the king and the parliament of Great Britain. I have also the honour of acquainting your excellency that his majesty, my most gracious sovereign, has been pleased to invest me with powers, political and judicial, to be exercised according to circumstances.

"At present I will only further request that your excellency will grant me, with my colleagues, the honour of a personal interview, when it will be my duty to explain more fully to your excellency the nature of the changes which have taken place, and upon which our present duties and instructions have been founded. Allow me to convey, through your excellency, to his imperial majesty, the high consideration of his majesty the king, my master ; and with the utmost respect for your excellency, allow me to subscribe myself your excellency's very faithful and obedient servant.

(Signed) "NAPIER (Chief Superintendent)." [1]

The whole tone and tenor of this letter was utterly foreign to Chinese ideas. The very word "king" would at once convey to a Chinese mind the idea of an inferior monarch, owning a suzerain, by no means comparable in rank or dignity with the ruler of the Celestial Empire, the Son of Heaven himself. It is not surprising that, when Captain Astell went to deliver the letter, no single Chinese could be found having sufficient temerity to take it to the Viceroy. The comedy enacted on that occasion is best described in the words of Lord Napier himself :—

"On the arrival of the party at the city gates, the soldier on guard was despatched to report the circumstance to his superior. In less than a quarter of an hour a soldier of inferior

[1] *Chinese Repository,* vol. xi, p. 26. *Correspondence Relating to China* (Blue Book, 1840), p. 10.

rank appeared ; whereupon Mr. Astell offered my letter for transmission to the Viceroy, which duty this officer declined, adding that his superior was on his way to the spot. In the course of an hour several officers of nearly equal rank arrived in succession ; each refusing to deliver the letter on the plea that 'higher officers would shortly attend.' After an hour's delay, during which time the party were treated with much indignity, not unusual on such occasions, the *linguists* and Hong Merchants arrived, who intreated to become the bearers of the letter to the Viceroy. About this time an officer of rank higher than that of any of those who had preceded him, joined the party, to whom the letter was in due form offered, and as formally refused. The officers having seen the superscription on the letter, argued 'that as it came from the superintendent of trade, the Hong Merchants were the proper channel for communication' ; but this obstacle appeared of minor importance in their eyes, upon ascertaining that the document was styled a *letter* and not a *petition*. The linguists requested to be allowed a copy of the address, which was of course refused.

"About this time the *kwang-hai*, a military officer of considerable rank, accompanied by an officer a little inferior to himself, arrived on the spot, to whom the letter was offered three several times, and as often refused. The senior Hong Merchant, Howqua, after a private conversation with the *kwang-hai*, requested to be allowed to carry the letter in company with the *kwang-hai*, and ascertain whether it would be received. This being considered as an insidious attempt to circumvent the directions of the superintendent, a negative was made to this and other offers of a similar tendency.

"Suddenly all the officers took their departure, for the purpose, as it was afterwards ascertained, of consulting with the Viceroy. Nearly three hours having thus been lost within the city, Mr. Astell determined to wait a reasonable time for the return of the officers, who shortly afterwards re-assembled ; whereupon Mr. Astell respectfully offered the letter in question three separate times to the *kwang-hai*, and afterwards to the other officers, all of whom distinctly refused even to touch it ; upon which Mr. Astell and his party returned to the factory."[1]

The boldness of this proceeding was sufficient to impress the Viceroy with the knowledge that it was useless to order Lord Napier to retire to Macao. He therefore contented himself with issuing to the Hong Merchants an edict stating that it was not expedient that "the barbarian eye" should remain long at Canton, and requiring him to retire, "when the commercial business regarding which he has to inquire and hold jurisdiction is finished." It is noticeable that throughout this controversy the Chinese never admit that the Chief Superintendent has come to exercise any but purely commercial functions. The edict was couched in that pompous and superior strain which, though extremely ludicrous to us, expressed quite seriously the Chinese view. The following passages show how the Viceroy regarded the matter :—

"As to the object of the barbarian eye's coming to Canton, it is for commercial business. The Celestial Empire appoints officers—civil ones to rule the people, military ones to intimidate the wicked. The petty affairs of commerce are to be directed by the merchants themselves. The officers have nothing to hear on the subject. In the trade of the said barbarians, if there be any change to be made in the regulations, in all cases the said merchants are to consult together, and make a joint statement to the superintendent of customs and to my office. Whether the proposals shall be allowed or disallowed must be learned by waiting for a reply publicly. If any affair is to be newly commenced, it is requisite to wait till a respectful memorial be made, clearly reporting to the Great Emperor, and his mandate received. Then it may be commenced, and orders may be issued requiring obedience.

"The great ministers of the celestial empire are not permitted to have intercourse by letters with outside barbarians. If the said barbarian eye throws in private letters, I, the Viceroy, will not at all receive or look at them.

[1] *Chinese Repository*, vol. xi, p. 27. *Correspondence Relating to China* (Blue Book, 1840), p. 8.

"To sum up the whole matter: the nation has its laws; it is so everywhere. Even England has its laws. How much more the Celestial Empire! How flaming bright are its great laws and ordinances. More terrible than the awful thunderbolt! Under this whole bright heaven, none dares to disobey them. Under its shelter are the four seas. Subject to its soothing care are ten thousand kingdoms. The said barbarian eye, having come over a sea of several myriads of miles in extent, to examine and have superintendence of affairs, must be a man thoroughly acquainted with the principles of high dignity. And in his person he sustains the duties of an officer—an eye. Then only can he restrain and control the barbarian merchants." [1]

With this edict the Hong Merchants waited on Lord Napier in a body, and suggested that the word *Pin* should be superscribed to the letter, and the designation of the Viceroy somewhat altered. To the first suggestion a firm refusal was returned, but the other, being but a matter of courtesy, was accepted. The following day the senior Hong Merchant, Howqua, announced his intention of calling with the other members of the Co-hong by sending in a ticket addressed to Lord Napier. On this ticket the Chinese characters used to denote "Lord Napier" were not those chosen by Dr. Morrison, but others, meaning, "laboriously vile." When asked for an explanation, Howqua could only say that he had been "so instructed by the pilot," whatever that might mean.[2] When the Hong Merchants called later in the day, they brought the message that the letter would not be received unless superscribed "*Pin.*" They were at once dismissed. On the 30th of July, the Viceroy issued another edict to the Hong Merchants, requiring them to ascertain why Lord Napier had come to Canton, and to order him to return to Macao. To this edict the Chief Superintendent paid no attention. On the following day yet another edict appeared, but this, too, was disregarded. As no member of the Commission would

[1] *Chinese Repository*, vol. iii, p. 188. *Correspondence Relating to China* (Blue Book, 1840), pp. 18-19.

[2] *Chinese Repository*, vol. xi, p. 27.

receive these edicts, they accumulated on the hands of the Hong Merchants.[1]

On the 1st of August the commission sustained an irreparable loss in the death of their interpreter, Dr. Morrison.[2] Fortunately there were by this time other British subjects at Canton well versed in the Chinese language, one being J. R. Morrison, the son of the deceased, who was chosen to fill his father's place. A few days after Dr. Morrison's death the Hoppo published an edict, reviving all the old regulations as to the formalities to be observed by ships and boats coming to Canton. There could be no doubt that this proceeding was occasioned by the fact of Lord Napier having reached Canton in violation of these ancient restrictions. On the 9th of August, the Chief Superintendent wrote to Lord Palmerston an account of his experiences, in which he thus justifies the course he had adopted :—

" My great object is to open and maintain a direct personal communication with the Viceroy ; so that I may be enabled to get redress from him in all commercial grievances connected with the Hong Merchants, or on criminal proceedings, connected with the duties of the *kwang-chow-foo*, or the criminal judge, instead of leaving myself at the mercy of those Hong Merchants, who, in fact, exercise no official powers whatsoever, and can never be depended upon for the transmission of complaints to the different heads of departments when circumstances require. I have reason to believe that His Majesty's subjects here have several causes of complaint. I forbear to trouble your lordship with these at present, as long as a chance exists, within a moderate time, of laying the same before the Viceroy, for his consideration and redress. In the meantime I shall endeavour to maintain harmony between all parties. Having now clearly explained to your lordship the position in which I stand, in respect to the Viceroy, up to the date hereof, I beg to acquaint your lordship

[1] For these edicts, see *Chinese Repository*, vol. iii, pp. 189-190 ; *Correspondence Relating to China* (Blue Book, 1840), pp. 17-21.

[2] For a short biography, see *Chinese Repository*, vol. iii, p. 177.

that all these measures have received the full support and concurrence of my two colleagues. Endeavouring also always to bear in mind the nature and spirit of H.M.'s instructions regarding my conduct towards the Chinese authorities, and enjoining respect towards the laws of the Empire, I conceive in adopting the line so approved, and which has given entire satisfaction to His Majesty's faithful subjects at this port, that I have, in fact, adhered most strictly to those instructions, without compromising the honour of His Majesty's commission, and without relinquishing that right of practice which has been so often exercised in times past by the presidents of the Select Committee, of enjoying direct communication with the Viceroy whenever circumstances might render such communication necessary or desirable." [1]

Having thus explained to the British Government the situation at Canton, Lord Napier next proceeded to strengthen his position by taking the British merchants into his confidence. Finding that they had been invited by the Hong Merchants to attend a conference, he convened a public meeting to discuss the whole question, and thus neutralized the attempt of the Chinese to create a schism among the British residents. By this time he could see clearly the error which his Government had made, in appointing him to his present office without some previous arrangement with the Chinese Government. On the 14th of August he wrote to Lord Palmerston, recommending that a commercial treaty be negotiated, by which the rights not only of British subjects, but of all Foreigners coming to Canton to trade, should be clearly defined. Lord Napier's idea was that we should demand the same personal privileges for the Foreign trader at Canton that every trader enjoyed in England, that we should acquire the right of settlement at every port, and that afterwards the trade should go on under the ordinary Chinese law, subject to a right to make diplomatic representations when the occasion needed. He suggested that the more courteous method of procedure would be to send an embassy, but pointed out that such a method would involve

[1] *Correspondence Relating to China* (Blue Book, 1840), p. 10; *Chinese Repository*, vol. xi, pp. 66–7.

delay. The words in which he refers to his own situation show that he had already realized the impossibility of carrying out his instructions. He said :—

"My present position is, in one point of view, a delicate one, because the trade is put in jeopardy, on account of the difference existing between the Viceroy and myself. I am ordered by His Majesty to go to Canton ; and there report myself by letter to the Viceroy. I use my best endeavours to do so ; but the Viceroy is a presumptuous savage, and will not grant the same privileges to me that have been exercised constantly by the chiefs of the Committee. He rakes up obsolete orders ; or, perhaps, makes them on the occasion ; but the fact is, the chiefs used formerly every year to wait on the Viceroy, on their return from Macao ; and continued to do so until the Viceroy gave them an order to wait upon him, whereupon they gave the practice up."[1]

In contrast with this it is interesting to see what the Viceroy had to say, when later he reported on the whole matter, in a memorial to the Emperor :—

"The said barbarian eye would not receive the Hong Merchants, but afterwards repaired to the outside of the city to present a letter to me, your Majesty's minister, Lu. On the face of the envelope the forms and style of equality were used, and there were absurdly written the characters, *Ta Ying Kwoh.*[2] Now it is plain, on the least reflection, that in keeping the central and outside peoples apart, it is of the highest importance to maintain dignity and sovereignty. Whether the said barbarian eye has or has not official rank there are no means of thoroughly ascertaining. But though he be really an officer of the said nation, he yet cannot write letters on equality with the frontier officers of the Celestial Empire. As the thing concerned the national dignity, it was inexpedient in the least to allow a tendency to any approach or advance by which lightness of esteem might be occasioned. Accordingly orders were given to Han Shau-king, the colonel

[1] *Chinese Repository*, vol. xi, p. 68. *Correspondence Relating to China* (Blue Book, 1840), p. 15.

[2] "Great English nation."

in command of the military forces of this department, to tell him authoritatively that, by the statutes and enactments of the Celestial Empire, there has never been intercourse by letters with outside barbarians; that respecting commercial matters, petitions must be made through the medium of the Hong Merchants, and that it is not permitted to offer or present letters. . . . On humble examination it appears that the commerce of the English barbarians has hitherto been managed by the Hong Merchants and tai-pans;[1]; there has never been a barbarian eye to form a precedent. Now it is suddenly desired to appoint an officer, a superintendent, which is not in accordance with old regulations. Besides, if the said nation has formed this decision, it should have stated in a petition the affairs which, and the way how, such superintendent is to manage, so that a memorial might be presented requesting your Majesty's mandate and pleasure as to what should be refused, in order that obedience might be paid to it and the same be acted on accordingly. But the said barbarian eye, Lord Napier, without having made any plain report, suddenly came to the barbarian Factories outside the city, and presumed to desire intercourse to and fro by official documents and letters with the officers of the Central Flowery Land; this was, indeed, far out of the bounds of reason."[2]

The quotations given above show very clearly the state of mind of both parties. Passages have been cited at length, so that the reader may know the kind of difficulties Lord Napier had to face in dealing with Chinese officials, and the kind of reasoning by which they sought to justify their actions. Allowing for the very strong leaven of hypocrisy in the Chinese character, which is manifested at its strongest in things official, it is possible, nevertheless, from the foregoing extracts to form a very accurate idea of the feelings of the Chinese on this particular question, and on the broader questions raised in connection therewith. The attitudes respectively assumed by the two parties to the dispute were in direct antagonism. Neither side would give way, and a deadlock

[1] That is, supercargoes. *Tai-pan* now means a Foreigner at the head of a Foreign hong.

[2] *Chinese Repository*, vol. iii, pp. 327-329.

resulted. Another public meeting of British merchants was held in Canton on August 16th, at which Lord Napier suggested that they should form a Chamber of Commerce to look after their interests in the way customary with such commercial associations. On the same day the Chinese, perceiving that stronger measures would be required to bring the Chief Superintendent into a state of submission, commenced to put in force the old expedient of stopping the trade by suspending the shipment of cargoes on British account. It happened that just at this time H.M.S. *Imogene* arrived off the Bogue from Singapore, and H.M.S. *Andromache* returned to Chuenpi from a cruise, so that Lord Napier found himself in a position to command the support of two frigates in case of necessity.

To show that his determination was unshaken, the Viceroy, on the 18th of August, issued another edict to the Hong Merchants, repeating his reasons for refusing to acknowledge the Chief Superintendent. He was at pains to point out that if an official from a foreign country were to proceed to England, he could not possibly neglect to have his coming announced beforehand. In further justification of the attitude he had taken up, he asserted that the "English barbarians" had no public business beyond their commerce, and that the officers of the Celestial Empire never took any cognizance of "the trivial affairs of trade,"—a declaration not altogether borne out by the experience of those who suffered from their exactions. In discussing the question of allowing official intercourse on a footing of equality he stated that, as other nations besides the English traded at Canton, it would be inexpedient to grant Lord Napier's request, and summed up the whole matter in the words: "The thing is decidedly impossible." This edict is perhaps more absurdly pompous than any other of the whole series. In it again we find traces of the evil wrought by Lord Macartney in allowing himself to be styled publicly a tribute-bearer. One of the most ridiculous passages is that in which the Viceroy discusses the proposed stoppage of trade; yet there can be no doubt that it accurately reflected the Chinese view of the situation. This passage runs :—

"The Hong Merchants, because the said barbarian eye

will not adhere to old negotiations, have requested that a stop should be put to the said nation's commerce. This manifests a profound knowledge of the great principles of dignity. It is most highly praiseworthy. Lord Napier's perverse opposition necessarily demands such a mode of procedure, and it would be most right immediately to put a stop to buying and selling. But considering that the said nation's king has hitherto been in the highest degree reverently obedient, he cannot in sending Lord Napier at this time have desired him thus obstinately to resist. The some hundreds of thousands of commercial duties yearly coming from the said country concern not the Celestial Empire the extent of a hair or a feather's down. The possession or absence of them is utterly unworthy of one careful thought. Their broadcloths and camlets are still more unimportant, and of no regard. But the tea, the rhubarb, the raw silk of the Inner Land, are the sources by which the said nation's people live and maintain life. For the fault of one man, Lord Napier, must the livelihood of the whole nation be precipitately cut off? I, the Viceroy, looking up and embodying the great Emperor's most sacred, most divine wish, to nurse and tenderly cherish as one all that are without, feel that I cannot bring my mind to bear it! Besides, all the merchants of the said nation dare dangers, crossing the seas myriads of miles to come from far. Their hopes rest wholly in the attainment of gain by buying and selling. That they did not attend when summoned by the Hong Merchants to a meeting for consultation, was because they were under the direction of Lord Napier; it assuredly did not proceed from the several merchants' own free will. Should the trade be wholly cut off in one morning, it would cause great distress to many persons, who, having travelled hither by land and sea, would by one man, Lord Napier, be ruined. They cannot in such case but be utterly depressed with grief." [1]

A few days later three Chinese officials, the *kwang-chow-foo*, the *kwang-chow-hai*, and the *chow-chow-foo*, were sent to

[1] *Chinese Repository*, vol. iii, p. 236. *Correspondence Relating to China* (Blue Book, 1840), p. 24.

"investigate and give verbal orders" to Lord Napier. They wished to know the cause of his arrival, the nature of his business, and when he intended to return to Macao. In reply they were referred to the edict of the 16th of January, 1831, requiring that in the event of the East India Company losing its monopoly, a chief should be appointed to preside over the English; the commission under which Lord Napier derived his authority from his sovereign was shown to them; the letter which Captain Astell had attempted to deliver was also mentioned, and they were asked to take it to the Viceroy. Advantage was taken of this visit to make the position of Lord Napier perfectly clear, so that no plea of ignorance should be afterwards set up. To prevent any misconception, the Chief Superintendent himself, two days later, on the 25th of August, published an open letter to the Chinese merchants reiterating what had been told to these officials, and pointing out that the Viceroy's lack of information and the stoppage of trade were entirely due to the obstinacy of the Viceroy in refusing to receive the letter. On the same day the British merchants, acting on the advice previously given by the Chief Superintendent, formed the Canton Chamber of Commerce, the first organization of the kind instituted by Foreigners in China.[1]

So far only the shipment of cargoes had been stopped; but on the 2nd of September, the Viceroy completely suspended the trade with British subjects. In the edict published for this purpose, he gave as his reason for not receiving the letter, that on examining the records he found that ministers of the Celestial Empire had no intercourse with outside barbarians. In utter disregard of what he knew to be the truth, he stated that, as Lord Napier was wholly without an official communication from the King of England, it could not be known whether he was an officer or a merchant; that even if he were a "barbarian eye," he could not have intercourse except by petition through the Hong Merchants; that he was stupid, blinded, and ignorant, and could not be made to comprehend reason; and that if he were left in control of British subjects

[1] *Chinese Repository*, vol. iii, p. 237; vol. xi, p. 69.

it would be impossible for the merchants to enjoy quiet. In this edict the Viceroy made it clear, beyond possibility of doubt, that he would in no way recognize the Superintendents of Trade.[1] To enhance the effect of the stoppage of business, it was ordered that all compradores, *linguists,* and servants should leave the Factories, and that no boatmen or workmen should do any work whatever for the English. The trade of the other nations was left undisturbed.

It happened that at this time Canton was unusually full of strangers. From all parts of the Empire candidates had come up for the triennial literary examinations ; soldiers had been brought in from all the surrounding districts ; and vagabonds from every quarter were crowding into the city. It is not surprising that the excitement rapidly grew in intensity. Chinese soldiers began to appear about the Factories, which were completely deserted by all Chinese servants ; Foreigners as well as natives were forbidden to supply provisions to any British subject ; and the passage of Foreign boats between Canton and Whampoa was strictly forbidden. Lord Napier, not knowing in what emergency he might find himself, had previously ordered the *Imogene* and *Andromache* to come within the river. These cruisers, on the 5th of September, cleared for action off the Bogue, and on the following day a small guard of marines reached Canton. On the 7th the cruisers moved up and anchored below Tiger Island, the forts firing on them as they passed. The fire was returned. On the 9th firing again took place, the British losing two men killed. On the 11th of September the cruisers reached Whampoa.[2]

Another edict was now issued by the Viceroy. On the 8th Lord Napier had written to the British merchants instructing them to inform the Hong Merchants in what respects the Viceroy's edict of the 2nd was inaccurate. He cited the examples of Weddell, Anson, Flint, Roberts, Staunton and others, as showing that the practice of communicating with the Viceroy on a footing of equality was no

[1] *Chinese Repository,* vol. iii, pp. 238-240.
[2] *Ibid.*, vol. xi, p. 70.

innovation. He further explained exactly what steps had been taken to apprise the Chinese authorities of his true position and his object in coming to Canton. This letter was evidently shown to the Viceroy, as appears from the comment thereon, which appeared in the edict issued by him on September 11th. There it was denied that officers of the great Ta Tsing Dynasty had ever had intercourse with barbarian officers, a qualification being added to the effect that, if there had been such occasions, they were exceptional ones when England had sent tribute and interviews were given to the tribute-bearers. From the language of the edict it was evident that the Viceroy was particularly angry at the presence of the cruisers and at the fighting which had taken place. These apparently had not been without good effect, for after bragging of the military strength of his own forces, he went on to indicate that, if the cruisers were withdrawn, he might be willing to negotiate. The exact words used were :—

"The soldiers and horses of the Celestial Empire, its thundering forces, guns, and weapons, assemble closely as the hills ; if it were desired to make a display of conquering chastisement, how could the petty little warships afford any protection ? Besides, I, the Viceroy, treat most liberally all the merchants trading here ; what need is there of protection ? By such ignorant and absurd conduct, entering far into the important territory, he is already within my grasp. Arrangements have been now made to assemble a large force, ranged out both by sea and land. What difficulty will there be in immediately destroying and eradicating ? Therefore that I am slow, dilatory, and cannot bear to do so, is because that I consider that such movements are not according to the wishes of the said nation's king, nor are they according to the wishes of the several merchants. I, the Viceroy, looking up, embody the benevolence of the Great Emperor. Only by reforming his errors can he avoid cutting himself off, and obtain reformation. If the said barbarian eye will speedily repent of his errors, withdraw the ships of war, and remain obedient to the old rules, I will yet give him some indulgence. If he still adhere to stupidity and do not arouse, maintain his wickedness and do not change, he will be sinning against the Great Emperor, and I, the Viceroy, will certainly find it difficult again to display endurance and forbearance: I apprehend that when the celestial troops once come, even precious stones will be burned before them. On no account defer repentance till afterwards."[1]

At this juncture the health of Lord Napier began to fail. A greater misfortune could not have befallen the interests of Great Britain, for the critical moment in the controversy had arrived. On the 9th of September he had beenseized with a fever, and so bad did this become that on the 14th he announced to the British merchants that he must leave Canton. In taking this course he was to some extent influenced by the consideration that the Hoppo had stated that negotiations would be opened as soon as Lord Napier retired to Macao. The Hong Merchants were already asking that the cruisers be sent down the river as a necessary preliminary to any discussion. After a valiant attempt to continue discharging his duties, the Chief Superintendent was obliged to give in, and on the 18th he assented to the suggestion of Colledge, the surgeon to the mission, that he should seek a change outside the Bogue. By this time the violent symptoms of fever had subsided, and it was thought that such a change was all that was necessary to complete recovery. Accordingly, on the 19th, Colledge agreed on behalf of Lord Napier with the Hong Merchants, that if they would get the necessary chop allowing a passage to Macao by way of Hëang-shan in a manner becoming to the Chief Superintendent's rank and dignity, the cruisers should be withdrawn from Whampoa, it being expressly stipulated that there should be no ostentatious display by the Chinese. It was not until the evening of the 21st, however, that Howqua and Mowqua, the senior Hong Merchants, arrived with the promised chop. As soon as it had been received, Lord Napier gave the order for the cruisers to withdraw, and he himself embarked on the boat that was to take him down the river.

[1] *Chinese Repository,* vol. iii, p. 288. *Correspondence Relating to China* (Blue Book, 1840), pp. 38-9.

The Chief Superintendent had not left Canton two hours when he was joined by a Chinese convoy of armed boats, and was informed that he could not proceed further than the Pagoda Fort that night. This delay was intensely irritating, as the state of the climate at that season of the year made it imperative that as little time as possible should be spent in the river journey. On the 22nd he was allowed to proceed slowly, still under convoy of eight armed boats, two transports carrying a civil mandarin, and another boat conveying a military official. They did not reach Hëang-shan until midnight of the 23rd, and there they were detained till 1.0 p.m. on the 25th, in flagrant breach of the arrangement made with Colledge. During the whole of this time the Chinese kept up an incessant beating of gongs, banging of crackers, and firing of salutes, in spite of the repeated remonstrances of those accompanying Lord Napier, whose fever increased to such a pitch that Colledge became seriously alarmed. The result was that, when on the 26th the expedition reached Macao, Lord Napier was completely exhausted. The change could do nothing for him, and it soon became evident that he would never return to Canton. He gradually sank until, on the 11th of October, 1834, he passed away. The news of his death was sent by J. R. Morrison, at Canton, to the Hong Merchants on the 13th, but no acknowledgment was received for five days when, after the Viceroy had been notified by the *foo-yuen*, the Hong Merchants intimated in a curt note that Morrison's letter had been received. On the 15th, Lord Napier was buried with military honours at Macao, the Portuguese furnishing a guard of honour from the troops forming the garrison.[1]

Thus closed the career of a man whom England could ill afford to lose. When Lord Napier left Canton he had just obtained a proper grasp of the situation, and had been long enough in China to have acquired, in some degree, that local knowledge requisite for dealing successfully with the officials. Throughout his stay he had maintained the dignity of Great Britain, refusing to attain the end he had in view by any means

[1] *Chinese Repository*, vol. iii, pp. 281, 347-9; vol. xi, pp. 73–4.

except such as were worthy of his position, though conscious that his instructions, if obeyed, were not such as would lead him successfully to fulfil his mission. When once he had determined to have nothing to do with the old method of procedure by petition, nothing could break down his resolution. His constancy is a precedent that we should do well to bear in mind in these days. Never for one moment did he relax his claim to be recognized as the King's minister, who must be received on terms of equality. It was natural that the Chinese should take up the attitude they did. In fact, neither side can be blamed for their course of action. We can only regret that, for lack of a little careful study and forethought, a sincere effort by the British to make friends with the Chinese should have failed so miserably. After Lord Napier had once taken his stand, there could be no going back to old ways. A change was inevitable, and a change of such radical importance does not take place in the polity of a great empire like the Chinese without tribulation. Lord Napier's death was the more regrettable in that he seems to have been eminently fitted to bring about the change that was bound to come. He was animated by the loftiest motives, and had conceived a broad and liberal policy to be applied to the settlement of the question of the intercourse between Foreigners and the Chinese. That policy he communicated in the letter to Lord Palmerston of August 14th. That we may better learn the kind of man he was, the line of action he advised, and the lessons he had learnt, it is important that we should read what he said[1]:

"I think I can have no hesitation at once in recommending His Majesty's government to consult immediately on the best plan to be adopted for commanding a commercial treaty, or a treaty which shall secure the just rights, and embrace the interests, public and private, of all Europeans--not of British alone, but of all civilized people coming to trade according to the principle of international law. I maintain that it will be as easy to open the whole coast as any individual port. It may possibly be advisable to go to Peking on the

[1] *Chinese Repository*, vol. xi., pp. 67-68; *Correspondence Relating to China* (Blue Book, 1834), pp. 13-14.

occasion, or perhaps only to send from the mouth of the Pei-ho river,[1] or any other point upon the coast. Sending an ambassador is the more courteous; but the presence of an embassy presupposes room for debates and long delays, alterations and amendments in plans proposed. Now, I should say, that we should propose nothing but what is fair and just towards all mankind; and avoid entering into minute details. Demand the same personal privileges for all traders that every trader enjoys in England. Having once acquired the right of settlement at every port, let the trade go on according to the established rules of the empire, good or bad—reserving always the common right to represent and negotiate when wrong prevails. Our first object should be to get a settlement on the same terms that every Chinaman, Pagan, Turk, or Christian, sits down in England.

"If your lordship should prefer making gradual propositions by an embassy, I would recommend none of that ostentation practised in the instances of Macartney and Amherst; leave all presents behind, all musicians and idle amateur gentlemen, literary and scientific; and go to work in a manner determined to carry what you mean. This is a vigorous measure which might possibly 'alarm the prejudices' of the Celestial Empire, were I to make my ideas commonly known among the hong. They are now thrown together for more special consideration; and till I have your authority to proceed upon more active principles, your lordship may rely on my forbearance towards a Government which is too contemptible to be viewed in any other light than that of pity or derision. What advantage, or what point did we ever gain by negotiating or humbling ourselves before this people, or rather before their Government? The records show nothing but subsequent humiliation and disgrace. What advantage or what point, again, have we ever lost, that was just and reasonable, by acting with promptitude and vigour? The records again assure us that such measures have been attended with complete success."

[1] This is a redundancy which should be avoided: "*ho*" means "*river*," and Pei-ho means "northern river." Similarly the word "river" is unnecessary after *Yang-tze-kiang*.

CHAPTER XI

A POLICY OF QUIESCENCE

THE death of Lord Napier placed both the English and the Chinese in a position of the greatest difficulty. Among the other members of the Commission there was no one comparable with the deceased Chief Superintendent, either in rank or ability. The British Government had chosen the assistant superintendents not with a view of having at Canton persons competent to fill Lord Napier's place in an emergency such as had arisen, but rather with the object of providing him with a staff, qualified by their local knowledge to advise him in matters in which his own experience might be deficient. A successor to Lord Napier could not be expected to arrive from London in less than nine months, yet the need was imperative that the negotiations, which had just been initiated, should be carried through without delay. The Chinese were apprehensive that the British community at Canton, if left without an authoritative head, might resort to such strenuous methods of improving their position as would be far worse than the measures taken by Lord Napier. The real condition of the official mind is shown by the fact that, only a week after the death of the Chief Superintendent, the Viceroy, Lu, who had treated him with such scant courtesy, was issuing an edict to the Hong Merchants instructing them " to order the British merchants to examine and deliberate what person ought to be made the head for directing the nation's said trade," and " to send a letter home to their country calling for the immediate appointment of another *taipan* to come to Canton, in order to direct and manage." The Viceroy's opinion was, that just as on the Chinese side responsibility in commercial matters was laid on the Hong Merchants, so on the British side the merchants should select " a commercial man acquainted with affairs " to take responsibility for the good behaviour of British merchants. He made it quite clear that he did not think it necessary that a " barbarian *eye* or superintendent " should be appointed.[1]

[1] *Chinese Repository*, vol. xi, pp. 74–5.

It is necessary here to go back a little and consider the effect produced at Peking by the news of what was happening at Canton. On the 8th September the Viceroy had reported to the Throne the arrival of Lord Napier and the coming of the British cruisers into the river.[1] So displeased was the Emperor at this news, that he wrote on the Viceroy's memorial with the vermilion pencil[2] the following words: "It seems that all the forts are erected in vain: they cannot beat back two barbarian ships: it is ridiculous, detestable. The military preparations being reduced to such a state as this, it is not surprising that the outside barbarians regard them slightingly. My further pleasure shall be given." It is evident that Chinese pride had been more severely wounded than on any occasion since the time when Captain Weddell first entered the Canton river. Not even Commodore Anson had dared to come up and fire on the Chinese batteries. This new development required that the Emperor should deliberate with the Grand Council before any further steps could be taken. When the Grand Council had considered the matter, two edicts were despatched to Canton.

The first of these was from the Emperor himself, and in it he announced his "further pleasure" in no uncertain voice. Kaou Eyung, the naval commander, whose business it was to guard the entrances to the river, was degraded from his office and ordered to wear the cangue in public at the maritime entrance; all the officers in charge of the forts were ordered to wear the cangue before their own troops; whilst Lu, the Viceroy, was deprived of his title of guardian of the heir apparent and of his two-eyed peacock's feather, and degraded from his office. The other edict proceeded from the Grand Council, and prescribed the measures that were to be taken to circumvent Lord Napier. Vessels were to be filled with stones and sunk across the channels of the river, which were to be

[1] *Chinese Repository*, vol. iii, pp. 327-336.

[2] The use of the vermilion pencil by the Emperor is confined to occasions when he desires to express his opinion in the most emphatic way. Instructions given in this way are equivalent to instructions under the Sign Manual in England.

further protected by cables and booms stretching from bank to bank ; a strong naval force was to cruise at the entrance, and troops with artillery were to be assembled on shore. When the barbarian vessels had been thus hemmed in, more than a hundred fire-ships, carrying saltpetre, firewood, straw, and other combustibles, were to be directed against them, and thus " the beast will then be taken, the fish caught," to quote the metaphor used in the edict itself. It was anticipated that in this way the barbarian *eye* would be " brought under," his schemes exhausted, and his strength wasted, so that he would " bow his head and confess his fault." When he had been reduced to this condition, then might " a light, trifling indulgence " be shown to him. It was absolutely necessary, continued the edict, to make the barbarian *eye* tremble and quake before the celestial majesty, and " penitentially arouse to reverential submission." [1] Both edicts were received at Canton on the 19th of October, eight days after Lord Napier's death.

If one can judge by the little attention paid to such matters, neither the Emperor nor the Grand Council cared one jot whether Lord Napier should be allowed to communicate with the Canton officials on a footing of equality, or be compelled to petition through the Hong Merchants. In neither of these edicts is there a single reference to this topic. It is the " negligence " of the Viceroy and his colleagues, not the temerity of the Chief Superintendent, that is the object of the imperial animadversion.

Davis, who by virtue of seniority, had succeeded to the office of Chief Superintendent for the time being, now wrote to Lord Palmerston describing the state of affairs at Canton, and enclosing a copy of the Viceroy's memorial to the Throne, in answer to which these edicts had been received. He suggested to the Foreign Secretary that perhaps the best course would be, that a despatch to the Emperor from the British Government, explaining their attitude, should be sent to the mouth of the Pei-ho, in the hope that a direct communication with the Emperor would have the effect of removing all difficulties. Davis stated as his reasons for

[1] *Chinese Repository*, vol. iii, pp. 336–8.

advocating this method of procedure, that it was well known that the officials at Canton kept the Court at Peking in complete ignorance of everything connected with Foreigners, that Chinese principles sanctioned and invited appeals against the distant delegates of the Emperor, and that Flint's visit to Peking in 1759 had been attended with marked success. He appears to have disregarded the lack of actual results, so far as any change at Canton was concerned, which had attended the embassies of Lords Macartney and Amherst.

Davis in this letter informed Lord Palmerston that he had resolved upon a policy of absolute quiescence, so far as it should be possible, until he should be instructed from England as to what line of action he should adopt. The instructions issued to the Superintendents of Trade under the Sign Manual, before the Commission left England, by which he was bound, were such as made it impossible for Davis to take on his own initiative any active measures to bring the Chinese officials to a state of reason, unless he assumed the boldness of his predecessor and disregarded them. By those instructions he was bidden to observe all possible moderation, cautiously to abstain from all unnecessary use of menacing language, or from making any appeal for protection to the British military or naval forces, unless, in some extreme case, the most evident necessity should require that such language should be used or such an appeal be made.[1]

In the meantime Lu had reported to Peking the withdrawal of the British cruisers and the retirement of Lord Napier to Macao, in the language characteristic of the Chinese on such occasions, attributing this unlooked-for development to an imaginary assemblage of Chinese military and naval forces and fire-ships, which had so terrified the " barbarian *eye* " that he had supplicated to be allowed to leave Canton in a "sampan."[2] The grounds on which this alleged supplication had been granted were thus stated :—

" At this time the naval and land forces were ranged out in order, arrayed as on a chess-board ; the fire vessels also were

[1] *Correspondence Relating to China* (Blue Book, 1840), p. 3.

[2] This is the smallest and meanest kind of boat known to a Chinese.

made ready ; were advantage taken of this occasion while the ships still found it impossible either to advance or recede, and an attack made on them on all sides, there would be no difficulty in instantly having their lives within our power. But our august sovereign cherishes those from afar virtuously, and soothingly treats outside barbarians, exercising to the utmost limit both benevolence and justice. If any be contumacious, they are corrected ; if submissive, they are pardoned ; but never are extreme measures adopted towards them. Although Lord Napier has entertained absurd visionary fancies, he yet has shown no real disregard of the laws : it would not be well precipitately to visit him with exterminating measures. Besides, the private merchants of the said nation, several thousands in number, all consider the barbarian *eye's* disobedience of the laws to be wrong. There is not one who unites and accords with him. Still more improper, therefore, would it be, to make no distinction between common and precious stones. Now, Lord Napier having acknowledged his error and solicited favour, and all the separate merchants having repeatedly made humble supplications, there certainly should be some slight indulgence shown, and he should be driven out of the port; to the end that, while the Foreign barbarians are made to tremble with terror, they may also be rendered grateful by the favour of the celestial empire, shown in its benevolence, kindness, and great indulgence." [1]

This version of the departure of the Chief Superintendent, and of the causes that conduced thereto, was at once accepted by the Emperor as correct. The course which Lu pretended to have taken was approved on the ground that, under the circumstances, it behoved him to extend to Lord Napier "a slight, trifling indulgence, and to drive him out of the port." For these valiant services Lu was restored to the office of Viceroy, and received back his double-eyed peacock's feather ; his degradation from official rank was, however, continued, in punishment for the neglect which had allowed the British men-of-war to enter the river. The term of punishment meted out to the officers who had been condemned to wear

[1] *Chinese Repository*, vol. iii, pp. 341–2.

the cangue was shortened to one month. The imperial edict dealing with these matters bearing date the 7th of October, was similar to those previously received, in that it made no complaint against Lord Napier for having demanded the right to communicate with the officials on a footing of equality. How futile was the contention that such a course was contrary to Chinese law is shown both by the imperial silence and by the admission in Lu's edict that Lord Napier had shown "no real disregard of the laws." The only part of the Emperor's edict that relates to the office of Chief Superintendent are the oft-quoted words in which he commanded that the English should send to their country to ask for the appointment of another person as *taipan* :—

"The English barbarians have an open market in the Inner Land; but there has hitherto been no interchange of official communications. It is, however, absolutely requisite that there should be a person possessing general control, to have the special direction of affairs. Let the Viceroy immediately order the Hong Merchants to command the said separate merchants that they send a letter back to their country, calling for the appointment of another person as *taipan*, to come for the control and direction of commercial affairs, in accordance with the old regulations. Respect this."[1]

As Davis had resolved to take no active steps towards establishing official relations with the Viceroy until further instructions should have arrived from England, the British merchants continued to carry on their business at Canton under the old conditions, hoping that a better state of things would soon be established. In this hope they were buoyed up by an announcement made by the Commission through the secretary, Captain Elliot, stating that a full report of events had been transmitted both to England and India, and requesting all British subjects to refrain from doing anything that might afford to the Chinese a plausible ground of complaint, and from making any comment on political occurrences.[2] Not being sure, however, that the Home Government was in

[1] *Chinese Repository*, vol. iii, p. 344.
[2] *Ibid.*, vol. iii, p. 472–4.

a position sufficiently to comprehend the gravity of the crisis that had arisen, they resolved, after some deliberation, to avail themselves of the old common law right of Englishmen to petition the King and lay before him a statement of their grievances in their own words. This right, though frequently used by British subjects in the Colonies, had never before been resorted to by British subjects in China, the reason being that so long as the East India Company had retained its monopoly, all complaints had been addressed to the Court of Directors.

A petition was drawn up stating very shortly the facts of the case, describing the undignified position in which the Superintendents were placed, and lamenting their powerlessness to demand reparation for the injury done to British subjects by the recent stoppage of trade. The petitioners asked that there might be no quiet submission to insult, or such unresisting endurance of contemptuous treatment as would compromise the honour of Great Britain; they deplored the fact that no such armed force had been placed at Lord Napier's disposal, as would have prevented the indignities to which that nobleman had been exposed; they asked that a plenipotentiary of suitable rank, discretion, and diplomatic experience be appointed to proceed with a sufficient naval force to some port as near as possible to Peking, to demand reparation for the insults offered to the late Chief Superintendent, and for the insulting language used in the official and imperial edicts; they suggested that some sort of treaty arrangement should be entered into regulating the intercourse between the two nations, and that Amoy, Ningpo, and Chusan should be opened to trade as of old; and they gave it as their opinion, that if forcible measures were needed, a small armed force should interrupt and cut off the imperial revenues in their progress to the capital, and capture all the Chinese war-junks, by which means not only would the Chinese Government be brought into a proper frame of mind, but a source of indemnity obtained for British subjects who had suffered loss.[1]

The petition, which was forwarded to England on the

[1] *Correspondence Relating to China* (Blue Book, 1840), p. 88: *Chinese Repository*, vol. iii, p. 354.

14th December, 1834, by the same ship that conveyed home Lady Napier and her two eldest daughters, is instructive as showing what were the views of the men whose interests were most directly affected by recent events, and who had the best means of judging the Chinese character. Taken in conjunction with Lord Napier's despatches, it shows that the unanimous opinion of those, who had come into contact with the Chinese, was that force of some kind must be used, if the position of the British community at Canton was to be ameliorated. Unfortunately, the persons responsible in England for our foreign policy took quite too pacific a view of the matter. The despatches of Lord Napier up to the 31st of August, 1834, were received in London on the 31st of January following, just at the time when Lord Palmerston, who had been Foreign Secretary since 1830, had retired on the formation of Peel's administration. In one of these despatches the deceased Chief Superintendent had recommended the destruction of the Chinese forts and batteries along the whole coast and on the river sides, if less violent means of bringing about a change of attitude on the part of the Chinese Government should prove unavailing. He considered that three or four frigates and brigs, with a few steady British troops, not Sepoys, would settle all difficulties in a space of time inconceivably short. The Duke of Wellington, who had succeeded Palmerston, was by no means pleased with the tenor of Lord Napier's communications. Not knowing that that nobleman was dead, he wrote on the 2nd February: "I avail myself of the opportunity earnestly to recommend to your Lordship's attention the instructions of Lord Palmerston. . . . It is not by force and violence that His Majesty intends to establish a commercial intercourse between his subjects and China, but by the other conciliatory measures so strongly inculcated in all the instructions which you have received."[1]

On the 24th of March, 1835, by which time all the despatches sent from Canton up to the 24th of the preceding October had arrived in London, the Duke drew up his celebrated memorandum on the state of affairs, and laid it before the

[1] *Correspondence Relating to China* (Blue Book, 1840), p. 13.

Cabinet. This document was to the effect that attempts, such as that made by Lord Napier, to force on the Chinese an unaccustomed mode of intercourse, must invariably fail and lead to national disgrace; that the time had come for the Cabinet to take into consideration the future direction of matters at Canton; that Lord Napier's high-sounding title was only the pretext for the Chinese jealousy, the real reason therefor being his attempt to establish himself at Canton without permission; that it did not matter much what we called our officer, but he must not go to Canton without the permission of the Chinese, or depart from the usual mode of communication; that for our sakes he must be a man of military, naval, or official rank and reputation, of great firmness and discretion, possessing great powers to enable him to control the King's subjects; and that there should be one Chief Superintendent, and a Second Superintendent, the latter to be a legal gentleman who should exercise the judicial powers conferred by the China Trade Act. He advised that the secretary should be entitled to succeed the Chief Superintendent in case of death or sudden departure, that alterations should be made in the instructions to the Superintendents, and that if necessary a communication should be made to Peking later. He also recommended that a stout frigate and a smaller man-of-war should always be within reach of the Chief Superintendent.[1] No steps, however, were taken to carry out these suggestions, probably because Peel went out of office a few weeks later.

Davis in the meantime had decided to resign from the Commission and to return to England. Having handed over Lord Napier's commission, the seals of office, and all official documents to Sir George Best Robinson, he left Canton on the 19th January, 1835. Captain Astell was promoted to be Second Superintendent, whilst the post of Third Superintendent was given to Captain Elliot, who was at that time only known as the secretary to the Commission, but was destined to occupy a very prominent position in the history of our relations with China. One of the last acts of Davis in his official capacity was to forward to Lord Palmerston a copy of an imperial

[1] *Correspondence Relating to China* (Blue Book, 1840), p. 51.

edict, which is valuable as showing that even at Peking it was recognized that there was a very real foundation to the grievances of which the Foreign community at Canton complained. This edict was in the following terms :—

"There are at Canton merchants who have of late been in the habit of levying private duties and incurring debts to barbarians ; and it is requested that regulations be established to eradicate utterly such misdemeanours. The outside barbarians' commercial intercourse with the Inner Land exists indeed by the compassion exercised by the celestial empire. If all the duties which are required to be paid can indeed be levied according to the fixed tariff, the said barbarian merchants must certainly pay them gladly, and must continually remain tranquil. But if, as is now reported, the Canton merchants have of late been in a feeble and deficient state, and have, in addition to the government duties, added also private duties, while fraudulent individuals have further taken advantage of this to make gain out of the custom-house duties, peeling off (from the barbarians) layer after layer ; and have also gone to the extreme degree of the government merchants, incurring debts to the barbarians, heaping thousands upon ten thousands, whereby are stirred up sanguinary quarrels : if the merchants thus falsely, and under the name of tariff duties, extort, each according to his own wishes, going even to the extreme degree of incurring debts, amount upon amount, it is not a matter of surprise if the said barbarian merchants, unable to bear their grasping, stir up disturbances. Thus, with regard to the affair this year of the English Lord Napier and others, disobeying the national laws and bringing forces into the inner river, the barbarians being naturally crafty and artful, and gain being their only object, we have no assurance that it is not owing to the numerous extortions of the Canton merchants, that they, their minds being discontented, thereupon craftily thought to carry themselves with a high hand. If regulations be not plainly established, strictly prohibiting these things, how can the barbarous multitude be kept in subjection and misdemeanours eradicated ?" [1]

[1] *Chinese Repository*, vol. xi, pp. 78-79 : *Correspondence Relating to China* (Blue Book, 1840), p. 77.

As soon as Davis had left Canton an incident occurred which showed that the Commission, as reconstituted, did not consider themselves bound by the conditions he had laid down for his own guidance. The British ship *Argyle*, when on a voyage from Bengal to Canton, was forced to put in for shelter at a point on the China coast near the island of Lien-chee. In the hope of getting a pilot the captain, Macdonald, sent ashore a boat with an unarmed crew of twelve men. The temptation to make pecuniary gain out of the misfortunes of the "foreign devils" was too great for the local Chinese, who seized the boat and held the crew to ransom, offering to release them on payment of five hundred dollars. When information of this occurrence was laid before the Commission, they resolved to bring the matter to the notice of the Chinese officials at Canton, with a view to obtaining redress and the release of the men who had been detained. A difficulty at once arose as to the means by which this resolution was to be carried into effect. It was decided to draw up a note setting out the facts and signed by all the Superintendents, and to hand this document in at the water-gate, following the precedent set by Captain Freemantle in 1831. The execution of this project was entrusted to Captain Elliot, who, accompanied by Macdonald and by the official interpreter, Gutzlaff, proceeded to the city on the 1st of February, 1835, but the only result was that after being treated with great contumely and having suffered many insults the party had to return leaving their object unaccomplished.[1]

No steps were ever taken to obtain an apology for this insult to the accredited representative of Great Britain. Captain Elliot remarks that two general officers, who were asked to receive his communication, replied that they only received *petitions;* nor did they stay long enough to give him an opportunity to complain of the treatment he had received.[2] In the existing circumstances any attempt by the Superintendents

[1] *Correspondence Relating to China* (Blue Book, 1840), pp. 82–86; *Chinese Repository*, vol. xi, pp. 124–126.

[2] *Correspondence Relating to China* (Blue Book, 1840), p. 82; *Chinese Repository*, vol. xi, p. 126.

themselves to obtain reparation would have been futile. They could only look to the British Government to vindicate their dignity. But Lord Palmerston, who was again installed at the Foreign Office, when the despatches giving an account of this affair reached England, was quite content to let it pass unnoticed, being apparently of the opinion that as the twelve detained seamen had been returned to Canton on the 18th of February, the matter deserved no further attention.

Whilst waiting for the appointment of a fresh *taipan* from England, the Chinese officials thought it advisable to impress upon the whole Foreign community the necessity of remembering that the arrival of Lord Napier was not regarded by them as inaugurating in any way a new era in the relations between Foreigners and Chinese. Conscious that the abolition of the East India Company's monopoly had worked a fundamental change in the position of British subjects at Canton, as determined by English law, and wishing to guard against any assumption that this change was effective to abrogate the conditions under which the Foreigners had theretofore been allowed to trade, the Viceroy and Hoppo determined to get those conditions re-affirmed by imperial edict. They therefore presented to the Throne a memorial to the effect that the rules of dignified decorum should be rendered awe-striking in order to repress over-stepping presumption ; the bounds of intercourse should be closely drawn, in order to eradicate Chinese traitors ; restraints on egress and ingress should be diligently enforced ; and investigation and supervision should be carefully attended to. The memorial further recited that in the years 1760, 1810 and 1831 regulations had been made "for the direction of the trade and of barbarians," and proposed for the imperial sanction eight "additional and altered regulations restrictive of the barbarians." These were very similar in effect to those recited, with the addition of a regulation against smuggling, which was undoubtedly introduced with the intention of stopping the trade in opium,[1] which had by this time assumed serious proportions. Foreign

[1] As to the opium trade, see *post*, chaps. xiii and xv.

ships of war were prohibited from sailing into the inner seas, and the Chinese naval commander-in-chief was ordered to cruise about and prevent any infringement of this regulation. Foreign ladies were forbidden to come up to Canton. The importation and use of arms by Foreigners was interdicted, except that each man might carry one sword, one rapier, and one gun. Pilots and compradores were not to be hired privately, but obtained under licence from the *tung-chi* of Macao. Two gate-keepers and four water-carriers were allowed to each factory, and each merchant might hire one man to guard his goods. With these exceptions the Foreigners were forbidden to engage Chinese servants. They were not to walk outside the Factories except on three days in the month, and then only in the neighbouring flower gardens and in the grounds of the Honan temple ; they were not to go about in parties of more than ten, and were to return to the Factories by five o'clock in the evening. If they wished to proceed to Whampoa on business, they might go in open boats, but were not to use boats decked over, or covered in, or flying a flag. All official communications were to be presented through the Hong Merchants, except that an accusation against a member of that body might be preferred before one of the local magistrates. Each Foreign ship was to be secured, not only by the Hong Merchant engaged for that purpose by the ship, but also by another, appointed in rotation, to keep watch over the one so engaged. Finally, the naval forces were to seize all Foreign vessels detected in selling contraband goods.[1]

The Viceroy, whilst waiting for the Imperial approval of these regulations, which he knew would be given as a matter of course, ordered them to be promulgated by the Hoppo, and this was done on the 8th of March, 1835. No notice of the edict was taken by the members of the Commission, who were still waiting for instructions from England. Indeed, until the beginning of the year 1836, the Superintendents of Trade displayed no public activity whatsoever, nor did the Home Government make the least sign that any other course of conduct should be followed. One of the strangest features

[1] *Chinese Repository*, vol. iii, pp. 579–584.

of the history of our relations with China is that from the death of Lord Napier to May, 1836, the crucial period, so far as the position of the Superintendents of Trade is concerned, not a single despatch, excepting that of the Duke of Wellington of the 2nd of February, 1835, mentioned above, appears to have been sent from the Foreign Office to Canton.

Hence it is that there is little, apart from the growth of the opium traffic, which is discussed in the next chapter, to record in connection with that period. On the 1st of April Captain Elliot was promoted to be Second Superintendent, in the place of Captain Astell, who had resigned, and was succeeded by Johnston, whilst Edward Elmslie was appointed secretary to the Commission. On the 7th of the same month, Mowqua, the senior Hong Merchant, died. He had taken a prominent part in opposing any extension of the rights or privileges of the Foreign community, and there was one universal expression of joy at his decease.[1] A few months later, on the 25th of September, Viceroy Lu died at the age of sixty-six years.

The difficulties of the Commission were not rendered less by the violent party spirit that prevailed among the mercantile community at Canton, of which Sir George Robinson speaks in a despatch to Lord Palmerston, dated the 13th of April, 1835. He there points out the necessity of putting the government officers as far as possible beyond the reach of these dissensions, and suggests that, to prevent their embarrassment, every British subject and every British ship should be removed from the river previous to any communication with the local authorities, and all British families at Macao be embarked on the merchant ships, so that the whole British community and shipping might take up a position in one of the beautiful harbours of Lantao or Hong-kong, until all political matters had been settled.

A curious episode of this period was the expedition of the *Governor Findlay* to the coasts of Fukien, carrying G. J. Gordon, an agent of the Bengal Government, to make enquiries into the cultivation and preparation of tea. The interpreter

[1] *Chinese Repository*, vol. iv, p. 47.

to this expedition was Gutzlaff, who had previously, in 1831 and 1832, explored the coast right up to the Gulf of Pe-chihli; and following the precedent set in 1832, the occasion was used for missionary as well as commercial enterprise, and a good deal of missionary literature was distributed. On arriving at the mouth of the river Min early in May, the party found themselves in difficulties through not knowing by what channel to proceed. The natives gave them a friendly reception, and at first there was no opposition from the officials; but as the expedition penetrated inland it was opposed by military force, and was more than once fired upon. Finding it impossible to proceed under these circumstances, the party returned, without having reached the hills of Wui, for which they were making. Later, when the matter came to the knowledge of the Viceroy at Canton, an edict was issued complaining of the distribution of literature on the coasts of Fukien and Chêkiang. It was quite clear that the Chinese authorities were strongly averse to Foreigners attempting to establish any sort of communication away from Canton. From what the expedition observed, it looked as though there was a feeling abroad in the maritime provinces that armed invasion might be sooner or later attempted. New forts were being erected, the old ones repaired, and deserted military stations being filled with troops.[1]

Another source of difficulty to the commission was that they found themselves incompetent to deal with civil disputes, owing to the fact that the powers conferred upon them by the China Trade Act, and the Orders in Council made thereunder, did not give them power to hear and determine civil causes, other than suits in admiralty. A firm called Turner & Co. claimed the sum of three hundred dollars from a British subject named Keating, and as he refused to pay they laid the facts before the Chief Superintendent. He enquired into the matter and came to the conclusion that the claim was a valid one, and requested Keating to discharge the obligation. The objection was taken by Keating that the Commission had no authority in the matter: in the first

[1] *Chinese Repository*, vol. iv, pp. 82-96.

place because they were entitled to exercise such powers as they had only at Canton, where they were not then residing; and in the second place because none of them were appointed directly by the Crown. On the Superintendents attempting to serve a written notice on Keating in respect of the matter, he appealed to the Viceroy as to their "right to attempt legislation" whilst resident at Macao. Finding that no civil process could be instituted against Keating, Sir George Robinson himself paid the three hundred dollars to Turner & Co., and then contended that that sum thereby became a debt due from Keating to the Crown. Keating still refused to pay, and the matter was referred to the Foreign Office.

At the same time another point of law arose, owing to the seizure of the property of a British subject named Innes on a charge of smuggling. Innes employed a pilot named Acha to transfer some goods from the ship *Orwell*, while passing up from Lintin to Canton, to another vessel bound for Manilla. Acha, instead of transferring the goods, proceeded to take them up the Canton river in a boat. The Chinese revenue officers seized them on the ground that Acha was attempting to smuggle them within the port of Canton. Innes thereupon petitioned the Viceroy for redress, but could get no satisfaction, being informed that the goods could not be traced. Happening one day to be engaged in business transactions, at which some of the Hoppo's officers were present, he noticed that one of them was carrying his papers wrapped in a handkerchief of the colour of those which formed part of the confiscated goods, a colour which had never before been imported into China. In his anger at this proof of official participation in the detention of the goods, he threatened to make reprisals against the Chinese shipping if the goods were not restored. The Superintendents warned him of the danger of taking such a course, whereupon he consented to abstain from carrying out his threat if the matter were submitted to the consideration of the British Government.

Accordingly the papers relating to both these matters were forwarded to Lord Palmerston. In due course a reply was received, dated 8th of November, 1836, in which it was stated that the opinion of the Law Officers of the Crown was, that if Innes carried out his threat, he would be guilty of piracy, and that the Superintendents had no authority to compel Keating to pay Turner & Co.'s claim. Lord Palmerston uttered a warning that if Innes persisted in his threat, he would be left by the British Government to his fate ; he further recommended the Commission to confine their interference in civil matters as much as possible to friendly suggestion and advice to the parties concerned. It had been suggested that the Superintendents might expel Keating from the port if he refused to carry out their injunctions, as they had vested in them all the powers of the supercargoes of the East India Company. In reference to this contention, Lord Palmerston took the view that, as the powers of the supercargoes had applied only to persons unlicensed by the East India Company, and as no license was now required to enable a British subject to reside in China, that power did not exist any longer.[1]

During the whole of the year 1835 Sir George Robinson continued to maintain his policy of quiescence, in which he was encouraged by the receipt, in the month of July, of the despatch dated the 2nd of February, from the Duke of Wellington.

[1] *Correspondence Relating to China* (Blue Book, 1840), pp. 95, 102, 126–7 : *Chinese Repository*, vol. xi, pp. 192–3. There was a power of expulsion vested in the British Consul at each port under the Order in Council of 9th March, 1865. A similar power is conferred by the Order in Council of the 24th October, 1904.

CHAPTER XII

THE OPIUM TRADE

MANY writers, and particularly those of philanthropic mind, who have taken upon themselves to discuss the relations between the Chinese and ourselves, have based their criticism of our conduct as a nation on the assumption that England is, and always has been, immensely superior to China in power, resources, and morality. In words by no means wanting in force, they have inveighed against the enormity and wickedness of our statesmen, in that they have not treated the Chinese with that solicitude and care which, they claim, should have been shown in such a case. Though not openly avowed, the analogies that have been present to the minds of such writers have been those of guardian and ward, trustee and *cestui que trust*, or even parent and child. England, in their opinion, should stand, and ought to have stood, to China in a position both fiduciary and tutelary ; and because they find that her behaviour has not always been in accordance with such an attitude, they wax indignant and hold her up to scorn, ridicule, and contempt. Particularly is this so with those who have written on the subject of the opium trade.

So far as the events discussed in the preceding chapters are concerned, such denunciation of our national behaviour is absolutely unfounded. With regard to more recent years it may be admitted that at times in our dealings with China a course of conduct might have been pursued, which would have afforded greater satisfaction to us and our descendants, than that of which history bears record. It may also be granted that the facts of the case are such as at first sight warrant, to some extent, the use of the analogies mentioned above. England is stronger than China : her resources are greater : and her code of morals is undoubtedly superior. But when we bear in mind that the intercourse between the two countries has been based on a totally different assumption—an assumption born of the pride and arrogance of the Chinese, that facts were quite different from what they were in reality—then we begin to see that the ground of condemnation is not so strong as might at first be supposed. It is true that England is stronger than China: but China has never yet acknowledged that simple fact; and until quite recently she believed that she was superior in power to all the nations of Europe combined.[1] It is true that England's resources are the greater; but to this day the Chinese comfort themselves with the belief that they have only to develop their national wealth and they will be able to defy the world. When it comes to morality, the merest Chinese coolie shows by his look of conscious superiority, as he passes us in the street, that to his mind the best of us are but outer barbarians.

Only those who have lived among the Chinese know how little ground there is in fact for these cherished beliefs; but they exist, and they have to be taken into account. We must not forget that in the early part of the nineteenth century, before Western powers had made their influence felt in China as it is felt at the present day, those beliefs flourished in an unpruned luxuriance. In the reign of William IV, and at the beginning of Queen Victoria's reign, Chinese self-complacency and self-satisfaction had received none of those shocks by which to some extent they have since been impaired. To the Chinese China was great and strong, England a despicable weakling; China the favoured of Heaven, England a dweller in outer darkness; China enlightened in culture and morals, England fast bound in misery and ignorance. The Son of Heaven was the indulgent father and benignant protector of the "foreign devils" who craved leave to dwell within his dominions; the King of England a tributary princeling, seeking the favour of being allowed to trade with the people of the Middle Kingdom of the earth. Founding on these ideas a policy of overbearing disdain, refusing to allow the nations, whose acts she disliked, to approach her on a

[1] This was strikingly shown by the support given to the Boxers by the Court at Peking in 1900. Nearly all the fighting during the Boxer troubles was done by the Imperial troops under express orders from the Empress-Dowager.

footing of equality, China involved herself in a contest from which she came out sadly humiliated.

The consumption of opium in China is undoubtedly a great national evil. Physically its effects are in many instances of the worst kind. Many Europeans summarily dismiss from their employ any servant they discover to be addicted to the practice of opium-smoking, so admittedly deleterious are its results. On the other hand, there can be no doubt that many Chinese partake of opium, by eating it, without harm to themselves, and probably with positive benefit. The controversy as to the physical effects of opium is one that still rages, and a mass of evidence might be cited on either side.[1] But such a discussion would here be out of place. Suffice it to say that the great mass of Chinese opinion is against the opium habit. There is another side, the economic side, which must be considered, as it was this side of the question to which the Chinese Government mainly devoted its attention when the opium traffic first became a subject of contention between England and China. It is this side of the question that presents the most practical difficulty to those who wish to suppress the export of opium from India.

Of a nation's imports and products, that part which remains stored up in the country in a permanent form is wealth which may be regarded as having a potential value ; it may, at any time, be converted by sale or exchange into other forms of wealth, or may be used in developing energy with which fresh wealth may be acquired. Wealth spent on necessary food or necessary pleasure may be regarded as having a kinetic value. That part which is consumed as necessary food serves to maintain the population in a state of efficiency ; and inasmuch as a certain amount of pleasure is conducive to

[1] Dr. A. H. Smith, in *Chinese Characteristics*, says opium is " a foe to the Chinese race, as deadly as war, famine, or pestilence " (5th edit., p. 145). This view is ridiculed by Dr. G. E. Morrison, in *An Australian in China* (3rd edit., pp. 41, 94), where instances of the beneficial use of opium are cited. De Quincey gives an instance of a Malay, who in his presence bolted at one mouthful a piece of opium big enough " to kill three dragoons and their horses," without suffering any harm. (See *Confessions of an Opium Eater*.)

efficiency, that part which is spent on what may be called necessary pleasure is also well spent. Wealth applied to any of these ends brings in, or is capable of bringing in, a return that is a benefit to the community. But when wealth is expended in the enjoyment of luxuries, for example, in such food or pleasure as is not necessary to maintain efficiency, it is, so far as the general advantage of the community is concerned, wasted; for it is thereby lost or destroyed. So long as a community produces or acquires more wealth than is requisite for the well-being of all its members, luxuries not essentially harmful in their nature may be indulged in without immediate hurt; but it is very seldom that a nation reaches such a pitch of economic development, because the tendency is to dissipate in war any actual or contemplated accumulation of resources. Even if a nation has an amount of wealth more than sufficient to maintain the whole of its population in a state of well-being, it will suffer in commercial competition with another which, other things being equal, consumes a less proportion of its wealth in luxuries; for the latter will have a greater capital, and can therefore, to obtain the same income, be content with a less rate of profit.

China is not a rich country,[1] and she is excessively over-populated. The average wealth per head of the population must be very small in comparison with that of other countries. The people, however, are hardy and able to live on food which, though coarse in its nature, is produced at a very small cost;

[1] This is contrary to the popular impression, but is found to be true on careful examination. The universal prevalence of infanticide is strong testimony of poverty. China has not enough wealth to develop her mineral resources without the aid of foreign capital. Apart from large deposits of coal, which are mostly at a great distance from the seaboard and do not occur in conjunction with iron, her mineral deposits are of little value. The poverty of her agricultural supplies, when her population is taken into account, is shown by the terrible famines that afflict the country so frequently. This to a considerable extent is due to bad administration; It is computed that in the city of Tientsin, which is the second port of the Empire, and has a population of about a million, there are not one hundred people with an income so high as £200 per annum. In the villages things are no better. (See Dr. A. H. Smith, *Village Life in China*, p. 310, 1st edit.; Matignon, *Superstition, Crime et Misère en Chine*.)

and this helps to alleviate their condition. Still, there is hardly a country in the world that could so ill afford to spend such a proportion of its wealth on luxuries as the Chinese spend on opium. The balance of trade is against her, and she has few sources of income on which to draw to pay for that balance. When we consider that of the goods imported a very valuable part simply disappears in the smoke of the opium pipe, we begin to realize to what an extent the opium trade is crippling the country. When nearly all the opium consumed was imported, the evil was greater than it is now; for then, in addition to the cost of production, the price included freight, insurance, interest on cost during transit from India, and the enormous profits of the Foreign merchant, all of which had to be paid for in wealth that went out of the country. Now that there is no restriction on the growth of the poppy in China, the same amount of opium as was formerly imported may be produced in China itself at a much less expense. It must be remembered, however, that there is still a large amount of foreign opium imported, owing to the demand for the best kinds. The cost of the native drug has to cover the labour and rent of the land employed in its production, both of which are very low, and the profit of the native dealer, which remains in the country. Thus the consumption of a given amount of home-grown opium involves a far less loss of wealth to the nation at large than the consumption of an equal amount of the imported drug. Nevertheless, for the reasons given above, the use of opium as a luxury, whether home-grown or imported, remains an economic evil. The place of production is relevant only in determining the degree of that evil.

Some people argue in favour of the opium trade, that if the consumption of the drug is an evil to one community, the production is beneficial to another that produces it. The answer to this is, that any benefit reaped by the producer is at the expense of the world at large, which is the poorer by the amount of wealth that would have been added to its store, had the producer spent the same amount of time and wealth and energy in producing some other article, the enjoyment of which would not have involved its absolute and immediate destruction. The fallacy is a familiar one. By breaking a pane of glass and thereby giving employment to labour one does not confer a benefit on the community. By burning opium the Chinese do not benefit the world at large. India reaps enormous profits from the sale of opium exported by her to other countries, chiefly to China.[1] In so far as that opium is consumed as a luxury, the world at large is poorer by the amount of wealth spent by the consumers in purchasing it. The purchasing power of China as a commercial entity, in respect of other commodities, is less than it otherwise would have been by the cost of production of the opium consumed by her as a luxury.

It cannot be stated with certainty when opium was first introduced into China. The compiler of the *Herbal*, who wrote early in the seventeenth century, speaks of the poppy and its inspissated juice, and says that formerly both were but little known.[2] As early as 1764 its importation had been prohibited. In that year a report reached the Court of Directors of the East India Company, that the trouble between Captain Affleck and the Chinese officials at Canton was due to the fact that the *Argo* had opium on board. The Court was careful to write to the supercargoes, pointing out that the importation of the drug was forbidden, and that its introduction could only be most detrimental to the Company's interests.[3] Before the year 1767 the annual import did not exceed 200 chests, but in that year it rose to 1,000 chests. The East India Company, who had obtained the right to cultivate the poppy as one of the results of Clive's great victory at Plassey, did not themselves import opium into China until the year 1773, the trade in the drug before that date having been entirely in the hands of the Portuguese.[4]

[1] India received in revenue from opium over £2,000,000 in 1840, and £7,657,000 in 1872. From 1862 to 1883 the revenue was always over £5,000,000 per annum. The figures for 1905–6 are £5,468,780 out of a total revenue of £62,621,929.

[2] Williams, *The Middle Kingdom*, vol. ii, p. 374.

[3] See *Factory Records of the East India Company* (MSS. in India Office No. 11, under *Memoir : Intercourse with China*, Part I, pp. 118–121).

[4] *Chinese Repository*, vol. v, p. 547.

In 1780 a depot for imported opium was established by the English on board two small vessels, which were stationed in a bay to the southward of Macao, called Lark's Bay. The price realized at this time was about $500 or $600 for a chest that in Bengal cost about 500 rupees, which shows a gross profit of about 100 per cent.[1]

In 1781 the East India Company found the whole of the annual crop left on hand in the warehouses at Calcutta. The Company's own shipping was engaged in supplying Madras with rice, and private ship-owners would not take the risk of buying, while the seas were infested with French and Dutch cruisers. Under these circumstances the Company determined to export it themselves, and consigned one shipload to the Indian Archipelago and another to China. The latter consignment was conveyed in one of the Company's armed vessels, which in those days appear to have been allowed to enter the Bogue free of measurement duty. The venture was not a particularly profitable one, though the Bengal Government twice drew against the shipment for 10 lacs, and were thus enabled to relieve the somewhat strained condition of their finances. The market was not a good one, and the supercargoes found some difficulty in selling. Ultimately the consignment was purchased by a Hong Merchant named Sinqua, who had previously conducted an extensive business at Macao. The Senior Hong Merchant, Pwankhequa, refused to have anything to do with it, apparently because even at that time the trade was looked upon with disfavour. Sinqua, who had purchased 1,600 chests, finding that 1,200 other chests had already been imported, and that the market was over-stocked, re-exported most of his to the Malay Archipelago.[2]

During the reign of Kien-lung,[3] and apparently for some time afterwards, opium was included in the tariff at Canton as a medicine, subject to a duty of 3 taels per hundred catties, with an additional charge of 2 taels 4 mace 5 candareens

[1] *Chinese Repository*, vol. v., p. 547.

[2] *Ibid.*

[3] 1736–1796 is the period of Kien-lung's reign.

(2·45 taels),[1] called charge per package. In 1793 the Chinese officials began to complain of the presence of the ships in Lark's Bay, of which, up till then, they had taken no notice. These vessels frequently suffered at the hands of pirates, and had made many attempts to obtain the protection of the Portuguese, who carried on an extensive trade in the drug at Macao. Finding these attempts fruitless, the parties concerned brought one of their ships, laden with nothing but opium, up to Whampoa in 1794, where she remained unmolested for fifteen months with about 300 chests of opium on board. The practice thus inaugurated of bringing Foreign ships having opium on board up the Canton river continued until 1820.

At the close of the eighteenth century the Chinese Government were beginning to view with alarm the extension of the opium traffic, and in 1799, three years after the accession of the Emperor Kiaking, the Viceroy of Canton, Keihking, presented a memorial to the Throne requesting that the sale of opium be prohibited. In 1800 the Emperor forbade its importation under severe penalties, whereupon the supercargoes of the East India Company recommended to the Directors that they should prevent any further shipment, whether in Bengal or England. But the Directors, finding the exportation of opium from India extremely lucrative, were loath to take such strong measures, particularly at a time when the trade at Canton was suffering under excessive impositions. They discontinued, however, the shipment of opium in the Company's ships, and from that time the traffic in the drug was carried on entirely by the private traders. In 1809 the Viceroy, who was then also acting as Hoppo, published a proclamation requiring the Hong Merchants, whenever they presented a petition that a ship might be allowed

[1] A tael is a Chinese ounce of unminted silver. One tael = 10 mace = 100 candareens. There are several kinds of taels in use, all of different weight. The tael in commercial use at Canton in those days was about 1⅓ oz. troy. In 1834 the dollar was worth 4s. 2d., and a tael about 6s. 8d.; silver being at 5s. per oz. See J. R. Morrison, *Chinese Commercial Guide*, p. 62. As to the present-day monetary system in China, see Lord Charles Beresford, *The Break-up of China*, p. 354

to discharge her cargo at Whampoa (this being the customary mode of procedure on the arrival of a merchant vessel), to give bonds that she had no opium on board. He also announced that, as everybody knew that opium was an article of contraband, any vessel found to have infringed the customs' regulations in respect thereto would not be allowed to land her cargo, and would be expelled from the port, while the security merchants who had given a bond in respect of her would be tried for misdemeanour.[1]

This edict was often repeated, by special orders from Peking, but the contraband traffic continued. In 1815 the Viceroy, Tsëang, reported to the Throne that some Chinese trading at Macao, Choomeiqua and others, had been convicted of buying and selling opium, whereupon the Emperor Kiaking issued the following edict :—

" When the Portuguese ships arrive at Macao, it is incumbent to search and examine each ship. And let the Viceroy widely publish a proclamation stating that as opium is an article produced abroad, and from thence flowing into China, and as every region has its usages and climate proper for itself, and differing from others, the Celestial Empire does not forbid you people to make and eat opium, or to diffuse the custom in your native place. But that opium should flow into the interior of this country, where vagabonds clandestinely purchase and eat it, and continually become sunk into the most stupid and besotted state, so as to cut down the powers of nature, and destroy life, is an injury to the manners and minds of men of the greatest magnitude ; and, therefore, opium is most rigorously prohibited by law. Often have imperial edicts been received, commanding a search to be made ; and it is absolutely impossible to suffer you people to bring it, in a smuggling manner, and disperse it by sale. Hereafter, when your ships arrive at Macao, they must all and each be searched and examined. If one ship brings opium, whatever other cargo the said vessel may contain, it will all be rejected ; and all commercial transactions with her

[1] *Chinese Repository*, vol. v, p. 548. This law was not enforced until revived in 1820.

be disallowed. If every vessel brings opium, then the whole cargo of every vessel will be rejected; and none of the ships be permitted to trade; and the ships in the state they come, will be driven out, and sent back to their country. As to you people who live in Macao, since you occupy the territory of the Celestial Empire, you therefore ought to obey the laws and regulations of the Celestial Empire. If you presume without public authority to act and frame rules for yourselves, and cherish schemes approaching near to grasp illicit gains, the laws are prepared to punish you; and just as in the case of those who in China clandestinely promulgate the Roman Catholic religion, they will assuredly severely punish your crimes, and will not show any indulgence. In this manner let an explicit and pointed proclamation be published to the said Foreigners, and no doubt they will every one of them, be afraid and yield implicit obedience, and not dare to oppose the prohibition, and to sell opium. And hereafter let a true and faithful search be made, as before, and so the source from which the evil springs will be cut off." [1]

This edict has the merit of being free from ambiguity as to its meaning. It clearly notified the Portuguese that, so far as Macao was concerned, the importation of opium was absolutely forbidden, and that the Portuguese settlement was not to be used as a means of evading the prohibition contained in the earlier edict. The Peking authorities soon found, however, that the trade continued, and that if it were to be suppressed there must be a more vigorous control of the Foreigners who traded at Canton. Accordingly, in 1818, the Emperor Kiaking published a fresh edict, which was directed to the Viceroy of Canton, laying down general principles to be applied in dealing with the barbarians. Reason was to be employed in the first instance to overcome them, and on no account was a violent demeanour towards them to be assumed. If this treatment proved unavailing, more stringent measures were to be adopted. Military force must be used if necessary, but never in a weak or indecisive

[1] *Chinese Repository*, vol. v., p. 549. As to the edicts against the Roman Catholic religion see *ante*, p. 141, and *post*, chap. xxiv, pp. 551-3.

manner. In this way the English must be made to obey the regulations as to their merchant ships and their naval convoys. The edict did not specifically refer to opium, but was directed against smuggling generally.[1]

Such vague denunciations as these were powerless to stop a traffic which was openly connived at by the officials at Canton. Both at Whampoa and at Macao the illicit trade was carried on without fear of interruption, so long as the many servants of the customs house received their wonted profits, and so long as the officials received a sufficient consideration. In 1820, however, the Viceroy, Yuen and the Hoppo, Ah, took up the subject.[2] They issued a joint proclamation to the Hong Merchants, reciting the imperial edict of 1815, and announcing that in future the law would be enforced and the Hong Merchants held responsible for its infringement. In true Chinese style the existence of the opium traffic was only hinted at. The contraband trade was spoken of as a thing that might possibly exist, and smuggling as a practice confined to a few vagabonds. Still, the proclamation was explicit in its terms, which were as follows :—

"Former proclamations were published, and stand on record ; and since that time four or five years have elapsed ; and it is feared that remissness may have crept in by length of time. It is probable, though not certain, that when the Portuguese ships anchor in Macao harbour, there may be avaricious vagabonds who smuggle opium into the port, and therefore the Macao deputy custom-house officers have been ordered to search very strictly and faithfully. With respect to Whampoa, it is the anchorage of all the foreign ships, and although I, the Viceroy, appoint to each ship an attending officer, and I, the Hoppo, also appoint tide-waiters, who watch the ship on each side, and make due search which seems as strict guard as can be kept ; still the seamen are not all good

[1] It was cited at a later date by Choo Tsun in his memorial against the legalization of the traffic. (*Chinese Repository*, vol. v, p. 394 : see *post*, p. 258.)

[2] This was possibly due to the activity of the Emperor Taoukwang, who ascended the throne in 1820.

men; it is impossible to be sure that they never connect themselves with native vagabonds, and seize opportunities of smuggling. Therefore strict orders are given to all the local military stations, to the deputy officer from the custom-house, and to the armed police at Whampoa, to be very strict in searching; and further, confidential soldiers are sent in all directions to search and seize. Besides these precautions, the Hong Merchants are required to promulgate to all Foreign Factory chiefs resident at Macao or Canton our commands to them, to yield implicit obedience to former imperial edicts, which disallow the clandestine introduction of opium, and which require the sources from which it comes to be cut off. If they dare to disobey this order, as soon as the discovery is made, the ship concerned will be expelled and not permitted to trade, and the security merchant will be seized and punished for the crime; if he dares to connive, he will most assuredly be broken and prosecuted to the utmost without mercy. Be careful, and do not view this document as mere matter of form, and so tread within the net of the law; for you will find your escape as impracticable as it is for a man to bite his own navel. Report the manner in which you execute these orders; and at the same time present a bond engaging to bind by the tenor of this. Delay not!"[1]

In reading Chinese official documents one is frequently struck by the excellence of their language and of the principles that they profess to seek to inculcate. Unfortunately, a closer acquaintance with official life makes us keenly conscious that with the publication of high-sounding phrases the effort to remedy an evil or effect a reform comes to an end. The weakness lies in the fact that no procedure is defined for enforcing the provisions laid down or recommended. In China there is no adequate machinery for the administration of the law, and no direct way of securing the proper discharge of official duties. When anything is ordered to be done, the responsibility of seeing the order carried into effect is delegated from one official to another, till by and by the force of the original command is completely spent in its passage

[1] *Chinese Repository*, vol. v, p. 550.

through the resisting media of various grades of officialdom. Moreover, the Chinese character is such, that any weapon, designed for enforcing a provision, which runs counter to the immediate self-interest of those who have to use it, is apt to become rusty through never being used from the moment of its creation. In other words, every Chinaman is open to a price, whether his rank be high or low, and if he can see in any course of action a chance of pecuniary profit, it takes a very strong application of the law, or any other force, to turn him aside from that course. For this reason, in spite of the Emperor's edicts, the opium traffic continued to be carried on without any attempt at concealment.

Of this edict public notice was given to the Foreign community, but owing probably to the connivance of the junior Hong Merchants it was not at first enforced. In November of 1821, however, the Viceroy wrote to the American consul, Mr. Wilcocks, informing him of the imperial commands, and stating that any ships bringing opium would be expelled from the port and not allowed to trade. As it happened there were at that time four ships at Whampoa with opium on board. This fact was reported by the Hong Merchants to the Viceroy, who threatened the severest penalties that the law would allow, but after some negotiation consented to deal leniently with them on the understanding that thereafter the law would be strictly enforced.[1]

The provision requiring the giving of a bond was from the year 1821 strictly enforced against every ship that came up to Whampoa.[2] The bond had to be signed in duplicate, one being given to the Viceroy, the other to the Hoppo. But a further precaution was taken. The security merchant of the

[1] *Statement of the Claims of British Subjects interested in Opium*, pp. 13–15.

[2] The form of the bond was: "This ship commanded by me has come to Canton with a cargo of . . . With it no opium is brought in the vessel. Should any at a future day be discovered, I will willingly await legal trial and punishment. As is reasonable, I give this bond to be held in testimony hereof." The bond had to be signed by the captain of the vessel. (See J. R. Morrison, *Chinese Commercial Guide*, p. 16.)

vessel concerned was required to sign a separate bond, stating that he had received from the captain an affirmation that there was no opium on board, and solemnly declaring that he had not conspired with the captain to smuggle in opium. This security merchant had further to obtain the guarantee of a Senior Hong Merchant that his statement was correct. Not until the bond was signed could a vessel get permission to unload. The East India Company protested that they could not acquiesce in the punishment of being for ever expelled from the port, if opium should be found on board any of their ships; they promised not to employ their vessels in the traffic at all; and by dint of firm opposition, based on these grounds, they managed to secure exemption from giving the bond. But all private traders were compelled to submit,[1] and the practice continued till 1843.

Just after the edict of 1820 had been published, the Viceroy was constrained to make some show of putting it into practice owing to the following circumstances. There was at Macao a Chinese of the lowest sort, a pettifogging native pleader,[2] the pest and terror of his neighbourhood. This man was the medium through whom the Portuguese paid the bribes, by which the connivance of the authorities at the smuggling carried on at Macao was secured. The cruelty of this wretch is shown by the fact that banditti, hired by him to attack one of his enemies, carried out their instructions by pouring quicksilver into the ears of their captive, so as to injure his head without killing him, and forcing him to drink tea mixed with the short hairs, which had been shaved from his own head. The native pleader had the misfortune in September, 1821, to incur the enmity of one of his official friends, who accused him in such terms to the Viceroy that the latter had him arrested and cast into prison. Immediately on his

[1] J. R. Morrison, *Chinese Commercial Guide*, p. 16.

[2] There are no lawyers, in our sense of the word, in China. No party to a suit or prosecution may appear otherwise than in person. The native pleaders only draw petitions and do such elementary drafting out of court as is possible under Chinese procedure. It is common for a newly-appointed official to publish an edict threatening to punish with beheading any who shall attempt to appear before him as advocates.

arrest he confessed what his occupation had been, and specified the exact sum paid by way of bribery to each of the officials. This confession showed, as the Viceroy must have known, that the corruption was not confined to the inferior officers, but extended to those of the highest rank, including the admiral himself. Statements of this kind could not be ignored, for if news of them reached Peking, without any attempt to punish the guilty having been made, the Viceroy would be in great danger of being degraded. Instead, however, of bringing to justice the real offenders, the Viceroy, in true Chinese fashion, seized on the senior Hong Merchant, who was known among the Chinese as " the timid young lady," as the person to be punished. The fact that the latter was a very rich man probably helped to bring upon him this fate. He was held liable for not carrying out the duties of his suretyship.

The senior Hong Merchant, in spite of his protestations, and notwithstanding his innocence, was forthwith disgraced at the command of the Viceroy, who then issued proclamations throwing all the blame of the contraband traffic on the English, American, and Portuguese merchants. In one of these publications the terrors of superstition were invoked, and the wrath of the infernal gods threatened against the smugglers. The Viceroy's estimate of republican institutions was such, that he attributed the boldness of the American captains to the fact that they had no king to reign over them. Though not attacking directly the Chinese officers who connived at the trade, he sent a spy to watch the revenue cutters, who surprised a party in the very act of smuggling. A struggle ensued in which one or two men were killed. Alarmed at this unlooked-for vigour, and finding that the prohibition of the trade and the giving of the bond were being strictly enforced at Whampoa, the Foreigners engaged in the illicit traffic removed the opium ships to Lintin, an island lying at the mouth of the Canton river, and north-east of Macao, which from that time became the centre of the smuggling trade. There the hulks in which the drug was deposited remained for most of the year, being removed only in the months from June to October, when the more sheltered anchorage of Kapshuy Moon was sought. In

1832 the anchorage of Kumsing Moon was substituted for that of Kapshuy Moon.[1]

From the establishment of the receiving ships at Lintin we may date the beginning of a fresh epoch in the opium trade. Thenceforward it was carried on with an utter disregard of edicts, proclamations, and all other impediments put forward by the Chinese Government in bar of its progress. Year by year the trade increased by leaps and bounds in volume and importance. In 1830 the illicit traffic was extended eastwards,[2] and the drug was cârried into the remote parts of Chih-li and Manchuria. So profitable was the trade that no expense was spared in extending and conducting it. "Opium clippers" were built in England, after the most approved designs, in the best shipbuilding yards and of the best materials, so as to be able to outsail any craft that might attempt to overtake them. These clippers, armed to resist interference, were the means by which the opium was distributed from Lintin to the ports along the coast. The local authorities at Canton, sharing in the immense gains that resulted from this branch of commerce, took no active steps to suppress it. Scenes of lawlessness ensued that the officials were powerless to check, owing to the fact that, being themselves implicated in the traffic, they were fearful that any vigorous action on their part would lead the parties proceeded against to give information at Peking of their own delinquencies. Cases of the shooting of Chinese from the receiving ships occurred in 1831,[3] and again in 1833, but the offenders were never brought to justice. One Englishman boasted in the papers of having set fire to a mandarin's house, but he was never punished. Towards the close of the year 1833, when it was known for certain that the authority of the East India Company was about to expire,

[1] *Chinese Repository*, vol. v, p. 551. The importation through Macao still continued. Until 1823 it was confined to the *moradores*, or citizens, but in that year a regulation was made by the Senate throwing it open to all alike, whether Portuguese or Foreigners, and securing to the latter "hospitality and the utmost freedom in their speculations." (J. R. Morrison, *Chinese Commercial Guide*, p. 27.)

[2] See *ante*, p. 167 (chap. viii).

[3] Auber, *Intercourse with China*, p. 340.

furious affrays occurred with the natives. In one of these which took place at Kumsing Moon, a Chinese was killed. In revenge his fellow villagers seized a Lascar belonging to one of the smuggling ships and put him to death. The ship's people retaliated by organizing an expedition in boats against the village, which they attacked. The Chinese, however, were prepared, and received the attacking party with so heavy a fire that they were obliged to retire. When news of this reached the Canton officials, they were, as usual, afraid to interfere, whilst dreading lest the matter should be reported to Peking. In this dilemma they were assisted by the Hong Merchants, who ingeniously proposed that someone should be hired to confess that he had been the author of the death of the Chinese, a proposal which was carried out by procuring a black man from Macao. On hearing of this proceeding, the Select Committee felt bound to protest against such a course, and a correspondence ensued with the Viceroy, who maintained that the black man had voluntarily delivered himself up.[1] Privately the Select Committee were assured, however, that the hired substitute would not be put to death. In the end he confessed to an offence which was held to be killing by misadventure, and was discharged.[2]

The public conduct of the contraband trade was entirely in the hands of Chinese, excepting in so far as the bringing of the drug to Lintin was concerned. The Foreign merchants did not openly engage in the active smuggling of the drug. On the arrival of a ship containing opium at Lintin, the agent at Canton negotiated a sale to native brokers, called by the Chinese "melters," to whom they handed a delivery warrant, on receiving the price in silver. The broker then engaged boatmen, who went down to the ship and presented the warrant, in return for which they received the quantity of opium specified in it. These boats were fine craft, well manned and armed, and carrying from twenty to thirty oars a side. They were commonly called by the Chinese "fast crabs," or "scrambling dragons." Some of the boats so engaged were

[1] *Chinese Repository*, vol. ii, pp. 513–6.
[2] Davis, *China and the Chinese*, vol. i, p. 110.

in the Government service. When the smugglers came alongside the vessel, their orders were at once attended to; the opium was taken out of the chests in which it was packed, and after examination was removed by the boatmen in matted parcels of a size that could easily be carried off if danger threatened. A fee of one dollar per chest was handed to the commander of the vessel by the boatmen, this being the price paid for the connivance of the revenue officials, who in due course collected it from the commander. In addition, a further fee of $5 per chest was frequently paid to the officers of the vessel, which was divided among them, or handed over to the owners, according to the custom of the particular vessel. In the newspapers at Canton the prices of opium were quoted in the same way as the prices of other imports, the names of the vessels arriving with consignments of the drug were openly announced, and the dealings in the drug chronicled.[1] Having transhipped their opium at Lintin, the vessels bringing it from India then proceeded to Whampoa, to unload the rest of their cargo.

In 1830 the Emperor made a determined effort to eradicate the evil of opium smoking, by enacting the penalty of death against anyone who should open a shop for the indulgence of this habit, and lesser punishments against dealers in the drug and their accomplices. The heinous nature of the offences to which the edict referred, is shown by the fact that responsibility for them was extended, as is often done in China in the case of serious crime, to all the members of the community to which the offenders belonged. The actual words of the provision inserted in the Penal Code were :—

" Those who deal in opium shall be punished according to the law against those who trade in prohibited goods (namely, military stores and weapons). The principal shall wear the cangue for one month and be banished to the army at a near frontier. The accomplices shall be punished with one hundred blows and banished for three years. He who clandestinely opens an opium-smoking shop, and seduces the sons and

[1] *Statement of the Claims of the British Subjects interested in Opium*, pp. 23–4; *Chinese Repository*, vol. ii, p. 467.

younger brothers of free families to smoke opium, shall be punished according to the law against those who delude the multitude by depraved doctrines. The principal, when his crime is proved, shall be strangled after the term of his imprisonment; the accomplices shall be punished with 100 blows and banished 3,000 *li*.[1] And the boat-people, constables, and neighbours shall receive 100 blows and be banished from the province for three years."[2]

This enactment was followed by measures designed to put an end to the smuggling that went on at Lintin. Strict commands were sent to the Viceroy, Li, at Canton, to investigate, consult, and exterminate by cutting off the source of the evil. The Viceroy then issued a proclamation to the Hong Merchants, commanding them to expostulate with earnestness with the barbarians of the several nations, and telling them that they must on no account bring opium concealed in the ships' holds, or appoint vessels to be opium depots at Lintin. If any ships should be found intentionally disobeying this injunction, their hatches should be sealed, their trading stopped, and they should be expelled from Chinese waters. In speaking of Lintin, the Viceroy thus describes the state of affairs at that island:—

"Opium is a spreading poison—inexhaustible; its injurious effects are extreme. Often has it been severely interdicted, as appears on record. But of late the various ships of barbarians, which bring opium, all anchor and linger about at Lintin, in the outer ocean, and exclusive of cargo ships there are appointed barbarian ships, in which opium is deposited and accumulated, and there it is sold by stealth. That place is in the midst of the great ocean, and to it there are four passages and eight communications. Not only do traitorous banditti of this province go there, and in boats make clandestine purchases, but from many places, in various provinces, vessels come by sea, under pretence of trading, to Lintin; and in the dark buy opium dirt, which they set sail

[1] i.e., 1,000 miles.

[2] Clause 14, sec. 225 of the *Ta Tsing Leu Lee* published in the tenth year of Taoukwang; *Chinese Repository*, vol. vi, p. 608.

with and carry off: as for example,[1] from Amoy in Fukien, Ningpo in Chêkiang, and Tientsin in Chihli provinces. And there are native vagabonds, who clandestinely open opium furnaces; then traitorous merchants from outside (or other provinces) first go to Canton shops, and secretly agree about the price; next make out a bond and buy; proceedings which are direct and gross violations of existing prohibitions."[2]

On the 13th of March, 1832, another edict was received from Peking, ordering the Viceroy and his colleagues to take measures for stopping the importation as well as the sale of the drug, and to prevent Foreigners using or having any ships except those employed in legitimate commerce. They were ordered to cut off the source of the trade, so that the evil might be eradicated, and not merely to punish the Chinese implicated in it. It is noticeable that the Emperor, to impress on his officials the urgency of the matter, subscribed with the vermilion pencil[3] the words: "If the said Viceroy and his colleagues can exert their whole mind and strength to remove from the centre of civilization[4] this great evil, their merit will not be small. To strenuousness let them still add strenuousness. Respect this!"[5] The publication of this edict was due to a memorial, which had been presented to the Throne, requesting the total eradication of the evil arising from opium, and describing in very graphic language the way in which the illicit traffic was conducted at Lintin. In this memorial the prevalence of opium smoking throughout the empire was brought to the notice of the Emperor, and it was stated that in all places, cities, villages, market-towns, camps, and stations, private establishments for smoking the drug existed.

[1] The trade to the Eastern provinces was commenced by the voyage of the *Merope* in 1830. It was carried on with the knowledge and connivance of the local officials just as at Canton. A permanent depot for opium was established at Chemoo in Fukien, where the local officials received a fee of 410 taels on every chest sold. One English commander lived there two consecutive years with his wife and family. (*Statement of Claims of British Subjects*, p. 29; Auber's *China*, p. 337.)

[2] *Chinese Repository*, vol. xi, p. 6.

[3] See *ante*, p. 211.

[4] i.e., China.

[5] *Chinese Repository*, vol. xi, p. 9.

Attention was drawn to the fact that some millions of sycee [1] were being exported every year as the price of imported opium, a proceeding of which it was truthfully said: "This is to take the useful wealth of the country and to exchange it for an injurious article from beyond the seas." [2]

Spurred on by the imperial behests the Hoppo Chung, on the 11th of April, 1832, issued a proclamation forbidding the opium ships to remain at Lintin, but with this effort his zeal seems to have come to an end. Not so, however, the imperial authorities at Peking, who, alive to the danger of the Empire, did not cease in their attempts to counteract what they considered a terrible evil. Conscious that the expenditure of money in the purchase of opium was a source of weakness and harm to his country, the Emperor consulted with the Board of Punishments to know what should be done to prevent the efflux of silver. The Board recommended that the penalty for exporting "yellow gold and white silver" should be the same as for exporting rice and other grains, but silver dollars should not be included in the prohibition, as they, being imported silver, could be exported without detriment. Against this recommendation, Hwang Tseotze, censor of the province of Fukien, protested on the ground that silver could easily be coined into dollars by native silversmiths, and thus the whole of the sycee in China might easily be shipped out of the country without detection. For this reason he asked that the coining of dollars be prohibited by law in the same way as the coining of cash. [3]

This question of the export of silver had not arisen before the year 1828. Until then, from the commencement of the European intercourse with China, the balance of trade had always been in favour of the Chinese, so that large quantities of silver, chiefly in the form of dollars, had been imported into the country. This result was very pleasing to them, as they

[1] *Sycee* are lumps of silver cast in moulds and stamped with an official stamp to show their fineness and weight. From their shape they are often spoken of as "shoes" of silver.

[2] *Chinese Repository*, vol. xi, p. 8.

[3] *Ibid.*, vol. ii, pp. 383–4.

imagined that their country was thereby made the richer. The silver thus imported they were anxious to retain, but there had been no need for legislation on the subject before 1829, when for the first time the volume of imports exceeded the exports. The only restriction on the export of silver before 1833 was a local regulation at Canton, promulgated in 1819 by the Viceroy Yuen, to whose edict relating to opium reference has been made above, by which silver was prohibited from being given in exchange for imports, except that three-tenths of the price might be paid in Foreign dollars.[1]

In spite of the vigorous efforts of the officials at Peking to put an end to the opium traffic, the use of the drug spread with the greatest rapidity. Of 1,000 troops taken by the Viceroy in 1832 to operate against the Yaou rebels, 200 had to be sent back as totally unfit for service, owing to opium smoking.[2] Several persons were brought to trial in Yünnan for growing the poppy. The local magistrate tried to acquit them, but was reported to the Throne and degraded. During Lord Napier's stay at Canton, the minds of the officials were occupied with other matters, but this did not prevent them from reporting to the Throne the increase in the trade, which they ascribed to the fact that the Foreigners had "a race of native banditti hooked together with them," and so were able to carry on the illicit traffic in spite of official attempts to prevent it. In reply to this report an imperial edict was received at Canton on the 3rd of November, 1834, commanding that an examination be made after the trading vessels had been sent away, and that if any receiving ships were then found, they should immediately be driven away by the naval forces. It was further directed that two cruisers should be

[1] From 1829 to 1840 the balance of trade continued to be against China, and in that period, so far as can be ascertained, only $7,303,841 worth of silver was imported, whilst there were exported $26,618,815 in foreign silver coin, $25,548,205 worth of sycee, and $3,616,996 worth of gold. In 1833 the exportation of silver was prohibited by imperial edict. (See *Statement of the Claims of the British Subjects interested in Opium*, p. 32.)

[2] *Chinese Repository*, vol. i, p. 31.

stationed among the Foreign shipping, to prevent *tanka* boats[1] and other Chinese craft from approaching them secretly. Any Chinese found resorting to the receiving ships, or smuggling opium, were to be severely punished, and those who detected them rewarded. The Hong Merchants were to inform the English that, if one ship should engage in smuggling, the whole of their vessels would be prohibited from trading. In conclusion, the Viceroy was commanded to keep the barbarians under very strict control, and to maintain strict guard with the revenue cruisers.[2]

About the time that this edict was received at Canton a number of smugglers were captured off Lintin with a considerable quantity of opium, the capture being made by an officer of the Hëang-shan district. In the following February another seizure was made, and it was rumoured that the captured boat belonged to the Viceroy himself. The Foreigners would not believe for one moment that these energetic measures were taken out of a genuine desire to enforce the law, but imagined that they were part of a plan to make the trade in the drug an official monopoly. Whatever the correct reason may have been, the Viceroy kept up the appearance of sincerity by ordering the captured opium to be publicly burned, which was done at the military parade ground on the east side of the city.[2] The Foreign community found it difficult to know exactly what policy was about to be adopted. Before the arrival of Lord Napier it had seemed plain that there would be no interference with the illicit trade, so long as a sufficiently large bribe was paid for official connivance. That the law would be enforced, if the bribe was not large enough, was shown by an occurrence that had taken place in July, 1834, a few days before the arrival of the Superintendents of Trade. Two brokers had refused to pay the Viceroy as large a sum for his connivance as he wished, whereupon a detachment of two hundred soldiers made a descent

[1] *Tanka* boats were small passenger boats, covered with an arched, or egg-shaped, shelter at the stern, whence their name. They were usually propelled by women.

[2] *Chinese Repository*, vol. iii, pp. 487–8.

on their houses. The brokers themselves had absconded, but their families and all their effects were carried off by the troops.[1]

Had Lord Napier's attempt to put the intercourse between the representatives of England and China on a proper footing been successful, it would doubtless have been followed by some investigation of the general conditions under which trade at Canton was conducted, which would have led to the careful consideration of the difficulties arising from the contraband traffic. His untimely death, however, deprived Great Britain of the one man on the spot who was capable of grappling with a question both intricate and requiring an extraordinary amount of care and tact. Up to this time the British Government had in no way condoned the traffic, or behaved with regard to it in any way deserving of censure. Indeed, it is doubtful whether they had any detailed information as to the manner in which it was carried on, as up to this time there had been no occasion for them to investigate the question. So far, Great Britain, as judged by the rules of international law, had behaved with perfect propriety. The modern doctrine, which throws on a state the duty of seeing that its subjects do not commit acts inimical to a friendly power was not then recognized. Even at the present day that doctrine does not apply to offences against revenue laws.

The residence of the Commission at Macao, whither Lord Napier had removed it, involved more than one difficulty of a practical nature. In the first place, all British subjects requiring to have their signatures to documents officially attested had to repair to that port for the purpose. Ships desiring a port-clearance had to anchor at Lintin on their way from Macao, until the necessary papers could be obtained from the office of the Superintendents. Reasons such as these, in conjunction with the feeling that the Commission could better discharge its duties, if outside the pale of the party feeling and factious criticism that was rife at Canton and Macao, led Sir George Robinson to take a step that can

[1] *Chinese Repository*, vol. iii, p. 142.

only be described as astonishing. On the 24th of November, 1835, he proposed to Lord Palmerston that he should make his headquarters at Lintin, stating that such a change was most anxiously desired by the British community as being in their interest. He appears not to have considered what effect would be produced in the minds of the Chinese, if the representative of Great Britain took up his abode in the very midst of the illegal traffic in opium; and without waiting for the sanction of the Home Government, on the 25th November he moved his office on board the cutter *Louisa*, and anchored at Lintin,[1] whence from that time all his despatches were dated, until he laid down his office some twelve months later. That this proceeding pleased the mercantile community would appear from the fact that the Canton Chamber of Commerce formally thanked him for making the change, as it obviated the need of the frequent stoppages, which ships had previously been obliged to make at Lintin, whilst communication was effected with Macao.[2] Nothing could show more clearly how habitually the British community regarded the traffic in opium as a perfectly legitimate branch of trade. How little Sir George Robinson suspected that his residence at Lintin could impair his prestige in the eyes of the Chinese, is shown by the fact that he does not mention such a consideration in the despatch in which some two months later he reviewed the situation. That despatch, dated January 29th, 1836, thus states the altogether inadequate reasons which induced him to take this step:—

"The Chinese seem to have but one object: that is, to prevent our establishing ourselves permanently in Canton. It appears to me, then, injudicious and vain to persist in the endeavour to place ourselves completely in their power and entirely under their control and thraldom, when the very locality of that place alone renders our residence there almost incompatible with the duties we have to discharge, and

[1] By this time the whole of the illicit trade was carried on through Lintin. The exactions of the Chinese officials at Macao had put an end to it at that port.

[2] *Correspondence Relating to China* (Blue Book, 1840), p. 109.

exposes British merchants in a tenfold degree, to inconvenience and danger, arising from our collision with the mandarins. I conceive the principal object of stationing a British authority in this country, is to exercise a salutary control over the safety, conduct, and perhaps property of the king's subjects in China; to arbitrate and assist in the adjustment of disputes and differences; and to prevent the occurrence of actions and proceedings, whereby the natives of China may be wronged or aggrieved; or to the prejudice of that high national character and reputation, which it is so desirable to uphold and maintain even for policy and interest alone.

"To these ends a full and efficient control over the shipping is the main point; little else seems requisite. While that power is retained in our hands and exercised when necessary, with judgment and discretion, little difficulty will exist in the management of other matters. No man can quit the country, or evade the fulfilment of just claims against him; and it cannot be doubted that the knowledge of our ability effectually to interpose our lawful authority, will check those evils which might be expected to result from the total absence of any officer of his majesty's government, unconnected with trade, unbiassed by party feelings, and ever vigilant over the safety, welfare, and bearing of the king's subjects. Feeling somewhat doubtful how far my residence at this anchorage, on board this little vessel of seventy-four tons, in conformity to the public notice under date November 21st, would answer the expectations I had long since formed of its utility and advantage, and being uncertain in what manner the Chinese would view the change of position I had assumed, trifling as it is, I delayed this despatch until the present period when the season is well advanced, and I am competent to speak with confidence and truth, on the efficient means I here possess to discharge at least a most important part of my duty. In this place I shall not enter into any argument on the mischiefs attendant on that disunion and opposition which I fear inevitably results from the existence of a Council or Board of three or more persons, but under the impression that the management of affairs would devolve infinitely better on a single individual, whose views and proceedings, not liable to opposition and counteraction, could be carried into effect on his whole and sole responsibility, I submit, with all due deference, that he should reside on some vessel in the vicinity of the shipping, completely out of the power, and free from the restraints of the Chinese. His situation should be centrical, for general communication, and his means of locomotion entirely unshackled. To this effect, and to afford him a comfortable habitation, I would suggest the purchase or hire of a small merchant vessel (about 200 tons) capable of accommodation for the chief superintendent, a secretary to his office in the event of death or absence, and one or two clerks; sufficient room for a master and crew of about twelve good steady seamen, two of whom might be sworn in as constables, to act as occasion required. Room might also be found for a medical man, whose presence in a large fleet is of the greatest advantage, and a space for the reception of a person under arrest, or whom it may be desirable to take out of his ship. The expense attendant on such an establishment would be trifling indeed, compared with that of the present commission, if permanently fixed at Canton, or elsewhere, and its utility and efficacy, in my opinion, beyond all calculation."[1]

From his post of observation, the Chief Superintendent was able to see how the opium traffic was conducted, and to form some idea of its magnitude. Apparently he became perfectly callous to its existence. On the 4th of February, 1836, he wrote to Lord Palmerston that he apprehended no fearful events from the extension of the trade to the north-east coast, as the scuffles between the smugglers and mandarins in those regions, both parties being engaged in and competing for the traffic, were not more serious or frequent than in the neighbourhood of Canton. Europeans, he said, had not so far been mixed up in any of these affrays, and he thought it was not likely that danger would arise from want of circumspection on the part of those "whose vital interests are so

[1] *Correspondence Relating to China* (Blue Book, 1840), p. 119; *Chinese Repository*, vol. xi, p. 187

totally dependent on its safety and continuance, and by whose prudence and integrity it has been cherished and brought into its present increasing and flourishing condition." If there was any danger that British ships would commit irregularities and crimes, that was a further justification for the establishment of a controlling authority within their midst at Lintin. If directed to prevent British vessels engaging in the traffic, he could enforce an order to that effect, "but," he added, "a more certain method would be to prohibit the growth of the poppy and manufacture of opium in British India."[1]

On the 12th of February, 1836, the newly appointed Viceroy, Tang Tingching, arrived at Canton, and on May 12th in the same year, he was followed by the new Hoppo, Wan. Whether due to the arrival of officials not used to the commercial ways of Canton, or whether due to some other cause, discussion of the opium question now took on a much more active form.

The energy of the Emperor Taoukwang, in exerting himself to suppress the evils induced by the opium traffic, had apparently produced a state of ferment throughout the whole nation. A great controversy arose between two schools of thought, one of which declared that the only cure was to legalize the traffic and so bring it under control, whilst the other maintained that the importation of the drug must be stopped at all costs. Of the former the most conspicuous protagonist was Hü Naitsi, a vice-president of the sacrificial court at Peking, who, having formerly been one of the salt commissioners at Canton, and for a short period in 1834 an acting judicial commissioner in the same province, had in the discharge of his official duties carefully examined into the whole question. The memorial which he presented to the Throne in July, 1836, in favour of the legalization of the traffic, is a remarkable product of the controversy. It is of considerable length, but the arguments advanced may be shortly summarized.

Starting with a brief survey of the legislation against opium, he pointed out that as the severity of the laws had been

[1] *Correspondence Relating to China* (Blue Book, 1840), p. 119; *Chinese Repository*, vol. xi, p. 187.

increased, the number of those who smoked the drug had grown, so that the practice now extended over the whole empire. As a result of the prohibitory enactments opium could only be purchased secretly, and so had always to be paid for in ready money. The annual import now amounted to 20,000 chests,[1] and the consequent waste of sycee that went out of the country exceeded $10,000,000 in each year.[2] Hence had resulted a scarcity of silver, and the tael was worth 1,200 or 1,300 cash, instead of 1,000 as formerly. The salt merchants, who conducted their industry on the basis of a cash currency, were consequently reduced to a state of serious embarrassment.[3] By way of remedy, Hü Naitsi placed before the Throne certain proposals, at the root of which lay the fallacy that, although the outflow of silver paid as the price of imported opium was an evil, the export of an equivalent amount of goods would involve no loss to the nation. He asked that the importation of the drug be legalized; that duty be levied on it as on a medicine; that it be allowed only to be bartered for merchandize, and not to be paid for in money; and that Foreign or coined silver equally with sycee should be prohibited from being exported. He drew attention to the practical difficulties, which were bound to be involved in any attempt to exclude the drug effectually; stating that, although the whole amount imported was brought in English ships, it would be necessary to cut off the whole Foreign trade, a measure that was both unjust to the other Foreigners and would bring ruin upon thousands of Chinese on the sea-board, who subsisted on Foreign commerce; that along so extensive a coast-line as that of China, smugglers could always find some island to which Chinese would resort to purchase the drug in secret; and that

[1] The figures are understated. In 1835–6 more than 26,000 chests were imported, and their value was over £3,000,000.

[2] The three qualities of opium known as "black earth," "white-skin," and "red-skin," sold respectively at $800, $600, and $400 per chest.

[3] Salt is in China a government monopoly under the care of a department known as the Salt Gabel. The monopoly is farmed by a certain number of licensed merchants. The price at which the salt is sold to the public is fixed by the government, and is paid in cash; but the farmers and collectors have to pay over to the government in sycee.

under the pretence of checking smuggling, lawless persons would engage in plunder and extortion, of which frequent instances had come under his notice, when he was acting as judicial commissioner. As to the contention that the increase in the contraband trade was due to official connivance and negligence, he cited instances where the law had been strictly enforced without producing any lasting result whatsoever. As to the physical evils resulting from the opium habit, it was true that of those who used the drug to excess the breath became feeble, the body wasted, the face sallow and the teeth black; that the power to control the habit disappeared;[1] and that the smokers of opium were idle, lazy vagrants, who had no useful purpose before them, were unworthy of regard or even of contempt, and were generally short-lived. "But," he added, with a frankness savouring of cynicism, "new births are daily increasing the population and there is no cause to apprehend a diminution therein."[2]

On the 2nd of July, 1836, the officials at Canton received from the Grand Council at Peking a short edict, issued in response to Hü Naitsi's memorial, commanding them to deliberate and report on the question of the proposed legalization. The Viceroy and Hoppo at once issued an edict to the Hong Merchants ordering them to investigate the matter, and before the end of July the Hong Merchants presented their report. In this document the Hong Merchants were careful to emphasize the necessity that the trade in opium, if legalized, should be conducted through themselves and not placed in the hands of a single individual, as had been suggested. They explained that no exertions on their part could prevent the efflux of silver, and suggested that a proportion of all sycee captured in the course of exportation should

[1] De Quincey, in the *Confessions of an Opium Eater*, gives an account of the struggle he went through in his determination to throw off the habit. He says, "I have struggled against this fascinating enthralment with a religious zeal, and have, at length, accomplished what I never yet heard attributed to any other man—I have untwisted, almost to its final links, the accursed chain which fettered me."

[2] *Correspondence Relating to China* (Blue Book, 1840), pp. 159–62; *Chinese Repository*, vol. v, pp. 138–42.

be paid as a reward to the captors, with a view to encouraging a stricter enforcement of the law. They further stated that the members of the Co-hong were so reduced in means, that they often could not pay even the duties on the goods imported in a season, much less could they lay in a sufficient stock of merchandise in advance, to barter for all the imports brought by the Foreign ships, much of which had frequently to be warehoused to await a market, after being paid for with money borrowed from the Foreigners themselves. In short, they considered the proposal, that each ship should be required to take nothing but export cargo in return for its imports, as "inapplicable, injurious, and impracticable." The question whether opium should be allowed to be imported subject to a duty was one for their excellencies' decision. If the existing law was to be maintained, the officers of the revenue cruisers should be made responsible for any smuggling that took place; the vessels and cargoes engaged in the contraband trade should be confiscated and handed over to the captors; and fresh edicts should be issued to warn the native merchants of the consequences of dealing in the drug.[1]

On the 7th of September, 1836, the Viceroy sent in his report to the Emperor on the proposals of Hü Naitsi, having been assisted in preparing it by the Hoppo and by the financial and judicial commissioners of the province of Kwangtung. In this report the provincial officials pronounced in favour of all the proposals of Hü Naitsi, and proposed regulations which, in their opinion, would serve to mitigate the evils arising from a legalization of the trade in opium. They suggested that, when a vessel was about to leave port, the security merchants should give a bond that she had no sycee on board; that opium should be subject to the same tariff as in the reign of Kien-lung; that only the common people should be allowed to use the drug, and that it should still be prohibited to all government officials, scholars, and soldiers; and that in this way a stigma of inferiority might be made to attach to all smokers of opium, who would thus be shamed into giving

[1] *Correspondence Relating to China* (Blue Book, 1840), pp. 159-62; *Chinese Repository*, vol. v, pp. 385-90.

up the habit. They further recommended that the old regulation, by which three-tenths of the price of imported goods might be paid in foreign silver, should be continued, owing to the difficulty of obtaining a sufficient amount of exports to counterbalance the import trade. In conclusion, they advocated that the restrictions against the growth of the poppy should be relaxed, as this would be the most effective way of shutting out the opium brought by the Foreigners.[1]

The appearance of this declaration of the policy favoured by the provincial officials was followed by the presentation of a memorial to the Throne by Choo Tsun, a member of the Council and of the Board of Rites at Peking, which is undoubtedly the most remarkable document produced by the controversy. It was directly antagonistic to the Viceroy's proposals, and asked that the severity of the prohibitory enactments be increased. Choo Tsun stated his views in the clearest manner. Whenever, he said, an evil exists, it should at once be removed, and the laws should never be allowed to fall into desuetude. The laws are not wanting in severity, but there are those in office who, for want of energy, fail to carry them into execution. The thing to be lamented is instability in maintaining the laws—the vigorous execution thereof being often and suddenly exchanged for indolent laxity. Because a law is sometimes relaxed and becomes ineffectual, that is no reason for its abolition. Neither is the fact that its enforcement has been made the cloak for extortion. When, he asked, have not prostitution, gambling, treason, and robbery, afforded occasion for extortionate underlings and worthless vagrants to benefit themselves? No one suggests that dykes built to prevent floods should be thrown down because they are old and out of repair. Yet the provincial officials think that a law legalizing the opium trade is better than one that does not absolutely prevent it. The fact that the English, by whom opium is sold, have been driven from Whampoa and Macao to Lintin shows what can be done. Having been driven away, should they be invited

[1] *Correspondence Relating to China* (Blue Book, 1840), pp. 163–8; *Chinese Repository*, vol. v, pp. 259–67.

to return? As to preventing the export of silver by insisting that tea be bartered in exchange for opium, there is not much doubt that if sufficient tea were not found, money would still be given in exchange for the drug. Besides, if the exportation of silver could be prevented, why could not the importation of opium? If the importation of opium were stopped, the exportation of silver would cease of itself.

The suggested relaxation in the restrictions on the growth of the poppy were, in Choo Tsun's opinion, useless. People, he said, would always prefer what was strange, and so would buy Foreign opium,[1] just as they bought Foreign broadcloths, camlets, and cotton goods. Besides, the poppy was already freely grown in China. From the provinces of Fukien, Kwang-tung, Chĕkiang, Shantung, Yünnan, and Kweichow, memorials had been presented requesting that its cultivation be prohibited, and in all those provinces, except Yünnan, he could say from his own knowledge the poppy was cultivated over all the hills and in the open country, and the quantity of opium annually produced therefrom could not be less than several thousand chests. Yet there was no diminution in the export of silver; on the contrary, the scarcity in Yünnan was twice as great as it formerly was. The cause of this was that the consumers of the drug were very many, and that those who were choice and dainty with regard to its quality always preferred the Foreign article. The loss to the country that would result from the extensive growth of the poppy was pointed out in graphic language. He said:—

"Those of your Majesty's advisers who compare the drug to the dried leaf of the tobacco plant are in error. The tobacco leaf does not destroy the human constitution. The profit, too, arising from the sale of tobacco is small, while that arising from opium is large. Besides, tobacco may be cultivated on bare and barren ground, while the poppy needs a rich and fertile soil. If all the rich and fertile ground be used for planting the poppy, and if the people, hoping for a large profit

[1] In this anticipation he was correct. To-day, when the cultivation of the poppy in China is allowed, much more opium is imported than was the case in 1836. China herself, however, produces about seven times as much as is imported.

therefrom, madly engage in its cultivation, where will flax and the mulberry tree be cultivated, or wheat and rye be planted? To draw off in this way the waters of the great fountain requisite for the production of food and raiment, and to lavish them upon the root whence calamity and disaster spring forth, is an error which may be compared to that of a physician who, when treating a mere external disease, should drive it inwards to the heart and centre of the body. It may in such a case be found impossible even to preserve life. And shall the fine fields of Kwangtung, that produce three crops every year, be given up to the cultivation of this noxious weed—those fields in comparison with which the unequal soil of all other parts of the empire is not even to be mentioned?"[1]

On the proposal that the use of opium should be forbidden only to the government officials, scholars, and soldiers, Choo Tsun was especially severe. He pointed out that these classes did not comprise more than one-tenth of the population; that the smokers of opium were mainly the relations and dependents of government officials, who would still have full licence to indulge in the habit, whilst an inducement would be held out to those who were free from it to imitate them; that the three classes mentioned were all recruited from the people generally, and if they had contracted the habit before reaching that status, what was to prevent them from continuing it afterwards; and that such a regulation would mean that, if an official secretly smoked opium, his clerks, his followers and his domestic servants would all have it in their power to make his failing their plaything, and by the knowledge of his secret to hold his situation at their disposal. Thus would the door be opened to falsehood and bribery. The discipline of the fathers of families would be destroyed. The rustic population, among whom a law always carries respect, would no longer be deterred by the shame of the thing from giving themselves up to a habit, which hitherto has been regarded as wrong.

In all the documents contributed to the controversy by Chinese writers, the main theme was how to prevent the

[1] *Chinese Repository*, vol. v, p. 393.

impoverishment of the people due to the loss of wealth arising from the opium trade, whether manifested in the export of silver, or in the diversion of agricultural resources to the production of a noxious luxury in the place of products of lasting value. Though the reasoning employed and the principles relied on were not always economically sound, yet it is evident that the economic evil was considered by the Chinese the most important. The Viceroy said in terms that the object, in proposing to repeal the interdict on opium, was to prevent the loss of specie occasioned by the sale of the drug for money.[1] The regulations which he recommended were aimed chiefly at preventing this loss. Hü Naitsi incidentally noticed the physical effects of opium smoking, but did not treat them as most deserving serious consideration. Choo Tsun was the only one who devoted any real attention to the moral effect on the nation. To him this aspect of the question was at least as serious as any other, and he called attention to it in the following passage :—

"To sum up the matter—the wide-spreading and baneful influence of opium, when regarded as simply as injurious to property, is of inferior importance ; but when regarded as hurtful to the people, it demands most anxious consideration ; for in the people lies the very foundation of the empire. Property, it is true, is that on which the subsistence of the people depends. Yet a deficiency of it may be supplied, and an impoverished people improved ; whereas it is beyond the power of any artificial means to save a people enervated by luxury. In the history of Formosa, we find the following passage : 'Opium was first introduced in Kaoutsinne, which by some is said to be the same as Kalapa (or Batavia). The natives of this place were at first sprightly and active, and being good soldiers, were always successful in battle. But the people called Hung-maou (Red-haired) came thither, and having manufactured opium, seduced some of the natives into the habit of smoking it ; from these the mania for it rapidly spread throughout the whole nation ; so that, in process of time, the natives became feeble and enervated, submitted

[1] *Chinese Repository*, vol. v, p. 262.

to the foreign rule, and ultimately were completely subjugated.' Now the English are of the race of Foreigners called Hung-maou. In introducing opium into this country, their purpose has been to weaken and enfeeble the Central Empire. If not early aroused to a sense of our danger, we shall find ourselves ere long on the last step towards ruin."[1]

Following close on that of Choo Tsun, another memorial against the legalization of the traffic reached the Throne. This was presented by Hiu-kiu, a sub-censor over the military department. He, too, dwelt on the scarcity of silver, which had now further appreciated, so that a tael was worth 1,400 or 1,500 cash. He stated that one method of evading the law against the export of sycee was to pretend that money had been left on deposit at Canton by the captain of some ship, which had visited the port a few years earlier, which money had to be repaid owing to the depositor's death. Frequently the name of the ship and of the captain were purely fictitious. The Hong Merchants would then present a petition in favour of the deposit being returned, and thus obtain official sanction to the export of sycee. He estimated the value of the annual import of all Foreign goods at $20,000,000,[2] and the total revenue arising therefrom at one million. He disagreed with those who advocated the cutting off of the whole Foreign trade at a moment's notice. The export of silver would not, he declared, be prevented by legalizing the importation of opium, as could be seen from the fact that the Spanish ships, which brought rice into Canton from Manilla, openly took silver away in payment. Notwithstanding all the imperial prohibitions, there had been only one case of late years of the capture of a boat containing opium. Strict regulations must therefore be made for the punishment of offences ; and then in turn attention must be directed to the natives who sold the drug, the Hong Merchants who arranged the transactions, the brokers who purchased

[1] *Chinese Repository*, vol. v, pp. 393–4.

[2] Apparently there had been an appreciation in value, for he takes the value of the best opium at from 800 to 900 dollars per chest, and the inferior quality at from 500 to 600 dollars per chest.

wholesale, the boat people who conveyed it, and the naval officers who allowed it to be smuggled, on all of whom must be inflicted the severest punishments of the law. The Foreigners, who had been engaged in the trade, should be treated at first with clemency, until they should have had time to send the receiving ships away, but after that they, too, should be visited with the full penalty of the law, namely, death. The passage in which the last proposal was made was thus worded :—

"The treatment of those within having been rendered severe, we may next turn to these resident Foreigners, examine and apprehend them, and keep them in arrest ; then acquaint them with the established regulations, and compel them, within a limited period, to cause all the receiving ships anchored at Lintin to return to their country. They should be required also to write a letter to the king of their country, telling him that opium is a poison which has pervaded the Inner Land, to the material injury of the people ; that the Celestial Empire has inflicted on all the traitorous natives who sold it the severest penalties ; that with regard to themselves, the resident Foreigners, the Government, taking into consideration that they are barbarians and aliens, forbears to pass sentence of death on them ; but that if the opium receiving ships will desist from coming to China, they shall be indulgently released and permitted to continue their commercial intercourse as usual ; whereas, if they will again build receiving vessels and bring them hither to entice the natives, the commercial intercourse granted them in teas, silks, etc., shall assuredly be altogether interdicted, and on the resident Foreigners of the said nation the laws shall be executed capitally. If commands be issued of this plain and energetic character, in language strong, and in sense becoming, though their nature be the most abject—that of a dog or a sheep—yet having the care for their own lives, they will not fail to seek the gain and to flee the danger.

"Some think this mode of proceeding too severe, and fear lest it should give rise to a contest on our frontiers. Again and again I have revolved this subject in my mind, and reconsidered how that, while in their own country no opium is smoked, the barbarians yet seek to poison therewith the people of the Central Flowery Land; and that while they bring us no foreign silver, they yet would take away our native coin; and I have therefore regarded them as undeserving that a single anxious or careful thought should be entertained on their behalf."[1]

To this memorial was attached a supplementary statement, describing the way in which Foreigners resident at Canton were concerned in the opium traffic. Nine names were given as of Foreigners so implicated. Of these, eight were British subjects, their names being Jardine, Dent, Innes, Turner, Whiteman, Framjee, Merwanjee, and Dadebhoy, the last three being Parsees. As soon as the memorials of Choo Tsun and Hiu-Kiu had reached Peking, the Emperor published an edict stating that the memorials had been received, and commanding the provincial officials to search for and apprehend "all those traitorous natives who sell the drug, the Hong Merchants who arrange the transactions in it, the brokers who purchase it by wholesale, the boat-men who are engaged in transporting it, and the marines who receive bribes." He further directed them to report on the steps that should be taken "to stop up the source of the evil" and to ascertain and report whether the charges made by Hiu-Kiu against Foreign residents were true.[2]

The appearance of this edict was the outward and visible sign that the anti-opium party had prevailed in the imperial counsels. Another sign was the banishment of Hü Naitsi to Tartary.[3] For once and all the Emperor had resolved to do his utmost to stamp out the use of opium in his dominions, and from that resolve Taoukwang never went back, though it involved him ultimately in war with Great Britain. The Viceroy Tang realized that the day had come when a real attempt to enforce the commands of the Emperor must be

[1] *Chinese Repository*, vol. v, p. 402; *Correspondence Relating to China* (Blue Book, 1840), pp. 173–8.

[2] *Chinese Repository*, vol. v, p. 405; *Correspondence Relating to China* (Blue Book, 1840), p. 178.

[3] Davis, *China and the Chinese*, vol. i, p. 125.

undertaken. From this date a fresh period begins in the opium traffic, a period of unrelenting opposition on the part of the Chinese Government to the continuance of the trade in any form. The Foreigners, however, did not believe that any change had taken place, and continued to engage in the contraband traffic without anticipating any untoward consequences, lulled into a false security by the knowledge that the imperial commands had for so many years been disregarded at Canton.

On October 23rd, 1836, the Viceroy issued a proclamation to the Hong Merchants, ordering them to make inquiries concerning Jardine ("the iron-headed old rat") and the other Foreigners mentioned in Hiu-Kiu's memorial, as to where they resided, of what nation they were, in what manner they continued stationary in Canton and stored up opium, from what year the commencement of the opium transactions dated, what quantity of the drug they annually stored up and disposed of, and whether they ordinarily insisted on payment of the price of it in silver. Why the particular names mentioned by Hiu-Kiu should have been chosen does not appear. Some of those were persons who were only slightly connected with the contraband traffic, whilst many others, who were deeply implicated, were left unnoticed.[1] In due course the Hong Merchants made their report, and on the 25th November, 1836, the Viceroy astonished the Foreign community by ordering all the persons named in Hiu-Kiu's memorial to leave Canton within half a month. Relying on the letter of the existing regulations, which in practice were never regarded, he asked why these Foreigners stayed continuously at Canton when they were forbidden to do so by law, and pointed out that they were not legally entitled to remain even at Macao. He asked what was the use of the Hong Merchants, if there was any force in the Foreigners' plea that their business made it necessary for them to reside continuously at Canton. He then ordered them in the most explicit terms to leave the port, whether they were implicated in the opium traffic or not, and forbade them to

[1] *Chinese Repository*, vol. v, p. 406.

remain even at Macao, justifying his action on the ground that the imperial commands were strict.[1] In the same month orders were issued that in future the anchorage at Kumsing Moon would be closed to Foreign ships.[2] None of these injunctions were taken by the Foreigners as meant seriously, and the proscribed merchants continued to carry on their business at Canton as usual.

[1] *Correspondence Relating to China* (Blue Book, 1840), pp. 182–5.
[2] *Chinese Repository*, vol. v, p. 336.

CHAPTER XIII

THE POLICY OF CAPTAIN ELLIOT

WHILST the controversy as to legalization of the opium traffic was being agitated among the Chinese, Sir George Robinson remained at Lintin, quietly pursuing the policy of quiescence, which had been inaugurated by Davis on the death of Lord Napier, and waiting in vain for further instructions from his Government. His stay in the vicinity of the opium hulks was not, however, one of untroubled tranquillity, for very shortly after his removal thither he found his authority again challenged by British subjects, who wished to enter upon a course of action of which he disapproved. The occasion of this difficulty was the arrival of the first steam vessel intended for use in Chinese waters, which certain Europeans, who had suffered much from the delays involved in getting from Macao to Canton by the ordinary passage boat, had introduced from Europe for the purpose of carrying mails and passengers between those two places. This small vessel, called the *Jardine*, whose dimensions were 85ft. length, 17ft. beam, and 6ft. draught, had arrived from Aberdeen under canvas on the 25th of September, 1835. Her machinery having been put together and installed at Lintin, she was ready to undergo her steam trials in the following December.

To avoid any trouble that might arise among the native population on the appearance of so unexpected a phenomenon as a self-propelled ship, a letter was addressed to Howqua, the Senior Hong Merchant, apprising him of the intention to use the *Jardine* on the Canton river, and to bring her up to the Factories. In this letter the new vessel was described as capable of moving against wind and tide, her measurements were given, and the purpose for which she had been brought out was carefully explained. It was further stated that she was not fitted with defensive weapons of any kind, and a general invitation was extended to the Chinese officials to make a personal inspection before she attempted to proceed up the river. The sending of this letter produced the very opposite effect from what was intended. The Chinese officials were thrown into a state of the greatest consternation and alarm. Edicts were issued to the Hong Merchants commanding them to expel the strange craft immediately, and ordaining that thenceforth " boats with holds and standing masts carrying flags " should never more be used.

Sir George Robinson, anxious to preserve the state of quiet which he so much favoured, was fearful that the contemplated voyage of the *Jardine* would lead to further complications between the Viceroy and himself. He therefore intimated to the owners, who had resolved to take her up to Canton in spite of the official prohibitions, that such a proceeding would be directly contrary to his wishes. Finding his remonstrances were unheeded, he wrote to Lord Palmerston to inquire whether his powers did not authorize him, as Chief Superintendent, to prevent the vessel from being used in the manner proposed. Long before he could possibly receive a reply, the *Jardine*, on the 1st of January, 1836, attempted to steam up the river. The Chinese, however, were determined that it should not be supposed that she did so with their approval. When she arrived off Chuenpi the little craft was met with a tremendous artillery fire, all the forts joining in the bombardment. Fortunately most, at any rate, of the guns were not shotted, so no immediate harm was done. Amidst the firing the captain of the *Jardine* sent a boat ashore to invite the military and naval officers to come and inspect the object of their warlike operations. Having made inquiries of the minutest character, they accepted the invitation, and came on board with an escort of about 100 soldiers. Reassured by a careful examination of the engines and fittings of the vessel, and failing to discover any cause for alarm, the Chinese admiral requested that his war-junk might be attached to the steam-boat and towed up and down the Bogue, a request that was promptly complied with, to his infinite delectation. Convinced by this signal proof of the harmlessness of the new product of European skill, he expressed his personal willingness to allow her to proceed, but stated that as his orders were peremptory that she was not to go up, he had no choice in the matter. Finding it useless to attempt to pass the Bogue, the captain was obliged to take her back to Lintin. It was not for some time that the panic which had prevailed on shore finally subsided, the Chinese forts and fleet keeping up a cannonade and firing rockets throughout the night.[1]

In addition to difficulties of this nature, the Chief Superintendent had to face dissensions among the members of the Commission itself. It was assumed at Canton that as no replies were received from the Foreign Office to the Chief Superintendent's despatches, that the policy of quiescence was approved among his Majesty's Ministers. Far different was the view taken by the British mercantile community in China. They openly complained of the inactivity of the Chief Superintendent and condemned his policy of keeping things quiet.

Captain Elliot, who had previously shown a disposition to take his own course, wrote on the 25th of January, 1836, a letter to Lord Palmerston stating plainly that the peaceful and conciliatory policy, by which the British Government appeared to desire to maintain and promote commercial intercourse with the Chinese, was not very generally approved among the fifty or sixty resident merchants at Canton, and that a determination to give it effect, so far as he himself was concerned, was the least popular task he could propose to himself.[2] Having initiated the practice of communicating direct, instead of through his chief, with the Foreign Secretary, the Second Superintendent, on the 14th of March, in the same year, again laid before Lord Palmerston his views on the situation, and suggested that the arrival of the new Viceroy afforded a good opportunity to the Commission to re-open communication with the Chinese officials through the Hong Merchants, that being, in his opinion, the only channel that would ever be open to them without what he regarded as a very hazardous and needless struggle. His view was that

[1] *Chinese Repository*, vol. iv., pp. 436–8.
[2] *Correspondence Relating to China* (Blue Book, 1840), p. 136.

if they once obtained a footing at Canton in this way, and conformed heartily to the spirit of their cautious and conciliatory instructions, they could soon make themselves so indispensable to the Chinese authorities, that the latter would not merely admit, but court direct communication with them.[1]

At a later date he proceeded in the same way to lay his views on the contraband trade before the Government. On the 27th of July he wrote to Lord Palmerston, discussing the legalization of the opium traffic, which he expected would result from the presentation of the memorial of Hü Naitsi. In this letter he said it was a confusion of terms to call the opium trade a smuggling trade, for though it was formally prohibited, there was no part of the commerce of China which had the more active support of the local authorities ; it had commenced and subsisted by means of the hearty connivance of the mandarins, and it could have done neither the one nor the other without their constant countenance. The proposal to legalize the traffic was a stroke aimed not at smuggling but at all trade carried on outside Canton, and was due really to the "tea and tract missions," which had engaged the anxious attention of the Court. So long as the Lintin trade was conducted quietly, the high officials had made no objection, though naturally averse to its extension to the coasts of neighbouring provinces. The memorial of Hü Naitsi was a public confession that the Chinese could not do without our opium. The regulation of the introduction of the drug in such a way as would render it least injurious to the policy of foreign exclusion was a skilful measure, but of questionable efficacy. The change had been delayed too long. Officers and people had become accustomed to the feeling that the government was false and feeble. Sooner or later, the feeling of independence engendered among British subjects in China would lead to grave difficulties. A long course of impunity would beget hardihood, some gross insult would be perpetrated, and the Chinese, terrified and irritated, would commit some act of cruel violence that would make armed interference imperative. The immediate effect of legalizing

[1] *Correspondence Relating to China* (Blue Book, 1840), p. 138 ; *Chinese Repository*, vol. xi, p. 138.

the growth of the poppy in China, he thought, would be to stimulate production in India, though eventually native opium would probably thrust ours out of the market.[1]

For some curious reason Captain Elliot had come to the conclusion that the proposed legalization of the opium traffic was certain to become an actuality within a very short period of time. It is difficult to know why he should have formed this opinion, unless it be that he gave too much credence to the Hong Merchants, who hoped that this profitable branch of trade would be made an acknowledged part of their monopoly. As early as August, 1836, they notified Innes that as soon as opium became dutiable there would be no need of the receiving ships at Lintin. Vague reports reached Canton from time to time that a policy of legalization had been resolved upon at Peking, but Captain Elliot himself tells us that little credit was attached to these rumours, though confessing that he was one of the few persons who thought they were well founded.[2] Even the presentation of the memorials of Choo Tsun and Hiu-Kiu did not make him waver in this belief, and on the 10th of October, 1836, he wrote to Lord Palmerston a letter discussing in the most sanguine strain the orders that were expected soon to arrive from Peking. He spoke of legalization as the most remarkable step which had been taken in respect to the foreign trade since the accession of the reigning dynasty, comparing it with the closing of the ports to Foreigners, which he erroneously supposed had taken place contemporaneously with the Manchu conquest.[3] Regarding this important change in the commercial policy of the Empire as virtually accomplished, he avowed his conviction that it wanted but steadiness of purpose to secure at no distant date important relaxations in other directions.[4]

[1] *Correspondence Relating to China* (Blue Book, 1840), pp. 137–8.
[2] *Ibid.*, p. 153.
[3] In this Captain Elliot fell into a common error, which has been repeated right down to modern times. The preceding pages show that it was Kienlung who confined the Foreign trade to Canton, and that before that date the difficulties in the way of the English trading at other ports were not due to the action of the authorities at Peking.
[4] *Correspondence Relating to China* (Blue Book, 1840), p. 138.

In December of 1836 several despatches of importance from England reached Macao. Lord Palmerston had at length broken the long silence of the Foreign Office, which, excepting the Duke of Wellington's despatch of the 2nd February, 1835, had remained uninterrupted since the departure of Lord Napier from London. One of these despatches, dated May 28th, 1836, announced that the jurisdiction of the Commission had been extended to Macao and Lintin, so far as British subjects were concerned. Another dealt with the question of the residence of the Commission at Lintin, a proceeding which Lord Palmerston refused to sanction, on the ground that his Majesty's Government were not in possession of sufficient information to enable them to form a final opinion on the merits of Sir George Robinson's plan. No censure was passed on the Chief Superintendent for the course he had taken. On the contrary, it was stated, that he was not to understand that the Government disapproved of his having resided there. At the same time, it was announced that, for reasons of economy, the Government had long intended to reduce the China establishment, though they did not quite know what form that establishment would ultimately take; they had resolved, however, that the office of Chief Superintendent should be abolished, hoping thus to put an end to the differences between the members of the Commission. Sir George was therefore requested to hand over all official papers to Captain Elliot, who would, from the date of the receipt of the despatch, consider himself the chief of the Commission.[1]

Captain Elliot, who now became the chief representative of Great Britain in China, was a nephew of the first Earl of Minto, and originally an officer in the Royal Navy, which he entered in 1815, at the age of fourteen. He served in the East Indies and on the coast of Africa, and in June, 1822, was appointed to the *Hussar* on the Jamaica station as lieutenant. He attained post rank in 1828, from which date he ceased to be actively connected with the service. From

[1] *Correspondence Relating to China* (Blue Book, 1840), pp. 111–4; *Chinese Repository*, vol. xi, pp. 188–195.

1830 to 1832 he was Protector of Slaves in British Guiana. In 1834 he was sent to China with Lord Napier as master attendant to the Commission. Thus it will be seen that he had no special training or experience that particularly qualified him for the post to which he was now appointed. The cutting down of the China establishment was due to a desire for economy, and it was no doubt thought that it would be cheaper to retain Captain Elliot as chief of the Commission at the same salary as he had received whilst Second Superintendent, than to appoint someone of more diplomatic experience who would require a higher remuneration. Later on, in a despatch dated the 8th of November, the final plans of the Government were made known. In future there was to be a Superintendent and a deputy Superintendent. The former post was to be held by Captain Elliot, the latter by A. R. Johnston. All salaries, except that of the Superintendent, were reduced, the surgeon's office was abolished, and the amount for contingent expenses reduced from £5,000 to £2,500.[1]

In another of the despatches which arrived in December, 1836, which was addressed to Captain Elliot himself, Lord Palmerston expressed the view that the Superintendent of Trade had no power to prevent the owners of the *Jardine* from using that vessel on such voyages as they might please, and recommended him to use great caution in interfering with the undertakings of British merchants, warning him not to assume a greater degree of authority over British subjects in China than that which he in reality possessed. In a third despatch, also directed to Captain Elliot, Lord Palmerston dealt with the suggestion that communication with the Chinese officials should be re-opened through the Hong Merchants. Of this proposal the Foreign Secretary expressed the strongest disapproval. His instructions to Captain Elliot on this point were conveyed in unequivocal language. He said :—

"I have to observe to you that it does not appear expedient to His Majesty's Government, that it would be expedient that

[1] *Correspondence Relating to China* (Blue Book, 1840), p. 130. Altogether a saving of £14,500 per annum was effected.

you should attempt to re-open communications with the Viceroy through the Hong Merchants, but on the contrary it is desirable that you should decline every proposition to receive official communications through that channel, whatever may be the quarter from whence such propositions may come. It might be very suitable for the servants of the East India Company, themselves an association of merchants, to communicate with the authorities of China through the merchants of the Hong ; but the Superintendents are officers of the King and as such can properly communicate with none but officers of the Chinese government. This is a point on which you should insist ; and I have therefore to instruct you, if any attempt should be made by the Hong Merchants to enter into communications with you upon matters of public business, to express your regret that you are not at liberty to receive any such communications, except from the Viceroy direct, through some responsible officer of the Chinese government. I have to add that His Majesty's Government do not deem it expedient that you should give to your written communications with the Chinese government the name of *Petitions*." [1]

It is evident from Captain Elliot's letter, to which this was a reply, that he thought that if he could once get into communication with the Chinese officials at all, he could by mere force of circumstances gradually and silently make his services so acceptable to them that they would soon receive him on a footing of equality with themselves. Such an opinion betrays great ignorance of the Chinese character, but it seems to have been honestly held. Indeed, so confident was Captain Elliot that his opinion was right, that he completely disregarded the prohibitions contained in Lord Palmerston's despatch, and on the very day of its receipt put himself in communication with the Hong Merchants, in order that no time might be lost in demonstrating the efficacy of his scheme. Before doing so, however, he wrote to Lord Palmerston on the 14th of December, 1836, acknowledging the honour conferred upon him in being made chief of the Commission, and outlining

[1] *Correspondence Relating to China* (Blue Book, 1840), p. 123; *Chinese Repository*, vol. xi, p. 189.

the policy he intended to pursue as the British Superintendent of trade, in these words :—

" I have this day assumed the chief place in the Commission. And with the expression of my thanks to your Lordship, I beg to convey my assurance that I shall endeavour to justify the appointment by a steady determination faithfully to discharge the duties entrusted to me. I apply myself to that purpose with a strong persuasion that a conciliatory disposition to respect the usages, and above all, to refrain from shocking the prejudices of this government, is the course at once most consonant with the magnanimity of the British nation, and with the substantial interests at stake, in the maintenance of peaceful commercial relations with this empire. Being thus impressed, my lord, I hope it will be a source neither of surprise nor dissatisfaction to you to learn that I do not propose to protract the actual interruption of our public communications upon the ground that we have a right to a direct official communication with the Viceroy. I will only add, that the very remarkable movements of this government, in respect to the foreign trade actually in agitation, and the critical state of uncertainty in which the results still remain, furnish me with a strong additional motive for desiring to place myself at Canton as soon as possible.

" The manner in which I propose to re-open the communications with the Viceroy, as the Select Committee was wont to conduct them, shall form the subject of an early despatch to your Lordship." [1]

Captain Elliot is here referring to his expectation that the opium traffic was about to be legalized, an expectation in which he was to be grievously disappointed. The probability of the Chinese officials seeking the co-operation of the Superintendent, in the event of such legalization taking place, was extremely small, and Captain Elliot, in regarding such a development in the situation as within the realm of practical politics, was singularly at fault in his judgment. Even if his plan were likely to meet with all the success he hoped, it

[1] *Correspondence Relating to China* (Blue Book 1840), p. 139 ; *Chinese Repository*, vol. xi, p. 196.

was one that ought never to have been adopted. The price at which he proposed to secure official recognition was far too high. It meant an admission by the accredited representative of Great Britain of inferiority to a Chinese Viceroy. This admission, it is evident, Captain Elliot was willing to make. He addressed a communication to the Viceroy announcing his appointment, and asking, as any ordinary trader would have done, for a passport allowing him to come up to Canton. This communication was in form a petition, it was superscribed with the character *Pin*, and it was presented through the Hong Merchants. Thus was thrown away at one stroke of the pen everything for which Lord Napier had contended. The language employed towards the Viceroy was of the most deferential kind, as appears from the following translation, all this being part of the plan by which Captain Elliot hoped the Chinese officials would be induced to receive him on a footing of equality :—

"The undersigned has the honour most respectfully to announce to his excellency the governor of the two provinces, that he has this day received despatches from the English Government appointing him to the station of chief English authority in China. In the actual condition of circumstances, with no English authority at Canton, and with great numbers of English ships in the river, having on board many hundreds of sea-faring persons and others, little acquainted with the laws and customs of this empire, the undersigned believes his excellency will be of opinion that he should be permitted to repair to Canton with as little delay as possible, for the purpose of fulfilling the duties confided to his management. The undersigned has therefore the honour to request that his excellency will be pleased to issue orders to furnish him with a passport to proceed to the provincial city. In using his most earnest efforts to maintain and promote the good understanding which has so long and so happily subsisted between this ancient and great empire and his own distant country, the undersigned can assure his excellency that he is only conforming to the strong instructions of his own government. The undersigned hopes he may permit himself to observe, in this place, that no task could be more agreeable to his own disposition than the duty of diligently seconding these wise objects, by the sincerest personal desire to conciliate the goodwill of his excellency. The undersigned has once more to offer his excellency the sentiments of his most profound respect, and will conclude with the expression of an ardent hope that his excellency's administration of these provinces may be long and prosperous."[1]

The Viceroy's reply is a manifestation of that seeming complaisance, which the Chinese official loves to use towards those who humiliate themselves to gain his favour, seeking to inspire the belief that he is inclined to grant their request, but knowing full well in his own mind that nothing is farther from his intention. A knowledge of the Chinese character would show that this is but a device for prolonging the state of humiliation from stage to stage, until the suppliant shall have been reduced to a state of absolute degradation. No thought of yielding what is asked under these circumstances ever enters the official mind. Captain Elliot's experience was only a particular instance in conformity with the general rule. In response to the "Petition" the Viceroy appointed officers to investigate, who were instructed to interview Captain Elliot personally, and promised to report the result to the Throne. He condescended to approve of Captain Elliot's attitude thus :—

"If on examination no covert purpose appear, then let orders be immediately enjoined on the said Foreigner to reside for a time at Macao, and wait there till I, the Viceroy, shall have sent in a memorial to the great Emperor. And as soon as I shall learn his Majesty's gracious pleasure, I will then address a communication to the superintendent of maritime customs, calling on him to grant a passport for the said Foreigner to come up to Canton, and oversee matters. When he thus comes up, he must comply with the old regulations, having a residence at Canton and another at Macao, and coming and

[1] *Correspondence Relating to China* (Blue Book, 1840), p. 142; *Chinese Repository*, vol. xi, p. 196.

going at the regular seasons. This is a law and ordinance of the Celestial Empire. The phraseology and subject matter of the said Foreigner's address are reverential and submissive. It seems that he understands matters and he will, therefore, doubtless be implicitly obedient in all things. During the residence of the said Foreigner, for the present, at Macao, the local officers should still keep a diligent and faithful watch on him, day and night; and they must not allow the said Foreigner to presume to leave Macao a single step, or to hold any communication or intercourse with people unconcerned. This is of the utmost importance. With trembling anxiety obey this, and oppose it not. A special order."[1]

Captain Elliot construed this edict as showing that an advance had been made towards establishing official intercourse on a footing of equality. Having signified to the Viceroy with what pleasure he had answered the inquiries of the officers deputed to interview him, and his intention of remaining at Macao until the Emperor's pleasure should be known, he wrote to Lord Palmerston a long despatch informing him of the course of events. From this document it is clear that the writer thought he had achieved a great diplomatic triumph. Had he been acquainted with the previous history of diplomatic intercourse with China,[2] he would have known how unlikely it was that his policy of seeking to propitiate the Chinese officials would meet with success. He was aware that the mode of communication, which he had employed, was that used by an inferior to a superior, as appears from the despatch, in which he relates to Lord Palmerston that he had used the character *Pin;* but that he had no conception that his policy was ill advised, is clear from the passage in which he thus justifies his conduct :—

"I have thus, my lord, once more opened the communications with this government; and I sincerely trust your lordship will see no reason to disapprove of my motives, or

[1] *Correspondence Relating to China* (Blue Book, 1840), p. 145; *Chinese Repository*, vol. xi, p. 198.

[2] See chap. vi, *ante*, p. 103.

of the manner of my proceeding. I have acted under a strong persuasion that all hope of peacefully carrying the point of direct official intercourse was futile; that the actual condition of circumstances was hazardous; that the instructions in my hand do not warrant the assumption that I have any high political or representative character; and, finally, that the course itself which I have pursued is neither derogatory to the national honour, nor at variance with sound principles of public propriety and utility."[1]

On the 20th of January, 1837, the Viceroy presented to the Throne a memorial reporting on the events to which reference has just been made. In this document he first gave a short epitome of the history of the relations between the English and China, then went on to describe the recent behaviour of Captain Elliot in asking to be allowed to come up to Canton, and finally recommended that the necessary permission be granted. An examination of this memorial fails to reveal any sign that the new policy had produced on the Viceroy any of those effects which the Superintendent of Trade had anticipated. There is no suggestion that Captain Elliot should be received on a footing of equality. He is described as a Foreigner who has "received credentials from his country appointing him to the general control of merchants and seamen," and it is proposed that he should be allowed to come to Canton just in the same way as, and in no other way than, the supercargoes of an earlier time. The Viceroy's estimate of his position is summed up in the words: "Though he is not precisely the same as the chief supercargo hitherto appointed, yet the difference is but in name, for in reality he is the same. And after all he is a Foreigner, to hold the reins of Foreigners; and, if not allowed to interfere in aught else, it would seem that an alteration may be admitted; and that he may be permitted to come to Canton and to direct

[1] This despatch was dated 30th Dec., 1836. He wrote again in January, 1837, and enclosed an extract from Dr. Morrison's Dictionary, translated by Gutzlaff, explaining the meaning of the word, and that Lord Napier had refused to use it. *Correspondence Relating to China* (Blue Book, 1840), pp. 139–142, 148; *Chinese Repository*, vol. xi, pp. 198–201.

affairs, according to the same regulations under which the chief supercargoes have hitherto acted."[1]

In reply to this memorial the Emperor issued an edict adopting the course suggested by the Viceroy and allowing the "said Foreigner" to repair to Canton "under the existing regulations applicable to chief supercargoes." He was to reside sometimes at Macao and sometimes at Canton "conforming to the old regulations"; he was not to be allowed to "loiter about" and gradually effect a continuous residence; and he was to be held responsible for the control of affairs, so that all disturbance might be prevented.[2] As soon as this edict was received at Canton, it was communicated by the Viceroy to the Hoppo, who on March 18th, issued a special edict of his own, incorporating that of the Emperor, and commanding the Hong Merchants to enjoin upon Captain Elliot the imperial "commands." This edict, received through the Hong Merchants, was acknowledged by the Superintendent on the following day, when he sent a note to the Viceroy assuring his excellency that it was at once his duty and his anxious desire to conform in all things to the imperial pleasure, and stating that he would "heedfully attend to the points adverted to" in the various edicts. On the 12th of April, 1837, Captain Elliot and his suite proceeded to Canton under the passport which had been furnished to him, and the Commission took up its residence in the provincial city after an absence of nineteen months.

By a despatch dated the 1st of April the Superintendent informed Lord Palmerston of the result of his efforts to re-open communication with the Chinese authorities. He described the imperial edict, which had granted permission for him to come to Canton in terms which expressly placed him on the same level as a supercargo, as "a very formal and unequivocal recognition" of his character as a British officer, and he further stated that no attempt had been made to evade the material distinction between his own position and that of the chief

[1] *Correspondence Relating to China* (Blue Book, 1840), pp. 151–2; *Chinese Repository*, vol. xi, pp. 242–4.

[2] *Chinese Repository*, vol. v, p. 527.

servant of the East India Company, or of any other Foreign functionary previously allowed to reside at Canton. He admitted that the communications of the authorities intended for him spoke " of " him and not " to " him, but he proposed to conform to instructions so conveyed, whenever he could conveniently do so. He hoped that when the Viceroy should find such communications rejected when points of importance had to be discussed, as might happen if he, Captain Elliot, were so minded, then some fresh means of intercourse would be devised.

How little progress had been made towards a proper understanding with the Viceroy is shown by an incident, unimportant in other respects, that happened just at this time. Some Chinese had been rescued from shipwreck by an English vessel homeward bound from Canton, and had been landed at Pulo Aor under an arrangement by which they were to be sent to Singapore. In informing the Viceroy of this occurrence, Captain Elliot referred to the many acts of kindness experienced by Englishmen at the hands of Chinese under similar circumstances, adding the words : " The interchange of these charities cannot fail to strengthen the bonds of peace and goodwill between the two nations." The Viceroy at once showed that he did not intend to be cajoled into any such barbarian exchange of civilities as betokened equality, and issued an edict laying down the principles which were at the root of all intercourse with Foreigners. He pointed out with some sternness that Captain Elliot had failed entirely to conform to the old rules in presenting such a document, and that in using such expressions as " your honourable country," and " peace and good-will between the two nations," he was guilty of an absurdity due to his own puffed-up imagination. He required the Hong Merchants to tell the Superintendent that he was to conform implicitly to all that was called for by the dignity of the Celestial Empire, and to render his expressions thoroughly respectful, in order that appropriate commands might be given in reply. In future all addresses intended for the Viceroy must be first perused by the Hong Merchants, who were to reject any that contained unsuitable language, and if any such address as that of Captain Elliot were again presented, they would be held personally responsible. How, asked the Viceroy, can there exist between the Emperor and "the small, the petty," anything like bonds of peace and goodwill ? [1]

An edict such as this could not be allowed to pass unnoticed, if Captain Elliot were to preserve any semblance of dignity. He at once wrote to the Viceroy saying that, though he could not presume to question the authority of the latter to issue such orders as he thought fit to the Hong Merchants, it was impossible for him to submit his addresses to their censorship. He further stated that under the circumstances he must cease to forward any "addresses," and that in future he could only receive official communications which were under the Viceroy's seal, and addressed directly to himself. In reply to this the Viceroy made a trifling concession, and instructed the Hong Merchants that the Superintendent might in future seal petitions from himself to the Viceroy, but must continue to forward them through the senior member of the Co-hong, whilst communications from the Viceroy would continue to be made in the same manner as before. This was Captain Elliot's opportunity to make a bold stand, but he at once gave way and wrote saying that he was humbly of the opinion that he would best evince his profound respect for the rules of the Empire by continuing to carry on the communications in the manner prescribed by the Viceroy, until further instructions should reach him from England.[2] When this correspondence was brought to the knowledge of Lord Palmerston he immediately forbade the continuance of official intercourse under such conditions. His prohibition, however, did not reach Captain Elliot until November, 1837, so for practically a whole year the British representative addressed petitions to the Viceroy superscribed with the character *Pin*, and

[1] *Correspondence Relating to China* (Blue Book, 1840), pp. 202–3; *Chinese Repository*, vol. xi, pp. 248–9.

[2] *Correspondence Relating to China* (Blue Book, 1840), p. 205; *Chinese Repository*, vol. xi, pp. 249–251.

received in reply "commands" communicated through the Hong Merchants in the form of edicts.[1]

Whilst these matters were being agitated the Viceroy had not relaxed his efforts to carry out the imperial commands with regard to the opium trade, as laid down in the edict of the 28th of October, 1835, to which reference was made in the last chapter. He kept on pressing for the departure of the Foreigners who had been prescribed in that document and showed such persistency that the foreign community at Canton began to fear that he might be in earnest. And not only against Foreigners were his efforts directed. Many natives engaged in smuggling were hunted out and exterminated. A striking incident took place on the 2nd of January, 1837, when Aming, a *linguist* who had been seized and tortured on a charge of aiding and abetting the export of fine silver, was brought in procession out of the city gate by an armed escort and placed with his neck in the cangue at the entrance to Howqua's hong. Having remained there in that condition for two days, he was taken away and placed for a similar period outside each of the hongs in turn, still wearing the cangue. By vigorous action of this sort the Viceroy, in the course of two or three months, worked a complete change in the conduct of the opium traffic, which it was evident would be killed if the viceregal efforts were left unchecked. At that time the amount of opium annually imported had reached the value of $18,000,000, and exceeded by $1,000,000 the total value of the teas and silk shipped on British account. Hence the enforcement of the prohibition with regard to the export of silver produced a stringency of money that resulted in complete commercial stagnation. The new crop of opium was due to arrive from Bengal towards the end of March, and it was plain that if the traffic were not legalized before that date a financial and commercial crisis must arise. Moreover, if the active measures of suppression were continued over that time, collisions between the smugglers and the revenue cruisers were bound to ensue.

[1] *Chinese Repository*, vol. xi, p. 264.

Captain Elliot, as appears from his despatches to Lord Palmerston, quite appreciated the gravity of the position, and in evolving his official policy he found himself forced to consider what in future was to be the attitude of the British Superintendent of Trade to the contraband traffic. On this subject he was entirely untrammelled by any instructions from his Government, and so had a perfectly free choice in deciding what line of conduct to mark out for himself. The choice that he made was not a wise one. Hitherto, as has already been explained, Great Britain as a nation had in no way abetted the contraband trade carried on in Chinese waters. It is true that that trade was mainly in the hands of British subjects, but no official countenance had been given to it in any shape or form by the British Government. Sir George Robinson's action, in taking up his residence at Lintin, was likely to be construed by the Chinese as an overt act showing an intention to give the receiving ships his official protection, but there is no evidence to show that his conduct in removing thither was prompted by any such motive. It was left to Captain Elliot to make the first advance in the direction of putting the opium traffic under the protection of the British Government. Having come to the conclusion that visits of British men-of-war to Chinese waters would have the effect, either of producing a relaxation of the restrictions which were being enforced by the provincial officials, or of hastening onwards measures of legalization, and so in one way or the other stimulating a revival of trade, he on his own responsibility wrote to the Governor-General of India and to the Commander-in-Chief of the British naval squadron in Indian waters, saying that at Canton there was a " pressing necessity " for naval assistance and asking that men-of-war be sent forthwith.[1] After taking this decisive step, he wrote to Lord Palmerston on the 2nd of February, 1837, discussing the position of the contraband trade, and enclosing copies of the memorials of Hü Naitsi, Choo-tsun, and Hiu-kiu, the Hong

[1] The inference that Capt. Elliot intended to protect the opium trade is supported by the language used in his own letters. See *Correspondence Relating to China* (Blue Book, 1840), pp. 210–1.

Merchants' report, the Viceroy's edict, and the imperial edict ordering investigation to be made into the facts alleged by Hiu-kiu.

The review of events contained in this despatch enables us to ascertain with tolerable clearness the state of mind of the Superintendent of Trade. Having remarked that the admission of opium might still be looked for, and that the system of law-breaking had been carried on under the sanction of the Emperor,[1] and with the connivance of the provincial officials, he said there was little reason to believe that Hü Naitsi's memorial would ever have been published, still less that the policy it recommended would have been worked out, if there had been "no more urgent incentives to its adoption than are to be found in the awakening spirit of public virtue upon the part of the Chinese Government." He stated that no portion of the trade of the country had more regularly paid its entrance than this, and the least attempt to evade payment of the fees of the mandarins was almost certain to be detected and severely punished. He added that a large share of these emoluments reached not merely the higher dignitaries of the Empire, but in all probability, in no very indirect manner, the imperial hand itself.[2] He attributed the proposal to legalize the opium traffic firstly to the political disquietude of the Court at the extension of Foreign trade to the north-eastern provinces, and secondly to the alarm felt at what was considered to be the irrecoverable disappearance of the real wealth of the country given in exchange for opium, and observed that the appearance of missionaries along the coast in 1835 and 1836 was, in the eyes of the Chinese, connected with the opium traffic. He prophesied that the counsels of those who advocated what was politically expedient would prevail over adverse reasoning founded on high principles

[1] This charge of connivance against the Emperor is entirely unsubstantiated. Apparently it rested entirely on a rumour, which Lindsay and Gutzlaff had heard when in the North, that opium was smoked in the Court at Peking. A more unsatisfactory basis of fact, than a rumour among the Chinese of what goes on in the Forbidden City, can hardly be imagined.

[2] There is no evidence to be found in support of this charge.

and remote mischief. The imperial edict, which had been published on the receipt of Choo Tsun's and Hiu-kiu's memorials, he regarded as "conclusive proof" that legalization had been determined upon.[1]

The writing of this despatch was contemporaneous with the appearance of an edict from the Grand Council at Peking, urging the Viceroy and Hoppo to take still more stringent measures to prevent the export of silver, and the circulation of a report that the Viceroy had been ordered to deliberate with regard to a duty to be levied on opium. It is absurd to suggest that the repeated imperial edicts against opium were due to the extension of the trade to the North-East, seeing that they commenced thirty years before the *Merope* first carried opium eastwards of Canton, which voyage was made more than ten years after the receiving ships had been driven to take refuge in the outer waters at Lintin. The suggestion, that the Emperor connived at the trade and received a direct profit therefrom, is contrary to every inference that may be drawn either from his public acts up to this time, or from subsequent developments in the imperial policy. Captain Elliot was right, however, in saying that the chief ground of hostility to the opium trade was the economic one; but that the moral objection had some weight, would appear from the fact that it was the presentation of Choo Tsun's memorial, in which this objection was for the first time urged at all strongly, which turned the scale against the party in favour of legalization. The Superintendent's anticipations as to the course of future events proved to be entirely erroneous.

A few days later Captain Elliot wrote to Lord Palmerston another despatch, dated the 7th of February, discussing the question of the proscribed merchants, on whose departure the Viceroy was urgently insisting. The objection to their proscription, as stated to the Foreign Secretary, was not that they were innocent, but that if the expulsion was allowed to be carried out it would produce great alarm among those who had invested capital in the trade at Canton. For this reason Captain Elliot avowed his intention to take active measures

[1] *Correspondence Relating to China* (Blue Book, 1840), p. 15.

GATE OF THE IMPERIAL CITY AT PEKING, WITHIN WHICH IS THE FORBIDDEN CITY

to protect them, if their dismissal from the country were attempted. From this one might infer that Captain Elliot regarded the opium traffic as worthy of the protection of the British Government, and his later policy strongly supports such a view. But if this was his opinion, it was not so firmly held as to be maintained with unswerving constancy, for on the 21st of March he again wrote to Lord Palmerston discussing the position of the trade generally, and pointed out that it could not be good that the conduct of a great trade should be so dependent, as was commerce at Canton, upon the steady continuance of a vast prohibited traffic in an article of vicious luxury, high in price and liable to frequent and prodigious fluctuation. In this letter he enclosed a copy of an imperial edict, dated January 26th, 1837, which had been recently received at Canton, utterly prohibiting the export of sycee.[1]

Whilst Captain Elliot was negotiating with the Viceroy on the question of re-opening official communication, the agitation with regard to the opium traffic continued, but did not occupy the attention of the provincial authorities so exclusively as it had before those negotiations were initiated. But when the Superintendent and his staff had arrived in Canton, the Viceroy again exerted himself towards the suppression of the illicit trade. In June, of 1837, an edict was issued forbidding the employment of decked boats as passage boats between Macao and Canton, it having been discovered that these vessels were being used for conveying opium up the river.[2] It was found that the smugglers of the drug no longer relied on Lintin as a sole distributing centre, but were bringing large quantities up to Whampoa, and even to Canton itself. In June, too, the *Raleigh*, one of the sloops of war attached to the British naval squadron in the East Indies, made her appearance under the command of Captain Quin, in response to the requests made by Captain Elliot to the Governor-General of India and to the naval commander-in-chief in the preceding February. Immediately on the arrival of Captain Quin in Chinese waters, Captain Elliot wrote to him

[1] *Correspondence Relating to China* (Blue Book, 1840), p. 191.
[2] *Chinese Repository*, vol. vi, p. 103.

pointing out that some British subjects, Lascars belonging to the crew of the brig *Fairy*, which had been wrecked off Fukien, were being detained in that province, and suggested an expedition to the river Min to request that they be released. In this letter the Superintendent confessed that he had no fears or anxiety as to the safety of these Lascars, but he thought that if such an expedition were made, and the request or demand granted, the effect on the officials at Canton would be "to help the uninterrupted progress of gradual relaxation" at that port and to impress them with the necessity of treating Foreigners with moderation and circumspection. Two days after receiving this letter, Captain Quin sailed for the river Min. In reality there was no reason for the *Raleigh* to make this expedition, the wrecked Lascars having been treated with the greatest consideration by the Chinese.[1] Captain Elliot's object was to induce the Viceroy of Foochow to communicate with Captain Quin by letter, and to use this as a ground for claiming that a similar means of intercourse should be employed between the Viceroy of Canton and himself.[2]

Owing to the request which had been made to the naval Commander-in-chief for protection, that officer wrote to the Lords of the Admiralty, that he should like some direction as to whether the instruction which had been issued, forbidding naval vessels to go to China, should be altered, and whether he himself should proceed to Canton. The Lords of the Admiralty communicated with Lord Palmerston on the matter, and on the 20th of September the latter embodied his views in a letter addressed to them in reply. In this letter he ordered that the existing instruction be cancelled, that in future one or more ships of the East India squadron, preferably a frigate, should visit the shores of China as frequently as possible, and that the rear-admiral himself should repair to Macao in a line of battleship to confer with the Superintendent on the situation. The object of this change in naval policy was stated to be that weight might be given to any representations

[1] *Chinese Repository*, vol. vi, pp. 201–7.

[2] *Ibid.*, vol. xi. pp. 253–5; *Correspondence Relating to China* (Blue Book, 1840), pp. 211–212. Gutzlaff, who went as interpreter, joined an American ship at the Loo-choo Is. and visited Japan. His report is set out in the Blue Book at pp. 223–230.

that the Superintendent might be under the necessity of making, in case any British subject should have cause of complaint against the Chinese authorities. The officers and men of naval vessels visiting Chinese waters were to be particularly cautioned to do nothing that would offend the susceptibilities of the Chinese. On the other hand, the use of such ships in defending British "property" was openly contemplated, and as the only British "property" which had so far been threatened was opium, the inference is that Lord Palmerston had at this time under consideration a policy of protecting the contraband trade by armed force.

Whilst the Foreign Office in England was arranging this change of policy with the Admiralty, the British representative at Canton was being required in no uncertain terms to send away the opium-receiving ships. The Viceroy, in a series of edicts[1] commencing on August 4th, instructed the Hong Merchants that the Emperor's will necessitated the utmost diligence on the part of the local authorities in repressing the contraband trade, and that they must issue orders to Captain Elliot that thenceforth no opium be imported. He stated that the King of England had theretofore been dutiful and respectful, and had sent Captain Elliot to hold a check on British subjects, lest their conduct should bring shame on their country. He therefore complained that although he had a month before commanded the receiving ships to leave, the Superintendent had taken no steps to see that his commands were obeyed, and he required Captain Elliot to report the matter to his sovereign in order that the receiving ships might be prevented by the British Government from coming to Chinese waters. To these edicts Captain Elliot returned answer that he knew an extensive trade was carried on outside the limits of the port, but as he only saw the papers of the ships which arrived within the port, he was without any means of knowing which of the ships that resorted to the outer anchorages were British, what was the nature of their pursuits, whence they came, or whither they went.[1] As an excuse

[1] *Chinese Repository*, vol. xi, pp. 257–262; *Correspondence Relating to China* (Blue Book, 1840), pp. 234–240.

for not reporting the matter to his sovereign, he put forward the fact that the imperial wishes had not been communicated to himself in a proper form, but by an edict addressed to the Hong Merchants. When it is borne in mind under what circumstances the official intercourse had been renewed, it is difficult to find any defence for the position thus taken up by the Superintendent. His own explanation to the Viceroy was, that in his ordinary intercourse he had deferred to that mode of intercourse, because the Viceroy had informed him that it was in accordance with the customs of the Empire, but in the transmission of messages to the King of England, it was necessary that the customs of England should be observed. At the same time he mentioned that the visit of the *Raleigh* to Fu-kien had resulted in the Viceroy of that province communicating direct with Captain Quin, and that if the Viceroy of Canton would conform to the same practice, all difficulty upon the subject would be removed.[1]

It is not surprising that the Viceroy characterized Captain Elliot's reply as "a specious document." Considering the matter of vital importance, the Chinese officials expressed their willingness to "adapt their proceedings to the occasion," determined that the Superintendent should have no excuse for not laying their views before the British Government. On the 29th of September, 1837, the prefect and chief military officer, acting under the Viceroy's instructions, issued a lengthy document under their seals direct to Captain Elliot, in which the imperial commands were set out at length, the failure of Captain Elliot to carry out previous commands was detailed, and fresh instructions were issued that the Superintendent should require the receiving ships to return home, and report the matter to his sovereign in order that they might never return. In the clearest terms it was intimated that if the opium ships were not withdrawn they would be treated with the utmost rigour of the law.[2]

Captain Elliot replied on the 17th of November that he

[1] *Chinese Repository*, vol. xi, p. 259.

[2] *Ibid.*, pp. 259–262; *Correspondence Relating to China* (Blue Book, 1840), pp. 237–240.

would transmit this document to his Government in the quickest possible manner. He added that the existence of any other than the regular trade had never been submitted to his sovereign, that the state of things described in the document he had received could not be heard without feelings of concern and apprehension, and that he hoped a sure and safe means of remedying a hazardous state of things would be speedily devised. He then wrote to Lord Palmerston describing the pitch to which the illegal traffic had attained, and expressing the opinion that the time had arrived when the British Government should interfere. He proposed that Queen Victoria (who had recently succeeded to the throne) should address a letter to the Emperor and send it by a special commissioner to Chusan, there to confer with officers deputed by the Court at Peking to deal with the matter. The Superintendent admitted that the opium traffic had so increased that there were no less than twenty vessels engaged in it on the coast of Fu-kien; that blood had been spilled in the affrays which were taking place between the revenue boats and the smugglers; that the vigilance of the authorities had led to a change in the manner of conducting the trade in the vicinity of Canton, it being now carried on in passage boats, belonging to British owners and slenderly manned by Lascar seamen; that the shipping at Whampoa was implicated in an increasing degree; and that if the Chinese authorities discovered that the ships, which gave a bond that they had no opium on board, were engaged in the illicit trade, "very embarrassing consequences" would ensue. He pointed out that the corruption prevailing among the officials was no guarantee that the law would not in future be enforced, and that in any case the carriage of so valuable a commodity as opium in small quantities invited piratical attacks and made the outbreak of another Ladrone War[1] a perfectly probable event.[2]

Two days after the Superintendent had thus reported to

[1] As to the Ladrone War, see Davis vol. i, p. 68 and *ante* p. 142.

[2] *Chinese Repository*, vol. xi, pp. 263–4; *Correspondence Relating to China* (Blue Book, 1840), pp. 241–2.

the Foreign Office, he received from Lord Palmerston a despatch dated 12th of June, 1837, setting out the Foreign Secretary's views on the plan of communicating with the Chinese officials through the Hong Merchants, and under the superscription *Pin.* Lord Palmerston instructed Captain Elliot forthwith to inform the Hong Merchants and the Viceroy that the British Government could not permit their officer to hold communications with an officer of the Chinese Government through the intervention of private and irresponsible individuals, to request that in future all official communications be sent to him direct, and to explain that his written communications would not thenceforth be superscribed with a character denoting inferiority, as the usages of England did not permit of such a method of communication.[1] These instructions were so clear and emphatic that Captain Elliot was forced to adopt at once a new mode of communication. On the 23rd of November he sent a document to the Viceroy superscribed with Chinese characters meaning "presented before the high place" instead of the usual *Pin.* The Viceroy, having opened and read it, wrote across it with his own hand in Chinese, "Cannot be permitted." Thereupon the Superintendent sent a second communication to the Viceroy, superscribed in the same way as the last, and explaining that in changing the style of address he was acting under the strictest instructions of "one of the great Ministers of his nation." The Viceroy replied by an edict issued to the Hong Merchants, which Captain Elliot refused to receive. A third attempt was made by the Superintendent to hold communication on a footing of equality, but in vain.[2] On the 29th of November he addressed a letter to the British residents in China informing them of the instructions received from his Government and the refusal of the Viceroy to receive his communications. On the 2nd of December he struck his flag and retired from Canton. Thus came to an end the long era in which the relations between England and China had

[1] *Chinese Repository*, vol. xi, p. 252; *Correspondence Relating to China* (Blue Book, 1840), p. 149.

[2] *Correspondence Relating to China* (Blue Book, 1840), pp. 246–8.

been based on the assumption that the Chinese were entitled to be regarded as a superior nation.

Captain Elliot was not even at this time disillusioned. He wrote to Lord Palmerston that his right to receive sealed communications direct from the Viceroy had been conceded in the clearest possible manner. Doubtless he was thinking of the exception made by the forwarding of the document of the 29th of September requiring him to send away the receiving ships and report on the matter to his sovereign. He told Lord Palmerston that on his departure from Canton it was easy to perceive that the Viceroy was prepared to communicate with him direct, if only he would waive the proposed change of superscription. He apparently did not perceive that in such a waiver was involved an abandonment of everything that the dignity of Great Britain demanded should be retained. In conclusion he expressed his conviction that a letter from the Foreign Secretary to the "cabinet" at Peking, written by Her Majesty's command and sent to the mouth of the Pei-ho by a ship of war, would at once draw from the Emperor an order for the concession of what was demanded on this point.[1] This optimistic opinion was never acted upon, and as events turned out, the right to communicate on terms of equality was only conceded after war had been waged and the treaty of Nanking negotiated.

[1] *Correspondence Relating to China* (Blue Book, 1840), p. 249; *Chinese Repository*, vol. xi, p. 265.

CHAPTER XIV

HONG MERCHANTS IN BANKRUPTCY

THE two great questions—official intercourse and the opium question—that were in dispute between the English and the Chinese at Canton when Queen Victoria ascended the throne of England, were in themselves sufficient to lead to hostilities. In addition to these there was a third question, of hardly less importance, that though little considered nowadays, largely contributed to the rupture between the two nations that ultimately occurred. This third source of difficulty was the monopoly of the Hong Merchants and the financial troubles arising from the existence of that monopoly. The discussion of this third question was not attended with any of those dramatic incidents that marked the controversy with regard to the other two, but in vital importance to the mercantile community it ranked at least as high as they. In earlier times there had been trouble arising from the occasional insolvency of a member of the Co-hong. Now the whole body of Hong Merchants was on the verge of bankruptcy, and some were suspending payment of their debts.

The opening of the trade at Canton to all British subjects alike was bound to lead to fundamental changes. It meant that in future not merely agents but principals would be the acknowledged representatives of the commercial interests of the British community, men who would be fettered by no such necessity of maintaining the trade at all hazards as had hampered the supercargoes of the East India Company. It very soon happened that independent British merchants residing at Canton began to rebel against the old-time restrictions on their commercial and personal liberty. For a few years, indeed, they submitted, induced so to do by the profits of the trade. But self-respect and regard for the good name of their country quickly asserted themselves and produced a state of discontent, that was certain to pass sooner or later from the smouldering stage. In short, the position in the year 1837 was that the British merchants found the conditions of commercial intercourse intolerable, the British Government found the conditions of diplomatic intercourse intolerable, and the Chinese found the opium traffic intolerable. In such a case there must be either a re-adjustment of relations or war.

The British merchants would probably have been content to obtain the relief they desired by an honourable arrangement with the Chinese, involving, if need be, a change with regard to the opium traffic. The British Government knew not what it wanted. Thus far it had only laid on Captain Elliot strict injunctions not to carry on official intercourse under the old style of petition, or to receive edicts issued to the Hong Merchants. No instructions had been given to the Superintendent as to what he was to demand of the Chinese authorities, who, so far from offering to make concessions, were becoming more overbearing every month. They refused to receive the British representative on such a footing as would make discussion possible; they professed themselves utterly indifferent to the continuance of the trade; and stoutly maintained that such liberty of commerce as had been allowed to the Foreigners was a concession made to barbarians by the commiserating tolerance of a superior civilization. It must be admitted that the situation was such as to leave the British Government in great perplexity. That, however, is a poor excuse for the policy of drift that was in fact adopted. The experience of English statesmen in sending embassies was hardly such as to lead them to try that expedient again. Their obvious course was to strengthen their position at every opportunity with the object of compelling the Chinese Government, by diplomatic means if possible, and by other means if necessary, to institute those changes which the well-being of the British traders and our national interests required.

In the midst of the controversy as to the opium traffic, and as to the mode of official intercourse, the evil conditions under which the trade was being carried on were brought into prominence by the bankruptcy of a Hong Merchant who traded under the style of the Hing-tai Hong. The nominal head of this hong was one Yen-Kechang, but the active management of its affairs was in the hands of his brother, Yen-Ketsëang. Early in 1837 their affairs were found to be in a most unsatisfactory condition, the liabilities being estimated at £200,000. The Foreign creditors, unable to obtain payment, found themselves face to face with some of the evils of the existing commercial system in a very disagreeable form.

In considering questions of Chinese law it is necessary to remember that in China political, and especially legal, ideas have not been developed to the extent with which we are familiar in England. To find a European analogy to the state of things which prevails in China at the present day, we should have to go back to the state of Rome at the time of the promulgation of the Law of the Twelve Tables, or even at an earlier date. Such civil law as obtains is of a very meagre kind. There is no commercial law as we know it. There are no schools of law or legal text-books : there is no legal profession ; there are no trained judges ; apart from the records of certain criminal trials there are no reported cases.[1] All is uncertainty and confusion. Bribery and corruption reign side by side with the grossest ignorance in such courts as are held. There is no law of bankruptcy at all in China : there is no statute of limitations. Once a debt always a debt may be taken as a fundamental conception of Chinese jurisprudence. There are no adequate means of obtaining payment of debts. The elaborate provisions designed by the English Law of Bankruptcy in the interest of creditors, have never been dreamed of by the Chinese. And even if they had, they would be unworkable in the present state of the national

[1] " Enquiry and research have failed to discover the existence of any code which governs or controls the decisions of Chinese tribunals in civil cases. Commercial disputes are submitted commonly for the arbitration of Chinese guilds ; and Chinese magistrates are believed to evolve out of their inner consciousness principles applicable to cases that are brought before them for decision."—Letter from the China Association to the Foreign Office. See *North China Herald*, 6th November, 1899.

character. The creditors of the Hing-tai Hong, at a loss for a means of enforcing payment of their just demands, resolved to lay the matter before the Viceroy, and accordingly, on the 21st April, 1837, they presented to that official a very temperate and business-like petition setting out their grievances. The hopelessness of such a proceeding was probably apparent to them at the outset, but, having no other remedy, they were willing to test the value of the only procedure open to them. On the 23rd April, the Viceroy, Tang, replied in a characteristic edict, full of high-sounding phrases, but affording little consolation to the creditors, which was thus worded :—

"I have examined the subject and find that heretofore Hong Merchants have always been forbidden to incur debts to Foreigners, and that in repeated instances on record they have been severely punished for so doing. And with regard to Yen-Kechang, of the Hing-tai Hong, he has been in the situation of Hong Merchant barely seven years, and has he in so short a time accumulated debts to the large amount of a million and upwards of dollars ? What degree of bad management must it have been that could run to this extent ! The thing is too absurd—too extravagant !

"If this matter be not faithfully and completely settled, where will be our compassion to Foreigners, and how shall we prevent similar and even worse conduct in future ? I issue therefore this order. When it reaches the said senior Hong Merchants, let them, in obedience to it, immediately convene a meeting of all the Hong Merchants, and examine the accounts of Hing-tai, to ascertain clearly what are the real sums owing by the hong to Foreigners ; and let them equitably and earnestly apply themselves to make some arrangement for the settlement thereof. Within ten days, let them send a joint report on the subject for my consideration. If they dare to regard this lightly, or to delay, and overstep the period, I, the Governor, will maintain the laws firmly as the solid mountains, and will assuredly direct the district magistrate to close the Hing-tai Hong, and, according to the law, apprehend the merchant, that he may be closely examined and punished. At the same time, the said senior Hong Merchants, together with all the other Hong Merchants, shall alone be held responsible. The property of the Foreigners cannot be left without an ultimate guarantee for its safety."

Though well aware of the futility of the measures suggested, the creditors went to work on the lines laid down by the Viceroy, but without avail. For two months they attempted to obtain some sort of satisfaction from the Hong Merchants, but the best reply they could get was: "Hing-tai has not finished his accounts, and objects to the sums claimed by Foreigners."[1] A second address was therefore presented to the Viceroy showing that the creditors had taken the steps recommended by him, but with no useful result.[2]

On the 23rd June, 1837, the Viceroy ordered Howqua, Mowqua, and Pwankequa, three of the Hong Merchants, to examine Yen-Kechang and see that he made out a clear and true statement of all debts owing by the Hong, and to report to himself in the matter. The statement sent in as a result of this order did not agree with the creditors' estimate of $2,850,000, and showed an utter ignorance of the affairs of Hing-tai. The creditors, therefore, on the 1st July, again petitioned the Viceroy, to the effect that a statement had been communicated to them by the Hong Merchants, in which all the accounts were disputed and objections raised apparently with no other object than to delay a settlement.[3] This drew from the Viceroy an edict dated 7th July, 1837. The whole series of edicts in connection with this matter is a splendid illustration of the exasperating methods of Chinese when faced with a difficulty. There is the inevitable appeal to "old custom," with a repetition of the orders that had already been found futile, coupled with delay after delay in enforcing those orders. In his reply to the creditors' second petition the Viceroy said that he had investigated the matter, and ascertained that balances of purchase money due for goods could not be classed under the same head as balances of borrowed money. The Hongs had, from time immemorial,

[1] *Correspondence Relating to China* (Blue Book 1840), p. 263.
[2] *Ibid.*, p. 263.
[3] *Ibid.*, p. 264.

been governed by precedents, which determined where interest was allowed and where it was not. He had compared the statements of the barbarian traders Jardine, Dent, and others with that of Yen-Kechang, and they differed widely, so that he was unable to decide which were reliable. He therefore ordered the senior and junior Hong Merchants to give their whole minds in conjunction with the two parties to examine the accounts and come to some suitable arrangement.

On the 17th July the creditors again petitioned the Viceroy, as literally nothing had been done towards a settlement, either of the accounts or of the terms of payment. The Viceroy promptly replied that the "barbarian traders" must wait till Yen-Këtseang made his appearance, when they must, in conjunction with the senior Hong Merchants and the two brothers, give their whole minds to the just and equitable settlement of the accounts and to determining the exact sums due. He admonished them not to throw impediments in the way of a settlement by their impatience, and plainly told them that they would reap no advantage by constantly presenting petitions.[1]

On receipt of this proclamation, the creditors adopted a sterner tone towards the Hong Merchants, and asked to be informed what steps they were taking to fulfil the Viceroy's orders. The only reply vouchsafed was that the requests in the letter were "of so weighty and deliberate a nature that we cannot reply to them without mature deliberation."[2] At the same time the Hong Merchants requested Messrs. Archer, Dent, and Green, on behalf of the creditors, to meet with them for examination of the accounts of the Hing-tai Hong. The request was granted, and these three, with Howqua, Mowqua, and Pwankequa, formed a committee of investigation, of which the first meeting was held at the Consoo House, on the 25th July, 1837. The examination of the accounts seems to have been unfruitful of any proposal for payment. On the 6th September, another petition was presented to the Viceroy, in which the creditors said that

[1] *Correspondence Relating to China* (Blue Book, 1840), p. 266.
[2] *Ibid.*, p. 267.

they could obtain no satisfactory reply from the Hong Merchants with respect to the liquidation of the debts. More procrastination by the Viceroy was the only result of this proceeding.

After this the Hong Merchants proposed to pay off the debts of the Hing-tai Hong in fifteen years. Justly regarding this as an unreasonable proposal, the creditors replied that they were not prepared to accept any such settlement. Receiving no acknowledgment of their reply they were forced again to have recourse to the Viceroy, and so presented a petition, which bears date 29th November, 1837, asking that the Viceroy would grant "that justice which the laws of China in such cases have hitherto given Foreigners." It was just at this time that Captain Elliot, in his negotiations for the re-opening of official intercourse with the Chinese authorities, reached the stage when Lord Palmerston expressly forbade him to use the term "Pin" in his official communications [1] and the Viceroy refused to receive any communication not so superscribed, with the result that Captain Elliot decided to leave Canton. On November 29th, 1837, the Superintendent addressed to the British merchants a letter informing them of his decision, and the reasons that made it necessary, pointing out to them that he considered it expedient that they should obtain from the Viceroy some definite explanation of his intentions with regard to the Hing-tai Hong, [2] which he might deal with in his report on the position of affairs to the Foreign Office. Thus the creditors, seeing that they were soon to be deprived of such support as the presence of Captain Elliot at Canton had hitherto afforded them, felt that no time must be lost in pressing their claims.

At this point of time the question of the Hing-tai Hong began to be confused by the Chinese authorities with that of the opium traffic. This appears from the following edict, which was issued by the Viceroy on December 1st, 1837 :—

"In reference to the several sums which the Hing-tai Hong is indebted to the said Foreign merchants, orders have been

[1] See *ante*, p. 292.
[2] *Correspondence Relating to China* (Blue Book, 1840), p. 249.

given for the apprehension of the said Hong Merchant, Yen-Ketsëang, imperatively requiring that he be discovered and, with Yen-Kechang, be subjected to severe punishment. Had they the power of repaying their debts, doubtless they should be, with strictness, compelled speedily to repay them in full. But if it rests on all the Hong Merchants to determine on a mode of repaying on their behalf, then, there being to each sum a creditor, how can these creditors beat down, as to time, those on whom the weight of suffering actually falls? The request made is indeed very far from being reasonable. In consideration for them, I, however, command that they wait while I instruct the Commissioners of Finance and Justice to hasten the senior Hong Merchants to come to a speedy determination as to the period to be prescribed, and to make representation to me, in order to obtain my final decision. It is my special desire that the said Foreign merchants should have guarantees to their debts, and also, that in effecting this the Hong Merchants should not be utterly ground down nor hindrance be thereby occasioned to the fulfilment of public duties.

"As to the Celestial Empire, in its cherishing tenderness towards men from afar, its benevolence is perfect, its justice without a flaw. But the depraved Foreigners twist awry the laws to subserve their private ends: and have thereby drawn from the Great Emperor reiterated and severe declarations of displeasure, that the receiving ships should be driven away. Yet, notwithstanding this, the Celestial terrors have not at once been displayed; but only the Superintendent Elliot has been commanded speedily to send them away, and order their return to their country. Is there aught so exalted or so substantial as the sacred favour herein manifested?

"Because the receiving ships in the outer seas have so long persevered in lingering out their stay, I lately limited the said Superintendent to a fixed period for faithfully paying obedience to the commands. If he still treat them with contempt and disregard, it will be in truth difficult in that case to extend indulgence, and put off the said Superintendent's expulsion. Whether the trade shall continue open or not, rests with the

Celestial Court to determine, and will depend on the line of conduct which all the Foreigners may adopt for themselves.

"To sum up, I, the Governor, reverently regard the sacred tenderness, and in conformity thereto, I carefully maintain the dignity of the government. I commit no act of tyranny or oppression. Neither do I seek surreptitiously to gain a name for liberality. The Foreign debts shall be fully paid to the uttermost mite. The receiving ships shall be with the utmost severity driven away. For each purpose, distinct measures are to be carried through. The two have no relation one to the other."

It is quite clear that introducing into the discussion the question of the opium traffic was a device of the Viceroy to confuse the issues. This is simply the customary Chinese method of meeting a difficulty. When your case is turning out badly, introduce some totally irrelevant topic on which you may have more chance of success. The Viceroy knew that in justice he ought to have compelled the Hong Merchants to pay Hing-tai's debts at the very outset. Those debts were perfectly well ascertained as far as the Foreign creditors were concerned. All the talk about "mature deliberation," "enforcing the laws," and the rest, is merely superfluous matter introduced for purposes of delay. The plea that the "weight of suffering" would fall on the Hong Merchants is worth nothing, for those merchants had received their monopoly expressly with a view to preventing disputes and on the condition that they were jointly liable for one another's debts. As for the proposal to liquidate the liabilities in fifteen years, such a period was sufficient at the rates of interest that then prevailed to more than double the capital sum in which the Hong Merchants were indebted.

The creditors replied to the Viceroy that they did not quite catch the Viceroy's meaning, in so far as in his edict their claims on the Hing-tai Hong were mixed up with transactions of a totally different nature, and their trade threatened to be stopped if Captain Elliot did not perform what they had no power to insist upon. They reminded the Viceroy that his repeated promises that their debts should be paid had so far produced no result, although the Consoo fund, which existed for the express purpose of meeting such engagements, had not been drawn upon for three years. With some bitterness they remarked: "We have been involved in these debts by trading with the merchants specially appointed by the Emperor for the avowed purpose of guaranteeing Foreign debts and guarding them against fraud, and with whom alone we are permitted to carry on business. If now we are put off from month to month, where is the use of such an appointed set of merchants, and where the celestial justice which, in restricting trade to a few men, prevents our dealing with others, yet refuses either to perform its own engagements, or to compel the Hong Merchants to perform theirs? We here remark, that the only wealthy merchants of the Co-hong will neither secure ships nor purchase their cargoes."

On the 17th December, 1837, the Viceroy acknowledged this address in an edict, which both evaded the point at issue and insulted the creditors. He pleaded that the caution contained in his former edict, against confusing the two topics there discussed was sufficient answer to the complaints of the creditors that they were threatened with a stoppage of the trade, if Captain Elliot did not carry out what the Viceroy had enjoined upon him. As regards payment of the debts, he said:—

"In the laws of the Heavenly dynasty [it is written]: 'If a man have received money improperly, such as stolen money, bribes, etc., he ought to repay it to its rightful owner, or he may be sued and sent to prison for six months; if, upon examination, it be found that with all his might he cannot repay, he may escape further prosecution, and on getting a bond from his friends certifying his inability to pay, etc., he may request forgiveness of his crime and such like.' Now Yen-Kechang and his brother, in owing a debt, having committed a much lighter crime than that of receiving bribes or stolen property, and they likewise being entirely unable to pay, it is plain that, their time of confinement in prison being expired, they also should be able to avoid further prosecution, and likewise sue for and obtain forgiveness.

But I, the Viceroy, having still further ordered the Hong Merchants to consult upon the subject, and to repay the debt in the stead [of the bankrupts] am truly looking up to the holy virtue of the Great Emperor as my model, in fostering the men from afar, not wishing that the said Foreigners should be deprived of their capital! This is goodness beyond the laws! Truly may it be called the extreme of benevolence and justice! How is it then, that so soon after the receipt of my reply [to your last petition] you again come with a mass of words, thus whining at and annoying me? If you say that the Hong Merchants who are to pay the debts instead [of the bankrupts] are in the place of the bankrupts, and as such are to be reprimanded for delay, then it is that the Hong Merchants are blamed by you for coming forward to pay the debt—so suppose that the Hong Merchants were to beg of you to excuse them bearing this blame, and on the other hand were to agree together not to pay this debt, I would like to ask you, whom would you go to beg it from? O, gross and ignorant that ye are, never was there stupidity equal to this!

"As to what you say about the Hong Merchants having received the Consoo Fund for three years without lifting arm [to pay any of it out], whether it is so or not, the Hong Merchants must state the fact, and if the money was applied for the benefit of the public, or if in [the Consoo treasury] there is any excess or not, stop till the Judge and Treasurer have examined and reported for my decision. As to whether the term or proposal to pay back in shares in fifteen years be too long or not, I again refer to my former edict, where I urged on the principal security merchants, without delay to consult together in justice, and determine with propriety. Wait till I get the document from the Judge and Treasurer for my investigation."[1]

On the 29th December the Judge and Treasurer presented their report, recommending that a period of twelve years be appointed for the payment of the debts. On the 30th, the creditors presented a petition to the Viceroy saying that in the

[1] *Correspondence Relating to China* (Blue Book, 1840), p. 271.

period suggested the usual interest would amount to twice the capital value of the debts, and that his Excellency's observation respecting "the fixed laws of the Heavenly Dynasty" were inaccurate, inasmuch as the laws quoted did not apply to Foreigners. The creditors went on to show that they had received repeated promises of payment, both from the Emperor and the Viceroy, and took up the position that the debt due to them from the Hong Merchants was the debt of the Celestial Empire. They concluded by pointing out that in former years large claims had been paid and that the claim they were now making was not of a kind previously unknown.[1]

On the 6th January, 1838, the Viceroy announced that "the compassion towards Foreigners consists in benevolently making arrangements for paying the capital, but there is no regulation for discharging the interest"; and told the creditors to wait while the ministers of Justice and Finance drew up a report to the Emperor. To this the creditors replied in a petition of 21st March, 1838, which recapitulated the various points previously urged. Nothing having been attained, except the receipt of an informal proposal from the Hong Merchants to pay in nine years, the creditors, on the 24th March, addressed a memorial to Lord Palmerston asking the aid of the British Government. This document is all that could be desired in the way of a lucid and temperate presentment of the case for the creditors, and, in addition to stating grievances, proposes remedies. It was signed by twenty-one British firms, of which two were Parsee. The following extracts show the difficulties under which the memorialists laboured :—

"Of the thirteen Hong Merchants which existed at the beginning of 1837, three or four are now avowedly insolvent. Their united debts, according to their own report, amount to upwards of $3,000,000, besides about $750,000, which they owe to the government for duties. One of these security merchants, named Hing-tai, has been formally declared bankrupt, and his debts to Foreigners proved by a committee appointed for the purpose by the Co-hong and Foreigners mutually at $2,261,439, exclusive of claims still in dispute.

[1] *Correspondence Relating to China* (Blue Book, 1840), pp. 273–4.

The Viceroy of Canton has declared in a public document, of which we transmit herewith a translation, together with all the correspondence upon the subject to your Lordship, that the debts should be paid, but has left the period for payment to be settled, as usual, between the security merchants and the Foreigners. The former began by proposing twenty years as the term for liquidation, but have subsequently reduced it, step by step, to nine years. The creditors have refused even the last proposition, on the ground, first, that it is impolitic to establish the principle of such a protracted payment in this first settlement of a debt under the free trade system, which debt arises entirely out of actual transactions of trade, and so far differs from all former debts ; and, secondly, because we wish to take this opportunity to procure a settlement of the debts of all the insolvent hongs, with a view to understand our exact position with them, and to endeavour to trade upon some safer system in future.

"The debts owing by the Co-hong, whether to the Government or to the Foreigners, have never been paid entirely out of their own resources ; but chiefly by means of extra duties levied upon the principal staples of the Foreign trade ; and the Hong Merchants propose to liquidate the debts now under consideration in a similar way. Such duties once imposed appear never to be taken off again, when the first occasion for them has ceased, but to be still levied under pretext of creating a fund, called the Consoo Fund, to meet future exigencies of the Co-hong, whether occasioned by debts to the Foreigners or by demands from the Emperor, to meet the expenses of the wars[1] or other extraordinary expenditure of the state. There is no reason to suppose, however, that such a fund has ever really existed, or that the Chinese authorities have ever recognized it ; but they have sanctioned the imposition of duties from time to time for the payment of specific

[1] According to the Hong Merchants' own statement, they contributed to the public funds $300,000 per annum, consisting of tribute, charges for the expenses of the new territory in Tartary, subsidies for repairs of forts, and purchases of ginseng. *Chinese Repository*, vol. iii, p. 425. See also *Correspondence Relating to China* (Blue Book, 1840), p. 287.

debts, and have connived at their continuance to feed, as is supposed, their own exactions. Independent of the extraordinary demands of the Emperor upon the security merchants, they are exposed to almost daily extortions on the part of the local authorities, chiefly the Hoppo, or Collector of Customs, and his subordinates, which have always impoverished them even when they shared in the large certain profits of the East India Company's trade. They have incurred heavy losses in their trading transactions since the expiration of the East India Company's charter; and seem likely to suffer still more severely since the same parties have now to conduct a more extended business, in competition with the intelligence and greater activity of the free-traders, to which neither their capital nor mode of conducting commerce seems adequate.

"We humbly submit to your Lordship's decision, whether the Chinese Government, so long as it shall insist upon confining our trade to so small a number of its merchants, is not bound to take care that those merchants have sufficient capital and probity for their trust; and whether on the transfer of our capital to them, in the shape of the debts in question, which becomes unavoidable in the conducting of an expensive commerce with a monopoly of such limited means, the imperial guarantee does not imply earlier repayment of such capital than has hitherto been or is now offered, or at all events, some compensation for the delay in the shape of interest. Our experience of the Chinese people and their rulers leads us confidently to infer, that the simple interposition of our own Government with the Cabinet of Peking in so just a cause, would facilitate the adjustment of our present claims; and if Her Majesty's Government would further require that any future debts incurred by the Hongs to British subjects should be paid immediately, or at all events, within a reasonable and defined time; and that the Hong Merchants should be protected from the extortions of the official subordinates, we feel assured that it would tend to lessen the hazards of our trade materially."

This document shows a degree of optimism as to the probable outcome of intervention by the British Government in Chinese affairs that can only be attributed to ignorance of the difficulties to be encountered. The sad experience of later generations of Englishmen has shown that "the Cabinet of Peking" is not easily moved to take any step on behalf of Foreigners, much less to perform that most difficult of all acts to a Chinese, namely, pay away money. The merchants themselves seem to have been in doubt as to the efficacy of the remedy they proposed, for, as will presently appear, without waiting for a reply from the Foreign Secretary, they agreed to terms of settlement, which covered all the debts owing by Hong Merchants.

The subsequent history of the Hing-tai case can be dealt with briefly. On the 31st March, 1838, the Foreign creditors, after patiently waiting for some satisfactory arrangement to be made, and finding that nothing was being done, again petitioned the Viceroy by a document, in which they took occasion to point out that in the preceding four years the Foreign merchants had paid upwards of a million and a half dollars to the Consoo Fund,[1] without receiving therefrom a single dollar. "And now," they said, "when the Hing-tai Hong by an act of swindling retains Foreign property to upwards of two million dollars, they, the Co-hong, propose paying the same back without interest in nine years. The proposal is so manifestly unjust, that we bring it once more to your Excellency's notice, in full confidence that orders for a more equitable settlement will emanate from your Excellency's sense of justice." Still nothing was done, and the matter

[1] It can hardly be supposed that the whole of this sum ultimately came out of the pockets of the Foreign merchants. In the natural course of trade it would be paid by the consumer under the guise of increased prices of imports, or diminished prices for the exports given in exchange under the system of barter which prevailed at Canton. Owing, however, to the fact that the trade was in the hands of the Co-hong monopoly, the Hong Merchants could compel the Foreign merchants to pay some part of these duties by refusing to deal on any other terms, with the result that the Foreign merchants would have to be content with less profits. It must be remembered that except in opium the Foreign merchants had not a free market, and there were no courts of law in which a recalcitrant Hong Merchant could be compelled to fulfil a bargain.

dragged for another six months. Then an offer was made by the Co-hong that was very little better than that previously made, and this was accepted.[1]

On November 26th the creditors wrote to Lord Palmerston explaining that the terms of this settlement were that Hing-tai's debts were to be paid off in instalments extending over eight and a half years, beginning from 30th November, 1837, and Kinqua's by instalments extending over ten years. Interest at six per cent. was to be paid on Kinqua's debts, but no interest was to be paid until the principal had been wiped out. No interest at all was to be paid on the Hing-tai liabilities. The creditors flattered themselves that the inclusion of Kinqua's liabilities made this offer one worth accepting, without waiting to see what the British Government could do for them. But when we take into consideration the fact that it had been agreed that the money for the payment of the debts was to be raised by fresh duties on the whole of the Foreign trade, an operation which could not fail to tend still further to produce commercial stagnation, it is difficult to see what there was in this scheme that made it acceptable. A scale of new duties to be imposed in accordance with this settlement was very soon drawn up, and it was not long before these duties became a source of loud complaint on the part of the Foreign traders.[2]

News of this settlement reached Lord Palmerston informally when he was acknowledging the receipt of Captain Elliot's despatches relating to the matter. Naturally, the Foreign Secretary was not very well pleased that the British merchants, after appealing to him, should have accepted terms which he found scarcely different from those previously rejected.[3] How ill-advised the creditors had been is seen when we examine the further history of this matter. A first dividend of four per cent. was paid on Kinqua's debts on January 14th, 1839; on the 27th a regulation that the debts of a single Hong Merchant to Foreigners was not to exceed 100,000 taels was ordered to be

[1] *Correspondence Relating to China* (Blue Book, 1840), pp. 302–6, 322.

[2] For the duties imposed on this occasion see *Correspondence Relating to China* (Blue Book, 1840), pp. 348–9.

[3] *Correspondence Relating to China* (Blue Book, 1840), p. 317.

engraven on stone and kept in everlasting remembrance. On February 4th, Hing-tai's creditors received a dividend of three per cent. in addition to four per cent. already paid,[1] and this is all that ever came of the settlement that had been arrived at. From that time the Foreign creditors received nothing, until in 1843, under the Treaty of Nanking, and as a result of the hostilities that had been waged, the balance of indebtedness was recovered from the Chinese Government. The whole story is a striking commentary on the commercial good faith which some attribute to the Chinese.

[1] *Chinese Repository*, vol. xi, pp. 352–4.

CHAPTER XV

FURTHER PROGRESS OF THE OPIUM TRAFFIC

WHILST all these proceedings were taking place with regard to the Hing-tai Hong, the Chinese authorities were paying increased attention to the evils of the opium traffic. Early in 1838 the officials at Canton went so far as to interfere with a European boat supposed to contain the contraband drug. This boat, which belonged to a man named Just, a watchmaker, afterwards made famous by Lord Palmerston, was stopped about two miles above the Factories by a search party, who demanded a bribe of £2,000 to release her. On Just refusing to pay more than half that sum, the matter came before a wider circle of officials, all of whom required to be propitiated as a condition of letting the boat off, with the result that in the end a total sum of $6,000 was demanded and refused. Captain Elliot, in reporting the incident to Lord Palmerston, wrote that this was the first instance for many years of a searching visit being paid to European boats; that he feared the practice might be inconveniently extended, the more so as several of the boats were armed; that if the seizure were publicly reported to the Viceroy, it would lead to some serious mischief; and, at all events, the Hong Merchant, who was the landlord of Mr. Just's house (and who had no more to do with the business than Captain Elliot himself), would be a severe sufferer.[1]

In the same month a native opium broker, Kwo Si-ping by name, a resident in the village of Mako, near Macao, where he had been settled since 1805, confessed under torture, the use of which is allowed in judicial proceedings by Chinese law, that he had clandestinely sent away sycee, and had carried opium on board Foreign ships to be sent to the province of Fu-kien. For this offence he was executed by strangulation,

[1] *Correspondence Relating to China* (Blue Book, 1840), p. 253; *Chinese Repository*, vol. xi, p. 298.

with the circumstantial barbarity customary in China. He was carried to the place of execution in a bamboo cage borne by two executioners, guarded by about one hundred of the Imperial Infantry, who were armed with boarding pikes and other weapons. Two matted bamboo sheds had been erected for the occasion about forty yards apart. One of these was furnished with chairs and tables, and there the officials had already taken their seats when the culprit arrived. The other contained only a slight wooden cross, about six feet in height, with a hole in the upper part immediately above the horizontal cross-piece. Three guns were fired as a signal to prepare for the execution. With his arms and legs heavily loaded with shackles of iron, the condemned man was literally shaken out of the cage, and lay there covered with the filth that accumulates in a Chinese prison, and so emaciated after his four months' incarceration as to appear more dead than alive. He was dragged to the cross, and placed with his back against it, standing upright on a piece of brick. The executioners first lashed a rope round his legs and under his arms, then through the hole in the upper part of the cross, after which it was passed through the loops of the cord and twisted round several times, for the purpose of tightening it in order to effect strangulation. No apparent signal, other than the removal of the piece of brick on which the culprit stood, was given for the fatal turning of the stick. The expression on the man's countenance did not change, nor was he perceived to make any struggle, the manner in which his arms and legs were shackled and bound to the cross making any movement impossible. About ten minutes after he had died, the officials departed with a salute of three guns. Shortly afterwards the executioners, when they had satisfied themselves by an examination of the eyes and mouth that the man was dead, left the scene, having first removed from his hands and feet the chains with which he had been bound.[1]

This terrible spectacle was not the only outward sign that there was a real determination on the part of the officials to enforce the law against opium. Coming so quickly after the

[1] *Chinese Repository*, vol. vi, pp. 607–8.

seizure of Mr. Just's boat, it showed that the law could no longer be regarded as a dead letter. Further evidence of this was afforded by another incident which took place on the 10th of January, 1838, when a European passage boat, the *Swift*, was boarded whilst at anchor in the river off the front of the Factories. Three chests of opium found on board were confiscated. A few days before this seizure was made, the three senior Hong Merchants had called on the Committee of the Chamber of Commerce and expressed their regret that the practice of smuggling opium had been revived at Whampoa and Canton, entreating the Committee to put a stop to these practices, since not only the whole Foreign trade, but they, personally, might suffer greatly if the smuggling continued. In the following month another passage boat, the *Alpha*, was stopped off Macao and twenty-three chests of opium found on board were confiscated. Other seizures were made about the same time. But the illicit traffic continued to grow. No longer was it confined to Lintin, but the whole river became the theatre of the smuggling operations.

In accordance with the change of policy propounded in Lord Palmerston's despatch of 20th September, 1837, to the Lords of the Admiralty, vessels of the British navy now began to visit Chinese waters. On February 5th, 1838, Vice-Admiral Capel had been relieved of the command of the British squadron in the Indian seas by Sir Frederick Maitland. The relations between England and Burmah at that time were in such a state as to render it necessary that the British fleet should remain in Indian waters, but as soon as circumstances permitted Sir Frederick sailed for Canton with his flag-ship, H.M.S. *Wellesley*, accompanied by the brig, H.M.S. *Algerine*. He arrived off the island of Lintin on 12th July, and on the 17th landed at Macao. His arrival was immediately reported to the Chinese authorities by the native pilots, who designated him a "barbarian eye" (*e-muh*), or head man, using the description applied to Lord Napier. The usual edicts, requiring the speedy departure of all vessels of war from the Chinese coasts, were at once issued, but inasmuch as this procedure had long since come to be regarded as a mere formality, it did not receive on this occasion any more attention than had hitherto been paid to it. The Chinese sent no officer to receive the Admiral, or to inquire the object of his visit, but contented themselves with questioning the native pilots, and with imprisoning the one who had brought in the *Wellesley* for not furnishing an explicit account of the purposes for which the Admiral had come.[1]

Admiral Maitland knew that his appearance in Chinese waters would be likely to arouse distrust, and therefore had forewarned Captain Elliot of his intended visit, in a letter sent under the care of Captain Blake of H.M.S. *Larne*, dated from Madras the 21st April, in which he said :—

" As it is possible the arrival of my flag-ship, as well as that of others which I may from time to time send into the China seas, may give some cause of jealousy and suspicion to the Government of China, I wish you clearly to understand that the trade, being no longer the monopoly of a company of merchants, comes under the immediate protection and care of Her Majesty's Government ; and that that Government considers itself bound to see that the ships and persons of Her Majesty's subjects are duly protected from injury or insult, as is the case in all other portions of the globe. This I communicate to you that the Chinese Government may, if necessary, be put at ease, and no suspicion arise of any hostile intention on the part of the British Government, which is the farthest from their views, by the more frequent visits of our ships now, as compared with former times.

"Though Captain Blake is commanded to assist you in maintaining order among the crews of the British merchant ships, you must be perfectly aware he, as captain of a ship of war, has no legal right to interfere, and must be very cautious in committing himself in the disputes between the masters and their crews." [2]

Evidently the Admiral was fully alive to the excitement which his visit would create, and it is not incorrect to say that,

[1] *Chinese Repository*, vol. vii, p. 175.
[2] *Correspondence Relating to China* (Blue Book, 1840), p. 312; *Chinese Repository*, vol. xi, p. 299.

as soon as his intention was known at Canton, it became the one topic of conversation, the English residents being as much in the dark as to its object as were the Chinese. Captain Elliott, since his withdrawal from Canton, had ceased to communicate with the Chinese authorities, who had shown no disposition to allow him to address them except by petition through the Hong Merchants. When on the 12th of July Admiral Maitland arrived off Macao, the Superintendent informed him of his intention to proceed to Canton to explain to the Viceroy the objects of the Admiral's visit, which he had had no opportunity of doing previously, owing to the cessation of official intercourse. The Chinese appear to have felt the difficulty of the situation, for on the 15th of July the *keun-min-foo* addressed a communication to Captain Elliot, but as it bore the character *yü*[1] it was returned unopened. Later they addressed an edict to him through the Hong Merchants, which was likewise rejected.

On the 21st July the Admiral arrived off Canton, and on the 28th an incident took place which led to some difficulty with the Chinese. The passage boat, *Bombay*, was proceeding from Canton to Hong-kong, when she was twice stopped by shots from the forts and boarded by Chinese officers, who inquired "whether Admiral Maitland or any of his soldiers, women, or men-of-war's men were on board." In reply to a question they stated that they would not seize opium, even if there were any on the boat. On receiving an answer in the negative to the inquiries respecting the Admiral, the boarding parties in each case allowed the vessel to proceed.[2]

On the 29th of July, Captain Elliot, having proceeded to Canton made one more attempt to open up an official correspondence on a footing of equality, and addressed to the Viceroy a note, superscribed *shusin*,[3] announcing that "an English officer of the first rank, Maitland, commanding the

[1] This is the character used as a superscription on a communication from a superior to an inferior.

[2] *Correspondence Relating to China* (Blue Book, 1840), p. 314; *Chinese Repository*, vol. xi, p. 301.

[3] *i.e.*, "letter of intelligence."

ships of his sovereign in the Indian seas, has arrived off these coasts by the command of his Government. The Superintendent Elliot has now received Maitland's instructions to signify to His Excellency the Governor that he desires to explain the peaceful purposes of his visit. It would be convenient, therefore, that the manner of intercourse should be clearly understood beforehand, so that all difficulties and misunderstandings may be prevented. For this reason Elliot requests that the governor will be pleased to send officers to communicate with him. And if they should come, His Excellency may be assured that they will be received in a manner consistent with their dignity." [1]

Captain Elliot left his communication to the Viceroy open, thinking thus to avoid the difficulty about the proper form of superscription. That official immediately returned it, with the remark that his orders from the Emperor were imperative, and the document could not be received unless it bore the character *Pin*. With this rebuff Captain Elliot left Canton and returned to the Admiral. On August 4th the Chinese Admiral, Kwan, styling himself "the potent and fear-inspiring," writing to the British Admiral, to ask the reason of the British ships being moved to the anchorage of Lungkect, thus expressed the official view of Captain Elliot's overtures: "On a recent visit of Elliot to Canton, he sought to effect a sudden change in the ancient rules by using, in place of the words 'humble address' (*pin*) the words 'letter of intelligence' (*shusin*). Hence His Excellency, our Viceroy, declined to receive, in disobedience of his regulations, his documents." The Chinese Admiral went on to admonish Admiral Maitland on the subject of Chinese official etiquette, suggesting that "humble address" would be the proper mode of styling his communications. [2]

Admiral Maitland replied to Kwan that the object of his coming was to demand an explanation of an insult offered to

[1] *Correspondence Relating to China* (Blue Book, 1840), p. 314; *Chinese Repository*, vol. xi, p. 300.

[2] *Correspondence Relating to China* (Blue Book, 1840), p. 315; *Chinese Repository*, vol. xi, p. 301.

the sovereign of his country in his own person, referring to the affair of the *Bombay*, and requested that officers be appointed to wait on him to whom he might more fully explain his meaning. Kwan seems to have acted with considerable tact, and at once sent officers to hold a conference with the English Admiral on his flag-ship, the *Wellesley*. Minutes of this and subsequent conferences forwarded to Lord Palmerston, show that all difficulties were soon smoothed over.[1] The Chinese officers explained that the stoppage of the *Bombay* was not due to any official command, they disavowed all intention of insulting the British flag, and promised that the persons actually responsible for the occurrence should be punished. This explanation was accepted by the Admiral, who, on his part, informed the Chinese that they must expect visits from British ships of war, now that the East India Company's monopoly had come to an end, as only in this way could British trade be protected. An exchange of civilities then took place, and the British ships returned to Tungku Bay, where they remained until, on October 4th, they returned to India.[2]

Notwithstanding the presence of Admiral Maitland and his ships, the Chinese authorities did not cease in their active operations against the opium traffic. They insisted on the stoppage of all boats running between Canton and Macao, and none were allowed to proceed up the river without passports which had to be countersigned at the Bogue.[2] The Hong Merchants seem to have regarded the activity of the authorities as a thing to be seriously reckoned with, for we find them writing to the Foreign merchants :—

" We beg to state respectfully that the number of the large boats belonging to the Foreigners of each nation, which sail between Canton, Lintin, and Macao, is great ; it is long since the larger boats have been forbidden to enter the port ; and as to the small boats, whether they come from Macao or Whampoa to Canton, or go from Canton to Whampoa or

[1] *Correspondence Relating to China* (Blue Book, 1840), pp. 309–317; *Chinese Repository*, vol. xi, pp. 303–7.

[2] *Chinese Repository*, vol. vii, p. 232.

Macao, a pass must always be applied for according to law, and they must be searched, and then they will be permitted to proceed; these have been hitherto the fixed laws. Lately we have repeatedly received edicts from the Viceroy and Hoppo, severely reprimanding us: and we have also written to you, gentlemen of the different nations, several times, giving you full information of the orders and regulations that you might perfectly obey them, and manage accordingly; but you, gentlemen, continue wholly regardless."[1]

The state to which the Chinese Empire was being reduced by the opium traffic is well shown by the memorial of Huang Tseo-tsze, president of the Sacrificial Court at Peking, who, in a document deserving careful attention, urged the Throne to adopt severer measures against all persons using the drug, and requested that for opium-smoking the penalty of death be substituted in place of those ineffectual punishments the cangue, the bastinado, and transportation.

Owing to the continued export of sycee, paid as the price of the imported opium, the rise in silver, measured by the market price of silver in cash, was so great as to be a serious evil. Huang called attention to these facts, and pointed out that the measures previously taken to stop the opium traffic were of no avail. He showed that the practice of requiring one of the Hong Merchants to give a bond on the arrival of a Foreign ship, stating that she had no opium on board, had become an empty form. He commented on the alarming way in which the use of opium had spread from the wealthy to all classes, "even to women, monks, nuns, and priests," and through the whole length of the Empire even to Moukden in Manchuria. He stated, as was undoubtedly the fact, that the importation was constantly increasing, that receiving ships were stationed at Lantao and the Ladrone Islands, and that the traffic had extended itself all along the coasts of Fu-kien, Chê-kiang, and Shantung, right to the city of Tientsin. The evil and difficulty of the situation were not overstated when he said:—

[1] *Canton Register*, 14th August, 1838; *Chinese Repository*, vol. vii, p. 232.

"In the province of Kwantung (Canton), the wholesale dealers in opium, having established large stores, maintain a good understanding with the custom-house officers along the various routes from that to the other provinces. The opium dealers in the several provinces, if possessed of capital, obtain the protection of these wholesale men; and the corrupt officers of the places of customs and toll consequently connive, and suffer them to pass; while, on the other hand, legitimate traders, passing to and fro, are, under pretence of searching for opium, vexatiously detained and subjected to extortion. The keepers of smoking houses, too, in all the departments and districts, are depraved and crafty under-officers, police-runners, and such like. These, acting in base concert with worthless young men of large families—families possessed of a name and influence—collect together, under protection of many doors, and in retired alleys, parties of people to inhale the drug; and the private officers and attendants of the local magistrates, being one half of them sunk into this vicious habit, are induced always to shield these their friends and abettors." [1]

This memorial had the effect of leading the Emperor to issue an edict commanding his high officials to lay their views on the question before the Throne. But among the high officials there was uncertainty. Opinion was divided as to the best means of combating the evil. At Canton severe measures were taken, scores of retailers being flung into prison and violent collisions taking place between the officials and the dealers. [2] All over the Empire seizures of dealers and smokers were made, and in Hu-peh smokers were punished by having a portion of the upper lip cut out, to prevent them using the pipe. [3] Among the Foreign merchants at Canton the opium trade was absorbing attention to the exclusion of more legitimate but less profitable pursuits. In November, 1838, the Committee of the Chamber of Commerce reported that their attempts to establish a proper postal service had been a failure,

[1] *Chinese Repository*, vol. vii, p. 275.
[2] *Ibid.*, p. 280.
[3] *Ibid.*, p. 392.

as " the boats, which were indispensable for the purpose, were suddenly employed in the opium trade, and no compensation that the Chamber could offer to the owners was equivalent to the profits which that traffic yielded them. The Committee are now of opinion that no adequate security can be obtained that any Foreign boats, which might be engaged for the post-office service, would not be in the same manner diverted to other employments.[1]

In the two years 1837 and 1838, as this passage shows, smuggling by means of passage boats had increased to an almost incredible extent. Owing to the vigorous action of the revenue authorities the native craft—the " scrambling dragons "—engaged in the illicit trade had been entirely suppressed. Foreign schooners and cutters were the vessels now employed. In a few months these had increased in number from eight or ten to thirty or forty. In some instances they brought to their owners thousands of dollars a week. As a rule, they were allowed to pass the Bogue unmolested; if fired upon, sometimes they were brought to and sometimes they managed to get away. Even the hospital ship was charged with being implicated, and was sold to the Chinese and broken up owing to the opposition raised against her by the officials. Matters came to a crisis on the 3rd of December, 1838, when twelve boxes, containing 203 catties of opium, were seized on board a tea boat anchored outside the Factories. The men in charge of the boat stated that they had been sent to Whampoa to fetch the drug from a vessel called the *Thomas Perkins*, and that they had been sent by an Englishman named Innes, a member of the Creek Factory, who shortly before had bargained and sold the opium to a Chinese broker. The Hong Merchant, Punhoyqua, who had become security for the *Thomas Perkins*, was forthwith arrested and placed in the pillory, and on the 5th of December an edict was issued ordering the hatches of the vessel to be closed, and commanding Talbot and Innes to leave the port within three days.[2]

Talbot, who was an American, at once replied that the cargo

[1] *Chinese Repository*, vol. vii, p. 386.
[2] *Ibid.*, pp. 437–8.

consigned to himself had consisted solely of rice, and that the vessel had brought no cargo consigned to Innes. The Viceroy refused to accept this disclaimer, and threatened punishment to all Hong Merchants whose houses were let to Foreigners engaged in the opium trade. The Hong Merchants, genuinely alarmed at this threat, wrote to the Chamber of Commerce, urging them to see that the law was obeyed, and the contraband traffic discontinued.

"If," said they, "any Foreigners attempt to smuggle up opium or any other contraband article into the Factories, we shall immediately petition the government that such may be dealt with according to law, and that the offenders may be turned out of our houses. If you consent to this, and give us a bond to that effect, we will continue to trade with you as usual; but if you refuse our conditions, we truly dare not continue to trade with you or to rent you our houses. You cannot say we have given you no warning. On receipt of this letter, we must beg you all to let us know whether you accept or refuse our terms, that we may frame the new agreement, after which chops[1] shall again be granted. We have established hongs for trading with you, gentlemen, in the hope of making a little money, and that all things may go on peacefully and to our mutual advantage; but by the Foreigners smuggling opium we are constantly involved in trouble. Ask yourselves, gentlemen, whether in our places you could be at ease. There are surely some reasonable men among you. Now we have been forced to demand some new conditions ere opening the trade, being determined no longer to suffer for others' misdeeds. We have resolved that hereafter not one large decked boat shall come up to Canton, and all small uncovered boats, whether coming from or going to Whampoa or Macao, shall, according to law, apply at the custom-house stations for passports and examination. As the security merchants and landlords are made answerable for any smuggling of opium, etc., these conditions are absolutely necessary, and we must request you, benevolent elder brethren, to give public notice that all gentlemen who, on consideration,

[1] *i.e.*, written permits to land goods.

determine to accept our terms for opening the trade, must give us a signed paper to that effect, when the trade shall instantly open, and we will continue to rent you our factories."[1]

The Hong Merchants also distributed far and wide a placard, of which they sent a copy to the Chamber of Commerce, pointing out that Innes, in dealing in opium, had disobeyed their most specific injunctions. They further notified the Chamber of Commerce that if Innes did not leave Canton within the appointed time, they would pull down his house.[2] This threat fairly roused the Foreign community, who were loud in their complaints that their exterritorial privileges would be violated by such a proceeding. The Chamber of Commerce wrote to the Hong Merchants :—

" It was imperatively necessary that we should draw attention to the threat of forcibly pulling down one of the Foreign Factories ; we therefore verbally pointed out to you the dangerous consequences which might result from such an act ; the inviolability of our personal dwellings being a point imperatively necessary for the security of our persons and the property under our charge. . . . Mr. Innes is not a member of the Chamber, nor have we any control or influence over his actions, even if he were. The Chamber of Commerce is purely a commercial body, and has no authority over persons residing in Canton. . . . In reply to your request, that we as a body should give you some pledge respecting the Foreign boats coming to Canton, we regret that we are unable to comply with it—these boats belong to a variety of persons, over whom we can exercise no authority."[3]

The period of three days named for the departure of Talbot and Innes had, at the request of the Hong Merchants, been extended by the Viceroy to eight days, which allowed time for further correspondence with the Chamber of Commerce. The Hong Merchants persisted in their demand for the written undertaking, but in vain. On the 12th of December the Chinese authorities attempted to give the Foreigners an object

[1] *Chinese Repository*, vol. vii, pp. 441–2.
[2] *Ibid.*, p. 443.
[3] *Ibid.*, pp. 442–4.

lesson in the consequences of disobeying the law by ordering a public execution before the Factories. A more impolitic step it would be difficult to imagine. No notice of this proceeding had been given, and it was therefore with intense surprise that the Foreigners saw the executioner take up his position outside the Swedish Hong, near the American flagstaff, with a tent, a cross, and the other instruments required for the infliction of capital punishment. As soon as the residents heard what was afoot, they crowded to the intended place of execution. The American consul at once ordered his flag to be struck ; the executioner was told that he would not be allowed to perform his office ; and as soon as he tried to raise his tent, it was pulled down and one of the poles broken. The officer in charge saw that it was useless to attempt to carry out his instructions in front of the Factories, and removed to Chaoyin Street, where the criminal was put to death.[1] It may be argued in defence of the Viceroy that such strong action on the part of the Chinese authorities had become necessary, in order to impress the Foreigners with the fact that the eradication of the opium traffic had been resolved upon in all seriousness. On the other hand it must be remembered that the Foreigners had from the earliest times regarded the land, on which their Factories were built, as reserved exclusively for their use, a view having no foundation in law, but one in which the Chinese had in practice acquiesced.

In the meantime some of the leading merchants had lodged a complaint with the senior Hong Merchant, and had persuaded him to proceed to the city in the hope of inducing the authorities to abandon their project. Whilst he was absent, crowds of Chinese assembled before the Factories. Word was raised by some rash Foreigner to "Clear the square," whereupon some of the residents, armed with sticks, charged the crowd and a serious riot ensued. The Chinese on the spot soon increased to some eight or ten thousand, who threw volleys of stones and brickbats at the small band of Foreigners. Very soon the mob were masters of the situation and were hurling missiles at the doors and windows of the Factories, pulling

[1] *Chinese Repository*, vol. vii, p. 445.

down the wall of one of them and tearing up the railings of three others. The situation was becoming critical, when a mandarin arrived with a small guard of soldiers. His retinue at once set to work to restore order. Very soon the storm was quelled and the Chinese had deserted the square.

It was not long before the Foreigners presented an address to the Viceroy complaining of what they regarded as a violation of their rights. " Foreigners," they said, " have now resided in Canton for more than 100 years, and it has always been recognized and allowed that the ground between the Factories and the river belonged to the houses rented by them. In former times, until the great fire in the second year of Taoukuang (1822), it was surrounded and enclosed by walls. In fact, it appertains to the Factories for which we pay a yearly rent. In proof of which we beg to point out, that above and below on both sides of the river the ground in front of a Hong belongs to the same and is enclosed; as regards the Dutch and English Factories this is the case, but in front of the others it has been kept open for mutual convenience, and to afford some place on which we might take exercise in peace and safety; such an event as its being turned into a public place of execution was never heard of or contemplated."

The Viceroy's reply cannot be called tactful. It shows the spirit in which these questions were being treated by the Chinese authorities, a spirit which could not fail to produce an outbreak of hostilities at some time, unless the Foreigners were prepared to live in a state of servitude to the Chinese officials. His reply commences with a statement that the law requires convicted prisoners to be executed in the market-place, in order that offenders may see and be warned; that this particular criminal had kept an opium shop and had been condemned to suffer death by strangulation for that offence, in accordance with the Imperial commands received through the Board of Punishments; and that as the introduction of opium into Canton was due to depraved Foreigners, he had decided to have this criminal executed before the Thirteen Factories.

"Thus it was designed," he continues, " to strike observation, to arouse careful reflection, and to cause all to admonish and warn one another. . . . that the good portion of the Foreign community might thereby preserve for ever their commercial intercourse, and that the depraved portion might be prevented from pursuing their evil courses. Those Foreigners, though born and brought up beyond the pale of civilization, have yet human hearts. How should they then have been impressed with awe and dread and self-conviction! Can they yet put pen to paper to draw up such insane whinings? The ground, whether in front or in the rear of the Foreign Factories, is all the territory of the Celestial Empire, and is merely granted by the Great Emperor from motives of extraordinary grace and clemency as a temporary resting-place for all the Foreigners who have been permitted to engage in trade here. What have you, Foreigners, to do with the question, whether convicted persons shall be executed there or not? Say you that the ground is used as a place of exercise by all the Foreigners? And is it not then a place of concourse also for the people—the natives of the land? . . . Now that zealous and diligent proceedings are in operation for the suppression of the clandestine traffic, it may be presumed that the executions, which will take place there on the spot referred to, of criminals convicted under the laws against opium will not in future be few."[1]

The English merchants, accustomed to the maxim, "An Englishman's house is his castle," to which nothing analogous can be found in Chinese law, felt that they had been openly insulted and outraged. They had to be content, however, with sending to the Viceroy a written protest against his reply, in which they asserted that he had violated the acknowledged custom and practice of 150 years. They undoubtedly felt that the attempted execution was a deliberate infringement of their legal rights. That the Chinese did not regard it in this light is evident from the Viceroy's edict, and it is a well-known provision of Chinese law that all executions shall take place in a public place where they can be seen by all the people and serve as an example to the spectators not to do wrong.

[1] *Chinese Repository*, vol. vii, pp. 449–450.

The opinion in England was in favour of the Chinese view, for as soon as an opinion could be obtained from the Home Government, Lord Palmerston wrote to Captain Elliot to know "upon what alleged ground of right these persons considered themselves entitled to interfere with the arrangements made by the Chinese officers of justice for carrying into effect, in a Chinese town, the orders of their superior authorities."[1]

Captain Elliot, who was at Whampoa when the riot took place, at once hastened to Canton, followed by armed boats for the succour of the inhabitants. He found on his arrival that so far as Innes was concerned the Chinese authorities were correctly informed as to the facts of the case. Innes himself forwarded a declaration to the Viceroy saying that the opium was his, that it came from his boat and not from the American ship, and that the two coolies were ignorant of the contents of the boxes. Having made this confession, he applied for a passport and left for Macao on the 16th of December.[2] On the evening of the 17th, Captain Elliot held a public meeting, at which he assured the assembled Foreigners that he regarded the recent occurrences with the same feelings of indignation as their own. He then pointed out to them that the root of all the trouble was the opium traffic, and that he intended to take measures, by sending the British owned vessels, engaged in the illicit trade, outside the river, to put a stop to the contraband trade. Knowing that it was very doubtful whether he was empowered, as Superintendent of Trade, to enforce measures of this kind, he added that he intended to take precautions to prevent their return, if necessary, by appealing to the provincial authorities for assistance. He explained that he hoped the general reprobation of the whole community would have the effect of relieving him from any such unpleasant necessity, and asked for the co-operation not only of the British residents, but also of all the Foreign community, so long as he advocated the principles of truth and justice.[3]

[1] *Correspondence Relating to China* (Blue Book, 1840), p. 325.
[2] *Chinese Repository*, vol. xi, p. 346.
[3] *Chinese Repository*, vol. vii, pp. 452–3.

The next day the Superintendent issued a further notice of the kind foreshadowed in his speech. The notice required that all British-owned schooners, cutters, and otherwise rigged small craft, either habitually or occasionally engaged in the illicit traffic within the Bocca Tigris, should proceed outside within three days and not return, and warned their owners that, if any such craft were seized by the revenue officials and confiscated, the British Government would not interpose to assist them.[1] It contained the further warning that, if any Chinese subject should come by his death feloniously at their hands, the guilty persons would be liable to trial and punishment, in the same way as if the crime had been committed within the jurisdiction of Her Majesty's Courts at Westminster. He also announced that the British Government would not interfere, if the Chinese authorities should think fit to confiscate opium belonging to British subjects, and that if any resisted Chinese officers in the execution of their duty, they would be guilty of a lawless act, as if they should forcibly resist the officers of their own Government in their own country.

British residents at once raised the question whether Captain Elliot's powers were wide enough to enable him lawfully to insist on the terms of this notice being obeyed. It was no crime by the law of England that the smugglers of opium were committing, and there was nothing in his commission that authorized him to legislate and create a new offence. There was further the diplomatic difficulty, that by attempting to control the illicit traffic within the river, he gave the Chinese very substantial reason to believe that he had authority from his sovereign to suppress the receiving ships at Lintin, an authority which he had previously assured them he did not possess. It is quite certain that, if his powers from the British Government enabled him to take any steps at all to suppress offences against the revenue laws of China, those powers did not restrict him to traffic carried on within the Bogue. The doubt as to the validity of his act was soon pressed upon the notice of the Superintendent, who, seeing how well it was founded, resolved to invoke the sanction of

[1] *Chinese Repository*, vol. vii, pp. 453–4.

the Viceroy himself, and thus give his notice a virtue, as being approved by the representative of the sovereign of China, that it would not otherwise possess. There at once arose the further difficulty as to the mode of communication with a Chinese official. But Captain Elliot did not hesitate. Throwing on one side all the injunctions of Lord Palmerston interdicting the use of the character *Pin*, he determined to have resort to the old and forbidden method of communication.

On the 23rd of December, 1838, Captain Elliot therefore addressed the Viceroy once more in an address superscribed *Pin*, and presented through the Hong Merchants. This document is of the greatest importance, because it shows what was put before the Chinese authorities as the view of the opium traffic entertained by the official representative of the British Government. There are passages in it which the Chinese officials must have found very difficult to explain, when later they roused the hostility of Great Britain by taking decisive measures to suppress the very traffic which it condemned. A noticeable feature of the address is an attempt to get the Viceroy to give an official intimation, that the character *Pin* was used by Chinese officials in such a sense, that in reality Captain Elliot had taken a perfectly proper and dignified course in reverting to this method of intercourse. The address was thus worded :—

"The undersigned, Chief Superintendent of the trade of British subjects in China, deliberating on those serious risks to which the lives and properties of many innocent men, both natives and Foreigners, are presently exposed, considers that it is his duty to lay his thoughts before Your Excellency. Seeking for the immediate source of this dangerous state of things, he finds it in the existence of an extensive opium traffic, conducted in small craft within the river.

"From one condition of undisturbed lawlessness to another and still more hazardous, the course is sure and rapid. Illegalities will be committed more and more frequently, the difficulty of distinguishing between the right and the wrong will daily become more difficult, the Foreign interests and character will suffer increasing injury, violent affrays will be of constant recurrence, life, and probably the lives of innocent men, will be sacrificed, some general catastrophe will ensue, and there will be employment, profit and impunity for none but the reckless and the culpable.

"The Government of the British nation will regard these evil practices with no feelings of leniency, but, on the contrary, with severity and continual anxiety; in proof of this, the undersigned has now to acquaint Your Excellency that he has already, on the 18th of this month, formally required all boats (owned by British subjects) engaged in this traffic, to leave the river within three days.

"He cannot faithfully declare that these injunctions have been fulfilled, and he has, therefore, now to request that Your Excellency will signify your pleasure through the honourable officers, the *kwang-chow-foo* and the *kwang-hai*, so that all those concerned in these pursuits may know that he has received Your Excellency's authority for this notice.

"The undersigned is without doubt that the continuance of this traffic in the inner waters will involve the whole Foreign community at Canton in some disastrous difficulty: and his Gracious Sovereign would not interpose for the protection of their property on behalf of those British subjects who continue to practise these dangerous disorders after Your Excellency's public warning shall be authentically made known to them, through the officers of their own nation. . . . .

"He can assure Your Excellency that he has not requested that the communications should be forwarded through the honourable officers from any vain or idle pretensions on his own part, but only that he may be able to impress on his own countrymen, in cases of emergency, that he is acting at Your Excellency's requisition, that his representations may be more effectual, and that his own government may see he has had proper authority, as well as urgent occasion, for his proceedings. Neither does the undersigned desire to trouble Your Excellency upon trifling affairs. So soon as the intercourse is renewed, all such matters can be conducted between the official Hong Merchants and himself, agreeable to Your Excellency's further arrangements. Influenced by motives of solicitude for the character of his countrymen, and the general protection of the interests of a good trade, the undersigned feels it right to submit his own views to Your Excellency of this moment; and he has therefore used the character *Pin* in the address; but he requests Your Excellency to signify through the honourable officers, that it is a mode of address used by native officers, even of the second rank, so that it may be seen by the Government of his own country that he has acted upon admissible principles. He can assure Your Excellency that there is no disposition to press inconvenient changes on the government of the Empire, but only such modifications as are needful for the conduct of authentic intercourse, so that peace and honourable trade may always subsist."[1]

So open and unreserved a condemnation of the opium traffic could not fail to impress the provincial authorities, and through them the Court at Peking, to whom it would undoubtedly be forwarded. From that time the Chinese Government were justified in assuming that the trade was such as all the best Englishmen despised, and that their efforts to suppress it would be heartily seconded by the British Government. At the same time, the complete abandonment of the position with regard to the use of the character *Pin*, and the presentations of petitions through the Hong Merchants, must have been extremely gratifying to the Viceroy. How Captain Elliot could ask for the declaration that the mode of communication was one that he might fittingly adopt, after the candid avowal of the Chinese admiral on the occasion of Admiral Maitland's visit, it is difficult to understand. It is a very significant fact, that he dared not announce to the British residents at Canton the sacrifice he had made in order to renew official intercourse.[2]

On the 26th of December the Viceroy acknowledged the receipt of the Superintendent's petition and issued his "commands" to the *kwang-chow-foo* and the *kwang-hai* in

[1] *Correspondence Relating to China* (Blue Book, 1840), p. 334; *Chinese Repository*, vol. vii, p. 455; vol. xi, p. 347.

[2] *Correspondence Relating to China* (Blue Book, 1840), pp. 362–7; *Chinese Repository*, vol. xi, p. 347.

reply. He pointed out that, as Captain Elliot had come to control the merchants and seamen of his country, and had received commands from his sovereign, he must needs also have powers; he further stated that it was inexplicable that the Superintendent should find it difficult to expel from the river boats which had entered it in defiance of the law. Relying on the terms of Captain Elliot's address, the Viceroy, protesting that the boats troubled him "not one iota," gave the necessary sanction in the following words:—

"Seeing he has now addressed me as above, and that in his address he has plainly stated, that the Government of the British nation will regard these evil practices with no feelings of leniency, but on the other hand with severity and continual anxiety—seeing this, it is clear that he yet has a distinct understanding of his duty as a repressor of the evil and protector of the good. Nor has he sought to excuse the difficulty he meets with by pleading inability. It is not then befitting to me to adhere obstinately to the letter of the law, and so to isolate him from the object for which he has come hither.

"The request is therefore granted."[1]

In the Viceroy's edict not a word was said that would enable Captain Elliot to state to his Government that in using the character *Pin*, and in communicating through the Hong Merchants, he was not acting in a manner derogatory to his dignity. On this point the Viceroy preserved a discreet silence. Captain Elliot was of opinion that his policy had been crowned with success, for had he not obtained an answer to his address through the *kwang-chow-foo* and the *kwang-hai* instead of through the Hong Merchants? This was the argument by which he justified to himself the course he had taken. His efforts at once bore fruit in the form of a re-opening of trade, which took place on the 1st of January, 1839. The pleasure which he felt at the results he had achieved is reflected in a lengthy despatch, dated the 2nd January, 1839, in which he recounted to Lord Palmerston the progress of events and explained the reasons which had induced him to disregard the instructions as to the method of communicating

[1] *Chinese Repository*, vol. vii, p. 456.

with Chinese officials. In referring to the opium traffic he said that it was obvious that, as the danger and shame attaching to it increased, it would rapidly fall into the hands of more and more desperate men ; that it would stain the Foreign character with constantly aggravating disgrace, in the sight of the whole of the better portion of the Chinese people ; and that it would connect itself more and more intimately with the lawful commerce, to the great peril of vast public and private interests. So far as the Chamber of Commerce was concerned, few of the members were connected with the illicit trade, though that trade was extending itself among the resident population and would soon bring to Canton the refuse of all the countries in the neighbourhood, so that within a year there would have been at least three hundred armed and lawless men carrying on this business in the very heart of the regular commerce. After paying a tribute to the remarkable vigour shown by the imperial authorities, Captain Elliot explained that, in these peculiar circumstances, he felt justified in resorting to the use of the character *Pin*, as only by that means could he take the measures which the situation demanded. He pressed upon the Foreign Secretary the assurance that the idea of the character *Pin* was that of respectful report, not of solicitation or petition, and that it was the manner of address used by Chinese officers even of the third rank. In conclusion, he hoped that this attainment of direct official intercourse, as he styled it, would be satisfactory to Her Majesty's Government, it being the first intercourse of the kind which had ever existed between China and the western world.[1]

[1] *Correspondence Relating to China* (Blue Book, 1840), pp. 326–9; *Chinese Repository*, vol. xi, 347–350.

CHAPTER XVI

THE HIGH COMMISSIONER LIN

WHEN the year 1839 opened every Foreign resident at Canton realized that a crisis was at hand. Reports from Peking told how the party opposed to opium had gained a complete ascendency in the imperial counsels. Three princes of the blood had been deprived of their honours, mainly because they were smokers of opium. Hü Naitsi, whose memorial in favour of legalizing the importation of the drug had excited so much comment, was degraded to the sixth rank and dismissed from the public service. Huang Tseo-tsze had presented a memorial to the Throne, asking that all who smoked opium should be punished with death. The several provincial governments had been ordered to deliberate and report on his proposals, and their representations in the matter had recently been laid before the Emperor, the Grand Council, and the Board of Punishments for final consideration. It was feared that the result of their deliberations would not be a mitigation of the severity of the existing law. The persistency with which the local officials had enforced that law against Chinese subjects, who had any connection with the contraband traffic, had excited not only surprise but genuine alarm. The direction in which the law was to be amended was shown by a proclamation published by the Viceroy at the end of the year 1838, warning the people of Kwang-tung that though the reports from the various provincial governments on Huang Tseo-tsze's memorial might differ, the only discrepancy would be in the degree of increased severity, which they all advocated should be shown against those who dealt in or smoked opium. None, said he, were in favour of lenient measures. In a few days the yellow rescript promulgating the new law would arrive, and all who violated it would be tried and condemned. With an unwonted earnestness he thus warned them of the impending danger to those who disobeyed the law :—

"As for those who open opium shops and sell opium, profit is out of the question, destruction is already at their door! Their wealth will be utterly spent, and their thread of life clipped at the same moment of time! We, the Viceroy and Lieutenant-Governor, truly feel for you the utmost alarm and pity! Try and reflect for a moment. Ye are all of you sons of China, and your wealth is the substance of the Central Land! But ye are now taking the substance of your native country, and giving it away to Foreigners from abroad; and ye, sons of China, are losing your property and your lives in the same instant! It was your wealth, but now Foreigners possess it: and your very lives the Foreigners are now about to deprive you of! This is the first reflection; and still to be duped and befooled by these Foreigners, and induced by them to carry on this trade! O monstrous folly! O stupidity unparalleled! Ye aim after profit, but to make profit is impossible: ye try to preserve your lives, but even to do that is equally difficult! Ye take your money and purchase *death*. . . .

"Ye must every one of you, who deal in opium, speedily awake to a sense of your danger, and cleanse yourselves of your previous crimes. Let each man exert himself to save his property and his life, and follow after some better means of livelihood. As for those who smoke the drug, after not many days the death-inflicting period will be at hand. Do ye also arouse yourselves, and get rid of the evil habit without delay, and thus save your lives—now within a hair's-breadth of the gulf of destruction."[1]

Whilst this proclamation was fresh in the minds of the residents at Canton, the Emperor arrived at his final resolution in regard to opium. He resolved to send to Canton a special imperial commissioner, having absolute power to deal with the evil in any manner he might think fit, and charged to stamp out both the trade in opium and the practice of smoking the drug, and not to return until the evil had been utterly exterminated.[2] This High Commissioner was to be superior even to the Viceroy himself, and was to devote his entire

[1] *Chinese Repository*, vol. vii, p. 499. The Lieut.-Governor is the *foo-yuen*.

[2] *Chinese Repository*, vol. vii, pp. 613–4.

attention to the opium question. For the office thus created the Emperor chose Lin Tsih-seu, Viceroy of Hankow, destined to become famous to English readers under the name of Commissioner Lin. The decree appointing him, which was delivered by the Emperor to the Inner Council on the 31st of December, 1838, was of the briefest. It simply invested him with the powers and privileges of an imperial high commissioner and directed him with all speed to proceed to Kwang-tung, to make inquiry and to act in regard to the affairs of the sea-ports. It also directed that the whole naval force of the province be placed under his control.[1]

This decree reached Canton on the 23rd of January, 1839, together with an imperial edict issued through the Grand Council. The latter document, after referring to the prevalence of the use of opium and the continually increasing loss arising from the exportation of silver, stated that Lin was invested with the powers and privileges of an imperial commissioner, to exert his utmost strength in inquiring and acting with the view of thoroughly removing the source of this evil. The buildings in which the opium underwent preparation, the smuggling vessels in which it was conveyed, the shops opened for its sale, or for indulgence in its use, were thoroughly to be uprooted. The Viceroy and Lieutenant-Governor, having so many other duties to attend to, were relieved from the responsibility of taking the special measures required by the exigencies of the situation, but were required to second the efforts of the High Commissioner with every means in their power, and so atone for their previous negligence. In conclusion, the hope was expressed that owing to the new policy the long indulged habit would be for ever laid aside, and every root and germ of it utterly eradicated, and China saved from the "dire calamity."[2]

On the receipt of these edicts, the Viceroy realized that a proceeding so unusual as the appointment of the High Commissioner, and the stringent enforcement of the law that must be expected on his arrival, needed to be notified to the public

[1] *Chinese Repository*, vol. vii, p. 600.
[2] *Ibid.*, p. 602.

in such a manner that no one found disobeying the law in future could plead ignorance. Perceiving that this was necessary with regard to Foreigners as well as in the case of Chinese, he departed from the usual practice of simply issuing an edict to the Hong Merchants, and published his " orders " in a proclamation addressed to the whole of the Foreign merchants direct. After the usual recital of the blessings derived from intercourse with the Celestial Empire, followed by a reminder of the many prohibitions which had been issued against the opium traffic, he upbraided the Foreigners for their disobedience to the laws, recounted the repressive measures that were being enforced against Chinese subjects, and explained the nature of the fresh instructions which had just been received. The naval authorities were to take every lawless boat engaged in the clandestine traffic, and drive forth all the Foreign vessels cruising about. The military were to search after and take possession of every building used for the preparation or for the smoking of opium, and to seize all persons found selling or inhaling the drug. All the warehousing vessels were to be sent away and the other vessels were to be brought under proper control. Any further participation in the contraband traffic on the part of Foreigners was to be punished by a stoppage of the whole trade. The language of this edict was so clear, that it is impossible to say that fair warning was not given of the measures that might be expected on the arrival of the High Commissioner. The following passages are sufficient to show this :—

" When you would come to Canton to trade, you all assumed to yourselves the name of good Foreigners. Could any then have conceived of the recent entrance of boats with opium into the river, which has been discovered by recent seizures, exposing to view all your impish trickery ? Can you now yet call yourselves good Foreigners, or say that you are pursuing each an honest calling ?

" At this time the Great Emperor, in his bitter detestation of the evil habit, has his thoughts hourly bent on washing it clean away. In the capital he has commanded the ministers of his Court to deliberate, and with severity to draw up plans for procedure. In the provinces he has commanded the administrators over his dominions to enforce vigorously the penalties prescribed by the laws. His Heaven-derived firmness will form its own resolves: and what his will determines, that surely shall be done. . . . Besides all this, the Great Emperor has just now appointed a high officer as his special commissioner to repair to Canton in order to examine and adopt measures in reference to the affairs of the seaports. From morn till eve his arrival may hourly be looked for. His purpose is to cut off utterly the source of this noxious abuse, to strip bare and root up this enormous evil: and though the axe should break in his hand, or the boat should sink from beneath him, yet will he not stay his efforts till the work of purification be accomplished."[1]

On the publication of these documents the mercantile community realized that great changes might be expected. Canton became full of rumours as to what the High Commissioner intended to do when he arrived. There was an almost complete stoppage of the contraband traffic on the coast, both at Lintin and further to the East. The receiving ships at Hong-kong, which had become a secondary depot for contraband opium, prepared to proceed to the "outside waters" for the greater security of their cargo.[2] A rumour arose that a search was to be made of every shop and house in Canton, and though this was officially denied, the inhabitants repaired the gates of the city, in order that, if such a search were attempted, they might first obtain assurances that it should be conducted in a lawful manner.[3] Howqua, the senior Hong Merchant, took particular pains to warn Captain Elliot that extreme measures were likely to be taken; and that this was fully understood by the British Superintendent appears from a despatch, dated the 30th of January, 1839, in which he apprised Lord Palmerston of the new development in the imperial policy. In this despatch he wrote:—

[1] *Correspondence Relating to China* (Blue Book, 1840), p. 347; *Chinese Repository*, vol. vii, pp. 602–5.
[2] *Chinese Repository*, vol. vii, p. 552.
[3] *Ibid.*, p. 504.

"The stagnation of the opium traffic at all points, however, may be said to have been nearly complete for the last four months. And it is now my duty to signify to your Lordship the expected arrival of a very high officer from the Court, to hold equal rank with the Governor, and specially charged, as I am this day informed by Howqua, with the general conduct of the measures lately determined upon at Peking, for the suppression of the opium trade. It must also be stated that the Emperor has recently been advised to command a total interruption of the Foreign trade and intercourse, till the introduction of the opium shall be sufficiently stopped: and an edict of great moment, evidently founded upon that policy, has just been issued to the Foreign merchants but not yet to myself. . . . There seems, my Lord, no longer any room to doubt that the Court has firmly determined to suppress, or, more probably most extensively, to check the opium trade. . . . In the excited temper of this extraordinary government it would be unsafe, indeed, to speculate upon the particular measures they may pursue: but, at least, I am sure that my own altered position, and the course I took last month, with respect to the forced trade within the river, will give much weight to my remonstrances, in any moment of emergency.

"Replying to Howqua's suggestion to-day, that such proceedings must be looked for, I said, I earnestly hoped not, because I was persuaded they would be regarded by my own Government to be unjust and hostile in the very last degree. I added, that I should be careful to clear myself of all responsibility, by signifying these convictions to the Provincial Government, in respectful, but most plain terms, directly that it adopted courses so certain, in my judgment, to tend to an interruption of the peace between the two countries. He met this observation by saying that I had experience enough of the Chinese Government to know that full time would be given before such extreme measures were adopted. I answered, that the lapse of no interval of time could justify aggression upon public and private interests embarked in this lawful trade, by reason of the acts of smugglers, in a high degree encouraged by the chief authorities of these provinces.

"He dwelt earnestly upon the manifold mischiefs of the trade, and particularly upon the alarming character of the late inside traffic, asking me what my Government would do under the circumstances! I said, that no such state of things could obtain in England, and he must give me leave to remark three things concerning that part of the subject: First, that it no longer subsisted; second, that it had been induced by the venality of the highest officers of this province; third, that it had been put down by the effect of my representations and proceedings, as soon as ever I was in a condition to take steps concerning it. . . .

"He anxiously entreated me to press, in my despatches to my Government, on the great and growing danger of this traffic to the lawful trade and peaceful intercourse; and he led me to understand that some official communication on the subject must be expected as soon as the High Commissioner arrived."[1]

This despatch shows a decided change of attitude towards the opium traffic on the part of Captain Elliot, when compared with his address to the Viceroy of the 23rd of December. To say that that traffic no longer existed, because the ships engaged in it had withdrawn from the Canton River, was a mere quibble. In his own mind the Superintendent seems to have drawn an artificial line across the entrance to the Bocca Tigris, and regarded everything that went on outside that line as not occurring in China. There was no foundation either in international law, or in the rules laid down by the Chinese for the control of Chinese waters, for any such distinction. The fact that the traffic had been induced by the venality of Chinese officials was no argument against the right of the Chinese Government to suppress it by any means they might think necessary. The statement that the traffic had been put down by Captain Elliot's "representations and proceedings" is not accurate. The Chinese had been frightened by the severity, with which the law was being enforced, from having any active dealings in the drug. Among the Foreigners there was a temporary stagnation induced by the uncertainty as to what the High Commissioner intended to do. That is

[1] *Correspondence Relating to China* (Blue Book, 1840), pp. 343–4.

as much as can be said in support of such an assertion. The visible evidence of the traffic had been removed from Canton, but although the opium boats had left the river, opium was being brought to Lintin as freely as ever. In February the shippers in India had 50,000 chests ready for the Chinese market, and there were 10,000 chests in Chinese waters.[1] In some way or another large quantities were finding their way to Canton, as is amply demonstrated by the amount delivered up a few months later, when the High Commissioner took the decisive measures of which mention will be made presently.

On the 1st February all the back doors of the Factories were blocked up.[2] On the 26th of the same month, when Captain Elliot happened to be away at Macao, the Chinese again asserted their right to execute criminals where they might choose. A native dealer in opium was suddenly brought down to the square before the Factories and there put to death by strangulation.[3] The British residents at once requested of Mr. Johnston, the deputy Superintendent, who had been left in charge at Canton, that the British flag might be struck as a protest against this fresh outrage. Two days later, having heard that H.M.S. *Larne* had arrived off Macao, they sent a written request that her services might be made available for the protection of British interests.[4]

The Superintendent, having received news of these occurrences, embarked for Canton, where he arrived on March 2nd. He at once notified the British community that he did not intend to hoist the British flag in the existing state of affairs, and that orders had been given to H.M.S. *Larne* to remain at Macao. On March 4th he issued a circular to British subjects having reference to the recent execution, in which he told them that "in his own judgment, the purpose of this most humiliating event was not only to intimidate but to degrade and render hateful the whole Foreign community in the sight of the native population." On the same day he sent a written

[1] *Chinese Repository*, vol. vii, p. 552.

[2] *Chinese Repository*, vol. xi, p. 354.

[3] *Ibid.*, vol. vii, p. 606.

[4] *Correspondence Relating to China* (Blue Book, 1840) p. 359; *Chinese Repository*, vol. vii, p. 606.

protest to the Viceroy, of which he distributed copies to the British residents.[1]

On 10th March Captain Elliot returned to Macao, "leaving the trade still proceeding, but with a state of gloom subsisting in the minds of all men, both natives and Foreigners," in order to consult with Captain Blake of the *Larne* as to the best course to be adopted. It had been rumoured that the High Commissioner, on his arrival, would commence operations from Macao. It was without surprise, therefore, that Captain Elliot found that a considerable military force had been assembled and numbers of ships and boats of war collected, while a display of old vessels, intended to serve as fire-ships, was made at the Bocca Tigris. By this time Captain Elliot's attitude towards the contraband trade had so completely changed that he had made up his mind to protect even the opium vessels. He himself says: "Resolved, in any pressure of emergency actually threatening the continued peaceful intercourse with this Empire, to incur most heavy personal responsibilities, concerning the ships engaged in the illicit traffic, I had also determined to resist sudden aggression on British life and British property at all hazards, and to all extremity, and I am well assured, your Lordship will be of opinion, that this was my capital duty as the Queen's officer."[2] On March 12th he notified the Viceroy that he was about to inform the British Government that the execution of a criminal before the Foreign dwelling-houses was "an outrage on the feelings and dignity of all Western Governments, whose flags were recently flying at Canton," and asked for "a calming declaration" in order that he might report to his official superiors "the needlessness of immediate and direct appeals to the Great Emperor for protection."[3]

Lin Tsih-seu was a native of Fu-kien. Having been born and bred in the maritime provinces, he had from his early days, as he tells us,[4] been intimately acquainted with the ways of

[1] *Correspondence Relating to China* (Blue Book, 1840), p. 360–1.
[2] *Ibid.*, p. 362.
[3] *Ibid.*
[4] *Chinese Repository*, vol. vii, p. 610.

Foreigners, and that was one of the reasons why he was specially chosen to deal with the opium question. At the time of his appointment he was holding the office of Viceroy of Hu-kuang.[1] His age at this time was about fifty-five years, but his appearance was that of a man about ten years younger.[2] Foreigners who saw him were favourably impressed with his personal appearance. He has been described as bland and vivacious, with nothing about him that was barbarous or savage. His countenance was that of a man habituated to care and thoughtfulness. The full round face and keen black eye, the clear voice and distinct utterance, showed a man of determination. The general impression left upon those who saw him was that in him the Emperor had found a great statesman.[3]

The High Commissioner received his instructions concerning the opium traffic direct from the Emperor himself. It is reported that his Imperial master, the father of the Chinese nation, having recounted to him the evils of the flowing poison that had long afflicted his children, burst into tears. "How, alas ! " he cried, " can I die and go to the shades of my imperial father and ancestors until these direful evils are removed ? " Then, turning to Lin, the Emperor put into his hand the seal of his high commission, invested him with such power as only thrice in their history had the monarchs of the Manchu dynasty delegated to a subject, and dismissed him with the words, " Go, examine and act."[4]

Thus charged, Commissioner Lin set out for Canton. No political passion prompted his mission. It was the outcome of a resolve by the Emperor to make one great effort to rid the empire of what he regarded as a national curse. Whatever our views of the opium traffic, whatever our opinion of the measures taken by the High Commissioner to effect his end, we must allow that there is something of the sublime in the spectacle of the Emperor thus rousing himself on behalf of his people.

[1] See *ante*, p. 186.
[2] *Chinese Repository*, vol. vii, p. 610.
[3] *Chinese Repository*, vol. viii, p. 77.
[4] *Chinese Repository*, vol. vii, p. 610.

On the 10th of March the High Commissioner arrived at Canton. For eight days he did nothing beyond making inquiries. Then, on the 18th, one of the Foreign interpreters, Mr. Thom, was summoned to Howqua's hong and asked to translate a paper, which proved to be an edict addressed to the whole of the Foreign residents, demanding that within three days all their opium be surrendered through the Hong Merchants to be burnt and destroyed. Admitting that smuggling had been possible owing to former prohibitions having been comparatively lax, the High Commissioner, in this document, announced that now the Emperor's wrath had been fearfully roused and would never be appeased until the evil had been utterly extirpated. Any Chinese found dealing in opium, or establishing houses for smoking it, would be punished with the extreme penalty of the law, and it was in contemplation to render capital the offence of merely smoking the drug Foreigners were to pay obedience to the laws and statutes of China equally with natives, and if they showed scornful or contemptuous trifling with the mildness of the Great Emperor, it would become requisite to comprehend them, too, within the course of punishment prescribed by the new enactments. Every particle of opium on the store ships was to be given up. Relying on the good faith which, as he said, he had learnt Foreigners practised, he demanded that they should each give a bond, written in English and Chinese, promising that their vessels would never again dare to carry opium, and acknowledging that, if thereafter any of the drug were brought to China, it should be forfeited to the Chinese Government, the persons bringing it punished with death, and to this punishment they would willingly submit. In the following terms he expressed his determination to carry out the imperial behests :—

"On this occasion I, the High Commissioner, having come from the capital, have personally received the sacred commands, that wherever a law exists, it is to be fully enforced. And as I have brought these full powers and privileges, enabling me to perform whatever seems to me right, powers with which those ordinarily given, for inquiring and acting in regard to other matters, are by no means comparable, so will I delay my return as long as the opium remains unexterminated. I swear that I will progress with this matter from its beginning to its ending, and that not a thought of stopping half-way shall for a moment be indulged."[1]

On the same day an edict was issued to the Hong Merchants[2] in which the High Commissioner upbraided them for that they, who had been specially charged in 1816 with the prevention of the illicit traffic, should have so signally failed in their duty. He pointed out that the bonds, given by them as security that the Foreign ships had no opium on board, were utterly worthless, being given without regard to the true facts of the case. The Hong Merchants themselves, their servants and assistants, had all participated in the unlawful trade. Moreover, they had got into the habit of abasing themselves before Foreigners, with the result that the latter had totally ceased to render that respect noticeable in earlier times. Their one desire was to grow rich. They had given Foreigners information on any topic on which it was desired, but they themselves, if questioned as to the affairs of the Foreigners, were found to have no information whatever. They had connived at the export of silver, by pretending that the money they sent away had been left in their custody by Foreigners, who had quitted Canton and afterwards died, and so had conspired to break the law. He exhorted them to carry out the imperial commands, and to see to it that the opium was delivered up within the three days. By way of stimulating their zeal, he concluded with these significant words :—

"Three days are prescribed in which they must obtain the required bonds and report in reply hereto. If it be found that this matter cannot be at once arranged by them, it will be apparent without inquiry, that they are constantly acting in concert with depraved Foreigners, and that their minds have a perverted inclination. And I, the High Commissioner,

[1] *Chinese Repository*, vol. vii, p. 614.

[2] *Correspondence Relating to China* (Blue Book, 1840), pp. 352–5; *Chinese Repository*, vol. vii, pp. 615–9.

will forthwith solicit the imperial death-warrant and select for execution one or two of the most unworthy of their number, confiscating their property to government, and thus will I show a lucid warning."

The excitement produced by these two edicts was intense. But the worst had not yet come. On the following day Mr. Wetmore, the chairman of the Chamber of Commerce, received through the Hong Merchants a notification from the Hoppo that, pending the stay of the High Commissioner in Canton, no one was to leave the city, and that no petitions to go to Macao would be granted during the investigations that had now begun.[1] In short, the whole of the Foreign residents were imprisoned in the Factories, and were to remain so confined until the High Commissioner had accomplished his purpose of extirpating opium and everything connected with it. A passage boat, the *Snipe*, which had no opium on board but only goods on which the duties had been paid, and for which a passport had been granted, was stopped in attempting to pass the Bogue. She was confiscated, and ultimately broken up.[2]

The 21st March, the last of the three days fixed by the edicts, arrived without any opium having been surrendered or any bond given. On that day the Chamber of Commerce wrote to the Hong Merchants informing them that the following resolution had been passed by the Chamber: "That the communications made by the Commissioner of the imperial will are of such vital importance, and involve such complicated interests, that a reply cannot be given to them without the greatest deliberation, and that a committee should now therefore be appointed to take the measures into consideration, and report their opinions to the Chamber at the earliest possible period. That in the meantime a deputation from this meeting do wait upon the Hong Merchants to state to them what has been done, who may at the same time state that there is an almost unanimous feeling in the community of the absolute necessity of the Foreign residents of Canton having no connection with the opium traffic." It was also stated that such

[1] *Chinese Repository*, vol. vii, p. 620.
[2] *Ibid.*

a committee had already been appointed.[1] This letter was conveyed by a deputation to the Hong Merchants, who took it to the High Commissioner.

Matters had now assumed a most serious aspect. All business was stopped. All intercourse with the outside world, even with Whampoa, was cut off, and boats that had come to the city were not allowed to return. Troops were assembled in the suburbs, and war-junks carrying armed men appeared on the river in front of the Factories. At ten o'clock at night a meeting of the Chamber of Commerce was summoned to receive the Hong Merchants, who had returned from the city. When asked what had happened before the High Commissioner they said : " We took the words of your letter to him, and he gave them to the prefect to examine ; on hearing them read, he said you were trifling with us, but you should not do so with him. He declared that if opium was not delivered up, he should be at the Consoo House at ten o'clock to-morrow, and then he would show what he would do." The Hong Merchants went on to declare that, unless some opium was given up, they felt assured two of their number would be beheaded in the morning! After considerable discussion it was decided that 1,037 chests should be surrendered to be destroyed, this being tendered not by the Chamber, but by individuals.[2]

On the following day the Hong Merchants communicated this offer to the High Commissioner, who assured them that the amount was by no means sufficient. Fresh demands were therefore made on the Foreign residents. Moreover, an invitation was sent to Dent, a merchant to whom reference has previously been made, to go to the city gates to meet his excellency. Dent expressed his willingness to go, on condition that the Commissioner would give him a safe-conduct guaranteeing his return within twenty-four hours. The Hong Merchants urged him to go, declaring that their lives would be in danger if he refused. But as the desired assurance was not forthcoming, it was decided that he should remain in the Factories. It was afterwards discovered that the High

[1] *Chinese Repository*, vol. vii, p. 621.
[2] *Ibid.*, p. 622.

Commissioner had engaged the services of two cooks, who had been in the service of Foreigners, from which it was inferred that there could be no doubt that it had been intended to detain him as a hostage. On the following day the Hong Merchants again repaired to Dent's house, Howqua and Mowqua appearing with chains around their necks and deprived of their buttons of rank.[1] They were met by most of the Foreign residents, who refused to allow Dent to go, except on a written and sealed guarantee that he should be treated with respect and allowed to return after the conference. After much discussion the Hong Merchants agreed to introduce to the *kwang-chow-foo* a deputation, who should explain to that official the objections to allowing Dent to go to the city.[2]

Messrs. Inglis, Thom, Fearon and Slade were chosen for this purpose. They were conducted by the Hong Merchants to the temple of the Queen of Heaven, where they had an interview with several of the local officials. These demanded that Dent should be given up and confronted with the High Commissioner, because, as they said, he was in possession of 6,000 chests of opium. They threatened that, if he did not consent, he should be dragged out of his house by force, and that the High Commissioner would most assuredly kill him. The latter part of the threat seems to have been invented by them for the occasion, for its ferocity was quite inconsistent with the fact that, after being detained about three hours, the deputation was allowed to leave with some trifling presents of silk and wine to the gentlemen who had acted as interpreters.[2] The deputation returned at nine o'clock in the evening. By midnight the Hong Merchants were back at Dent's house, again urging their request; but when it was suggested to Howqua that the next day, being Sunday, was the Foreigners' day for religious worship, the discussions were at once suspended. At the usual hour the residents did in fact engage in public worship in their chapel, and continued to do so on every Sunday during their forced stay at Canton.[3]

[1] *i.e.*, the buttons worn by officials on their caps.
[2] *Chinese Repository*, vol. vii., pp. 623–4.
[3] *Ibid.*, p. 625.

The news of what was happening at Canton reached Macao on March 22nd. Captain Elliot at once sent a letter to the Viceroy, demanding to know in the name of his Sovereign, whether the warlike preparations going on around him and the unprecedented events at Canton meant that the Viceroy was about to make war upon British subjects. This he forwarded through the *keun-min-foo*, there being no Hong Merchants at Macao. On the same day he issued a circular to British subjects, requiring all British shipping lying at the outer anchorages to remove to Hong-kong, and to be prepared to resist any act of aggression on the part of the Chinese Government. The next day he published a notice saying that owing to recent events he was without confidence in the justice and moderation of the provincial government; that he considered it impossible to continue peaceful intercourse with safety, honour, or advantage till satisfactory explanations had been received; that he intended to demand forthwith passports for all British subjects who might wish to proceed "outside"; and that British merchants should lodge with him without delay their claims in writing for loss or damage arising out of the present condition of affairs. He further announced that the Portuguese authorities had pledged themselves to afford protection to all British residents at Macao, so long as their business was not at variance with the laws of China. The Superintendent then wrote to Captain Blake that in the interests of British subjects he felt it necessary to proceed to Whampoa, and that if no news of him should be received within six days of his departure, Captain Blake might assume that he was detained as a prisoner with the British subjects at Canton, unless satisfactory assurances were forthcoming from the Chinese admiral at the Bogue. With these preliminaries he set out for Whampoa, having first despatched to Lord Palmerston an account of the steps he had taken, stating that he should take the most prompt measures to meet "the unjust and menacing dispositions of the High Commissioner and the provincial authorities."

At four o'clock in the afternoon of the 24th of March the Superintendent reached Whampoa, where he learnt that no communication had been allowed with the Factories for two days. Moved by "the reflection of the natural unfitness of a commercial community to take any consentaneous course respecting the delicate and momentous question in hand," and by the belief that unless he reached the Factories some desperate calamity would ensue, he decided to go right up to Canton. Arrayed in his official uniform, he embarked in the gig of H.M.S. *Larne*, which he had brought with him, and with four men at the oars managed by pulling and sailing to reach the Factories in safety at six o'clock that evening. Immediately on landing he ordered the boat's ensign to be hoisted to the lower mast-head of the Factory flag-staff, the topmast having been struck after the execution. He then went straight to Dent's house and walked with him arm-in-arm to the hall. Having sent word to the Hong Merchants that he was willing to proceed into the city with Dent, on receiving a written assurance, sealed with the signet of the High Commissioner, that Dent should never for an instant be removed from his sight, he assembled the whole Foreign community, read to them the circular he had issued at Macao, and exhorted them all to be moderate, firm, and united.[1]

As far as the Chinese were concerned, Captain Elliot's arrival did not improve the situation. No sooner had he landed than they were seized with alarm, and orders to close every pass around the Factories were shouted from one police post to another. In a few minutes the Factory square was deserted by the natives, and the entrances thereto closed and guarded. The few coolies, who on the preceding nights had watched the doors of the Hongs, were replaced by large companies of men armed with spears and furnished with lanterns. A triple cordon of boats, filled with armed men, formed a crescent in the river along the whole front of the Factories, and soldiers were stationed on the roofs of the neighbouring houses. As night drew on, patrols, sentinels, and officers hastened hither and thither, adding to the confusion with the blowing of trumpets and the beating of gongs. To crown all,

[1] *Correspondence Relating to China* (Blue Book, 1840), pp. 355–8; *Chinese Repository*, vol. xi, pp. 372–3.

orders were given by the High Commissioner that all compradores and coolies should leave the Foreigners, with the result that by nine o'clock not a servant remained in the Factories.[1] Only those who have lived in the East can appreciate the misery and discomfort that this last measure entailed.

The next day the Chinese constructed two rafts across the river to prevent the Foreigners escaping, or help coming to them from Whampoa. No parcels or letters could be sent down the river, except at the risk of life to those who carried them. In short, the residents at Canton were as completely cut off from the outside world as they would have been in a beleaguered city. Then, as on many an occasion since, the Chinese seem to have discovered that their regular soldiers existed only on paper, for coolies without any military training were promptly converted into men-at-arms, and provided with swords, spears, and shields. Some of these were boatmen, others labourers, others porters. Under the command of subaltern officers they marched round and round the square before the Factories, like boys at a mock training.[2]

On the 25th March Captain Elliot wrote to the Viceroy, asking that he would issue passports for all the British residents within three days, and grant them boats for the removal of their persons and property, with a guard to protect them from the violence of the lower orders. In this letter he ignored the real reasons why the residents were detained in Canton, and observed that he could not conceal from His Excellency his conviction that the peace between the two countries was placed in imminent jeopardy by the late unexplained and alarming proceedings of the government. On the same day the Superintendent sent a second letter, asking that the Viceroy would appoint an officer to visit him, "to the end that all matters may be peacefully adjusted," and promising that, if he were permitted to communicate with his countrymen at Whampoa, none should attempt to force their way up the river. He further requested that the native servants might be allowed to return, that

[1] *Chinese Repository*, vol. vii, p. 627.
[2] *Ibid.*, p. 628.

provisions might be supplied and the barriers removed from the Factories. He stated that he was sincerely anxious to fulfil the pleasure of the Great Emperor, as soon as it should be authentically made known to him, and that he had always manifested his desire to keep the peace and fulfil the pleasure of the Viceroy. He apologized for any unsuitable expressions that might appear in his communications, on the ground that they were due to his imperfect acquaintance with the Chinese language, and not to any intention to manifest disrespect.[1]

These letters were forwarded by the Viceroy to the High Commissioner with a covering despatch, which recommended that the passports should be granted when the opium should have been surrendered. The Viceroy, in this document, professed not to understand what was meant by the phrase "the two countries," which Captain Elliot had used, and expressed the opinion that it might be intended to denote England and America! Lin adopted the viceregal recommendation, and on the 26th March issued through the *kwang-chow-foo* "commands" to the British Superintendent, to the effect that he should speedily take the opium laid up on board the store-ships and surrender it at once, promising that if this were done the passports should be issued without delay. At the same time, he made severe comment on Captain Elliot's omission to refer to the real cause of the present troubles.[2]

On March 26th the High Commissioner issued a further proclamation, exhorting the Foreigners to surrender their opium, and giving under four heads the reasons why they should do so. First, the reason which heaven hath implanted in all should show them that the opium traffic was one which heaven looked upon with disgust, and that in cutting it off the Emperor was actuated by the exalted virtue of heaven itself. Second, because they would be obeying the law of the land, which was in harmony with the laws of their own country, that prohibited the smoking of opium.[3] Third,

[1] *Chinese Repository*, vol. xi, pp. 360–1.

[2] *Correspondence Relating to China* (Blue Book, 1840), pp. 368–9; *Chinese Repository*, vol. xi, p, 362.

[3] This was and is true so far as India is concerned.

because of their feelings as men, which should make them see that the advantage to be gained in being allowed to continue their trade was infinitely greater than any temporary loss they might suffer by delivering up the opium in their possession. Fourth, because the necessity of the case demanded it. As an awful warning he cited the case of Lord Napier, who " bolted through the Bocca Tigris, but being overwhelmed with grief and fear almost immediately died." He reminded them of their boasted sense of honour, and sarcastically observed that now that the Chinese officials were appealing to it, not the slightest particle of honour could they find. He warned them that a total suspension of trade would be the result of further delay.[1]

This threat was put into force the next day, when the Hoppo issued an edict, dated the 27th of March, prohibiting all ships then at Whampoa from opening their holds or leaving the port during the stay of the High Commissioner in Canton, and so long as his measures against opium were in operation.[2] By this time the merchants were beginning to waver in their opposition to the High Commissioner's demands. On the 25th of March they had presented a petition stating that, having now been made fully aware of the imperial commands for the entire abolition of the traffic in opium, they pledged themselves not to deal in the drug, or to attempt to introduce it into the Chinese Empire. They pointed out that as individual merchants they did not possess the power of controlling the whole trade, and requested that a final settlement might be arranged through the representatives of their respective nations.[2] Influenced, no doubt, by the conduct of the merchants in presenting this petition, and impressed with the firmness shown by the High Commissioner, Captain Elliot resolved that the opium should be surrendered without further resistance.

The 27th March, 1839, was an eventful day. The British Superintendent sent an address to the High Commissioner asking that His Excellency would be pleased to indicate the

[1] *Chinese Repository*, vol. vii, pp. 628–33.
[2] *Ibid.*, p. 636.

point to which the ships of his nation having opium on board should proceed, in order that the whole might be delivered up. A reply was received through the *kwang-chow-foo*, stating that there were twenty-two ships with opium on board, and requiring Captain Elliot to ascertain what was the precise amount of their consignments, and to present a written report setting out the exact details.[1]

Captain Elliot forthwith issued a notice to British subjects, requiring them to surrender to him, as representing the British Government, all the opium under their control, to hold the British ships engaged in the opium traffic subject to his immediate direction, and to forward at once a sealed list of all the British-owned opium in their possession. He announced that he would be responsible, for and on behalf of Her Majesty's Government, to all British subjects who should comply with this demand, and that he would accept no liability in respect of British-owned opium that was not surrendered by six o'clock that evening. Another document that appeared on the 27th of March was the High Commissioner's reply to the merchants' petition of the 25th, in which he announced that he would direct the superintendents and consuls of the various nations, who must forthwith send in their names for his information, to manage the business of arranging a final settlement of the opium question.[2]

One merchant, a Mr. King, had written to the High Commissioner to say that, during the many years he had been engaged in trade at Canton, he had never bought, sold, received, or delivered one catty of opium or one tael of sycee silver, and that he was ready to promise to pursue the same course in future under the penalties desired by the Chinese Government. Having made this declaration, he asked that the restrictions on his business might be removed and his servants allowed to return to his factory. The High Commissioner, in reply, commended his previous conduct, but pointed out that, as the opium had not yet been delivered up, he could not for the sake of a single case, " change his great

[1] *Chinese Repository*, vol. vii, pp. 635-641.
[2] *Ibid.*, pp. 637-9.

plans." The reason given in this edict for the withdrawal of the compradores and servants was that it was feared that, if allowed to remain with the Foreigners, they might point out a way of escape.[1]

Notwithstanding Captain Elliot's promise that the opium should be surrendered, and the efforts he was making to that end, the Chinese continued to keep the Foreign residents in even closer confinement, but in other ways gave proof of a desire to treat them without severity. On the 28th of March three of the four streets leading into the square before the Factories were walled up, and as a military guard was stationed at the fourth, no way of egress was left. In the afternoon some sheep, pigs, and poultry and other provisions were sent to the Consoo-house by order of the High Commissioner. These were on the following day "graciously bestowed" on the Foreign residents, most of whom refused to accept them. Coolies were also sent to the Factories with water.[2] On the same day Captain Elliot notified the High Commissioner that he was prepared to deliver up 20,283 chests of British-owned opium, but could not hold himself responsible for that belonging to the subjects of other nations. As a good deal of this opium was not at Canton, and so could not be surrendered forthwith, Captain Elliot requested that the Chinese authorities would accept his solemn pledge to deliver it up as it came into his possession, adding that, if he dared to break his pledge in the least degree, he would assuredly draw upon himself the severest displeasure of his sovereign.

Commissioner Lin was evidently pleased with the success that had attended his measures. In acknowledging the Chief Superintendent's communication he made it quite clear that all the opium, whether stored or lately arrived, and wherever it might actually be, must be surrendered. He expressed the conviction that Captain Elliot's behaviour was absolutely sincere, and promised a complete amnesty to all who had violated the law, provided the whole of the opium were delivered up. He appointed the 29th of March as the date

[1] *Chinese Repository*, vol. vii, p. 638.
[2] *Ibid.*

on which his officers would receive the opium actually lying in the Factories, and the 30th as the day on which the ships at Whampoa should be inspected and the opium lying there surrendered. As to the twenty-two store ships outside the Bogue, the High Commissioner himself, accompanied by the Viceroy, would visit them between March 31st and April 2nd, and accept the surrender of their cargoes. To the American, French, and Dutch Consuls he intended to issue orders similar to those addressed to the British Superintendent, but as Captain Elliot had been specially permitted to remain as Superintendent in the Factories, he was required to spread abroad his monitions, so that all might speedily deliver up whatever opium they had.[1]

This date, the 28th March, 1839, was a memorable one for edicts. In addition to that just mentioned, the High Commissioner, on that day, issued through Chu, the *kwang-chow-foo*, rules for the delivery of the opium, in which he made it clear that he meant to get into his hands every particle of the drug controlled by the Foreigners within his jurisdiction. That in the Factories and at Whampoa was first to be surrendered; then the receiving ships at Lintin were to proceed to Chuenpi and there await the arrival of the High Commissioner and the Viceroy; then that at Macao should be taken to the same point and surrendered. The precaution was taken to include opium that might happen to be in transit, and it was ordered that ships which arrived with any on board should proceed to Sandy Head and there surrender it.[2] On this same day the High Commissioner issued an edict to the American, Dutch, and French consuls, whose names he had ascertained from the Chamber of Commerce, requiring them to see that the residents of their respective nationalities delivered up all the opium in their possession. This document is remarkable for the statement that the traffic in opium carried on by the American and other Foreign merchants, had not been

[1] *Chinese Repository*, vol. xi, pp. 367–8.

[2] *Ibid.*, pp. 368–9; *Correspondence Relating to China* (Blue Book, 1840), p. 377. The point at Chuenpi chosen for unloading the opium was Sandy Hook.

less than that of the English.[1] Throughout the negotiations for the surrender of the opium the Chinese regarded Captain Elliot as responsible for all the Foreigners, partly because in his communications with the Chinese officials he held himself out as the champion of all foreign interests, and partly because the British at this time enjoyed so pre-eminent a position at Canton.[2] Captain Elliot thus found himself in the very unenviable position of being regarded as personally responsible for the delivery up of all the opium in Canton or the neighbourhood, however owned. This was a wider responsibility than he could possibly accept, but he determined to see that all that happened to be in the control of his countrymen, whether British-owned or not, was surrendered. Accordingly, on the 28th March he issued to the British residents a notice requiring any of them who might have opium in their factories, without particularizing its ownership, to acknowledge the same to him within two hours of the publication of the notice.[3]

The next day, the 29th, was Good Friday, when at Captain Elliot's request the usual services were held in the chapel. This day was marked by the confinement being made a little closer, access to the Consoo House being prohibited and Old China Street closed. The British Factory was now closely guarded day and night by scores of coolies under the superintendence of the Hong Merchants. On this day two buckets of spring water were brought to each house by the Chinese. The Superintendent sent a request to the High Commissioner that the servants might be allowed to return, and the passage boats resume their running. In reply, the High Commissioner complained that Captain Elliot had not taken the necessary steps for the delivery of the opium, and requested him to prepare letters immediately, which the Chinese authorities might hand to the store ships, as orders for the delivery of the opium contained on board.[4] On the 30th Captain Elliot

[1] *Chinese Repository*, vol. vii, p. 639.
[2] See *ante*, pp. 176, 182, 326.
[3] *Chinese Repository*, vol. vii., p. 638.
[4] *Ibid.*, vol. vii, pp. 643–5; vol. xi, pp. 369–370; *Correspondence Relating to China* (Blue Book, 1840), pp. 378–80.

asked that the passage boats might be permitted to run again, as he wished Mr. Johnston, the deputy superintendent, to proceed outside the Bogue and assemble all the British shipping at Lintin, with a view to superintending the delivery of the opium. To this the High Commissioner replied, that as Captain Elliot had taken on himself the power, entrusted to him by his sovereign, of requiring the people of his nation to surrender their opium, it was plain that there could be no difficulty in giving orders direct to the store-ships, and that there was no need of " multiplying the twists and turns of the transaction " by sending Mr. Johnston.[1]

The Chinese authorities were beginning to show their gratification at the success that so far had attended their policy. On the 30th of March the local magistrates came into the square before the Factories on a tour of inspection. Supplies of food were sent by the High Commissioner to Captain Elliot, who thought best to refuse them and hand them over to the *linguists*. The same day an American, named Wetmore, who held the position of Chairman of the Chamber of Commerce, received from the High Commissioner an edict acknowledging the receipt of the information as to the names of the American, French, and Dutch consuls, supplied by him some few days before. In this edict Wetmore was asked why the non-British residents had not surrendered their opium, and was requested to urge them to comply with the High Commissioner's demands forthwith. Another edict of the same date, addressed to the United States' consul, asked for a full and true statement as to the opium in the possession of American citizens. To this request the answer was given that 1,540 chests had been handed over to Captain Elliot, to be delivered up by him. The High Commissioner retorted that this was greatly at variance with Captain Elliot's statement that he had no control over people not under British rule, and a mere pretext, and required that a full and true statement be made out without concealment.[2]

The Dutch consul, also on 30th March, informed His Excellency that neither he nor any of his nation held any

[1] *Chinese Repository*, vol. vii, p. 645.
[2] *Ibid.*, pp. 646–7.

opium ; that the Hoppo had refused him leave to go to Macao, or to give a port clearance for the one Dutch ship at Whampoa ; that he therefore considered he and the people of his nation had been forcibly detained ; and that he wished leave to depart.[1] To this the High Commissioner replied, that for the sake of a single vessel of the Dutch nation, it was impossible to break in upon the preventive measures, and that although the Dutch consul had no opium, he ought to induce the other Foreigners to give up theirs, and that when all the opium had been given up the ordinary trade would be resumed.[2]

On April 2nd the mode in which the Chinese authorities should receive the opium was agreed upon after much discussion. It was also stipulated that when one-fourth had been delivered, the servants should be allowed to return to the Factories ; that when one-half had been delivered, the passage boats should resume their running ; that when three-fourths had been received, the trade should be re-opened ; and when the delivery of the whole was complete, everything should "proceed as usual." Breach of faith was to be punished by cutting off the supplies of water after three days of "loose performance of engagements"; by the stoppage of the food supply after three days more ; and "with the last degree of severity" on Captain Elliot himself after three days more of such conduct.[3] Captain Elliot issued a notice to British subjects on the 3rd April, informing them of the terms that had been agreed upon, asking that they would scrupulously fulfil the obligations he had entered into, and thanking them for the patience and kindly feeling that they had shown under very trying circumstances.

On April 3rd arrangements were made by which Mr. Johnston was allowed to leave Canton to attend to the delivery of the opium from the receiving ships outside the Bogue. This was the first opportunity of sending letters "outside" that had been afforded since the 22nd March, a period of twelve days. The Superintendent took this opportunity

[1] *Chinese Repository*, vol. vii, p. 647. Whether a mistake had been made does not appear.

[2] *Ibid.*, p. 647. [3] *Ibid.*, p. 648.

of sending to Lord Palmerston a short despatch, the purport of which was, that confidence in the Chinese could never be restored to the same degree as that at which it had stood before the recent events, and that it was unsafe for the British community to remain on the mainland of China separated from their ships. He expressed the hope that the British Government, on receipt of this despatch, would make such a declaration of its general intentions as would uphold confidence. What course he wished taken it is impossible to say. Judging from the despatches that succeeded this, his opinion as to the most suitable policy varied from time to time. His one fixed thought was how to get free. For another month, however, the Foreigners were destined to spend weary days and nights shut up in the Factories, "close and safe as a fish in a tank," as the Chinese very aptly phrased it, though not so closely confined as before. Day by day the confinement became less rigorous. The vigilance of the guards was relaxed, till by and by the sentries' cries degenerated from the alert "Kang-cho" to a feeble utterance, scarcely audible and given out with no regularity.[1]

On the 5th of April there was a new development. The High Commissioner, relying on the merchants' statement that they would bring no more opium into China, determined to obtain a further assurance to this effect in the form of a bond. Having made out a draft of the kind of instrument that would be acceptable, he sent it by Howqua and Mowqua, the senior Hong Merchants, to the British Superintendent. This bond was expressed to be given by "the English Superintendent Elliot, and the deputy superintendent Johnston, at the head of the English Merchants," as well as the various British, Indian, and other traders whom it was sought to bind. It contained recitals of an extremely humiliating kind, in which the parties were made to acknowledge that they had long continued to enjoy "the dewy influences of the favour of the Celestial Court," and to rejoice in the acquisition of unbounded gains. It further recited that opium had been

[1] *Chinese Repository*, vol. vii, p. 649.

stored on board warehousing ships in the waters of Kwang-tung, and had been sold contrary to the laws; that owing to the appointment of a special commissioner the signatories had now begun to have knowledge of the severity of the prohibitory enactments, and were filled with unutterable dread and terror, and so, having delivered up their opium to the Government, intreated and implored that a memorial be presented to the Throne, requesting the Great Emperor to show clemency beyond the bounds of law, and remit their past offences. By the operative part of the bond Captain Elliot was to undertake to address the sovereign of his nation, that she might proclaim to all British merchants that they must obey the laws of China, not introduce any opium there, and not manufacture opium at all. The bond further provided that, in future, if any ships brought opium, they and their cargoes should be confiscated, and the guilty persons should readily submit to suffer death at the hands of the Celestial Court; but that, as regards ships arriving with opium before the ensuing autumn, they would simply be required to surrender it on arrival.[1]

On the 8th of April the Chamber of Commerce, who, in discussing the opium question with the Chinese authorities, had gone outside the scope of the objects for which they were constituted, resolved that they would not be involved any further in correspondence of a political or personal nature, nor would they commit themselves to any promises or engagements that might become impossible of fulfilment, and that the functions of their committee should cease till the restoration of the trade should come about.[2] On the 9th a meeting of representatives of the Chinese and of the Foreigners was held at the Consoo House to discuss the terms of the proposed bond. The former consisted of the *kwang-chow-foo*, the chief magistrates of Nanhai and Pwanyu, the Hong Merchants, *linguists*, and a deputy from the High Commissioner, while among the latter were the American and Dutch consuls and three or four private persons. After a long and tedious

[1] *Chinese Repository*, vol. vii, pp. 650–9.
[2] *Ibid.*, p. 652.

discussion the meeting broke up at midnight without any conclusion having been reached.[1]

This day also witnessed the departure of the Hoppo, who went down the river to the Bogue, being followed the next day by the High Commissioner and the Viceroy, to witness the delivery of the opium. All these officials, in making this journey, passed right through the Foreign vessels, twenty-four in number, without any guard beyond the usual retinue of a Chinese official. This was a bold step to take, as they might easily have been captured by the commanders of the vessels; but the latter, having received from Captain Elliot the strictest injunctions to keep the peace, allowed them to pass on their way undisturbed. No better proof could be forthcoming that these officials were not conscious of any desire to destroy the lawful trade or to provoke hostilities. It should be mentioned here that, during the whole period of the detention of the Foreigners at Canton, everything had remained quiet at Whampoa. Indeed an English lady, the wife of one of the commanders, remained on board ship there the whole time. The supplies of food, too, continued uninterrupted, the compradores in the customary manner furnishing their ships with what was necessary.[2]

On April 13th coolies returned to several of the Factories, with some of the compradores and domestic servants. On the 15th Captain Elliot issued a notice inviting tenders for the supply of a fast clipper to be chartered by him on Her Majesty's service for the carrying of despatches, it being a condition of the charter that she should not be required to proceed round the Cape of Good Hope. He intended that news of the recent occurrences should go *viâ* the Isthmus of Suez, in order that it might reach England as soon as possible. Meanwhile the opium was being surrendered, and by the 16th April, 7,000 chests had been delivered up. On the 19th an edict was issued allowing compradores and servants to return to the Factories. Difficulties arose as to the deliveries at Chuen-pi, but these were settled after some discussion. On

[1] *Chinese Repository*, vol. vii, p. 653.
[2] *Ibid.*, p. 653.

the 4th May the guards were removed from the Factories and the passage boats allowed to run. The ships at Whampoa were allowed to open their holds, and Captain Elliot received permission to pass to and fro as usual. He, however, publicly announced that he intended to remain at Canton till his public obligations to the Chinese authorities had been fulfilled. On May 5th the Chamber of Commerce received a notification that, for the present, no Foreigners would be allowed outside Old China Street, but all restrictions would be removed when the delivery of the opium was complete. That same day the companies of soldiers were disbanded, and the large boats of armed men withdrawn, and the next day the first passage boats left for Macao, taking in all some fifty passengers. Thus, after lasting forty-six days, the confinement of the Foreigners in the Factories came to an end.

CHAPTER XVII

SURRENDER AND DESTRUCTION OF THE OPIUM

THE conclusion that the Chinese Government was sincere in its efforts to suppress the traffic in opium and the use of the drug by Chinese subjects is irresistible. The unusual persistency and energy displayed by the imperial authorities at Peking; their continual revision of the law with regard to opium; their admonitions to the local officials at Canton urging them to a stricter enforcement of that law; the appointment of the High Commissioner with his extraordinary powers; all these show in the strongest manner that the authorities at Peking were in earnest. The manifestation of imperial approval that followed the drastic measures described in the last chapter, coupled with the fact, to which reference will presently be made, that the Emperor absolutely refused to receive any material benefit from the result of those measures, is sufficient to destroy any doubt that might remain. Viewed impartially the line of conduct adopted by Lin must be regarded as just, particularly when judged by the standard in use among the Chinese, the only standard with which at that time he could possibly have had any real acquaintance. He has been blamed because he did not distinguish between the innocent and the guilty, because the policy of constraint, by which he compelled a surrender of the contraband drug, was exercised against all the residents in the Factories alike. In view of the difficulties that experience had already shown to stand in the way of a suppression of the opium trade, in view of the imperfections of Chinese law and the corruption rampant among those who had to administer it at Canton, it is not easy to suggest a policy which would have commended itself to the Foreign traders and at the same time have produced the results desired by the Chinese Government. Nearly every Foreign resident at Canton was implicated in the contraband trade. Examination of each of them by Chinese process would have been impossible, as well as hateful to the Foreign community. As things stood at that time the method in fact adopted was in all probability the least unpleasant that could have been successful. Finally, it must be remembered that all the property seized consisted of smuggled goods, forfeit to the Government by the law of the land.

The chief factor in producing the local opinion, that Lin had behaved unjustly, was surprise that he should have dared to grapple with the opium question at all. The ordinary British resident had never taken the edicts and decrees and proclamations against the contraband trade as even intended to be serious. They thought that the connivance of the local officials in the illicit importation of the drug afforded a sufficient ground for disbelieving that the Emperor could possibly be in earnest. The official element among the Foreigners at Canton, represented by Captain Elliot and the few consular representatives of other nations, were equally at fault in not discerning the trend of events. Captain Elliot found some difficulty in excusing himself to his Government for having been taken unawares by the High Commissioner's vigorous policy, which he stigmatized as one of public robbery and wanton violence. His despatches of the beginning of April, 1839, contradict the statements he had made at an earlier date, as to his impression of the policy that the imperial authorities intended to follow. In them he says that he had come to the conclusion some months before that the determination of the court to put down the trade was firmly adopted, but he had not supposed they could effectually accomplish that object. It was his fixed purpose, he said, when he left Macao, to afford every reasonable satisfaction concerning the immediate withdrawal of the opium ; and it was only when he got to Whampoa that he abandoned his plan, because he saw that there was no hope that it would be acceptable to the High Commissioner.[1]

It is interesting to compare the different views on the High Commissioner's policy expressed by the British Superintendent

[1] *Correspondence Relating to China* (Blue Book, 1840), pp. 385–391 ; *Chinese Repository*, vol. xi, pp. 402-9.

at different times. Whilst confined at Canton, he made no protest to the Chinese authorities, not even when surrendering the opium. On the contrary, he told them that in promising to deliver up the contraband drug he was acting in pursuance of commands which he felt bound to obey, and that he would incur the displeasure of his sovereign if he failed to carry out that promise to the letter. To Lord Palmerston he described the enforcement of the demand for surrender as an act of spoliation of the very worst description, and the confinement of the residents as a state of restraint, insult, and dark intimidation. The general policy of the Chinese Government towards the opium trade he summarized as being "the utmost conceivable encouragement, direct and indirect, upon the one hand, and sudden violent spoliation on the other."[1]

In other despatches to Lord Palmerston he went on to say that the destruction of the surrendered opium, which the Chinese officials had at first pretended was their object, had been abandoned and Commissioner Lin was having it sorted and packed with a care that showed that it was intended to be preserved. Captain Elliot thought it was to be sold by the Chinese Government, under a scheme for legalizing the trade in the form of a Government monopoly. As opium was at that time fetching $1,200 per chest in Canton, and $600 outside, such a scheme would have brought great gain to the Government, and out of the profit so made it was supposed the owners of the 20,283 chests would be compensated. Lord Palmerston was urged to make a strong declaration that the British Government would exact an indemnity for all manner of loss to British subjects, and so hasten the purposes of the Chinese Government and extend the measure of remuneration. Four conclusions were drawn by the Superintendent from the existing state of affairs. The first was that an immediate extension of the peaceful and profitable intercourse with China was as certain as any event dependent on human agency could be said to be; the second, that this could be attained by immediate vigorous measures founded upon the most moderate ulterior purposes; the third, that

[1] See his despatch of 13th April, 1839.

a more favourable or necessary conjuncture for action had ver presented itself; and fourth, that every man's just indemnity could surely be recovered from the Chinese Government.[1]

Another question discussed by the Superintendent in his despatches at this time was that of the bond. As first proposed, the form of bond was particularly hateful to Captain Elliot. A second request for such an instrument, a request sealed by the High Commissioner and Viceroy, filled him with such anger that he tore the letter to pieces and told the Hong Merchant who had brought it, that they might take his life before he could consent to any such instrument being executed by British subjects. The view which he finally expressed to the Chinese, both of the surrender of the opium and of the bond, was couched in much milder language than that used by him at the same date in his despatches to Lord Palmerston. To the High Commissioner he wrote :—

"It has been a great satisfaction to Elliot to know that the merchants of his own and other Foreign nations at Canton, have sincerely pledged themselves to your Excellency to discontinue a trade which the Emperor has strictly forbidden. And, assuredly, they will faithfully fulfil their obligations. For honour, though with poverty, is of far more value than shameful life and disgraceful profit; and their characters are gone for ever if they violate their solemn pledges to this Government.

"In the matter of bonds, however, Elliot can consciously declare, that it is not in his power, according to the laws of his country, to meet the pleasure of your Excellency.

"The opium is a thing in actual possession: and therefore it has not been impossible to Elliot, assuming very heavy responsibilities, to require it in the name of his Sovereign and render it up to your Excellency on behalf of his Government. But the bonds have relation to the future, and would involve terrible responsibilities in any possible case of disobedience to the prohibitions. They would involve, too, not alone parties

[1] *Correspondence Relating to China* (Blue Book, 1840), pp. 390–1; *Chinese Repository*, vol. xi, pp. 408–9.

themselves but others also. Such bonds, then, it is impossible even for his honoured Sovereign to require: and how much more must it be out of the power of Elliot himself to require them!

"Nay, were he so far to forget his duty as to require them of the people of his country, they themselves too well know the laws of their country to venture on giving bonds that would render them highly criminal."[1]

It is hardly necessary to say that these legal arguments did not convince or satisfy Commissioner Lin. What foundation in English law the Superintendent had for saying that the giving of such a bond by a British subject would be a criminal offence, it is impossible to imagine, though he was right in saying that he had no authority to compel the giving of such an instrument. His general attitude, however, with regard to the bond is one that must be commended, for it would have been a monstrous thing, if the official representative of the British Government had consented to British subjects being tried and condemned to death by Chinese tribunals. The nature of the offence was not such as demanded so severe a punishment, and a still more formidable objection was that the administration of what is euphemistically called justice in Chinese courts then, as now, was such that no Chinese, much less a British subject, could ever be sure of a fair trial.

Finding himself in something of a difficulty, desiring to bring force to bear on the Chinese, and having none at hand, Captain Elliot, whilst shut up in the Factories, bethought himself of the expedient of trying to draw the Portuguese into the contest, on the ground that their interests were incidentally being attacked. He first disclosed this project to Lord Palmerston in a despatch dated 13th April, which was not forwarded from Canton until May 6th. Having remarked that the Portuguese had taken advantage of the High Commissioner's engagement with the concerns of the British to embark their opium and send it to Manilla, he proceeded to demonstrate that the safety of Macao, though an object of secondary moment to the Portuguese Government, was to the British Government

[1] *Correspondence Relating to China* (Blue Book, 1840), p. 394.

"indispensably necessary." The garrison at that time consisted of about 400 men recruited from India and 500 Kaffir slaves. The Governor was well supplied with rice and ammunition and the forts were in an efficient state of defence. Having pointed out these facts, he advised that a treaty should be concluded with Portugal for the cession of her rights over Macao and for the effectual defence of that port, stating, with a view to showing the advantage that might be expected to spring from such an arrangement, that already the larger British ships were in the habit of remaining at Macao and sending their cargo over to Hong-kong in small vessels.[1]

Ignorant, in all probability, of the events of 1808, he wrote to the Governor of Macao a despatch placing "all Her Britannic Majesty's subjects, ships, and property presently in Macao, or hereafter proceeding there, under the protection of Her Most Faithful Majesty, and offering all possible help on behalf of the British Government to put Macao into a state of defence, and for the equipment of a sufficient number of vessels to keep the coast clear." He enclosed for circulation a notice ordering all British subjects in the outer seas to place themselves under the command of the Governor for the defence of Macao, and the general protection of the lives, liberty, and property of all the subjects of Christian Governments, then or thereafter resorting to that port. The Governor, however, was not to be drawn into any such entanglement. He at once replied thanking Captain Elliot for his offer, "an offer, however, of which he is not at liberty immediately to avail himself, feeling that his very peculiar situation imposes on him the bounden duty of observing a strict neutrality, so long as powerful reasons shall not constrain him to a different line of conduct, or until there shall be evidence of the imminent peril, which the Superintendent seems to fear, as being about to happen ; and in this case he will frankly take advantage of the generous facilities presented to him."[2]

Macao was not the only source to which the Superintendent looked for assistance. About the same time he determined

[1] *Correspondence Relating to China* (Blue Book, 1840), p. 405.

[2] *Ibid.*, p. 408. "Her Most Faithful Majesty" is the Queen of Portugal.

to have recourse to India, and on the 16th of April wrote to the Governor-General, Lord Auckland, asking that a naval force might be immediately despatched to the China seas. The situation was not so serious as the Superintendent supposed, but the alarmed state of his mind is clearly demonstrated by the following passage from the despatch: "Immediate countenance and protection are necessary for the safety of life and property: and I am sensible your Lordship will not require any importunities on my part to do whatever may be in your Lordship's power in that respect. As many ships of war as can be detached, and armed vessels, to be employed under the command of the naval officer (the whole to be instructed to conform to my requisitions), seems to be the most suitable means of protection available at this moment."[1] It was in response to this request that at a later date Captain Smith arrived with the two vessels that took part in the first hostilities.[2]

As soon as the confinement of the Foreigners had come to an end, it became apparent that there was to be no return to the easy conditions, which had obtained before the arrival of the High Commissioner. Detailed regulations[3] for the control of the passage boats were issued by the Hong Merchants, which were in part designed to prevent the departure of sixteen Foreigners, who were specially mentioned as being the chief offenders in respect of the contraband trade. These were being detained as hostages for the due performance of the promise to surrender the opium. At the same time, the trade was re-opened to the extent that ships at Canton were permitted to load. To Captain Elliot permission was given "to pass to and fro as usual," in order that he might superintend the delivery of the opium.[4] He preferred to remain at Canton, however, until the whole amount promised had been surrendered, and sent Captain Johnston down the river to supervise matters outside. Speaking of the additional precautions that were being taken

[1] *Correspondence Relating to China* (Blue Book, 1840), pp. 408–9.
[2] See *post*, p 396.
[3] *Chinese Repository*, vol. viii, pp. 17–18.
[4] *Ibid.*, pp., 15–17.

for the control of Foreigners, he wrote to Lord Palmerston: "A strong paling has been run round the square, no doubt with the purpose more easily and suddenly to shut the Foreigners from access to the river-side; their pleasure boats have been taken from them; and a variety of novel regulations, inconsistent with any possibility of carrying on trade at Canton, have been established. . . . The measures of the Government are not confined to Foreigners alone. The whole trade of the province is to be broken down under a new and rigorous system."[1]

On the 8th of May the *kwang-chow-foo*, acting on the instructions of the High Commissioner and the Viceroy, issued an edict in reply to a request of the British Superintendent and other Foreign representatives for leave to depart with their countrymen and their shipping. Though proclaiming in the usual strain that China had no need of commercial intercourse with outward barbarians, this document betrayed a certain amount of alarm at the thought of the Foreigners withdrawing altogether. They were reminded that they had enjoyed the overshadowing benevolence of the Great Emperor, had eaten of the herbage and trodden the soil of the Celestial Empire equally with the people of the land, and by their buying and selling had acquired very rich advantages. They were admonished that it was their duty to rest in their stations, observing the laws, but that the prohibitions against opium must be enforced. In conclusion, it was left to them to remain in China or to return to their own countries as they might choose, but they were warned that, if the latter course were adopted, they would never be allowed, to come back again, and if they were found bringing opium they would suffer capital punishment.[2]

This edict was first transmitted to Captain Elliot through the Hong Merchants in an unofficial manner, but being rejected by him was thereupon retransmitted under the seals of the *kwang-chow-foo* and the *kwang-hai*. As soon as it had been thus received, the Superintendent issued a notice to British

[1] *Correspondence Relating to China* (Blue Book, 1840), p. 410.
[2] *Chinese Repository*, vol. viii, pp. 19–20.

subjects informing them of its contents and pointing out the danger of confiding to the Chinese authorities any administration of judicial process. In his opinion, the enforcement of the law against dealing in opium would place the lives, liberty, and property of the whole Foreign community at the mercy of any reckless person outside the Bogue, and more especially at the disposal of the Hong Merchants, *linguists*, compradores, and their retainers, as it would be mainly on the testimony of such persons that judgment in a dispute heard before a Chinese tribunal would be given.

Everybody at Canton was now anxiously awaiting the day when the surrender of the whole of the opium would be accomplished. In the meantime the Europeans learnt how irksome were many of the new restrictions. No Foreigners were allowed to go to the warehouses of the Hong Merchants, and so merchants, who wished to buy goods for export, had no opportunity of inspecting their prospective purchases. An edict was published ordering all the streets leading into the square before the Factories, excepting Old China Street, to be closed up, and the shopmen living in them to remove. All the back doors of the Factories were to be closed up. The one thoroughfare leading into the square was to be guarded by soldiers, in the same way as the land approach to Macao. Constabulary were to be stationed in every street "in order to separate good from bad subjects." All sign boards painted with Foreign words were to be taken down.

These irritating measures confirmed Captain Elliot in his determination to withdraw all his countrymen. On the 19th of May, knowing that the surrender of the opium was almost complete, he issued a notice charging all British subjects to abstain from bringing or assisting to bring any ship into the port of Canton, and threatening that the British Government would disregard any claim for compensation that might be put forward by any British subject who should disregard such notice.[1] The Chinese, ill pleased at the publication of this document, made some attempt to impede the departure of British ships, by taking the unprecedented step of refusing

[1] *Chinese Repository*, vol. viii, pp. 24–25.

pilots to a large Indiaman and two other vessels that wished to proceed to Second Bar, alleging, by way of excuse, that these vessels were not taking away so much weight of export cargo as they had brought of imports.

On the 21st of May, 1839, the surrender of the 20,283 chests of opium was completed at two o'clock in the morning. The whole of it was stored in godowns at Chinkow, near the Bogue, to await the Emperor's special orders. Feeling that he was now free to take his own course, Captain Elliot, on the same day, issued a further notice to British subjects animadverting on the course of recent events, and repeating that he was without confidence in the justice or moderation of the provincial government. He explained that it was only under duress that he had called for the surrender of the opium, that in so doing he had acted on behalf of the British Government, which thereby incurred immense liabilities, and that the right of exacting indemnity was now vested in the Crown. He then enjoined on all British subjects to be prepared to leave Canton either before, or at the same time with, his own establishment, the date of which would be announced at the earliest convenience, and once again he charged those having any connection with shipping not to be requiring, aiding, or assisting in any way in bringing British vessels within the port of Canton. In conclusion, he uttered a warning that such sudden and strong measures, as it might be necessary to take thereafter for the honour and interests of the British Crown, could not but be prejudiced, if any British subject should continue in Canton after his own departure.[1]

On the 23rd May the Chinese authorities issued an edict ordering ten of the prescribed Foreigners, among whom were some British subjects, to leave Canton. Having been made to sign a bond that they would never again return, all the sixteen left with Captain Elliot on the following day. As soon as the Chief Superintendent had departed, the guards of coolies were removed from before the Factories and access was afforded to the streets in the neighbourhood.

The British merchants thought this a suitable opportunity

[1] *Chinese Repository*, vol. viii, pp. 29–30.

for laying their grievances before the Home Government. On the 24th May, they addressed a memorial to Lord Palmerston setting out the " acts of aggression " on the part of the Chinese Government to which they had been subjected. The grounds of complaint, as put forward in this memorial, were the stoppage of trade in the case of vessels against which no complicity with the opium trade was alleged ; the forcible detention of the British residents at Canton, in order to compel the surrender of the opium ; the threat to hold Foreigners responsible with their lives for any future infraction of the Chinese customs' laws ; the attempt to force them to sign bonds rendering not only themselves but also all others coming to China, over whom they had no control, liable to a penalty.

In this memorial the merchants related for the information of the Foreign Secretary the circumstances under which the opium trade had come into existence : that it had increased from 4,100 chests in 1796 to 30,000 chests in 1837 ; that no penalties had ever been enforced against Foreigners bringing the drug into China ; that the prohibitory laws had never been a rule to the functionaries of the Chinese Empire, who should have administered them, nor to the Chinese people, on whom they were intended to operate : that the laxity in the administration of the law had been admitted by the High Commissioner : that the peculiar character of the opium trade had been distinctly recognized in the report of the Select Committee of the House of Commons in 1830 ; and that in the subsequent report made in 1832 the Committee expressed their opinion " that it does not seem advisable to abandon so important a source of revenue as the East India's monopoly of opium in Bengal." This allusion to the East India Company's monopoly was evidently inserted in the belief that it would touch the Home Government in a sensitive spot. At this time the Government of India was drawing a revenue of over £1,000,000 per annum from the sale of opium, and anything which tended to show a danger to the continuance of this revenue, might possibly have a far greater effect with Lord Palmerston than any sentimental considerations, such as the indignity suffered by the Superintendent, or the degrading conditions under which British subjects had been trading at Canton. The memorialists admitted in the latter part of their memorial the right of the Chinese Government to demand the surrender of the opium, alleging on the other hand that they could not willingly have complied with the demand, or given the required bond, as the "great bulk" of the opium was the property of others in India and elsewhere. They also paid a strong tribute to the public spirit and courage of the British Superintendent.[1]

To show his approval of the course the High Commissioner had been taking, the Emperor now created him Viceroy of the Liang-Kiang, which post, next to that of Viceroy of Chih-li, is the most important administrative position in the Empire.[2] Shortly afterwards the imperial commands with regard to the disposal of the surrendered opium were received at Canton, and on the 29th May an edict was published, stating that the Emperor's order was that the whole amount, which was found to be 20,291 chests, should be destroyed where Chinese and Foreigners alike could "both see it and hear of it." The 3rd of June was appointed as the date on which the work of destruction should be begun. These commands were carried out to the very letter. For this purpose the High Commissioner chose an open site, on the brow of a hill, near the village of Chunhow, to which access might readily be had by boat from Canton and the neighbourhood. An area some 500ft. square was marked out on the north of the village as the place of destruction, and anyone who pleased might be a spectator.

A party of Europeans, who went over from Canton with Mr. King, have left on record an account of what they saw of the process that was adopted. On landing at the creek, on which Chunhow stands, they were saluted by the war-boats and junks with the beating of gongs. Two divisions of troops in full uniform were drawn up guarding the area mentioned above, which had been enclosed with a strong

[1] *Chinese Repository*, vol. viii, pp. 32–34.

[2] The holder of this position is usually spoken of nowadays as the Viceroy of Nanking.

palisade of bamboos and was shaped like a Malayan camp. On each side, except the east, was a gate, and at each gate sentries were posted to prevent anyone entering without a written permit. All persons coming out of the enclosure were carefully searched in order that none of the opium might be taken away. Towards the west of the enclosure were three large vats or trenches, running east and west, about 150ft. long, 75ft. wide, and 7ft. deep, flagged with stone and lined at the sides with heavy timbers. Each trench was surrounded with an inner fence having a single entrance. Close at hand, in separate enclosures, was stored the surrendered opium.

The mode of destroying the drug was briefly this. Each trench was first filled about two feet deep with water from the top of the hill. Planks were then laid across every part of the trench at distances of a few feet. Along these the opium was distributed in baskets by coolies. The balls of opium were then lifted out, placed on the planks, and stamped on and trodden under feet till broken in pieces, which were then kicked into the water. Other coolies, standing in the trench, were busily engaged with hoes and similar implements in beating and turning up the opium from the bottom of the vat, whilst other coolies again brought salt and lime and strewed it profusely about the trench. Having been thus operated upon, the contents of the vat were allowed to stand in a state of slow decomposition until ready to be drawn off, which was done through a sluice that opened into the creek. The sluice was two feet wide, somewhat deeper than the floor of the trench, and furnished with a screen, which acted as a sieve and prevented the large pieces of opium from passing into the creek.

In this way from 1,000 to 1,300 chests of opium were destroyed each day. About 500 coolies were employed in the task, under the supervision of sixty or eighty civil and military officers, and a number of clerks and attendants. Some of the superintending officers sat on elevated seats placed under mat sheds, from which they kept every part of the enclosure under observation. Day and night they took turns at keeping watch, lest any of the opium should be abstracted. Every time a chest was brought out to the trenches, special care was taken to see that it corresponded with the entry that had been made in a list, prepared at the time when the surrender took place. The whole business was carried out with the greatest strictness and fidelity. The guard kept over the enclosure was much stricter than that kept over the residents in the Factories during the period of confinement. One wretched man, who attempted to carry off some small pieces of the drug concealed about his person, was at once arrested and beheaded before the eyes of Mr. King and his companions.

On the east of the enclosure were the special apartments of the High Commissioner, built of bamboos like a temporary theatre. The hall of audience was about 20ft. square, a little elevated and open on the west side, so as to command a full view of the trenches and of the landing-place at the creek. The floor was laid with carpets, and the walls decorated with the customary Chinese scrolls. At the east end of the hall was the seat of the High Commissioner. Into his presence the party of Foreigners was ushered. They found, sitting on his right, the commander of the naval forces of the province, whilst to his left sat the Hoppo and the Minister of Justice, all of whom received them in the most friendly manner. In the course of conversation the recent occurrences were discussed, and the Foreigners inquired as to the terms on which ships would in future be allowed to enter the port. Commissioner Lin, in reply, said the evils had grown gradually and secretly because their authors had been treated so leniently, but now the time had come when forbearance was no longer possible; it was solely for the repression of opium that the late severe measures had been prosecuted; the illicit trade must now be stopped, but the other should be protected. After speaking at length and with great animation on this point, he gave them the following written statement :—

"Vessels engaging in the regular and honourable trade, and really having no connection with the hurtful practice of introducing opium, shall assuredly receive additional favour, and shall in no way be involved in difficulties.

"Vessels engaging in the clandestine sale of opium shall assuredly be examined and treated with great severity, and no degree of favour or leniency shall be shown to them.

"In brief, the good are good for themselves, and the evil are evil for themselves. Let the good, dismissing all anxiety of heart, prosecute their commerce freely, without any apprehensions of difficulty. As for those who are evil, it only remains that they early turn about, change their practices, and abandon their vain expectations."[1]

The Chinese officials, before bidding Mr. King and his party farewell, inquired as to the best method of communicating with the Queen of England and other European sovereigns, in order that an attempt might be made to secure their co-operation in the suppression of the opium trade, and also for maps, geographies, and other books. It would seem that Commissioner Lin was already contemplating writing those letters to the Queen of England, which afterwards aroused so much interest. On their departure the Foreigners were presented with a large number of gifts. The whole tenor of the reception accorded to this party of sightseers, as well as of the written declaration made in their presence by the High Commissioner, indicates a complete absence of that hostile spirit, which Captain Elliot supposed was animating the Chinese officials. The work of destruction going on at Chunhow showed also that his prediction as to the ultimate destiny of the surrendered opium was completely falsified. Nothing could be more significant of the earnestness of the Chinese in their crusade against the opium traffic than the fact that the Emperor's commands were carried out with such stringency. There is nothing that appeals so strongly to the Chinese mind as wealth. It speaks volumes that they were willing to destroy, and did destroy, so great a quantity simply for the good of their country.

[1] *Chinese Repository*, vol. viii, pp. 75–6.

CHAPTER XVIII

THE BEGINNING OF HOSTILITIES

Released from confinement, Captain Elliot was pressed with the necessity of putting into practice the declarations of policy made by him whilst still shut up in the Factories at Canton. But a very casual survey of the situation was sufficient to show that, without some sort of armed force, it was impossible to take steps towards punishing the Chinese officials for their contumacy, or vindicating his own outraged dignity. From the language employed in his despatches and notices, one would have expected him to have withdrawn entirely from the jurisdiction of the Chinese authorities, and to have taken with himself as many British subjects as were willing to protest, by some action of that kind, against the treatment meted out to them at Canton. Whether it was that his countrymen could not be persuaded that they had suffered wrongs that called for so strong a protest, or whether it happened that on further reflection the Superintendent himself was in doubt as to the necessity of taking such a course, cannot now be determined. We only know that, having proceeded to Macao with all the residents who were amenable to his control, and induced practically all the British shipping to retire to the sheltered anchorages at Hong-kong, he decided to wait in a state of passive resistance, until such time as he should receive further instructions from his Government. H.M.S. *Larne*, the only British man-of-war left in Chinese waters, put to sea on the 29th of May, and was immediately followed by the clipper *Ariel*, which had been chartered to carry, with all speed, the despatches that were to put Lord Palmerston in full possession of the facts of the case. With no military or naval force to support him, the Superintendent was obliged to persist in a policy of quiescence until a reply to these communications could be received.

There can be no doubt that the Chinese would have been much more impressed with the determination of the Superintendent to obtain reparation, had he withdrawn completely from Chinese territory. So far from doing anything of this kind, Captain Elliot continued within the jurisdiction not only of the Imperial but of the provincial authorities. Again, he seems to have drawn an imaginary line across the mouth of the Bogue, and to have persuaded himself that, once beyond that line, the British community was beyond the reach of the Chinese officials. If this was his impression, it was entirely erroneous. At Macao, where the *keun-min-foo* and the *tsotang* exercised a perpetual jurisdiction on behalf of the Chinese authorities, Portugal was far from having an absolute dominion.[1] As to the anchorages around Hong-kong, less than two years before, the Viceroy in an edict relating to the opium traffic, had been careful to point out that his jurisdiction extended as far as the Ladrone Islands, and that the "outer waters," in which Lintin and the Nine Islands are situated, were part of the province of Canton.[2] To the High Commissioner and the Viceroy it must have been unthinkable that the Superintendent had in any degree emancipated himself, or those on board the ships, from their control by the withdrawal that had taken place.

By the 1st of June only twenty-five or thirty Foreigners remained in Canton. The loss arising from the cessation of business, consequent on the exodus of the English merchants, soon made itself felt to Foreigners and Chinese alike. On the 9th of June the Hoppo, alarmed at the decrease in revenue, issued, at the bidding of the High Commissioner and the

[1] See *ante*, chap. i, p. 6.

[2] The passage to which reference is here made is as follows: "Having carefully examined the charts of the inner and outer seas, we find that the Ladrone Islands constitute the boundary. Beyond them is the wide and boundless ocean, the black water of the foreign seas, which are not under the control of the Central Land. Inside them, at the offings for instance of Lintin, the Nine Islands, and other places, are the outer seas, which are under the jurisdiction of Canton. Where the sea washes the shores of the interior districts it is called the 'inner sea,' and of such inlets Kumsing Moon affords an instance."—*Chinese Repository*, vol. vi, p. 474.

Viceroy, a proclamation urging the newly arrived ships, that were waiting in the outer seas with their cargoes, to come up to Whampoa and unload. He complained that Captain Elliot kept them "loitering about," until they should hear from the sovereign of their country, whilst his duty was "to secure Foreign merchants from loss, and think anxiously how they may enjoy their blithesome profits," and not to "set about producing thorns and briars which will choke up business and prick himself." Having reminded him that the surrender of the opium was proof enough that he was respectful and submissive, the Hoppo exhorted him not to be ashamed of being called a Superintendent of Trade, but to perform his duties in unison and with propriety ![1]

The position had resolved itself into a contest between the Chinese officials and the Superintendent to secure the adhesion of the British merchants. To the ordinary plain business man, indifferent to the question of the form of bond, there was no reason why the invitation to resume business at Whampoa should not be accepted. The state of crisis, which had been somewhat too graphically described in Captain Elliot's despatches, had completely disappeared, and to all outward appearance the Chinese officials were perfectly friendly. Two American captains did not hesitate, and on the day, on which the Hoppo's proclamation appeared, took their ships, the *Paris* and *Nantasket*, up the river. This action put the British merchants in a difficult position. Either they must forego the opportunity of trade and spend many months in unprofitable idleness, or they must ignore the Superintendent's prohibitions and injunctions. The only other courses open to them were to ship their cargoes by American ships, or place their own vessels under the American flag, and so assist in the aggrandizement of their commercial rivals. Under these circumstances they wrote to Captain Elliot, asking him whether they were to understand his notice as placing a positive embargo on British ships, and whether he considered the present tone of his negotiations with the Chinese authorities warranted a belief, that at no distant date

[1] *Chinese Repository*, vol. viii, p. 62.

such a settlement of existing differences might be expected, as would admit of British property being sent within the Bocca Tigris. To this they received the formal reply that an embargo was an act of the government of a country prohibiting the departure of the ships and goods of another, so nothing done by him could place an embargo on British ships and goods; that he had not transgressed his lawful powers in issuing the notices in question; and that disobedience to the terms of those notices might, and most probably would, involve consequences of the most serious nature. Apart from considerations of danger, such a step would, he said, be intensely humiliating and mischievous, as showing confidence in the justice and moderation of the provincial authorities, and a willingness to be tried by Chinese tribunals.[1]

On the receipt of this reply, the British merchants decided that the public notices of the Superintendent were to be considered as conveying a positive order from him, as the agent of his Government, that British ships and goods should not be sent within the Bogue, and that it was necessary to make some proper arrangement for the present disposal of vessels and cargoes that were in the outer anchorages. They further resolved that the interests of all concerned in the China trade would be best promoted by a strict adherence to the Superintendent's orders. These conclusions were submitted to Captain Elliot, who was thus assured of the confidence and support of the British mercantile community. The only question left open was as to the payment of demurrage for the detention of the ships, and this was arranged by agreeing a rate and fixing the date from which demurrage should run, all with the approval of the Superintendent, and leaving it to the Courts in England to decide on whom the liability for payment should fall. The consequent abstention of British ships from the trade provoked the issue of another edict by the Chinese, which emanated from the *kwang-chow-foo* and the *keun-min-foo*, in which they pointed out that two American ships had applied for permission to enter the port, and that there was no reason why the sixteen British merchantmen, whose

[1] *Chinese Repository*, vol. viii, pp. 63–5.

cargoes were still undischarged, should not do likewise.[1] Captain Elliot at once issued a counter-proclamation, exhorting British subjects to respect his injunctions, and setting out the terms of a declaration, which he had caused to be sent to these officials. This declaration was a statement of the motives which had induced him to surrender the opium, and was in form an imitation of a Chinese edict. The document is of value as showing the view Captain Elliot took of the state of affairs, a view which may be gathered from the following passage :—

"On the 24th of March last, Elliot repaired to Canton and immediately proposed to put an end to the state of difficulty and anxiety then existent, by the faithful fulfilment of the Emperor's will : and he respectfully asked that he and the rest of the Foreign community might be set at liberty, in order that he might calmly consider and suggest adequate remedies for the evils so justly denounced by his imperial majesty. He was answered by a close imprisonment of more than seven weeks, with armed men day and night before his gates, under threats of privation of food, water, and life. Was this becoming treatment to the officer of a friendly nation, recognized by the Emperor, who had always performed his duty peacefully and irreproachably, striving in all things to afford satisfaction to the Provincial government ? When it thus became plain that the Commissioner was resolved to cast away all moderation, Elliot knew that it was incumbent upon him to save the imperial dignity, and prevent some shocking catastrophe on the persons of an imprisoned Foreign officer, and two hundred defenceless merchants. For these reasons of prevailing force he demanded from the people of his nation all the English opium in their hands, in the name of his Sovereign, and delivered it over to the Commissioner, amounting to 20,283 chests. That matter remains to be settled between the two courts.

"But how will it be possible to answer the Emperor for this violation of his gracious will, that these difficult affairs should be managed with thoughtful wisdom, and with

[1] *Chinese Repository*, vol. viii, p. 67.

tenderness to the men from afar? What will be the feelings of the most just prince of his illustrous dynasty when it is made manifest to him by the command of Her Britannic Majesty, that the traffic in opium has been chiefly encouraged and protected by the highest officers in the Empire, and that no portion of the foreign trade to China has paid its fees to the officers with so much regularity as this opium? Terrible indeed will be his imperial majesty's indignation when he learns that the obligations into which the High Commissioner entered, under his seal, to the officers of a foreign nation were all violated! The servants were not faithfully restored when one-fourth of the opium was delivered; the boats were not permitted to run when one-half was delivered; the trade was not really opened when three-fourths were delivered; and the last pledge, that things should go on as usual when the whole was delivered, has been falsified by the reduction of the Factories to a prison with one outlet, the expulsion of sixteen persons, some of them who never dealt in opium at all, some clerks, one a lad, and the proposal of novel and intolerable regulations."[1]

It is difficult to say at this distance of time what foundation existed for these charges of breach of faith against the Chinese officials. The events narrated above show that the confinement at Canton came to an end long before the whole of the opium had been yielded up. When it is remembered how slowly things move in China, and how utterly regardless of time is the Chinese mind, the more accurate view would appear to be that, judged by Chinese standards, the High Commissioner was unusually punctilious in the fulfilment of his pledges. The changes that had been made at the Factories were hardly of such importance as to deserve the attention bestowed upon them in the Superintendent's declaration. The complaint that the promulgation of new regulations was another breach of faith hardly merits serious consideration. To it no heed whatever was paid by the Chinese officials, and on the 23rd of June they promulgated fresh regulations for the prevention of smuggling by Foreign ships. The prophecy of displeasure on

[1] *Chinese Repository*, vol. viii, pp. 68–9

the part of the Emperor must have provoked a smile when discussed in the Viceroy's yamên.

The chief feature of this new enactment was the elaborate care that was to be taken in future in keeping Foreign vessels under surveillance. It was provided that every Foreign ship, on anchoring in the outer waters, should be measured in such a way as to show her draught, which should be certified in writing. On her arrival at Whampoa she was to be measured again, and if the draught then shown did not agree with that stated in the certificate, she was to be fined. In this way it was hoped that any secret unloading, which might have taken place outside the river, would be detected. Presumably some allowance would have to be made for the difference in specific gravity between salt and fresh water, but there was no mention of this in the regulation. At Whampoa a revenue officer was to anchor on her right, and custom-house runners on her left, and keep her under constant observation. For each ship a high civil official was to be sent down from Canton, to superintend the whole body of those keeping watch on her, for which purpose it was ordered that the candidates for civil appointments should be employed. Military and police were to assist the customs' officers, and the whole preventive force was to be in charge of a specially appointed official. The penalty for receiving bribes was at least dismissal and deprivation of rank. Finally, a bond was to be given by the captain of the ship that he had not infringed the laws against opium.[1]

To prevent any hitch arising in the trade which was being done by the Americans, the Chinese officials ordered the Hong Merchants, Mowqua and Ponkhequa, forthwith to secure the *Nantasket* and the *Paris* in accordance with the new regulations. Acting under these instructions they drew up a form of bond, which was so mild in its terms, that no exception could possibly be taken to the requirement that it be signed as a condition of trading operations being allowed. The bond was very short, and was thus worded :—

"The foreign captain, ————, belonging to the United States of America, has now received the commands of the

[1] *Chinese Repository,* vol. viii, pp. 77–81.

Heavenly Dynasty rigidly prohibiting opium; and he has had it clearly proclaimed to him that certain new regulations have been proclaimed to that effect, and the said Foreigner, holding the same in great dread, will not dare to oppose or violate them.

"Now the said ship just arrived brings no opium, and I now give this as a true certificate of the same."[1]

It will be seen at once that this was a much less onerous instrument than that which had been tendered to Captain Elliot at Canton, and the fact that it was settled in this form shows that the Chinese authorities, in their desire to restore the trade of the port, were not above making concessions. The captains were made to append their signatures between the Chinese and English versions, to show that they had signed the bond in both languages. Since this wording had now been accepted by the Americans, the British merchants found themselves in a still more difficult position, for it was no longer possible to maintain that the form of the bond in itself justified a refusal to sign it. Very soon ten or eleven American captains had subscribed to the new conditions, all of whom found no difficulty in carrying on their trade as formerly,[2] in spite of the great changes that were apparent at Canton. With two or three exceptions the only Foreigners left there were Americans. Considerable alterations had taken place in the Factories, which in respect of promenade space were better off than before the troubles, but in other respects had suffered considerably. The terraces on the tops had been removed and the balustrades taken away. Most of the pleasure boats remained drawn up on the shore, where they had been placed by the Hong Merchants' orders. Most of the Hongs were without an inhabitant, and generally there was an air of desolation about the place that spoke of calamity. Captain Elliot was still at Macao, awaiting instructions from his Government, where many of the British merchants were carrying on their businesses. The British ships were at Hong-kong anchored in idleness.

[1] *Chinese Repository*, vol. viii, p. 82.

[2] *Ibid.*, p. 83.

Commissioner Lin was experiencing the old difficulty in obtaining efficient interpreters, who could accurately translate the documents published by the English relating to the matters in dispute. On the English side there were excellent interpreters, who could translate with perfect accuracy all the edicts and proclamations that emanated from the Chinese officials, but on the Chinese side the only persons possessing any knowledge were the *linguists*, whose jargon of "pidgin" English had never advanced beyond the crude state described in an earlier chapter.[1] Under these circumstances the High Commissioner looked about for Chinese who had received some kind of English education, and ultimately was able to add to his staff one who had been educated in Penang and Malacca, a second who had been educated in Singapore, a third who had been in a school at Cornwall (Conn.), in the United States, and a fourth who had received some English education in China. How far they were able to give him the assistance he needed is doubtful. If we may judge of their capacity by an edict issued by the High Commissioner and Viceroy at this time, the first ever published by Chinese officials in the English language, the merit of their performances was not far above that of the *linguists*. The intrinsic interest attaching to this document makes it worthy of reproduction. It was in these terms :—

"Great imperial commissionary's governor's of two Kwang province lieutenant-governor's of Canton earnest proclamation to foreigners again issued.

"For the managing opium on the last spring being stopped trade for present time till the opium surrendered to the government than ordered be opened the trade the same as before.

"The American vessels are ready to continually enter into the port ten and more ships have been examined by the hupos officers are bringing no opium on board and the hong merchants and foreign merchants give bond for the same then captain Remmond's ship loaded and filled with cargo sailed and returned to her country but English country ships get anchored

[1] See *ante*, chap. v, p. 82.

in outside sea not get information coming into the port must being deceived by rumours of bad persons saying you are being ready selling opium now if you go into the port should be put you into the punishment therefore you are still retain and expect some other chance why you are never think celestial empire treat natives and foreigners all equal in the world if any to be found out bad merchant dealing with opium will be brought into punishment if honest merchant from whatsoever may come into the port should be allowed to trade the same as was and will not intend to say being do a kindness to one and to another never will treat you foreigners by two manners of ways therefore another proclamation.

"Now you are whose persons had any opium on board the celestial empire law as strictly should be not allow such opium bring into the port if any honest merchant without any opium the great imperial commissionary the governor and lieutenant-governor must be to representate cherishing favor of emperor the great and valiantly protect you and to make no separate black and white put you into boat you must taking in good purpose get your formation enter to the port all the constitutions of examine and bond will be according American ships managed and not to be deceived by rumour when you did not intend come into port and quickly sail back to your country and not allow to be continue these proclamation."[1]

Whatever may have been the precise meaning intended to be conveyed by this document, it is clear that the general purport was an invitation to the English merchants to follow the example of the Americans and bring their ships into port. These repeated overtures would possibly have resulted in some better expedient for the continuance of their trade being devised by the British merchants, than the one to which they had been compelled to resort, namely, transhipping their goods into American bottoms and so sending them up to Canton. But when things had come to this pass, there occurred at Hong-kong, on July 7th, that unfortunate affray which was the proximate cause of the outbreak of hostilities. It seems that a party of British and American seamen went

[1] *Chinese Repository*, vol. viii, pp. 77, 167.

ashore on a Sunday afternoon for the purpose of bathing and taking exercise on the beach. Some of them appear to have got drunk, but, whatever the cause, a serious riot arose between the sailors and the villagers, in which several of the Chinese were beaten, one of whom, named Lin Wei-hi, died on the following day. As soon as news of this occurrence reached the Superintendent, he hastened to Hong-kong to investigate the matter, where he arrived on July 10th. He at once offered a reward of $200 to any person, who would adduce evidence leading to the conviction of the person responsible for the death of Lin Wei-hi, and $100 for information leading to the conviction of the ringleaders in the riot, provided the guilty persons should turn out to be British subjects. He also advanced $1,500 on his private account as compensation to the family of the deceased, another $400 to them to protect them against the extortion of the lower officials, and $100 he ordered to be distributed among the villagers.[1] In this respect Captain Elliot, with the best motives, allowed his zeal to outrun his discretion, for the Chinese afterwards represented that he had given bribes to get the matter hushed up.

The Chinese authorities at Canton, as soon as they received news of the affair, sent officers to Captain Elliot to make inquiries. He replied in a note telling them of the rewards he had offered, promising that the offender, if a British subject, should be tried by the laws of his country, and stating that his Government would hold him deeply guilty, if he failed to prosecute the affair with the utmost severity. He added that the family of the deceased attributed his death to accident and not to wilfulness.[2] A week later he again wrote to them, assuring them that he was doing everything in his power to discover the author of the death of Lin Wei-hi. He used this opportunity to point out the inconsistency of first advising the British merchants to defy his authority, and then calling

[1] *Chinese Repository,* vol. xi, p. 458; vol. viii, p. 213; *Correspondence Relating to China* (Blue Book, 1840), p. 432. In cases of this kind two or three hundred dollars would be a sufficient and five hundred an ample compensation.

[2] *Chinese Repository,* vol. xi, 459; *Correspondence Relating to China* (Blue Book, 1840), pp. 431–2.

on him, as they now were, to exert that authority by punishing the commission of crime. He stated that he would receive no further papers from them, until he should be satisfied that there would be no repetition of these inflammatory practices and that the higher officers would receive his sealed addresses "agreeably to custom."[1]

It had been ascertained by this time that the British sailors who had participated in the riot belonged to two merchant ships, the *Carnatic* and *Mangalore*, which belonged to Jardine, Matheson & Co. To them Captain Elliot had written on the 15th of July, stating the measures he had taken to compensate the relatives of the deceased, and suggesting that the firm should refund the expenses he had thus incurred.[2] In accordance with his promise to the Chinese officials the Superintendent resolved to put these men on their trial without further delay. On the 26th of July he published a notice, setting out the rules of procedure, under which he proposed to exercise the criminal jurisdiction conferred upon him by statute. These are of interest as being the first manifestation of the exercise of judicial authority over British subjects in China by a representative of the Sovereign of Great Britain, an authority which has since been recognised by treaty, and is now vested in the Supreme Court for China and Corea.[3]

Apparently at this time Captain Elliot did not anticipate that the incident of Lin Wei-hi's death would assume the importance that afterwards attached to it, for he makes no mention of it in a despatch addressed to Lord Palmerston on the 18th of July. In this letter he confined himself to discussing the difficulties in which Commissioner Lin was reported to be involved, owing to the fact that he could not venture to leave Canton until able to report to the Throne that trade with the

[1] *Chinese Repository*, vol. xi, p. 460; *Correspondence Relating to China* (Blue Book, 1840), p. 441.

[2] *Chinese Repository*, vol. xi, p. 458; *Correspondence Relating to China*, p. 432.

[3] This Court was created by order in Council in 1865, and exercised jurisdiction in Japan until our ex-territorial rights in that country were surrendered by the treaty of 1894. It was originally called the Supreme Court for China and Japan. See Chapter xxiv, *post* p. 560.

British had been resumed, and to the fact that his repressive policy had resulted in a great increase of smuggling along the whole of the rest of the coast. Discussing the opium traffic he expressed the opinion, that the late crisis would enable the British Government to interpose for the establishment of regular and honourable trade on a firm basis, as well as " for the effectual check or regulation of a traffic, which by the present manner of its pursuit must every day become more dangerous to the peace of this ancient empire, and more discreditable to the character of the Christian nations, under whose flags it is carried on." The only alternative that he could see was that the coast should be delivered over to a state of things, which would rapidly pass from the character of forced trade to plain buccaneering.[1]

Having now made the preliminary arrangements necessary for the proper constitution of a court of criminal procedure, the Superintendent fixed August 12th as the date on which the accused sailors should be put on their trial. The place of trial was fixed at Hong-kong and the Chinese officials, who were invited to send a representative, were informed that the charge would be one of participating in the riot. But to this courteous invitation they returned no response. The day before this notification was sent, an edict had appeared from the High Commissioner and the Viceroy, in which they roundly abused the Superintendent for his conduct in the matter. Their view was that Captain Elliot should have apprehended the offender and handed him over to them for punishment. In this edict the source of the trouble was traced to the fact that the English ships had neither come into Canton nor gone wholly away. It was declared that, at an inquiry held by a Chinese official, it had been clearly proved to what ships the offending sailors belonged, that they struck Wei-hi with clubs till he dropped down, that a Foreign ship's surgeon came to attend him, that bribes had been paid and a promissory note given for the payment of more money, and that it had been proved who had given such promissory note. From this

[1] *Chinese Repository*, vol. xi, 459. *Correspondence Relating to China* (Blue Book, 1840), p. 431.

they argued that it was clear that the murderer had been identified. The edict went on to abuse Captain Elliot for having wished "most unreasonably to throw the blame on the Americans," for wishing "that the Foreign murderer may escape capital punishment, and that the dead man may still be longing for revenge in the regions below and his vengeance be unappeased," and for unjustly oppressing the ghost of a murdered man by depriving him of his expiatory victim! It pointed out that, had a Foreigner been killed by a Chinese in like circumstances, the latter would have been at once executed, and instances were cited in which this had been done. The edict ended with a command that in future no food was to be supplied to the Foreigners, or any communication had with them, till the murderer should be delivered up to be tried and executed, and that the edict should be posted on the Praya Grande at Macao, in a spot secure from wind and rain.[1]

There is something almost humorous in the idea of entrusting the administration of justice, under conditions of such delicacy as had arisen on the death of Lin Wei-hi, to an ordinary British naval captain, who had received no legal training whatsoever. It is the English way to put men into positions for which, by their training, they were never intended. Sometimes it works well, owing to the latent ability of the individual; sometimes the results are disastrous. In this particular case it cannot be said that any ill consequences followed. Captain Elliot, in order that he might efficiently discharge his duties as judge, prepared himself with the greatest care. His charge to the Grand Jury shows that he had read up the law from the works of Stowell, Coke, Blackstone and Hale.[2] The number of grand jurors was twenty-three, of petty jurors twelve.[3] Two bills were preferred, one charging

[1] *Chinese Repository*, vol. viii, pp. 212–5.

[2] His charge to the Grand Jury, together with the Rules of Procedure, are given in full in the *Chinese Repository*, vol. viii, pp. 180–194. The names of the jurymen are also given.

[3] A petty jury in China now consists of five persons only. The change was introduced by Order in Council in 1865, and upheld as valid by the Privy Council in the case of *Carew v. Japan Crown Prosecutor* (1897), App. Cas. 719.

a seaman with wilful murder, and the other charging five sailors with "riotously and unlawfully and injuriously entering certain dwelling houses, in a village on the Eastern shore of the anchorage of Hong-kong, in search of spirits, and for then and there riotously assaulting the inhabitants, men and women, cutting, beating, and otherwise dangerously ill-using them."

The Grand Jury ignored the charge of murder, but found a true bill against the five seamen. After a careful trial the whole five were found guilty. In passing sentence the Superintendent said he could find no extenuating circumstances, and that the prisoners had acted under the incitement of a vicious motive. Nevertheless, he pronounced a "mitigated sentence," mainly on the ground of the "inexcusable negligence" (presumably on the part of the captains of the ships) "of permitting so many persons of your station to go on shore, particularly at such a moment as the present, without regard to your personal steadiness and with no officer to control you, in spite of the dictates of common prudence, and contrary to my recent instructions."[1] The sentences imposed were, on some, three months' imprisonment and a fine of £15, and on others six months' imprisonment and a fine of £20, the sentences to run from the date of confinement in one of Her Majesty's gaols in Great Britain. The convicted men were sent at the earliest opportunity to England, where they were set at liberty immediately on their arrival.[2]

The result of the trial was officially communicated to the Chinese authorities on the 16th of July, in a note informing them that the Superintendent had not been able to discover the actual perpetrators of the deed.[3] Whether they appreciated the differences between the English and Chinese law of homicide it is difficult to say, but smarting under the disappointment of seeing so many richly laden ships remaining outside, whose arrival in the river would at once have caused

[1] *Chinese Repository*, vol. viii, pp. 193–4.

[2] The Law Officers were of opinion that they could not lawfully be detained in custody. See Hansard: *Parliamentary Debates*, vol. 53, pp. 1133–4.

[3] *Chinese Repository*, vol. xi, p. 461: *Correspondence Relating to China* (Blue Book, 1840), p. 441.

a revival of the trade of Canton, they used the fact, that the "murderer" had not been discovered, as a pretext for venting on Captain Elliot their anger at his success in securing the allegiance of the British merchants. To the local officials at Macao, whither the Superintendent had returned on the conclusion of the trial, the High Commissioner and the Viceroy sent an edict, ordering them to prohibit the English from having any access to that port by sea and to cut off their supplies of food. The reasons given for this drastic proceeding were that Captain Elliot had "obstinately declined to give up the murderer," had kept the newly arrived ships "loitering about," had not sent back the empty opium ships to their country, and had allowed the proscribed Foreigners to remain with the British shipping. Acting on these instructions the *keun-min-foo* and the *tsotang* issued, on the 15th of August, 1839, a proclamation which, in effect, placed under a ban of excommunication and anathema every British subject in China. By it the Procurador was commanded to make out a list of such provisions as would be needed by the Foreigner residents other than British at Macao, and the shopkeepers were commanded to supply nothing beyond what was enumerated in that list. All compradores and servants in British employ were ordered to return to their homes within three days, under penalty of being punished with the utmost rigour of the law. Placards containing these injunctions were posted on boards and carried through all the principal streets and the markets of Macao.[1]

These measures showed that the Chinese officials were becoming careless of consequences. If the thousands of seamen assembled at Hong-kong were deprived of food, trouble was bound to ensue. Appreciating the gravity of the situation the British Superintendent wrote to the *keun-min-foo* pointing out the nature of such action and asking that the servants be allowed to return. For some days no reply was vouchsafed, and the British who were at Macao managed to obtain provisions through their Portuguese servants. Prices, however, were high, as the country people had been forbidden to send

[1] *Chinese Repository,* vol. viii, pp. 216-221.

their produce into the town. On the 23rd of August, Captain Elliot withdrew to Hong-kong, hoping thereby to induce a relaxation of the prohibitions. In this he was disappointed. On the very next day the Chinese officials signified their view of his protest by calling on the Portuguese to eject all British residents from their houses, and to drive all British subjects from Macao.[1] The Governor, powerless to disregard such an order, announced that he could no longer answer for the safety of British subjects, and requested that they would leave on the following day, promising to attend and protect them with troops under arms. Accordingly, on the 26th of August, men, women, and children, hurried from their residences and embarked on schooners, lorchas, and such small craft as could be collected for the purpose, only the invalids and one other, a gentleman who acted as Prussian consul, being left behind. Some repaired to Hong-kong; others, under the supervision of Captain Askell, sought the anchorage in the Typa.[2]

The excitement caused by these events both at Macao and Hong-kong was intense. The excitement grew to alarm when it became known that an Englishman named Moss had been attacked at Lantao and barbarously wounded. For this outrage the Chinese officials were not responsible, it being the work of Ladrone pirates, but in the prevailing confusion it was ascribed to the malevolence of the Viceroy and High Commissioner. The *Black Joke*, on which Moss was a passenger, had left Macao early on the morning of the 24th, and anchored off Lantao in the evening. About ten o'clock that night an alarm was given by the Lascar crew that boats were approaching, and in a few minutes five boatloads of Chinese pirates were swarming on deck. Moss, seeing three of the Lascars cut down and having himself received a cut in the face, sought refuge below; but hearing the dreaded cry of *Ta! Ta!*[3] he

[1] *Correspondence Relating to China* (Blue Book, 1840), p. 438.

[2] *Chinese Repository*, vol. viii, pp. 223, 439.

[3] *Ta*[1] is the Chinese for "Kill!" and when raised by a mob is the signal for violence. It shows to the experienced European that the persons using it have got beyond control.

again made for the deck, in the hope of finding a way of escape. On putting his head out of the companion he received an ugly wound with a pike. The pirates then seized him and stripped him naked, giving him three cuts in the arm as he raised it to protect his head. One of them cut off a finger to gain possession of his ring ; another laid hold of his ear and called to a third, who, coming up with a sharp knife, cut off the ear and a large piece of scalp, and crammed it into his mouth. Having beaten him about the body they left him for dead, first making an attempt to blow up the vessel with gunpowder. They then fled, leaving all the crew dead, excepting only the tindal, who had managed to save his life by hanging on to the rudder under water. Shortly afterwards a British vessel arrived on the scene and rendered such assistance as was possible.

Whilst these things were going on at Macao, the High Commissioner with the Viceroy was at Hëangshan, about midway between the former place and Canton. A small detachment of troops had been quartered just outside the Barrier to keep the Portuguese under surveillance. Many of the Chinese residents had fled to the villages, in the fear that fighting was about to begin. The provincial officials, however, were not desirous, now that matters had come to such a point, that there should be an actual outbreak of hostilities. Indeed, in their edict to the Procurador, they had stated that so soon as the English should be brought to repentance, should deliver up the "murderer," should bring up their ships to Whampoa, and should send away the opium ships and the sixteen proscribed persons, they would be allowed to resume trading operations. With a view to re-establishing confidence, they announced by a public proclamation that for six months the death penalty would not be imposed on those who surrendered their opium, and that ships having any of the contraband drug on board might either yield it up, in which case they would be allowed to trade, or return home. The demand for the surrender of the murderer of Lin Wei-hi was repeated, and in conclusion the warning was given that, if the English presumed on their numbers and opposed, it would be impossible to "discriminate between the gems and the pebbles," and all must be punished.[1]

In this condition of affairs, when the Superintendent might well have despaired of overcoming the difficulties with which he was surrounded, H.M.S. *Volage* arrived in Macao Roads. Never was the advent of warship more opportune or more welcome. The date of her arrival, the 30th of August, was the turning point in the misfortunes of the British community. Having remained a few hours at Macao, she proceeded to Hong-kong, where some days later she was joined by H.M.S. *Hyacinth.*[2] Both these vessels had been despatched by the rear-admiral commanding the Indian squadron, to render such assistance as might be required, and, if necessary, to co-operate in the defence of Macao, it being supposed, at the time of their departure, that the Governor would continue to afford protection to the British community under any circumstances that might arise. On the 1st of September, Captain Elliot informed the Portuguese of the arrival of the *Volage*, and that he was now able to place a force of from 800 to 1,000 men at His Excellency's disposal, should he be desirous, as Captain Elliot imagined he was, to see the British community once more under the protection of the Portuguese flag.[3]

It must have been with some surprise that the Superintendent received the reply of the representative of a nation, with which Great Britain was connected with ties of amity and friendship, ties which had been cemented with the blood of the British soldiers who fell in the Peninsular War. With great politeness the Governor, having acknowledged the offer of assistance, explained that he was bound to repeat what he had officially declared more than once since the arrival of the High Commissioner at Canton, that without receiving from his Government express and definite orders, he could

[1] *Chinese Repository,* vol. viii, p. 224; *Correspondence Relating to China* (Blue Book, 1840), pp. 438–9.

[2] *Chinese Repository,* vol. viii, pp. 224, 439.

[3] *Chinese Repository,* vol. xi, p. 463; *Correspondence Relating to China,* p. 443.

not cease to preserve the most strict neutrality between the two nations, the English, with which his own had been so long and so intimately allied, and the Chinese "from motives well known to all." He added that the British had retired of their own accord from Macao, with a view to not compromising that establishment, and by that step had placed themselves under the necessity of not landing there until all difficulties with the Chinese were terminated. He had, he said, represented to the Chinese that the British residents had retired of their own free will, and therefore judged that the British subjects and the dignity of the Portuguese Government would be equally satisfied.[1]

The truth was that the High Commissioner, who had issued an edict thanking the Portuguese for driving the British out of Macao, had determined to honour the Procurador with a personal visit, and had, in fact, done so on the very day when the Governor's reply was despatched. Early in the morning he had been received by a company of Portuguese troops, with a band of music, at the Barrier, and had been escorted to the temple of Lienfung, just north of the hill beyond the village of Mongha. There, in company with the Viceroy, he was received by the Procurador, the *keun-min-foo*, and the *tsotang*, and made the recipient of presents of silver, silk, tea, pigs, and bullocks decorated with scarlet ribbons. On the conclusion of the interview, which lasted half an hour, the procession was re-formed and moved towards the town, which it entered to a salute from the guns of the Portuguese forts. The Chinese inhabitants had erected triumphal arches, adorned with festoons and laudatory scrolls, and as the High Commissioner passed their houses they set at the doors tables decorated with vases of flowers, to show, as they said, "their profound gratitude for his coming to save them from a deadly vice, and for removing from them a dire calamity by the destruction and severe interdiction of opium."[2]

It was putting the Governor to a high test, to ask him to

[1] *Chinese Repository,* vol. xi, p. 464; *Correspondence Relating to China,* pp. 445–6.

[2] *Chinese Repository,* vol. viii, pp. 268–9.

give permission to British troops to put Macao into a state of defence against the very officials, who were being entertained at the moment of replying to Captain Elliot's letter. Knowing the precarious tenure on which the Portuguese settlement was held, and conscious that he had received no instructions from his Government, that would have justified him in taking sides against the Chinese, the Governor could not be expected, perhaps, in the circumstances, to offer the British community shelter at Macao. A personal desire not to imperil his charge by taking a bold step was probably the motive that influenced him most. It would be unfair to attribute to his Government any wish not to afford to the subjects of a friendly Power such succour as they needed.

Forced to remain at Hong-kong, the British were at a loss to know what course to take. The naval force at the disposal of the Superintendent was not sufficient to enable him to take the aggressive, even had he wished to do so. On the other hand, the prospect of an indefinite residence on board the merchant ships was not pleasing to those who had placed themselves under his care. Whilst this state of doubt continued, a fresh source of alarm arose from a report that the wells on shore had been poisoned, a rumour which arose owing to the discovery of a notice in Chinese at one of the springs, warning natives not to drink, as the water contained poison that would destroy the bowels. Thinking it hopeless to appeal to the officials on such a point, Captain Elliot published a notice in Chinese, setting out the reasons why he was compelled to remain at Hong-kong, and asking the villagers not to draw on themselves punishment by using against the Foreigners any such barbarous treatment.[1] This seems to have had the effect desired, as no further complaint on this head occurs in the despatches. Possibly a complaint made to the High Commissioner, in a communication dealing with the affair of the *Black Joke* as well as the poisoning of the water, was also instrumental in preventing any recurrence of trouble of this kind.

[1] *Chinese Repository,* vol. xi, pp. 464–5; *Correspondence Relating to China,* p. 448.

So far sufficient supplies of food had been obtained, though with some difficulty, to satisfy the needs of the British at Hong-kong. But now a change was experienced in this respect, and they began to be threatened with the fear of starvation. To remedy this state of affairs, the Superintendent, on the 4th of September, wrote to the native officials at Kowloon,[1] pointing out that frequent conflicts would ensue if his people were left without food. On the same day, feeling that the situation was becoming desperate, he determined to go in person to the war-junks that were riding at anchor in the harbour, and whose presence had caused the cessation of supplies, in order to obtain formal permission to purchase supplies from the villagers, who were in dread of being punished if they allowed the British to obtain food. Setting out with Gutzlaff, his interpreter, in the *Pearl*, the armed pinnace of H.M.S. *Volage*, he spent some five or six hours in vain endeavours to gain his end. The officers on the junk pretended that they must consult those in the fort, and these again said they could do nothing until they had communicated with the High Commissioner's deputy and obtained his sanction. Having obtained from Gutzlaff a list of the articles most needed, they said that some of these would be supplied as a present, to relieve immediate necessity, but none could be allowed to be sold. It was evident that the Chinese were prolonging the negotiations with a view to manning the fort, into which numbers of soldiers were by this time crowding. Seeing that nothing was to be gained by parleying with the officers, Captain Elliot sent a boat ashore with money to purchase supplies. The natives were willing enough to bargain, as they always are, but on the arrival of some police runners they were obliged to take back what they had sold, and to cease from further trading.

Captain Elliot was waiting in the pinnace for the provisions which he expected to have been bought. But, when his men returned with the news that the natives had been forcibly prevented from trading, he lost his self-control. From the

[1] Kowloon is the mainland adjoining the island of Hong-kong. See chap. xxiv *post*, p. 543.

pinnace, the cutter, and another vessel he opened fire on the three junks. It was answered by the junks and by the fort with great spirit. For half an hour the cannonade continued, when the British were obliged to draw off through failure of ammunition. The junks, which had suffered considerably, after a delay of three-quarters of an hour, weighed anchor, and attempted to escape under protection of the batteries. By this time the British had made cartridges, and were in a position to renew the action. Whilst Captain Smith proceeded to bring in the *Volage*, the Superintendent, supported by the *Cambridge*, a merchantman whose captain had purchased twenty-two eighteen pounders at Singapore, bore up and again engaged the junks, forcing them back to their original position. When this had been accomplished evening was closing in, so the fight was suspended. Captain Smith, who had now brought in his ship, wished to renew the attack in the morning and to destroy the three junks, as well as assault the fort. But now that his ardour had cooled, Captain Elliot was averse to further fighting. It is probable that on reflection he perceived the grave nature of the action he had taken. In his report to Lord Palmerston he gave, as his reason for not continuing hostilities, the fact that he considered sufficient damage had been done to serve as a salutary lesson to the Chinese. He added that it did not appear to be judicious, or indeed becoming, to use a man-of-war for the destruction of three small junks; there had been no act of aggression against the *Volage*; her active interference was unnecessary for the support of the honour of the flag; and he thought it his duty only to use her services in defence against attack.[1]

The Superintendent did not fail to realise that his attack on the junks was not consistent with a state of peace. At the same time he was anxious that it should not be construed as a declaration of war. If the Chinese should interpret it in this way, he would have to bear the onus of having provoked a conflict, unless by some means he could show that the responsibility did not rest on himself. He therefore published on the

[1] *Chinese Repository*, vol. xi, pp. 446–7; *Correspondence Relating to China*, p. 449.

following day a notice in Chinese, stating that the English desired nothing but peace, but they could not submit to be poisoned and starved; that they had no wish to molest or impede the imperial cruisers, but these must not prevent the people from selling food; and that to deprive men of food was the act only of the unfriendly and hostile.[1] The High Commissioner was equally reluctant to be involved in a state of actual war. He could not, however, allow the attack to pass unnoticed. Quick to seize an advantage, he at once issued an edict,[2] in which he stated that Captain Elliot had come forward to seek a quarrel, and so had necessitated that the naval and land forces should be assembled, to combine in "an attack of extirpation," and to place the Superintendent's life in the hands of the Chinese. Permission was given to the villagers to kill any English troops that might be landed, but it was made clear that the merchants were not to be extirpated. To them an invitation was issued to throw off their allegiance to the Superintendent, lest they all be consumed together. Apart from publishing this edict, the High Commissioner showed no disposition to indulge in measures of retaliation.

Captain Elliot was now in the position that he must either take the offensive, or tacitly admit that he had committed a blunder. The terms of his commission, so far from giving him power to declare war, enjoined in the strictest language that the utmost forbearance should be shown towards the Chinese. In this dilemma he had recourse to the semi-warlike expedient of a blockade, though he exceeded his powers in taking even that course. Another consideration that made him pause was the knowledge that measures of active hostility might easily be construed as amounting, in effect, to a vindication of the cause of the opium traders by force of arms. Indeed, the High Commissioner had publicly stated, as a justification for his conduct towards the British, that many of the merchants at Hong-kong were still engaged in the illicit traffic. For this there seems to have been some ground, as Captain Elliot issued a notice saying that he considered it his

[1] *Chinese Repository*, vol. xi, p. 467.
[2] *Ibid.*, vol. viii, p. 269.

duty to leave no room for the inference that Her Majesty's flag was flying in protection of such persons, and requiring all commanders of British ships not having opium on board to repair to him within forty-eight hours and make oath to that effect, and all British vessels engaged in the opium trade to leave " this harbour and coast."

Here again he was faced with the difficulty that he had no more right to prevent opium ships remaining at Hong-kong than to restrain them from infringing the revenue laws of China. But the weakness of his position was not merely a legal one. He could not alter the fact, that the main reason for the presence of the British community at Hong-kong was, that he had withdrawn from Canton as a protest against the seizure of the contraband drug. The intimate connection of the present troubles with opium was at this moment further demonstrated by the destruction of the *Bilbaino*, a Spanish ship anchored in the Typa, which the High Commissioner, mistaking her for the *Virginia*, a British vessel from which opium had been surrendered in the spring, ordered to be burnt at her moorings.[1] To prevent the recurrence of any incident of this kind, the senate of Macao passed an ordinance decreeing the confiscation of any vessel that should anchor in the Typa with opium on board, and ordering the fitting out of an armed cruiser to enforce the decree.

The Superintendent now determined to make an effort to come to terms with the Chinese authorities. On the 14th of September he sent to the *keun-min-foo* through the Governor of Macao a note saying that all he desired was peace and quietness, with a view to negotiating some sort of *modus vivendi*. Two days later he instructed Captain Smith to suspend the blockade so long as negotiations should be in progress.[2] Commissioner Lin thought it would help him if at first he treated any such overtures with disdain. He therefore issued instructions to Kwan, the Chinese admiral,

[1] For this act the Spaniards demanded an indemnity, but obtained nothing until in 1841 the British troops were in possession of the heights around Canton. Apparently some British subject had an interest in the vessel.

[2] *Chinese Repository*, vol. viii, p. 271.

to drive the British ships away, and threatened what he would do if the ships did not depart. The latter was content to issue a proclamation blazoning forth his own prowess in the most approved Chinese style. He said that, as admiral, he ruled over the whole seas, and his especial duty was to sweep them clean of the depraved and reprobate; that his family dated back two thousand years, and his ancestor was a deified emperor; that the mind of this godlike warrior was grand and powerful as the winds and clouds, his heart genial and refulgent as the sun by day or the moon by night; that he, the admiral, flew like an arrow to recompense the goodness of his country, but did not covet the bloody laurels of the butcher. In the most picturesque language he called on the opium ships to take their departure, and exhorted the merchants not to engage in the contraband trade. As a reason for not treating them at once with more severity, he explained that he entertained for them a mother's heart.[1] The real reason was more probably a natural hesitation to pit his forces against the *Volage*.

The admiral's proclamation concluded with threatenings of the most terrible kind, but having thus satisfied the rules of propriety, he was content to do nothing further towards expelling the English. When, after a short interval, the Chinese authorities found that the Superintendent did not mean to make war, they responded to the desire for negotiation. On the 9th of October the High Commissioner and Viceroy issued a joint edict saying that Captain Elliot had petitioned them to examine and search each individual ship to see that she had no opium on board, and had offered to give a bond to that effect, covering all the ships that should be therein specified. This proposal was approved, and the manner in which the search should be conducted was carefully prescribed. Chuenpi was named as the place of examination, which was to be conducted with the greatest strictness. If any opium was found on board, the "smuggling criminal" was to be put to death, and the whole of the ship's cargo confiscated. Ships having no opium might either go up to Whampoa to trade, or send their cargoes up to Canton to be sold by the Hong

[1] *Chinese Repository*, vol. viii, pp. 426–8.

Merchants on account of the British owners. But the demand for the signature of the bond was reiterated, and it was declared that a refusal to sign the bond or to submit to be searched would be regarded as proof that there was opium on board. Three days were allowed in which such ships might leave Chinese waters, after which time fire-ships would be sent among them to destroy them. The responsibility for the failure to surrender the " murderer " of Lin Wei-hi was laid on Captain Elliot alone, and it was expressly declared that this affair had no connection with and did not involve any ship or other persons. This edict, which was issued on the 23rd of September and was described by its authors as " a double *quantum* of kindness and compassion," concluded with the following words :—

" Summing up the whole, then, we the imperial commissioner and Viceroy, tell you one thousand times, and ten thousand times, that the opium trade must be cut off for ever. Every day that opium continues to come, every day shall we not rest employing our hands against you. Therefore after this, do ye Foreigners take your smuggling of opium ideas and give them to the winds to all eternity. If ye dare again to scheme after this clandestine traffic, we shall most certainly put you to death according to the new law, and what then will your after-repentance avail you ? And, moreover, after the issuing of these commands we have nothing to say to you."[1]

It is strange that, in the face of language so precise, a misunderstanding as to the terms actually agreed should have arisen only some two weeks later. This edict clearly indicates the nature of the terms the Chinese were disposed to accept as a *minimum*. On October 12th two minor officials, to whom Captain Elliot had also intimated his wish to come to a peaceful arrangement, issued a proclamation, at the command of the higher officials, of precisely the same tenor.[2] Three days later the Superintendent announced that on the 14th October he had accepted conditions from the High Commissioner and the Viceroy, involving the opening of British trade outside the

[1] *Chinese Repository*, vol. viii, pp. 379–380.
[2] *Ibid.*, pp. 429–430.

port of Canton.[1] But he did not state what were the actual terms.

When on September 16th the notice of blockade was suspended,[2] nothing remained to prevent British merchants from following the example of the Americans, except loyalty to the Superintendent, whose influence had been sufficient to detain at Hong-kong the sixty British vessels that were now assembled there. On the very day of the announcement that terms had been arranged, there arrived in the river the British ship *Thomas Coutts.*[3] Her captain, when at Calcutta, had taken a legal opinion as to the validity of the notices issued by the Superintendent, and had been advised that they had no binding force.[4] Without demur he signed a form of bond which satisfied the Chinese authorities, and proceeded up to Whampoa to trade, regardless of all prohibitions to the contrary. The bond signed by him was much more stringent than that signed by the Americans, but shorter than the form previously submitted to Captain Elliot. It bound the captain, for himself, his officers and crew, " dreadfully to obey the new laws " and, if the least opium was found in any part of his ship, to deliver up the culprit to be punished according to Chinese law, in which case the ship and her cargo were to be confiscated.

This proceeding showed Captain Elliot that he might have difficulty in restraining much longer his countrymen from accepting the conditions demanded by the Chinese officials. He therefore hastened to make public the terms that had been agreed for the re-opening of trade, and on October 20th issued a notice setting them out, as well as an abstract of the correspondence that had passed in the course of the negotiations, which had been conducted through the Hong Merchants.[5] From these documents it appears he had made it clear that he could not agree to allow British merchants to proceed to

[1] *Chinese Repository,* vol. viii, p. 440.
[2] *Ibid.,* p. 271.
[3] *Ibid.,* p. 440.
[4] Hansard : *Parliamentary Debates,* vol. 53, p. 728.
[5] *Chinese Repository,* vol. viii, pp. 321–4.

Whampoa, or enter into more than a provisional arrangement, until he should receive from his Government further instructions. In one of these documents he proposed that the commander and consignee of each vessel should, on the day of its arrival, hand in a solemn declaration that it had brought no opium and would have nothing to do with opium, and that unless such a declaration were given the vessel should not be allowed to trade. As announced by him, the conditions agreed were, that the British trade might be carried on outside the Bogue without the necessity of signing the bond, provided the vessels were subjected to examination ; that the place of resort should be the anchorage between Chuenpi and Anunghoy ; that the measurement duty, pilots' and *linguists*' fees should be paid in the same manner as though the ships had gone up to Whampoa ; and that vessels proceeding to Anunghoy would transport their cargoes in chop boats, which would be searched by Chinese officers.[1] In promulgating these conditions the Superintendent observed that he did not pretend to deny the right of the Emperor to make such laws as he thought fit, but no responsibility for their administration should be laid on the shoulders of British subjects ; the affair of the *Bilbaino* had shown how liable to error were Chinese officials ; and that if in the trial of a British subject before a Chinese tribunal any injustice were done, it would be impossible to intervene on behalf of the accused, after he had signed a bond consenting to be tried by Chinese law.

On the 22nd of October a meeting took place between certain British merchants and the members of the Co-hong for the purpose of framing detailed regulations for the re-opening of trade which had now been arranged. It was soon discovered, in the course of the discussion, that the interpretation likely to be put upon the conditions by the Chinese was different from that entertained by the English.[2] The latter maintained that the arrangement was to apply to all ships that might arrive in China, until the wishes of the British Government should become known to the Superintendent, and

[1] *Chinese Repository*, vol. viii, p. 324.
[2] *Ibid.*, pp. 324–6, p. 440.

that the return of the British merchants to Macao was essential to a resumption of commercial relations. To neither of these contentions would the Hong Merchants accede. This difference of opinion would probably have caused considerable trouble, but any necessity for its further consideration was set aside by the action of Commissioner Lin, who by edicts of the 25th[1] and 26th of October repudiated the whole arrangement. Both these documents were issued through the *keun-min-foo*, who incorporated them in proclamations of his own, that were even stronger in their terms than those of his superiors. There is some ground for supposing that the Chinese officials at Macao had exceeded their powers in agreeing to terms not sanctioned by the officials at Canton, particularly in dispensing with the requirement that a bond be signed, under which any person found importing opium would be delivered up to be tried and punished by the Chinese tribunals. It is also very probable that the Hong Merchants never fully or correctly transmitted to one party the proposals of the other, and it may well have happened that the Superintendent and the High Commissioner were never really at one, though each supposed a definite agreement had been reached.

The motives which influenced the Viceroy and the High Commissioner in repudiating the arrangement for the reopening of trade are plain from the edicts. The reasons assigned are multifarious, but it is not difficult to pick out those of most weight. The truth would seem to be that just when the negotiations had been concluded, a despatch arrived from the Emperor insisting on the bond being given, before trading operations could be resumed.[2] At any rate, the receipt of such a despatch at Canton was synchronous with the publication of an edict by the High Commissioner saying that this requirement could not possibly be waived.[3] Other reasons given

[1] *Chinese Repository*, vol. viii, pp. 430–1.

[2] *Ibid.*, pp. 380–4, 433–4.

[3] *Ibid.*, pp. 433–4. The terms of the "new law," prescribing decapitation for principals, and strangulation for accessories, against bringing opium into Canton had been received by the High Commissioner on July 19th. See his letter to Queen Victoria, *Chinese Repository*, vol. viii, p. 503.

for repudiating the agreement were that the rush for permits to unload had been premature; that the British merchants had returned to Macao without permission; that Captain Elliot had been guilty of deceit in saying that no British captain could sign a bond; that the British had traded secretly through the Americans; that the trade in opium continued; that the murderer of Lin Wei-hi had not been surrendered; and that it had never been intended that commercial relations should be re-opened until the whole of the ships had been searched, which could not happen in less than six months. It was admitted that a search of the ships had been agreed upon, as a substitute for the signing of the bond,[1] and the reason put forward for repudiating this part of the arrangement was, that Captain Elliot had induced the High Commissioner to yield this point by representing that if the signing of the bond were insisted upon as a necessary preliminary, the trade could not be re-opened until he had received the instructions of his Government, a representation which was shown to be false by the action of the captain of the *Thomas Coutts.*[2]

The tenor of the edicts was in consonance with the acts of their authors, who forthwith caused all native servants to be again withdrawn from British employ, forbade the supply of provisions, ordered all British subjects to leave Macao, and stationed a body of some four or five hundred soldiers at the Barrier to intimidate the Portuguese from rendering any assistance to their fellow Europeans.[3] Captain Elliot at once issued a notice to his countrymen, stating that the High Commissioner and the Viceroy had been guilty of a breach of faith, and had violated the arrangement which had been approved under their signets, and calling on all commanders of British vessels to repair to Tungku, an island near Lintin, as the anchorage at Hong-kong was liable to a surprise attack by fire-ships or war-junks. He instructed

[1] *Chinese Repository*, vol. viii, p. 383.

[2] The edicts by which the arrangement was repudiated are given in full in the *Chinese Repository*, vol. viii, pp. 379–84, 430–84.

[3] *Chinese Repository*, vol. viii, p. 328.

Captain Smith to take such steps as to him seemed best calculated to prevent the entrance of British shipping within the Bogue, and to warn British subjects of the danger of putting themselves within the grasp of the Chinese authorities.[1] In this letter he attributed the existing state of affairs to "the shameless proceeding of the Government, to the entrance of the ship *Thomas Coutts*, and the belief of the mandarins that their possession of hostages will enable them to constrain us into the acceptance of conditions incompatible with the honour of the British Crown, and the safety of the Queen's subjects."

The view that fresh commands had been received from Peking is corroborated by the fact that from this time all American ships desirous of trading were required to give a bond, in the same terms as those accepted by the captain of the *Thomas Coutts*. In making this change the High Commissioner said that it was necessary that all should be placed on the same footing, for by the "new law," which had been "received," any Foreigners bringing opium to the Inner Land were to be immediately executed, the principals by decapitation, and the accomplices by strangulation.[2] The American merchants did not show any hesitation in complying with these new conditions, being willing apparently at all costs to retain the commercial advantage that fortune had so unexpectedly bestowed. The result was that, in spite of an express prohibition against the carriage of British goods in vessels of other nationalities, there was a marked increase in the practice of freighting American ships with the goods of English traders. In fact, so great was the anxiety of British ship-owners and consignees to clear their vessels, the freight from Hong-kong to Whampoa on a bale of cotton rose to $6, whilst as much as $10 was paid for bringing a ton of tea down from Canton. The commercial value of the British flag was reduced to nothing. Ship after ship was sold at a merely nominal price to American or other traders, to supply neutral tonnage, which would be protected in the hostilities, that all expected were on the point of breaking out. The American consul,

[1] *Chinese Repository*, vol. viii, p. 327.
[2] *Ibid*., p. 432.

disregarding all provisions of American law to the contrary, recognised with the greatest eagerness the transfer of British ships to the flag of his country.[1]

Finding that the Chinese were threatening the destruction of all British shipping, and seeing how hopeless would be the position of his countrymen, if he acquiesced in the violent measures that were being taken against them, the British Superintendent on the 29th of October proceeded to the Bogue, with H.M.S. *Volage* and H.M.S. *Hyacinth*, to demand an explanation. On November 2nd, Captain Smith forwarded through Admiral Kwan a request to the High Commissioner, that he would withdraw his edict threatening the destruction of the British shipping and expelling all British subjects from Macao, until such time as the British and Chinese Governments could arrange matters. The next day this letter was returned unopened, and it was observed that the Chinese war-junks, twenty-nine in number, were manœuvring to attack, whilst thirteen fire-ships had been placed between them and the British vessels. Without more ado the *Volage* and the *Hyacinth* were cleared for action, and Captain Smith opened fire. The first shot was directed at a fire-ship that was passing the *Volage*, and in a few minutes she was sunk. The next vessel to suffer was a junk, which was soon blown up. The fight then became general, and after a short time three more junks were sunk. The rest thereupon fled. Practically no damage was done to our ships. The Chinese guns were not fitted for elevation or depression, so their shot could take effect only among the spars and rigging. The loss of life on the part of the Chinese was considerable, but among the British there were no casualties.[2] This engagement, which took place off Chuenpi on the 3rd of November, 1839, was the beginning of the contest commonly called the Opium War.

[1] *Chinese Repository*, vol. viii, p. 457. On the 6th of August, 1839, the U.S. frigate *Columbia* and the sloop-of-war *John Adams* left Macao Roads, where they had been visiting. The American commodore expressed himself strongly against the manner in which the trade was being carried on by his countrymen, and said they could not expect the assistance of American men-of-war if any misunderstanding should arise. See *Chinese Repository*, vol. viii, pp. 455, 458.

[2] *Ibid.*, pp. 491–3.

CHAPTER XIX

A WASTED YEAR

At the beginning of the year 1840 the situation at Canton was anomalous in the extreme. From England and India merchant ships had continued to arrive, many of them with opium, intending to proceed to Whampoa, and trade as usual. These all found themselves detained below Macao, unable to let their owners know of the difficulties that had arisen. A few British subjects were in the Factories; some were at Macao; the majority were with the shipping, which now by Captain Elliot's express orders was gathered together at Tungku. Two British ships, the *Thomas Coutts* and *Royal Saxon*, whose captains had signed the bond required by the Chinese authorities, were peacefully trading at Whampoa. The latter vessel had taken advantage of the engagement off Chuenpi to slip by the *Volage* and *Hyacinth* and enter the river.[1] In Canton not a single flag floated over the Factories, but some fifty or sixty Foreigners were there, including the American consul, Mr. Snow. On the coast the number of ships engaged in merely distributing opium, which was not less than twenty, was probably greater than it had ever been before, and many of these were so manned and armed as to be able to set all native craft at defiance. The demand for the drug was so great, that the price had risen to $1,000 and $1,200 per chest, although a full crop had been gathered at Patna, Malwa and Benares in the preceding year, and the Indian Government was about to make advances for a full crop for the next season.[2]

British prestige and influence in China were at their lowest ebb. Even the Portuguese did not spare the Superintendent in his humiliation, who, driven to ask permission in the name of Her Britannic Majesty to deposit the remainder of British cargoes in the warehouses at Macao, found his request refused.[3]

[1] *Chinese Repository*, vol. viii, p. 491.
[2] *Ibid.*, pp. 441–5.
[3] *Ibid.*, p. 494.

The Viceroy and his colleagues warned the other Foreigners, by special edict, that if they dared to convey up to Canton goods brought in British ships, or to dispose of such goods, their trade, too, would be cut off. It was plain from the language used on this occasion that the provincial authorities, owing to instructions received from Peking, were no longer able, had they been willing, to come to terms with the Superintendent. Still there seems to have been no very bitter feeling on their part. The crew of the British barque *Sunda*, which was wrecked off the island of Hainan at about this time, were treated with great kindness by the High Commissioner. who told them that he had no ill-will against the British, but only against those of them who dealt in opium, and these he should treat as he would treat Chinese offenders. In proof of the absence of any animosity on his part, he sent them back to their countrymen at Tungku, where they arrived in safety.

On the 14th of January there arrived at Canton an edict from the capital declaring the will of the Emperor. The language used in this document is such as would be interpreted in any European country as a declaration of war. Whether it was intended in this sense by the Chinese Government it is difficult to say. Possibly it was meant to be only an order of the most stringent kind for the cutting off of all intercourse with the British. The truth probably is, that the Emperor and his advisers did not pause to consider whether it would or would not be interpreted as a signal for the commencement of hostilities, caring only that all British subjects should be driven out of the Chinese Empire, and leaving it to the provincial officials to choose the means by which that end might be attained. In any case its language is of interest, as showing in what spirit the Court at Peking entered on the first war ever waged by China with a Western power. The following extract sufficiently illustrates the spirit of the whole edict :—

"The Foreigners of the English nation, from and after the time that it was agreed upon to prohibit opium, have been continually shifting backwards and forwards. On a previous occasion they had the hardihood to fire off great guns, and afterwards, under false pretence of respect and obedience, they leagued themselves with ships of war and clandestinely schemed after revenge and reprisals. At that time, although we awarded them the chastisement due to their rashness, yet did not we immediately cut off their commercial intercourse, not deeming their faults hitherto worthy of so stern a display of celestial dignity. But this time the Foreign ship *Smith*,[1] having again dared to be the first to fire off his great guns, and having further seized upon the neighbourhood of Hong-kong as a stronghold or fastness, this is quite enough to show that these said Foreigners cherish dark and unfathomable designs in their hearts. Thus even granting that they were at this time prepared to give the duly prepared bond, yet it is difficult to secure that they would not be turning and twisting again, and if, they having so often shown us opposition and defiance, we were still to permit them to hold commercial intercourse with us, this would be a very improper way of managing affairs. As to the little petty amount of duties, this is a subject not worthy a monarch's consideration. We of the heavenly dynasty cherished these Foreigners from afar with the utmost kindness and benevolence, but these said Foreigners know not how to feel grateful! They, on the other hand, act the part of the unfilial *shi* bird (which attacks and tries to destroy its mother as soon as hatched). That they are in the wrong, and we in the right, is a fact known alike to those of the Inner Land, and to those from beyond the seas! Since, then, these said Foreigners, by their own act, have put themselves out of the pale of the laws, what occasion is there for us to feel any sorrow or regret about them? Cause therefore that the trade of the English nation be immediately put a stop to, and let every one of the ships belonging to the said nation be forthwith driven out! Cause at the same time that it be clearly proclaimed and made known to all nations, and let the crimes [of the English] be duly and specifically drawn up in order, and disseminated among the people of all countries, showing how that the English Foreigners have cut themselves off from communion with the celestial dynasty, and that this affair has no reference to you (the good) Foreigners of other countries. Do ye then, O all Foreigners of

[1] *i.e.*, H.M.S. *Volage* (Captain Smith).

all other nations, be respectful and submissive as hitherto, and you will be permitted to continue your commercial intercourse as of old! But if you dare to shelter or protect the English, or clandestinely to convey them into our harbours, so soon as found out then shall your crime be visited with the most severe punishment."[1]

Before putting into execution the imperial commands as thus conveyed, the High Commissioner, the Viceroy, and the *foo-yuen* resolved to put on record their statement of the causes that had produced the present crisis and, possibly, to make one last effort for peace, by writing to Queen Victoria a personal letter urging her to intervene and put a stop to the opium traffic carried on by her subjects in China. The statement of the case, as there set out, contains no reference at all to the many grievances under which the British residents at Canton had so long laboured, and ignores the fact that those grievances had much to do with bringing about the existing troubles. But in so far as those troubles were due to the contraband trade, and as an exposition of the ethics of the opium question, its main propositions are difficult to refute.

The letter commenced with an exordium of the usual kind on the benevolence and goodness of the Emperor. He was described as one who, if a profit exists anywhere, diffuses it over the whole world—who, if the tree of evil takes root anywhere, plucks it up for the benefit of all nations. The Queen of Great Britain was complimented, as occupying a throne whose previous occupants had through successive generations been styled respectful and obedient. She was reminded that her predecessors had sent "tribute," accompanied by documents expressing gratitude to the Emperor for the most perfect justice and the kindest treatment. For this reason the Heavenly Dynasty had nourished and cherished her people, and bestowed upon them redoubled proofs of urbanity and kindness, and it was entirely through intercourse with the Celestial Empire that Great Britain had become the rich and flourishing kingdom it was said to be. This preamble, it must be confessed, is in the worst vein of Chinese arrogance

[1] *Chinese Repository*, vol. xi, p. 523.

and disregard of facts, and can scarcely be described as politic. But apart from the introduction, the document offers little scope for serious criticism. It consists of a succinct narrative of the circumstances under which the High Commissioner had been appointed to suppress the opium traffic, of the surrender of the 20,283 chests, and of the reasons why Foreigners should respect the law and cease to import the drug. It concludes with an appeal, in the flowery and superior language habitually used by the Chinese officials, that "her highness" would punish her subjects who broke the law, and thus secure peace and quietness to her possessions. The nature of the arguments advanced is shown by the following passages :—

"Let us suppose that Foreigners came from another country and brought opium into England, and seduced the people of your country to smoke it, would not you, the Sovereign of the said country, look upon such a procedure with anger, and in your just indignation endeavour to get rid of it? Now we have always heard that your highness possesses a most kind and benevolent heart; surely then you are incapable of doing or causing to be done unto another that which you should not wish another to do unto you.

"Moreover, we have heard that in London, the metropolis where you dwell, as also in Scotland, Ireland, and other such places, no opium whatever is produced. It is only in sundry parts of your colonial kingdom of Hindostan, such as Bengal, Madras, Bombay, Patna, Malwa, Benares, Malacca, and other places where the very hills are covered with the opium plant, that tanks are made for the preparing of the drug: month by month, and year by year, the volume of the poison increases, its unclean stench ascends upwards, until Heaven itself grows angry, and the very gods thereat get indignant! You, the Queen of the said honourable nation, ought immediately to have the plant in those parts plucked up by the very root! Cause the land to be hoed up afresh, sow in its stead the five grains, and if any man dare again to plant in these grounds a single poppy, visit his crime with the most severe punishment. . . .

"Suppose the subject of another country were to come to England to trade, he would certainly be required to comply with the laws of England, then how much more does this apply to us of the Celestial Empire! Now it is a fixed statute of this Empire, that any native Chinese who sells opium is punishable with death, and even he who merely smokes it, must not less die. Pause and reflect for a moment: if you Foreigners did not bring the opium hither, where would our Chinese people get it to re-sell it? It is you Foreigners who involve our simple natives in the pit of death, and are they alone to be permitted to escape alive? If so much as one of those deprive one of our people of his life, he must forfeit his life in requital for that which he has taken; how much more does this apply to him who by means of opium destroys his fellow men? Does the havoc which he commits stop with a single life? Therefore it is that those Foreigners, who now import opium into the Central Land, are condemned to be beheaded and strangled by the new statute, and this explains what we said at the beginning about plucking up the tree of evil, wherever it takes root, for the benefit of all nations."[1]

The imperial commands that the English be driven out resulted in an immediate change of attitude towards the Portuguese, who, up to this time, at the cost of some sacrifice of independence, had preserved perfectly friendly relations with the Chinese. The provincial officials suspected, probably not without reason, that the people of Macao would not be adverse to reaping any commercial advantages that might flow from the misfortunes of the British. For this reason they appointed a new official, with the rank of *Taotai*, to regulate the affairs of that port, in addition to the *tsotang* and the *keun-min-foo*. His duties were to observe and regulate foreign affairs; to keep watch over the licensed vessels, and prevent any transactions under false names on behalf of the English; to search after and apprehend any Chinese who might furnish them with supplies, and to have control of the military guard stationed outside the Barrier. In the memorial asking the

[1] For the whole of this letter see *Chinese Repository*, vol. viii, pp. 497–503. Apparently it never reached the Royal hand. It is not mentioned in the *Letters of Queen Victoria*.

Emperor to sanction this appointment, the Portuguese were described as Foreigners who "though declaring themselves respectfully obedient, yet they neither plough nor spin, but diligently pursuing schemes of improper gain, abound in ever varying tricks."[1]

At this juncture Captain Smith, of the *Volage*, as senior naval officer, took a bold step for the protection of those British subjects who were still in Macao. On the 4th of February, 1840, without any diplomatic preliminary, H.M.S. *Hyacinth* moved into the Typa and dropped anchor. This proceeding, of which no intimation had been given, at once aroused the resentment of the Portuguese. The Governor sent a despatch to Captain Smith pointing out that it had hitherto been an unbroken rule that no man-of-war should enter the harbour of Macao, and that the entry of H.M.S. *Hyacinth* was an act of declared hostility. To this Captain Smith replied that, if the Governor would protect British subjects then at Macao from the harassing treatment to which they had been experienced by them in the last six months, the sloop should be withdrawn and the Governor's sentiments made known to the British residents. To this the Governor answered, with some dignity, that he should continue to give such protection as he was able, and that it must be remembered that he had to consider the welfare of the 5,000 Portuguese subjects who had exposed themselves to some hardship, in order to maintain their friendship with the British. The Senate drew up a protest, and issued a proclamation notifying the inhabitants of Macao that the *Hyacinth* had entered the harbour without their permission or consent, and calling on them to remain quiet. Captain Smith had no alternative but to comply with the formal request to withdraw sent by the Governor, which he did, after expressing a hope that the same treatment would be meted out to any Chinese force that might enter Macao as had been shown to himself, and offering to assist the Portuguese if at any time they should request him to do so.[2]

[1] *Chinese Repository*, vol. viii, p. 504.
[2] *Ibid.*, vol. viii, pp. 543–7.

The Imperial Government at Peking was steadily preparing to meet the coming storm. To prevent the dual control, which had existed at Canton since the appointment of the High Commissioner, from becoming a source of weakness, the Viceroy Tang was removed from his office and Lin appointed to fill both positions. Thus Commissioner Lin was placed in sole and supreme authority over affairs at Canton, and the policy of the provincial government from this time on was purely his policy. He at once began to prepare for hostilities. Seeing that Chinese war-junks could never hope to compete with the British men-of-war, he conceived the idea of forming a Chinese navy on British lines, but in the realization of this plan he was no more successful than those latter-day Chinese officials who have attempted a similar undertaking. Thinking that the easiest way to accomplish his object was to obtain European vessels and convert them to the uses of a Chinese navy, he seized three merchantmen and appropriated them by force. This method of procedure was found to excite too much opposition. He then set to work to build ships of the required type, and in April, 1840, two or three schooners, built after European models, were launched on the Canton river. But the difficulties were found to be insuperable and the plan was abandoned.[1]

Captain Elliot now found himself in the unenviable position of having provoked hostilities, for which he was unprepared. There can be no doubt that neither at this time, nor at any subsequent period, did he correctly estimate the degree of forcible constraint that would have to be brought to bear on the Chinese before they would yield to the British demands; but, ignorant as he was, he could yet perceive that he must wait for some sort of reinforcements, before he could take the offensive. Another thing that prevented him from taking any decisive action was his utter ignorance as to what were the intentions of the Home Government. He therefore waited. Soon there were signs that Lord Palmerston contemplated some sort of warlike demonstration. On the 24th March, H.M.S. *Druid* (44), Captain Lord John Churchill,

[1] *Chinese Repository*, vol. viii, p. 648; vol. xi, p. 524.

arrived at Tung-ku, and on the 2nd of April the *Ariel* returned with despatches from England, from which it was clear that the British Government had decided to coerce the Chinese authorities into adopting a policy more congenial to the wishes of the British community. This decision was not openly avowed, but was apparent from the language of the despatches.

Reference has already been made to the burning of the Spanish brig *Bilbaino*. On the 1st of April two of her crew, the mate and a boy, who had been captured by the Chinese, managed to get back to Canton. The account they gave of their experiences was anything but calculated to induce the British to consent that British subjects, charged with offences against the laws of China, should be tried by Chinese tribunals. They had been carried in chains to Canton, where they were led in a triumphal procession to the residence of the High Commissioner. There they were kept for twenty-five days, and on thirteen of these underwent an examination lasting for many hours, during the whole of which they had to kneel. Every means was tried to induce them to say that the vessel was English. The officers declared that they knew she was a smuggling vessel, and promised instant liberation as the reward of a frank confession. At one time a drawn sword was held over the mate, who was threatened with instant death if he did not confess. Then they were separately confined, and before each of them was placed a box of dollars, it being explained to each that the others had confessed and had received such a box and had returned to Macao. They were then imprisoned in a small dark apartment in a temple, lighted only with two small apertures opening on to a court-yard, and there they were kept for six months and fed on the coarsest food, no change of clothes being allowed to them nor any means of communicating with their friends. Ultimately, through the mediation of the American consul, they were released, and sent to Macao, where one of them, in a fit of mental derangement, brought on by the confinement, tried to commit suicide by jumping out of the window.[1]

It must not be supposed that those members of the Foreign

[1] *Chinese Repository*, vol. viii, p. 648.

community in China, who were not British subjects, had taken up the quarrel of the Chief Superintendent as their own. On the contrary, they took every precaution to dissociate themselves from the controversy, and to secure a continuance of commercial intercourse with the Chinese. At the end of April the American consular authorities presented a petition to the Viceroy on behalf of the subjects of the United States, asking that American ships might be allowed to come direct to Whampoa to discharge their cargoes, lest in the event of a stricter blockade being undertaken by the British, while those vessels were still waiting outside the Bogue, they should be altogether prevented from being able to trade. The Viceroy was annoyed at the suggestion that such a possibility might arise. It is clear from his reply that he did not anticipate that the British Government really meant to use force. "It is an egregious mistake," he says, "analogous to a falsehood, that the English contemplate putting on a blockade." So distasteful to him was the idea of such a course being adopted, that he returned the petition to the petitioners, in order that it might not be filed among the official records.[1]

The British naval squadron in Chinese waters now began to amount to an effective force. Just at this point, however, it sustained the loss of its senior officer, Captain Lord John Churchill, who died on June 3rd, 1840, at Macao. He was the fourth son of the Duke of Marlborough, and was but forty-three years old at his death. Six days later the Chinese made an unsuccessful but determined attempt to destroy the British shipping at Kapshuy Moon, by sending into its midst ten fire-ships. Shortly after this the steamship *Madagascar* arrived, to the no small excitement of the Chinese, who had only once before seen such a vessel. On 21st of June H.M.S. *Wellesley*, bringing Commodore Sir James John Gordon Bremer, the commander-in-chief of the ships on the Indian station, anchored off Hong-kong.[2]

Three days after his arrival Commodore Bremer established a blockade of the Canton River by all its entrances. For the

[1] *Chinese Repository*, vol. ix, p. 53.
[2] *Ibid.*, vol. xi, p. 525.

convenience of such British shipping as might resort to China in ignorance that this had been done, the anchorages at Kapshuy Moon and Macao Roads were appointed as a rendezvous. For some reason, which is not explained, Captain Elliot seems to have thought that this action needed some justification in the eyes of the Chinese. He accordingly published a special address for the information and instruction of the native population. A few days later he published a translation in English, the following extracts from which show the reasons put forward by the Superintendent as justifying his own course of action, and the hostile operations that were now to be commenced :—

"Twelve months since the Emperor was graciously pleased to depute Lin, the Commissioner, to come to these provinces and suppress the traffic in opium. He found it stagnant; he has made it flourish here and along the whole coast of the Empire. . . . The Commissioner disregarded the immediate offer of Elliot to fulfil the imperial pleasure, which he was ready faithfully to do, in a manner consistent with the dignity of the Empire, with the preservation of peace, and with obligations of justice to innocent and absent men, unconnected with the traffic in opium. But on the contrary he forthwith confined Elliot a close prisoner at Canton, and so detained him for several weeks, proceeded to constrain the whole Foreign community, by the stoppage of their supplies of food and fresh water, and under these circumstances of lawless and most violent constraint, required Elliot to deliver up all the opium in the possession of his countrymen, under pain of death. . . .

"And which would have been the most effectual means of accomplishing the imperial pleasure? Those that Elliot had offered and was ready to take, founded upon the separation of the innocent from the offending, and accompanied by securities and precautions that would have given permanent efficacy to such distinctions? Or those of senseless violence, casting upon the whole transaction the character of shameful spoliation? The Commissioner preferred a career of needless and spoliatory constraint, which has made amplest reparation a duty of highest obligation in the government of England, which has broken to pieces all sense of confidence in the wisdom or justice of the provincial government, and which has had the effect of immediately reviving the opium traffic at all points of the coast with utmost vigour. The Emperor admonished the Commissioner to maintain the honour and dignity of the Empire. He has over and over again violated his pledges under the seal of the Empire, and left the word of a high officer without weight in the eyes of all men, native and Foreign. . . . He causes vessels engaged in lawful pursuits, or in carrying away some of these innocent fugitives (Spanish as well as British) to be cowardly attacked by overwhelming force in the night time, and burnt. Nine or ten innocent persons, some Spanish and some English, lose their lives, some are cruelly mutilated; some still detained in captivity upon the most false pretences, and under circumstances terribly disgraceful to the empire. Poison is put into the springs of water. The English people were driven to conflict to procure supplies of food; worthy officers and soldiers of the empire have fallen a sacrifice to the violence of the Commissioner; and falsehood upon falsehood has been reported to the Emperor, and proclaimed to the people, to cover these bloody and disgraceful proceedings. . . .

"When the Commissioner came to Canton, the empire was at peace and respected by the whole world. His first act was one of the most unprovoked wars against the English nation, by the imprisonment and wanton insult of the English officer, who had already offered to fulfil the imperial pleasure.

"The gracious Queen and the people of the English nation venerate the Emperor, and cherish the people of the empire. But great injuries have been perpetrated, and the truth must now be made known to his imperial majesty, to the end that the evil-doers may be punished, and that all things may be re-established on a sure and honourable basis. Let the natives of the land pursue their ordinary occupations in peace and security, in the assurance that no violence will be offered to them or their property, whilst they are opposing none of the forces of the Queen of England."[1]

[1] *Chinese Repository*, vol. ix, pp. 110–111.

It is very doubtful whether it was good policy to issue any such notice, much less one abounding in rhetoric of the kind here employed. What could be gained by stating that the High Commissioner, in his efforts to stop the opium traffic, had disobeyed the behests of the Emperor and brought insult to his name? Every Chinese knew that such was not the fact. Again, why pretend that the English sovereign and people venerated the Emperor? There was no shadow of truth in such a statement, as it would be construed by the Chinese. The history of the failure of Lord Amherst's mission, and of Lord Napier's attempts to communicate with the authorities at Canton on a footing of equality, were a direct contradiction of any such contention. The probability is, that if any Chinese read the notice, he regarded it as only one more sign of barbarian inferiority. An honest avowal by the Superintendent that his Government meant to insist upon compensation for the loss of the opium surrendered at Canton and on new conditions of intercourse, and to secure those ends by force, would have impressed Chinese readers with a feeling of respect. Force they could understand. The desire for money they could understand. But utterances of the kind contained in this notice were unintelligible.

Not content with this notice, however, the Superintendent, some three months later, issued another, addressed to the inhabitants of the coasts of the province of Kwangtung, which both in tenor and language was very similar to the previous one. In this he states that as Lin and Tang have visited the English with perfidious violence, "it has been determined by the gracious sovereign of England to send royally appointed officers to the coast of China, to the end that the truth may be made manifest to his imperial majesty, and lasting peace and honourable trade firmly established." He repeats the sentiments about venerating the Emperor and cherishing the Chinese people; and, in consideration of the fact that their lives and property are to be spared, if they do not oppose the English, he calls on them to "bring their supplies and commodities to the several stations of the British forces without fear, in the certainty that they will receive kind protection and just payment." He concludes by announcing a blockade of the port of Canton.[1]

By this time the command of the British forces in China had been taken over by Rear-Admiral the Hon. George Elliot, a cousin of the Superintendent. These forces had reached a respectable total. In July, 1840, there were sixteen men-of-war, one troopship, four armed steamers, and twenty-seven transports assembled off the Bogue. The number of men available for military operations was about 4,000, made up of the 18th (Royal Irish), the 26th (Cameronians), the 49th (Bengal Volunteers), and a corps of Madras Sappers and Miners.[2] What object the British Government had in view in sending them to China no one seemed to know. After some discussion between the Admiral and the Superintendent, it was decided that the best course would be to proceed to the North and deal directly with the imperial authorities at Peking, instead of with the High Commissioner at Canton. Accordingly, on the 30th June, Admiral Elliot and Captain Elliot left Macao Roads on board H.M.S. *Melville*, bound for the Pei-ho and Tientsin, in the hope that as joint plenipotentiaries they might arrive at an amicable settlement of the difficulties between England and China.[3] Commodore Bremer had preceded them by some days, with most of the military and naval forces.

Before leaving for the North, Captain Elliot left instructions that in his absence an attempt should be made, by that part of the naval forces which remained behind at Macao, to communicate with the Chinese officials at Amoy, by means of an official communication not superscribed with the character *Pin*. He instructed Captain Bourchier, of H.M.S. *Blonde*, and Mr. Thom, who had been appointed official interpreter, to deliver the document into the hands of the Chinese Admiral at Amoy, or in his absence to the highest Chinese official at that port. This despatch was called a "letter," and was addressed in terms of official equality, as coming "From

[1] *Chinese Repository*, vol. ix, p. 111.
[2] *Ibid.*, p. 221.
[3] *Ibid.*, p. 112; vol. xi, p. 526.

the imperial appointed naval commander-in-chief of the Great English nation to His Excellency the imperial appointed admiral of the Chinese, for his Excellency's inspection."[1] Why Captain Elliot should imagine that he would be allowed to communicate on terms of equality with the Chinese authorities at Amoy, after all that had taken place in that connection at Canton, it is impossible to explain. All that is known is, that he left orders that the attempt should be made, and that measures of a most extraordinary kind were taken to carry out those orders.

By way of a preliminary announcement, Mr. Thom drew up a curious document in Chinese, purporting to be an explanation of the use of the white flag as sanctioned by the rules of international law. As a good deal was afterwards said about the Chinese not respecting flags of truce, it is well that the reader should know what were the terms of this singular publication, in order that he may judge as to the sufficiency of their means of knowledge. It was thus worded :—

"Behold! it hath been said by the ancient sages—the ten thousand kingdoms of this earth form but one house, and all mankind are but one great family of brothers; thus although they may at times have their differences yet in the end all hope to drop their enmity and love each other as before—this is a principle of human nature, applicable alike to all countries. The object of this, then, is to say, that a misunderstanding having unfortunately arisen between the two great nations of England and China, in order to restore their brotherly harmony as of old, it will be necessary for quiet, peaceable people to be continually coming and going between both parties for the purpose of speaking kind words, or delivering letters or such like. These people go utterly unarmed, and carry a white flag, which, with the exception of savages, is looked upon by all nations as a sacred sign. No violence is ever offered to their persons: on the contrary, all mankind look upon them as good men, and treat them accordingly: it answers very much the same purpose as a *meen chen pae* (board having the characters "avoid fighting"

[1] *Chinese Repository*, vol. ix, p. 222.

on it) in your own honourable country. We therefore beg that you communicate the same to all your fellow-officers that they may know accordingly. At the same time, distinct warning is hereby given, that if any of your people fire off guns or muskets at such white flag, it will be impossible for me, the great English chief, to prevent my people exacting a most fearful vengeance! Beware, therefore, Beware!"

A better parody of a Chinese edict it would be impossible to find. As a serious diplomatic document the whole thing is ludicrous. The language employed speaks for itself, the sentiments are those of a philanthropist engaged in an enterprise which he knows is not quite in accordance with the principles he professes, while the description of the operations that would be necessary to effect the policy of Lord Palmerston, as making it necessary "for quiet, peaceably-disposed people to be continually coming and going between both parties for the purpose of speaking kind words," reads like a delightful satire, which would have been appreciated by no one more than by that eminent statesman himself. The description of Captain Elliot as "the great English chief" must have particularly appealed to the Chinese sense of humour when they thought of the communications superscribed with the character *Pin*.

As soon as the *Blonde* had cast anchor at Amoy, a boat containing about half-a-dozen yamên runners came alongside, to inquire who the Foreigners were and what they wanted. Mr. Thom's document was handed to them open, having first been read aloud for their instruction. They were asked if they understood its purport, to which they replied that they understood perfectly that the white flag was to be held sacred. They were then told to take it to the *fun-fu* and the *chung-ying*, the highest officials that then happened to be in Amoy. Presently they returned with the message that the officials had taken a copy of it, but as they could not hold communication with outside Foreigners they begged to return the original whence it came. The runners were told that they must take it back, whereupon the head man among them said a few words to the others, and quietly put the paper in his bosom, doubtless intending to destroy it, rather than run the risk of being punished for returning with such a missive. The whole of the Chinese then returned to land, having been informed that Mr. Thom and his party would call on the mandarins ashore after dinner. It had been decided that the letter from Captain Elliot should be delivered to the Chinese officials by a British officer in person. Accordingly Mr. Thom and a second lieutenant put off in the cutter, flying a white flag at the bows. So far from meeting with the kind reception they seem to have expected, they found two or three hundred soldiers drawn up on the beach to oppose their landing, who warned them that if they dared to set a foot on shore they would kill them, or bind them hand and foot and send them to Foochow. Expostulations were in vain, and Mr. Thom and his party had to retire. Captain Bourchier in the meantime seized a junk, the captain of which was ordered to carry a note to the Chinese officials; but in the night time the junk got away and no reply was ever received to this communication.

The next day a second attempt to deliver Captain Elliot's letter was made. The frigate was taken close in shore, and a notice was prepared stating in large Chinese characters, so as to be legible at a great distance, that "the Foreign *employé*" had been ordered by his superior officer to deliver a despatch into the very hands of the honourable officers of the district, and that if they declined to receive it they would bring upon themselves a great calamity. Mr. Thom proceeded in the jolly-boat to deliver the letter, with this notice displayed so that it might be read by all on shore. When about five or six yards from the beach, Mr. Thom placed the notice at the stern and requested the officials to peruse it. The fury of the latter at this proceeding knew no bounds. Evidently it had caused them to lose face before the whole of the immense crowd of Chinese, who had collected together out of curiosity, as well as the naval and military forces that had been assembled evidently with the most hostile intentions. To Mr. Thom's friendly overtures they replied with threats and curses, making at the same time the well-known sign of cutting off the head. Finding the enterprise hopeless, the boat's crew started to return to the frigate, and making the boat spring to the oars, they caused Mr. Thom to lose his balance and fall. At that very moment an arrow flew over the place where he had been standing, and struck the bottom of the boat with such force as to shiver the arrow-head to pieces. The Chinese then discharged firearms at the retreating craft, and Captain Bourchier, seeing the peril in which the occupants were, opened fire with two thirty-two pounders, which scattered the Chinese in all directions and killed outright about ten or a dozen. The frigate then bombarded the fort for about two hours, after which Captain Bourchier despatched another landing party to paste on the wall of the fort a large notice vindicating his action, as having been necessitated by the conduct of the Chinese in firing on the white flag. But this party, too, were attacked and forced to retire; so after capturing and setting fire to a junk, the expedition returned to Canton with its purpose unaccomplished.[1]

Mr. Thom was of opinion that good consequences were bound to follow this incident, because the Chinese saw their own military forces put to flight and panic by a single barbarian ship, which they had defied. He regretted that there was no steamer available, by which the *Blonde* could have been towed into such positions, that she could have battered down every public office in turn, and thus convinced the ordinary Chinese that the quarrel was with their rulers and not with them. He thought that, the trouble having originated as it had, a white flag would in future be recognised all over the empire as the emblem of peace. Mr. Thom must have been an optimist to come to these conclusions. He is more accurate when he says that "but for the merciful Providence of God and the well-directed fire of H.M.S. *Blonde*, myself and every individual in this jolly-boat had without doubt been most barbarously murdered." The Viceroy of Fu-kien reported to the Throne that the Foreigners, under the pretence that they wished for peace, had insisted on landing and had fired off their guns, whereupon their "principal person" had been shot through

[1] *Chinese Repository*, vol. ix, pp. 222–8.

the breast with an arrow, three other Foreigners killed, and an immense number wounded, and made out that a great victory had been won. The Emperor was so pleased that he promoted all the Chinese officers who had taken any part in the fighting, and pensioned the relations of soldiers who had been killed. The officer who fired the arrow at Mr. Thom was specially rewarded with a peacock's feather.[1]

These events did not tend to promote good feeling between the Chinese officials at Canton and those British subjects who had taken refuge in Macao. Early in August great alarm was caused by the abduction of Mr. Stanton, the officiating clergyman at the English Chapel, who was carried off when bathing and detained at Canton, as well as by an attack on two British officers when walking on the Praya Grande at nine o'clock at night. At the same time it was noticed that there was a movement of troops going on, which seemed to indicate fresh measures of hostility. The newly appointed Taotai of Macao had taken up his abode about 500 yards on the south side of the Barrier with a guard of some 200 troops, while outside the Barrier he had stationed some 100 more. In the harbour, which had been regarded as a sort of neutral ground, there were eight large war-junks, so that altogether he had at his disposal some 2,000 men of the land and sea forces together. Gradually these were augmented, till on the 19th of August they amounted to 5,000 men of all arms. The total Portuguese garrison did not consist of more than 500 men, distributed over six forts which mounted 150 guns. In this state of affairs, Captain Smith, the senior British naval officer, determined to attack the Chinese before they should have concentrated further. On the 19th of August, H.M.S. *Larne* and *Hyacinth*, with the steamer *Enterprise* and the cutter *Louisa*, advanced to within 600 yards of the Chinese camp and opened fire, while a landing party of 380 with a single gun raked the Barrier from the south. The fire was returned and a general engagement ensued, as a result of which the whole of the Chinese were put to flight. The British casualties were four wounded; the

[1] *Chinese Repository*, vol. ix, pp. 227–8; vol. x, pp. 443–4.

Chinese were supposed to have lost about a hundred. Throughout this affair the strictest neutrality was maintained by the Portuguese, who for several nights organized patrols not only of the soldiery, but also of the Governor and citizens, for the maintenance of peace and safety.[1]

At about the time that the attack on the Barrier was taking place at Macao, Captain Elliot was waiting in the North for a reply to Lord Palmerston's letter, which he had induced the Chinese officials to receive. When he left Canton with Admiral Elliot, he did not proceed direct to the Pei-ho, but made for Tinghai, a strongly fortified town on the Chusan islands, at the mouth of the Yang-tse-kiang, whither Commodore Bremer had preceded them. The date of Sir Gordon Bremer's appearance before Tinghai was July 4th, 1840. He at once invited the Chinese officials on board the *Wellesley*, pointed out to them that the Chinese defences could not possibly offer any real resistance to a vessel of her armament, and demanded the surrender of the town. To this demand the Chinese admiral replied that he knew he was weak, but as the servant of the Emperor he was bound to fight. Thereupon he was told that he would be allowed till 2.0 p.m. to surrender, when a gun would be fired from H.M.S. *Wellesley*, and, if there was any reply, the British squadron would bombard the town. At 2.0 p.m. the *Wellesley* fired, and was answered by the guns on shore. The bombardment was then undertaken by H.M.S. *Wellesley*, *Conway*, *Cruizer*, and *Alligator*. In about one minute all the Chinese forces had disappeared, and the British effected a landing without opposition.

The chief product of the Chusan Islands is the Chinese wine, or rather spirit, called *sam-shu*, very similar to the Japanese *sake*. The first duty of the British officers on landing was to prevent their men looting this spirit and drinking too much of it. The outer city of Tinghai seemed to be nothing but a *samshu* depôt, so great was the quantity found there. Thousands of jars were broken open at the officers' commands, till the liquor flowed through the streets in sounding torrents. The men of the transport service, seconded by the Chinese

[1] *Chinese Repository*, vol. ix, pp. 234–9.

boat-people and peasantry, could not resist the temptation to break into the remaining stores and help themselves to the contents. In the end the whole of the outer city was literally gutted. For days the spirit lay about in stagnant pools, emitting a stench that was simply intolerable. It is not surprising that subsequently sickness broke out among the troops with such violence as to cause the climate, somewhat unjustly, to earn a most unenviable notoriety. Moreover, Chinese robbers seized the opportunity, as they always do when a town is taken in war, to pillage and burn, so that the general condition of affairs at Tinghai immediately after its capture was deplorable. In such circumstances as these the British flag was hoisted with a royal salute. On the 6th July, Admiral Elliot arrived with the Superintendent, a blockade was established of the coast from Ningpo to the mouth of the Yang-tsze river, and it was determined to organize a provisional government. Major-General Burrell was appointed Governor, and to him was assigned the duty of evolving order out of the prevailing chaos. This was the first time that Chinese territory had ever been occupied by British troops.

The *Blonde* arrived at Chusan on July 7th. Three days later the Superintendent, again failing to profit by his experiences at Canton, and, it is to be presumed, knowing of the fiasco which had just occurred at Amoy, attempted to communicate with the Chinese officials at Chusan on a footing of equality. Having seized a small trading-junk he sent a note by her desiring that officers might come off to see him. The lieutenant-governor and *tituh* sent a polite answer, promising that a deputation should be sent, after one had first waited on them. Captain Elliot thought fit to receive in meekness this lesson in etiquette, and to comply with the intimation that it was his place to make the first overtures. The same day Messrs. Morrison, Clarke, and Astell, and Captain Bethune, were sent on shore with a Chinese translation of Lord Palmerston's letter, which they delivered open into the hands of officers wearing blue buttons. The following day, the document was returned, but as the plenipotentiaries were not then on board, it was refused. Later the document was sent back by the trading-junk which had conveyed it.[1] The efforts to deliver the letter here were as fruitless as those at Amoy.[2]

Having spent about twenty-five days at Chusan, the British plenipotentiaries resumed their journey northwards, and passing the Shantung Promontory on August 5th, arrived off Taku, at the mouth of the Pei-ho, on the 9th of the same month. On the 10th the steamship *Madagascar*, with Captain Elliot on board, proceeded towards the shore, and on the next day anchored within the river. Although drawing 11ft. 9in. she was only just able to cross the bar, on which she found 12ft. of water, which shows that even in 1840 the navigation of the Pei-ho was not free from the difficulties that are experienced there to-day. Kishen, the Viceroy of Chih-li, had come down to Taku to receive any despatches of which Captain Elliot might be the bearer, which showed that the Chinese officials of the northern provinces were ready to deal with the barbarians in a more conciliatory spirit than those of Canton. In fact, throughout Captain Elliot's stay in the North, they were under the greatest apprehension as to what use he would make of this opportunity to obtain the concessions required. Their one thought, as it afterwards appeared, was to get him to withdraw as soon as possible, so that in some more distant region negotiations might be carried on in the dilatory spirit dear to the Chinese mandarin, without fear of any unpleasant consequences to the Court and its immediate surroundings. In this object, as will be seen, they succeeded with the greatest ease, and the British expedition returned to the South absolutely empty-handed.

Kishen was a diplomatist of no mean order. His first endeavour was to prevent any tinge of hostility from creeping into the negotiations. On August 13th he sent an officer to the British squadron to enquire what provisions were needed. Cattle, sheep, and food were brought off in plenty, and offered as a gift, but the British insisted on paying for

[1] For a more detailed account of the occurrences at Tinghai, see *Chinese Repository*, vol. ix, pp. 228–233, 408.

[2] *Chinese Repository*, vol. ix, p. 420.

them. At the same time arrangements were made for the reception of Lord Palmerston's letter. On the 16th this document was delivered on board H.M.S. *Wellesley* into the hands of the Chinese officer who had been specially deputed to receive it. As Kishen had stated that he must have ten days in which to prepare an answer, the British squadron, as soon as the letter had been delivered, sailed away to the coast of Manchuria, which now, for the first time, came within the purview of our foreign politics. At the island of Chang-hing on the east of the Gulf of Liao-tung, H.M.S. *Blonde, Modeste,* and *Ernaad* succeeded in obtaining supplies of water, and cattle. It was noticed that some native boats were carrying coal, specimens of which were given to British officers as having been obtained near Fuchau, a town not far from the site of the modern Port Arthur. H.M.S. *Wellesley* was driven by a gale to one of the Miao-taou islands off Chefoo. H.M.S. *Volage* and *Pylades*, failing to cross the Gulf of Liao-tung, proceeded up the western side and reached Kien-ho, with the troopship *David Malcolm* and the steamship *Madagascar*, where they were joined later by the *Wellesley*.

On August the 27th the squadron re-assembled at the mouth of the Pei-ho. No reply having been received from Kishen on the 28th, a menacing letter was despatched to the shore, when it was discovered that the reply had reached Taku on the 24th, before there was any British vessel to receive it. It was then arranged that a conference should take place on land between Kishen and Captain Elliot, attended only by their interpreters. A piece of ground in the shape of a parallelogram near the mouth of the river was fenced off with cords stretched on poles, over which cloth was hung, after the manner of a Tartar encampment, and within this enclosure were pitched two tents, one for each plenipotentiary. The meeting took place and passed off just as Kishen wished, with a display of the utmost affability on both sides. The Superintendent was treated as being on a footing of equality with the Viceroy, and everything done to keep him in a pleased state of mind. For three days talking went on, an ominous sign in any negotiation under such circumstances.

Kishen again asked for time in which to refer to Peking, and six days from September 3rd were granted for this purpose. In the meantime a party was sent to explore the Great Wall at Shan-hai-kuan. On the 9th the plenipotentiaries again met, but history does not record what passed between them. The talking went on till the 15th, when it was announced that the expedition would return southwards, but no mention was made of any concession having been obtained from the Chinese authorities.[1] We now know that the only reason for returning was, that Kishen had persuaded Captain Elliot that the Chusan Islands were better suited for diplomatic operations than the metropolitan province of Chih-li. On the departure of Captain Elliot, Kishen reported to the Throne that the Foreigners had listened to and received his "instructions" and "orders," and had returned southward, having by memorial declared "that along the whole coast they will make no disturbance, provided they be not first fired on, but that, if they are attacked, it will be hard to stay the hand from retaliation; also, that of the soldiers at Tinghai, one half shall be withdrawn early."[2]

As a reward for his successful diplomacy in getting rid of the British from the neighbourhood of the Pei-ho, Kishen was promoted to the office of High Commissioner at Canton, in place of Lin, whose degradation was now imminent. The latter, all unconscious of the fall that awaited him, was busy taking further measures for the extinction of the traffic in opium. In September he published a special edict, warning those who dealt in or smoked opium that the penalty of strangulation would be strictly enforced when the period of eighteen months' grace from July, 1839, should have expired,[3] and urging all who used the drug to reform while the opportunity still offered itself. The presence of the British men-of-war had paralysed the efforts of the Chinese admiral to deal with the receiving ships and the smugglers. Had he attempted any active measures there can hardly be

[1] *Chinese Repository*, vol. ix, pp. 418–421.
[2] *Ibid.*, p. 412.
[3] *Ibid.*, pp. 267–274; 404–8.

any doubt that it would have been resisted by the captains of the British cruisers.

On the very day that Lin published this proclamation the Emperor, enraged at the arrival of the English ships in the Pei-ho, issued the edict dismissing him from office. The language of the edict is unusually severe. Nothing gives so bad an impression of the Chinese as their utter lack of gratitude for past services or favours. This is particularly manifested in the relations between the Emperor and his servants. If they fail to secure the end that he has in view, whether through their own fault or owing to circumstances over which they have no control, disgrace and degradation are the almost invariable reward. It is for this reason that all Chinese officials prefer to pursue a course of dilatory procrastination rather than take any decided step. The former course is the safe one; the latter may lead to an unsuccessful issue and ruin. No Chinese official ever served his imperial master more faithfully or with more earnestness than the High Commissioner Lin. Even his enemies admitted his integrity and single-mindedness. Yet the outcome of it all was to be dismissed by an edict couched in the following terms:—

"Lin Tsihseu! You received my imperial orders to go to Canton to examine into and manage the affairs relating to opium; from the exterior to cut off all trade in opium, and to terminate its many evils and disgraces: as to the interior, your orders were to seize perverse natives, and thus cut off all supplies to Foreigners: why have you delayed so long in the matters connected with these small, petty, contemptible criminals, who are still ungratefully disobedient and unsubmissive?

"You have not only proved yourself unable to cut off their trade, but you also proved yourself unable to seize perverse natives! You have but dissembled with empty words, and in deep disguises in your report [to the Emperor]: and so far from having been of any help in the affair, you have caused the waves of confusion to arise, and a thousand interminable disorders are sprouting: in fact, you have been as though your arms were tied, without knowing what to do: it appears you are no better then than a wooden image: when I think to myself on all these things, I am filled at once with anger and melancholy: we shall see in what instances you can answer to me."[1]

Lin preferred his defence to the Throne through the medium of a censor named Wang. This official presented a memorial asking that severer measures be taken against the English, and stating the difficulties that the ex-Commissioner had found in his way. Opium, he said, must be exterminated root and branch. The English in disposition resemble fiery and untameable horses. Had not the English been compelled to surrender the opium at Canton in the way they were, it would never have been given up. All the Foreigners signed the bond willingly, except the English. These barbarians of the English nation have actually dared to sail their ships into the inner waters, to fire off their guns and muskets, and to kill an incalculable number of Chinese officers and sailors. As regards the *Bilbaino*, she was under the control of the English, supplying them with provisions and aiding the rebels in their wickedness: she was in one moment therefore exterminated.

The concluding words show that even though degraded Lin favoured no half measures. His final words of advice to his imperial master were:—" Last year an imperial envoy received the royal commission to enquire into and regulate the maritime affairs of Canton. The Foreigners were left without a spot of ground whereon to lay their heads, and the country was nearly freed of the opium pest. They had then not the smallest chance of carrying into effect their diabolical schemes. Some time afterwards their dormant wickedness burst forth: they hurried to, attacked and usurped Chusan, opposed and ruined thousands of our people, and killed our officers and soldiers who were fighting in your majesty's service. Gods and men view this conduct with intense ire, and every man may follow his bent and slay the Foreigners. The object of this memorial is to request your majesty to ordain that our English prisoners be forthwith taken back to Chê-kiang and there beheaded;

[1] *Chinese Repository*, vol. ix, p. 412-3.

and their heads suspended as a warning : that their trade be cut off for ever ; and that all the Foreign obedient nations be allowed to trade as formerly, with the proviso that if any ship be discovered carrying cargo for the English, the said ship and her cargo shall be confiscated."[1]

Thus fell Commissioner Lin. He had not achieved the end he had in view, but he had done as much as was humanly possible under the circumstances. In spite of his efforts the opium traffic was flourishing vigorously. Sixteen ships and barques, each of from six to sixteen guns, and carrying crews of from thirty to ninety hands, and twenty-seven brigs and schooners, each mounting from four to twelve guns, and with crews of from twenty to sixty men, were engaged in carrying on the contraband trade.[2] All this shows that the task which had been allotted to the High Commissioner was an impossible one, unless indeed the co-operation of the despised barbarian English could be secured. We cannot blame Lin for his failure. He had, in the main, behaved with perfect justice. In him we see the Chinaman at his best, which after all is a long way behind the Englishman at his best. Whatever his failings, and however difficult it may be for us properly to appreciate his character, the fact remains that even his bitterest enemies had to admit in him the existence of the rarest of all virtues in China—that his actions were prompted by the sincerest patriotism and that his hands were free from bribes.

The negotiations at Chusan, which were entered upon as soon as Captain Elliot had returned from the North, were conducted on behalf of the Chinese by Ilipu, the Viceroy of Min-chêh (more commonly known as the Viceroy of Ning-po), a man of great ability and one destined to play a conspicuous part in the settlement of the difficulties between England and China. It was soon apparent that Captain Elliot was being beguiled into further inactivity by the cunning of this new representative of Chinese diplomacy. On the 6th of November a truce was signed, of which public notice was given by Admiral

[1] *Chinese Repository*, vol. ix, pp. 535–6.
[2] *Ibid.*, p. 328.

Elliot as having been agreed upon "pending the negotiations between the two countries." The English boundary was defined as taking in the island of Chusan and the small adjacent islands, and British subjects were prohibited from passing beyond it.[1] Having thus reduced his opponent to a condition of harmlessness, Ilipu's next care was to remove him still further from the capital, and back to the regions to which it had been customary hitherto to confine barbarian intercourse. This object was soon accomplished, Captain Elliot being induced to retire to Canton itself, as the most convenient place for resuming the negotiations with Kishen, who, as we have seen, was about to take up his abode at that port.

On the 15th of November the British plenipotentiaries left Chusan, and on the 20th of the same month reached Macao. So complaisant was the Chief Superintendent that he had agreed to transmit by the steamer *Queen*, possibly as being the quickest means of communication, a despatch from Ilipu to the new High Commissioner. In pursuance of this agreement the *Queen* on the 21st approached the Bogue, flying a flag of truce. But no sooner had she come within range of the first fort—a new one, which had been built round the Chuen-pi watch-tower—than the Chinese, quite regardless of the white flag, opened fire and discharged at her some twenty shots, one of which struck one of her paddles. A small boat which had been launched, also flying the white flag, was hastily recalled, and the steamer returned the fire by throwing some 68lb. shot and a few shells into the fort. She then retired to Tung-ku.

Most men in Captain Elliot's position would have regarded this as an insult, that demanded some sort of explanation. But he was far from taking that view of the matter. On the contrary, he at once landed at Macao, and forwarded the despatch to Kishen through the sub-prefect of Canton the same evening, apparently without protest or remonstrance. The next day some of the heavy shot discharged at the fort from the *Queen* were presented to the authorities at Canton,[2]

[1] *Chinese Repository*, vol. ix, p. 531.
[2] *Ibid.*, pp. 531–2.

whether as souvenirs or what does not appear. A week later Kishen arrived, and negotiations were at once resumed.

The British merchants, who were beginning to get impatient at the delay in arriving at anything certain, as soon as the plenipotentiaries arrived in Macao, wrote to Admiral Elliot asking him to obtain redress for the abduction of Mr. Stanton, to which reference has already been made. They also sent a second letter, inquiring as to whether the blockade at Canton was to be continued, and if so whether trade might be temporarily carried on at Macao. To this they received the reply, that the Admiral could only deal with the one part of their inquiries, and that the truce concluded at Chusan did not extend beyond the jurisdiction of the Viceroy of Ning-po. It is difficult to account for the course of conduct pursued by Captain Elliot, if the Admiral's view was correct. Apparently there was not that harmony between the two plenipotentiaries which is desirable in such a case. To this cause must be ascribed the resignation of the Admiral, which was announced a few days after his reply to the merchants had been received. "Sudden and severe illness" was the reason publicly given for this step. On November 29th, Commodore Sir J. J. Gordon Bremer formally succeeded to the command of the expedition.[1] On the 7th of December Admiral Elliot sailed for England.

This change did not interfere with the negotiations, which continued to drag slowly along, and by means of which Captain Elliot was hoping to obtain all that he wanted. The suavity of the High Commissioner—a fatal sign in a Chinese—fostered these hopes. This official went so far, it was stated, as to correspond on terms of equality with Foreign officers.[2] He issued an edict exhorting his forces to respect the white flag, and declared that the firing on the *Queen* was "exceedingly improper." He ordered Mr. Stanton to be released, and restored that gentleman to his countrymen. But as to the future no promise would he give. We know now that all the time he was working to obtain from the Superintendent

[1] *Chinese Repository*, vol. ix, pp. 535–6.
[2] *Ibid.*, p. 645.

some undertaking that there should be no dealing in opium, although he knew that the demand for a bond had been steadfastly refused. These are the words he used to the Emperor, in communicating his account of the progress of events at Canton :—

" Night and day have I considered, and with a sincere heart examined, the state of our relations with the English. At first, moved by the benevolence of his majesty, and the great severity of our laws, they took the opium, and made an entire surrender of it, evincing thereby good hearts unperverted. The business being indeed thus well begun, it were the more requisite that it should be well completed. Commissioner Lin accordingly commanded them to give bonds, that they would never more deal in opium—really a most excellent plan for securing future good conduct. This the English, still cherishing vain expectation, refused to give; and thus they trifled with the laws; and so obstinate were their dispositions, that they could not be made to submit. Hence, it becomes necessary to soothe and admonish them with sacred instruction, so as to cause them to change their mien, and purify their hearts (lit., skin face, wash hearts), after which it will not be too late for their commerce to be renewed." [1]

[1] *Chinese Repository*, vol. ix, p. 645.

CHAPTER XX

PARLIAMENT AND THE WAR

THE responsibility of a nation for those acts of its statesmen, over which it is able to exercise control, varies as the means of knowledge, which the nation has at the time when it authorizes or ratifies such acts. If it has not perfect control of its rulers, the measure of its responsibility is less in the proportion that its power of control is deficient. In discussing the responsibility of the people of Great Britain for the policy pursued with regard to China up to the year 1842, we must consider what was their knowledge at different periods of events at Canton, and what was their power of controlling the acts of British statesmen in matters of foreign policy. It is essential that we should not judge them by so high a standard as we should have to employ, were the same acts to be done at the present day. The length of time required in those days for the transmission of news, the slowness with which such news was diffused when received, the imperfect representation of the people in Parliament, and the nature of the control exercised by Parliament over foreign affairs, have all to be borne in mind when we attempt to arrive at a just conclusion on this subject.

It is a defect of the constitution of Great Britain that Parliament has in reality very little voice in deciding what shall be the foreign policy of the nation. The will of the English people, in matters that arise between other countries and their own, is the will of the Sovereign for the time being, as exercised on the advice of the responsible Ministers of the Crown, in particular of the Secretary of State for Foreign Affairs. Even in the making of peace and war Parliament has no initiative. It may censure, or refuse to support, a ministry that adopts a course of conduct of which it disapproves, and it may even go so far as to refuse to vote the necessary funds for carrying out a policy which it dislikes. But in practice these checks on the freedom of Ministers to adopt such policy as they please are of less value than in theory they would appear to be.

It is almost impossible for them to be brought into operation until after the event has happened against which they are sought to be directed. By that time it is, in most cases, worse than useless to attempt to recede from the course of conduct, which has excited the nation's disapproval.

Suppose, for example, that on some occasion after war had been declared, Parliament showed its disapprobation, in either of the ways mentioned above, of the conduct of Ministers in having entered on hostilities. The only course open to the Government would be to make peace forthwith, or to request the Sovereign to dissolve Parliament, in the hope that a newly elected House of Commons would give them support. If the latter expedient failed, peace must be made at any price. But the discontinuance at short notice of a war lately begun could not fail to put a belligerent, who so discontinued, at such a disadvantage, that greater injury would be sustained than would probably result from a continuance of the hostilities. Thus it is that Englishmen usually take the view that a war once begun must be carried through to the bitter end, even though the conscience of the nation disapprove of the war having been commenced. Against this view, it may be urged that what is ethically wrong cannot be politically expedient. With no wish to controvert that proposition, it must be admitted, as a matter of fact proved by experience, that the view expressed above is the one usually taken.

It is in the light of such considerations as these, that inquiry must be made into the responsibility of the English people for the First War with China, and for the way in which the matters in dispute between the two countries were settled. The responsibility of the Ministers and servants of the Crown, who were directly concerned, is another question. It is the responsibility of the English people themselves that has now to be considered. It has been said that, in discussing the rulers of a nation, we must assume that they are as good as is warranted by the condition of the people they govern. This proposition is often predicated of China, but with doubtful accuracy. Applied to England, there is no doubt of its untruth. The war with China is one that, arising when and in the manner it did, would have been forbidden by the people of Great Britain, had they been able to exercise a veto before it was commenced. Even with such imperfect means of control as they possessed, they would have made it impossible for the Government to continue in office, had they known the facts of the case and what were Lord Palmerston's intentions. This opinion is corroborated by the fact that, in the light of fuller knowledge, the war has been condemned by every impartial man of thought. So little information was before the country at the time when hostilities were begun, that the English people had but scanty means of judging whether the course about to be taken was one to be disapproved or commended. A few of the salient facts, such as the detention of the British community at Canton, had been noised abroad; but even in regard to this episode there was very little exact knowledge.

The way in which the ordinary Englishman looked at the matter is very fairly summed up by a modern writer in these words: "It is not surprising if the English people knew little of the original causes of the controversy. All that presented itself to their mind was the fact that Englishmen were in danger in a foreign country; that they were harshly treated and recklessly imprisoned; that their lives were in jeopardy, and that the flag of England was insulted. There was a general notion, too, that the Chinese were a barbarous and a ridiculous people, who had no alphabet, and thought themselves much better than any other people, even the English, and that, on the whole, it would be a good thing to take the conceit out of them. Those who remember what the feeling of ordinary society was at the time, will admit that it did not reach a much loftier level than this."[1]

When affairs in China had come to the pass described in the last chapter, questions began to be asked in Parliament as to the intentions of Ministers. It began to be suspected that we were drifting into war. Until after war had become inevitable, the answers to such questions showed an almost complete ignorance as to Captain Elliot's proceedings at Canton. Even so late as March 12th, 1840, Lord John Russell,

[1] McCarthy: *History of Our Own Times*, vol. i, pp. 175–6.

Secretary for War and the Colonies, stated that he had received no official intelligence amounting to a declaration of war, and that he presumed the rumour to that effect was due to some directions given or act done by the Government of India, to whom instructions had been sent "to make active preparations." Sir Robert Peel then inquired whether, in the event of hostilities being resolved on, any formal message would be sent down to the House of Commons; to which Lord Palmerston replied that "the *communications*, whatever they might be, which took place between this country and China, would be carried on in the name of the Queen of Great Britain and not of the Governor-General of India." To this Sir Robert retorted that that was the very reason why he had asked the question, and if hostilities were to be carried on at the charge of this country and in the name of Her Majesty, some formal communication should be made to Parliament. It was then that Lord Palmerston made the reply, which afterwards was the subject of so much sarcastic comment, "I used the word *communications*, not *hostilities*."[1]

It is a remarkable fact that up to this time no papers relating to the state of affairs at Canton had been laid upon the table of the House. There was a rumour that, to make up the complement of opium promised to be surrendered, Captain Elliot had been obliged to make purchases in the open market, but even on such a point as this no official statement had been made. Now, in answer to a question by Sir James Graham, Lord Palmerston admitted the truth of the rumour, and stated that such a purchase had been rendered necessary through one of the opium ships, whose cargo had been included in the list of consignments handed to Commissioner Lin, having sailed away in disobedience to the orders of the Superintendent. But how slight was the knowledge of the Government as to recent events in China is shown by the fact that at this date the Foreign Secretary did not know what had become of the surrendered opium,[2] which had been publicly destroyed in June of 1839.

[1] Hansard: *Parliamentary Debates*, vol. 52 pp. 1155–6.
[2] *Ibid.*, p. 1222.

On March 19th, the public learnt for the first time what were the objects of the expedition that was being fitted out in India. Lord John Russell, in answer to a question in the House of Commons, thus stated them: "In the first place, they were to obtain reparation for the insults and injuries offered to Her Majesty's Superintendent and Her Majesty's subjects by the Chinese Government; and, in the second place, they were to obtain for the merchants trading with China an indemnification for the loss of their property, incurred by threats of violence offered by persons under the direction of the Chinese Government; and, in the last place, they were to obtain security that the persons and property of those trading with China should in future be protected from insult and injury.[1] This statement, vague as it was, made it abundantly clear that the British Government regarded the conduct of the Chinese authorities, in compelling the surrender of the opium, as a proceeding that could not be allowed to pass as legitimate. Captain Elliot's views had been completely adopted by the Home Government, and the responsibility for making the war an opium war rests in the fullest degree on the then Ministers of the Crown.[2]

Under these circumstances Sir James Graham (Member for Pembroke), on the 7th of April, 1840, moved a resolution in the House of Commons to the effect "that the interruption in our commercial and friendly intercourse with China, and the hostilities which have since taken place, are mainly to be attributed to the want of foresight and precaution on the part of Her Majesty's present advisers, in respect to our relations with China, and especially to their neglect to furnish the Superintendent at Canton with powers and instructions calculated to provide against the growing evils connected with the contraband traffic in opium, and adapted to the novel and difficult situation in which the Superintendent was placed." It will be seen at once that this was really a motion of want of confidence in the Government, which, if carried, must lead to their resignation. The immediate cause of the debate was

[1] Hansard: *Parliamentary Debates*, vol. 52, p. 1223.

[2] This is made clear in the despatches given in *Letters of Queen Victoria*, 1837-1861, at pp. 327, 333.

the publication of the first China Blue Book, to which free reference has been made in this work. Moved by the complaints of the lack of official information, the Government had had this volume prepared and published in the greatest haste. Lord Palmerston stated that in its preparation he had literally broken through one of the floors of the Foreign Office with the weight of the types accumulated in the printing of these papers.[1]

The various speeches made in the course of this great debate, which was twice adjourned, are even at this distance of time of the greatest interest. It gives food for reflection, if we examine, in the fuller knowledge that we possess to-day, the assertions that were made, the arguments that were put forward, and the prophecies that were uttered. Many men who were then, or afterwards became, distinguished in English public life, made their contributions to the discussion. To make the position clear, and to explain some of the allusions in the speeches, it is necessary to recall some of the changes of Ministers that had occurred in the preceding ten years. It will be remembered that, in spite of those changes, Lord Palmerston had been Secretary of State for Foreign Affairs for a continuous period of eleven years, with the exception of four months at the beginning of the year 1835, when the Duke of Wellington held that position. It would be a mistake, therefore, to assume that changes of Government were to any appreciable extent the cause of the weakness of our policy in China.

Shortly after the death of George IV, Lord Grey in 1830 formed the Government that in 1832 passed the great Reform Bill and in 1833 abolished the East India Company's monopoly of trade with China. With him were associated Lord Melbourne as Home Secretary, Lord John Russell as Paymaster of the Forces, Lord Palmerston as Foreign Secretary, and Sir James Graham as First Lord of the Admiralty. It was this Government that sent out Lord Napier as the first Superintendent of Trade. In 1834 Lord Grey resigned, and Lord Melbourne became Prime Minister, Lord Palmerston

[1] Hansard : *Parliamentary Debates*, vol. 53, p. 947.

remaining Foreign Secretary. At the end of that year Lord Melbourne was succeeded by Sir Robert Peel, and it was then that the Duke of Wellington took Palmerston's place. In this Government Mr. Gladstone held office for the first time, he having been appointed a junior Lord of the Treasury. Peel, who did not command a majority in the House of Commons, found his task an impossible one, and after six months Lord Melbourne again became Prime Minister, and formed the Government which continued in office until the year 1841. Lord Palmerston was again Foreign Secretary, and Lord John Russell was at first Home Secretary and afterwards, in 1839, Secretary for War and the Colonies, whilst Macaulay held the office of Secretary at War.[1]

Thus we see that Sir James Graham, the mover of the resolution, had been identified in its inception with the policy he now condemned. The explanation of this is, that he had in the meantime changed his political opinions and gone over to the other party. Then, as nowadays, resolutions moved by the Opposition were framed rather with a view to an immediate tactical advantage in party politics than to raising a discussion on the real merits or demerits of a question, and Sir James Graham's motion was no exception to the general

[1] Before the changes which were made in the organization of the army in 1855, consequent upon the Crimean War, the system of administration was one of decentralization, having for its object the maintenance of guarantees against the army becoming a menace to the constitution. The Commander-in-Chief was responsible to the Crown for the discipline of the army, for appointments, promotions, rewards, and punishments. The Secretary at War, who was not a Secretary of State, nor often a member of the Cabinet, was responsible to Parliament for the money voted for the army, for the security of the citizen against the soldier in person and property in respect of the fairness of the rules of military discipline, which were embodied or authorized in the Mutiny Act. The Secretary of State for War and the Colonies was responsible for the numbers of the army, for the general policy respecting it, and for the movement of troops on foreign or colonial service. The Secretary of State for the Home Department was responsible for the Reserves and for the forces on the Home Establishment. By Burke's Act, passed in 1783, the Secretary of War was to prepare the estimates for Parliament, to transmit the money when voted to the Paymaster of the Forces, and to receive and settle annually the accounts of expenditure.—See Anson: *Law and Custom of the Constitution*, Part II, chap. viii, sec. ii.

rule. Thus it came about that the House of Commons was concerned more with the question, whether Ministers had or had not been negligent or foolish in not giving wider powers to the Chief Superintendent, than with deciding, whether the objects of the expedition then being fitted out, as recently announced by Lord John Russell, were good or bad. The House of Commons, when considering executive matters, is not in practice a deliberative assembly that thinks out the best line of policy to be pursued. It is a body by which the people of England express through their representatives their opinion of the policy of the Government as it strikes them at the moment. It is easy to criticise such an assembly and to point to its defects. Englishmen value it because by its means they can enter on an unfettered discussion of the actions of those who, in fact, control the affairs of their country. Not many nations are free to indulge in such discussion.

The mover of the resolution began by alluding to the magnitude of the interests involved in our relations with China. One-sixth of the whole revenue of Great Britain and India depended on those relations. The duties on tea alone amounted to £3,660,000, out of a total revenue of £4,200,000 derived from the imposts on China products brought to this country. Of the gross revenue of India, which amounted to £20,000,000 per annum, one-tenth was derived from China, of which £1,700,000 was shipped in specie. He then proceeded to criticise the wide powers and jurisdiction given to the Superintendents of Trade under the China Trade Act by Lord Grey's ministry, and dwelt on the fact that the instructions given to Lord Napier were emphatically pacific. He recalled the prophecies of the Duke of Wellington, that an attempt to force upon the Chinese authorities a mode of communication distasteful to them must end in failure, and alluded to the fact, though there was nothing to show it in the papers laid before the House, that the successors in office of Lord Napier had all insisted in the strongest manner on the propriety of opening up some communication with Peking. In conclusion, he denounced the policy of the Government as impolitic and erroneous, in that greater preparations had not been made or wider powers conferred on the Superintendents before the commencement of hostilities.[1]

Lord Macaulay (Member for Edinburgh), who then as plain Mr. Macaulay held the office of Secretary at War, which must not be confused with that held by Lord John Russell,[2] rose to defend the Government. The general tenor of his speech was to the effect that, owing to the distance of China from England, and our ignorance of that country, " the Secretary of State for Foreign Affairs could not be expected to give the same precise instructions to the representative of his sovereign, as he could to our ministers at Brussels or the Hague."[3] Dealing with the various points raised by Sir John Graham, he dwelt on the omission to give the Chief Superintendent fuller powers, particularly in reference to the suppression of the illicit trade. He stated that the reason why these powers had not been given was that the Foreign Secretary down to May, 1838, had very strong reasons to believe that it was in the contemplation of the Chinese Government immediately to legalize the traffic in opium, which he admitted had been carried on in disobedience to the existing law. Even when it was found that this belief was false, it was not desirable that such powers should be conferred. He doubted whether the withholding of those powers was the cause of the unfortunate circumstances that had arisen in China. Had such powers been conferred we should still have found ourselves involved in hostilities. It would have been impossible to put down the opium trade except by the exertions of the Chinese themselves. The difficulties experienced in England in the prevention of smuggling showed " that a traffic supported on the one hand by men actuated by the love of a drug, from the intoxicating qualities of which they found it impossible to restrain themselves, and on the other hand by persons actuated by the desire of gain, could not be terminated by the publication of a piece of paper signed Charles Elliot."

His next contention was that measures to suppress the

[1] Hansard : *Parliamentary Debates*, vol. 53, pp. 669–704.
[2] See *ante*, p. 447 *note*.
[3] Hansard : *Parliamentary Debates*, vol. 53, p. 707.

traffic at Canton would have produced the worse result of spreading it along the whole coast. "If under the eye of an English society—consisting certainly of persons some of whom were suspected of being concerned in the trade, but many of whom were of the highest respectability—the traffic could not long be carried on without producing acts having some appearance of piracy, what could they expect when no man would have any judge of his own conduct but himself ?

If the smuggling trade had been removed from Macao and scattered along the coast, in the manner which he had described, hostilities with China would have been the inevitable consequence. Commissioner Lin had not hesitated to inflict severe punishment upon men whose characters were totally unsuspected, and was it likely that, if the events which he had endeavoured to describe had occurred along the coast of China, Lin would have been more scrupulous ? He then proceeded to state what he imagined would have been the charges made by Commissioner Lin against Captain Elliot, and that any failure by the latter to prevent the trade along the whole coast would have been made a pretext by Lin for a seizure of all Englishmen as hostages. He said that this country must have provided a preventive service for the whole coast of China, and it was impossible that we should incur such an expense. In his opinion the present rupture was not due to any of the omissions, of which the Government were alleged to have been guilty.

His next ground of defence was that, if any other course than that which had been followed had been adopted, the existing evils would only have been exaggerated. He continued thus :—

"They had seen it asserted, over and over again, that the Government was advocating the cause of the contraband trade, in order to force an opium war on the public ; but he thought it was impossible to be conceived that a thought so absurd and atrocious should have ever entered the minds of the British Ministry. . . . If, after having given fair notice of their intention to seize all contraband goods introduced into their dominions, they seized our opium, we had no right to complain; but when the Government, finding that by just and lawful means they could not carry out their prohibition, resorted to measures unjust and unlawful, confined our innocent countrymen, and insulted the Sovereign in the person of her representative, then he thought the time had arrived when it was fit that we should interfere. The people at Canton were seized: they were driven from Macao, suspected or not. Women with children at the breast were treated with equal severity, were refused bread, or the means of subsistence: the innocent Lascars were thrown into the sea: an English gentleman was barbarously mutilated, and England found itself at once assailed with a fury unknown to civilized countries."

The peroration to his speech was a description in the most grandiose language of the might of Great Britain. England, conscious of her power, could bear to overlook petty provocations, but there was a limit to her forbearance. Her might must be exerted to protect her citizens. "He begged in conclusion to declare his earnest desire that this most rightful quarrel might be prosecuted to a triumphant close—that the brave men to whom was entrusted the task of demanding that reparation, which the circumstances of the case required, might fulfil their duties with moderation but with success; that the name not only of the English valour but of English mercy might be established; and that the overseeing care of that gracious Providence which had so often brought good out of evil, might make the crime which had forced us to take those measures which had been adopted the means of promoting an everlasting peace, alike beneficial to England and China."[1]

The pious aspiration expressed in the last sentence has not been fulfilled. It has met with the fate a sentiment framed in such language deserves. The reader may judge for himself, in the light of the information already set before him, how far Macaulay's observations were well founded.

The attack on the Government was next taken up by Sir William Follett (member for Exeter), who had been Solicitor-General, and in 1844 became Attorney-General under Sir

[1] Hansard: *Parliamentary Debates*, vol. 53, p. 720.

Robert Peel. Worthy of the great lawyer that he was, his speech was a masterly analysis of the hard facts of the case, as shown by the evidence contained in the Blue Book. He could not, he said, help thinking that the effect of the member for Edinburgh's speech was to draw off the attention of the House from the real question it was called upon to decide. He maintained that, with the exception of the period of Sir Robert Peel's administration, which gave rise to the invaluable memorandum of the Duke of Wellington, there was no trace to be found in the papers before the House that the affairs of China had occupied the attention of Her Majesty's Government for even an hour. He pointed out that the charge was not that the Government had failed to employ a preventive force to check the trade in opium, when that trade had become a menace to the whole community, but that they had left their officer without powers to deal with the evils that had arisen. There was no evidence in the despatches that at any time it had been reasonable to suppose that the opium trade would be legalized. If there was any want of energy or any vacillation on the part of the Chinese Government, that formed no excuse for the policy of the British Government. He asked, with some reason, whether we could seek to impose upon the Chinese our ideas of international law in this respect, when at the same time in all our other dealings with them we proceeded on the supposition that they were not subject to international law at all. "Although the British were violating continually the laws of that empire, yet they said now that the violation on the part of the Chinese of international law was a just reason for war. He must say that he was averse to letting loose against such a people the horrors of war without the certainty of the justice of it."[1]

Sir George Staunton, who, as having a first-hand knowledge of China, was listened to with the greatest respect, exhibited the spectacle of a man who tries to reconcile his political sympathies with an antagonistic moral sense. He regretted that the motion entirely omitted the consideration of the

[1] Hansard: *Parliamentary Debates*, vol. 53, pp. 720–38.

great question which was agitating the country, whether the important contest in which we were about to engage was a righteous and just one, or a cruel and iniquitous one. He noticed that none of the speakers, who had attacked the Government, had ventured to take up the attitude of many of the newspapers and say that the war was atrociously unjust and dishonourable. "Considering, as he did, though very reluctantly, that this war was absolutely just and necessary, under existing circumstances, he rejoiced to find that it had received the tacit approbation of that House." He admitted that to the resolution of the Select Committee appointed by the House in 1832, which declared that it was not expedient to relinquish the revenue arising from the cultivation of the poppy in India, could be traced all the consequences which had taken place down to the present interruption of the trade with China. He confessed that he yielded to none in his anxiety to see the opium trade put down altogether: but he felt that as Parliament had approved that resolution, it was unjust to visit on the present Ministers the responsibility for its consequences. He acknowledged that since 1837 the opium traffic had become connected with every branch of British trade in China—constituting nearly three-fifths of that trade—and that the existence of the rest of the trade had become dependent on it. He regarded as the immediate cause of the rupture the fact that Commissioner Lin's conduct had been of such a kind as no one could have expected.[1]

Mr. Thesiger (member for Woodstock), who, as Lord Chelmsford, in 1858 became Lord Chancellor of England, in a maiden speech continued the attack on the Government. He complained that, if the war were now necessary, it was only necessary because of the neglect of Her Majesty's Ministers. He pointed out that the initial mistake consisted in changing the mode of intercourse at Canton, and sending out Lord Napier without any previous communication with the Chinese Government. He commented on the fact that, throughout the whole of the despatches laid before the House, there was not in connection

[1] Hansard: *Parliamentary Debates*, vol. 53, pp. 738–45.

with Lord Napier's death one word of sympathy, not one word of regret, not the slightest expression directed towards this event, and that no attempt had ever been made to obtain redress for the contumely and insult to which that nobleman had been subjected. Dealing with the forced surrender of the opium at Canton, he contended that the Chinese were justified in the course which they adopted. He regarded the Chinese as a "simple and unsophisticated people," who were surprised at hearing that the Chief Superintendent had no powers to put down the trade in opium.[1]

Mr. Gladstone (member for Newark) attacked the Government in a speech of great vigour. He complained that though authorized to confer on the Superintendents even wider powers than those possessed by the old supercargoes of the East India Company, Lord Palmerston had refused to listen to the advice of Mr. Davis and Sir George Robinson, or to comply with the requirements of the Act. It was a just charge against the noble lord, that no steps had been taken to carry out the intentions of Parliament. As to the contraband traffic, the Chinese had declared in the most positive terms that they would no longer allow it to be carried on. Up to 1836 the Chinese authorities had connived at the opium trade, but in that year an imperial edict was published ordering, in the most strict and positive terms, that a stop be put to the traffic. The connivance on the part of the Chinese authorities was confined to the subordinate officials: there was no reason for saying that the Government itself connived at the corruption of its officers, or at the contraband trade which was carried on in consequence of that corruption. Captain Elliot could not be blamed. His errors were those of the noble lord, while it would be difficult to show that his merits were ascribable to his instructions from the Foreign Secretary. The Chinese Government had trusted in the first instance to Captain Elliot's statement—a statement which, he must say, he did not consider a very open or straightforward one—that his Government had no knowledge of the existence of any but the legal trade, and that over an illegal trade he

[1] Hansard: *Parliamentary Debates*, vol. 53, pp. 756–79.

could exercise no power. If they were judging the conduct of Chinese, not of British officers, they would call that a miserable equivocation.[1]

He then replied directly to Macaulay's speech. What was the value, he asked, of the right honourable member's declaration, that he deplored the prevalence of the opium traffic as much as any member on the other side of the House, when the agent of the Government (for such Captain Elliot was) exhibited himself at Canton as the supporter of the British merchants engaged in the contraband trade, and the opponent of the Chinese Government in their attempt to remove the offending ships? The Chinese Government had adopted every means during a period of two years and a half to stop the opium trade, and had resorted to every proper means of making their intentions known to the British Government. Yet they had been treated with contempt and neglect, with the same contempt by the noble lord at home as by the British Superintendent at Canton.

Dealing with the events that led up to the arrival of Commissioner Lin at Canton, Mr. Gladstone showed that there was no ground for Captain Elliot's assertion that this measure of the Chinese Government was sudden and violent.

"For two years and a half the Chinese Government were continually remonstrating, continually announcing their firm determination to suppress the trade, though through all that time not the slightest notice was taken of their remonstrances by Her Majesty's Government. They were told that the Chinese ought not to have taken possession of the persons of the British residents at Canton. This was a subject upon which the right honourable gentleman, the member for Edinburgh, had become very indignant, and demanded what proof the Chinese officers had of these individuals being concerned in the prohibited traffic. What proof? Why, it was a matter of universal knowledge. The seizure of the opium was recorded regularly in a printed form at Canton. Captain Elliot had no power to arraign and judge those engaged in the opium trade. On the other hand the Chinese had no

[1] Hansard: *Parliamentary Debates*, vol. 53, p. 808.

power to try them. There were no means, therefore, of legally establishing the guilt of these parties. Yet they were to be told that it was a matter of complaint against the Chinese Government that they should have seized their persons. The Chinese Government had acted in accordance with their fixed determination to put a stop to the opium smuggling. Had they not a strict moral right to put a stop to it? Was it not mere mockery to affect—to pretend—indignation as to the pernicious consequences of the opium trade, and yet exhaust all the armoury of ingenuity and eloquence to prove that the Chinese Government were not justified in taking effectual means for crushing that trade? Her Majesty's Government would have unquestionably evinced a more sincere desire to discharge their duty satisfactorily had they manfully encouraged those efforts of the Chinese Government, instead of systematically taking measures to defeat those efforts.[1] Another theme of the indignant denunciation of the right honourable gentleman opposite was, that the Chinese should have indiscriminately confined the innocent with the guilty. He owned that when the news of this transaction first reached him, he did think it a cruel and a monstrous act. But from further and more accurate information, he found that the whole British community, almost to a man, had been engaged in that illegal traffic. What were the facts? Two hundred persons had been confined. Had the right honourable gentleman inquired how many were innocent and how many were guilty? Did he suppose that five out of the two hundred were innocent? If so, what of his charge? The circumstances being so notorious, the guilt being so undeniable, the Chinese Government were justified in acting against the entire community, the more especially because there was no possibility of fixing the guilt on individuals. . . . In the month of August, 1838, Mr. King stated that he proposed a pledge to the foreign merchants resident at Canton, which went to bind them not to take any further part in the opium trade. And what did the House think was the reply which the press at Canton gave to his proposition? The press

[1] Hansard: *Parliamentary Debates*, vol. 53, p. 811.

replied that no merchant could give this pledge, as they were one and all more or less interested in the sale of the drug. . . .

"The right honourable gentleman opposite asserted that it was quite impossible for us to put down the opium trade in China ourselves. Admitting that to be the fact, still we might have shown a desire to co-operate with the Government of China; and if we had done so, we should have put down the traffic to a great extent, though we might not have succeeded in abolishing it. We might have sent away the receiving ships—we might have refused them the protection of our flag. . . . Did the right honourable gentleman opposite know that the opium smuggled into China came exclusively from British ports, that was from Bengal and through Bombay? If that were the fact—and he defied the right honourable gentleman to gainsay it—then we required no preventive service to put down this illegal traffic. . . . He knew that the interference of Parliament would have been necessary. . . . The noble lord would only have had to declare the difficulties that were before him to establish the necessity for the interference of the Legislature."

Continuing, Mr. Gladstone said it was contended that our Sovereign had been insulted in the person of her representative. But how was he her representative? Was it because he was unable to control her subjects? It was clear the Chinese authorities had never formally acknowledged him. Captain Elliot had been placed in a position in which he could not, from lack of the necessary powers, fulfil the task that was imposed upon him. But whenever he showed a disposition to check the opium traffic, Lord Palmerston had prevented him. When he implored the noble lord to interfere one way or the other, and to prepare measures either for the legalization or suppression of the traffic, he was met by a contemptuous silence. In the course of 1839 Captain Elliot had completely identified himself with the opium traffic. He had notified the Foreign Office that he had made up his mind to resist any attacks that might be made on the opium ships at Lintin, and that act had been recognised by the Foreign Secretary, who must therefore take the responsibility. Mr. Gladstone went on to discuss the conduct of the Chinese after they had driven out the British from Canton. He referred to the poisoning of the wells in language which, at first sight, looks as though he thought that such conduct was justifiable. For this he was severely taken to task by some of the speakers who followed. With that exception his attack was allowed to pass almost unchallenged. He concluded a very powerful speech with a peroration, in which occurs the following passage, which has often been cited as showing that at an early age his opinions on questions of this kind were not different from those of his later years.

"The Chinese," he said, "gave you notice to abandon your contraband trade. When they found that you would not, they had a right to drive you from their coasts on account of your obstinacy in persisting in this infamous and atrocious traffic. You allowed your agent to aid and abet those who were concerned in carrying on that trade, and I do not know how it can be urged as a crime against the Chinese that they refused provisions to those who refused obedience to their laws whilst residing within their territories. I am not competent to judge how long this war may last, or how protracted may be its operations, but this I can say, that a war more unjust in its origin, a war more calculated in its progress to cover this country with permanent disgrace, I do not know, and I have not read of. The right honourable gentleman spoke last night in eloquent terms of the British flag waving in glory at Canton, and of the animating effects produced on the minds of our sailors by the knowledge that in no country under heaven was it permitted to be insulted. . . . But how comes it to be that the sight of that flag always raises the spirit of Englishmen? It is because it has always been associated with the cause of justice, with opposition to oppression, with respect for national rights, with honourable commercial enterprise; but now, under the auspices of the noble lord, that flag is hoisted to protect an infamous contraband traffic, and if it were never to be hoisted, except as it is now hoisted on the coast of China, we should recoil from its sight with horror, and should never again feel our hearts thrill, as they now thrill with emotion, when it floats proudly and magnificently on the breeze."[1]

Dr. (Sir Stephen) Lushington (member for the Tower Hamlets), now chiefly remembered as Judge of the Court of Admiralty, a position which he filled with great distinction from the year 1838 to the year 1867, spoke in support of the Government. His opinion on the legal aspect of the questions under discussion is bound to carry great weight. He said there could not be a shadow of doubt that China had a perfect right, he would not say by the law of nations, but by every principle of justice and equity, to prohibit the opium trade, if she so thought fit. She had a right to do more. She had a right to say, " If you persist in your endeavours to carry on the trade which we have prohibited, we shall exclude you from all other trade : and after due warning of her intentions with respect to that trade, she had a right to seize and punish according to her own laws every British subject whom she detected in the act of carrying on that trade." But we could not interfere to stop the opium traffic. Such a course would have been against all precedent, as well as impossible to produce any effective result. At Canton the innocent had been punished with the guilty. The opium had been seized to enrich the Chinese Government. The wells had been poisoned; an attempt had been made to set fire to the dwellings of the British. In that state of things, " England was by every principle of right and justice entitled, and had authority by the law of God and of man, to demand redress; but, be it understood, not for a war of blood and reprisals." [2]

After Sir Robert Peel had summed up the arguments advanced against the Government, begging the House to remember that, although it had received no formal message to that effect, we were on the verge of hostilities with a nation of 350,000,000 people, Lord Palmerston replied for the Government. [3] His speech was an extremely clever debating effort, but his method of argument effective in

[1] Hansard : *Parliamentary Debates*, vol. 53, p. 818.
[2] *Ibid.*, pp. 855–867.
[3] *Ibid.*, p. 925.

exposing the weakness of his opponents rather than in disclosing any inherent strength in his own position. At this distance of time we are unmoved by the train of reasoning which carried the House of Commons with him. He seems to have evaded giving a direct reply to his strongest antagonist, Gladstone, and to have contented himself with reproving that young politician for having said that of course the Chinese had poisoned the wells. Similarly, with regard to the other speakers, who attacked the Government for demanding satisfaction from the Chinese authorities, because it compelled the surrender of opium, he was content to let their attacks pass with general rhetorical pronouncements on the necessity of upholding the prestige of Great Britain, and with the assertion "that the friends around him had refuted the arguments of those on the opposite side."

He began by denouncing the resolution as feeble in conception and feebly supported. If it were desired to obtain support from the enemies of the opium trade, or from the enemies of war, the resolution should have been more direct. It was shaped for a peculiar end, and that end was the transference of political power from one side of the House to the other. The charge against him was one of omission: therefore, the resolution should have stated distinctly and definitely what ought to have been done. There was, he was glad to say, no censure of Captain Elliot, with one exception. From first to last that officer had endeavoured to discontinue the opium traffic to the utmost of his power. He had not made preparations to protect the opium ships, but the cargo ships. And even had he done so, the authorities of China had no right by its law to seize vessels stationed outside the harbour. He had heard Mr. Gladstone's speech with deep regret and sincere pain.

As to the charge of having neglected to answer the Chief Superintendent's official communications, he denied that there was any truth in it. The Duke of Wellington had been prompt in answering despatches. So had he. The despatches desiring his opinion were answered immediately. As to the failure to give sufficient powers and instructions to the Chief

Superintendent, he would ask, What were the instructions that ought to have been sent? The Order in Council[1] did establish in China that court of criminal and admiralty jurisdiction which the Government were accused of neglecting to establish. It had even been called into action. A trial had taken place in it, the proceedings of which he had felt it his duty to place before the Law Officers of the Crown. The court had been constituted, and continued to exist down to the present time. The China Courts Bill of 1837 was introduced to give, in addition to the criminal and admiralty, a civil jurisdiction, capable of enforcing a debt due from one British subject to another. That bill had not passed, because Sir James Graham and his friends had objected to the principle of establishing any court in the territory of an independent sovereign, without having the previous consent of that sovereign. The memorandum of the Duke of Wellington had in many respects been carried out, but it fell into the same error of supposing that no court had been established by the Order in Council of 1833. The only part of that memorandum which had not been acted upon was that relating to rules of practice for the courts, but this was of no importance, as it had been ordered that their practice should conform to that of the courts in England. "Gentlemen who made long speeches thought that he ought to write long letters. They imagined that precise instructions contained in few but significant words were not proportioned to the length which they had to travel: they imagined that when you write to China, your letter should be as long as the voyage."

As to the opium traffic, it would, he said, have been totally at variance with British law, totally at variance with international law, to put down the opium trade by arbitrary acts against British merchants. It would have been a forced interpretation of the Act to have done so. If he had come to Parliament for additional powers, he would have been opposed. Such powers, in any case, would have been ineffectual. To enforce a prohibition the Chief Superintendent must have had

[1] *i.e.*, the Order in Council issued in 1833 on the passing of the China Trade Act.

armed men at his disposal, an idea not very palatable to the Chinese. If Elliot had expelled the opium trade from the Canton river, it would have taken refuge in other places. "He would be the last to defend a trade which involved the violation of the municipal laws of the Chinese, and which furnished an enormously large population with the means of demoralization, which tended to the production of habits inconsistent with good order and correct conduct. But he put it to any man opposite, whether he could with a grave face say that he honestly believed the motive of the Chinese Government to have been the promotion of the growth of moral habits. The answer to such a supposition was, Why did they not prohibit the growth of the poppy in their own country? The fact was, that this was an exportation of bullion question, an agricultural interest-protection question. It was the poppy interest in China, and the practical economists who wished to prevent the exportation of the precious metals, that led the Chinese Government to seek to put down this contraband trade in opium. He wondered what the House would have said to Her Majesty's Ministers, if they had come down to it with a large naval estimate for a number of revenue cruisers to be employed in the preventive service from the river at Canton to the Yellow Sea for the purpose of preserving the morals of the Chinese people, who were disposed to buy what other people were disposed to sell them. . . . And yet without such instructions, and without such a preventive force, the instructions which Ministers were ridiculed for not sending, would have been nothing more than waste paper."[1] Instead of thinking himself liable to the censure of the House, he claimed merit for not having given to the Superintendent at Canton such powers and instructions as the right honourable member of Pembroke recommended.

"But it had been said that we ought to send an embassy to China. . . . But considering what had passed when other embassies had been sent, knowing the disinclination of the Chinese to enter into diplomatic relations with Foreign states, reflecting that we had not any practical measure to propose

[1] Hansard: *Parliamentary Debates*, vol. 53, p. 941.

to their Government for consolidating friendship or alliance, he thought it would have been an unwise policy to send an ambassador to China, when the only practical measure which we could have proposed to the Chinese Government was to join them in putting down the trade in opium. Another objection to this plan was, that when our mission and cruisers and coastguard had arrived in China, we might have found the trade in opium legalized by the Chinese Government." The American merchants at Canton had presented to their Government at Washington in January, 1840, a memorial in which they avowed their opinion that the course pursued by the High Commissioner was unjust and no better than robbery, and that if satisfaction was not yielded to the demand of the British Government, then England and America and France should join in blockading the China coast and obtaining from the Chinese such acknowledgments and treaties as would place the Foreign commerce upon a safe and advantageous footing. The memorialists further asked that, if their government would not interpose itself in the affairs of American and British citizens in Canton, an agent or commissioner should be appointed to reside at Canton, with a sufficient naval force to protect American commerce, and also to secure participation in such advantages as might be granted to other powers. Then again, thirty London firms had sent him a letter saying that unless the measures of the Government are followed up with firmness and energy, the trade with China could no longer be conducted with security to life and property, or with credit and advantage to the British nation. For these reasons he felt justified in believing that the Government policy was proper and just.

Sir James Graham, in his reply on the whole debate, pointed out that the opinion of London firms in this matter might not be altogether unbiassed, as £2,000,000 worth of bills had been protested in the city owing to the seizure of the opium. He was proceeding to deal at length with the various points raised during the discussion, but was cut short by repeated cries of "Divide!" On the motion being put, there voted, Ayes 262, Noes 271, so that the Government policy was approved by the narrow majority of nine. The arguments in support of the Government policy are best set forth by Macaulay and Palmerston, but both these speakers assumed as fact in many instances what was nothing more than the product of their imaginations. It is absurd to talk of a poppy interest, as the latter did, when we know under what strict penalties the cultivation of opium was forbidden in China at that time. The chief protagonist on the opposition side, judged by matter of his speech, was undoubtedly Mr. Gladstone, who was then at the beginning of his career and still in the state of being the "hope of the stern and unbending Tories." He had a clearer insight into the true issues at stake than any other speaker. His condemnation of the Government policy, and his prediction of the view that would be taken by posterity of the war on which we were about to enter, have been fully justified by the subsequent course of events. It was his wish—a wish which he should have carried into effect—to raise a second debate, challenging the Government on the justice of demanding from China compensation for the surrendered opium. The following entry appears in his diary under date 14th May, 1840. "Consulted (various persons) on opium. All but Sir R. Inglis were on grounds of prudence against it being brought forward. To this majority of friendly and competent persons I have given way, I hope not wrongfully: but I am in dread of the judgment of God upon England for our national iniquity towards China. It has been to me a matter of most painful and anxious consideration. I yield specifically to this: the majority of the persons most trustworthy feel that to make the motion would, our leaders being in such a position and disposition with respect to it, injure the cause."[1]

Although Mr. Gladstone was on this occasion content to subordinate his idea of what was right to considerations of political expediency, he could not let the matter rest. In Committee of Supply an opportunity occurred of again referring to the matter. On 27th July a resolution to grant £173,442 for the expenses of the China Expedition came up for

[1] Morley: *Life of Gladstone*, chap. i, p. 227.

consideration. His argument on this occasion was so precise and well conceived that no apology is needed for referring to it at length. He said :—

"The Secretary for the Colonies had in the earlier part of the session stated that the objects of the expedition were, (1) Reparation for insults offered to the English flag ; (2) Compensation for injuries inflicted on the property of British subjects ; (3) Security for our commercial intercourse for the future. The second of these meant compensation for the surrender of the opium into which they had been coerced. If he were not contradicted, he should assume that he was right in his interpretation. This had affected the price of opium, which had risen nearly forty per cent. If compensation were obtained from the Chinese, they would recoup themselves by a tax on tea and silk. Thus the British public would be taxed twice. The commercial houses in England, who had lost by the surrender, claimed compensation against the British Government, not against the Chinese. The parties interested in the surrender of the opium contended first that its value was guaranteed by Captain Elliot, and they were therefore entitled to the recognition of their claim. He must say that he could not understand, how it was possible for the Government to continue Captain Elliot in the situation which he held, and to give its approbation of the line of policy which he had adopted, and at the same time to disown an act of his not trifling or of secondary importance, but the corner stone upon which the maintenance of his whole system depended. . . .

"The demand for compensation for the opium which had been surrendered rested, he concluded, upon this foundation, that the act was an unjust one. It was said that a system of connivance had been carried on by the Chinese governors, by the bribery of the inferior authorities. We, however, were only the *offerers* of the bribe, and had little right to take advantage of our own misconduct. Mr. Marjoribanks, before the Committee of 1832, attributed the system to the lower and not to the higher Chinese authorities: but he still maintained that even this had ceased long before the occasion which the House was now considering. It was argued next, that the confiscation of the opium was a penalty not justified by the Chinese law, or by usage. In point of fact, however, when they looked into the real circumstances of the case, they found that the law of China rested upon edict only; and that whatever was declared by edict was law, and that no other law was known. The argument upon the law of China therefore failed. Then, with regard to custom, no one could deny that confiscation was the usual, as well as the most natural and appropriate, punishment for smuggling, and so far from this custom not being recognised and acted upon in China, it appeared from statements made on behalf of the persons interested in the seizure that, from the year 1821 down to the present time, all Foreign ships entering the Canton river with opium were deemed and held liable to confiscation, or to be expelled the river and to be constantly interdicted from trading there. Then it would be a narrow ground, indeed, to take, that although the right of confiscation extended to the Canton river, it was not to be carried beyond that. It was not a question of legal jurisdiction, but if it were, the maritime jurisdiction of China was not confined to the Canton river."

Mr. Gladstone further commented at some length on the allegation that the opium had been seized without due notice that the trade was prohibited. He showed that Mr. Jardine, a member of one of the chief British firms which traded at Canton, expressed the opinion, in December of 1838, that the Emperor was in earnest. It was clear, in his opinion, that every means had been adopted which could possibly be taken to convey a knowledge of the determination of the authorities to put the law in force, as it had frequently been declared. As to the detention of the merchants at Canton, they had only been surrounded by a species of cordon, which in fact amounted to nothing more than a refusal of a passport to leave that place. The contention that the Queen's representative had been insulted was ill-founded, as Captain Elliot had never been acknowledged as a diplomatic agent. "Because Captain

Elliot placed himself in a false position, were the Chinese to be debarred from taking any steps which they might think fit in order to put an end to the smuggling on their coasts? . . . He would not stop to enquire whether or not the Chinese had technically put themselves in the wrong. They might have done so in their subsequent proceedings, but what he contended was, that at the time when Captain Elliot threw himself into Canton, the policy of the Chinese was not bloody: that their confiscation of the opium did not involve any substantial injustice: and that we had no right to make that confiscation either the subject of a war, or the ground of a demand of the value of the opium confiscated."[1]

Two or three other speakers followed Mr. Gladstone in this onslaught on the Government, which called forth a spirited reply from Lord Palmerston, who used to great advantage the fact that his antagonist had not ventured to raise the question of compensation as a direct issue in the House of Commons. He taunted Mr. Gladstone with having reserved "this strong expression of his disapprobation to the end of the Session, when it could be attended with no other practical result than to throw discredit on the cause of England." He further maintained that had the Chinese Government given notice of their intention to seize opium brought into Canton, "it could not have altered the character of the proceedings which had been resorted to, and which were alike contrary to the law of nations, to the law of nature, and to every principle which should guide the intercourse between man and man." In reply to the argument based on the non-reception by the Chinese of Captain Elliot as a diplomatic agent, the noble lord continued:—

"When the British Government appointed an agent to protect the interests of British subjects, and to urge their claims against the Government of the country to which the agent was sent, whether he were called a diplomatic or commercial agent, he was equally entitled to respect, and if outrage were offered to him, the nation was outraged in his person,

[1] Hansard: *Parliamentary Debates*, vol. 55, pp. 1029–37.

and was entitled to demand satisfaction, reparation, and redress. The honourable member said, that according to writers on the law of nations, consuls were not protected: but there were many instances in which they had been considered entitled to protection. He need hardly refer to the dispute between the French Government and the Barbary chief, when the French consul, being threatened with execution for some offence,

'Quoted Wicquefort
And Puffendorf and Grotius,
And proved from Vattel
Exceedingly well,
Such a deed would be quite atrocious.'

"The honourable member had timed the expression of his sentiments rather ill, for if he thought the measures taken against the Chinese for the purpose of obtaining compensation unjust, he ought to have acted on his opinions when there was yet time for them to be of some effect, either on the occasion to which he had already adverted, or on the debate which had taken place upon the motion of the right honourable Baronet, the member for Pembroke."[1]

Sir Robert Peel replied to Lord Palmerston by asking, how he reconciled the views he had expressed about the conduct of the Chinese in seizing the opium with his own action in seizing the ships of Neapolitan subjects, in order to obtain redress from their Government in the matter of the sulphur question. After Sir Robert Peel had spoken, the vote was agreed to without a division. This was the last occasion on which the rights and wrongs of our First War with China were discussed in the House of Commons, or, for the matter of that, in Parliament. In the House of Lords very little attention was paid to the matter at all. A short debate took place on the 12th May, on which occasion the Duke of Wellington, after very few speeches had been delivered, moved the previous question, which was carried without a division.

[1] Hansard: *Parliamentary Debates*, vol. 55, pp. 1046–9.

For all practical purposes there was no discussion at all in the House of Lords of the China Policy of the Government.[1] Under these circumstances the English people engaged in the war with China, which was destined to be the commencement of a new era for the whole of the Far East.

[1] Hansard : *Parliamentary Debates*, vol. 54, pp. 1–48.

CHAPTER XXI

CHANGES OF *PERSONNEL*

LOOKING back over the twelve months which came to an end in December, 1840, there can be no doubt that a whole year had been completely wasted. The occupation of Chusan, the expedition to the Pei-ho, the demonstrations at Amoy had effected nothing. The state of affairs at Canton in the beginning of the year 1841 was practically the same as at the beginning of the preceding year. So far as there had been any change, it was favourable to the Chinese and adverse to the British. The former had learnt by experience that their strength lay in diplomatic rather than in naval or military action. The latter had satisfied themselves that in open warfare they were irresistible: they had not realized their inferiority in diplomacy. To the Chinese Peking had been preserved from the hand of the invader, when it seemed to be at his mercy; to the British community were the losses arising from the stagnation of trade and the misery of having no place to call their home. For nearly two years the British merchants had talked of the beginning of a new era, when commerce should be carried on under conditions of enlightened freedom. When the year 1841 dawned, the realization of their hopes appeared as distant as when the High Commissioner held them shut up in the Factories at Canton. Ship after ship arrived outside the Bogue and stayed for the re-opening of trade. But still the blockade went on, and the suspension of trade continued.

The explanation of all this was not far to seek. It lay in the fact that the Superintendent had such a passion for negotiation, such a belief in his powers as a diplomatist, that the Chinese officials were able to play with him as they willed. In January, 1840, he was negotiating with Commissioner Lin; in January, 1841, with Kishen. The purport of the negotiations in the one case are as little known as in the other. Simply keeping up the appearance of being desirous to settle the controversy by peaceable means, the Viceroy was able to attain his object, which was to keep the British forces in a state of inactivity. In the hope that the future would reveal some way of bringing the English under control, which would not involve the necessity of fighting them in open warfare, Kishen persevered with the pretence of negotiating. For many months he induced Captain Elliot to believe that he was actuated by the most perfect sincerity. At length something occurred, we know not what, that roused the suspicion of the Superintendent. Without any notification to the British community the negotiations were broken off and offensive operations were resumed against the Chinese. The forts at Chuen-pi and Tai-kok were simultaneously attacked by sea and land on the morning of the 7th of January, and in a few hours both had fallen to the British arms.[1]

The action by which these two forts were captured lasted little more than an hour. The Chinese are supposed to have lost some 500 men killed, and 200 or 300 wounded, together with sixteen junks destroyed. Of the British none were killed, and only thirty-eight wounded.[2] Elated with this success, Captain Elliot fell into the fatal mistake, a mistake which was repeated afterwards with disheartening frequency, of believing that the enemy, by being defeated, had been vanquished, and were ready to grant all that he required. Failing to profit by his experience of the futility of negotiation, he granted an armistice without demur, at the request of the Chinese admiral, Kwan, just when the British squadron was in readiness to attack the remaining forts. The object of this concession, as officially announced, was "to afford the High Commissioner time to consider certain conditions now offered for his acceptance."[3] It took some days to actually arrange terms, but on January the 20th, 1841, the Superintendent announced that preliminary arrangements had been arrived at between the High Commissioner and himself, which were thus epitomized :—

[1] *Chinese Repository*, vol. ix, p. 648.
[2] *Ibid.*, vol. x, pp. 37–44.
[3] *Ibid.*, vol. ix, p. 648.

1. The cession of the island and harbour of Hong-kong to the British Crown. All just charges and duties of the Empire upon the commerce carried on there to be paid as if the trade were conducted at Whampoa.

2. An indemnity to the British Government of $6,000,000 of which $1,000,000 were to be payable at once, and the remainder in equal instalments ending in 1846.

3. Direct official intercourse between the countries upon equal footing.

4. The trade of the port of Canton to be opened within ten days after the Chinese New Year,[1] and to be carried on at Whampoa till further arrangements should be practicable at the new settlement.[2]

In announcing these terms the Superintendent gave expression to that spirit of liberality which, it may justly be said, has always marked our policy in China. "The plenipotentiary," he announced, "seizes the earliest occasion to declare that Her Majesty's Government has sought for no privilege in China exclusively to the advantage of British ships and merchants, and he is only performing his duty in offering the protection of the British flag to the subjects, citizens, and ships of foreign Powers that may resort to Her Majesty's possession. Pending Her Majesty's further pleasure, there will be no port or other charges to the British Government."[3] This declaration, which amounted to saying that Hong-kong was to be a free port, was re-affirmed at a later date by Sir Henry Pottinger, the successor of Captain Elliot, when the island was finally ceded to Great Britain by the Treaty of Nanking, and its spirit has continued to guide our administration of the colony to the present day.

It will be noticed that nothing was said in these terms about compensation to the British merchants for the loss of the opium, or about payment of the debts due from the Hong Merchants. Possibly the sum agreed upon as an indemnity was intended

[1] The Chinese year, being dependent on the completion of twelve lunar months, does not always begin on the same day in our year. Roughly speaking, their new year is about the middle of our February.

[2] *Chinese Repository*, vol. x, p. 63.

[3] *Ibid.*

to go towards the expenses of the expedition, as well as compensation for these other matters. This view is borne out by the fact that the Superintendent, on the 20th of January, 1841, issued a notification "assuring the commercial community that he will use his best efforts with Her Majesty's Government to secure an early and entire advance of their claims for indemnity," and promised to use his efforts to get the Governor-General of India to second his efforts to this end.[1] Another matter of importance, left unnoticed in the Superintendent's announcement, was that the evacuation of Tinghai and the Chusan Islands formed one of the terms agreed with the Chinese.

Apparently the Superintendent had previously communicated to the Home Government the terms he intended to propose to the Chinese when an opportunity should offer itself, for as early as March of this year, before any news of the arrangement actually made with Kishen could have reached England, it was announced in Parliament that he was to be recalled, as the preliminary arrangements made by him with the Chinese were not agreeable to the Home Government.[2] When the actual terms were made known in England, Lord Melbourne, the Prime Minister, stated in the House of Lords that instructions had been sent to Captain Elliot, that if a definite treaty had been come to based on these preliminary articles, it would not be ratified by Her Majesty's Government.[3] On the 10th of April, by which time the terms agreed must have been known in England, Lord Palmerston expressed in a despatch to Queen Victoria his disappointment and mortification at the sequel of the operations. He stated that Captain Elliot seemed to have disregarded his express instructions, that the compensation for opium was too small, that his orders had been that Chusan should be retained as a security, and that the condition attached to the cession of Hong-kong would make the tenure of the new possession as much one of sufferance as that on which the

[1] *Chinese Repository*, vol. x, p. 63.
[2] Hansard: *Parliamentary Debates*, vol. 57, p. 1491.
[3] *Ibid.*, vol. 58, p. 6.

Portuguese held Macao.[1] In ignorance that he was about to be superseded, Captain Elliot continued to act as Superintendent for some months longer, until, in fact, a very few days before his successor arrived, but his tenure of office in reality came to an end when the news of the preliminary arrangement of January 20th was received in England.

The chief result of the negotiations with Kishen was the handing back of Chuen-pi and the evacuation of Chusan by the British,[2] which took place on the 24th February, 1841, and the cession of Hong-kong, the first piece of territory acquired by Great Britain in China. Putting on one side the treaty of Nerchinsk, made between Russia and China in 1689, we may say that this was the first occasion on which the Chinese Government allowed a European Power to take territory, over which it had exercised jurisdiction. By way of taking effective possession of the newly ceded territory, the Superintendent proclaimed the sovereignty of the Queen of Great Britain on the 1st of February, 1841, and stated in his proclamation that, pending Her Majesty's pleasure, the government of the island would be exercised by the Chief Superintendent for the time being. It is doubtful whether Captain Elliot's powers, as defined by Act of Parliament and Order in Council, were wide enough to authorize such a proceeding; but inasmuch as his action in this respect may be taken to have been ratified later by the British Government, though the other terms made by him were repudiated, we must regard Hong-kong as having become a part of the British dominions from this time.

Kishen, in reporting to the Throne the loss of the forts at Chuen-pi and Tai-kok, omitted all reference to the fact that an armistice had been concluded. In this document he guardedly intimates that the plan he has in his mind is to grant to the British commercial intercourse, and so lull them into a state of security, in which they may the more easily be managed, a plan which was afterwards put into execution in the most treacherous manner by his successor in the control

[1] *Letters of Queen Victoria*, 1837-61, vol. i, pp. 327-8.
[2] *Chinese Repository*, vol. x, p. 184.

of affairs at Canton. His exact words were: "Some, giving their advice on this matter, express it as their opinion that, if the whole defensive and preventive guard be maintained, that will suffice in time to weary them out. Or, it is said, if they only be granted commercial intercourse, a restraining cordon may be kept around what they have. Whether or not these schemes are worthy of confidence, your Sacred Majesty's wisdom and thorough knowledge will determine—and to escape it would be impossible. These Foreigners, now, having dared to commence this attack, and having begun troubling and disturbing, the present quarrel is then of their own creation; in their behalf nothing can be said."[1] In a supplementary memorial, which was received in Peking on January 30th, he informed the Emperor that he had "devised a scheme of temporary expediency" and "pretended to promise what was requested," and gave this as his excuse for not having restrained and seized the English. This was the man of whose "scrupulous good faith" Captain Elliot had testified in his official notice, which announced the cession of Hong-kong.[2]

On the receipt of these memorials the Emperor's wrath knew no bounds. He ordered the Board of Punishments to take into its "severest consideration the conduct of Kishen." Admiral Kwan was deprived of his button and all his insignia of rank, and was declared with a naïve accuracy to have "shown himself at all times devoid of talent to direct, and, on the approach of a crisis, perturbed, alarmed, and resourceless." A second edict was issued the same day reproaching Kishen with having neglected to make any defensive preparations whatsoever. Both officials, however, were retained at Canton until their places could be filled up. Against the British a war of extermination was ordered. The language of the imperial edicts left no doubt on this point, but thus denounced them:—

"The rebellious dispositions of these Foreigners being now plainly manifested, there remains no other course than, without

[1] *Chinese Repository*, vol. x, p. 109.

[2] *Ibid.*, p. 63.

remorse, to destroy and wash them clean away, and thus to display the majesty of the empire. What room can there yet be left for showing them consideration and exhibiting them to reason! . . .

"Our ruling dynasty has kept in good order and discipline the exterior Foreigners wholly by the perfect exercise of good favour and justice. So long as those Foreigners have been truly compliant and dutiful, they have unfailingly been treated with generous liberality, in the hope that all might rejoice together in the blessing of peace.

"Some time back, owing to the daily increasing prevalence of the poisonous opium, introduced by western Foreigners, commands were issued to make vigorous endeavours to arrest the growing contumacy. But the English alone, staying themselves upon their pride of power and fierce strength, would not give the required bonds; and for this it was commanded that they should be cut off from commercial intercourse. But, in place of repenting themselves, they daily increased in boastful arrogance. And suddenly, in the month of August of last year, they went so far as to invade with several tens of vessels the district of Ting-hai, seizing and occupying its chief town. And they further came and went, as they would, along the coasts of the several provinces of Fu-kien, Chê-kiang, Kiang-su, Shantung, Chih-li and Moukden, causing disturbance and trouble in many ways. The violence, presumption, and disobedience of these rebellious Foreigners having reached to such a degree, it would have been no hard thing to array our forces, and to exterminate them and cut them off utterly. But considering that these Foreigners had presented letters, complaining of what they called grievances and oppressions, it was deemed unsuitable to refuse to make investigations for them, and thus to fail of displaying the perfect justice of our rule. Hence special commands were given to our minister, Kishen, to proceed with speed to Canton, and to examine and act according to the facts. . . . After the arrival of Kishen at Canton, when he proceeded plainly to admonish and point out the right course, they still continued insatiable in their covetous desires. Having first thought to extort the cost of the opium, they further requested that places of trade should be given them.

"We had anticipated finding them changeable and inconstant, and had estimated them as persons not to be influenced by truth and justice: we had therefore made provision, last year, for the selection of veteran troops, of the provinces of Sze-chuan, Hu-nan, and Kiang-si to be ordered for service in Kwangtung; and we had ordered forces from Hu-nan, Hu-peh, and An-hui to proceed to Chê-kiang as a precaution against attack. And now the report received by express from Kishen is that on the 7th of January these Foreigners, in combination with Chinese traitors, proceeded on board many vessels, directly for the offing of the Bocca Tigris; and that, having opened the thunder of their fire, they inflicted wounds upon our officers and soldiers, and also destroyed the fort of Tai-kok, and possessed themselves of that of Sha-kok. Thus rebellious have they been against heaven, opposers of reason, one in spirit with the brute beasts—beings that the overshadowing vault and all-containing earth can hardly suffer to live—obnoxious to the wrathful indignation alike of angels and of men. There can only remain one course, to destroy and wipe them clean away, to exterminate and root them out, without remorse. Then shall we manifestly discharge our heaven-conferred trust, and show our regard for the lives of our people.

"The various forces that have been ordered for service must now speedily reach their posts. Let Ilipu instantly advance with the forces under him, and recover Ting-hai, that he may revive its people from their troubles. And let Kishen on his part stir up the soldiery and with energy and courage proceed right on, making it his determined aim to compel these rebellious Foreigners to give up their ringleaders, that they may be sent encaged to Peking, to receive the utmost retribution of the laws. The base and vile fellows among those Foreigners, and the Chinese traitors who abet their rebellious practices, are yet more to be sought after. Measures must be devised for seizing them, nor must proceedings cease till they be utterly slain.

"Regarding the coasts of all the maritime provinces, it has

repeatedly been declared our pleasure, that strict and well arranged measures of precaution be everywhere taken. Let all the authorities—generals, governors, lieutenant-governors—with increased diligence maintain a constant plan of observation, and, as soon as any come, attack them. And let them also proclaim it to all, whether officers or people, that it becomes them to regard these Foreigners with a hostile spirit, to cherish towards them the asperity of personal enemies. Speedily report perfect victory, and all shall enjoy rewards from their sovereign. That it will be so we indeed cherish strong hopes."[1]

It is usual in China not only to threaten punishment for wrong-doing, but also to encourage meritorious service to the state by the promise of reward. Thus by the law of China anyone who goes up to the general of the enemy and cuts off his head, and performs a few other warlike exploits demanding equal courage, is entitled to claim a place among those who enjoy the "privilege of illustrious actions."[2] Whether the services promised to be rewarded are possible or probable of performance seems never to be taken into consideration. Acting in accordance with this principle of Chinese jurisprudence, and moved by the exhortation contained in the imperial edict quoted above, I-liang, the *foo-yuen* of Canton, published a proclamation offering rewards for the capture of the English leaders, and indeed of all British subjects, based on a scale proportioned to their importance. This curious document, which incited the patriotic Chinese to such feats of valour as sinking a British man-of-war by boring a hole in her bottom, was thus worded :—

"I-liang, lieutenant-governor, issues the following scale of rewards :—

"1. If the native traitors can repent of their crimes, and

[1] *Chinese Repository*, vol. x, pp. 113–115.

[2] *Ta Tsing Leu Lee* (Staunton's translation), pp. 5–6. "Privilege of illustrious actions : Those are entitled to privilege under this class, who pursue the enemy to the distance of 10,000 li, cut off the head of the general of the hostile army, tear down his standard, and break his sword."

quit the service of the (English) Foreigners, come before the magistrates and confess, their offences will be forgiven; and those who are able to seize alive the rebellious Foreigners, and bring them before the magistrates, as well as those who offer up the Foreigners' heads, will be severally rewarded according to the following scale.

"2. On the capture of one of the line-of-battle ships, the ship and guns will be confiscated, but all that the ship contains, as clothes, goods and money, shall be the reward of the captors, with an additional reward of $100,000; those who burn, or break to pieces, or bore holes through a line-of-battle ship's bottom, so that she sinks, upon the facts being substantiated shall be rewarded with $30,000; for ships of the second and third class, the rewards will be proportionately decreased.

"3. The capture of one of the large steamers shall be rewarded with $50,000; for the smaller, one-half.

"Those among the brave who are foremost in seizing men and ships, and who distinguish themselves by their daring courage, besides receiving the above pecuniary rewards, shall have buttons conferred on them, and be reported for appointments in the public service.

"4. Fifty thousand dollars shall be given to those who seize either Elliot, Morrison, or Bremer, alive; and those who bring either of their heads—upon the facts being ascertained—shall get $30,000.

"5. Ten thousand dollars shall be given to those who seize an officer alive, and $5,000 for each officer's head.

"6. $500 shall be given for every Englishman seized alive; if any are killed and their heads brought in, $300 will be given.

"7. $100 will be given for every Sepoy or Lascar, and $50 for their heads.

"8. As to those among you who, in their efforts to seize the English rebels, may lose their lives, on examination and proof of the facts, a reward of $300 shall be given to your families."[1]

These edicts were known to Captain Elliot in February. One would have supposed that their language was sufficient to show that no permanent arrangement was likely to be

[1] *Chinese Repository*, vol. x, p. 175.

reached, until the Chinese had been taught by actual experience in war that it was useless to oppose the demands of the British Government. But the effect produced on his mind does not appear to have been of this nature. At the time when these edicts were received in Canton, he was waiting for Kishen to conclude the promised treaty. So far from there being any indication of such a consummation being reached, it was apparent to ordinary observers that the zeal, which the Chinese were exhibiting in strengthening their defences, showed that before long hostilities would again break out. Indeed, so serious did the outlook become, that Commodore Bremer, on the 19th of February, returned with his forces to the Bogue, to be ready for any eventuality. On the 20th the Chinese were discovered engaged, under the protection of a masked battery, in blocking up a channel at the back of Anunghoy. As this proceeding was a flagrant breach of faith, they were attacked and dislodged by the British forces. On the 24th Captain Elliot announced that, as the imperial minister and High Commissioner had failed to conclude the treaty of peace within the allotted period, hostilities had been resumed.[1] The British fleet moved up to the Bogue, and on the 25th of February, seized the forts of Tai-kok, and Sha-kok, and re-took Chuen-pi.

The capture of these forts, which is sometimes called the Battle of the Bogue,[2] was accomplished without any loss to the British forces. On the other hand, the Chinese fought with more bravery and determination than they had hitherto shown. Some hundreds of them were killed and wounded, and over a thousand were made prisoners. Two hundred and fifty guns were taken and destroyed. The British steamships proved of the greatest use in this encounter. As soon as the forts had been occupied, they pushed on up the river. On the 27th of February the advance force came upon some 2,000 Chinese, whom they attacked and routed. They captured

[1] *Chinese Repository*, vol. x, pp. 116, 176.

[2] This title is sometimes applied to the fight that took place in 1816, when Captain Maxwell, in the *Alceste*, forced a passage up the river. See *The Fanqui in China*, vol. i, p. 59.

and disabled a hundred guns, burnt the encampment and a large quantity of ammunition, and blew up the *Cambridge*, an old British ship which had been converted by the Chinese into a man-of-war. On arriving at Whampoa the British forces attacked and captured a masked battery, which had opened fire on them as they proceeded up the river. They were preparing to attack Howqua's Fort, when the *kwang-chow-foo* came out under a flag of truce and asked for a suspension of hostilities, which was at once granted by Captain Elliot.[1]

Nothing in the way of proposals for peace came of this truce, which had been arranged to last for three days. Accordingly, on the 6th of March, 1841, hostilities were re-commenced by Sir Hugh Gough, who had arrived from Madras four days previously to take command of the land forces.[2] Howqua's Fort was taken and occupied, and the expedition pushed on till it was in such a position that Canton was at the mercy of the guns of the British ships. Captain Elliot now had the opportunity of regaining the advantage he had lost by the evacuation of Ting-hai; for if Canton were taken he would have in his possession an asset of the utmost diplomatic value. But again he displayed an ill-timed leniency. Instead of allowing the troops to attack, he decided to try the experiment of showing mercy, in the hope that by such a policy he would gain the good opinion of the Cantonese and range them on his side as advocates for the granting of his demands. He therefore published the following proclamation :—

" People of Canton,

" Your city is spared because the gracious Sovereign of Great Britain has commanded the high English officers to remember that the good and peaceful people must be tenderly considered. But if the high officers of the Celestial Court offer the least obstruction to the British forces in their present stations, then it will become necessary to answer force by force, and the city may suffer terrible injury. And if the merchants be prevented from buying and selling freely with

[1] *Chinese Repository*, vol. x, pp. 120, 176–9.

[2] *Ibid.*, p. 180.

the British and foreign merchants, then the whole trade of Canton must immediately be stopped. The high officers of the English nation have faithfully used their best efforts to prevent the miseries of war; and the responsibility of the actual state of things must rest upon the heads of the bad advisers of the Emperor. Further evil consequences can only be prevented by wisdom and moderation on the part of the provincial government."[1]

The immediate result of this exhibition of clemency was that the Chinese officials, disregarding the fact that there was no cessation of hostilities, granted chops to the ships of various nationalities to proceed to Whampoa to trade. This necessitated an announcement by Captain Elliot, that no one would be allowed to enter the river without the permission of the British commander-in-chief. A further result was that the Chinese again resumed the construction of defensive works. These Sir Hugh Gough, compelled to resume hostilities within a week of Captain Elliot's pacific proclamation, attacked and carried on the 13th of March, capturing 105 cannon and nine war-junks. On the 16th the Chinese fired on the white flag, whereupon the whole British squadron advanced further up the river and carried all the works immediately in front of Canton, so that that city was again brought directly under the guns of the men-of-war. Again Captain Elliot failed to profit by the success of the forces at his command, and resorted to futile parleyings. He announced on the 20th that a suspension of hostilities had been arranged between the imperial commissioner Yang and himself, that it had been agreed that the trade of Canton was open, and that merchants of any nationality, who might proceed thither to trade, would be protected.[2]

On this occasion the Superintendent would appear to have represented to the Chinese officials that his only object was to open the trade. It is difficult to know why they should have disregarded the commands of the Emperor that the British should be exterminated, if the Superintendent's demands amounted to more than this. The commissioner

[1] *Chinese Repository*, vol. x, p. 180. [2] *Ibid.*, p. 181.

Yang, one of three who had arrived to take over the office held by Kishen, announced by special edict that Captain Elliot had "officially represented that it was his desire to maintain peace, and he demanded nothing else but only immediate permission for the trade to be carried on as usual."[1] Apparently there was to be no mitigation of the old burdensome conditions, which had been one of the chief causes of the present rupture. Captain Elliot issued a public notice, that the merchants would have to pay "the usual port charges and other established duties," pending a final settlement of affairs. No bond, however, was to be required by the provincial government, but smuggling was to be punished in the same way as in England, "detention of the person or penal consequences of all kinds excepted."[2] A further proof that the conditions under which trade was to be carried on were to be much the same as in the old days was afforded by the Hong Merchants, who gave notice on the 12th of April that the Consoo charge would be the same as in the preceding year. Still, everybody indulged the hope that peace had been obtained at last. The trade at Canton revived. The river became crowded with shipping, that had long been waiting outside the Bogue and in the Macao Roads. The Foreign merchants began to return to the Factories. On the 5th of April, Captain Elliot returned to Canton and took up his residence in the British Hall, where he remained till the 17th of the same month.[3]

In the meantime Kishen received news of his degradation. On the 12th of March he left Canton, to be put on his trial at Peking for "traitorous conduct."[4] In his place the Emperor had appointed a commission of three, consisting of Yihshan, with the title of "general pacificator of the rebellious," and Lungwan and Yangfang as assistant ministers, "to repair to Canton to co-operate in the work of extermination." Their instructions from the Emperor were to "all act together in

[1] *Chinese Repository*, vol. x, p. 182.
[2] *Ibid.*, p. 181.
[3] *Ibid.*, pp. 184, 233–4.
[4] *Ibid.*, p. 184.

perfect harmony, with combined strength advance to the work of extermination, recover back the lost points, clearly display the vengeance of heaven, and achieve for themselves great merit."[1] These three officials are generally spoken of as the "three commissioners," and in practice they appear to have exercised jointly the powers which had previously been vested in the High Commissioner.

It was not long before even Captain Elliot saw that nothing had been gained by his forbearance towards the Chinese. The warlike preparations that went on made it evident that more hostilities were bound to come. Fresh troops were daily arriving in Canton, but the excuse was made that they had been ordered thither by the Emperor, and that there had not been time to countermand the order. These were quartered in the city, because, said the officials, the temples there afforded protection from the rain. In a similar strain the casting of new cannon was explained on the ground that the old had become useless! It was known to many of the Chinese that treachery against the British was at the bottom of all this, but they gave no warning. Then it was observed that large numbers of natives began to leave the city, a sure sign of trouble at any time in China. Anxiety and alarm spread throughout the whole Foreign community. On the 10th of May the Superintendent, slow to believe that his diplomatic efforts had miscarried, went to Canton with his wife to re-assure the British, and to show the Chinese that he entertained no suspicion against them.

This visit served to make it clear to the Superintendent that matters were coming to a dangerous pass, and he began to take precautions. An expedition to Amoy, which had been resolved upon, was abandoned, and Sir Hugh Gough and Sir Le Fleming Senhouse, the latter of whom had succeeded to the command of the naval forces, moved towards Canton. They found numerous batteries erected along the river bank from one end of the suburbs to the other, fully manned with soldiers, while the temples and warehouses near the river had been converted into arsenals and barracks. At this juncture

[1] *Chinese Repository*, vol. x, p. 119; vol. xi, p. 580.

The Iron War Steamer "Nemesis" rounding the Cape of Good Hope in a gale on her voyage from England to China

(Reproduced from an aquatint print by kind permission of Messrs. Maggs Bros.)

men, women, and children fled from the city in crowds. Foreign merchants hastened away, leaving their effects unprotected. Yu, the acting prefect, whether to allay what he believed to be an unfounded state of panic, or whether as part of a deep laid scheme of treachery, issued, on the 20th of May, an edict promising protection to merchants of all nationalities. But the ambiguity of the language of this document only served to increase the general alarm, and on the day following its publication Captain Elliot recommended all Foreigners to retire from Canton before sunset.[1]

That same night at about eleven o'clock, without a moment's warning, the advanced British squadron was attacked with fire-rafts. Simultaneously a cannonade commenced from every point where the Chinese could bring guns to bear on the British forces. The cutter *Louisa* and the schooner *Aurora*, which were anchored off the Factories, were attacked by a battery of guns, which had been secretly erected abreast of them, as well as by fire-ships, but managed to get away down the Macao passage. The British squadron at the Bogue now included more than one steamer, as well as the East India Company's iron steamship, the *Nemesis*, the first ironclad to make the voyage round the Cape of Good Hope, which had arrived in Chinese waters late in the preceding year. Thus the British naval forces were easily handled in face of such an attack. In reply they opened fire and poured in upon the Chinese a storm of shot, shell, and rockets. The *Modeste*, *Pylades*, *Algerine*, and *Nemesis* accounted for the fire-ships, as well as thirty-nine war-junks and fishing boats. The Chinese kept up their fire during the whole of the night, but no great damage was done. Altogether 200 fire-ships had been got ready for this attack, and some of them came so near the *Modeste*, that the water braves on abandoning them were shot down by the musketry fire from her deck.[2] Of these engines of destruction about one-half were destroyed in three or four hours, and the rest were either run on shore, abandoned, or hidden in the shallow creeks of the river.

[1] *Chinese Repository*, vol. x, pp. 293–4.
[2] *Ibid.*, vol. x., pp. 294, 340–5.

Early in the morning Yihshan sent 2,000 soldiers to search the Factories for guns. Entering the Creek, Dutch, and English Factories, these men made havoc of all the rooms, some fifteen or twenty in number, looting or destroying everything they could find. Not a door, hinge, window, or lock was spared. Chinese officers were seen returning to the city with their horses loaded with the spoils of the Foreign devils' hongs. In this work of destruction the soldiers were joined by the rabble. The large mirrors and chandeliers in the British Hall were smashed to pieces, the clock was pulled down, and even the weather-cock on the top of the belfry was overthrown. In the chapel everything of value was destroyed, not excepting a monumental tablet erected to the memory of a former chief supercargo.[1] A boat belonging to the American ship *Morrison*, containing an officer and four seamen with three passengers, left the Factories for Whampoa, displaying a notice in large Chinese characters stating who they were. Before she was out of sight of the Factories the Chinese fired on her, and the whole party, excepting one seaman who was killed, were captured and taken to Canton. A similar fate befel an Englishman named Coolidge, who with a few others had stayed in the Factories all that night.[2]

For three days the British squadron were harassed with attacks from fire-vessels. In the meantime Sir Le Fleming Senhouse was engaged with General Gough in concentrating the British forces for an assault on Canton city. During the whole day of the 26th active operations were rendered impossible by the rain, which fell in torrents. That night preparations were made for the final assault in the morning. Guns, mortars, rocket apparatus, and troops were got into position. The escalading parties were detailed. The infantry was so placed as to be able to prevent the enemy from working their guns. Early on the morning of the 27th all was in readiness. The guns were loaded and primed: the port fires were lit: the general and commodore were giving a last look round before giving the signal to commence

[1] *Chinese Repository*, vol. x, pp. 295, 343.
[2] *Ibid.*, p. 295.

firing. Suddenly an unlooked for messenger arrived. He brought despatches from Her Majesty's plenipotentiary. The despatches were opened and read. Without a word of warning, with no consultation with the commander-in-chief, Captain Elliot had again spared Canton. He had agreed to accept a ransom of $6,000,000. The commodore could not restrain himself, but publicly protested against the terms of the treaty *in toto*. The feeling of disgust on the part of the naval and military forces was intense. That Captain Elliot could be guilty of such folly, weakness, and want of courtesy could hardly be believed. Still there was no doubt about it. To make matters worse he had arranged that the British forces should remain in their position on the Heights, soaked with rain as they were, until the ransom should have been paid.

The actual terms arranged with the Chinese were announced a week later. The three imperial commissioners and all the troops, other than those of the province of Kwang-tung, were to quit the city within six days. The ransom was to be paid within a week, the first instalment of $1,000,000 being paid before sunset on the 27th. If the whole ransom was not paid within the agreed time, it was to be increased by $1,000,000 for the seventh day, and another $1,000,000 if there should be a delay as long as fourteen days, and another $1,000,000 if the delay should extend to twenty days. When the whole ransom had been paid, the British forces were to retire outside the Bocca Tigris, and the captured forts were to be handed back, but these were not to be re-armed until affairs had been settled between the two nations. Losses occasioned by the destruction of the Factories, and of the Spanish brig *Bilbaino*, were to be paid within one week. Even then the limit of Captain Elliot's complaisance had not been reached, for he subsequently arranged that, when two-thirds of the money had been paid, security should be taken for the rest. What this security was to be it is difficult to imagine, and history does not inform us.[1]

It was rumoured that the delay in payment was due to an expectation that reinforcements were coming, for whose arrival

[1] *Chinese Repository*, vol. x, p. 397.

the Chinese officials wanted to gain time. Captain Elliot refused to believe any such rumour. In this state of things the Cameronians and the Madras Native Infantry received orders to drive off a large force of Chinese, who were found to be advancing against the British encampment! This operation was successfully accomplished, and the troops returned to the spot whence they had set out, but not without difficulty and discomfort, as it again came on to rain in torrents, and soon a violent thunderstorm was raging. In retiring they had been much annoyed by the enemy, who, perceiving that their muskets were useless owing to the rain, attacked them with long spears and hooks attached to bamboo poles. Little resistance could be offered by the British. Not a musket would go off. The enemy had surrounded and could have annihilated the whole of them, had they possessed sufficient determination and courage. Fortunately the rain ceased for a while, and the Sepoys, tearing the lining from their turbans, the only dry thing about them, washed and dried their muskets sufficiently to be able to fire a few volleys. This compelled the enemy to retire, but on the rain coming on again the British in self-defence were once more compelled to form a square. Shortly afterwards a relief party of marines arrived with percussion muskets, which were not affected by the rain, and the Chinese were driven back. The Sepoys had lost one killed, and one officer and fourteen men wounded.[1] Whether Captain Elliot thought this the normal result of his proceedings does not appear. We only know that the British troops were kept outside the city, and Canton and its inhabitants, together with all the Chinese officials, left to enjoy a comfort and peace denied to the soldiers who had the misfortune to serve Her Majesty the Queen, the insults to whose representative they were supposed to have come out to avenge.

It is possible that this Chinese force was not part of the regular troops. The people of Canton had begun arming on their own account, and the natives of the country round about were following their example. From 118 villages the whole

[1] *Chinese Repository*, vol. x, pp. 399–400.

of the male population between the ages of sixteen and sixty had joined this movement, which was not unlike the Boxer rising of more recent years, though on a much smaller scale. There is this further similarity, that both in 1841 and in 1900 these irregular forces appeared only as auxiliaries of the imperial troops. Another point of resemblance between these Cantonese volunteers and the Boxers is that both styled themselves the soldiers of righteousness. The former were known as the *I Ping*, the latter as the *I Ho Ch'uan*. The character *I* was the same in both cases, and was inscribed on the banners of each of these bodies of irregulars.[1] Sir Hugh Gough was in some doubt as how best to deal with these Cantonese irregulars, and forcibly protested to the Chinese authorities against the manner in which they were behaving. Thereupon they were suppressed by the Viceroy, or at least prevailed upon to cease from active hostilities.[2]

Disease had been the greatest enemy of the British soldiers who had been engaged at Chusan, and now at Canton the climate began to tell on the health of the troops. When Captain Elliot so unexpectedly made terms for the ransom of Canton city, the British forces, as we have seen, were already in occupation of the neighbouring heights. This position they continued to hold for seven days, until the terms of truce were settled. This period was sufficient to allow the miasma, that arose from the marshy flats, to sow the seeds of sickness throughout the army, and no sooner had the troops begun to retire than disease broke out in their midst. One of the

[1] It is interesting to observe that the word Boxer, which, since the stirring events of 1900, has passed into all the languages of Europe, originated in the slang of the Treaty Ports, where it was used as a convenient equivalent of the "Righteous Harmony Fist" denoted by the characters *I Ho Ch'uan*.

This may be accepted as the correct translation of the three Chinese characters (see Smith: *China in Convulsion*, vol. i, p. 154). There has been a good deal of controversy as to the exact translation, due to the fact that the Chinese, when asked for an explanation of the *I Ho Ch'uan*, adopted the English term volunteer as the nearest equivalent. A careful analysis of the term shows that the analogy is of the slightest. (See *North China Herald*, vol. lxv, pp. 115, 192.)

[2] *Chinese Repository*, vol. x, p. 350.

first to succumb was the commodore, Sir Le Fleming Senhouse, who died on board H.M.S. *Blenheim* at Hong-kong on the 18th of June, 1841. He was buried at Macao, and over his grave a monument was erected at the joint subscription of the army and navy.[1] The climate of Hong-kong, indeed, seemed no less unhealthy than that of Canton. Much of the sickness, however, which prevailed there in the first years of the life of the colony was due to temporary causes, and particularly to the lack of proper sanitary precautions. So bad was the state of affairs in June, 1841, that many of the men were re-embarked, with the object of giving them a better chance of recovery, a measure which at once proved beneficial. But among those left on shore sickness increased to an alarming degree. Hospital gangrene was one of the worst evils. The slighest abrasion of the skin degenerated into a foul and malignant ulcer. Of 600 men in the 37th Madras Infantry, scarcely 100 were fit for duty. To make matters worse, a terrible typhoon overturned the field hospital, and when the sick had been removed thence into the barracks for safety, these too were levelled with the ground by the force of the storm.[2]

In this state of affairs the *régime* of Captain Elliot came to an end. Lord Palmerston seems to have realized that to retain him longer in the position of plenipotentiary could entail nothing but delay, disappointment, and diplomatic defeat. No special announcement was made, but in answer to a question in Parliament, it was admitted that the Government were about to recall him from Canton. Early in August the news reached China that there was to be a change in the office of Superintendent, and on the 10th of that month a successor to Captain Elliot arrived in the person of Sir Henry Pottinger. By his commission Sir Henry, who had been a major-general in the service of the East India Company, was appointed Her Majesty's special plenipotentiary and Chief Superintendent of Trade, a combination of offices which the British Minister to China continues to hold to the present

[1] *Chinese Repository*, vol. x, p. 619 ; vol. xi, p. 583.
[2] *Ibid.*, vol. x, p. 620.

day. To him were given full powers and authority to negotiate and conclude, with the properly authorized representatives of the Emperor of China, "any treaty or agreement for the arrangement of the differences now subsisting between Great Britain and China."[1] With him came Rear-Admiral Sir William Parker, K.C.B., commander-in-chief of the British naval squadron in the East Indies, to command the sea forces. Commodore Bremer, who had returned from Calcutta as recently as June 18th to act as joint plenipotentiary with Captain Elliot, returned to India on the 24th of August, 1841, in his company.

At the time when Captain Elliot was leaving Hong-kong under recall, Kishen, his old antagonist, was being examined at Peking as to his conduct of affairs when High Commissioner. Under the necessity of explaining to his imperial master the situation as it was when he left Canton in March, he had presented a memorial to the Throne, which set out the sequence of events from the time of his arrival in Kwang-tung to the date of his recall. This memorial, couched in language of the greatest humility, showed how hopeless from a military point of view was the struggle in which his country was engaged. With great boldness, and a candour patriotic but perilous in the extreme, he described the disadvantages under which he had carried on operations against the British forces. On the one side, he explained, were the Emperor's express commands that the defences of Canton be strengthened; on the other, the might of the enemy, which was exerted in overwhelming manner as soon as the defences were increased, or troops assembled. The Chinese means of defence, he pointed out, whether as regarded forts, ships, or men, were all inferior to those of the enemy, and it was useless to carry on warlike operations in the hope of success. Such forts as did not stand completely isolated in the sea, were compassed about with channels on every side, so that the barbarians were able to blockade them, or to get round them and proceed up the river with the greatest ease. As soon as the Foreigners

[1] *Chinese Repository*, vol. x, p. 476. He had distinguished himself in the recent operations in Afghanistan.

had passed the Bocca Tigris, there were waterways open to them in every direction. As to guns, the total number available were but enough to fortify the fronts of the forts, so the sides had to remain undefended. Moreover, they were cast from a bad design, being so small in the bore that they could only carry half-way across the channels they were meant to protect, and were placed in embrasures "as wide as doors, so that people might almost pass in and out."[1]

The troops under his command were practically useless. The only way to oppose the British was by fighting them at sea. The troops that had been ordered to Canton by the Emperor were all land forces and could not be utilized without the co-operation of a strong naval support. Of the available marine force, the whole of which had been enlisted from the province of Kwang-tung, he said, with a delicate meiosis, "their quality is very irregular." After the battle of the 7th of January, the whole of the naval force had gone to their commander-in-chief and demanded money, under threats that they would immediately disband if not paid, so that that officer "was obliged to pawn his clothes and other things, by which means he was enabled to give each of them a bonus of two dollars and thus only could get them to remain until now at their posts." It would have been most disastrous to have given battle, when he was not certain that the marine force would stand firm. Moreover, the ships of war were not of sufficient size or strength to carry large guns, and could never cope with the British men-of-war. In short, the forces at his disposal were altogether insufficient for the task to which he had been designated.[2]

Again, the people of the province of Kwang-tung had become accustomed to seeing Foreigners through many years of intercourse, and so had become intimate with them. In this respect they were far different from the people of Ting-hai, who felt a natural hostility to Foreigners. In these circumstances he took the course he thought best in the interests of the empire.

[1] *Chinese Repository*, vol. x, pp. 237–8.
[2] *Ibid.*, pp. 238–9.

"Your slave has again and again," he said, "resolved the matter in his anxious mind. The consequences, in so far as they relate to his own person, are trifling: but as they regard the stability of the government, and the lives of the people, they are vast and extend to distant posterity. Should he incur guilt in giving battle when unable to command a victory, or should he be criminal in making such arrangements as do not meet the gracious approbation of his sovereign, he must equally bear the offence: and, for his life, what is it that he should be cared for or pitied!

"Entertaining these views, a council has been held of all the officers in the city . . . all of whom agree that our defences are such as it is impossible to trust to, and that our troops would not hold their ground on the field of battle. Moreover, the troops ordered from the different provinces by your Majesty, having yet a long journey to come, time is necessary for their arrival: nor can they all arrive together. The assemblage of a large body of troops, too, is a thing not to be effected without sundry rumours flying about. Our native traitors are sure to give information; and the said Foreigners will previously let loose their contumacious and violent dispositions. Your slave is so worried by grief and vexation that he loathes his food, and sleep has forsaken his eyelids. But for the above reasons he does not shrink from the heavy responsibility he is incurring, in submitting all these facts, the result of personal investigation, to your Celestial Majesty. And at the same time he presents for perusal the letter of the said Foreigners, wherein they make the various restorations before enumerated. He humbly hopes his sacred sovereign will with pity look down upon the black-haired flock, his people, and will be graciously pleased to grant favours beyond measure, by acceding to the requests now made. Thus shall we be spared the calamity of having our people and land burnt to ashes, and thus shall we lay the foundation of victory, by binding and curbing the Foreigners now, while preparing to have the power of cutting them off at some future period."[1]

[1] *Chinese Repository*, vol. x, p. 240.

The account of his negotiations with Captain Elliot is characteristic. He says :—

"Now after that these said Foreigners had despatched a person to Chê-kiang to restore Ting-hai, and had delivered up all that had been captured by them in the province of Kwang-tung—after, too, their ships of war had all retired to the outer waters—it so happened that Elliot solicited an interview: and as your slave had not inspected yet the entrances of the port, and the fortifications of the Bocca Tigris, and as the troops ordered from the several provinces had not yet arrived, it did not seem prudent to show anything that might cause suspicion on the part of the Foreigners, and so to bring on at once a commencement of troubles and collision from their side. Therefore the occasion of visiting for inspection the Bocca Tigris was taken advantage of to grant an interview. . . .

"Elliot presented a rough draft of several articles on which he desired to deliberate—the major part having regard to the troublesome *minutiæ* of commerce: and he agreed that for the future in any cases of the smuggling of opium, or of other contraband traffic or evasion of duties, both ship and cargo should be confiscated. Among the number of his proposals were some highly objectionable, which were at the moment pointed out and refused: upon which the said Foreigner begged that emendations should be offered and considered of. It has now accordingly been granted him that alterations and emendments be made, and when these shall be determined on and agreed to, the whole shall be presented for your majesty's inspection."

It is very unusual for a Chinese, when he memorializes the Throne, to speak the truth so plainly as did Kishen on this occasion. The fear of capital punishment is a strong deterrent from such a course. It therefore redounds the more to his credit that he was sufficiently patriotic to set before the Emperor the true state of the defences of Canton. Nor is it less creditable that he openly stated that his policy in dealing with the British plenipotentiaries was not prompted by any desire to grant their demands, but by the desire to gain time, in which to prepare to crush them the more effectually. In this latter respect Kishen showed the same disposition that has at many subsequent times been manifested by Chinese statesmen towards the Western peoples. Indeed, it is well to recognise that this is the same disposition in which they work at the present day, much as it may wound our self-esteem to know that sixty years of intercourse have not sufficed to work any change.

The Emperor, on receipt of the memorial, was furious. He forbade the discussion among Chinese of the relations between his country and England. Death was decreed against anyone who should talk of making peace. A Chinese who was found to have been commenting on the state of affairs was visited with exemplary punishment. Two small sticks, each bearing a mimic flag, were stuck one through each ear, so as to stand upright at the sides of his head. With his hands tied behind his back, he was marched through the streets of Canton in this array, guarded by soldiers, preceded by a man beating a gong, and followed by another beating his bare back with a rattan.[1] As to Kishen himself, the Emperor commanded that he be handed over to the Board of Punishments, in order that they might examine and report on his case.

In the autumn of 1841 the Board presented their report to the Throne. They were not satisfied with the information obtained from the degraded minister, for after stating that he had replied to all their questions, they respectfully requested that the sacred glance might be cast upon the case and torture added to the examination. Having summarized the events that had occurred during his period of office, they concluded with the words :—

"We, the ministers, have examined Kishen on the whole of the foregoing charges, and at the close of the third examination Kishen could only tremble with fear and acknowledge his own unpardonable crimes. At the time he and the barbarian eye[2] held their negotiations, he without delay fully delivered Hong-kong over to the English for the time, not

[1] *Chinese Repository*, vol. x, p. 292.

[2] *i.e.*, Captain Elliot.

daring to deceive them nor persevering to receive the things they had to offer, but his entire policy was decidedly bad, and he now requests that we, the ministers, would on his account memorialize and implore that the celestial favour might be manifested in inflicting upon him the heaviest punishment."[1]

It must not be supposed that Kishen was undergoing any exceptional fate in being thus treated. As already pointed out in the case of Lin, he was only suffering the ordinary experience of a Chinese official, who finds circumstances too strong for him, and is unable to direct the course of events as the Emperor would wish. But in the degree of punishment that was meted out, both he and Lin fared worse than is usual in such cases even in China. On receiving the report, the Emperor referred it back to the Board, to determine the precise punishment that should be inflicted on the fallen minister, and the Board then made a further report in the following terms:—

"Kishen, when sent as a high commissioner to Canton to examine into and arrange the affairs of the barbarians should have applied the most attentive care and thorough ability and devised plans for the full settlement of every point. When the barbarian English became refractory towards his clear commands for arrangement, and manifested their wolfish dispositions, he ought straightway to have memorialized the Court, requesting troops to be prepared in order that at an early day they might be exterminated. But he incoherently presented them a place to dwell at, and for the time being gave Hong-kong to them, which is the excuse they give for taking possession of it. In all matters where it was necessary to guard and watch, he made no previous preparations, and consequently the barbarians have attacked and destroyed the forts in succession, and the very important place (the Bogue) cannot now be guarded. He has throughout been guilty of the greatest political errors, and it is in accordance with the laws that his case should be inquired into and

[1] *Chinese Repository*, vol. x, p. 591.

deliberated upon, for it is owing to his not making previous preparations that we have lost our important passes, the city fortifications and encampments. The law decrees imprisonment and decapitation, and we hereby sentence him to be beheaded, but to be imprisoned until after autumn and then to be executed."[1]

Lin and Kishen were not the only officials to suffer degradation through their want of success in keeping out the English. Very soon after the latter had reached Peking, an edict reached Canton ordering Ilipu to return to the capital, and appointing Yu-kien in his stead. In the middle of June, 1841, Ilipu arrived at Peking, and was at once handed over to a special commission including three princes of the blood, the members of the cabinet, the presidents of the Six Boards, and the members of the Board of Punishments.[2] This commission reported after a few months to the effect that the conduct of the accused was at first commendable, he having induced the British to leave Chusan and repair to Canton. Of his subsequent behaviour, however, they spoke in the severest terms, as though it were through some fault of his own that he had been unable to drive out the enemy's forces. Said they :—

"Ilipu did not, in obedience to the imperial will, forthwith advance and slaughter, and make a thorough extermination of them. The whole of his proceedings being improper and really marked by imbecility, he, being unworthy to bear so high an office, earnestly besought that his crimes might be visited with heavy punishment. The imperial will was repeatedly transmitted, that he should proceed to exterminate the enemy; but on every occasion he delayed, and idly looked about him, and through excessive timidity did not go forward, and thus for every purpose he proved himself weak and useless. We therefore jointly solicit the imperial will, that Ilipu may forthwith be disgraced from the office he formerly held as Viceroy of the Liang-Kiang provinces, and be sent to

[1] *Chinese Repository*, vol. x, p. 592.
[2] *Ibid.*, p. 447.

Ili, that by strenuous exertions he may make amends for his offences." [1]

This recommendation was adopted by the Throne, and Ilipu was banished to the hard labour of making roads or some similar task in Chinese Turkestan, where so many of China's ablest men have ended their careers. He appears to have been reduced to a condition of actual slavery. But a better fortune awaited him, for in March, 1842, he was recalled to advise the Emperor again in the troubles that beset him. In April of the same year the Manchu Kiying, who was on his way to Canton to take the place of Yihshan, was appointed to act as joint plenipotentiary with Ilipu, and in August of the same year these two acted as plenipotentiaries in the negotiation of the Treaty of Nanking. [2]

[1] *Chinese Repository*, vol. x, pp. 633–5 ; vol. xii, p. 329.
[2] *Ibid.*, vol. xi, p. 571 ; vol. xii, p. 329.

CHAPTER XXII

WAR IN EARNEST

WITH the appointment of Sir Henry Pottinger a new order of things had begun, an order of vigorous and energetic measures destined to accomplish in a single year all that was gained by the signing of the Treaty of Nanking. Actions, not words, was the watchword of the new policy. It was a fortunate thing that Sir Henry, on his arrival, found Sir Hugh Gough visiting Macao. The opportunity was used to make arrangements forthwith for the prosecution of the campaign. That the mercantile community might know what to expect, the plenipotentiary, in announcing his appointment as Captain Elliot's successor, stated that it was his resolve to devote his undivided energies and thoughts to the primary objects of securing a speedy and satisfactory close to the war, and that he could allow no consideration, connected with mercantile pursuits and other interests, to interfere with the strong measures which he might find it necessary to authorize and adopt towards the government and subjects of China. with a view to compelling an honourable and lasting peace.[1] To the policy thus enunciated he adhered with the utmost steadfastness, so that in twelve months he achieved more towards placing the relations between Great Britain and China on a firm and satisfactory basis than had been effected by his predecessors since the death of Lord Napier.

Sir Henry Pottinger was accompanied by Major Malcolm as Secretary of Legation, who was at once despatched with letters to the Chinese officials at Canton, a proceeding which caused no small astonishment in the minds of the native population. The officials themselves seem to have been surprised at this unwonted boldness, but not knowing what such a step might portend, they deemed it best to despatch the *kwang-chow-foo* to Macao to solicit an interview with the plenipotentiary. Sir Henry, not to be led into any action that might lessen his dignity in the eyes of the Chinese, refused

[1] *Chinese Repository*, vol. x, p. 477.

the request, but the visitor was allowed to see Major Malcolm. No time, however, was wasted in negotiation. On August 21st the two commanders-in-chief left Hong-kong in command of a second expedition to the North, with the purpose of effecting what the previous expedition, under Captain Elliot, had so signally failed to accomplish. With them went Sir Henry Pottinger and his staff, which included J. R. Morrison as Chinese secretary, and W. H. Medhurst as a clerk, both of whom have achieved some distinction in the history of English intercourse with China. The expedition was made up of thirteen men-of-war, a surveying vessel, fifteen transports with troops, and six provision transports.[1]

On the 25th the expedition arrived in the outward anchorage of Amoy. Although found to be strongly fortified, the port and its defences were captured without serious opposition.[2] A garrison was left on the island of Kulangsu, which is separated from the mainland by a channel some 600 yards wide leading to the Inner Harbour, but the rest of the troops were re-embarked as soon as possible. Kulangsu soon became the site of a British settlement, and on it at the present time is situate the British Concession at Amoy. As soon as the troops were re-embarked, the expedition left for Ting-hai, where it arrived on September 29th. The batteries on this island had been much strengthened, since the withdrawal of the British forces in the preceding February, the brass guns being quite new and admirably constructed. On October 1st the city was taken by storm, but not without some loss. A provisional government was formed and a proclamation was published by Sir Henry Pottinger, announcing that the city and the Chusan Islands generally would be retained until the demands of the British Government had been not merely acceded to, but carried into effect. On the 10th October Chin-hai was bombarded and captured, and shortly afterwards Ningpo was peacefully occupied.[3]

[1] *Chinese Repository*, vol. x, p. 524.

[2] For the official despatches relating to the capture of Amoy, see *Chinese Repository*, vol. xi, p. 148.

[3] *Chinese Repository*, vol. x, pp. 623–33.

It was too late in the season for the expedition to push on to the North, as the Pei-ho freezes up about the middle of December, and from then till the beginning of March access to Tientsin is impossible.[1] Nevertheless the Chinese, not knowing what these terrible English might do, began at once to put the defences of that river in order, by building two new forts on the south bank at Taku, and repairing the three on the north side of the river. They also collected vast quantities of stores and assembled a special corps of "water-braves," or Chinese marines.[2] When Captain Elliot had visited the north in the preceding year the whole coast was defenceless, there not being a single gun in the forts at Taku. Now, however, a far different state of things prevailed. The Chinese were making every effort to be ready for the expedition when it should arrive. So alarmed were the authorities at Peking that they even recalled Lin, in order that he might be at hand to advise them how best they might deal with the terrible barbarians. He was appointed as a Commissioner to repair the banks of the Yellow River, which had recently undergone one of its periodical overflowings and laid the capital of Honan in ruins.[3]

In the meantime the relations between the British and Chinese at Canton had assumed an appearance of perfect amity, the scene of hostilities having been shifted further north. In August the Emperor received from "the imperial appointed great rebel-quelling general, Yihshan, and his colleagues Lungwan and Yang Fang," a memorial stating that the English had given them back the forts, that their militia and volunteers had slaughtered a great many traitors and Foreign robbers who were raising disturbances, and that they had restored tranquillity to the provincial city. Thc

[1] It is now possible to get to Tientsin in winter by proceeding to the harbour of Chin Wang Tao, some 150 miles north of Taku, and thence by rail.

[2] *Chinese Repository*, vol. x, p. 686.

[3] A curious parallel to this incident is the appointment of Li Hung Chang to the same office in 1899, when he was just beginning to regain his influence at Peking and shortly before he was made Viceroy of Canton.

excuse, which is always given by the Chinese in similar circumstances, that the success of the British had been due to native traitors, finds a place in this document. Of course there was no truth in this statement, in the sense in which it was made by the Chinese officials who presented the memorial. But unconsciously they, as also their successors who at different periods have sheltered themselves behind the same plea, put their fingers on one of the causes of the invariable success of military operations against the Chinese, that is, the ease with which supplies and labour may be obtained by an invader from the native population. It is a curious thing that the Chinaman in a normal condition is absolutely devoid of patriotism. He is willing to render any services to the enemies of his country in return for an adequate consideration in cash. It is only when some wave of fanaticism sweeps over the country, as in the Boxer movement of 1900, that he allows any other feeling to override the desire to get money. Even then it is not for long that he withstands the dominant passion. The Chinese of Tientsin, who in June, 1900, were doing their utmost to exterminate the Foreigners that were besieged in the British Concession, in August were willing helpers of the column that was organized to relieve the Legations at Peking. And in Peking itself there were lulls in the hostilities, when the native soldiery gave up fighting for the more attractive pursuit of selling melons and eggs to the besieged.[1] So in 1841 the *foo-yuen* of Canton was so struck by the extent to which his countrymen were helping the English, that he issued a most sarcastic edict pointing out to them their folly and want of patriotism.[2]

When in May of 1841 Captain Elliot had consented to Canton being ransomed, it was agreed by the Chinese that none of the fortified places within the river should be re-armed, nor any fresh preparations for defence made, and it was on the faith of this stipulation that the British merchants had to some extent resumed commercial operations at Canton.

[1] See *China Blue Books*, No. 4 (1900), p. 30, and No. 3 (1901), pp. 24, 25.

[2] *Chinese Repository*, vol. x, pp. 533–5.

The Chinese in reality never intended to be bound by this condition, but agreed to it with the intention of breaking it at the first convenient opportunity. That this was so is evident from Yihshan's memorial to the Throne, in which he communicated the terms of ransom to the Emperor. In that document he had stated that as soon as the ships of war should have retired, he meant to block up the course of the river at every important point, beginning with the river in front of the city and continuing down to the Bocca Tigris itself, and at each of such points erect forts and place guns in position. He avowed that his object in so doing would be to secure "the door of entrance," and make it possible to oppose the progress of the British forces, and to maintain the Chinese defences.[1]

When, in August of 1841, Sir Henry Pottinger first arrived in China and heard of the terms that had been arranged in May, he suspected that the Chinese did not mean to keep faith. He had, therefore, before starting for the North, notified the local officials that the slightest infringement of the stipulations arranged with his predecessor would lead to a resumption of hostilities. The result was that until he was fairly on his way to the Pei-ho the Chinese refrained from making any defensive preparations. But when they thought he was at a sufficient distance from Canton, they at once renewed their efforts to fortify the river. Whilst the expedition waited at Chusan for the opening of the Pei-ho, he, in January of 1842, returned to Macao and discovered that during his absence there had been a real breach of the agreement. Four new forts had been raised between Canton and Howqua's Fort, and another was being erected at the Macao passage. The provincial officials, who had not expected this visit, sent the Hong Merchants to ask that the stipulation as to defences might be waived. But the days of interviews between the representative of Great Britain and Hong Merchants were gone for ever, and the request for a meeting was at once refused. To prevent unnecessary hostilities, however, Sir Henry caused it to be made known to the deputation that

[1] *Chinese Repository*, vol. x, p. 404.

the conditions arranged by Captain Elliot would be strictly enforced, and that any further infringement would be punished with a stoppage of trade and the renewal of hostilities. He also, at this time, put a stop to the seizure of merchant junks, that during his absence had been going on by order of the senior naval officer in charge, in accordance with the ordinary usages of war.[1]

On the 27th of February the British plenipotentiary moved the whole of the establishment of the Superintendent of Trade from Macao to Hong-kong, which now, for the first time, became the seat of the British diplomatic agency in China. He further published a notice to the effect that from that time Hong-kong and Tinghai and their dependencies would be considered free ports; that no duties, customs, or other charges would be levied at either of them on vessels or cargoes of any nationality whatever; and that the protection of the British flag would be afforded to all ships desirous of trading at Amoy.[2] He further informed the British community of the steps he had taken to prevent the Chinese adding to their defences, and requested any person who might notice the assemblage of workmen in the neighbourhood of the forts, or any other suspicious circumstance, to inform him of the fact at the earliest opportunity.[3] His next step was to take measures for the development of Hong-kong as a British possession, by appointing a committee to sell and allot plots of land and to mark out roads and lay out the site of a settlement, as well as choose sites for barracks, cantonments, and a naval depot and dockyard.[4] To facilitate trading operations he arranged for the opening of a market, and published a proclamation declaring that the Mexican dollar should be the standard coin, and fixing the rate of exchange at 1,200 cash to the dollar and 533 cash to the rupee.[5] Altogether during his stay at Hong-kong, which lasted until

[1] *Chinese Repository*, vol. xi, pp. 64, 119, 182.
[2] *Ibid.*, vol. xi, pp. 119-120.
[3] *Ibid.*, p. 182.
[4] *Ibid.*, pp. 184, 240.
[5] *Ibid.*, pp. 240, 296.

13th of June,[1] he laid the foundations of a well-organized British community.

At Peking the war party and the peace party had long been striving for the mastery. By the end of 1841 the former had prevailed and the imperial commands had gone forth that the fighting should be continued. An imperial edict was issued announcing that Yihking had been appointed "majesty-bearing generalissimo," and Tih-e-shun and Wan-wei, "joint assistant high ministers to lead and direct the veteran troops from every region, and with promptitude to advance and exterminate." Strict orders were given that the troops in passing through the country should not be allowed to molest the inhabitants in the smallest degree, and the villagers were exhorted to combine together for self-defence against robbers and disorderly persons. The avenues of official promotion were thrown open to those who should distinguish themselves in serving against the enemy, and a general amnesty and pardon was promised to all who had aided the British if they returned to their allegiance.[2] This last provision was especially directed at the large numbers of Chinese, who were settling in Hong-kong and placing themselves under British protection. Even at that early date the native population realized that there were advantages attending residence under British jurisdiction that they looked for in vain from their own Government.[3]

The ascendancy of the war party at the capital bore immediate fruit in the neighbourhood of Ningpo, where the British expeditionary forces were spending the winter. Garrisons of Tartars and Chinese were thrown into the cities of Yuyau, Tsz'ki, and Funghwa, to deter the villagers from furnishing supplies to the British or acknowledging their authority. At the end of December, the weather having

[1] *Chinese Repository*, vol. xi, p. 397.

[2] *Ibid.*, vol. x, pp. 683–4.

[3] By the end of May, 1842, the population of the new British town on Hong-kong had reached 12,000, and £6,000 had been received for the sale and leasing of plots of land. When the island was first occupied the population of the three Chinese villages was about 4,000. (Loch, *Events in China*, p. 19.)

become frosty and better suited to military operations, Sir Hugh Gough led an expedition against these three places, all of which were captured, after some fighting, without any loss to the British. The alarm created by this advance was shown by the fact that the imperial commissioners, who were at Hangchow, some 100 miles distant, fled incontinent to Soochow, some ninety miles further to the north.[1] This success deterred the Chinese from active hostilities for the next two months, but during the whole of February intelligence kept reaching the British commanders that active operations were under consideration. On the 10th of March, when General Gough and Admiral Parker had gone over to Chusan to make arrangements for a forward movement, which the advent of spring now rendered possible, some 10,000 or 12,000 Chinese troops attacked Ningpo and Chinhai, but were repulsed with great loss.[2] The British followed up this success by storming the heights of Sagaon, near Tsz'ki, twenty miles from Ningpo, where they destroyed the enemy's camp and barracks and a great quantity of military stores. In this engagement the Chinese lost a thousand killed, whilst the attacking force had only three men killed and twenty-two wounded.[3] On the 18th of May the offensive operations were extended to Chapu, which was captured with the loss of nine killed and fifty wounded. Here again the Chinese losses must have been very heavy, as the British buried from 1,200 to 1,500 of their dead. A vast quantity of warlike material was taken and destroyed, including eighty or ninety guns, as well as a gunpowder factory and several arsenals.[4]

At this time the British forces in China consisted of the 18th (Royal Irish), 26th (Cameronians), the 49th and 55th, the Madras Rifle Company (36th N.I.), the 37th Madras Native Infantry, and a detachment of the Bengal Volunteer Regiment, besides sappers, miners, and artillery. The naval

[1] *Chinese Repository*, vol. xi, pp. 179–81.
[2] *Ibid.*, pp. 233–4.
[3] *Ibid.*, pp. 235, 496–504.
[4] *Ibid.*, pp. 342–4.

force was made up of the *Blenheim* (72), *Herald* (26), *Nimrod* (18), *Cruizer* (18), *Royalist* (10), *Young Hebe* (schooner), and the two armed steamers *Hoogly* and *Ariadne*, all of which were off the Canton river early in 1842; the *Druid* (44), *Pylades* (18), *Chameleon* (10), and *Starling* (6), off Amoy; *Cornwallis* (72), *Clio* (16), and *Jupiter* (troopship), off Chusan; the *Blonde* (44), *Modeste* (18), *Hyacinth* (18), *Pelican* (18), *Columbine* (18), *Algerine* (10), *Lady Bentinck* (surveying vessel), and the armed steamers *Nemesis*, *Queen*, *Sesostris*, and *Phlegethon*, off Chinai and Ningpo. These were being added to by rëinforcements,[1] until in June there were reported to be 10,000 bayonets, several companies of artillery, one of cavalry, and one or two of riflemen on the military side, whilst on the naval were 100 sail of all kinds, of which twenty were steamers and forty or fifty men-of-war.[2]

Having destroyed the stores captured at Chapu, the expeditionary forces advanced to the Rugged Islands, and thence to Woosung, where they arrived on the 13th of June. Here they found immense lines of works, which had been erected by the Chinese to defend the entrances to the Yang-tsze and Whangpoo rivers. On the 16th of June, when the British ships were taking up their positions for the attack, the Chinese opened fire. For two hours the cannonade was of the fiercest, but, as the enemy's fire then began to slacken, the British landed parties of seamen and marines, and these in a very short time had taken the batteries by storm. Two hundred and fifty-three guns were captured, of which forty-two were of brass, all well mounted and fitted with bamboo sights. Proceeding up the river the expedition captured many other guns. No real resistance was made by the Chinese. Altogether 364 guns, seventy-six of them being of brass, and most of them large and handsome pieces of ordnance, were taken at and above Woosung. Some of these bore in Chinese characters the name "Tamer and Subduer of the Barbarians." One

[1] A brigade under Lord Saltoun had reached the Cape of Good Hope in March. (Loch, *Events in China*, p. 1.)

[2] *Chinese Repository*, vol. xi, pp. 114, 296, 344.

was designated simply "The Barbarian."[1] The importance of this defeat was fully realized by the Chinese. They summed up the situation in the words, "The Great Wall of China is broken down."[2]

On the 19th of June the expedition moved forward against Shanghai, which now, for the first time, came within the scope of our activity in the East. The Chinese did not attempt to hold it, and very shortly after the advance had been begun, Sir Hugh Gough was able to occupy the native city. With three regiments he took up his quarters in the gardens of the Ching-huang Temple. The Viceroy Niu, to whom fell the duty of reporting to the Throne the progress and successes of the British, was careful in his despatches not to minimise his own efforts on behalf of his country. In his memorial to the Emperor he described how he had braved the hottest of the fight "on the battle-field, where cannon balls innumerable, flying in awful confusion through the expanse of Heaven, fell before, behind, and on either side of him, while in the distance he saw the ships of the rebels, standing erect, lofty as the mountains. The fierce daring of the rebels was inconceivable. Officers and men fell at their posts. Every effort to resist and check the onset was in vain, and a retreat became inevitable."[3]

When Shanghai had been occupied, the expedition moved towards the Grand Canal and attacked Chinkiang.[4] The fighting here was more severe than on any previous occasion, and owing to the intense heat was carried on under the greatest difficulties. The gate of the town was blown up with gunpowder and the fortifications carried by storm on July 21st. Thirteen days later the British fleet got under way for Nanking, which is regarded by the Chinese as the capital of the whole of Southern China. On the 9th of August Nanking was

[1] *Chinese Repository*, vol. xi, pp. 397–8. The despatches relating to this action will be found in the *Chinese Repository*, vol. xii, pp. 287–94.

[2] *Ibid.*, vol. xiii, p. 256.

[3] *Ibid.*, vol. xi, pp. 455–6.

[4] The despatches relating to the occupation of Shanghai and Chinkiang will be found in the *Chinese Repository*, vol. xii, pp. 341, 464.

surrendered without resistance, and the Chinese authorities signified their readiness to discuss terms of peace. It has already been mentioned that in March, after the unsuccessful attacks by the Chinese on Chinhai and Ningpo, the Emperor had re-appointed Ilipu to office, having by this time learnt that the misfortunes of that official might have been due not altogether to "excessive timidity."[1] Hence it was that on reaching Nanking Sir Henry Pottinger found Ilipu joined with Kiying as representing the Emperor. With them and the Viceroy, Niu Kien, negotiations for peace were opened at their request. On the 13th of August these two officials memorialized the Throne that the demands of the British plenipotentiary be granted. The terms of the memorial are very instructive, as showing the circumstances (as they were represented to the Emperor) under which our first treaty with China was signed. Those terms were as follows :—

"1st. The said barbarians begged that we should give them twenty-one millions of dollars. On examination it is found that the said barbarians originally wanted to extort thirty millions of dollars ; but Chang and his colleagues argued the point strongly again and a third time, and at length the sum was fixed at twenty-one millions of dollars. They said that six millions was the price of the opium, three millions for the Hong Merchants' debts, and twelve millions for the expenses of the army. The *shiwei*[2] Changhi and his colleagues repeated that the price of the opium, six millions of dollars, had already been paid by the city of Canton : how could payment be extorted a second time ? And the debts of the Hong Merchants should be liquidated by themselves : how could the officers of government be called upon to pay them ? As to the necessary expenses of the army, why should China be called upon to pay them ? And these matters were discussed again and again. The said barbarians exclaimed that opium was not produced in England, but that it was all sent forth from a neighbouring country : that upwards of twenty thousand chests had been destroyed, and it required no small sum to

[1] *Chinese Repository*, vol. xi, p. 570.
[2] An officer of the Emperor's body-guard.

pay for them; the six millions that had been paid did not amount to half the prime cost; and therefore the deficiency must now be supplied."[1]

Having despatched this memorial, the commissioners appointed the following day for a preliminary discussion of terms of peace. Accordingly, on the 14th August, Major Malcolm went ashore with Morrison and Thom, and having inspected the Emperor's commission to satisfy himself as to its genuineness, he produced his own patent, by which he had been appointed Secretary of Legation, and the discussion of the terms began. A skeleton treaty was drafted in duplicate, one being kept by the Chinese and the other by Major Malcolm, who returned to Sir Henry and laid the draft before him for his approval, after arranging for an interview between the Commissioners and the British plenipotentiary, at which the draft might be considered.[2]

On the 26th of August, the day set apart for discussing the terms of peace, Sir Henry with his suite, among whom were the three interpreters Morrison, Gutzlaff, and Thom, proceeded up the river to Nanking in the admiral's barge, and was received by the Chinese Commissioners with all the courtesy of which they were capable. The place of meeting was decorated with scarlet cloth, in the manner customary with the Chinese, and bands of Chinese musicians discoursed Chinese music, while tea and sweetmeats were served as a preliminary to the business on which those present had come together. Sir Henry had to submit to that embarrassing feature of the best Chinese hospitality, namely, being fed by the host himself. The scene is thus described in the words of a British naval officer who was present:—

"A more tolerable band than we had yet heard commenced, as we sat down, a tune resembling a pibroch, and continued to play throughout the repast. Young white-buttoned officers handed round tea, hot wine, and sweetmeats, while a conversation upon general subjects was maintained between

[1] *Chinese Repository*, vol. xi, pp. 571–2.
[2] Captain Loch: *Closing Events of the Campaign in China*, p. 152.

the Commissioners and Sir Henry through the medium of the interpreters.

"Numerous patties of minced meat, pork, arrowroot, vermicelli soup with meat in it, pig's-ear soup, and other strange dishes, were served in succession, in small china and silver basins, and in proportion to our various capabilities in making these messes disappear we seemed to rise in the estimation of the beholders. But human nature could not support this ordeal long, and, as a *coup de grâce*, Kiying insisted upon Sir Henry opening his mouth, while he with great dexterity shot into it several immense sugar-plums. I shall never forget Sir Henry's face of determined resignation after he found remonstrances were of no avail, nor the figure of Kiying, as he stood planted before him, in the attitude of a short-sighted old lady threading a needle, poising the *bonne bouche* between his finger and thumb preparatory to his successful throw.

"After this the tables were cleared, and the business commenced. The demands, written in both languages, were again read: and, with the exception at first of a slight demur to our detention of Chusan as a guaranty until the full payment of the 21,000,000 of dollars, and a wish to exclude Fuchau-fu from free trade, were unanimously agreed to. The Commissioners were made perfectly to understand that the final settlement of the tariff, residence of English families in the various towns and their vicinities, the future management of commerce through our own consuls, and the entire abolition of the Hong monopoly, were points only delayed in consequence of the time it would require to discuss their minutiæ in detail, but that they were of such vital importance that if, when they were brought forward, any procrastination or refusal should occur, it would effectually interrupt the amity so auspiciously commenced between the two empires.

"None of the critical examination into phrases or expressions, so keenly canvassed and suspiciously viewed by European diplomatists, occupied a moment of their attention. All their anxiety, which was too powerful to be concealed, was centred upon the one main object, our immediate departure; in consequence, almost in the same breath with their assent, they requested the plenipotentiary to remove the ships away from the canals, and to send them down the river. To this the envoy replied that, upon the treaty being signed the blockade would be removed, and when the last dollar of the first instalment of six millions was paid, every town and fort within the Yang-tse-kiang would be delivered back into their hands."[1]

Without waiting for the Emperor's sanction, the Imperial Commissioners signed a treaty. This auspicious event took place on the 29th of August, 1842, at Nanking, on board the British flag-ship, H.M.S. *Cornwallis*. "It was expected," says an eye-witness, "that Ilipu would not attend, as he was very sick. Their Excellencies Kiying and Niu Kien arrived without him, and were conducted into the after-cabin, where a grand tiffin was laid out. After they had been seated about half an hour, Ilipu made his appearance in his own boat, and was obliged to be carried up the side of the ship in a chair. Their Excellencies, Sir Henry, the Admiral and General, went out and met him, and supported him into the cabin (for he could not walk by himself) and laid him on a couch, and they forthwith set to work, that he should not be tired. The treaty was first sealed with Sir Henry's seal by Mr. Morrison as his secretary, and by Wang Tajin, Kiying's secretary, with the seal of the Imperial High Commissioners. The table was then drawn up for each of their Excellencies to put his signature to the treaty. This was done—Kiying, Ilipu, and Niu Kien each signed it; and lastly, Sir Henry. The signature of the three former personages was not done with characters, but with a private mark or rubric.[2] After they had signed it, they sat down to the table and took refreshments; and then a royal salute of twenty-one guns was fired: and a yellow flag for China, and the Union Jack for England, were hoisted at the main and mizzen of the *Cornwallis*."[3]

[1] Captain Loch: *Closing Events of the Campaign in China*, pp. 170–3.

[2] This must mean with their private seals. In China sealing is effected by first placing the seal on a red pad and then printing off an impression in red on the document to which the seal is to be set.

[3] *Chinese Repository*, vol. xi, p. 575.

The treaty was at once despatched to Peking for ratification by the Emperor, which was immediately given. An exchange of prisoners was sanctioned, and an amnesty declared in favour of all Chinese who had assisted the British forces.[1] As soon as the ratification was received from Peking the treaty was sent to London to be ratified by Queen Victoria.[2] But although concluded with much expedition, it was not by any means accepted with feelings of joy by the Chinese. A sense of humiliation was the prevailing feeling in the capital. The lower classes, who form the vast majority of the population of China, appeared to regard it with the indifference they usually display towards matters of state. The better class, to whom the term "gentry" is applied by some English and American writers, who miss the exquisite humour of such an application of the word, gave vent to their opinion in no uncertain terms. In a manifesto published at Canton they thus expressed themselves :—

"We have been reverently consulting upon the empire, a vast and undivided whole! How can we permit it to be severed in order to give it to others? Yet we, the rustic people, can learn to practise a rude loyalty; we too know how to destroy the banditti and thus requite His Majesty. Our Great Pure dynasty has cared for this country more than two hundred years, during which a succession of distinguished monarchs, sage succeeding sage, has reigned; and we, who eat the herb of the field, and tread the soil, have for ages drunk in the dew of imperial goodness, and been imbued with its benevolence. The people, in wilds far remote beyond our influence, have also felt this goodness, comparable to the heavens for height, and being upheld by this bounty, like the earth for thickness. Wherefore peace being now settled in the country, ships of all lands come, distant though they be from this for many a myriad of miles; and of all the Foreigners on the south and west there is not one but what

[1] *Chinese Repository*, vol. xi, p. 629.

[2] The Ratifications were exchanged at Hong-kong on the 26th June, 1843.

enjoys the highest peace and contentment, and entertains the profoundest respect and submission.[1]

"But there is that English nation, whose ruler is now a woman and then a man, its people at one time like birds and then like beasts, with dispositions more fierce and furious than the tiger or the wolf, and hearts more greedy than the snake or hog—this people has ever stealthily devoured all the southern barbarians, and like the demon of the night they now suddenly exalt themselves. During the reigns of Kienlung and Kiaking these English barbarians humbly sought entrance and permission to make a present; they also presumptuously requested to have Chusan, but those divine personages, clearly perceiving their traitorous designs, gave them a peremptory refusal. From that time, linking themselves in with traitorous traders, they have privily dealt at Macao, trading largely in opium, and poisoning our brave people. They have ruined lives—how many millions none can tell; and wasted property—how many thousands of millions who can guess! They have dared again and again to murder Chinese, and have secreted the murderers, whom they refuse to deliver up, at which the hearts of all men grieved and their heads ached. Thus it has been that, for many years past, the English, by their privily watching for opportunities in the country, have gradually brought things to the present pass."[2]

[1] The reference here is to such countries as Siam, Burmah, Thibet, etc.
[2] *Chinese Repository*, vol. xi, p. 630.

CHAPTER XXIII

THE TREATY OF NANKING

It has been the wont of the nations of Christendom to insist that those of their subjects who reside within the territorial limits of countries of imperfect civilization shall be exempt, in certain respects, from the operations of the laws to which the natives of those countries render obedience. To the extent of this exemption such subjects are governed by the laws of their own nation, administered through tribunals constituted by the sovereign to whom they naturally owe allegiance, who thus enjoys an increase of jurisdiction, exercised beyond the limits of his own dominions, and obtained at the expense of the sovereign in derogation of whose authority such exemption has been claimed. In law the persons so governed are regarded as outside the territory in which they, in fact, have their residence, and for this reason the rights enjoyed by them are said to be exterritorial. The term exterritoriality, or extra-territoriality,[1] is used to denote the general principle on which such rights are based.

In all but savage countries, ambassadors and diplomatic persons have now received exterritorial rights, which in most cases have been accorded by the comity of nations.[2] As regards persons, who have no diplomatic status, exterritoriality, where it now exists, is founded in almost every case on special treaties called capitulations, to the terms of which we must look, if we wish to know the exact nature of the exterritorial rights enjoyed in the countries with which such treaties have been negotiated. Still, it must not be supposed that these

[1] Some writers use the term exterritorial only in describing the rights enjoyed by such subjects, and reserve the term extra-territorial to describe the increase of jurisdiction so acquired by their sovereign (see Pigott: *Exterritoriality*). The two words are commonly used by writers on International Law as convertible terms. (See the works of Wheaton, Holland, and Hall.)

[2] In China these were not conferred until 1860, when the Treaty of Tientsin was approved.

peculiar privileges had their origin in definitive conventions. Historically the principle can be traced back to simple grants, made by sovereigns of their own motion to foreigners, who came to reside within their dominions for the purposes of trade. The first known instance of such a grant is that made by the Greek Emperors of Constantinople to the Warings, or Varingians, in the ninth or tenth century. Later, similar grants were made to the Venetians, the Amalfians, the Genoese and the Pisans at that capital. These grants were not revoked when Constantinople was taken by the Turks in 1453.[1] The first capitulations were the treaties made between France and Turkey by Francis I with Soliman the Magnificent in 1528 and 1535, the provisions of which seem in some measure to be founded on usages, that had been in vogue in the ports of the Levant since the time of the Crusades.[2] The treaties between Great Britain and China, in so far as they grant or confirm to British subjects exterritorial rights, must be classed among the capitulations; but in China, too, such rights have their origin in the simple grants of the "usual privileges," made in the early days of British intercourse.

The Treaty of Nanking was not the product of scientific draughtsmanship. Its provisions were thrown together without regard to logical sequence. Hence a discussion of those provisions is best conducted, if the various matters, to which they relate, are noticed in an order different from that in which they there appear. The Treaty commences with one of those harmony clauses, which are common form in agreements signed on the termination of hostilities between two powers. It declared that thenceforward there should be peace and friendship between the Queen of Great Britain and the Emperor of China, and between their respective subjects, a declaration which, in the light of subsequent events, can hardly be considered to have been literally fulfilled. It also laid down that the subjects of each sovereign should enjoy

[1] Ilbert: *Government of India*, chap. vii, p. 416; Introduction by J. Theodore Bent to *Early Voyages and Travels in the Levant* (published by the Hakluyt Society).

[2] Rivier: *Principes du Droit des Gens*.

full security and protection for their persons and property within the dominions of the other. Though we may claim that this stipulation has been faithfully observed on our part, the breaches on the part of the Chinese, even if sometimes excusable, have been many and flagrant. It is in virtue of this stipulation that the British Government claims the right to demand reparation in cases of injury to British subjects or their property in China.

The next provision of the Treaty was one of the utmost importance. By it the whole system of intercourse previously in vogue, the degrading conditions under which trade had been carried on, and the restriction of British commerce to the single port of Canton, were swept into oblivion. The five ports of Canton, Amoy, Foochow, Ningpo, and Shanghai, selected as being the most suitable and profitable centres of trade, which had come under the notice of the few Englishmen who had obtained a knowledge of China outside the province of Kwang-tung, and all of which, except Shanghai, had before the year 1760 been the resort of Foreign merchants, were thrown open to trade. It was provided that British subjects, with their families and establishments, might reside for the purpose of carrying on their mercantile pursuits at each of these cities and towns without molestation or restraint. Thus the old system under which continuous residence at Canton had been forbidden, and the wives and families of Foreigners compelled to remain at Macao, was for ever abolished. In its place was substituted the free and unrestrained residence at the five Treaty Ports, as they came to be called, which has resulted in the settlement of European communities at the many Open Ports where they are found to-day.[1]

[1] The number of the Treaty Ports has since been increased by the addition of Newchwang, Chefoo, Taiwan (in Formosa), Swatow, Kiungchow, and Tientsin, which were thrown open under the Treaty of Tientsin, and the Convention by which that treaty was confirmed in 1860. Various other places, some on the coast and some inland, have since been opened by the Chinese Government, either in pursuance of treaty stipulations or voluntarily, and put on the same footing as the original Five Ports. As some of these, viz., Woosung, Santu-ao, Yochow, Chin-wang-tao, Chinan-fu, Wei-hsien and Choutshu, have been voluntarily thrown open, it is becoming more common to employ

By one of the later articles of the Treaty, which should be noticed here, it was provided that the Emperor of China should establish at the Five Ports a fair and regular tariff of export and import customs and other dues. Such a tariff, together with a set of General Regulations under which British trade at the Treaty Ports was to be carried on,[1] was drawn up after discussion between the Chinese Commissioners and Sir Henry Pottinger, and in order that there might be no cause of dispute left over, the tariff and General Regulations as thus agreed were confirmed by a Supplementary Treaty, which was signed at the Bogue on the 8th of October, 1843. In discussing the rights acquired by British subjects in China at the close of the First War, we have, therefore, to take into account the provisions of this Supplementary Treaty, as well as those of the Treaty which was signed at Nanking. It must be borne in mind, however, that there is this difference between the two documents: the Treaty of Nanking is binding on the high contracting parties to-day, having been confirmed by the Treaty of Tientsin in 1858. The Supplementary Treaty was abrogated in 1858, though many of its provisions still obtain by virtue of having been incorporated in the Treaty of Tientsin.[2]

The conditions under which British subjects were allowed to reside at the Five Ports were elaborated in the Supplementary

the term "Open Ports" to denote all those places in China at which Foreigners can trade or reside. Of course among these are not included such places as Hong-kong, Port Arthur, Wei-hai-wei, Kiao-chao, and Macao, which have passed from the dominion of the Emperor. See *post*, p. 548.

[1] These are given in Hertslet: *Commercial Treaties*, vol. vi, pp. 234–43.

[2] The Chinese and the English versions of the Treaty of Nanking and of the Supplementary Treaty will be found in the *Chinese Repository*, vol. xiii, pp. 438–46; 449–66. The English versions are given in Hertslet: *Commercial Treaties*, vol. vi, pp. 221–7; 262–70. The English version of the Treaty of Nanking is given in Mayers: *Treaties between China and Foreign Powers*: also in the *Hong-kong Chronicle and Directory for China, Japan, and the Straits Settlements*. The Treaty of Tientsin is given by Hertslet and by Mayers, and in the *Hong-kong Chronicle and Directory*. Of the above only Hertslet gives the *General Regulations*.

Treaty, where it was specifically laid down that they should not resort to any other port or place in China, and that the Chinese at other ports and places should not trade with them. It was agreed that the British plenipotentiary should publish at Hong-kong a proclamation, calling on British subjects to observe these conditions, and that the Chinese officers should be at liberty to seize and confiscate any British vessels with their cargoes found guilty of infringing them.[1] It was further provided that British merchants and others, residing at or resorting to the Treaty Ports, should not go into the surrounding country beyond certain short distances to be fixed by the local officials in concert with the British consul, and on no pretence for the purposes of traffic. With a view to preventing any such disturbance as that in which Lin Wei-hi lost his life, it was agreed that seamen and others belonging to ships should be subject to special regulations with regard to landing, which should be drawn up by the consul in conjunction with the local officials. Any person found infringing these stipulations and wandering into the country might be seized and handed over to the British consul for suitable punishment.[2]

In arriving at a settlement of the vexed question of the means of communication between British subjects and Chinese officials, it was decided to extend to each of the Treaty Ports the system which the China Trade Act had created for Canton. In the language of the Treaty, it was agreed that "Her Majesty the Queen of Great Britain will appoint Superintendents or Consular officers, to reside at each of the above-named cities

[1] *Supplementary Treaty*, Art. v.

[2] *Supplementary Treaty*, Art. vi. Hence it has become customary when a fresh port or place is thrown open to Foreigners, for the Chinese officials to confer with the Foreign Consuls at the nearest Open Port, or with the Foreign Ministers at Peking, in fixing the limits within which the privileges granted by treaty as to residence and the acquisition of land may be enjoyed. These limits no longer mark the bounds beyond which Foreigners may not go into the surrounding country, for by the Treaty of Tientsin it was agreed that British subjects might travel to all parts of the interior for the purposes of pleasure or trade, under passports issued by their consuls and countersigned by the Chinese authorities, and that no passport need be applied for by a person going on an excursion from any of the ports open to trade to a distance not exceeding 100 *li* (33 miles) and for a period not exceeding five days.

or towns, to be the medium of communication between the Chinese authorities and the said merchants."[1] If any British subject had a complaint against a Chinese, he was to proceed to the Consul at his port and state his grievance. The Consul would then inquire into the merits of the case and do his best to arrange it amicably. If it were necessary that the British subject should address the Chinese authorities, he was to do so through the Consul, who must either see that becoming language was employed, or refuse to convey the address.[2] Thus in the person of the British consular officer was combined, so far as his particular area was concerned, functions similar to those of the Superintendent of Trade and of the Hong Merchants combined.

The system thus inaugurated, of making the British Consul at each Treaty Port the medium of communication between British subjects and the Chinese officials, has been maintained to the present day, and has been copied by every nation that has consular representatives in China. In this respect the subjects of each of the high contracting parties to the Treaty of Nanking do not enjoy like privileges in the dominions of the other. In every part of the British Empire[3] Chinese may sue British subjects in the Courts of Justice, and the necessity for the intervention of any official is avoided. In China there are no tribunals, with the exception of the Mixed Court at Shanghai, to which British subjects have access.[4] Any complaint against a Chinese subject, any claim for debt or damages preferred by a British subject, has to be laid before

[1] *Treaty of Nanking*, Art. ii.

[2] *General Regulations*, Art. xiii. Hertslet: *Commercial Treaties*, vol. vi, pp. 243–248.

[3] For the time being there is an exception in the Transvaal. Labourers imported under the Ordinance of 1903 have to lay their complaint before the inspectors of the mines, who report to the Superintendent of Labour. The latter has a discretion as to whether he will or will not make the complaint the subject of proceedings in the Courts.

[4] During the Boxer troubles the Tientsin Provisional Government, which was organized for the administration of the territory occupied by the European troops, instituted a Court for Chinese defendants, presided over by an American, which worked with great success.

the Consul, who then makes a representation on the subject to the Taotai, the Chinese official of equal rank. The Taotai then takes such steps as he thinks proper in the interest of the complainant. If these are not of such a nature as to obtain satisfaction, the only remedy is to get the Consul to make further representations, either personally or through the British Minister at Peking. When the latter course is adopted the Minister, if he thinks the matter deserves his intervention, brings it before the Wai-wu-pu,[1] who may or may not see that justice is done. It must be confessed that this system has curious defects ; but so long as China continues to be without tribunals worthy of the name of courts of justice, it is difficult, if not impossible, to devise something that would work better.

The provision, which granted to the Sovereign of Great Britain extra-territorial jurisdiction over her subjects in China, was not contained in the Treaty of Nanking proper, but for some unexplained reason was relegated to the General Regulations. It was there laid down that, if a Chinese have reason to complain of a British subject, the Consul shall listen to his complaint, and endeavour to settle it in a friendly manner, and if the Consul is unable to determine it in this way, he shall request the assistance of a Chinese official, that they may together inquire into the merits of the case and settle it equitably. The same article[2] provided that as regarded the punishment of criminals, the British Government would enact the laws necessary to that end, and the Consul should be empowered to put them into force. Thus the whole principle of exterritoriality, which was the real issue involved in the dispute as to the punishment of the murderer of Lin Wei-hi, was conceded in a few words.[3]

[1] This is the Board of Foreign Affairs, which now exercises the functions of the old Tsung-li-Yamên.

[2] *General Regulations*, Art. xiii.

[3] This question was not left so clear as could have been wished. It seems not to have occurred to anyone, that where a British subject was defendant to a civil claim, it was advisable that the matter in question should be determined by English law. Nothing was said about civil claims brought by one British subject against another, or between British subjects and subjects of some other European state. These defects have since been made good. See *post*, pp. 557–8.

Although a means of communication between British subjects and Chinese was provided for in the Treaty, by the establishment of a system of Consuls at each port, no adequate steps were taken to inaugurate a proper system of diplomatic intercourse between the sovereigns of Great Britain and China.[1] It was only in defining the mode in which intercourse between British and Chinese officials should be conducted that, by implication, the right to communicate with the authorities at Peking was conceded. By the article of the Treaty which deals with this question,[2] it was agreed that "Her Majesty's Chief Officer in China," by which presumably was meant the Plenipotentiary and Chief Superintendent of Trade at Hong-kong, should "correspond" with the "Chinese High Officers, both at the Capital and in the Provinces," under the term "communication," and that subordinate British officers, by which presumably was meant Consular representatives, should communicate with Chinese High Officers in the Provinces under the term "statement" on the part of the former and "declaration" on the part of the latter. The subordinates of both nationalities were to communicate on a footing of equality. Merchants and others having no official position were to use the term "representation" in all documents addressed to or intended for official perusal. Thus the old controversy which had raged round the use of the character *Pin* was satisfactorily settled, and the right to use terms denoting an absolute equality between British and Chinese expressly recognised. The Hong Merchants were abolished, and communications from the officials of one country to those of the other were to be sent direct to the officers to whom they were addressed.

It next became necessary to decide what was to be done

[1] It was not until the Convention confirming the Treaty of Tientsin was signed in 1860, that Great Britain, or any Foreign Power, obtained the right to have at Peking a diplomatic representative properly accredited to the Emperor of China. Until that time the Chief Superintendent of Trade carried on from Hong-kong as best he was able such intercourse as took place between the two Governments. (See *Treaty of Tientsin*, Arts. ii and iii, and *Convention*, Art. ii.)

[2] *Treaty of Nanking*, Art. xi.

with Hong-kong. It was not likely that the British, who were still in possession, would wish to hand it back to China: it was equally improbable that they would be content to hold it on some such tenure as that on which the Portuguese were allowed to hold Macao. Moreover, it was foreseen that steam power was destined to revolutionize maritime commerce, and that if British trade were to be carried on in the future to the utmost advantage, the possession of a coaling station in the China seas was indispensable. The success of the iron steamers, such as the *Nemesis*, in the recent hostilities had shown, too, that the days of the old three-decker, and of wooden ships and sailing ships generally, in naval warfare were numbered, so that for strategic purposes it was necessary that Great Britain should have a naval base somewhere in the China seas. There was this difficulty, however, in the way of a cession to Great Britain, that to yield up a piece of Chinese territory, as having been acquired by the barbarians by right of conquest, would have entailed an irreparable "loss of face"[1] to the Emperor and his ministers. It therefore became the duty of the British plenipotentiary to demonstrate to the Chinese commissioners that in the altered circumstances of peace and friendship, which were to prevail between Great Britain and China in the future, it would only be natural and in accordance with this spirit of amity that the British merchants, who would be trading in China, should have some place to call their own and to use as a commercial centre. It was for reasons such as these that the clause of the treaty dealing with the cession of Hong-kong was drawn in the somewhat curious form in which we find it, which is as follows: "It being obviously necessary and desirable that British subjects should have some port whereat they may careen and refit their ships when required, and keep stores for that purpose, His Majesty the Emperor of China cedes to Her Majesty the Queen of Great Britain the island of Hong-kong, to be possessed in perpetuity by Her Britannic

[1] As to "loss of face," and the importance attached to that consideration in China, see Dr. Arthur Smith: *Chinese Characteristics*, p. 16.

Majesty, her heirs and successors, and to be governed by such laws and regulations as Her Majesty the Queen of Great Britain shall see fit to direct."[1] Thus the face of the Chinese was saved, while disputes such as had arisen, as to the tenure on which the Portuguese held Macao, were for ever obviated.

Some of the most important provisions of the Treaty are those that regulate the manner in which trade between British and Chinese merchants was to be conducted. The grievances under which the former had laboured in trading at Canton were of very long standing, and were of such a nature that they would probably in course of time have led to hostilities, even if the question of the opium traffic had never arisen at all. Now that war had been entered upon and concluded, the opportunity was used to deal with these grievances in a manner satisfactory to those having commercial interests in China. The terms in which this was done amount to a complete emancipation of the Foreign merchants. As indicated above, the Co-hong monopoly was abolished, and the method of communicating with Chinese officials, when difficulties arose, was determined by the treaty in a manner that was agreeable to both parties. Moreover the Consoo charge, the measurement duty, and all the other impositions that had burdened commerce at Canton were abolished, as well as the practice of requiring a security merchant for every vessel that came into port. In their place was introduced a system of port regulations, customs and duties, of such a kind and administered in such a manner that Englishmen could conform to them without loss of self-respect.

The abolition of the Co-hong and the payment of the debts of the bankrupt Hong Merchants were dealt with in one and the same article of the Treaty. The Chinese Government was made to acknowledge that it had compelled the British merchants trading at Canton to deal exclusively with certain merchants, called Hong Merchants, or Co-hong, who had been licensed by the Emperor for that purpose. With this prefatory declaration the Emperor undertook to pay to the British Government $3,000,000, on account of the debts due to

[1] *Treaty of Nanking*, Art. iii.

British subjects from those Hong Merchants who had become insolvent. By way of precaution against any survival of the conditions that had obtained at Canton, it was further stipulated that the Emperor should abolish at all ports, where British subjects might reside, the practice of licensing such a body as the Co-hong, and would allow British subjects to carry on their mercantile transactions with whatever persons they pleased.[1] On the other hand, as a protection to the Chinese Government against any liabilities that might in future be incurred, it was expressly provided in the General Regulations that, from that time forward, if a Chinese debtor absconded, or died, or became bankrupt, the English merchants in such a case could not expect to have their losses made good.[2] Thus the old controversy as to the debts of Hingtai and the other bankrupt Hong Merchants was determined in favour of the British Merchants.

The recovery of debts is bound to present difficulties in a country that has no properly organized judicial tribunals. Some attempt was made to deal with such difficulties in the General Regulations, where it was provided that if a Chinese merchant absconded, the Chinese authorities would do their best to bring him to justice: if, however, the defaulter could not be found, or were dead, or were bankrupt, no responsibility would be assumed for his debts.[3] This was embodied in the Chinese version of the Supplementary Treaty in these words: "Henceforth the cases of debtors—whether of the Chinese merchants to the English, or of the English merchants to the Chinese, if the accounts and vouchers be well authenticated, the persons present, and the property in existence,—shall all be settled by the proper English and Chinese authorities, according to the principles of justice, so as to manifest perfect equality. And according to the original stipulations, both these authorities shall prosecute on behalf of creditors; but in no case shall they be made responsible for them."[4] This is one of those typically Chinese pronouncements

[1] *Treaty of Nanking*, Art. v. [2] *General Regulations*, Art. iv.

[3] *General Regulations*, Art. iv. See Hertslet: *Commercial Treaties*, vol. vi, pp. 234–43.

[4] *Chinese Repository*, vol. xiii, pp. 451–2.

that sound well and mean nothing. In actual experience it is found that no Chinese accounts or vouchers are well authenticated. Chinese arithmetic and book-keeping are not of such a kind as tend to elucidate the accounts between traders. The evidence on which a claim for debt against a Chinese would have to be rested is usually anything but clear. Hence the practice has grown up among Foreign merchants of requiring their compradores, through whom all business is transacted with Chinese, to give security, to which the compradore's employer may have recourse in case of loss arising out of transactions conducted through the compradore, without any appeal to courts of law or any kind of official. This means that commercial intercourse between Foreign merchants and Chinese is still carried on under a system similar in principle to that on which the Co-hong was founded, but without the evils attendant on a monopoly.

One of the evils that had afflicted the trade at Canton was the difficulty of ascertaining what were the duties and customs that merchants were legally bound to pay. It was therefore provided by the Treaty, as already mentioned, that the Emperor should "establish at the Treaty Ports a fair and regular tariff of Export and Import Customs and other dues, which tariff shall be publicly notified and promulgated for general information."[1] Such a tariff was, in fact, drawn up and confirmed by the Supplementary Treaty. It set out a list of articles subject to pay duty, and the rate of the duty was given opposite each of such articles. It further provided that all articles unenumerated in the tariff were to be subject to a duty of five per cent. *ad valorem.*[2] At the end of this tariff was appended a note, which dealt with the question of the measurement duty that had been charged on ships. In this note it was provided that the old system should be changed, and that in future ships should be charged according to the registered number of tons that the ship could carry,

[1] *Treaty of Nanking,* Art. x.

[2] Hertslet: *Commercial Treaties,* vol. vi, pp. 234–43. This was superseded in 1858 by the tariff drawn up in accordance with Articles 26 and 28 of the Treaty of Tientsin. See *post,* p. 541.

at the rate of five mace per ton (reckoned equal to the cubic content of 122 *tow*), and that all the old charges of measurement, entrance, and port-clearance fees, daily and monthly fees, were abolished.[1]

There was one provision of the Treaty of Nanking that has been a constant source of trouble to Foreign merchants, that which recognized the *likin*, or transit duties, levied on imports in the course of their passage into the interior of China. As difficulties still arise in relation to this question, it is important to observe the exact force of the language used, of which the English version runs thus : "The Emperor further engages that when British merchandise shall have once paid at any of the said ports the regulated customs and dues, agreeable to the tariff to be hereafter fixed, such merchandise may be conveyed by Chinese merchants to any province or city in the interior of the Empire of China, on paying a further amount as Transit duties, which shall not exceed — per cent. on the tariff value of such goods."[2] Now it is one thing to set such a restriction on the power of an independent sovereign to impose taxes as he pleases within his own territory, and another to enforce the stipulation in which such a restriction is contained. An obligation of this kind is devoid of sanction, save in so far as the sovereign promisor considers himself in honour bound to carry his undertaking into effect. But in such a country as China, where underpaid magistrates have to supplement the meagre pittances paid to them as official salaries by taking toll of such produce or persons as come within their power, it is impossible to prevent abuses in the levying of a duty of this kind. Thus it happens that over and over again Foreign merchants have had to complain that goods, imported by them and forwarded to consignees up country, are detained as security for some illegal exaction, levied by a local magistrate

[1] Small craft plying between Canton, Hong-kong, and Amoy, were to pay no tonnage dues if they carried only passengers and letters ; if they carried cargo they were to pay one mace per ton on a tonnage between 75 and 150 tons. (*Supplementary Treaty*, Art. xvii.)

[2] *Treaty of Nanking*, Art. x.

under the pretence that he is collecting *likin*. In 1903 an arrangement was made with the British Government for the abolition of the whole system, on condition that the other Foreign Powers consented to be bound by the same arrangement.[1] It will be noticed that in the Treaty of Nanking the rate of transit duty was not specific. This omission was made good by a declaration of the British and Chinese plenipotentiaries dated the 26th of June, 1843, which provided that the future amount of such duty to be levied on British merchandise should not exceed the rates then existing, which were declared to be on a moderate scale.[2]

A proper system of customs and duties having been established, it became necessary to devise customs, regulations for their collection, and to prevent smuggling of all kinds. The Chinese accepted the contention that it was their duty to keep out opium and other contraband goods, and to enforce their own revenue laws, and the demand that the British merchants, before being allowed to trade, should give a bond that they had no opium on board, was not put forward. All

[1] See *Treaty of Shanghai*, Art. viii. *Parliamentary Papers, Treaty Series No.* 17 (1903).

[2] Hertslet: *Commercial Treaties*, vol. vi, p. 231; *Chinese Repository*, vol. xiii, p. 655. Nothing could have been more favourable to the growth of abuses in the collection of *likin* than leaving it in this nebulous state. As soon as trade at the Treaty Ports was established, disputes began to arise. One source of difficulty was that British merchants could never obtain any accurate information as to the amount of *likin* payable on a given consignment of goods, before despatching such consignment into the interior. To remedy this cause of complaint the Treaty of Tientsin provided that at any open port the authority appointed to superintend the collection of duties shall be obliged, upon an application by a Consul, to declare the amount of duties leviable, in the case of exports, between the place of production and the place of shipment, and in the case of imports between the consular port in question and the inland markets named by the Consul; and that every British subject should have the option of paying a single sum in commutation of all transit duties, in the case of exports at the first barrier they should pass, and in the case of imports at the port where they are landed. (Art. xxviii.) In 1903 the Chinese Government undertook to abolish the whole system of *likin*, the Foreign Powers consenting in return to the imposition of a surtax on Foreign imports and Chinese exports, and to a consumption tax on Chinese products not intended for export. See *Treaty of Shanghai* (1903), Art. viii.

such matters were dealt with in detail in the General Regulations, which were promulgated in July, 1843.[1] The first matter adjusted in this connection was the granting of pilots, about which difficulties had so frequently arisen at Canton, owing to the refusal of the Chinese authorities to supply them, in proper time or on suitable terms. It was provided that, whenever a British merchantman should arrive off any of the five Treaty Ports, pilots should be allowed to take her in, and that on her departure pilots should be granted without delay, as soon as all legal duties and charges should have been settled. To enforce the payment of the legal duties and charges, a Chinese Superintendent of Customs was to be appointed at each of the Five Ports, and to him was assigned the task of adopting proper precautions to prevent the revenue from suffering through fraud or smuggling.[2] It was agreed that when a ship came into port this official should depute one or two "trusty officers" to keep watch over her and to prevent frauds on the revenue.

On the part of the British it was agreed that instructions should be given to the consuls to strictly watch over and scrutinize the conduct of all British subjects trading under their superintendence, and if any instance of smuggling came to their knowledge, to apprise the Chinese officials instantly. All smuggled goods might be seized and confiscated by the Chinese authorities, who might also prohibit from trading or send away any ship from which smuggled goods had been landed.[3] It was further agreed that the master of any British ship trading at a Treaty Port should deposit the ship's papers at the British Consulate within twenty-four hours of arrival, and that the penalty for non-observance of this regulation should be $200. The British Consul, having taken possession of the ship's papers, was to send forthwith a written communication to the Superintendent of Customs, specifying the registered tonnage of the ship and particulars of her cargo, after which permission would be given to unload and the

[1] Hertslet: *Commercial Treaties*, vol. vi, pp. 243–8.
[2] *General Regulations*, Art. ii.
[3] *Supplementary Treaty*, Art. xii.

duties would be levied. For presenting a false manifest the penalty was to be $500 ; for breaking bulk before permission had been granted the penalty was payment of $500 and confiscation of the goods so landed.[1] No vessel would be allowed to leave port until export and import duties had been paid in full, together with the tonnage dues. When these had been paid the Superintendent of Customs would grant a port-clearance, and the British Consul would thereupon return the ship's papers and permit the vessel to depart.[2]

The way in which the amount of the duties to be paid was to be ascertained was thus laid down. An English merchant having cargo to discharge must first hand particulars of the same to the British Consul, who would thereupon send a recognized *linguist* of his own establishment to communicate these particulars to the Superintendent of Customs. The latter would then appoint an official to examine the goods proposed to be landed.

The British merchant was to have a duly qualified representative present, when the examination took place : if no such representative were present, no complaint afterwards made by the merchant would receive attention. If any dispute arose in connection with the examination, the British merchant might appeal to his consul, provided he did so the same day, who would then endeavour to settle the matter amicably with the Superintendent of Customs.[3] To facilitate the payment of duties when levied, it was agreed that "the Superintendent of Customs will select certain shroffs, or banking establishments, of known stability, to whom he will give licences, authorizing them to receive duties from the English merchants on behalf of Government, and the receipt of these shroffs for any money paid them shall be considered as a Government voucher." To prevent disputes as to the rate of exchange between Foreign and Chinese currency, it was provided that this should be fixed by the Superintendent of Customs.[4]

[1] *General Regulations*, Art. iii.
[2] *Ibid.*, Art. vi.
[3] *Ibid.*, Art. vii.
[4] *Ibid.*, Art. viii.

As a precaution against fraudulent weights and measures, which abound in every branch of commerce in China, it was provided that standards "in exact conformity to those hitherto in use at the Custom-House of Canton, and duly stamped and sealed in proof thereof, will be kept in possession of the Superintendent of Customs, and also at the British Consulate at each of the Five Ports, and these shall be the standards by which all duties shall be charged, and all sums paid to Government." In this way it was made certain that the rate of duty fixed by the tariff should not be surreptitiously increased by lessening the standards of weight and measure for goods, or increasing those for silver, a contingency that the British community knew, from experience, might easily happen.

The other matters dealt with in the General Regulations were of minor importance. It was agreed that there should be no transhipment of goods at any Treaty Port without permission of the Customs authorities. The reason for this provision was that the Chinese officials, who regard commerce primarily from the point of view of men who have to miss no opportunity of raising a revenue, tax both exports and imports, in defiance of all the laws of political economy, and, when goods are transhipped, they insist on both import and export duties being charged at the port of transhipment. If after being so transhipped the goods are carried on to another Chinese port and there landed, import duties are again charged; if the same goods are consigned to the interior, *likin* also has to be paid. Thus the revenue benefits to the maximum extent consistent with commerce being not entirely killed.

Seamen and persons connected with ships were not admitted to the same privileges as other British subjects in China. They had not the same unrestricted right of landing at the Treaty Ports. By the General Regulations it was further provided that whenever sailors landed, they must be accompanied by officers, who would be held responsible for any disturbance in which they might take part on shore. At any place selected for the anchorage of British ships, there was to be a subordinate British consular officer, who should exercise control over the seamen and prevent quarrels between them and the natives. If any such disputes should arise, this officer was to do his best to settle them amicably. As a sanction to the regulations provided for the control of British subjects, it was provided that at each of the Treaty Ports should be stationed a British cruiser, so that the Consul might have the power of restraining and preventing disturbances.[1] Finally, it was agreed that, as the old system of having a security merchant for each vessel, through whom duties and port charges were paid, had been abolished, the British Consul should be security for all British ships entering any of the Treaty Ports.[2]

In the Supplementary Treaty the relation, in which Hong-kong was to stand to the dominions of the Emperor of China, as regarded matters of commerce and jurisdiction, was further particularized. It was provided that all persons, whether Chinese or otherwise, who might wish to convey goods from any of the Treaty Ports to Hong-kong, should be at liberty so to do, on paying the export duties and obtaining a port-clearance from the Chinese authorities.[3] It was further laid down that natives of China might freely resort to Hong-kong for the purpose of purchasing goods, and if they required a Chinese vessel to carry away their purchases from Hong-kong, they must obtain a port-clearance at the port of destination, which would be available for one voyage only.[4] An English officer was to be appointed at Hong-kong to examine the registers and port-clearances of all Chinese vessels that might resort thither, and if any were found not to have a port-clearance or register from one of the Five Ports, such vessel was to be regarded as a smuggler, and a report of the circumstances sent to the Chinese authorities.[3] By this regulation it was hoped to prevent piracy and contraband trade. All

[1] *General Regulations*, Art. xiv ; *Supplementary Treaty*, Art. x.

[2] *General Regulations*, Art. xv.

[3] *Supplementary Treaty*, Art. xiii and xiv.

[4] In the Chinese version this permission was stated to be obtainable only at the Treaty Ports, but no such limitations are contained in the words of the English version. (See *Chinese Repository*, vol. xiii, p. 460.)

debts incurred by Chinese in Hong-kong were to be recoverable in the courts of the Colony. If a Chinese debtor absconded and was known to have property within Chinese territory, the matter was to be dealt with in the manner already described for settling the affairs of absconding bankrupts. On the other hand, if an English debtor incurred debts at any of the Treaty Ports and fled to Hong-kong, the British authorities, on receiving an application from the Chinese authorities, accompanied by statements and full proof of the debts, were to investigate the claims and oblige the defaulting debtor to settle such as were established.[1]

The only provisions of the Treaty, which have been left unnoticed above, are the stipulations dealing with questions of amnesty and indemnity. The Chinese Government agreed to pay the sum of $3,000,000 in liquidation of the Hong Merchants' debts. In addition to this, it undertook to pay $6,000,000 as the value of the opium, which was surrendered at Canton in March, 1839,[2] and another $12,000,000 on account of the expenses incurred by the British Government in sending out the military and naval forces. Against these obligations the Chinese Government was to be allowed to set-off any sums paid as ransom for cities or towns in China after the 1st of August, 1841. Of this total of $21,000,000, $6,000,000 were to be paid on the ratification by the Emperor of the Treaty of Nanking, $3,000,000 on the 30th of June, and another $3,000,000 on the 31st of December, 1843, $2,500,000 on the same days of 1844, and $2,000,000 on the same days of 1845. Interest at five per cent. was to be paid on any of these instalments not punctually discharged.[3] On the payment of the first sum of $6,000,000, the British forces were to retire from Nanking and the Grand Canal, the trade of China was to be no longer molested, and the military post at Chinhai was to be withdrawn. As security for the due performance of their treaty obligations, the Chinese agreed that Kulang-su (Amoy) and the Chusan Islands should be continued to be

[1] *Supplementary Treaty*, Art. xv.
[2] *Treaty of Nanking*, Art. iv.
[3] *Ibid.*, Art. vii.

held until the completion of the money payments and of the arrangements for opening the Five Ports to British merchants.[1] For the protection of those Chinese who had afforded supplies or otherwise rendered assistance to the British forces, it was stipulated that the Emperor should grant a general amnesty and indemnity to all Chinese subjects, who had had dealings with, or had entered the service of, the British, and should release all persons who were in confinement on such charges.[2] This undertaking was faithfully performed.

The only provision of the Treaty, to which exception can be taken, is that which compelled the Chinese to pay an indemnity for the opium, which had been surrendered at Canton in 1839. In an earlier chapter reasons have been given to show that the course adopted by Commissioner Lin on that occasion was perfectly justified. For the same reasons the insertion of this stipulation in the Treaty is the one disfigurement in a piece of work, that in all other respects is fair and honourable. The framers of the Treaty seem to have realized that future generations might call in question the justice of insisting on such a payment, and, as if to put the Chinese out of court in any inquiry that might thereafter be held, the Emperor was made to declare expressly, that the opium had been delivered up "as a ransom for the lives of Her Britannic Majesty's Superintendent and subjects, who had been imprisoned and threatened with death by the Chinese high officers."[3] The value of such an admission can be ascertained only by investigating the circumstances under which it was made. When we remember that the Chinese had been hopelessly defeated both by land and by sea, that things had come to such a pass with them that they were obliged to accept whatever terms the victors might think fit to impose, we are bound to say that the words quoted above are worse than useless, if they were intended to show that the demand for payment of the price of the surrendered opium was just.

[1] *Treaty of Nanking*, Art. xii.
[2] *Ibid.*, Art. ix.
[3] *Ibid.*, Art. iv.

The Treaty of Nanking must, as pointed out earlier in this chapter, be classed among the capitulations. It is not, however, merely a capitulation, as the foregoing analysis of its provisions shows. It is that and something more. It is the record of the terms of settlement, agreed between England and China, with reference to all the matters that were in dispute between the two countries from the year 1834 to the time when the Treaty was signed. In the form and nature of its provisions we can trace the effect of each of the forces, that had contributed to bringing about the rupture between the two nations. Taken as a whole, it is the product of the resultant of those forces. It is also the title-deed of the Sovereign of Great Britain to the island of Hong-kong. Last, but not least, it is the instrument by which the Chinese Empire, and indeed, the Far East generally, was thrown open to the influences of Western civilization.

CHAPTER XXIV

SOME TREATY DEVELOPMENTS

THE success of Great Britain, in obtaining for her traders an entry into China at five of the principal ports, on the favourable terms conceded by the Treaty of Nanking, totally changed the attitude of the civilized world to the countries of the Far East. Other Powers at once bestirred themselves to secure some benefit from the hostilities which had been waged by our forces, and hastened to send out plenipotentiaries, who might obtain for their subjects like advantages to those conferred on the British. Profiting by China's fear, that a refusal might entail a war with some other Western power, and by the Chinese view that all Foreign nations were on the same footing, these plenipotentiaries succeeded in procuring in some cases even slightly better terms than had been granted to Sir Henry Pottinger. Now that the pioneer work had been done, they found far less difficulty than he had experienced in negotiating satisfactory terms. That which he had to extract in instalments, embodied in three distinct documents drawn up at different dates, they were able to secure in the form of a single treaty, so much easier was it to obtain concessions now that a precedent had been established.

The first country to succeed in this direction was the United States of America, by whose representative, Mr. Caleb Cushing, and by Kiying on behalf of China, a "treaty or general convention of peace, amity and commerce" was signed at Wanghia, near Macao, on the 3rd of July, 1844.[1] This was immediately followed by a treaty between France and China, which was signed by M. de Lagrané at Whampoa on the 24th of September, 1844, ratified on the 25th of August,

[1] This treaty was ratified at Canton on the 31st December, 1845. For its terms see Mayers: *Treaties between the Empire of China and Foreign Powers*, p. 76. The Chinese text, together with the English version, is given in the *Chinese Repository*, vol. xiv, pp. 558-83, and a translation of the Chinese version at p. 30 of the same volume.

1845, and proclaimed by Louis Philippe at the Tuileries on the 22nd of November in the same year.[1] Belgium had to be content with a rescript of the Emperor permitting her subjects to trade in China on the terms of the treaties already concluded with Great Britain, France, and America, the terms of which were on the 25th of July, 1845, communicated to M. Lannoy, the Belgian Consul-General, by a joint edict of Kiying and the Viceroy.[2] Commissioner Liljewalch, acting on behalf of Sweden and Norway, negotiated a treaty which was signed at Canton on the 20th of March, 1847, and is almost identical in terms with that concluded by America. This was accepted and confirmed by Sweden on the 28th October, 1847.[3] Later on, Russia followed the example of these other powers and negotiated a fresh treaty, which was signed by the Russian plenipotentiary, Kovalevsky, at Kuldja, on the 25th of July, 1851, and ratified by the Czar on the 13th of November.[4] This document, however, is in no sense comparable with the other treaties, to which reference has been made. It dealt only with frontier questions and the overland trade through Siberia, in respect of which Russia was able to obtain for her subjects more favourable conditions than they had previously enjoyed. It conferred no right to trade or reside at any of the Treaty Ports, nor any of the privileges ancillary thereto.

By the French and American treaties the rights of persons residing or sojourning at the Treaty Ports were more clearly and somewhat more largely defined than in the treaties with Great Britain. The provisions of the British treaties, which dealt with this question,[5] were very vaguely worded, and only gave a right to British merchants to reside, with their families and establishments, for the purpose of carrying on their

[1] For the terms of the treaty with France see Mayers: *Treaties between the Empire of China and Foreign Powers*, p. 49. The Chinese text, together with the French version, will be found in the *Chinese Repository*, vol. xv, pp. 10–38, and a translation in English in the *Chinese Repository*, vol. xiv, pp. 41–51.

[2] *Archives Diplomatiques* (1861), T. 1, p. 319.

[3] The terms of this treaty are given by Mayers at p. 128.

[4] The terms are given by Mayers, p. 97.

[5] *Treaty of Nanking*, Art. ii; *Supplementary Treaty*, Art. vii.

mercantile pursuits, without molestation or restraint, whilst providing that ground and houses, the rent of which should be equitably arranged for, should be set apart for this purpose. By France and America it was expressly stipulated that residents should enjoy all proper accommodation in obtaining houses and places of business, as well as in hiring sites from Chinese on which to construct not only dwellings and warehouses but also hospitals, churches, and cemeteries;[1] that they might rent houses and shops and establish hospices and schools;[2] and that Chinese violating churches or cemeteries should be punished with all the rigour of the law of China.[3] These treaties further provided in stringent terms for the protection by the local Chinese officials of the subjects of the contracting powers resident in China and of their property. The local authorities were to give such subjects special protection; to defend them from all insult or injury on the part of the Chinese; and, in the event of attack by mobs, incendiaries, or other violent or lawless persons, to despatch, on the requisition of the consul, a military force to disperse the rioters and apprehend the offenders, who should be punished with due severity.[4] All this was to be without prejudice to the right, on the part of the persons aggrieved, to be indemnified against such loss as should be proved to have been suffered.[5]

To the benefit of all these provisions in the French and American treaties British subjects became entitled as soon as those treaties were ratified. The reason for this was, that on the signing of the Supplementary Treaty in 1843 it was stipulated, that if the Emperor of China should thereafter, from any cause whatever, be pleased to grant additional privileges or immunities to any of the citizens or subjects of countries other than Great Britain, the same privileges

[1] *American Treaty*, Art. xvii.

[2] *French Treaty*, Art. xxii.

[3] *Ibid.*, Art. xxii; *American Treaty*, Art. xvii; *Swedish Treaty*, Art. xvii.

[4] *American Treaty*, Art. xix; *French Treaty*, Art. xxvi.

[5] *French Treaty*, Art. xxvi.

MONGOLIAN CARAVAN FROM KIAKHTA, OUTSIDE PEKING

and immunities should be enjoyed by British subjects.[1] By virtue of this provision Englishmen became entitled to enjoy all such rights as might be obtained by the subjects of other countries subsequent to the Treaty of Nanking, but privileges conferred by treaties anterior in date were reserved to the subjects of those countries by which such treaties had been negotiated. Now the only nation with which China had entered into treaty obligations before 1842 was Russia, with whom she had concluded the treaties relating to overland trade, which have been discussed in an earlier chapter.[2] All the other treaties and conventions now in existence between China and Western powers have been negotiated since that date, and any right, privilege, or immunity granted in any of these—and there are many of them—enures in favour of British subjects from the moment of the grant.

The benefit of this principle of construction, commonly known as "the most favoured nation treatment," which was first enunciated in the Supplementary Treaty, was confirmed and amplified by the Treaty of Tientsin in 1838. The clause of the Treaty of Tientsin, which relates to this matter,[3] expressly states that "the British Government and its subjects will be allowed free and equal participation in all privileges, immunities, and advantages that may have been or may be hereafter granted by the Emperor of China to the Government or subjects of any other nation." Thus it comes about that, to obtain a comprehensive view of our Treaty rights in China as they exist to-day, one has to examine, not merely the compacts, to which the British Government has been a party, but also the whole of the treaties and conventions that have at any time been concluded between China and other powers. It follows that since 1860, when the Treaty of Tientsin was ratified, Great Britain has been entitled to claim for her subjects rights with regard to the overland trade and to an establishment at Peking similar to those granted to Russia. So far we have not asked to be allowed to enjoy any

[1] *Supplementary Treaty*, Art. viii.
[2] Chap. vi *ante*, pp. 109–116.
[3] *Treaty of Tientsin*, Art. liv.

such privileges, but the day may come when it will be of advantage to British statesmen to bear in mind that in this respect we have dormant rights of some diplomatic and even commercial value.

Some brief mention may here be made of the circumstances under which the Treaty of Tientsin was negotiated. As early as 1844 difficulties began to arise with regard to the right of entry into the native city of Canton, a right claimed by the British in virtue of the treaty provisions, but resisted by the inhabitants and the provincial authorities with great vigour. On the death of Taoukwang, in 1850, his son adopted a policy of cutting off all communication between British and Chinese officials, except through the Viceroy of Canton, who maintained an attitude of contemptuous seclusion within the walls of his city. The success of the Tai-ping rebellion led to an independent revolt in Kwang-tung in 1852, and when this began to be suppressed by the imperial troops, thousands of the insurgents became pirates and took refuge in the islands and bays along the coast. Yeh, the Viceroy, shut himself up in Canton and refused to see any Foreign minister in connection with the many difficulties that ensued. The seizure in 1856, by his command, of the lorcha *Arrow*, flying the British flag, brought matters to a crisis. England despatched Lord Elgin with armed assistance to act as a British plenipotentiary; the French Government sent out Baron Gros with a like expedition. The Viceroy refused the ultimatum presented by the two plenipotentiaries, with the result that Canton was stormed and taken, Yeh himself captured, and a provisional government set up. Lord Elgin and Baron Gros then proceeded towards Peking, in order to enter into direct negotiation with the Chinese Government.

At Taku their forces were joined by the American frigates *Minnesota* and *Mississippi*, and the Russian gunboat *Amerika*, but these were under instructions not to use force. The British and French forced the defences of the Pei-ho and made their way to Tientsin, where ultimately the British Treaty was signed on the 26th of June, 1858, and the French Treaty on the following day. America and Russia had concluded treaties a few days previously. On the 6th of July, Lord Elgin left Tientsin, having arranged that ratifications should be exchanged within a year at Peking, and, after sailing up the Gulf of Pe-chi-li to the end of the Great Wall, returned to Shanghai, where fresh customs' regulations and a tariff of duties on imports were drawn up and signed as part of the Treaty. He then proceeded to Japan, whence he returned to Shanghai at the beginning of October. During the winter nothing of importance occurred, except that in the North the Chinese used every effort to fortify the Pei-ho against any further incursion by the "barbarians." When in June, 1859, Lord Elgin and Baron Gros returned to Taku for the exchange of ratifications, they found that new fortifications had been erected, the appearance of the forts entirely changed, and the mouth of the river barred by an elaborate boom of timber and chains. A combined attempt by the British and French forces to enter the river proved unsuccessful. It was during this fighting that Commodore Tatnall, of the U.S.S. *Toeywan*, seeing that the attack of the allies was failing, rendered them assistance by towing boatloads of British marines into action, a breach of international law which he defended with the famous declaration that "blood is thicker than water." In the following year a combined British and French force of 10,000 men assembled off the Pei-ho, who, having effected a landing at Pehtang, defeated the Chinese army and stormed and captured the Taku Forts. The expedition then forced its way to Peking, where the Treaty of 1858 was ratified, and the Convention of 1860 signed.

The Treaty of Tientsin renewed and confirmed the Treaty of Nanking. It also incorporated the main provisions, with many amendments and improvements, of the Supplementary Treaty and General Regulations of 1843, whilst abrogating both of those documents. It further contained several entirely new provisions dealing with the opening of fresh ports, the establishment of a British Legation at Peking and the reception of a diplomatic representative of China in England, the administration of justice, the treatment of missionaries, and many points of commercial detail too numerous to be mentioned. By the Convention of 1860 the Kowloon peninsula was ceded as a dependency of the colony of Hong-kong, Tientsin made an open port, and the emigration of Chinese placed on a legal footing. It was agreed that an indemnity of 8,000,000 taels should be paid by China towards the cost of the British expedition and the losses sustained by the British mercantile community at Canton, and that the British troops should evacuate Chusan, the Taku forts, and other places occupied by them, on the payment of this sum.[1]

The Treaty of Tientsin and the Convention of 1860 have remained in their main features and most of their details unaltered down to the present day. In respect of our Treaty rights in China, these two documents stand to the Treaty of Nanking in a relation, which may be compared with that occupied by the Bill of Rights and Act of Settlement towards the Great Charter. The subsequent conventions between England and China need a brief mention.[2] In 1866 a Convention was signed to regulate the engagement of Chinese emigrants by British subjects, which dealt with the evils arising out of the coolie traffic.[3] The attack on the Bhamo expedition and the murder of Margary led to the negotiation of the Chefoo Convention in 1876, by which terms of indemnity for the outrage were agreed, the trade between Burma and Yünnan put on a legalized footing, and regulations drawn up for the administration of justice in mixed cases, that is to say, cases in which one party was British and the other Chinese. This Convention also contained further provisions with regard to *likin*, and for the demarcation of residential areas for Foreigners at Open Ports, the number of which was increased by the opening of six new ports on the Yang-tsze river and

[1] As in 1843 Chusan became the security for the due performance by the Chinese of the Treaty. Chusan had been evacuated in 1846 when China paid up the last instalment of the indemnity stipulated for in the Treaty of Nanking. On the arrival of the joint expedition of 1858 it had been again occupied.

[2] A very good collection of the Treaties between England and China will be found in the *Chronicle and Directory for China, Japan, and the Straits Settlements*.

[3] For the terms of this Convention see Mayers : *Treaties between the Empire of China and Foreign Powers*, p. 32.

four other towns for the purposes of Foreign trade. The provisions of the Chefoo Convention relating to opium were modified by a supplementary agreement made the 18th of July, 1885, at London, and not until this had been done was the Convention ratified. The date of ratification was the 6th of May, 1886, but on the 11th of September in the same year, the Opium Convention was signed, by which the importation of opium into Hong-kong was further regulated. In 1891 the Chunking Agreement was signed, by which the rights of Great Britain to trade on the Yang-tsze river were further defined.[1] Overland intercourse between India and China was regulated by the Sikkim Convention of 1890 and the Burmah Convention of 1897. The Powers, after the suppression of the Boxer movement in 1901, obtained the right to have the Legation Quarter at Peking exclusively reserved to their use, to erect fortifications round it, and to maintain a garrison.[2] On the 5th of September, 1902, the Treaty of Shanghai was signed, by which the commercial relations between China and Great Britain, which had been sorely disturbed in the two preceding years, were re-adjusted and five fresh towns thrown open to trade.[3] This was ratified at Peking on the 28th of July, 1903. There only remains to be noticed the Convention signed at London on the 13th of May, 1904, respecting the employment of Chinese labour in British Colonies and Protectorates, by which detailed regulations were drawn up in accordance with Article V of the Convention of 1860.[4] By the Kowloon Extension Agreement of 1898, territory on the mainland adjoining Hong-kong was leased for ninety-nine

[1] The position in Yünnan and the question of the Burmah frontier were settled by the Burmah Convention signed at Peking on the 4th of February, 1897.

[2] Protocol of the 7th of September, 1901. See Hertslet: *Commercial Treaties*, vol. xxiii, p. 363; *Correspondence Respecting the Affairs of China* (China Blue Book), No. 1 (1902), pp. 237–245.

[3] For the terms of this treaty see Hertslet: *Commercial Treaties*, vol. xxiii, p. 403; *Parliamentary Papers*, Treaty Series, No. 17 (1903).

[4] It was under this Convention that Chinese labourers were imported into the Transvaal to serve in accordance with the terms of the Transvaal Labour Ordinance, 1903. Its terms are contained in *Parliamentary Papers*, Treaty Series, No. 7 (1904).

years, and in the same year a Convention was signed by which Wei-hai-wei was leased to Great Britain for so long as Port Arthur should continue in the occupation of Russia.[1]

The way in which the provisions of the Treaty of Nanking and of the Supplementary Treaty, in virtue of which British subjects reside at the Open Ports, have been interpreted, deserves particular notice. In some cases the local Chinese officials selected a piece of ground, approved by the British Consul, and conveyed it by deed of grant to him as representing the British Government, to hold as a place where British subjects only might reside, under such government and administration as the British authorities might determine, "saving the sovereign rights of the Emperor of China." The form of conveyance in such cases is a lease in perpetuity, which to all intents and purposes is the same as a grant in fee simple in English law. When this course was adopted, a money consideration for the grant was paid by the British Government, and a further sum was paid in commutation of the land-tax ordinarily levied by the Chinese Government on all land in the Emperor's dominions, or an annual sum paid as rent in place of that tax. There was a provision in the deed, that all private ownership of land by Chinese, within the area leased, should at once come to an end, and the native owners be compensated at a specified rate before the British Consul might take possession. When such compensation had been paid, the Consul was to have the right to sub-let the land to British subjects, in such lots as he might choose. An area so granted to the Crown was called, and is still called, at each of the ports where such a grant was made, the British Concession.[2]

The operative influence, which induced the Chinese authorities to adopt this construction of the Treaty provisions, was undoubtedly the remembrance of the old Factory system at

[1] See *Correspondence Respecting Affairs in China* (China Blue Book, No. 1, 1899), *passim*. *Chronicle and Directory of China, Japan and Straits Settlements*; Hertslet: *Commercial Treaties*, vol. xxiii.

[2] The terms of grant were not identical at every port where a British Concession was constituted. For the deed of grant by which the British Concession at Hankow was extended, see *Correspondence affecting the Affairs of China* (China Blue Book, No. 1, 1899), pp. 320-1.

Canton, and the feeling, freely acknowledged, that Foreigners, like wild beasts, are safest when caged up. The wording of the Supplementary Treaty[1] was certainly capable of this construction, and no objection seems to have been raised by the British officials, though the course adopted has been the subject of much criticism in more recent times. At none of the original Five Ports were strict grants made in the first instance. At Canton the Foreigners continued to live in the Factories, under conditions and restrictions that were nearly as bad as those that obtained before the war, until in 1859 the British and French authorities, with the Viceroy's consent, at a cost of $325,000, of which four-fifths was paid by the British, levelled up a mud bank, known as the Island of Shameen, and partitioned it into French and British Settlements, having an area of forty-four and eleven acres respectively. In 1861 the Chinese Government granted the British portion of Shameen to the British Government as a concession under a lease in perpetuity at a yearly rent of 396,000 copper cash. At Foochow a portion of the island of Nantai was allotted to Foreigners generally as a Foreign Concession, which has no definite legal status. At Amoy a portion of the island of Kulangsu was appropriated to a similar use, but in 1851 a definite area was granted as a British Concession. At Ningpo an area known as the Campo was set apart in 1844, and of this the boundaries were defined in 1862. In that area Foreigners have continued to reside, but its exact status is still undetermined.

After the events of 1860 British Concessions were granted

[1] This wording was as follows: "The Treaty of perpetual peace and friendship provides for British subjects and their families residing at the cities and towns of Canton, Foochow, Amoy, Ningpo, and Shanghai without molestation or restraint. It is accordingly determined that ground and houses, the rent of which is to be fairly and equitably apportioned, arranged for, according to the rates prevailing among the people, without exaction on either side, shall be set aside by the local officers in communication with the consul, and the number of houses built or rented will be reported annually to the said local officers by the consul for the information of their respective viceroys and governors, but the number cannot be limited, seeing that it will be greater or less according to the resort of merchants." (*Chinese Repository*, vol. xiii, p. 453.)

at some of the newly opened ports, such as Tientsin, Newchwang, Hankow, and Chinkiang, whilst at others no such course was adopted. At these latter the Foreign residents, who commenced to reside and carry on trade in pursuance of their treaty rights, bought or rented, for the erection of residences and places of business, plots of land in close contiguity, as was natural and convenient, and thus there gradually came into existence a group of dwellings and warehouses built on land, the whole of which, or nearly the whole of which, was in the possession of Foreigners. Imitating the form of government authorized for the Concessions at other ports, the members of these communities organized a form of municipal administration for the areas thus occupied, and voluntarily submitted themselves to the regulations promulgated by the authority thus brought into being. To this practice, so long as it was kept within reasonable limits, the Chinese authorities raised no objection, and thus at some of the Open Ports, such as Chefoo, where there is no Concession at all, we nevertheless find what is called a Foreign Settlement having a carefully organized municipal government. These settlements are now so firmly established that no interference on the part of the Chinese authorities would be tolerated.

Shanghai is in a category by itself. There an area was agreed upon for a British Settlement, in which all Foreigners should have to reside, between the British Consul and the Chinese Taotai in 1843. The land-renters in this area were chiefly British subjects, and thus the municipal administration was in British hands. From 1851 to 1853 there was a great influx of wealthy Chinese residents, driven thither by the Taiping troubles. Numbers of these settled in the French Settlement, which had been set apart in 1849, and in the United States' Settlement, which, had also recently been allotted. In 1854 an international code of Land Regulations was agreed upon for the three settlements, which thus came under one municipal administration, but the French Government withdrew from this arrangement in 1862 and in 1868 declared the French Settlement to be a "Concession," over which France had exclusive control.

The form of administration that has been set up by the British authorities within the Concessions is very simple. The Crown has sub-let the land in lots on lease for ninety-nine years at a low rent; a Council, elected by the lessees, who are known locally as the land-renters, is the authority for the municipal government of the Concession. This Council is presided over by a Chairman chosen by the other members, and the only part taken by the British Consul in the municipal administration is, that he convenes and presides over the annual meeting of the land-renters, at which the Council is elected. The raising of a revenue for municipal purposes has been sanctioned, power being given to the Council to levy dues on all merchandise brought within the Concession, and on all vessels using the Bund, and to impose a land-tax.[1]

It will be seen at once that there is nothing to prevent Chinese, or subjects of countries other than Great Britain, from residing in settlements such as that at Chefoo. But from a British Concession the Crown may exclude all but British subjects, and this is effected by the insertion in the leases, on which the lots are let to the land-renters, of a covenant against sub-letting or assigning to persons, who are not of British nationality. In the same way are excluded from the British Concessions the wealthy Chinese, who would otherwise crowd within their borders. With the consent of the Consul, alien Europeans and Americans are usually allowed to reside within the British Concessions, but in their leases a covenant is inserted to the effect, that they will obey the municipal regulations and, if sued by a British subject in the British Courts, will submit to the jurisdiction. Where, however, the defendant in a judicial proceeding is the subject of a state having a properly organized tribunal within the consular district, compliance with this covenant is generally waived.

The first additions to the original Five Ports were those

[1] At some of the Treaty Ports the regulations have been revised and householders admitted to the franchise. See for example the new Regulations for the British Concession at Kiukiang, given by Hertslet, *Commercial Treaties*, vol. xxiv, pp. 210–219; and the Land Regulations of the British Concession at Hankow approved in 1905. *Ibid.*, pp. 311–326.

specified in the Treaty of Tientsin, namely, Newchwang, Chefoo, Taiwan (in Formosa), Swatow, and Kiung-chow (in Hainan), together with Chinkiang and Hankow and two other ports on the Yang-tsze below Hankow.[1] To these was added Tientsin by the Convention of 1860; and since that date many other places, seaports, river-ports, and inland towns, have been thrown open to Foreign trade.[2] The practice of granting Concessions has not, however, been followed at all these places, and the Chinese have never recognised a right in any Power to receive such a grant at any port that might be thrown open. In 1896, however, Japan obtained the right to have settlements "at the places newly opened to commerce," and by the most favoured nation treatment Great Britain obtains an equal right. In the Treaty of Shanghai of 1903, by which it was agreed that five fresh places should be opened to Foreign trade, it is expressly declared that Foreigners residing at any of those places are not to be entitled to establish municipalities of their own or police of their own, except with the consent of the Chinese authorities.[3]

It should be mentioned that the term "settlement" is frequently used in a general sense to include both Concessions and Settlements proper. Thus, at Newchwang there are British, Japanese, and Russian Concessions, as well as a Settlement, all of which are often spoken of as the Foreign Settlements.[4] At Tientsin nearly every European country has

[1] *Treaty of Tientsin*, Arts. x and xi.

[2] By the Chefoo Convention alone Ichang, Wuhu, Wênchow, and Pakhoi were opened, and it was declared that Chungking should be opened as soon as steamers should succeed in ascending the Yang-tsze so far. In addition six others were made ports of call on the Yang-tsze, viz., Tatung, Nganching, Hukow, Wusuëh, Lu-chi-kow, and Shashih. Wuchow-fu and Samohin were opened by the Burmah Convention of 1897, by which also Kongmoon, Komchuk, Shinking and Takhing were made ports of call on the Yang-tsze River. Soochow was opened by the Treaty of Shimonoseki in 1896. By the Treaty of Shanghai in 1903 Kongmoon became a Treaty Port, and fresh ports of call were constituted on the Yang-tsze and West rivers. For ports voluntarily thrown open not under agreement, see *ante*, p. 517.

[3] *Treaty of Shanghai*, Art. viii (12).

[4] The rise of the Settlement proper at Neuchwang is due to the fact that the British authorities have allowed the whole of their Concession, with the exception of two lots, to be washed away by the River Liao.

a Concession, and in addition the British have an anomalous area, known as the British Municipal Extension, which for purposes of administration has been placed on a footing very similar to that of a Concession, with the consent and authority of the Chinese Government, but for purposes of land tenure is on a different legal basis. All these are known as the Foreign Settlements at Tientsin. At Shanghai the position is particularly complicated. Originally there were British, French, and American Concessions lying side by side, but the British and the American Governments have to some extent retroceded their rights, and the areas previously held by them were in 1863 amalgamated into an International Concession, organized on a municipal basis approved by the Chinese Government. France still retains at Shanghai a Concession in the strict sense of the word, which was granted in 1849.[1]

The practice of granting Concessions has been severely attacked by some writers. Thus Dr. Wells Williams speaks of it as "vicious."[2] If he speaks from the Chinese point of view, possibly he is correct. But from the English standpoint it has been a great boon. The plan adopted, though meant to be a restriction, has given British subjects in China a freedom and independence they would not otherwise have possessed. Moreover, it has rendered much easier the task of the Chinese authorities, in giving that protection to person and property promised in the treaties. One has only to compare the position of a land-renter in the British Concession at Newchwang, with that of a dweller in the Settlement at the same port, to see how infinitely preferable is the condition of the former, with its freedom from the dirt, filth, noise, and other disgusting concomitants of residence in a Chinese city.

The provisions as to churches, hospitals, schools and hospices, in the French and American Treaties of 1843, mark the formal introduction of what is now known as the missionary question into the relations between China and the Western Powers.

[1] In a short account of the origin of the Concession at Shanghai see *Correspondence Respecting the Affairs of China* (China Blue Book, No. 1, 1899), pp. 268–9.

[2] *The Middle Kingdom*, vol. ii, p. 626.

As already mentioned, difficulties had arisen in the early days of European intercourse owing to the methods adopted by Roman Catholic missionaries, which had resulted in the expulsion of all Christian missionaries from every part of the Empire, except Peking, and the prohibition of the Roman Catholic religion. In 1728 Russia obtained the right to maintain a mission of the Greek Church at Peking for the benefit of her merchants resorting to the capital, and the traders that occupied Factories at Canton had been accustomed to have their resident chaplains. In 1808 Dr. Morrison had founded the first Protestant mission in China, and gradually a small band of assistants had grouped themselves around him. Of these some at times made journeys along the coast and attempted mission work at places East of Canton. But they had always found themselves received with disfavour, and often with active opposition.

Now that Five Ports had been thrown open to trade, the supporters of missions in England expected that a much wider field would be available for missionary operations, and that an entrance would soon be gained into the interior itself. Their joy at this development was unbounded and unconcealed. One school of philanthropists showed what can only be described as an unseemly delight, that any cause, even one so intimately connected with the opium trade as the warlike operations of 1841 and 1842, should have given them an opportunity to send out a larger number of mission workers. At a meeting held at Exeter Hall in 1843 by the London Missionary Society, one of the largest of its kind that had ever been assembled, Dr. Liefchild moved a resolution, " expressive of thanksgiving to God for the war between China and Great Britain, and for the greatly enlarged facilities secured by the treaty of peace for the introduction of Christianity into that empire." This resolution was seconded by the Reverend Dr. Adler, and carried unanimously.[1] As a matter of fact, the treaties negotiated by Sir Henry Pottinger contained no reference at all to the question of missionary enterprise, nor

[1] See the *Examiner* for 21st January, 1843, and Hildreth: *Japan as It was and is*, p. 494.

was there any clause relating to churches, such as is found in the French and American treaties. It was the French plenipotentiary, M. de Lagrené, that forced this question into the region of diplomacy. Whether the lively interest, taken by him in all that concerned the operations of the Roman Catholic Church in China, arose from a desire to promote religious toleration and the spread of Christianity, it is difficult to say. The attention subsequently paid by the French Government to this question would seem to be not entirely unprompted by political considerations. Whatever the cause, M. de Lagrené, having obtained the insertion in his treaty of a clause protecting ecclesiastical property, prevailed upon Kiying to present a Memorial to the Throne, asking that the prohibition against Roman Catholicism be withdrawn, and that toleration be extended to "the religion of the Lord of Heaven." This document throws a curious light on Chinese ideas as to the reasons why Yungching had issued his prohibitory edict. It was thus worded :—

"On examination it appears that the religion of the Lord of Heaven is that professed by all the nations of the West ; that its main object is to encourage the good and suppress the wicked ; that, since its introduction to China during the Ming dynasty, it has never been interdicted ; that subsequently, when Chinese practising this religion often made it a cover for wickedness, even to the seducing of wives and daughters,[1] and to the deceitful extraction of the pupils from the eyes of the sick,[2] government made investigation and

[1] This idea is doubtless due to the excesses committed by the Portuguese at Liampo (Ningpo) where they had a Settlement before the English appeared in China. Some writers attribute the Chinese dislike of Foreigners to the same cause, but though probably accentuated by this behaviour, its roots would appear to lie deeper. (See *Chinese Repository*, vol. xiii, p. 340.)

[2] The Chinese believed that it was a custom with the Roman Catholic priests, when a man was about to die, to take a handful of cotton with a sharp needle concealed in it, and then, while rubbing the eyes of the dying man with the cotton, to introduce the needle into the eye and puncture the pupil, so that the humours of the pupil might saturate the cotton and afterwards be used as a medicine. This belief had its origin in their inability to understand the administration of extreme unction (*Chinese Repository*, vol. xiv, p. 198). At the

inflicted punishment, as is on record; and that in the reign of Kiaking special clauses were first laid down for the punishment of the guilty. The prohibition, therefore, was directed against evil-doing under the cover of religion, and not against the religion professed by Western Foreign nations.

"Now the request of the French ambassador, Lagrené, that those Chinese who doing well practise this religion, be exempt from criminality, seems feasible. It is right, therefore, to make request, and earnestly to crave Celestial favour, to grant that henceforth all natives and Foreigners without distinction, who learn and practise the religion of the Lord of Heaven, and do not excite trouble by improper conduct, be exempted from criminality. If there be any who seduce wives and daughters, or deceitfully take the pupils from the eyes of the sick, walking on their former paths, or are otherwise guilty of criminal acts, let them be dealt with according to the old laws. As to those of the French and other foreign nations, who practise the religion, let them only be permitted to build churches at the Five Ports opened for commercial intercourse. They must not presume to enter the country to propagate religion. Should any act in opposition, turn their backs upon the treaties, and rashly overstep the boundaries, the local officers will at once seize them and deliver them to their respective consuls for restraint and correction. Capital punishment is not to be rashly inflicted, in order that the exercise of gentleness may be displayed. Thus peradventure the good and the profligate will not be blended, while the equity of mild laws will be exhibited.

"This request, that well-doers practising the religion may be exempt from criminality, he (Kiying), in accordance with reason and his bounden duty, respectfully lays before the Throne, earnestly praying the august Emperor graciously to grant that it may be carried into effect."[1]

When, on the 28th of December, 1844, this memorial was

present time Chinese women frequently snatch their children in horror from the presence of a Foreigner with a photographic camera, as they believe that children's eyes are used for the preparation of developing fluid.

[1] *Chinese Repository*, vol. xiv, pp. 196–8, where also the Chinese text is given.

laid before the Emperor, he wrote in his own hand with the vermilion pencil the words: "Let it be according to the counsel of Kiying." Thus Kiying's memorial became the foundation on which religious toleration in China rests to-day. With it must be read the proclamation addressed by him to the American Consul on the 22nd of December, 1845, by which it was made clear that the benefit of the imperial rescript extended to Roman Catholics and Protestants alike. The expression used in the memorial for "the Religion of the Lord of Heaven" was *Tien Chu Kian*, the term usually applied to Roman Catholicism. There was some dissatisfaction among the Protestants that the term *Yesu Kian*, meaning "the Religion of Jesus," had not been used in the memorial, and the proclamation was issued to remove any misapprehension that might arise on this score. The words employed in the latter document for this purpose were: "Now with regard to the religion of the Lord of Heaven—no matter whether the crosses, pictures, and images be reverenced or not reverenced—all, who acting well, practise it, ought to be held blameless. All the great Western nations, being placed on an equal footing, only let them acting well practise their religion, and China will in no way prohibit or impede their so doing. Whether their customs be alike or unlike, certainly it is right that there should be no distinction and no obstruction."[1] Thus early in the new era were thrust upon the notice of the Chinese the incomprehensible distinctions between conflicting schools of Christianity. A final confirmation to the religious toleration thus sanctioned was given by an imperial edict of the 20th February, 1846, which, after reciting the imperial rescript of the 28th of December, 1844, ordered that the churches of the Roman Catholics built in the reign of Kanghi, which had been subsequently confiscated, should be restored to their rightful owners, except those that had become temples or dwelling-houses.[2]

[1] For the Chinese text and a complete translation see *Chinese Repository*, vol. xiv, pp. 588–9.

[2] For the Chinese text and a translation see *Chinese Repository*, vol. xv, pp. 155–6.

The permission thus given to missionaries to work and reside in China was in terms confined to the Five Ports. It was not until 1860 that the restriction against operations outside those areas was removed, and the Emperor's dominions thrown open to missionary enterprise. For this enlargement of their privileges missionaries are again indebted to the French.[1] The English version of the Treaty of Tientsin simply provided for the liberty to teach or profess Christianity, and for the protection of those, who exercise such liberty.[2] The permission to travel in the interior, which is granted by the next article of the Treaty, is confined to those, who travel for the purposes of trade or for pleasure. The English version of the Convention of 1860 does not contain any allusion to the question. It is in the French version of the Treaty of 1858 that the words are found, on which missionaries rely in support of their contention, that they are entitled to go to any part of the Empre as they please and to carry on their missionary work. Those words provide, that the members of all Christian communities shall enjoy complete security for their persons, their property, and the free exercise of their religion, and an efficient protection shall be given to missionaries, who betake themselves peaceably to the interior of the country under the protection of passports, such as the Treaty provides shall be furnished to all French subjects who wish to travel in the interior.[3] There is further an express

[1] The Russian treaty signed on the 13th of June, 1858, twelve days before the French, contains a similar provision. (See Art. viii, of Russian Treaty, Mayers, *Treaties*, etc., p. 103.)

[2] Article viii of the Treaty of 1858 is in these terms: "The Christian religion, as professed by Protestants or Roman Catholics, inculcates the practice of virtue, and teaches man to do as he would be done by. Persons teaching it or professing it, therefore, shall alike be entitled to the protection of the Chinese authorities; nor shall any such, peaceably pursuing their calling, and not offending against the laws, be persecuted or interfered with."

[3] Art. xiii: "La religion Chrétienne ayant pour objet essentiel de porter les hommes à la vertu, les membres de toutes les communions Chrétiennes jouiront d'une entière sécurité pour leurs personnes, leurs propriétés, et le libre exercice de leurs pratiques religieuses, et une protection efficace sera donnée aux missionaires qui se rendront pacifiquement dans l'intérieur du pays, munis des passeports réguliers dont il est parlé dans l'article viii.

provision, that everything which had previously been written, proclaimed, or published in China against the Christian religion was completely abrogated and rendered void in all the provinces of the empire. The French version of the Convention contained a clause not found in the English, by which it was provided, that the religious and philanthropic establishments, which had been taken from the Christians during the persecutions to which they had been subjected, should be restored to their rightful owners through the French Minister, to whom the Chinese Government would cause them to be delivered with the cemeteries and buildings belonging thereto.[1]

Owing to some cause that has never been explained, there crept into the end of the Chinese text of this article words not found in the French version, or in any treaty with any other nation, that gave to French missionaries permission to rent and purchase land in all the provinces, and to erect buildings thereon at pleasure. It is quite certain that the Chinese Government never distinctly contemplated any such concession, and the existence of the passage in question has been the subject of bitter controversy.[2] In the first place, a

" Aucune entrave ne sera apportée par les autorités de l'empire chinois au droit qui est reconnu à tout individu en Chine d'embrasser, s'il veut, le Christianisme et d'en suivre les pratiques sans être passible d'aucune peine infligée pour ce fait."

Tout ce qui a été précédemment écrit, proclamé ou publié en Chine par ordre du gouvernement contre le culte Chrétien, est complètement abrogé, et reste sans valeur dans toutes les provinces de l'empire.

Art. viii of the French Treaty gives the right to travel in the interior under passport to *all* French subjects.

[1] Conformément a l'Édit Impérial rendu le vingt Mars, mil huit cent quarante-six, par l'auguste Empereur Tao-Kouang, les établissements religieux et de bienfaisance qui ont été confisquées aux Chrétiens pendant les persécutions dont ils ont été les victimes, seront rendus à leurs propriétaires par l'entremise du Ministre de France en Chine, auquel le Gouvernement Impérial les fera délivrer, avec les cimetières et les autres édifices que en dépendaient." (Art. vi of the Convention of 1860.)

[2] The translation of the Chinese text runs as follows: " It shall be promulgated throughout the length and breadth of the land, in the terms of the Imperial Edict of the 20th February, 1846, that it is permitted to all people in all parts of China to propagate and practice the 'teachings of the Lord of Heaven,' to meet together for the preaching

difficulty arose as to which version was to be considered binding. In the French Treaty of 1858 it is provided, that where there is a discrepancy between the "original text" and the "translation," the former is to prevail;[1] but, as neither of these terms is defined, that does not dispose of the difficulty. In the English Treaty of the same date there is no corresponding provision, and the inference from the facts is that the English and French versions are both translations from the original text, which must in that view be the Chinese version. In the Russian Treaty of 1858 it is provided that the Manchu text is to prevail, but in the Convention of 1860 the Russian is described as the text and the Chinese as the translation,[2] whilst no declaration is made as to which is the binding version. Under these circumstances not much assistance can be derived from contemporaneous documents, and as the various European Powers and America, in virtue of the most favoured nation treatment, have long since claimed for their respective missionaries the right to own land in the interior and thereon to erect buildings, the point would have but an academic interest, were it not for the fact, that the Chinese still regard themselves as the victims of an injustice in this particular.[3]

Until this clause in the Chinese version came to light, no Foreigner could hold land in the interior of China. Prior to the Treaty of Nanking alien ownership of land was not allowed in any part of the Emperor's dominions, and the

of the doctrine, to build churches and to worship; further, all such as indiscriminately arrest (Christians) shall be duly punished; and such churches, schools, cemeteries, lands and buildings, as were owned on former occasions by persecuted Christians, shall be paid for, and the money handed to the French Representative at Peking, for transmission to the Christians in the localities concerned. It is, in addition, permitted to French missionaries to rent and purchase land in all the provinces, and to erect buildings thereon at pleasure." (Mayers: *Treaties between the Empire of China and Foreign Powers*, p. 73.)

[1] Art. iii.

[2] Art. xv. (See Mayers: *Treaties between the Empire of China and Foreign Powers*, p. 111.)

[3] So recently as March, 1898, the British Minister asserted this right. See *Correspondence Respecting the Affairs of China* (China Blue Book, No. 1, 1899), pp. 60-61, where the form of title-deed for such land is discussed.

leasing of the Factories at Canton, prior to the date when it was sanctioned by Kienlung, was an exception to this rule, that had been sanctioned only on the representations of the local authorities. There is no such notion, as that which we call a trust, known to the Chinese law, so that the means by which the law against alien ownership in England, which obtained till 1870, was evaded in our own country, is lacking in China. To this day the Chinese Government has been most strict in preventing any further infringement of the law in this direction, though many attempts have been made by Foreigners to acquire land in the interior in the name of missionary owners. In cases where Foreigners in the employ of Chinese corporations, or of the Chinese Government, have been obliged to reside outside the limits of an Open Port, a kind of dispensing power has been exercised in their favour.[1]

Another question with which the American Treaty dealt more carefully than either the Treaty of Nanking or the Supplementary Treaty, was that of judicial tribunals and their jurisdiction. It was expressly stipulated that disputes, whether of property or persons between Americans should be settled by American authorities, and between Americans and other Foreigners in such a manner as might be arranged between the United States and the sovereign of the persons concerned, and that there should be no interference whatever on the part of the Chinese.[2] By the most favoured nation

[1] On the Gulf of Pe-chi-li there is a flourishing seaside resort, known as Pei-tai-ho, which has its origin in the fact that a few missionaries acquired land and built houses, to which they might remove their families in the rainy season. Other Foreigners, wishing to avail themselves of the amenities of so pleasant a locality, sought to acquire land in the same neighbourhood. For the most part they did so by taking land on lease from missionaries, in whose name it was registered. Some entered into contracts with Chinese owners, purporting to be conveyances direct from the Chinese vendors. The authorities objected to the whole course of these proceedings and refused to recognise title in any but missionaries. Great difficulties arose in connection with registration, without which a valid title cannot be acquired according to Chinese law. In the end, the difficulty was solved by the inclusion of the area most suited to be a seaside resort within the limits of the port of Chin-wang-tao, which was declared an Open Port in 1899.

[2] *American Treaty*, Art. xxv.

treatment, Great Britain at once obtained similar privileges as to any disputes in which British subjects were concerned. With regard to our own country, the matter was made perfectly clear by the Treaty of Tientsin, which expressly provided, that all questions in regard to rights, whether of property or person, arising between British subjects, should be subject to the jurisdiction of the British authorities, and that crimes committed by British subjects should be tried and punished by British tribunals.[1] Even after this, difficulties occasionally arose, and, in order that every doubt on the subject might be removed, it was declared in 1876 by the Chefoo Convention, that mixed cases, that is to say, cases in which one party was British and the other Chinese, should always be tried in the Court of the defendant, an officer of the plaintiff's nationality merely attending to watch the proceedings in the interests of justice.[2]

In one important respect the United States and Sweden and Norway obtained for their subjects narrower exterritorial rights than those conferred by the British and French treaties. Both these countries consented to the trial and punishment by the Chinese authorities of any of their subjects, who should attempt to trade clandestinely with such of the ports of China as had not been thrown open, or should trade in opium or any other article of contraband. It was further declared that subjects guilty of any of these offences should not be entitled to any countenance or protection from their respective Governments,

[1] *Treaty of Tientsin*, Art. xv and xvi.

[2] Section II (iii) of the Chefoo Convention provides: "It is further understood that so long as the laws of the two countries differ from each other, there can be but one principle to guide judicial proceedings in mixed cases in China; namely, that the case is tried by the official of the defendant's nationality, the official of the plaintiff's nationality merely attending to watch the proceedings in the interest of justice. If the officer so attending be dissatisfied with the proceedings, it will be in his power to protest against them in detail. The law administered will be the law of the nationality of the officer trying the case. This is the meaning of the words *hui t'ung*, indicating combined action in judicial proceedings, in Article xvi of the Treaty of Tientsin: and this is the course to be respectively followed by the officers of either nationality." (Mayers: *Treaties between the Empire of China and Foreign Powers*, p. 46.)

and that these countries would take measures, to prevent their flag from being abused by the subjects of other nations, as a cover for the violation of the laws of the Empire.[1] Thus the American Government conceded the point of substance in the demand for a bond against the introduction of opium, which was one of the main themes of controversy between Captain Elliot and Commissioner Lin before the outbreak of hostilities. This concession was in perfect harmony with the conduct of the American merchants, who had voluntarily given such a bond and so been allowed to continue to trade.

Neither the successful negotiation of a treaty by the British plenipotentiary, not its ratification by the Crown, made its provisions binding on British subjects. It was necessary that Parliament should embody the terms of the Treaty of Nanking in a statute, or otherwise provide for their enforcement. This was done by the Act for the Better Government of Her Majesty's Subjects in China, [2] which received the royal assent on the 22nd of August, 1843. This statute empowered the Crown, by Commission under the Great Seal accompanied by Instructions under the Sign Manual, to authorize the Superintendent of Trade at Hong-kong to enact laws and ordinances for the government of British subjects in any part of the Chinese Empire. Up to that time the Sovereign of Great Britain had never exercised any extra-territorial jurisdiction, and a doubt arose as to how far the statute was effective. To remove this doubt a second statute was at once passed, [3] which

[1] *American Treaty*; Art. xxxiii; *Swedish Treaty*, Art. xxxiii; Mayers; *Treaties*, etc., pp. 83, 135.

[2] 6 & 7 Vict. c. 80. This statute was repealed in 1878.

[3] 6 & 7 Vict. c. 94. This Act was intituled : "An Act to remove doubts as to the exercise of power and jurisdiction by Her Majesty within divers countries and places out of Her Majesty's dominions, and to render the same more effectual." It is generally known as the Foreign Jurisdiction Act, 1843. Amending statutes were passed in 1865, 1866, 1875, and 1878, but the whole of these have now been repealed, together with the 6 & 7 Vict. c. 94, and their provisions re-enacted in the amending and consolidating Act known as the Foreign Jurisdiction Act, 1890 (53 & 54 Vict. c. 37). This last named statute is the only statute under which the orders in Council are issued at the present day for the government of British subjects in China. The 6 & 7 Vict. c. 80 was repealed by the Foreign Jurisdiction Act, 1878.

expressly gave to the Queen power to exercise jurisdiction outside her own dominions, where permission to exercise such jurisdiction had been acquired by treaty, grant or sufferance. In virtue of the statutory powers thus conferred, the Crown at once issued a Commission to Sir Henry Pottinger, authorizing him to make ordinances for the government of British subjects in China. Acting under this authority the Superintendent of Trade, early in 1844, published the ordinance conferring on the Court at Hong-kong jurisdiction over all British subjects.

Thus was constituted at Hong-kong a Court having cognizance over all actions and prosecutions brought against British subjects within the Chinese Empire. When, however, in 1860 the Superintendent of Trade became the British Minister at Peking, Hong-kong ceased to be the centre of British influence, so far as the Treaty Ports were concerned, and it was felt that a change was desirable in the system of judicial administration. Accordingly a new Court was formed, called Her Majesty's Supreme Court for China and Japan,[1] to which was transferred all the matters of which the Court at Hong-kong had had cognizance, except those arising within the colony itself. This was done by an Order in Council dated the 9th of March, 1865, and issued under the two statutes of 1843 mentioned above.[2] By this Order the new Court was invested with an original jurisdiction over all matters arising within the consular district of Shanghai, where it was to sit under the presidency of a Judge aided by an Assistant-Judge, both appointed by the Crown. At each Treaty Port was constituted a Provincial Court, having jurisdiction over matters arising within the consular district and presided over by the local Consul. From these provincial courts there was an appeal to the Supreme Court at Shanghai, but this latter also had an extraordinary jurisdiction extending

[1] Japan, too, by this time had been opened to Western influence, and Great Britain had acquired exterritorial privileges there under the Treaties of 1854 and 1858.

[2] This Order in Council has been repealed by that of 1904, which enacts new rules of procedure and defines afresh the constitution and jurisdiction of the Court.

over the whole of China and Japan, in virtue of which the Judge was empowered to proceed to any Treaty Port and hear cases arising there. From the Supreme Court there is an appeal to the Privy Council. Under the Order in Council the Judge had power to frame rules of procedure, subject to the approval of a Secretary of State, and such a body of rules was promulgated on the 4th of May, 1865. These have now been superseded by the new rules, that came into force under an Order in Council of the 24th of October, 1904. The jurisdiction thus constituted extends to every kind of cause of action, civil and criminal, known to English law except matrimonial causes in which a decree of dissolution, nullity or jactitation of marriage is asked.[1]

In virtue of these provisions a British Consul exercises in China, in addition to the commercial functions exercised by consuls elsewhere, not only the varied functions described in the preceding chapter, but also those of Judge of his Provincial Court. The cases that he has to try are often difficult and important, but it is customary for him to notify the Judge at Shanghai of the more important matters that are about to come before him, and the Judge, or Assistant-Judge, if he conveniently can, proceeds, as it were on circuit, to the Treaty Port and tries such cases himself. In this way a more experienced judge, than the Consul can possibly be, is made available, and the expense to the parties of a possible appeal to Shanghai is saved: there is, of course, in such a case a direct appeal to the Privy Council. The existence of the Courts thus constituted has largely contributed to the success of British mercantile enterprise in China, by reason of the feeling of security that has been engendered among all whose commercial operations might result in an action against a British subject.

One other matter remains to be considered, and that is

[1] See Hertslet, *Commercial Treaties,* vol. xxiv, pp. 250–306. The Court is now called the Supreme Court for China and Corea, our ex-territorial rights in Japan having been retroceded by the Treaty of London signed in 1894. The jurisdiction of the Supreme Court outside the consular district of Shanghai is declared by the new rules to be concurrent and original.

the manner in which the British Government dealt with the claims of the owners of the opium, which had been surrendered at Canton in 1839. Peel's Ministry, which succeeded that of Lord Melbourne in 1841, has been hotly attacked on the ground that it failed in its duty in this respect, and used the misfortunes of the opium merchants to enrich the public treasury. Careful investigation shows that this charge is without foundation. It is true that when the drafts, given by Captain Elliot on the Treasury as the price of the opium surrendered, were presented for payment, they were dishonoured. No other result was possible in view of the stringency of the law by which Treasury payments are regulated. Until the necessary sum of money had been voted by the House of Commons in Committee of Supply, and appropriated to this purpose by statute, it would be impossible for the officials of the Treasury to honour drafts given without the authority of Parliament. When the war had been brought to a close, and the $6,000,000 opium indemnity paid over by the Chinese, the British Government at once took steps to see that the sum thus received was properly expended. It was proposed in Committee of Supply on the 4th of August, 1843, that the sum of £1,281,211, being the product in sterling of $6,000,000 less £33,977 paid for the 500 chests purchased by Captain Elliot in the open market, should be appropriated to paying for the opium at the price of £66 7s. 2d. for Patna, £61 11s. 3¼d. for Benares, £64 11s. 2d. for Malwa, and £43 3s. 5d. for Turkey. It was objected by the Opposition of the day that the invoice price was the proper measure of compensation, but Peel and his Chancellor of the Exchequer, Goulbourn, had no difficulty in showing that, so far as actual value was concerned, these prices were liberal. It appeared from a letter sent by Captain Elliot to Lord Aberdeen, the new Foreign Secretary, that on the 5th of March, 1839, three weeks before the surrender of the drug, the prices quoted at Canton had been $300 for Patna, $280 for Benares, and $250 for Malwa;[1] that at that time there were no buyers; and that the market depreciated between the 5th and the 27th, the day on which

[1] The price of the silver dollar was then a little over four shillings.

Commissioner Lin reached Canton. Moreover, in a lawsuit tried in the High Court at Calcutta,[1] in which this very question was raised, in the form of a claim by the plaintiff for the value of opium which the defendant had contracted to sell immediately on arrival at Canton, the Court found the value to be £40 per chest.[2] The prices actually paid by the Treasury were based on an average taken up to the end of November, 1838, at which time the market had not been depreciated by the expected arrival of the High Commissioner, and the surrendered opium would be leaving India.[3]

It has been asserted that the merchants had paid to the Indian Treasury, as the price of the surrendered opium, double the amount received in compensation. It is impossible to find any evidence to support such a statement, and the figures showing the quotations at Canton are strong evidence to the contrary. If the statement is true, it shows bad trading on the part of the merchants, which must have resulted in a great loss, if the surrender had never been made. In any case, they were only entitled to be compensated for the loss arising from the surrender, and this they received so far as actual value is concerned. It is true that they received no interest on their lost capital, but neither did the British taxpayer receive interest on the capital spent in the prosecution of hostilities. Seeing that the whole of the opium consisted of smuggled goods, the merchants were extremely fortunate in receiving back the cost of those goods at all, especially as the expense of recovering that cost was not borne by themselves. Captain Elliot's promise of indemnity was made without authority, and the British Government might have repudiated it. Then it has been urged that the money should have been paid over in China, and the cost of freight and interest during the transit saved. It may be pointed out that the machinery available for a just distribution at Canton or Hong-kong in 1843 was altogether wanting, and as the ownership was for the most part not in the consignees who

[1] Ramsabuck Mullick *v.* De Souza.

[2] Hansard : *Parliamentary Debates*, vol. 71, pp. 252, 266.

[3] For detailed figures, see *Chinese Repository*, vol. xiii, pp. 54–6.

had made the surrender, the Treasury acted not unwisely in making payment in England. The Treaty of Nanking was signed on the 29th of August, 1842, and ratified on the 26th of June, 1843. On the 25th of August, 1843, the Treasury announced that payment was to be made.[1] Not a penny of the $6,000,000 went into the public treasury, and the dollar was exchanged at its full value. If, as is asserted, the silver was coined into money, the profit to the mint is one that would have been made whether this or any other silver had been used for the purpose.[2]

After the signing of the treaties the opium traffic took a new lease of life. The law against the importation of the drug remained unaltered, and though we did not force the Chinese to legalize the traffic, still our conduct, in forcing them

[1] For form of Notice see Hertslet, *Commercial Treaties*, vol. vi, p. 254. The drafts given by Captain Elliot had been made out in quadruplicate, and the Treasury naturally required that all four parts should be presented, or the missing parts satisfactorily accounted for. This was the only way to prevent claims being made twice over.

It is impossible in the face of the facts set out above to accept as either just or accurate the following criticism: "The conduct of the Ministry in remunerating the merchants who had surrendered their property to Captain Elliot was appropriate to the character of the trade. The $6,000,000 instead of being divided in China among those who were to receive it—as could have been done without expense—was carried to England to be coined, which, with the freight, reduced it considerably. Then by the manner of ascertaining the market value at the time it was given up, and the holders of the script got their pay, they received scarcely one-half of what was originally paid to the East India Company, either directly or indirectly, thereby reducing it nearly a million sterling. Furthermore, by the form of payment they lost one-fifth even of the promised sum, or about $1,200,000. Then they lost four years' interest on their whole capital, or about $4,000,000 more. What the merchants lost the Government profited. The Company gained during these four years at least a million sterling by the increased price of the drug, while Sir Robert Peel also transferred that amount from the pockets of the merchants to the public treasury. It was an undignified and pitiful haggling with the merchants and owners of opium, whom that Ministry had encouraged for many years in their trade along the Chinese coast, and then forced to take what was doled out." (Dr. Wells Williams, *The Middle Kingdom*, vol. ii, pp. 563–4.)

[2] The chief sufferers by the payment of this indemnity were the Hong Merchants, who were made to pay to the Chinese Government some $4,000,000. (See *Chinese Repository*, vol. xiii, p. 53.)

to pay an indemnity for the surrendered drug, had a paralyzing effect on the attempt to root out the evil. The intimate connection between the war and the support afforded to the opium merchants, has led to the name "Opium War" being used to describe the hostilities not only throughout the English-speaking countries, but also in France.[1] In China the reproach, of having conducted a campaign in support of a contraband trade, is one that attaches to England at the present day, as strongly as when the Treaty of Nanking was signed. And though we did not insist on any alteration in the law, the impartial student must admit that the reproach is not without foundation. From the time that Captain Smith arrived with British men-of-war, the Chinese dared not attack the smuggling ships, which thenceforth carried on their operations with impunity. The effect of the war was as though all restrictions on importation had in fact been removed. The Chinese feared that any attempt to suppress smuggling might provoke a fresh conflict with some Foreign Power. At every Treaty Port a flourishing trade in opium arose, connived at by the officials and openly prosecuted by the Foreigners. The new colony of Hong-kong became the centre of illicit trade, the smugglers finding no difficulty in transporting across the frontier goods that could lawfully and openly be taken into the port. So great became the scandal, that in 1858 Lord Elgin came to the conclusion that legalization was the only remedy. In this view the Chinese acquiesced, and opium was admitted subject to a duty of 30 taels per chest, on the same footing as general imports under the Treaty of Nanking. After importation it was to pass into Chinese hands and become subject to such duties as the Government should think proper.[2] Since that date opium has been more and more

[1] Cordier in his excellent bibliography of works on China (*Bibliotheca Sinica*) classifies those relating to this period under the heading, "Guerre d'opium."

[2] This has been the cause of difficulties with the Customs, and has resulted in the enactment of special regulations in connection with opium. The documents which deal with this matter are the Chefoo Convention of 1876, and the additional Article of 1885; the Opium Convention of 1886; and Art. viii. of the Treaty of Shanghai, ratified

grown in China, with the result that the importation from abroad is but a fraction of the whole. A change, however, would appear to be imminent. By the Treaty of Shanghai, the importation of morphia was, in 1903, made illegal, with the express consent of Great Britain, and China pledged herself to prevent its manufacture on Chinese territory.[1] The late Emperor, Kwang-Hsü, showed a clear determination to grapple with the opium evil. It remains to be seen, when the ten years of grace allowed by him have expired, whether those who have recently succeeded to the reins of power will attempt to perfect the work which he began.

in 1903. All but the last will be found in Mayers' *Treaties between the Empire of China and other Foreign Powers*, at pp. 44, 251, and 253.

For an account of the discussion in 1858 on the opium question, see Oliphant, *Lord Elgin's Mission to China and Japan*, vol. i, pp 278–282.

[1] Art. xi of the Treaty of Shanghai. See *Parliamentary Papers*, Treaty Series, No. 17 (1903), p. 12.

CHAPTER XXV

PROBLEMS TO BE SOLVED

At the close of an account of the circumstances, in which the foundations of our interests in China were laid, some discussion of the problems of the immediate present and of the future may not be out of place. First and foremost of these is the opium question, which, owing to the edicts of the late Emperor Kwang-hsü, has recently entered on a new and most interesting phase. One of the questions which Great Britain will have to decide is, what shall be her attitude towards the new policy of prohibition, by which a fresh attempt is being made to eradicate the opium evil. Different answers will be given to this inquiry by persons of different ethical and political views. So far the British Government has shown very considerable sympathy in trying to assist the Chinese executive in carrying out the new policy.[1] A careful study of the opinions prevailing among the governing classes in China, and of the edicts that have been issued during the last few years,[2] cannot fail to give the impression that, in this effort to suppress the opium traffic, the Chinese Government is sincere. However much conflict there may be between those who regard the consumption of opium as a great national vice on the part of the Chinese, and those who think that the opium habit is not an evil at all, or one that has been greatly exaggerated, there can be no doubt that the view of the Chinese people themselves is, that the smoking of opium is both morally and economically a source of national weakness, misery, and poverty. Rightly or wrongly, they regard themselves in this respect as the victims of the national policy of Great Britain, a policy enunciated in the time of Lord Palmerston and maintained to the present day. If, in taking this view, they are

[1] For particulars on this matter see *Correspondence Respecting the Opium Question in China*, issued as a Parliamentary Paper, China, No. 1 (1908), in February, 1908.

[2] See Parliamentary Paper, No. 2 (1908), *The Opium Question in China*.

acting on a wrong assumption, one thing, which we as a nation can do, is to bend our policy in a direction that will disabuse the minds of the Chinese of that error, and show that any attempt on the part of China to improve the conditions of her people in this respect will at least meet with our sympathetic support, and will not in any way be hindered by an insistence on trading rights and privileges, conferred on British subjects at a time when China believed that any such attempt would meet with active opposition on our part.

To put these ideas into a more practical shape involves, in effect, suggesting some definite line on which the British Government may co-operate with the Chinese in attempting to prohibit the importation of opium, to suppress opium dens, and to take restrictive measures for suppressing what may comprehensively be called the opium evil. It may be taken for granted that, for the enforcement of revenue enactments directed to this end, the Chinese Government must, generally speaking, look to its own executive. But, under the treaties described in the preceding pages, many ports and towns have been thrown open to Foreign trade, at which British subjects have the right to reside, enjoying the exterritorial privileges conferred by those treaties. One of the most important of these privileges is that conferred by the stipulations, that they are subject only to the law of their own country, that they cannot be tried elsewhere than in a British court, and then only in accordance with English law. In spite, therefore, of the severest prohibition against the importation or smoking of opium, that the Emperor of China might enact, any British subject, as English law exists to-day, might defy such prohibition at pleasure, because on being tried in his own court it would be shown that he had not been guilty of any offence under the law, which that Court was competent to administer. So far as the existence of opium dens and warehouses within the Concessions and Settlements is concerned, action has already been taken in some of these by the withdrawal of licences, which prevents such places from being conducted openly, or with the assent of the municipal authorities. British subjects may, however, carry on a flourishing trade in importing the drug without fear of consequences, until such time as legislation shall have been enacted, that will make binding on British subjects the law with regard to opium as laid down by the Chinese Government.[1] This is a defect which can easily be cured. The British Government may inform itself as to the state of the Chinese law, and thereupon by Act of Parliament forbid, on the part of British subjects, all those acts which would be offences or breaches of the law if committed by Chinese. The only distinction, that need be made, would be in the penalty and punishment for breach of such a statute, as it would certainly be a sufficient deterrent to make the infringement of such a law by a Foreigner entail considerably less severe consequences than should befal a Chinese subject, who had done a similar act. Possibly such legislation might be enacted by Order in Council under existing statutory powers, but probably the opposition that will be excited, among those who make a profit out of opium, against any such attempt on the part of the British Government to deal with this question, will be so great, that it is preferable that the matter should be dealt with by special statute, so that the validity of any such enactment may be assured, and ample opportunity be given for discussion in Parliament.[2]

How necessary is some such enactment may be shown by reference to the Treaty, which was signed at Shanghai in 1902.[3]

[1] Possibly by this time local regulations have been sanctioned with regard to some of the Concessions, which tend to restrict these evils. The sale of prepared opium has been prohibited in the Concession at Chinkiang.

[2] It is doubtful whether the Privy Council has power under the Foreign Jurisdiction Act, 1890, in virtue of which it issues Orders in Council for the government of British subjects in China, to create a new criminal offence. The Order in Council of the 24th October, 1904, s. 155 (1) *b*, provides that the British Minister at Peking may make regulations for securing the observance of any Treaty for the time being in force relating to any place or of any native law or custom whether relating to trade, commerce, revenue or any other matter. It is very questionable whether the Privy Council itself has so wide an authority, and it is difficult to find ground for believing that it can delegate such power to His Majesty's Minister at Peking.

[3] Treaty of Shanghai, signed 5th Sept., 1902, ratified at Peking 28th July, 1903.

It is there provided[1] that the British Government agrees to the prohibition of the general importation of morphia into China, excepting on payment of the import duty and under special permit for medical purposes. The medical practitioners, chemists and druggists, who alone are to be allowed the benefit of this exception, are to sign a bond before a British Consul, guaranteeing that they are duly qualified within the meaning of the exception, that they only intend to sell in small quantities, and that they have received a requisition in writing for morphia signed by duly qualified Foreign medical practitioners. The only provision in the Treaty against a breach of the conditions of the bond is a statement, that the offender will not, after such a breach, be allowed to take out a further permit. There is no mention at all of any punishment or penalty to be inflicted on a person who, not being a medical practitioner, chemist, or druggist, is nevertheless found engaged in importing the drug. The only way, in which this treaty provision can be legally and adequately enforced, is by the enactment of a statutory prohibition, sanctioned by the sovereign power of Great Britain, that will make it an offence on the part of a British subject to do such acts as would amount to an infringement of the treaty, and will also provide appropriate penalties for any breach of such statute. Until such legislation has been passed, either by order in Council or special statute, a treaty provision of this kind remains a dead letter, and the Chinese Government remains unconvinced of our sincerity in professing a desire to assist them in so small a reform as the prohibition of the importation of morphia, the use of which, as a means of self-indulgence, is rapidly becoming popular with the opium-smoking Chinese.

In the minds of some people the chief difficulty in dealing with the opium question is that which will arise in India, if a source of considerable revenue is suddenly cut off. For the year 1905-6 out of a total revenue of £62,621,929 no less than £5,468,780 was received by the Indian Government as the product of its opium monopoly. If a policy of prohibition

[1] Article xi.

were really enforced in China, there would immediately result an immense falling off in this source of income. In such a case it would be the duty, both of the Indian and the British Governments, to find some means of recouping this loss. It may be that this could not be done immediately, but after the lapse of a few years it should not be beyond the powers of British statesmen to find some other means of using the land, that would thus be thrown out of cultivation, as well as the labour which would be thrown out of employment, in the production of other articles, which would at least bring in an equivalent amount of wealth to the people of India, and possibly a not less income to the Indian exchequer. The mere fact that China had succeeded in prohibiting the importation of opium, should at once stimulate the demand for other commodities, and in supplying such demand India would probably stand in a better position than any other country. One of the most striking features in the recent commercial development of China is the fact, that the import of cotton from India has immensely increased, and so far as can be judged is about to expand to very large extent. The probability is that a less consumption of opium in China would at once result in a far greater demand for cotton, and such a demand could not fail to benefit India. Nearly a hundred years ago it was shown that the demand for imported cotton increased or diminished, broadly speaking, as the importation of opium was less or more.[1]

[1] The following figures, taken from *Papers Relating to Trade with India and China*, presented to the House of Commons, June, 1829, are very eloquent to this effect. They show the imports into Canton and Macao together.

Season.	Raw Cotton.	Opium.	Other Imports.	Total Imports.
1817-8	$6,556,600	$2,957,100	$1,567,900	$11,081,600
1818-9	5,784,916	4,393,000	1,821,356	11,999,272
1819-20	4,271,601	4,464,000	724,331	9,459,932
1820-1	1,898,781	6,486,000	1,742,937	10,127,718
1821-2	3,113,942	4,166,250	1,890,102	9,170,294
1822-3	2,295,939	9,329,000	1,643,310	13,268,249
1823-4	2,283,550	7,288,600	1,500,860	11,073,010
1824-5	3,378,315	4,515,000	3,131,244	11,024,559
1825-6	4,275,826	9,782,500	1,642,552	15,700,878
1826-7	5,153,561	9,269,826	1,285,845	15,709,232
1827-8	3,480,083	11,243,496	1,122,066	15,845,645

The cessation of the opium traffic would certainly result in loss of capital, and probably the labour at present employed in raising the poppy would be thrown out of work. The British Government might guarantee the Indian Exchequer against loss, until such time as the Indian finances could be adjusted to meet the deficiency created by a falling off in the revenue from opium. The return to the people of Great Britain alone, in the form of an increased export of manufactures consequent on the improved purchasing power of the Chinese people, should make such an expenditure an investment of the most profitable kind to the nation at large. The Indian Government is apparently prepared to meet any such loss, if spread over a period of ten years, for it has agreed with the Chinese Government to reduce its total export of opium by 5,100 chests every year, commencing from 1908.[1]

The mention of cotton raises another question in connection with our commercial relations with China, that deserves attention. Until the close of the war between China and Japan it had been strenuously contended by the Chinese Government that the privileges, previously granted to Foreigners by treaty in respect of commerce, conferred only a right to engage in purely trading operations, and not to engage in manufacturing enterprise within Chinese territory. Hence it was that, by the treaty of Shimomoseki, Japan in 1895 insisted on the recognition of a right in her subjects to engage in all kinds of manufacturing industries at the Open Ports of China, and to import machinery for such purposes. By the most favoured nation treatment British subjects at once acquired a similar right, and since that date several attempts have been made by British capitalists to develop the cotton industry in China. For the most part these were until lately a failure. It is wonderful that, with all the natural advantages of a cotton growing country and of a teeming population, from which labour may be obtained at a very small cost, China has been quite unable, even with

[1] *Correspondence Respecting the Opium Question in China* (Parliamentary Paper, China, No. 1, 1908), p. 47. That is, roughly, one-tenth of its total export of opium.

the assistance of Foreign capital, not only to develop any large manufacturing industry in piece goods, but even to compete with other countries in the production of cotton yarn.[1]

It is a surprising fact that for the production of this yarn much of the raw cotton is grown in China itself and then exported. The many natural advantages enjoyed by China in regard to this industry appear not to help her. On the Foreign yarn, freight and insurance both ways have to be paid, and, in the case of imports carried beyond the limits of an Open Port, a further duty has to be added to the ordinary tariff payable at the port of importation on all goods brought into China.[2] The low price of Chinese labour should make an enormous difference in favour of China, but here it is, in the opinion of some people, that we touch the secret of the failure of the cotton enterprise. Chinese labour is so unreliable, that in this respect alone India and Japan have a great economic advantage. Another cause is that combinations of native traders are directed against the success of the mills established in China, and so in spite of the fact, that in many cases a monopoly for very large districts has been given by the Chinese

[1] The following figures show the number of pounds weight of cotton yarn imported into China for the six years ending 1903 :—

	1898	1899	1900	1901	1902	1903
British	9,145,333	7,827,100	4,122,100	7,007,500	4,313,500	2,244,000
Indian	186,657,333	254,190,100	131,465,200	228,931,000	251,611,467	250,788,000
Japanese	64,699,200	103,960,000	62,870,800	66,415,467	69,654,400	110,854,000
Hong-kong	—	—	—	694,000	816,800	1,230,000
Tongkinese	—	—	—	—	—	10,000
Total	260,501,866	365,977,200	198,458,100	303,048,367	326,396,167	365,126,400

[2] Since 1903 the following stipulations contained in Art. viii, sec 9. of the Treaty of Shanghai have been in force with regard to cotton :—

An excise equivalent to double the import duty as laid down in the Protocol of 1901 is to be charged on all machine-made yarn and cloth manufactured in China, whether by Foreigners at the Open Ports, or by Chinese anywhere in China.

A rebate of the import duty and two-thirds of the import surtax is to be given on raw cotton imported from Foreign countries, and of all duties, including consumption tax, paid on Chinese raw cotton used in mills in China.

Chinese machine-made yarn or cloth having paid excise is to be free of Export Duty, Export Tax, Coast-trade Duty, and Consumption Tax.

Government to the owners of Chinese mills, still to-day a very large part of the capital that has been embarked in this industry is either unproductive or has been absolutely lost.[1]

This question of the reliability of the Chinese character is one that is bound to arise in many important ways in connection with all commercial enterprise in China. British merchants are very much in the habit of proclaiming the fact that in commercial integrity the Chinese are very superior to the Japanese and very seldom fail to fulfil their contracts. So far as the respective merits of the two races are concerned this may be true. But it must not be forgotten that, from the time of the foundation of the feudal system in Japan[2] to the commencement of the New Era in 1868, commerce was relegated to the lowest classes of the community, whereas in China the military profession has always been that least esteemed. When we come to compare Chinese commercial morality with that to which we are accustomed in England, it must be confessed by any impartial student that it does not deserve the laudatory comments, which are so freely bestowed upon it by some. The custom is for most business houses in China to place the whole of their Chinese staff under the control of a kind of Chinese manager, called the compradore,[3] who alone is responsible to the Foreign merchant for any defalcation on the part of any member of the Chinese staff. Usually a large sum is deposited as security by the compradore, to which his employer may have recourse in the event of any default being made by any person employed by the compradore, or accepted as a customer on his introduction. It is expressly provided by a written contract of employment, that such recourse may be had without appeal to a court

[1] For further information on this subject see Diplomatic and Consular reports, *Cotton Mills of China*, Miscellaneous series, No. 629, published in March, 1905, by the Foreign Office. *Report for the year* 1907 *on the Foreign Trade of China*, published in October, 1908, in the Diplomatic and Consular Reports, No. 4152, Annual Series.

[2] The feudal system was founded by Yoritomo about 1190 and consolidated by Iyeyasu, who was shogun from 1603 to 1605.

[3] Compradores, in the old days at Canton, were the purveyors who contracted to supply ships with provisions. Nowadays they are the managers of the Chinese staff in the Foreign business houses.

of law or the intervention of any tribunal whatsoever. In addition, the compradore frequently has to provide written guarantees from well-known Chinese merchants for the faithful discharge of his duties and liabilities. When such precautions as these are taken, it is not surprising that a compradore seldom makes default, and, if any of his clients fail to fulfil their contracts, the compradore covers up the failure, and his employer lives in the happy belief that everything has gone smoothly. Very few British merchants speak Chinese at all well, and most of them are absolutely at the mercy of the compradore, when they seek for information as to the manner in which their business has been conducted. Now that competition is increasing on the China coast, it is becoming essential that a person who wishes to engage in large commercial enterprises should have a knowledge of the language and be able to deal direct with his Chinese customers. In short, the time has come when the compradore system should be superseded by something better.[1]

A question which will demand careful consideration in the near future, particularly if there should occur in China any such national change as has been recently witnessed in Turkey, is the question of how long Foreigners are to continue to enjoy exterritorial privileges. This is a subject which divides itself into two branches, the one being concerned with the status of the Concessions and Settlements, the other arising out of the existence of the various Foreign tribunals, which exercise judicial functions within Chinese territory. So far as the former branch is concerned, it will probably be a great many years before China seeks to bring about any change, provided that the existence of these favoured areas is not used as a means by which Foreigners may evade perfectly just provisions of Chinese law, such, for example, as might be enacted for the restriction of the opium trade, which in their tendencies run counter to the interest of some Foreign traders. In relation

[1] For a discussion on Chinese commercial integrity see Dr. A. H. Smith, *Chinese Characteristics*, ch. xxv, pp. 279–285, 5th ed. For a discussion of the Compradore system, see *Report of the Mission of the Blackburn Chamber of Commerce* (Neville and Bell's section), pp. 323–330.

to the Concessions and Settlements it should be our aim to preserve and consolidate all that we now have in the way of material interests. In considering this matter we have to pay regard to the loss of prestige that would follow if we neglected these interests. In the face of competition by other Powers, it is well to remember that we cannot afford to make a retrocession until other Powers are willing to take a similar course.

The care and development of our Concessions at the Treaty Ports is a matter of great commercial importance. In many instances the form of administration needs to be thoroughly revised, and the old system of government by land-renters needs to be swept away and replaced by an administration controlled by all those, who pay rates or duties towards the maintenance of the municipal government. This has been done in some ports, and thus a good precedent has been set for introducing a similar reform at the others. Some fifty years hence the question will arise, as to what is to become of the land held by the Crown at ports where British Concessions exist. Some land-renters are of the opinion, that their leases should be converted into perpetual tenancies, with no increase of rent. In favour of such a course it is difficult to advance any logical argument. The land so let rapidly increases in value, and this, to a large extent, is due to the fact that the income derived from duties paid by the whole of the residents, whether land-renters or not, is applied in improving the Concessions, where the land so leased is situate. Thus automatically the lots held by the land-renters are bound to increase in value, so long as the trade of the port continues to progress. Seeing that the very existence of the mercantile communities, which carry on the trade in these Concessions, is dependent on the protection afforded by the naval, military, and diplomatic services, it is only fair that some of the benefit, arising from an increase in the value of land so protected, should be secured in the future to the taxpayer, at whose expense those services are maintained. The opportunity of obtaining a substantial benefit in this way will arise, when the existing leases come to an end, and care should be taken that that opportunity is not thrown away, and that the interests of all concerned are taken into consideration.

As to the British Courts in China, it would be the highest folly to think of abolishing them for many years to come.[1] They are one of the chief sources of that feeling of security, without which great commercial operations cannot be carried on. In them the Chinese have the utmost confidence, and, so long as the British Government takes care that the persons appointed to exercise judicial functions are properly chosen and efficient for the purpose, the continued existence of these Courts cannot be other than a great advantage to English and Chinese alike. It will be very many years before China can evolve a bench of judges, having the requisite training to administer justice in such a way as to secure the confidence of British residents, or even of the Chinese themselves. Even in Japan, where the spirit of reform has been working unchecked for forty years, it is very doubtful whether the substitution of Japanese for British Courts, which took place in 1898, has made for the advantage of the subjects of either nation. It must be remembered that in Japan the advance made in recent years, in such branches of knowledge as law and jurisprudence, is nothing like so great as that which we all know to have been made in military and naval science. The probability is, that the progress of China in any of these directions, when it shall have commenced, will be very much slower than that witnessed in the dominions of the Mikado.

The Chinese Government has itself recognised, in the Treaty of Shanghai, the necessity of reforming her own legal institutions. Not only does she need a reformed judiciary and a new system of procedure, but in substantive law great improvements are imperative, before she can pretend to be on

[1] By Art. xii of the Treaty of Shanghai (1903) Great Britain bound herself with the following stipulation :—"China having expressed a strong desire to reform her judicial system and to bring it into accord with that of Western nations, Great Britain agrees to give every assistance to such reform, and she will also be prepared to relinquish her extra-territorial rights when she is satisfied that the state of the Chinese laws, the arrangement for their administration, and other considerations warrant her in so doing."

an equality with the lowest of Western powers. Her case is not like that of Turkey, where there is an admirable body of substantive law badly administered. China in many respects has no substantive law at all, and one of her most difficult tasks will be to create a code sympathetic with the genius of the Chinese people, and at the same time adequate to regulate the intercourse between Chinese and Foreigners, and to enable the latter to feel that in all matters of business and kindred relations their interests are as well protected as under the jurisprudence of a Western state.

In effecting this reform China is likely to find Roman law more adaptable to this double need, as the basis of such a code, than the modern law of any European state. With regard to the law of the family in particular, there is a very strong resemblance between the ancient law of Rome and the present law of China.[1] On to this would have to be grafted many branches of English law for the regulation of matters of commerce. With these latter Chinese merchants and officials at the chief Open Ports already have some acquaintance, and English company law has already, to some extent, become the source of similar legal ideas among the Chinese. The position is not unlike that at Rome in the time when the *jus gentium* came to be regarded as a source of new principles. Owing to the predominating influence enjoyed by the English in commerce for so many years, the vast body of the *jus gentium* available in China is derived from English Law. So far as the law of procedure is concerned, China has never yet, except at Shanghai, properly constituted those "Mixed Courts," for the trial of suits brought by Foreign plaintiffs against Chinese defendants, which she promised to consider under the Chefoo Convention,[2] and she might well attempt some further advance in this direction before the question of the abolition of our own courts is again so much as discussed.

With regard to the general question of the preservation and development of our interests in China, we should consider

[1] As to the Chinese Law of the Family see Von Mollendorf.

[2] Section II (ii). The Regulations for the Mixed Court at Shanghai were agreed to in 1869. For their terms see Mayers, *Treaties, etc.*, p. 236.

whether, apart from the persons appointed to exercise purely judicial functions, the services which have the care of those interests are now adequate for all the purposes they have to fulfil. Speaking generally, one has only praise for the diplomatic and consular services in China as they now exist.[1] But it is necessary that the Home Government should see that the staff, who have to administer those services, is not inadequate in numbers. In training, too, some changes might with advantage be introduced. For example, it is now a vital necessity that a Consul at any of the larger ports should have had a good legal education, and though the Government encourages men, when on furlough, to acquire a knowledge of law, the system does not provide that a man appointed as Consul to a port, where he may have to determine questions of great legal difficulty, must of necessity have had the peculiar training that alone can fit him to exercise functions of that kind.

A further matter worthy of consideration is whether the office of Superintendent of Trade should continue to be held by the British Minister at Peking. Under the present system the diplomatic representative of His Majesty's Government in China has to exercise all sorts of functions, many of a purely commercial nature, that are not imposed upon our diplomatic officials in any other part of the world. This question is one of peculiar nicety, and can only be rightly solved after careful consideration. The suggestion here made is, that His Majesty's Government should now appoint an official separate from the Minister at Peking to act as a Superintendent of Trade. He should exercise no diplomatic function: his duty should be to visit in turn the various Open Ports and study the needs of the residents, and to inform himself as to all questions of a commercial nature, so that he may be able to advise the Home Government as to what new developments or modifications are necessary in our foreign policy, for the advancement of our commercial interests in China. Questions of changes in the

[1] For the China Consular service there is an entrance examination conducted by the Civil Service Commissioners. Candidates, who must be under twenty-four years of age, have to obtain a nomination from the Foreign Secretary.

tariff, enforcement of customs regulations, protection of shipping, development of Concessions, and generally the further advancement of our interests under the commercial privileges secured to us by Treaty, should be particularly within his province. If such an official were appointed, it would be necessary to have a man of broad views and wide experience, and by preference one whose training has not taken place entirely in the Far East. He should in no sense interfere with the functions of the Minister at Peking, and any representation he might make would be addressed to the Foreign Office.[1] If, owing to information received from the Superintendent of Trade, the British Government wished to communicate with the Chinese, such communication would be made through the Minister at Peking, who would remain the sole channel of diplomatic intercourse. Our interests at Shanghai and Tientsin alone have now grown to such an extent, and involve questions of such intricacy and difficulty, that a more careful study of them than can possibly be made by the Minister at Peking is necessary to their preservation and continued prosperity.[2]

Another matter, and one of peculiar difficulty, which will require the attention of not only British but all European statesmen in the near future, is the problem of missionary activity. In 1903 Great Britain pledged herself to join in a Commission to investigate this question,[3] and it is extremely probable that a few years hence China will request that this

[1] Or perhaps to the Board of Trade, as being the more suitable department to deal with matters of the kind on which he would have to report. The existence of a commercial attaché is a recognition that some such official is needed.

[2] The International Settlement at Shanghai has now become a great commercial centre. The population in 1905 consisted of British, 3,713; Japanese, 21,517; Portuguese, 1,331; American, 991; German, 785; French, 393; Russian, 354; Indian, 568; Total, 11,497. In addition 452,716 Chinese live in the Settlement.

[3] *The Treaty of Shanghai*, Art. xiii, provides: "The missionary question in China being, in the opinion of the Chinese Government, one requiring careful consideration, so that, if possible, troubles such as have occurred in the past may be averted in the future, Great Britain agrees to join in a Commission to investigate this question, and, if possible, to devise means for securing permanent peace between converts and non-converts, should such a Commission be formed by China and the Treaty Powers interested."

pledge be redeemed. No solution of this question, that does not provide for the cessation of an influx of missionaries into all parts of the Empire at their pleasure, can ever be acceptable to the Chinese, or operate as a cure for the evils that have arisen since the year 1860. Some Powers use the missionary question simply as a political weapon. Under diplomatic pressure in March, 1899, the Emperor conferred official rank on missionaries, by which a bishop ranks with the Governor of a province. The presence of the Foreign missionary element acts as an irritant to the whole body politic in China, and produces such terrible maladies as the Boxer movement of 1900. The reasons for this are somewhat intricate, but when it is remembered that the same treaties which record the humiliation of China, the payment of compensation for the surrendered opium, and the free admission of the drug into the "Flowery Land," are also the basis of what the missionaries regard as their "rights," it will be seen how different is the aspect of this question to the Chinese mind from that which presents itself to the conventional Englishman. Opium, missionaries, men-of-war are the agencies of European civilisation that have most impressed themselves on the Chinese imagination. Except at Canton these agencies have first presented themselves in this sequence, and generally in intimate connection. It is not surprising that Christianity, as thus introduced to the Chinese, has not been welcomed with open arms.

For nearly fifty years the missionary bodies have now had free scope throughout the Empire; for sixty-five years they have been countenanced and tolerated at the Five Ports. If, by this time, they have succeeded in establishing a healthy organisation, no harm can be done by gradually diminishing the influx of Foreign evangelists. If such a point has not yet been attained, and if the vast expenditure of life and money has not yet resulted in the creation of a living church, then surely the time has come to terminate what must be regarded as a failure. The great missionary bodies are fond of proclaiming the success of their work. That being so, they might leave the further propagation of Christian ethics to the native converts. The two broad remedies for existing conditions that suggest themselves are, first, a time-limit, after which no fresh European missionary should be allowed to proceed to those parts of China which are outside the limits of the Open Ports; and, secondly, the establishment outside the Chinese dominions of colleges, where Chinese converts can be trained to carry on the work which the Foreign missionaries claim to have successfully inaugurated. The whole principle of forcing religious emissaries on an unwilling people is so repugnant to common sense, so contrary to the great examples in imitation of which the modern missionary movement is supposed to have been established, that no intelligent Englishman can want any further reason for insisting that no longer shall his Government be required to lend its sanction to a proceeding such as this.[1] We need only imagine how Englishmen would treat a similar incursion of Buddhist missionaries from Japan, for example, into our own country, supported by armed force and maintained by vast contributions on the part of the Japanese people, to appreciate the frame of mind in which the ordinary Chinese look upon this question of missionary enterprise.

One more question remains to be considered, and that is the relation between British subjects as a whole and the nations of the Far East. This is the most difficult of all. Under present circumstances it cannot be treated as a whole, but has to be subdivided into a number of subordinate issues, owing to the fact that the relations between any one of our self-governing colonies and the nations of the Far East must be regarded as an independent question. That each colony has the right, for example, to restrain the immigration of the Yellow Races into its territory is generally conceded. The function of the Home Government is to supervise the manner in which that right is exercised, and to take care that due consideration has been paid to the interests of the Empire at large, in the mode of maintaining this right adopted in each case. Australia, for example, has the right to resolve on a

[1] For a very able discussion of the problems presented by the Missionary Question, see Michie: *Missionaries in China*.

policy of absolute exclusion ; but if in the future, as China and Japan develop, either or both of these countries should assert the right to a similar policy of exclusion as against such a Colony, it must not be expected that the people of Great Britain would in such a case insist on the Chinese, or Japanese, Government renouncing any claim to such a right. So in matters of fiscal policy, those parts of the Empire which proceed on different lines from those adopted by the Mother Country, must be prepared to receive from the nations of the Far East correspondingly different treatment from that accorded to Great Britain herself. The right of entry on equal terms to all British subjects alike has been granted by China without complaint, and has been accepted as one of the commonplaces of commercial intercourse. How far a re-organised China would be content to continue that policy is a matter of grave doubt.

Looking back over the whole history of our intercourse with China we are confronted with the question, what has China gained by reason of that intercourse ? If we answer truthfully, we must admit that she has gained very little. Depleted of much of her wealth, paid as the price of opium, or to defray the cost of military operations undertaken by Western Powers in their own interest, or as indemnity for outrages against Foreigners and their property, whose presence has been forced upon her, her loss in material wealth must have been immense. Compelled to admit all British subjects on favourable terms, under treaties that have never been modified, she has to watch in silence whilst her own subjects are rigidly excluded from many parts of the British dominions. The generous language of the letters of Tudor monarchs and the flowery language of treaties is, indeed, in striking contrast to the immigration ordinances sanctioned by the British Crown.[1] Against these

[1] It must not be supposed that this is written in any spirit of censure on the self-governing colonies, but rather to explain the Chinese point of view and to indicate what substantial grounds the Chinese consider they have for treaty revision. There is not much doubt that the people of the United Kingdom would demand similar legislation for themselves, if there were any danger of an influx of Chinese workers into their midst. For the immigration ordinances passed by various British colonies see Blue Book of July, 1904, on Admission of Immigrants into the self-governing Colonies.

losses and disadvantages may be set off the introduction of new ethical ideas to her notice, of which few countries stand in greater need than China, and an acquaintance with those ideas of good government, good administration, and sound finance, that would do so much to advance the prosperity of the Chinese people, if their rulers would once make up their minds to use them as a model for reform. In addition, the knowledge of medicine and hygiene that could, if properly applied, do so much for the immense proportion of suffering humanity included in her population, would never have been available but for the incursion of Europeans within her borders. These gifts the Chinese Government has so far refused to accept, and the failure to enjoy the potential good, of which they might be the source, is attributable only to pride and incompetence. The actual material loss, which she has suffered through her acquaintance with Europeans, is one of which the proximate cause is not entirely her own conduct. On the other hand, she has the benefit of Foreign capital invested in various enterprises, that conduce to the material prosperity of the country. When, however, the balance is struck between losses and advantages, the former appear to predominate.

In conclusion, let us consider for one moment what principle should guide us in our policy towards China in the future. We have reached the point where we may properly consider how to make amends for any injustice we may have done her in the past. An occasion for reparation now presents itself, in the form of an opportunity to assist her in the struggle to eradicate the opium evil. The access of prestige that would come to us as a nation, if we adopted such a course, could not fail in the long run to bring a material reward. The power of sentiment and of gratitude in commercial matters has been witnessed in Turkey. A reformed China, which the world may yet see, might not be less appreciative of any magnanimity we may show. It is true that to take such a course means the adoption of a higher standard of national ethics than is demanded by international law. But has not Great Britain now advanced to a position where it would become her to set up such a standard? If she has not, we may find, when an awakened China shall assert her will, that the pre-eminent position, which was ours, has passed to some competitor, whose record is not stained with the blot that the opium traffic has left upon our own.

INDEX